Imagining the Past, Remembering the Future

BLACK LIVES IN THE DIASPORA: PAST / PRESENT / FUTURE

BLACK LIVES IN THE DIASPORA:
PAST / PRESENT / FUTURE

EDITORIAL BOARD

Howard University
Clarence Lusane, Rubin Patterson, Nikki Taylor, Amy Yeboah Quarkume

Columbia University
Farah Jasmine Griffin, Frank Guridy, Josef Sorett

Black Lives in the Diaspora: Past / Present / Future is a book series that focuses on Black lives in a global diasporic context. Published in partnership with Howard University's College of Arts and Sciences and Columbia University's African American and African Diaspora Studies Department, it builds on Columbia University Press's publishing programs in history, sociology, religion, philosophy, and literature as well as African American and African Diaspora studies. The series showcases scholarship and writing that enriches our understanding of Black experiences in the past, present, and future with the goal of reaching beyond the academy to intervene in urgent national and international conversations about the experiences of people of African descent. The series anchors an exchange across two global educational institutions, both located in historical capitals of Black life and culture.

Nicole M. Morris Johnson, *The Souths in Her: Black Women Writers and Choreographers and the Poetics of Transmutation*

Jamall A. Calloway, *Imagining Eden: Black Theology and the Search for Paradise*

Wendell H. Marsh, *Textual Life: Islam, Africa, and the Fate of the Humanities*

Jarvis McInnis, *Afterlives of the Plantation: Plotting Agrarian Futures in the Global Black South*

Lauren Coyle Rosen and Hannibal Lokumbe, *Hannibal Lokumbe: Spiritual Soundscapes of Music, Life, and Liberation*

Laura E. Helton, *Scattered and Fugitive Things: How Black Collectors Created Archives and Remade History*

Sarah Phillips Casteel, *Black Lives Under Nazism: Making History Visible in Literature and Art*

Aïssatou Mbodj-Pouye, *An Address in Paris: Emplacement, Bureaucracy, and Belonging in Hostels for West African Migrants*

Vivaldi Jean-Marie, *An Ethos of Blackness: Rastafari Cosmology, Culture, and Consciousness*

For a complete list of books in the series, please see the Columbia University Press website.

Imagining the Past, Remembering the Future

Forms of Knowledge in the Afro-Brazilian Diaspora

Isis Barra Costa

Columbia University Press

New York

Columbia University Press
Publishers Since 1893
New York   Chichester, West Sussex
cup.columbia.edu

Copyright © 2026 Columbia University Press
All rights reserved

Library of Congress Cataloging-in-Publication Data
Names: Barra Costa, Isis author
Title: Imagining the past, remembering the future :
forms of knowledge in the Afro-Brazilian diaspora / Isis Barra Costa.
Other titles: Forms of knowledge in the Afro-Brazilian diaspora
Description: New York : Columbia University Press, [2026] |
Series: Black lives in the diaspora : past / present / future |
Includes bibliographical references and index.
Identifiers: LCCN 2025024325 | ISBN 9780231212625 hardback |
ISBN 9780231212632 trade paperback | ISBN 9780231559485 epub |
ISBN 9780231564960 PDF
Subjects: LCSH: Brazil—Civilization—African influences |
Black people—Brazil | Brazil—Civilization—European influences
Classification: LCC F2659.B53.B376 2026
LC record available at https://lccn.loc.gov/2025024325

Cover design: Elliott S. Cairns
Cover image: Cleiri Cardoso, *Sem folhas não tem nada
(Without leaves, nothing exists)*. Metal engraving (drypoint) on
Hahnemühle paper and crochet, 2023. Photo: Paulo Pereira /
Teia Documenta.

GPSR Authorized Representative: Easy Access System Europe,
Mustamäe tee 50, 10621 Tallinn, Estonia, gpsr.requests@easproject.com

In memory of

Maria Teresa Barra Costa (1938–2021)

Luiz de Oliveira Costa (1935–2013)

and

Kamau Brathwaite (1930–2020)

Contents

Acknowledgments ix
Road Opener: Òsanyìn's Bird: The Triumph of the Small xv

Introduction: Entering Other Forests 1

PART I

The Euro-Afro-Brazilian Archive:
European Civilization in Brazil

1. Visual Art Images:
"I See... I Narrate. But What Is It That I Am Seeing?" 41

2. History:
A Gold Medal for the Best Story 48

3. Literature:
Heroes, Monsters, Giants, and the Canon 52

4. Poetics:
Two Giants and Two Prophecies 74

5. Social Sciences:
Three Founding Moments of Euro-Afro-Brazilian
Studies (Separating the Wheat from the Chaff) 86

6. Law:
Peace Without a Voice Is Not Harmony 106

PART II
The Kongo-Angola-Yoruba-Ewe-Brazilian Archive: African Civilizations in Brazil

7. Mundiongo: Ancestral Languages:
Entering Other Forests 119

8. Aruanda: Ancestral Geographies:
A Map to Aruanda and Other Realms 154

9. Ìtàn: Ancestral Genealogies:
Obatala Came Before Us 234

Final Considerations: Dikenga and Opón Ifa:
Ancestral Times and Technologies 309

......

Notes 321

Works Cited 379

Index 399

Acknowledgments

Opening a book is an ancient ritual. The leaves of books, like the leaves of trees, are portals, carrying long-intersected histories we know very little about. Without trees, there would be no codices. I thank the histories of materials and processes involved in the creation of the object you hold. I thank the tiny pixels that come together to emit light and form the eco-friendlier digital pages you read. I thank the unborn sources of reading technologies we have yet to encounter. I thank *you* for approaching these pages, for creating the time to decode these leaves. I thank the leaves that heal, that allow us to breathe, and that provide us with the path to the sacred. *Kò sí Ewé, kò sí Òrìṣà. Láróyè, Ẹlẹ́gbá. Máfẹrẹ̀fun, Ọ̀ṣọ́ọ̀sì, Yemọjá. Oníbèbè, a júbà. Ìyá mi, a júbà. Máfẹrẹ̀fun, gbogbo Òrìṣà. Máfẹrẹ̀fun, gbogbo Egún.*

The history of this book is long. It is longer than mine. I thank all those who transmitted some of their histories to me, those I met only in books, and those I met only in dreams. I thank those who were present and visible throughout the journey of assembling this printed microcosm. It would be impossible for me to properly acknowledge everyone who made this possible. May this text fully fulfill its mission to honor all those, and all that, involved in its creation.

I thank the *comadres* and *compadres*, the doulas and midwives of this book. I thank Wendy Lochner, RASP (Religion, Animal Studies, and Philosophy) editor at Columbia University Press, to whom I am deeply indebted. I have only known her through letters. Her very first message to me read, *"Thank you for persevering!"* and her emails always close with Pythagoras's line, *"Astonishing! Everything is intelligent!"* Wendy understood and championed this book in a way no other editor ever did. I thank her for her steady support, enthusiasm, and insight. To Alyssa Napier, editor at Columbia University Press, and to all members of the editorial boards at Columbia University and Howard University, I extend my gratitude for including this book in *Black Lives in the Diaspora: Past / Present / Future*. This series, born of collaboration between these institutions, testifies to the power of collective effort in enriching global diasporic studies of Black experience. I am honored to be part of this initiative. I thank everyone at Columbia University Press who worked with Wendy Lochner and me—Emily Simon, Marielle Poss, Zachary Friedman, and Elliott Cairns—for guiding this project, designing its cover, and bringing it to readers. I thank the editing team at Knowledge Works Global—Kalie Hyatt, Cole Bowman, and Marcella Munson—for shepherding the manuscript to its finished form. I also thank Doreen and Eric Anderson, as well as Cynthia and Robert Swanson at Arc Indexing, for their expert oversight of the index.

To Cleiri Cardoso, the artist whose illustration graces the cover of this book, I am deeply grateful for her accepting my invitation and joining this circle. I came across her etching and crochet art pieces in an exhibit at the Afro Brasil Museum of São Paulo in the summer of 2024. I photographed them in the haste of a traveler, in the anguish of an immigrant who cannot carry her home on her back, as land and sand snails can.

To those who took up the task of editing the text written in this language that will always be foreign to me, I offer my heartfelt thanks. To Charles St-Georges and Marisa Pagano, my deepest gratitude for being the editors and very first readers of this long manuscript. Thank you for your stamina, gentleness, and enlightening feedback. To my two colleagues at Ohio State University who read and refined the proposal for this book, Laura Podalsky and Lisa Voigt, thank you for your discerning energy that fueled the launch of this project. To Lúcia Costigan, my lifelong gratitude for being a model of the woman, scholar, and sage I can only aspire to emulate. Thank you for welcoming me to these green lands baptized by Iroquoian nations and for embodying how a scholar can sustain her womanhood, enlightened by joy, humor, and kindness.

Thank you to the old and young masters, those from whom I have learned most of the little I know; those who have taught and initiated me through a wide range of pedagogies; those who worked with me for years and those I only encountered very recently and for shorter spans of time. To Ọbaíkọ́í, Ìlárí, Adéòkùn, Ànhábè, Makota Valdina, and Mãe Beata de Iemanjá: may I have your blessings; may I do justice and live up to a fraction of what you have taught me. My gratitude to the masters I have been following since the beginning of this journey, who have helped me to develop deeper seeing and hearing—Kamau Brathwaite, M. Jacqui Alexander, Myrna Bain, Ngũgĩ wa Thiong'o, C. Daniel Dawson, Edimilson de

Almeida Pereira—and to those I have only recently met—Rafael Galante and Lorraine Mendes.

Thank you for the blessings and teachings of my godmothers—Marilyn Mastrandrea, Arethuza Pompéia Sturm, Ọmìládé, and Ọmítọwá; the grandmothers—Diva da Cunha Barra and Carolina de Oliveira Costa; the grandaunts and uncles—Maria do Carmo Mastrandrea and Mário Vieira da Cunha; the godfathers—Wilson Mastrandrea, Àláìbọ̀ọ̀dẹ Kòfútónàdé; and the grandfathers who followed my arrival to the world of the living from Ku Mpèmba—Guaracy Ribeiro Barra and João Abílio da Costa.

My gratitude to the members of my nuclear family, those who followed me from an infancy marked by rickets, through the healing with Oshosi's sun on Yemaya's waters, the many rites of passage, the departure from Brazil, the promises, gifts, trips, and the stories that shape who I am. To those already in Ilé Ọ̀run—my parents and brother, Luiz, Teresa, and Marco; and to those who stand with me, Caio, Kátia, and the one who shall continue to stand in this world after we cross the Kalûnga—my niece, Lys Limongelli Costa, the first to learn that I had completed the journey of this book.

My gratitude to the family I have formed with my partner in the adventure of life, whom I met in these lands of the Great River, Andy McNally, and those he brought into my life—Diann, Beth, Callan, Alex, and Charlotte Rose. Thank you for joining me and for supporting me through the ups and downs of completing this long, challenging project.

Thank you to my extended family—Diracyr and Murta; Henriqueta and Oscar; Will and Iris; Vicki and Paulo Sérgio; Margarida and Maurício; Rick and Angelina; Laura and Kevin; Jeferson, Raquel, Luiz Fernando, Luciana and Tainá; Carla, Rafa, Alex, Adriana, Célia, Lúcia, Denis, Bruno, Paul, Priscilla, Monica, Marie, and the many more.

Thank you to the older, younger, and twin sisters that life has given me outside the walls of academia—Cláudia Sodré, Cláudia de Fátima Silva, Creuza Gomes, Daniela Ervolino, Dilma Alves do Nascimento, Katerina Dimitrova, Mindy Meyers, Regina Foster Ribeiro, Tae Jung Chang; and my feline siblings—Capitão Rodrigo Amoroso, Catalina, Eliot, and Minerva.

Thank you to all those with whom I have shared the academic realm, who followed the gradual development of the stories and reflections contained in these pages, who cheered for me even when I couldn't, who inspired me, and who brought beauty, joy, and purpose to my journey. *Salve, salve*, Alexandra Isfahani-Hammond, Alison Crocetta, Ana Paula Alves Ribeiro, Ana Puga, Anna Babel, Arturo Matute Castro, Bárbara Copque, Carla Beatriz Melo, Camila do

Valle, Carolin Overhoff Ferreira, César Braga-Pinto, Cida Salgueiro, Cláudia Maria Ceneviva Nigro, Claudia Sadowski-Smith, Cristina Pinto-Bailey, Eduardo Muslip, Elizabeth Horan, Emanuelle Oliveira-Monte, Giséle Manganelli Fernandes, Kit Danowski, Kwasi Konadu, Lance Gharavi, Leonardo Tonus, Luciana Namorato, Maria José Somerlate Barbosa, Michelle Wibbelsman, Paloma Martinez-Cruz, Pamela Espinosa de los Monteros, Patrícia Pinho, Paulo Dutra, Pedro Pereira, Peggy Sharpe, Rebecca Haidt, Rebeka Campos-Astorkiza, Rick Santos, Sandro Barros, Selma Vital, Susan Canty Quinlan, Vânia Penha-Lopes, Zeca Ligiéro, Zelideth María Rivas, and all those I am sure I forgot to include.

Thank you to my students and advisees who brought and continue to bring me wisdom, challenges, and joy, including Ana Carolina dos Santos Marques, Andrew Gantt, Ayodeji Olugbuyiro, César Alves dos Santos, Clara Fachini Zanirato, Jacqueline Sampaio, Jaret Waters, Jean Carlos Carniel, Julián Marcel Baldemira, Laurelann Porter, Maria Vitória de Rezende Grisi, Marla R. Goins, Megan Anne Todd, Mohamed A. Gabal, Raphael Palermo, Romeu Foz, Sheneese Thompson, Terra Rothpletz, and Vitor Vilaverde Dias. Last but not least, thank you to those who organize and lead the department of Spanish and Portuguese at Ohio State University, who have supported me and helped disentangle my projects and ventures, especially Adam Keller, Christiana Whitesel, Connie Knoechel, Dana Renga, Elizabeth Wigal, Gary Hayward, and Rachel Sanabria. This publication was made possible in part by an Arts and Humanities subvention grant from Ohio State University.

Obrigada a todas, todos e todes, que este livro tenha valido a espera, e que o Tempo continue a dançar no ritmo e passos que bem entender.

All translations from sources originally in Portuguese are my own unless otherwise indicated. Original-language excerpts are provided only for poetic texts.

Road Opener

Òsanyìn's Bird: The Triumph of the Small

*To Makota Valdina Oliveira Pinto (1943–2019),
Guardian of Parque São Bartolomeu.
In memory of a day long gone but always yesterday.*

They hopped off a bus in a suburb of Salvador and started walking the narrow trail along the highway. The sun was still asleep. Two small women. One half the age of the other. The younger one kept looking down at the bushes fighting against the concrete. Zigzagging along her path, struggling against unwanted thoughts, she sighed, tightened up her head tie, and rubbed her eyes. The older one, head held high, with a steady gaze and pace, looked beyond this world. From where the sun sets in the water to where the sun sets behind the mountains, she knew all the roads and yet she seemed too slim-shouldered for certain burdens. She shook her head and sucked her teeth as she approached the police station at the entrance of São Bartolomeu.

São Bartolomeu: once home to maroons, now the backyard to thousands of destitute slums. Each and every herb that one might need for the healing of the body and the strengthening of the soul was there. A bundle of sacred medicine waiting to be untied, combined, and activated. But the agony of destitution demands immediate relief. A quick fix. Illusions of conquest: a blade, a cutlass, a gun. Manhood denied. Raping young bodies of girls—your daughter, sister. Womanhood denied. Spirits amputated by man-made chemicals. Life: not as a gift but as an incursion into the darkest alleys of hell. Denied light and potential destinies. The sole north: possession. By force. Of bodies and lands and anguished spirits. A cynical smile. A minute of pleasure. Coming, coming, into further—and yet further—destruction.

São Bartolomeu: for centuries, touching, sheltering, opening up, and speaking to the sprouting spirits of new initiates; a healing ground for priests and priestesses of Salvador; a living library and archive for all who could read between stems. São Bartolomeu: now bordered by the highway, secured by military forces. Osayin's sacred realm encroached upon by modernity, urban violence, and fear. Katende's healing cosmos misunderstood, abused, violated. Ancestral maroon ground obscured by engendered disorientation.

The two women were greeted by a policeman. He touched the ground and asked for blessings from the older one. From inside the improvised police station came the sounds of guns being loaded. The younger one clenched her teeth. "*Alafia.*" Wishing for peace almost felt like a contradiction. The policeman stood still, looking down. With her gently piercing eyes, the older woman lifted his head, captured his gaze, and smiled. He thought his mission was to protect us. She knew her mission was more complicated than that.

"*Kò sí Ewé, kò sí Òrìṣà*—without herbs there are no Orishas."

Three policemen followed the two women. Loaded guns stuck out from their belts. They kept a distance from them—out of respect, out of fear of unknown forces immune to bullets or uniforms. As concrete turned into dirt, the women opened their bags. They placed some coins and tobacco leaves on the ground, poured some honey, and spit some rum. Chewing on a shared kola nut they started singing, almost in a whisper, asking for permission to enter those grounds:

Àwa dágò l'ójú Ewé, àwa dágò l'ójú ẹmọ̀ òògùn,,
àwa dágò l'ójú Ewé, àwa dágò l'ójú ìmọ̀ òògùn..

On behalf of our eyes, we ask Your permission, Herb,
we ask permission for our eyes to look into Yours
to see and take shelter in all Your wisdom.

The younger woman offered her arm to the older one. They had arrived in good time, well before sunrise, and they walked into the woods slowly and carefully, as if they didn't yet wish to awaken that world. The boots of the policemen echoing in unison behind them made the older one stop and look back. With her gaze, she froze them for a moment before they turned back and walked away.

"When I was a child," the older one began in a low, slow voice, "we didn't have so much concrete, we didn't have so many walls. When my grandmother was a child, she didn't keep the Orishas in rooms, framed by walls; this is where she would come to be with them. And as she greeted them, her forehead would touch the warmth of the earth. I don't know, child. I see diseases today that didn't exist before, and people know less and less about these herbs. Everything that exists on this earth—everything that sprouts from this bundle of coiled energy, looking at us from inside out even when we cannot see them, eyeing us the way they do—everything here was given to us with a purpose. The loss of knowledge about the world we dwell in is what creates the imbalance. So, what we are dealing with is not the disease of one individual, not the physical or spiritual imbalance of one body, not something one individual brought on himself or a part of his journey in this world. It is much more complicated than that—and much deeper, child. Much deeper."

The younger woman stopped and picked a small leaf from the ground. She licked it and stuck it to her forehead as if parading a third eye, as if showing the winning card in her hand, as if saying, "It's better than it seems, here she is, *ètípónlá*, right on our path." And she sang in a smile: "*ètípónlá àwa fi pà burúrú, à fi pà burúrú*." Etiponla: the herb that pushes away all that is evil. The eyes of the older woman brightened as she continued: "So, as you walk in this world of the living and see what you see, and hear what you hear, beyond this *àiyé* there is an *òrun*, the source of the reflections of everything you may feel over here. Everything is connected, like each grain of corn tied to its husk by a string. Now, the umbilical cord for each *Ará àiyé* to each *Ará òrun* is an *Ewé*. Without these herbs the connection between us, the living, and them, our ancestors, is lost."

"*Kò sí Ewé, kò sí Òrìṣà*" said the younger one.

"*Béè ni, ọmọ òde. Béè ni*. Each herb offers a map that directs us to one ancestral family. Their wind, their strength, is all around us. Before receiving, we need to attract. Before attracting, we need to have clarity. To have clarity, we need to listen to this silence and understand it. Everything has a counterpart in this world, *omo ode*. You, child of the hunter, child of the King of Ketu, you are part of him, as he is part of you. *Alékèsí* is one of the leaves that allows you to exist inside each other. It is the one that allows us to be with him, and him with us. For these shores of Salvador to remain at arm's reach from Dahomey, for your feet to remain on this *àiyé* and your head launched to the mysteries of the *òrùn*, *Alékèsí* must sprout from the earth without the help of men. Agriculture feeds the body, the touchable flesh—that's Òkò's wisdom. But no man can plant the road to his own belly. Only the wind, the rain, the kindness of Olódùmarè. The herb is what creates the paths that lead us to the *òrùn*. As this highway expands, potential paths are shattered; spirits yet to come already shipwrecked; unimaginable diseases, like curses, weakening and destroying strong men and women."

The younger woman turned her face from the path toward the first arrows of light shooting up on the horizon. She looked for a soothing word, an answer, an affirmation of alternatives—an *affir*-nation. She chose to remain quiet, to look into the eye of the hurricane, breathe it in, give it time.

In the sky a small *òpèrè* took flight, direct as an arrow.

Òpèrè Òsanyìn ni í ṣ'ibú,
Kùkúrú ìdè àkàkà.

Osányin's little bird makes its nest deep in the forest,
a small ring rippling wider and wider.
Greetings to the tiny one who crosses endless distances.

Imagining the Past, Remembering the Future

Introduction

Entering Other Forests

How have the cultures of ancient civilizations of the African continent—those that crossed the Atlantic—transformed themselves over the centuries in the Americas? Which elements of their millenary archives are visible and acknowledged in the Western Hemisphere? When archives are visible, can they be given the same respect granted to those of Roman and Greek civilizations?

Aspects of the artistic and philosophical practices of these African civilizations have shaped life in Brazil, Cuba, and the United States. But what is known today, in the twenty-first century, in the Americas, about the Yoruba pantheon of Nigeria and the Republic of Benin; the cosmologies of the Bakongo of the Republic of the Congo and Angola; the canon of oral traditions of the Fon and Ewe of Benin and Togo; or the musical corpus of the Baka of Cameroon, Gabon, and the Central African Republic?

When recently asked in an interview how I describe my research to people outside my field, I explained how it often feels like trying to discuss a poem with an interlocutor who might not be sure which languages are spoken in Europe, or whether Europe is a country, or whether Sicilians and Calabrese consider themselves Italians—or what, exactly, a flute, an iambic pentameter, a pipe, a family, a soprano, a god, a week, or an umbrella even are. Where does one start? At times, in class, I ask my students to imagine a reverse hypothetical in which the enslaved would have been Europeans barred from bringing their bibles, masterpieces, or foundational artifacts to the African continent. How would these enslaved European cultures have persevered?

It was during my first years of living in the United States that I became intrigued by how African Americans and Caribbean Americans imagined

Brazil. I sensed that Brazil seemed to exist as a secular myth, a name to be uttered with a certain reverence. I realized Brazil had become an icon protected by fictitious, yet believed, concepts: an illusory metonymy for the Creole Americas. And, as with all icons, it had a basis in elements of truth. Under the guidance of Barbadian poet and historian Kamau Brathwaite, I started to develop my main area of research: African Brazil.[1] The fact that we, living in countries established and dominated by Western philosophies and cosmologies, remain so illiterate in aspects of life on the African continent has often led us to refer to Africa or sub-Saharan Africa as a uniform whole. Scholarship that overlooks the legacy of African civilizations—their sociopolitical organization, histories, cultures, arts, technologies, and philosophies—in the formation of the Americas, despite good intentions, cooperates in this all-too-common impoverishing exercise. Without an understanding of the structural racism that informs such scholarly practice, we remain stuck in a vicious cycle. This type of oversimplification reflects a tendency to connect the African diaspora to a Pan-American/European universe rather than a Pan-African one. It continues to produce historical and political views in which Africans are perceived as half-agents or nonagents of their own history, acting and reacting exclusively according to what was (is) happening in Europe and North America. Historical studies that follow this propensity tend to portray Africans as ancient creatures, extraterrestrials perhaps, who drifted toward the shores of the New World and suffer from irreversible historical amnesia.

In an interview on the Black Atlantic, Robert Farris Thompson, preeminent scholar of African art history, commented with indignation: "How dare people patronize Africa?" He went on: "Those people stand like giants in teaching us how to live. There is a moral voice imbedded in the Afro-Atlantic aesthetic that the West can't grasp. They don't see the monuments, just barefoot philosophy coming from village elders. But the monument is a grand reconciling art form that tries to morally reconstruct a person without humiliating him."[2] "Barefoot philosophy," a concept that recalls the term "subjugated knowledges" employed by Foucault in a different context, refers to low-ranked knowledges "disqualified as inadequate to their task or insufficiently elaborated: naïve knowledges, located down on the hierarchy, beneath the required level of cognition or scientificity."[3]

Imagining the Past and Remembering the Future: Forms of Knowledge in the Afro-Brazilian Diaspora is written from the standpoint of someone who has been researching and teaching African-Brazilian literature and culture for years and who recognizes the need for studies that address historiographic changes and offer frameworks informed by nonhegemonic scholarship. *Imagining the Past* responds to the Malawian historian Paul Zeleza's call to recognize Brazil's centrality in the history and culture of African diasporas in the Americas. Writing about the dominance of African American scholarship in the study of global African diasporas, Zeleza warns that Brazil's African diaspora—the largest in the Americas, and in the world—"is often lost in the clamor of exceptionalisms, of America's Anglo-Saxon multiculturalism and Brazil's Lusotropical 'racial democracy.'"[4] With an awareness of the emblematic historical and social role Brazil has played in the African diaspora, and of its intrinsic place in racial debates and the history of the Americas, this book engages sacred and secular African diasporic expressions in the literature, performance, visual arts, and philosophy of Brazil to remake, root and branch, current debates and scholarship.

RE-MEMBERING THE FUTURE

Imagining the Past and Remembering the Future works in concert with the aims of the United Nations International Decade for People of African Descent (2015–2024), which seeks new perspectives and broader lines of inquiry for African diaspora studies. Expressing concern that contemporary forms of racism are regaining political, moral, and even legal recognition, the UN declaration urges research and educational projects that redress Africa's seminal contribution to humanity and—paying particular attention to the thoughts and actions of the victims of the transatlantic slave trade in their quest for freedom and justice—build upon the efforts of the Slave Route Project of the United Nations Educational Scientific and Cultural Organization (UNESCO).[5] In a moment marked by the rise of authoritarianism, deepening social disparities, the denial of science, misogyny, and racism, the saving grace is the potential for reevaluating and repositioning ourselves. Studies informed by hemispheric intersections of artistic processes and literacies that redefine individuals, retell histories, and connect communities across the Americas and continents present themselves as political projects with the potential of healing, liberation, and enchantment.

Previously, the United Nations' 1978 Declaration on Race and Racial Prejudice placed on instructors the responsibility of ensuring that curricula and textbooks include ethical considerations concerning humankind, and it called on specialists in the natural and social sciences, as well as in cultural studies, to undertake "objective research on a wide interdisciplinary basis."[6] Nothing in the hegemonic study of civilizations, as we know it, has encouraged humankind to understand itself as a community of equally contributing peers in a worldwide historical trajectory. In recent decades, we have witnessed significant revisions and developments in the humanities as a result of the implementation of affirmative action policies. Yet the understanding of an African diasporic corpus—and the reevaluation of the Euro-American corpus—remain incipient projects.

Imagining the Past is, first and foremost, a project aimed at revisiting the past, reenchanting the present, and shedding new light on the future. Through an exploration of oral historical archives, it analyzes how iconic Afro-Brazilian historical realms and protagonists, in an interconnected diasporic network spanning thousands of miles and centuries, are remembered, told, poeticized, sung, danced, prayed to, and evoked in stories, chants, and performances. The poetic features of orally performed texts can inform not only *what* is remembered but also *how* history is re-membered. These evocations of the past, as the performance scholar Joseph Roach has pointed out, "suggest alternatives for the future."[7]

"Remembering the future" is both reference and homage to Toni Morrison's (1931–2019) legacy and her conceptualization of "rememory" as a fictional practice of recollecting and reassembling members of families, bodies, and pasts. In the novel *Beloved* (1987), Morrison reimagines histories silenced in the official historical record. Re-membering the fractures, transcending supposedly absent and haunted spaces and beings, rebuilding the past in the present, Morrison proposes the challenges of a reconstructive historiography. In her words: "If my work is to confront a reality unlike that received reality of the West, it must centralize and animate information discredited by the West—discredited not because it is not true or useful or even of some racial value, but because it is information held by discredited people, information dismissed as 'lore' or 'gossip' or 'magic' or 'sentiment.'"[8]

In a similar operation, the cultural historian Saidiya Hartman, responding to imagining the past within the limitations of the official archive, elaborates the concept of critical fabulation.[9] Hartman proposes redressing history through reconstruction—by means of a speculative narration of what could have been. At the crossroads of past and future, she probes the seemingly inevitable and impossible past and amplifies the chances for liberation contained within this fictional-historical exercise. *Imagining the Past* is an invitation to continuously revisit, re-memorize, and recognize what we were once unable to; to claim the inheritance of different processes of knowing; and to reassemble the present as the coming wave crashes down, diluting our certainties and transforming mirrored pasts.

Pondering whether we are forever consigned to repeat the same restricted stories, Hartman recently commented on the need for our liberation from the confinement imposed by the violence and power that produced these deficient official archives.[10] In the context of growing and increasingly strong antiracist social movements, Hartman identifies both the need and the urgency for new and different structures.

BLINDING PARADIGMS AND THE CANON

If you are intellectuals and artists who belong to a subordinated group, you are necessarily going to be educated in the scholarly paradigms of the group who dominate you.

Sylvia Wynter

Through case studies of sacred and secular performances, *Imagining the Past* examines concepts and practices of Afro-Brazilian cultural expressions and how these expressions sustain and renew an ever-evolving corpus of African diasporic history, arts, and philosophies. It focuses on spaces and beings, kingdoms and heroes, philosophers and historians, integral members of a nonhegemonic canon. Informed by the archives and transformative processes of oral literature—ritual iconography, popular music, festivals—this book reveals protagonists of the Black Atlantic who have longed served as an orienting compass, a repository of memory and imagination, for members of the diasporic epistemic universe of Afro-Brazil and beyond. As detailed in the chapter descriptions, the book analyzes diverse forms of cultural production, including: the evocation of Aruanda in "dictated" Spiritist novels and parades of Black royal courts; the construction of heroic genealogies and cultural lineages by Carnaval performing groups; and sacred concepts of space and time expressed in oracular literature, music, and performance.

One of the central claims of *Imagining the Past* is that in order to conceptualize the great African diasporic archive, we must recognize a different historical dynamic—one that leads us to multiple spheres of convergences. Such recognition only becomes possible through the weaving of paradigms that delineate the inclusive epistemological hermeneutics Africans brought to and developed in the Americas. Following the Barbadian historian Kamau Brathwaite, my claim is that as multidisciplinary scholars we need to "undertake an investment in the veracity of our oral traditions," enlisting these in the reconstruction of a "broken legacy."[11] In this historical reconstruction one must, according to Brathwaite, above all, "listen to and learn from the history of his people," because in doing so, history "becomes not an account or analysis of events only; but something nearer, more urgent, part of the blood and dream."[12]

RE-LEARNING THE WORLD

In an essay on the role of image, image making, and image control in Caribbean societies, M. NourbeSe Philip, a literary critic and poet from Trinidad and Tobago, points out the potential intrinsic power of all artists: "If allowed free expression, [they] succeed in altering the way a society perceives and, eventually, its collective consciousness."[13] The imagination that informs literature—its concepts and processes—has attracted me ever since I enrolled as a graduate student in a New York University Comparative Literature course entitled "Topics of Imagination." The name of the instructor was unknown to me—Kamau Brathwaite—yet through my studies and interaction with this poet and historian from Barbados I began to forge tools to gain access to personal archives that had been forbidden to me. I embarked on an academic and personal journey in search of new literacies and new knowledge—especially about the construction of time and space in African-Brazilian philosophy. My research was ultimately triggered by questions such as: How were enslaved Africans orienting, situating, defining themselves in the New World? How were they interpreting their unforeseen adversities? How did the *Babalawos*, *Tata Nkissi*, and other religious men and women interpret God—or the gods—amid such unprecedented conditions? How did the cosmological concepts of various African nations arrive in and transform themselves within the New World?

With Kamau Brathwaite I came to see the slave ship (*tumbeiro*) as a kind of space capsule. In his study of Afro-Jamaican popular culture, Brathwaite analyzes the decisive role played by the immanent character of African cultures transported to the Americas. According to his analysis:

> What contemporary white commentators saw was what they wanted to see (and hear), what they were trained by prejudice and education to see and hear.... To try to understand the nature and reality of the slave's religion in Jamaica (and the Caribbean/New World), we have to begin with an understanding of the nature and reality of religion in Africa, where, as Herskovits and others have

conceptualized it, *the culture focus is religious*; i.e., that African culture, like most pre-literate/oral, pre-industrial folk culture is what Europeans call theocentric: all aspects of life have religious reference and meaning; all artifacts and customs are based on or come out of religious belief, practice and symbolism; there is no real distinction between "secular" and "sacred," and the priest, who is essentially the center of the culture, is concerned with and/or is capable of more than "priestly" (sacerdotal) function, but is/can be healer/physician (physical and psychological), artist (as, among other things, dancer/choreographer), the maker/designer of symbolic cloth (*adire, adinkera*), the carver of stools, statutes and "fetishes," historian (the griot's function is a religious one), storyteller/poet, diviner/prophet, politician (the chief and *okomfo* (priest) are always closely associated, often indistinguishable), warrior, philosopher, etc.[14]

It was the power of cultures sustained in cultural archives invisible to the European world that allowed agents involved in this long process to maintain the power of their civilizations' legacies. As Brathwaite explains:

The significant feature of this African (religious) culture was that it was (is) *immanent*: carried within the individual/community, not (as in Europe) existentially externalized in buildings, monuments, books, "the artifacts of civilization;" so that in a sense, African societies *did* appear to European observers "to have no culture," because there is no externally visible signs of "civilization." That dance was African architecture, that history was not printed but recited, contemporary Prospero could not understand. And yet it was the immanent nature of this culture which made it amazing and successful ("miraculous") transfer from Africa to the New World/Caribbean, even under the extraordinary conditions of slave trade/slavery, possible.

The slave ship became a kind of psycho-physical space capsule, carrying intact the carriers of the kind of invisible/atomic culture I have described; so that every African on those ships had within him/herself the potential of reconstruction; every mortal individual African (now slave), blessed with religious gift, carried within himself the potential of explosion: the ability to use, starting with nothing more than his nakedness and breath, a whole wide range of remarkable resources.[15]

In order to begin envisioning African diasporic literary archives, we must undergo a process of re-education (or de-education). We must be able to recognize a millenary artistic repertoire that colonial and contemporary Prosperos have never been able to acknowledge.

In a text dedicated to Kamau Brathwaite (among others), Charles Daniel Dawson, a scholar of African diasporic philosophies, creates the image of "treasure in the terror" to describe what I refer to as a literary and cultural archive. Regarding the "extensive arsenal" mentioned by Brathwaite, Dawson explains:

> Africans brought with them to the Americas their most important possessions, their minds. Those minds were and are essential in the formation of the world we now inhabit. Those minds, functioning under the terror of slavery and continued oppression, also contained the treasure of African (i.e., Yoruba, Kongo, Mande, etc.) art, philosophy and spirituality. This treasure, although often unacknowledged, misattributed or seen as only popular culture without specific historical or cultural connection to an African root, has become the vibrant enlivener of world culture. As we shall see, much of the planet thinks, prays, plays, dances and sings using the models created, established and disseminated by Africans and the African Diaspora.[16]

This rich legacy has never gone unclaimed. That the African-Brazilian archive remains largely invisibilized and unacknowledged by the canon does not translate into its nonexistence. If nothing else, as Edimilson de Almeida Pereira—Brazilian prolific writer and specialist in AfricanBrazilian oral literature—points out, this characteristic allowed it to blossom according to its own volition.[17] The potential for reconstruction that Brathwaite refers to manifested itself in continuous developments, creations, and re-creations of artistic (as well as philosophic, medicinal, culinary, and cultural) expressions.

Learning to see what has been made invisible is part of confronting what Dawson elucidates as "a continuous generational amnesia regarding Africans and their place in American societies."[18] Using a concept elaborated with Robert Farris Thompson in lectures and conversations, Dawson aptly describes our condition:

> Much of the scholarship concerning Africans in the Americas has functioned under the myopia of the "Deficit Model," a term frequently used by Robert Farris Thompson to explain the tendency of scholars to view African cultural contributions as nonexistent, or at best, deficient. The Deficit Model presumes that because of their lack of material goods and deprived social conditions under the yoke of chattel slavery, Africans were unable to contribute in any significant way, other than their labor, to the formation of the cultures in the Americas.[19]

To access African diasporic textualities—written, verbal, and visual—one must develop an understanding deep enough to grasp the prolific amplitude and ingenuity of what shapes and informs the expressions of this nonhegemonic canon. *Imagining the Past* focuses on the formation of Afro-Brazilian philosophies from the perspective of iconic historical realms and protagonists, and on how these are remembered and modernized as part of the ever-evolving corpus of a diasporic network spanning thousands of miles and centuries.

Afro-Brazilian identities are forged at the crossroads of codes and symbolic systems that confront and weave into each other. As Leda Maria Martins, a leading scholar of Afro-Brazilian performance, analyzed in *Afrografias da memória* (*Afrographies of Memory*), we are dealing with an "identity that can be thought of as a fabric and a texture in which the mnemonic gestures and speech of African oral archives, in the dynamic process of interacting with one another, continuously transform and update each other in newly differentiated rituals of language and expression, choreographing the singularity of Black alterities."[20]

TWO HALVES OF A CALABASH
CRUDELY STITCHED TOGETHER

Imagining the Past and Remembering the Future is divided into two major parts—related, though not mutually dependent. The first covers aspects and imagery associated with the processes of **Euro-*Afro*-Brazilian** national and cultural formation. "Euro-Afro-Brazil" refers to the official cultural configuration of Brazil as a nation that has drawn extensively on African mythological, musical, performative, medical, scientific, philosophical, and religious frameworks. The second part of the book focuses on the **Afro-(*Euro*)-Brazilian** dimension of this civilization formation. "Afro-(*Euro*)-Brazil" refers to the African-Brazilian civilization that has incorporated and re-created European arts and sciences while maintaining a predominant Pan-African configuration. The use of parentheses for "Euro" is deliberate. It emphasizes the enduring and predominant role of Pan-African articulations that predate the European era of maritime expansion, as well as the limited role played by Europeans and their culture in these co-creations—despite the imposition, in the past and its aftermath in the present, of widely intelligible Eurocentric cultural concepts and languages that shape the lives of most.

The backbone of Euro-Brazil is Afro-Brazilian. It does not stand on its own. It can only exist as Euro-Afro-Brazil. Afro-Brazil supports itself with its own vertebrae. Its relation to Euro-Brazil, by force or by choice, is mostly extraneous. Afro-Brazil responds to Euro-Brazil by selecting aspects and constructions that may appear worthy, relevant, or pragmatically necessary. Because Afro-Brazilian philosophies address and reinterpret national Euro-Afro discourse and ideologies, the official hegemonic archive is presented first and probed through snapshots of its own disciplinary frameworks. Once this contextualization is established, other, more relevant and less familiar paradigms can take center stage. Euro and Afro configurations now stand on equal footing, each with its respective mythologies and narratives. One is as exotic and primitive—and as scientific and modern—as the other.

Part 1 of the book—"The Euro-Afro-Brazilian Archive"—is subtitled "Those We Have Been Trained to See (Featuring Caravels, Oxen, Giants, Curses, a Bonfire, and a Trial)." Part 2—"The Kongo-Angola-Yoruba-Ewe-Brazilian Archive"—bears the subtitle "Those Which Were Never Unheard or Unseen (Featuring Ngomas, Nzimbus, Gungas, Bambas, Milonga, and Orikis)." While the chapters in part 1 are organized according to areas of study informed by Western disciplinary fields, the chapters in part 2 follow Yoruba-Kongo-Brazilian philosophical concepts.

The objects, beings, symbols, and concepts alluded to in the subtitle of part 1 are emblematic of the Western world and widely comprehensible. Conversely, the references in the subtitle of part 2 are largely unknown to those informed by Eurocentric epistemologies. It is only when basic references—such as some of the concepts alluded to in the subtitle, and geo-historical landmarks such as Mbanza Kongo and Pungo-a-Ndongo—attain the same level of recognition as Lisbon and London that we will start to envision an Afro-Euro-Hemispheric world characterized by some degree of equity.

ANCESTRAL TEXTS

The opposite of life is not death, but disenchantment.
Luiz Antonio Simas and Luiz Rufino

The Afro-Brazilian trailblazing philosophers Lélia Gonzalez (1935–1994) and Beatriz Nascimento (1942–1995) situated Brazil within the expansive, transnational network of the Black Atlantic. Their work—which gained increased visibility in the United States in the 2020s—transcended frameworks that typically divide hemispheres and center on the Anglophone Black Atlantic.[21] Gonzalez, in particular, redefined identity markers: by reversing "Afro" and "American" and proposing the term "Amefrican" instead of "Afro-American," she emphasized

African centrality in a culture shaped by connections across the Americas.[22] For Gonzalez, the Americas serve as "an ethnogeographic reference system," described as "both our creation and that of our ancestors, inspired by African models."[23] Her hemispheric vision of Amefricanity challenges fragmented perspectives and surpasses Western epistemological boundaries, highlighting African diasporic commonalities and solidarities as a unifying force within the Black radical imagination. As Bryce Henson elucidates, Gonzalez's concept of *amefricanidade* reorients core identity and belonging, ritualizing Black meanings and behaviors within a transnational context.[24]

Following a Pan-African orientation as envisioned by Lélia Gonzalez and Beatriz Nascimento, and building on the conceptualization of the Black Atlantic as envisioned by Robert Farris Thompson, as well as by William Bascom and Melville Herskovits, *Imagining the Past and Remembering the Future* broaches the Portuguese colonization of Brazil and the former African kingdoms of Central and West Africa through careful readings of various artistic and historical narratives as they unfolded on both sides of the Atlantic in continuous intercultural processes and influxes. Investing in "the veracity" of African diasporic oral traditions, this book attempts to leap over apparent discontinuities.[25] Indebted to Farris Thompson, Kamau Brathwaite, and Joseph Roach, *Imagining the Past* is a testament to the belief that performances tend to reveal what texts may conceal and can revise "the yet unwritten epic" of the fabulous cocreation of circum-Atlantic cultures.[26] *Imagining the Past* proposes an exercise in seeing the past, a poetics of memory, through different angles. It offers a history not guided by statistics but, as the Nigerian historian Elizabeth Isichei writes, "concealed in legend, symbol, and ritual"—a history as it was perceived and is remembered.[27]

Oral literatures, or orature, imbued with historic and cosmological references and associations, reflect specific knowledge-creating processes.[28] In either their sacred or secular renditions, oral literatures carry alternative worldviews that both challenge hegemonic, exclusionary values and redefine identities and priorities. Afro-diasporic literatures are rooted in oral literature. The same can be—and has been—said of all literatures, for that matter. Epic poems such as the eighth-century *Beowulf* have been perceived as literary landmarks of the particular traditions they came to represent and, supposedly, inaugurate. Such early writings stand as quasi-divinized literary ancestors. T. S. Eliot and Joseph Roach, through different perspectives, elaborated on the construction of the English canon as a Western ancestral ritual.[29] The canon formation, according to Roach, "serves the function that 'ancestor worship' once did" and the English classics "help control the dead to serve the interests of the living."[30] One of the questions this book raises pertains to a quest for roots: which texts might we perceive as the original ancestors of Afro-Brazilian literature? If the cantos of *The Lusiads* (1572) of Camões became the Portuguese epic of a nation defined by its ultramarine visions and anguishes, and the letter to King Manuel I composed by the embedded reporter Pero Vaz de Caminha (1500) became the birth certificate of Brazil as a Portuguese colony, which texts might we now contemplate as the ground zero of Afro-Brazilian literary traditions?

Oral literatures reflect on and magnify beings and realms through specific creative processes of supposedly unavailable registers. The fabulations explored in this book serve as poetic, political, and historical cores of cultural resistance for African diasporic subjects—and for all those who can envision how official fictions might be restructured to reflect the multifaceted truths of intrinsically intersecting histories. In recent decades, movements to recognize and make recognizable) heroes of the African diaspora (understood and praised as heroes by the people) have been gaining force. Following Kamau Brathwaite's understanding of heroes as symbols of transformations devised on human and national terms, *Imagining the Past* proposes an alternative approach to dealing with the challenge of comprehending and recognizing the heroes of the African diaspora.

Besides the scarcity of formal written official archives during the slavery period, one must consider the specific contradictions of multidimensional heroes living in Afro-diasporic contexts. To overcome Western prejudices and lack of skill and preparation to access the true achievements of these heroes, one must achieve literacy to access the unwritten and apparently invisible historical archive and canon of oral textualities. In his study of Afro-Jamaican Maroon heroes Nanny and Sam Sharpe, Brathwaite remarks that heroes before the abolition of slavery in Jamaica (1834) and elsewhere remain suspect, since "in terms of the written tradition of which we are part, the history of slavery could not contribute in any significant way to our sense of worth or nationhood; and, in any case, any heroes from within this period could be little more than myth or legend since there could be no worth-while verifiable historical record of them."[31] Heroes are not only participants in a struggle for freedom anchored in a particular moment of history but also an expression of "an entire moment of history; so that though anchored in a specific period, he or she illuminates the meaning of the whole, establishing correspondence with each step and stage of the past, and linking these through his or her individual achievement with our sense of nationhood."[32]

In the groundbreaking study *Cities of the Dead: Circum-Atlantic Performance*, Joseph Roach approaches performance as practice that invents, creates, and restores genealogies and history. Roach introduces the concept of studying the performative archive of oral literature as a field of "kinesthetic imagination" of evoked absent times, places, actions, and characters that are transmitted and transformed as shared practices.[33] Such a historical archive, often referred to as erased or forgotten, remains very much alive and protean. As Brathwaite reminds us: "There could be no 'forget' since there was 'nothing' to forget. The gods therefore do not 'survive.' They wait they listen they remain as ancient and as modern as the morning star."[34]

In *Afro-Caribbean Poetry and Ritual*, Paul Griffith identifies in the oral culture of the Caribbean "a grammar of mythic forms" and the structures of a "mythic geography concerning psychocultural processes in the region."[35] As he delineates a theory for Caribbean imaginary archetypes, Griffith elaborates on concepts such as "psychospiritual speculation" and "imaginative architecture."[36] Influenced mostly by the semantic conventions of Brathwaite's "tidalectics"—the cyclical restorative vision of time and events as tides—and Antonio Benítez-Rojo's repeated rhythmic identity and syncretic interparticipation, Griffith reaffirms the importance of myth and symbol as a mode of imaginative conceptualization.[37] According to Griffith, history is thus "reimagined or redeemed in visionary frameworks of sacred reference."[37] The psychospiritual speculation and mythic intentionality incorporated into Afro-Caribbean culture suggest "primary interests in action and thought as means through which human beings define their understanding of themselves and seek to illuminate the world in which they live."[39] Like Griffith, the historical mythic consciousness and the propelling forces and media for the reenactments of these ethnopoetics are central to the main thesis of this book.

AN EXTENDED FAMILY TREE

Fact is simply fiction endorsed with state power to maintain a fidelity to a certain set of archival limits. Are we going to be consigned forever to tell the same kinds of stories?

Saidiya Hartman

Drawing from secular and sacred archives, *Imagining the Past and Remembering the Future* analyzes the interconnected diasporic network of Afro-Brazilian historical embodied references. In an imagination exercise to chart and visualize diasporic family trees, one can observe the intersection of roots and branches in multilayered processes of exchange and communication. The metaphor of trees for extended family histories gains special depth and beauty in light of recent scientific discoveries. Technology can now map images of the subterranean collaborative network of trees, which allows us to better understand the functioning of global ecosystems. This underground cartography reveals fungi as the agents for transactions in the "Wood Wide Web."[40] Emitting a mass of rootlike structures, fungi—acting as messengers like the Greek Hermes or the Yoruba Elegba—branch out, spanning thousands of miles in and beneath the soil.

Imagining the Past, as a product of its time, builds on the historiographic turn that has resituated Diasporic studies since the end of the twentieth century. A possible historiographic landmark could be the scholarship developed by Ira Berlin, a historian who worked with the complexity of African American history according to different times, geographies, and economic states. In the early 1980s, Berlin argued that time and space formed "the usual boundaries of historical inquiry," and that "the last generation of slavery studies in the United States has largely ignored these critical dimensions but has, instead, been preoccupied with defining slavery, especially as compared with racial bondage elsewhere in the Americas."[41] Commenting on existing studies, Berlin observes that despite advances in representing the sociohistorical conditions of slavery, these accounts remain limited, offering "a static and singular vision of a dynamic and complex society."[42]

A decade later, Caribbean anthropologist David Scott proposed a line of inquiry that transcended the anthropological "sustained preoccupation with the corroboration or verification of authentic pasts."[43] Proposing a "theoretical relocation" of the analysis of the "complex discursive field we may usefully call 'tradition,'" he ponders that this field of discourse "resides not in anthropologically authenticated traces, but in its being constructed around a distinctive group of tropes or figures, which together perform quite specific kinds of rhetorical labor."[44] The questions that guide Scott's model of analysis include:

> What are the varying ways in which Africa and slavery are employed by New World peoples of African descent in the narrative construction of relations among pasts, presents, and futures?... What is the rhetorical or, if you like, ideological, work that they are made to perform in the varied instances and occasions in which they are brought into play?.... What space do Africa and slavery occupy in the political economy of local discourse? To what kinds of authority do they make their appeal? From what kinds of audience do they seek their support? What are the conditions—discursive and nondiscursive—of reception that facilitate their persuasiveness?.... How are the figures of Africa and Slavery employed in the fashioning of specific virtues, in the cultivation of specific dispositions, specific modes

of address, specific styles—of dress, of speech, of song, of the body's movements; how, in other words, do these figures participate in those techniques by means of which the construction of appropriate bodies and selves are effected?[45]

By the early twenty-first century, Africanist historian John Thornton presented an "inclusive, multicentric, and multiregional" approach to the study of the Atlantic world and the cultural heritage and collective memory created from the encounters of Europe, Africa, and the Americas.[46] Arguing that the traditional approach to Western civilization is often unilaterally anchored in Europe, he proposed a comparative approach that recentered Africa and the Americas as protagonists of a more representative Atlantic history. *Imagining the Past* follows the path opened by these historiographic revisions as well as a long trajectory of publications informed by quite different ideologies, disciplines, eras, and regions.

Janheinz Jahn's *Muntu* (1961) was one of the first studies to provide an overview of African and Pan-African philosophies warranting the recentering of Africa as a protagonist in the history of the Atlantic world. Informed by Rwandan philosopher Alexis Kagame, Jahn delineates four Bantu categories or forces that served him as axes, namely: *Muntu*, beings (living, dead, deified); *Kintu*, forces and materials that may be perceived by the senses; *Hantu*, space and time; and *Kuntu*, modalities of experiencing and expressing. Grounding himself mostly within Bantu, Dogon, and Yoruba knowledge, Jahn explores these epistemological forces through the study of Pan-African arts, music, dance, literatures, religions, and philosophies. The structure and philosophical orientation of *Imagining the Past* are highly indebted to Jahn's *Muntu*.

Farris Thompson's masterpiece on the study of Black Atlantic civilization, *Flash of the Spirit* (1983), following the path charted by Melville Herskovits in 1941, was another game-changing publication in the field of African diasporic philosophy. Practicing what he referred to as "guerrilla scholarship" (a combination of anthropology, sociology, and ethnomusicology), Thompson explored the originating philosophies of the Yoruba, Kongo, Fon, Mande, and Ejagham, and portrayed how interlocking expressions of these civilizations kept on flourishing in the United States, Cuba, Haiti, Trinidad, Mexico, and Brazil.[47] It is with *Flash of the Spirit* that his concept of the Black Atlantic gained wider currency. Ten years later, Paul Gilroy would adopt the term—without much acknowledgement—and, despite celebrated contributions, shift and restrict the magnitude of Thompson's original perspective. *Imagining the Past* follows the conceptualization of Thompson's Black Atlantic. My "guerrilla scholarship" follows different strategies informed by a poetic/historic background in comparative literature and a mode of inquiry that makes use of history, anthropology, sociology, and ethnomusicology as fictional narratives that reflect moving perspectives informed by times, beliefs, and various subjectivities.

After the lines of inquiry opened by Farris Thompson, Joseph Roach's *Cities of the Dead* (1996), though anchored on the cities of London and New Orleans, further conceptualized the "geohistorical matrix of the circum-Atlantic world" or the "insufficiently acknowledged cocreations of an oceanic interculture."[48] Roach incorporated the "postdisciplinary agenda" of performance studies to explore how Black performances are complex evolving archives of the unwritten past that can organize present identities and reimagine the future.[49] Building on Roach's model and method for reading performances on both sides of the Atlantic, *Imagining the Past* focuses on encounters triggered mostly by the expansion of the Portuguese Empire and is driven more by the search for a spiritual and philosophical (rather than historic) epistemology.

Two other publications closely related to *Imagining the Past* are Paul Griffith's *Afro-Caribbean Poetry and Ritual* (2010) and Mary Lorena Kenny's *Deeply Rooted in the Present: Heritage, Memory, and Identity in Brazilian Quilombos* (2018). Griffith, Barbadian scholar of philosophy and literature, analyzes archetypal patterns of Caribbean oral traditions and their role as imagination sources, along with their conceptualization and cultural and artistic expressions. Kenny, through an anthropology of heritage and memory, explores the Maroon (*Quilombo*) movement that has, since colonial times, dealt with politics of race and land. The works of Griffith and Kenny, leading to connections beyond the Caribbean and Brazil, explore how archives of oral literature illuminate present literary and political movements.

Imagining the Past follows parallel and at times intersecting routes. Focusing on the cocreations that have taken place in the Southern Hemisphere, it reflects on the content and trajectory of philosophical denominators. It examines the poetics (broadly construed) of the development of Afro-Brazilian history, arts, and philosophy through axes established along routes connecting Central and West Africa to Brazil and the Americas. Embracing a long repertoire composed of diverse textualities, *Imagining the Past* investigates this epistemological circuit in its continuous transformative dynamics, from contemporary African diasporic digital circuits of communication, moving back to previous exchanges that took place during the period of voluntary mass migrations and further back to the period of the transatlantic slave trade, as well as the return of formerly enslaved Africans to the African continent.

Imagining the Past is an intervention that seeks to study transcontinental African artistic traditions according to their own languages, structures, and values; to build on the reconceptualization of African diasporic religions as philosophical, historical, and literary constructions; to shed light on largely unacknowledged African diasporic artistic sources, processes, histories, and philosophies; to provide different angles of thought and perception for activists, scholars, and artists; and to contribute with the reframing of African Diaspora studies by opening up further paths of inquiry and action.

CHAPTER OUTLINES

Part 1 of this volume—"The Euro-Afro-Brazilian Archive—European Civilization in Brazil: Brazilian Cosmology: Kingdoms and Heroes We Were Trained to See"—is divided into six segments or chapters, each titled according to areas of study informed by Western disciplinary fields: Visual Art Images, History, Literature, Poetics, Social Sciences, and Law. These units structure the preliminary contextual argument and serve as textual compartments focusing on representations and elaborations of the Brazilian national imagery, as well as the place of European (and African) cosmologies and disciplinary perspectives within it. The brevity of chapters 1 through 4 is connected to the Eurocentric context of the first part, which, unlike the second part, will be familiar to most readers. Because of the familiarity, they dispense with much contextualization and focus on the specific images and narratives essential to this study. Part 2—"The Kongo-Angola-Yoruba-Ewe-Brazilian Archive: African Civilizations in Brazil: Pan-African Cosmologies: Kingdoms and Heroes Never Unheard or Unseen"—is divided into four chapters, which include the "Final Considerations." These are titled according to four key interrelated Yoruba-Kongo-Brazilian philosophical concepts: Mundiongo, Aruanda, Ìtàn, and Dikenga, which embody ancestral languages, geographies, genealogies, and time, respectively.

In part 1 of the book, I "entangle" the taken-for-granted *legible* foundations of the Euro-Brazilian nation. I trace these formulations from the birth of Brazilian historiography in the nineteenth century to the twenty-first-century legal challenge to official narratives, as enacted by the 2015 Truth Commission on Black Slavery in Brazil. Before addressing African and Afro-Brazilian historical icons, heroes, and their secular and sacred geographies and genealogies, I examine the Portuguese and Eurocentric development of the icons and metaphors that underpin Brazil's national identity. My goal is to place the fabulation of images and that of histories on equal footing—as if sitting across from each other at a bar. Euro and Afro configurations, each with its respective mythologies and narratives, one as exotic and primitive as well as scientific and modern as the other. Because African-Brazilian philosophies address and reinterpret national Eurocentric discourse and ideologies, I first presented the fabulations of the hegemonic archive, probing it through the lens of its own disciplines. Once this contextual foundation was established, other, more relevant, yet less familiar paradigms could take center stage.

The introduction you are now reading—"Other Forests"—is intended as a roadmap for a journey into a largely unfamiliar forest. The epigraph or road opener introduces metaphorical key images that tell us the "other forest" has a name; that it exists on the map of an urban center; that its distance from the center merely entails a bus ride and some steps away from paved roads. This other forest was and remains sacred. In other words, this academic and scientific center was and remains prestigious and respected. This center of knowledge has been misunderstood, violated, taken over by brutality, cynicism, greed, death, and destruction. And yet, it has not been destroyed; it stands. It is bordered by the highway and patrolled by military forces. As you approach, the first sound you hear is that of machine guns being loaded. To enter the forest, you must pass the sentry box, acknowledge the presence of its guardians, and walk past them, away from their power and gaze. Part 1 of this book is, symbolically, the first half of the narrative of the epigraph. After crossing it, we can enter the other forests of part 2. We begin by situating the trajectory of Afro-Brazilian arts and philosophies within their transcontinental Pan-African, American, and European orbits, and by outlining a rationale for developing an epistemological model to study African (re)conceptualizations of nations, heroes, and meanings, before walking toward—and through—an initial Euro-Afro-Brazilian archive.

Chapter 1—"Visual Art Images: 'I See . . . I Narrate. But What Is It That I Am Seeing?'"—opens with the image of a chief of the Suruí Nation pulling back his bowstring, with the arrowhead hovering inches away from the face of Brazil's Federal Senate President. Representing a coalition of Indigenous nations and challenging the celebratory climate surrounding the 500th anniversary of the Portuguese arrival in Brazil, Henrique Iabaday demanded the approval of the Statute of Indigenous Societies, which had been pending in Congress for nine years. In parallel with the grand festivities organized by the Brazilian government, an alliance of Indigenous, Black, and Landless Workers movements convened to resist the artificial commemorations and present their manifesto. The military police were summoned, and a solemn request for pardon by the Catholic Church was denied. This chapter examines two canonical paintings from the end of the nineteenth century that depict a hegemonic vision of the birth of Brazil and its society. The brief analysis highlights marginalized figures and seemingly minor details in these works, and begins delineating characters—such as ox drivers—who will emerge as protagonists. These canonical images—part of a corpus currently being resignified by contemporary Black and Indigenous Brazilian artists—offer visual elaborations of a historical past and a projected future that haunt the present and call for intervention.

Chapter 2—"History: A Gold Medal for the Best Story"—introduces the historical narratives that inform the visual narratives of the first chapter. It moves back in time to Brazil's gradual independence from Portugal and the founding of the Brazilian Geographical and Historical Institute under the Brazilian Empire, tasked with creating a national narrative, a glorious shared past, and an envisioned national future. In 1842, a Bavarian botanist won a contest promoted by the institute for a treatise that laid the foundation for how the historical narrative of Brazil should be told. Unlike other nations that achieved independence in that era, Brazil was to be imagined as an inheritor of Portuguese civilization with a commitment to carry forward the objectives set forth by Portuguese colonization. This commitment was, to a certain extent, fulfilled. If Brazil is officially deemed an heir, what foundation myths did it inherit?

Chapter 3—"Literature: Heroes, Monsters, Giants, and the Canon"—investigates the Portuguese cosmological model and imagery inherited by Brazil. The foundation of Brazil's official collective identity was built upon literary and historical narratives that function as a mythical genesis, celebrating the present, glorifying the past, and articulating a sense of purpose for the future. This chapter is subdivided into six sections that explore the Portuguese foundation myth from an epic ancestral text—Camões's 1572 *The Lusiads*—to its reinterpretation in a Eurocentric Brazilian genesis. Like Shakespeare's *The Tempest*, the narrative of *The Lusiads* centers on the European classical binary of hero-colonizer and colonized-monster: namely, the dyads of Vasco da Gama–Adamastor and Prospero–Caliban. These texts depict an explorer and a castaway, respectively, endowed with magical powers as the protagonists and narrative owners of their foundational texts.

Following his expedition around the Cape of Good Hope and along the Eastern African coast, including encounters with Khoisan and other peoples in Mozambique, Kenya, and Tanzania, Camões's fictionalized Vasco da Gama acquires an enchanted fetish and becomes further empowered. A sea goddess, destined to bear a son more formidable than his father, hands da Gama the "World-Machine" ("a grande máquina do Mundo"). Departing from Greco-Roman mythologies and European tales of monsters in uncharted lands, Camões, we see, came to shape Adamastor—the titan who would transform Portuguese explorers into heroes as they encountered and conquered the Luso-African monster.

While Adamastor is the mythical guardian of the Cape, Caliban is the heir to the island belonging to his mother. They share similarities as victims of territorial violations; yet unlike Caliban, who is an heir by birthright, Adamastor—a former sea captain—was transformed into the Cape as divine punishment. Emblematic of a nation that would later elaborate a Lusotropical exceptionalism, Adamastor embodies aspects of both Prospero, who commands the ocean, and Caliban.

The images crafted by Camões and Shakespeare resonate in the shaping of the Brazilian nation. Prospero's unrelinquished farewell to Caliban's realm echoes in the historical memory of two Portuguese kings who left Brazil and returned to Portugal during the transitional era of Brazilian independence. Amid prophecies and curses, and images of future and present enchantments rooted in past or present injustices and resentments, Euro-Brazil would draw inspiration from the mythos of its progenitor nation.

Adamastor and Caliban are also intrinsically connected to rocks: the former turned into a seaside cliff, the latter kept captive "in this hard rock" where Prospero "styed" him.[50] A Brazilian iconic titan would later be refashioned to represent not a nemesis but a symbol of self-identity or reflection. Through various Brazilian visual and poetic elaborations, this character assumed a central place in the Brazilian national anthem, appearing as a beautiful and strong giant—a fearless colossus whose future is mirrored in its own greatness. National anthems, like the mythical Janus, possess a twofold character, gazing simultaneously into the past and the future.[51] In Luso-Brazilian cosmology, Adamastor is reacclimatized and reshaped through Brazilian poetic texts introduced in chapter 4.

Chapter 4—"Poetics: Two Giants and Two Prophecies"—picks up from chapter 1 the topic of visual canonical national representations from the end of the nineteenth century; from chapter 2, the foundational role of the Geographical and Historical Institute in shaping national narratives and the canon; and from chapter 3, Portuguese literary cosmology with its gods, monsters, and rock giants—and their tales of an extraordinary past, present curses, and future prophecies. After the 1842 contest that selected the winning historical narrative for Brazil, another contest, in 1922, nominated the official lyrics for the national anthem. From then on, the image of a peaceful and fearless giant symbolizing the Brazilian nation would become as powerfully emblematic as that of the green and yellow national flag. The elaboration of the Brazilian heroic giant evolves through mid-nineteenth century poetic texts that sought to represent and reflect on Brazilian geography, sociology, and ideologies marking the transition from the era of slavery.

While the lyrics of the national anthem include and acknowledge a poem by Gonçalves Dias entitled "Song of Exile" ("Canção de exílio"), they also refer to two lesser-known poems of his: "The Stone Giant" ("Gigante de pedra") and the prose poem "Meditation" ("Meditação"). Januário da Cunha Barbosa, another member of the Geographical and Historical Institute, explores Adamastor even more directly in his related poem "Niteroi or the Metamorphosis of Rio de Janeiro" ("Niterói: metamorfose do Rio de Janeiro"). Cunha Barbosa's anthropomorphization of Rio de Janeiro's iconic Guanabara Bay dramatizes the curses involved in the vengeance of the Brazilian titan Niteroi for the murder of his father by Mars, as well as Glaucus's prophecies of Brazil's future glories. The protagonists of both Dias and Cunha Barbosa are giants who were struck down by lightning and have since remained in perpetual slumber. This image reemerges in Dias's prose poem "Meditation," where not a giant but a king lies in perpetual slumber amid chaos and a despotic takeover. Dias's prose poem presents the Portuguese legacy of chattel slavery as a Brazilian curse. A fourth poem in this chapter, Bento Teixeira's "Prosopopoeia" ("Prospopéia"), from an earlier period, employs the anthropomorphism of nature like some of its successors. It also emulates Camões's classic text, employing hegemonic devices to protest the status quo and to prophesy. Teixeira, through the prophecies of Proteus, glorifies Pernambuco as a safe haven for persecuted converted Jews and prophesies the rise of a new kingdom for warriors of justice and hard-won peace.

These four foundational Brazilian texts, blending Greco-Roman mythology and Luso-European forms of expression, were composed by three poets, two of whom were born in Brazil but not considered *reinóis* (i.e., "born in the kingdom," or Portuguese). Of these poets, one was a mestizo and the other had left Portugal as a boy with his family, fleeing the Inquisition. Under the auspices and constraints of the Portuguese monarchy and subsequent Luso-Brazilian empire, all three poets created representations of the past, present, and projected future of an emerging nation. Their lyrics echo the goals and premises established by the Geographical and Historical Institute and reflect on the present through metaphysical and political readings of the past, offering forecasts of glory or doom. Subtly altered European stylistic devices serve as tools to forge cosmologies and the character of a nation that would be celebrated across time through the collective singing of the national anthem. The presence of Indigenous, African, and Jewish peoples and cultures appear in the undertones of these constructions. Like the paintings explored in chapter 1, they embody a central concoction: a stone giant as the protagonist of a nation, an entity ranging from fear-striking and monstrous to glorious, peaceful, or sedated, yet extraordinary.

Within Eurocentric lore, other disciplinary fields gradually built upon the 1842 imperial institute's winning narrative and, unlike their poetic counterparts, claimed to address Africans and their descendants directly. Although social science narratives significantly affected the lives of African descendants in Brazil, their primary focus was not Africans but rather European descendants confronting a context that challenged their European ideologies and standards of modernity and civilization and threatened their place within the eccentric realm that determined their citizenship.

Chapter 5—"Social Sciences: Three Founding Moments of Euro-Afro-Brazilian Studies (Separating the Wheat from the Chaff)"—traces the timeline of an official narrative that has evolved since before Brazil's independence. Recalling the image of the Indigenous chief holding an arrow to the face of the Senate president that opens chapter 1, chapter 5 begins with an account crafted not by the chief's or the president's ancestors, but by a foreign observer—a visitor reporting on the fauna, flora, curiosities, and opportunities of a realm yet to be explored. This chapter is divided into three sections, each delineating a distinct period and some of its defining characteristics. The timeline of these narratives reveals paradigm shifts within recurring motifs of national ideologies. They encompass the study—insights, oversights, and rationale—of Africans and Africanities, the compilation of records and archives, and the manipulation and eventual legal confrontation of their hegemonic composite.

The subtitle "Separating the Wheat from the Chaff" emphasizes the high value of elements within these archives for the re-membering of African-Brazilian civilizations. It also suggests a research method akin to sorting beans or separating husks from grains. This patient approach acknowledges the significance of these archives despite the limitations of their nature and creators, while emphasizing the need to remain vigilant during their examination to avoid getting caught in obvious traps of anachronistic interpretations. The significance of these archives is *not* that, even with their deficiencies, they constitute the only historical registers available. As will be explored in part two, there are richer archives of a different nature that have never been incorporated into or acknowledged by the established canon. However, dismissing Eurocentric archives as worthless and repeating the exclusion or erasure of other alien or objectionable epistemologies would mean relinquishing power fiercely earned under unprecedented coercion and brutality.

The timeline proposed in chapter 5 starts with von Spix as a representative of colonial travelers and their travelogue legacies. It includes some of the narratives concerning the makeup of the society and its relationships as well as, to my knowledge, the oldest comprehensive description of a Congada performance—an epistemology that is central to part 2. It then discusses Brazilian researchers Sílvio Romero and Nina Rodrigues and their early insights into Brazilian literary, artistic, and protoanthropological traditions and compositions, including investigations that, to various degrees, explore Africans, African descendants, and their cultures. The third subsequent "founding moment," informed by social-psychological approaches, marks the apex of a more solid Euro-African-Brazilian worldview. Arthur Ramos brings an early psychological-ethnological reinterpretation of miscegenation as a "psychic constraint." Among other scholars of the period, Gilberto Freyre epitomized, translated, and registered an existing narrative that can be traced back to von Spix's portrayal of Brazil "as the land of broad amnesty, accompanied by a glass of *cachaça*," or Camões's Adamastor, the former European explorer transformed into the guardian of Africa. From a sociological perspective, Freyre's writings became metonymic of a larger entrepreneurial movement of ideological, political, artistic, linguistic, and literary updates taking place in the 1920s and '30s.

The final segment of chapter 5 traces back to celebrations marking the 100th anniversary of Brazilian independence, the moment when the Brazilian national anthem became official. It also revisits the production of the first two founding moments of Euro-African-Brazilian culture, which served as both inspiration and foundation for multiartistic formulations of a Brazil seeking to cut the umbilical cord with Portugal. The proclaimed liberated self-identity of this elite group was largely shaped by secondhand readings of some Indigenous—and mostly African—representations. The three foundational moments of this chapter close with a 1937 convention on Afro-Brazilian studies held in 1937 in Salvador, a rare crossroads where academic and community intellectuals met. The scholars who built on this initial era of Euro-Afro-Brazilian studies make their appearance throughout the subsequent chapters and receive a more exclusive spotlight in chapter 9, in the subsection entitled "From Dahomey-Oyo Conflicts to Jeje-Nago Collaborations."

Chapter 5 closes with reflections on how the multi-artistic formulations of the 1930s legitimized, and were legitimized by, recurring long dictatorships in the twentieth century. These regimes further appropriated elements of African-Brazilian philosophical expression—such as Capoeira, Umbanda, Samba, Candomblé, and Carnaval—to be explored in part 2. The fact that the sociological narratives of Eurocentric lore were less motivated by the study of Africans than by that of European descendants in Brazil is symbolized in one of the chapter's final images: Freyre's discomfort at the sight of African-Brazilian sailors leaving their footprints in the snow in Brooklyn. It was this sight—described as incongruent, akin to a mirage, hallucination, or nightmare—that prompted an account of the eccentric context he and those he stood with uneasily occupied: a context shaped by enduring relationships with Africa and Africans and by projected futures constrained by established frameworks.

Euro-Brazilian and Afro-Brazilian epistemologies have processed the larger contexts within which they exist and evolve in radically different manners. The transatlantic trade era inescapably influenced Afro-Brazilian epistemologies through force and coercion, compelling examinations, interpretations, incorporations, and adaptations of African, Indigenous, and European concepts. The very nature of African epistemologies already had a millenary history of integrating and transforming what is foreign, regardless of mutually societal engagements. These cultural frameworks allowed for more than survival; they enabled re-creation and regeneration despite past and ongoing naturalized violations and assaults.

The Euro-Brazilian ideologies and constructs made official in the 1930s have undergone intense scrutiny and reassessment over recent decades. As we approach 2030, disarticulation and rearticulation "from the bottom up" have become increasingly visible and effective. The final chapter of the first part of the book opens with an epigraph excerpted from a well-known song by a group that blends funk, hip-hop, rock, and reggae. Its refrain echoes the initial image of a weapon aimed at someone's face—here, the face of the oppressive peace of the privileged or the feigned peace of those living in fear.

Chapter 6—"Law: Peace Without a Voice Is Not Harmony"—focuses on the culminating achievements of social movements' articulation and demands. It begins by examining the implementation of affirmative action in Brazil at the turn of the twenty-first century and the challenge it posed to the myth of racial democracy—a challenge that encountered resistance, including from scholars now positioned as advocates for social justice. In an era empowered by new media, the growing awareness of entrenched racial disadvantage and structural racism, bolstered by manifestos urging individuals, organizations, and the public sector to take a stand against racism, has gradually produced a paradigm shift. Racism is widely recognized to be continuously evolving, and what has been referred to as "Afro-pessimism" can be better understood as Afro-realism. Yet it is through navigating this well-known minefield that policies of inclusion have effectively begun to change the makeup of academia and promote the emergence of new individual and group identities.

The other major movement explored in chapter 6 concerns the 2015 establishment of the Truth Commission on Black Slavery in Brazil, which petitioned Brazil's Supreme Court (Supremo Tribunal Federal) to address the constitutive violence of the nationalist imaginary from a legal perspective. Evidence included narratives developed since the inception of the Brazilian Historical and Geographic Institute. In ongoing studies stemming from these investigations, a group of constitutional law scholars has conducted legal analysis of the narrative surrounding the burning of slavery archives by Ruy Barbosa—a landmark in

Brazilian national historical mythology. Chapter 6 examines how these lawyers have deconstructed the received narrative of the burnt archives from multiple angles, challenging the normalization of violations against Black and Indigenous peoples' rights by questioning the significance of the past in the present.

Chapter 6 closes with a section entitled "That Which Could Never be Burnt," which serves as a transition to part 2 and shifts to perspectives that view the material presented so far from a different vantage point.

The main section of the book (chapters 7–9) revisits icons and realms explored in previous chapters but now viewed from a different perspective. Tertiary characters and antagonists become protagonists, bandits transform into heroes, and the illiterate are recognized as possessing fully dimensional practices and technologies of literacy. The unseen becomes evident and perceivable through all the senses. This challenges long-held concepts that have been inappropriately applied to non-European structures—from basic interpretations of what literacy is and does; to organizational concepts inaccurately translated as equivalents to European figureheads and concepts (such as kings and queens, or kingdoms); to relationships among beings, their ancestors, the unborn, their environment, and their perceptions of time.

Part 2—"The Kongo-Angola-Yoruba-Ewe-Brazilian Archive: African Civilizations in Brazil"—is divided into four chapters and runs parallel to part 1. It can be thought of as a wide and deep-reaching Afro-Brazilian River basin with tributaries of varying visibility and strength that intersect and collide with those of Euro-Brazil. This complex network reflects the historical interplay of different civilizations, in which ancestral and engineered water systems metaphorically represent cultural exchanges and transformations. Historically, institutions such as the Brazilian Historical and Geographic Institute have upheld European dominance and monopolized national narratives. Establishing alternative centers and perspectives, however, challenges these hegemonies and envisions different truths. But if Euro-Afro-Brazilian narratives dominate the physical spaces of libraries, universities, courts, and governmental offices, where can we uncover the Pan-African archives?

The section opens with an epigraph, a poem-chant recorded in 1976 by Maria Aparecida Martins, a singer born in Minas Gerais and raised in Rio de Janeiro, whose poetry, music, and dance performances are part of the corpus of Bakongo-Brazilian philosophical expressions. Martins's song highlights the presence of other knowledge centers, underscoring that unrecognized does not mean invisible, silent, or nonexistent. Her song, entitled "Diongo, Mundiongo," exemplifies how Afro-Brazilian cosmologies are transmitted, often eluding mainstream understanding and control. *Mundiongo*, from Kimbundu, can be explained as a Western equivalent to an assembly, an educational, religious, or legislative center. It is a center of knowledge that does not exclude pleasure, movement, music, and joy, unlike some of its Western compartmentalized versions.

Chapter 7—"Mundiongo: Ancestral Languages: Entering Other Forests"—explores instruments, languages, codes, and processes that inform learning and cultural transmission. It draws parallels between the familiar concept of the codex—with its associated images of pages, books, and libraries—and other "containers" of knowledge, such as musical instruments and dance. It begins with Afro-Brazilian traditions known as Congadas. Their "book" is expressed in numerous ways: visual narratives; symbolic oral and inscribed accounts; chants; and body performances that convey a network of social and political praxis, reinterpreting history, nations, family, and community relations. The philosophies expressed in and through Congadas are often understood as mere symbolic coronations of African kings in the Americas. Through quotes from community scholars, this chapter expands upon a dialogical understanding of Afro-Brazilian knowledge as the unfolding of social praxes. An initial excerpt from a poem by Edimilson de Almeida Pereira, an academic as well as a community scholar and philosopher, alludes to the limitations of Western languages—or, more precisely, to the limited understanding of what foreign languages are as framed by basic curriculum-based disciplines.

Chapter 7 introduces the three primary—simplified yet useful—cultural-geographic centers of African-Brazilian civilization, as defined by scholars who were introduced in chapter five: the Nago-Ketu (which encompasses present-day Benin and Nigeria, home to speakers of Yoruba); the Jeje-Mina (covering present-day Togo and Benin, inhabited by speakers of Ewe, Fon, Gun, and Mahi); and the Angola-Kongo group (consisting of Central Africans, speakers of Kikongo and Kimbundu). It further presents helpful concepts such as "African extensions" in the New World, "Neo-African cultural zones," and African "matrices" and the kinetics of "m(o)trices"—as explained by scholars such as Gerhard Kubik and Zeca Ligiéro. It is through this initial framework that the converging concept of languages and their role in elaborating philosophical concepts, establishing shared worldviews, and nurturing spiritual and artistic traditions are examined.

Some African-Brazilian sacred and secular linguistic systems are introduced, especially the languages articulated through musical instruments and performative bodies. Musical instruments serve as crucial tools for human and spiritual connection, encompassing not only the physical objects and their symbolic meanings but also those who wield them—players, singers, or dancers—who possess specialized knowledge of their technology. The music they produce constitutes narratives—ancestral vocalizations—conveyed through a coded language, demanding skill and proficiency for effective production (coding) and interpretation (decoding).

Chapter 7 investigates the royal commanding language of bells, expressed for instance in the Candomblé *adjá* or in the bitonal *agogô* and *gã*, and their legacy as instruments once part of African tonal languages. It also explores the philosophical language communicated by harps and instruments such as the *berimbau*, which trace their roots back to Central African origins. It examines the Bakongo tripod metaphor, which translates into the tripod structure of Afro-Brazilian harps and drums, such as Candomblé's *rum-rumpi-lé* drum trio and the Capoeira trio formed by the *gunga*, *berimbau médio*, and the *viola*. In Capoeira, *gungas* are the larger *berimbau* musical bows, but in Congada perfomances, *gungas* are smaller gourds or metallic rattles fastened to dancers' ankles, often filled with seeds known as Tears of Our Lady ("Lágrimas de Nossa Senhora")—the same seeds often used as rosary beads.

While the seventh chapter explores the "how," the next two chapters—dedicated to what I refer to as ancestral geographies and geologies—explore the "where" and the "who." The eighth and ninth chapters form the book's apex. They reiterate and begin to answer the question I posed at the beginning of this introduction: how would it feel to talk about a sonnet with an interlocutor who isn't sure of *where*, or even *what*, Italy is? How would you discuss the metaphors of this hypothetical sonnet with someone who doesn't know what a pipe, a God, a week, or an umbrella are? One of the Dahomean-Brazilian meanings for "umbrella" is actually explained in chapter 9, in the section entitled "Dahomean Divine and Royal Twins."

We have limited and inadequate tools at our disposal. Our understanding and interpretation of concepts such as towns, families, and wealth often differ from the perspectives of civilizations across various places and time periods. A lack of proficiency in the languages that played pivotal roles in the multiethnic and multilinguistic processes of colonization in the Americas—coupled with a tendency to prioritize European languages, structures, and disciplines—makes it easy to oversimplify and homogenize differences. When referring, for example, to English, Portuguese, Yoruba, Fon, or Kongo empires and kingdoms, it is crucial to remember that that these labels do not map neatly onto modern understandings of political organization, governance, or their complex relationships. The concept and characteristics associated with a king or emperor, for instance, do not quite capture the nuanced notions and historical significance that have evolved over centuries for a Yoruba Oba, a Fon Fia, a Kongo Mani, or a Ndongo Ngola.

Chapter 8—"Aruanda: Ancestral Geographies: A Map to Aruanda and Other Realms"—looks into the resignification of spaces and realms of Central Africa in the Afro-Brazilian collective memory. Drawing from stories, chants, and performances, it analyzes the fabulation of ancestral divinized geographies—the poetic construction of symbolic spaces in the African diaspora. It focuses on the case study of Aruanda—a reference not only to the slave port of São Paulo de Luanda, but also to a mythical ancestral Africa, a repository of divinized force and the home of deified ancestors within Brazilian-Kongo-Yoruba cosmologies. Chapter 8 also explores performances of foundation myths that continue the royal cultural traditions of Central African kingdoms; Capoeira chants, movements, and symbols; praise chants of Afro-Brazilian religions; and overlooked media such as Brazilian Spiritualist novels, said to be dictated by spirits.

The island of Luanda was once part of the largest and wealthiest of the twelve provinces that formed the Kingdom of Kongo. Luanda served as the analog of a Federal Reserve, the source of *nzimbu* spiraled shells—the most widely used form of currency in the kingdoms of the area. The center of financial stability for the kingdom was gradually destabilized by Portuguese interventions, their definitions of wealth, and their inflation of the market with counterfeit currency (importing shells from other shores). As a diasporic cosmology, Aruanda contains and is contained by the memory of the kingdoms of Angola, Kongo, and Mozambique. As memory anchors, these navigation omens are landmarks for mapping routes and layouts of the protean cartography of Afro-Brazilian history.

Through the centrality of Aruanda in Afro-Brazilian imagery, other realms and figures from colonial Brazil and Central Africa come into focus. Among these are the Angolan *Kilombos* and the Brazilian Maroon *Quilombos*—human sanctuaries that proposed alternative nations and the regeneration of the torn social fabric of families ripped apart by slavocracy—along with their leaders: Queen Nzinga Mbandi Ngola Kiluanji (c. 1582–1663), ruler of the states of Matamba and Ndongo, and Zumbi dos Palmares (c. 1655–1694), the last leader of an African republic inside colonial Brazil, Angola Janga or Quilombo dos Palmares (c. 1605–1695). Nzinga—celebrated even today in Brazil as Rainha Jinga—and Zumbi, quintessential icons of colonial resistance, open the path for the Black diasporic heroes who take center stage in this and the following chapter. Some historical figures introduced include Ndongo Prince Lourenço da Silva Mendonça (1620–1698), a political exile in Brazil; the Congada Captain João Lopes (1930–2004); and the philosopher Beatriz Nascimento (1942–1995). Iconic realms—such as Pungo-a-Ndongo, Mbanza-Kongo, and Matamba—are described with varying degrees of detail. Some narratives involve members of the royal lineage of these realms, such as Zimbo (the first Ngola, or king of the Ndongo) and Temba-Ndumba (the first chief of the Kasanje).

In preparation for a discussion of the Central African-Brazilian universe of symbolism and metaphors, this chapter historically contextualizes the states that have significantly influenced African-Brazilian civilization. Chapter 8 provides an overview of the struggles, alliances, and interplay of military, cultural, and political engagements among the Kingdom of Kongo, the state of Ndongo, the Dutch, and the Portuguese. It traces the Kingdom of Kongo from the encounter between King Nzinga-a-Nkuwu (1440–1509) and the Portuguese to the death of Mvemba-a-Nzinga Afonso I in 1543, an event that marked the beginning of the end for this unified state. It explores the shifting trajectories of dominant power—from the Kingdom of Kongo in the fifteenth century to the Mbundu state of Ndongo (or Angola) in the sixteenth century, then to the prominence of the Kingdom of Kasanje—culminating in the Scramble for Africa (1884–1914) and the European-imposed partitioning of the continent.

Without some knowledge of the history and significance of cultural practices, such as the coronation ceremonies and performances of the Kongo, it is impossible to discuss their resignification in Brazil or anywhere else. The Central-African legacy in Brazil is framed through the lens of historical realms and figures to allow for analyses of expressions such as the Congadas, their dynamic expressions of cultural memory, and the sacred and political symbolism of the choreographies of their Congo and Moçambique performers ("Guarda de Congo e Moçambique").[52] To reflect on Afro-Brazilian Aruanda, it is necessary to contemplate the intertwined narratives of geography, history, and cosmology that illustrate how places such as Pungo-a-Ndongo became epicenters of Central African cultural and spiritual memory. To think about Maroon societies in their historical structures and ideologies, one has to consider their origins. To understand the Brazilian Republic of Palmares and the significance of Zumbi and Quilombismo as an ideology, one has to go back to Nzinga's Kilombos and how she adapted a worldview and structure from her ancestor, Temba-Ndumba. What were the legal and ethical principles, the power hierarchy, the existential philosophy, and the military and architectural structures of the Kilombos and Quilombos? How was this epistemology and political structure transmitted across centuries and across the Atlantic—from Temba-Ndumba to Nzinga, to Zumbi, and to the present? How do performative expressions such as Congadas and Capoeira communicate, register, and evolve these movements?

As Jan Vansina reminds us, "migration stories should be understood as cosmologies."[53] The Bakongo cosmogram of the Dikenga is introduced in chapter 8 with a focus on migration and spatial movement. In the foundation myths of the Kongo, the perspective centers less on the concept of original spaces and more on the notion of a foundational direction or pathway between established coordinates. At the end of this chapter, through a conceptual representation of multiple narratives of contemporary Afro-Brazilian cosmological values and references, I propose a visual conceptualization of the imaginary contours of Pan-African-Brazilian configuration of foundation myths.

While the core of chapter 8 focuses on the fabulation of divinized geographies (the "where"), chapter 9—"Ìtàn: Ancestral Genealogies: Obatala Came Before Us"—is dedicated to ancestral genealogies. This is the "who": symbolic heroes and historical, mythological, and sacred figures—ancestors from family trees who were rarely protagonists in the fictions of official history. For the analysis of the fabulation process of these embodied references, one main focus is on unsuspected archetypes of Afro-Brazilian imagery—such as Mahatma Gandhi in Brazilian Carnaval—as case studies illustrating the development of a multifaceted cast of characters within diasporic historiographies.

From the kingdoms or federations of Central Africa, mainly the Kongo and Ndongo—a cultural area referred to in Brazil as Congo-Angola—chapter 9 moves to the Gulf of Guinea, focusing primarily on the empire and kingdom of Ọyọ́ and Dahomey, referred to in Brazil as Nago-Jeje (Yoruba-Fon). The Central-African-Brazilian epistemologies are less visible and understandable to those who have not lived and intentionally studied them. The epistemologies from the Gulf of Guinea, due to historical factors and more direct and intrinsic similarities to Western political and civilization configurations, became more visible in Brazil and the diaspora. When comparing the cultural expressions from these two major regions, Congo-Angola is subtle and can entirely escape untrained eyes and ears, while Nago-Jeje—though not always fully understood—has taken center stage under the spotlight of cosmopolitan centers. Some of its nonexclusivist cultural expressions feature massive 40-foot floats with celebrities, glitter, and epic tales of kings and queens, set to the beat of more than 300 percussionists who shake the ground and stir the soul, accompanied by the voices of 72,000 audience members singing along. Carnaval, in general, is an evolution of both Congo-Angola and Nago-Jeje sacred and secular parades, though some of its genres are specifically rooted in Nago-Jeje expressions. While the epistemologies of both Congo-Angola and Nago-Jeje connect the future to the past and the present, one might venture a rough generalization: Congo-Angola embodies the "Sankofa's head turned backward," looking into the past, while Nago-Jeje symbolizes the "Sankofa's feet planted forward," about to move into the future.

In these epistemological elaborations, the main geographical spiritual and resistance icons of the African-Brazilian civilization—Aruanda, Palmares, and other Quilombos—are Congo-Angola contributions. Their cultural expressions move from less to more visible: from the members-only Candombe to the Jongo, the Congada, and Capoeira. The Nago-Jeje elaborations also reference ancient states, but perhaps due to their public-engaged performances, power negotiations, and processional reconfigurations, the celebration of ancestral and contemporary heroes and celebrities acquires greater centrality. In the reading of the corpus of these two main epistemologies, we move from the Congadas of the countryside to the Carnaval of the cosmopolitan centers. Carnaval (in its various forms of expression, including the Afoxés of Bahia), serves as an artistic platform to restore, update, and reinterpret history. In chapter 9, we examine the poetic and political processes of the formation of heroes and historical figures within sacred and secular Nago-Jeje African-Brazilian civilization. As Elizabeth Isichei posits, the study of heroic embodiments of multiple-layered narratives across centuries and spaces is a challenge resembling the study of a poetic text—"their interpretation is not unlike literary criticism."[54] As previously argued, any analysis of such expressions entails some familiarization with the cultural-historical-philosophical context that informs them; in other words, one cannot interpret resignifications without knowledge of the original signification.

To approach not Aruanda but Ilé-Ifẹ̀ from an African-Brazilian vantage point, a different cultural group—one not descended from Our Lady of Rosary, as discussed in chapter 8, but from ancestors such as Obatala and Gandhi—will come to the forefront. The Children of Gandhy performers, like their counterparts in the Moçambique Children of the Rosary, are renowned for their ability to bring the sacred from afar. Mahatma Gandhi (1869–1948), the pioneer of *satyagraha*, the principle of nonviolence as a form of protest and revolution, was assassinated in New Delhi in 1948. At that time, in Salvador, a group of stevedores was drinking and chatting under a mango tree when the wind blew a newspaper page announcing Gandhi's death into their path. The following year, this group brought a Carnaval performance paying tribute to the Mahatma to the streets, inaugurating the Carnaval group "Sons of Gandhi."[55] According to Yoruba cosmological principles, every person is intrinsically connected to and descends from an Orisha god. Personality traits are understood as archetypical characteristics shared by Orishas and their human protégés. Physically as well as ideologically, Gandhi presents aspects of the sacred archetype of a Yoruba god—the oldest Orisha, King of the White Cloth, creator and coder of humankind, Obatala—and can be read as Obatala's son or human embodiment. This interpretation is enforced by the parade choreographed by this Carnaval group, which follows quasi-sacred aspects of a Brazilian-Yoruba religious processional cycle of feasts that recall the battles between Ile-Ife and the Oyo empire as well as the mythological voyage of Obatala. These festivities are centered around the same motifs as those that take place in Nigeria, such as in the Itapa festival in Ife. The development of the Brazilian "Sons of Gandhi" performing group presents multiple layers of historical and philosophical interpretation that offer an epistemological model for studying the creative processes of African diasporic manifestations as moving archives.

The history of the Carnaval group "Sons of Gandhi" reflects a long and multifaceted process of interaction and reinterpretation, shaped not only by intercontinental traditional practices and ongoing political and economic transformations but also by non-Western understandings of gender. In her analysis of the socially constructed and historically gendered corporeality that dominates Western interpretations of the social world, the Nigerian sociologist Oyèrónkẹ́ Oyěwùmí explores how physical attributes or gender markers do not always serve as the foundation for, or legitimization of, social positions.[56] According to Oyěwùmí, in Yoruba society—particularly in pre-nineteenth-century Oyo culture—it was impossible to classify individuals into social categories merely by their appearance.[57] Instead, Yoruba social classifications are non-gender-specific, relational, and dynamic: "society was conceived to be inhabited by people in relation to one another."[58] Oyěwùmí critiques Western scholarship for its tendency to prioritize "body-based categories," such as men and women, over "non-body-based categories," such as societal roles like traders, rulers, or diviner-priests.[59]

The founding Bahian "Sons of Gandhi" group was initially characterized by a standard of masculinity primarily associated with the professional identity of dockworkers. During a time when loading and unloading shipments was a particularly perilous form of manual labor, male "body-based categories" became intrinsically intertwined with societal roles. However, the archetype of the virile, brave male existed within the context of African-centered sacred and secular relational models of masculinity. Afro-Brazilian sacred models encompass the roles of men, women, gays, lesbians, and transsexuals, fostering standards for relationships among individuals and their environment. Candomblé understands masculinity as connected to spirituality, ancestry, and religious practice—elements that define masculinity primarily as a form of spiritual (not physical) resilience.

Over time and across different regions, the "Sons of Gandhi" gradually distanced themselves from the context experienced by the dockworkers who founded the group. The modernization process of port labor and the life experiences of those working in this sector further reconfigured symbolic values and patterns related to masculinity.[60] In her study of the Sons of Gandhi group in Rio de Janeiro, the anthropologist Roberta Sampaio Guimarães explores how the group responded to modernity by further incorporating and readapting the roles of women and LGBTQIA+ members into its activities amidst polarized internal tensions.⁶¹

Chapter 9 introduces interrelated icons of Afro-Brazilian ancestral genealogies and geographies that are also celebrated in Carnaval and popular music. To visualize these other protagonists, we move away from Gandhi in Bahia to Rio de Janeiro, and along the way encounter another slave-port realm: Ouidah, known to the Portuguese as São João Batista de Ajudá. To consider the resignification of the realm of Ouidah, we turn to Yoruba-Fon processes of philosophical and historiographical elaboration. Among the interconnected historical figures of this realm are King Gezó (ruler of Dahomey from 1818 to 1859); the king's mother and/or co-ruler, Queen Na Agontimé (sold as a captive); and Brazilian-born slave trader Francisco Félix de Souza (c. 1754–c. 1849), who, over a span of around thirty years, controlled all commerce that Dahomey maintained with Europe and the Americas. Through the analysis of performances that pay homage to these historical figures, chapter 9 proposes an alternative approach to addressing the challenges of recognizing the multidimensional heroes of the African diaspora.

In 2003, the Rio de Janeiro Carnaval group (*escola de samba*) Unidos da Tijuca chose as their "plot-theme" (*samba-enredo*) the performance titled: "Agudas: Those Who Carried Africa in Their Hearts and Brought Brazil Back to Heart of Africa" ("Agudás, os que levaram a África no coração, e que trouxeram para o coração da África, o Brasil"). The Agudas, known as the Brazilians in Benin, are the descendants of Brazilian-African deportees, mostly Muslim, who were arrested during the thirty-year period of urban guerrilla resistance in Salvador. As the jails overflowed with prisoners, an 1841 decree established that all freed Africans imprisoned in Bahia were to be deported.⁶² Some were sent to Porto Novo and Ouidah, others to Agué (Benin), Lagos (Nigeria), Lomé (Togo), and Accra (Ghana). Those who landed in the slave port of Ouidah—the main point of operation of the former Kingdom of Dahomey (c. 1620–1904)—had the protection of Félix de Souza, a free-born Brazilian-African who had been active in the area since around 1810 and was in charge of the harbor.⁶³ Dahomean King Gezó conferred upon this Afro-Brazilian returnee tycoon the title of Chacha, granting him the right to represent the king on the shore. During his reign, Gezó repeatedly sent expeditions to Havana and Bahia in search of Queen Na Agontimé. Two centuries later, French scholar Pierre Verger (1902–1996) traced Na Agontimé to the founding of one of the most important Afro-Brazilian Vodun religious centers, the Casa Grande das Minas, or Querebentã de Zomadônu, in São Luís do Maranhão.

Carnaval groups have continuously celebrated and reformulated the histories of Na Agontimé, Gezó, and Félix de Souza. In 2022, Belo Horizonte's samba school Grêmio Recreativo Império do Rio Belo depicted Na Agontimé in a Candomblé Jeje ceremony surrounded by Vodun gods. Rio de Janeiro's Beija-Flor samba school, in 2007, paid joint tribute to Queen Na Agontimé, Queen Nzinga, Zumbi dos Palmares, and other historical and legendary figures such as Tia Ciata (1854–1924) and the eighteenth-century icon Chico Rei. The Aguda community has been celebrated by samba schools across Brazil, including Rio de Janeiro's Unidos da Tijuca in 2003 and Beija-Flor de Nilópolis in 2001. In the latter, the homage focused on Queen Na Agontimé with the theme "The Saga of Agontimé, *Maria Mineira Naê*" ("A Saga de Agotime, *Maria Mineira Naê*")—referring to the name Agontimé received before departing from Africa (Maria), her generic geographical origin (Mina), as well as her title of spiritual mother in Fon (Naê).

Less understandable at first is the homage paid to Félix de Souza. The refrain of the 2003 Carnaval poem-praise-song-narration of Unidos da Tijuca announced: "Long live the Chacha! Long live all negritude." Félix de Souza became one of the most celebrated slave traders in the history of the African diaspora. To this day in Benin, his descendants and their community call themselves Brazilians or Agudas and are led by a Chacha, a descendant of de Souza—currently the ninth, Chacha IX Roger Moise de Souza. Félix de Souza's spirit became Dagoun, a Fon ancestral deified entity protected by a high priest titled Dah Dagoun-non.[64] In Brazil, he became the image of Afro-Brazilian royalty and a contradictory icon of negritude. During the recent commemoration of the 500th anniversary of Columbus's arrival in the Americas, the legacy of the Agudas and Félix de Souza was confronted in Benin within the context of UNESCO's Slave Route Project, ongoing debates about the memorialization of the slave trade's history, and shifting narratives surrounding victims and perpetrators.

Chapter 9 considers the relationships between the Ọ̀yọ́ Empire and Dahomey; their political capitals—Ọ̀yọ́-Ilé, Abomey, and Allada; their spiritual capitals—Ilé-Ifẹ̀ and Cana; the concepts of kingship, such as Ọ̀yọ́'s Aláàfin and the Dahomean King with the co-king "King-as-Prince"; and some of their Orisha and Vodun Gods. These include—in addition to Obatala, Oduduwa, and Eshu-Elegba—the mighty Xangô (Shango), the Aláàfin, owner of all palaces, and Mawu-Lisa, who travels with the serpent Dan Ayido Hwedo and organizes the universe. Through various perspectives, it is possible to observe aspects of centuries of transformations. The doppelgänger Dahomean governance model revived by King Gezó (r. 1818–1850) is presented as one such formulation that blended tradition with innovation, and foundation myths with political systems. This model allowed for a degree of stability and the reinforcement of community ties while adapting to the demands of statecraft in the era of transatlantic slavery. The Fon ideology of doubling extended from religious practices to military and political structures. The male-female complementarity of the Vodun creation deity Mawú-Lisà was part of the worldview that informed Gezó in the re-creation of an organizational framework that mirrored Queen Nzinga's ancestral adaptations in her revival of the Kilombos. The king-and-prince rulers Gezó-&-Gaakpé were Gezó's reinterpretation of a recognizable institution from the past, creatively modified to meet the challenges of his time, with the goal of ensuring survival and maintaining continuity.

Chapter 9 features kingdoms such as Ejigbo, Allada, and Whydah, as well as transcontinental realms such as Punjab and Pakistan. It also follows trading posts built as forts and castles along the Guinea coast between the fifteenth and sixteenth centuries, which were leased to Europeans—such as the early Elmina Castle in Ghana, the Castle of Saint Francis Xavier of Accra, the Fort Saint Sebastian of Porto Novo; and, later, in the eighteenth century, the fort of São João Baptista de Ajudá in Ouidah. Characters from Brazil and the Gulf of Guinea are brought into focus: Dahomean royal lineages such as that of Aladaxonou, and some of their kings, including Dakodonu (r. c. 1620–1645), Agaja (r. c. 1718–1740), Agonglo (r. 1789–1797), and Adandozan (r. 1797–1818); as well as the Oyo rulers they engaged with—Alaafin chiefs such as Ojigi (r. 1724–1735), Abiodun (r. 1770–1789), and Awole (r. 1789–1796). These lineages can be traced to Brazil mostly through religious-philosophical centers of knowledge—such as the Casa das Minas in Maranhão, which evolved from Benin royal worship practices known as Kevioso, Dambirá, Savaluno, and Davice—and the Axé Opô Afonjá in Salvador, which extended from, among others, the Asipà lineage of the former Oyo Empire. These Casa das Minas narratives in Maranhão are told through the life experiences and artistic expressions of contemporary figures such as singer Gilberto Gil and sculptor Mestre Didi (1917–2013). The history of the latter traces back to his great-great-grandmother Marcelina da Silva, or Obá Tossi (c. 1812–1885), and his great-great-great-grandmother or godmother, Ìyá Nàsó, or Francisca da Silva (c. 1780–1859).[65]

Grasping the complexities of African heroes of the diaspora, especially those from the Atlantic slave trade era, is inherently challenging. The ongoing negotiation of the historical memory of Na Agontimé, Francisco Félix de Souza, Nzinga, Zumbi, Obá Tossi, Iyá Nassô, and other protagonists operates through a symbolizing process that relies on mnemonic codes grouping together "unrelated materials with similar attributes."[66] Vansina elaborates on this mnemonic process, describing heroes who endure over long periods as "logical constructs."[67] Joseph Roach employs an approach similar to Isichei's in his analysis of the Indian performance at Mardi Gras in New Orleans, reminding us that metaphors such as bricolage or patchwork both capture the core of constructing collective memory and exchange and do not imply "anything haphazard."[68] The Mardi Gras performer inhabits an "ambulant architecture" possessed of its social memory, occupying and transforming the streets of New Orleans.[69] Invoking Fu-Kiau Bunseki, Roach points to the main achievements of such performed accounts: "Parades alter truth. Parades see true meaning."[70]

If Nzinga can be perceived as a contradictory heroic icon, and Gandhi as having no place in the history of Afro-Brazil, how then can we interpret the celebration of Félix de Souza? Oral archives introduce history as it was (and is) felt and interpreted. As such, they remain the richest and most vital archives for political orientation and for the historical and identity construction of Pan-African communities and traditions. *Ìtàn*—cosmological narratives involving Orishas, Voduns, and members of the royal lineage of Yoruba and Fon realms—form the core of chapter 9. The concept of *ìtàn*, which will be reviewed in the final chapter, can be broadly understood as history. It encapsulates cosmological and foundation narratives, historical accounts, mythology, and philosophical concepts, and is communicated through not only literary, musical, sacred, and performative expressions but also through visual arts and various multimodal textualities.

Nine is a number associated with Orisha Oya-Yansan. She is the Mother of Nine, due to her connection with the Egugun ancestral masqueraders; with principles of transformation and revolution; with dynamics of negotiation and the marketplace; with *eguns* and graveyards; with her knowledge of transforming into a water buffalo or embodying and launching winds, tornadoes, and hurricanes that can spread seeds, life, and ideas, as well as destroy all that was once built. Oya-Yansan is ultimately connected with the first breath we inhale and the last we exhale.[71]

While the previous chapters explored *how*, *where*, and *who*, the final considerations—"Dikenga and Opón Ifa: Ancestral Times and Technologies"—explore *when*. The chapters in part 2 explore ways of knowing through icons (languages, spaces, and beings) that serve as existential coordinates for the human odyssey of the African diaspora in Brazil. Following reflections on these coordinated systems, the closing segment turns to the fourth axis—the most elusive—addressing motion, direction, and rotation; that is, time and its applied processes and technologies.

What metaphors capture African concepts of time in the continent and its diaspora? How did these concepts travel to and transform themselves in the New World? How have they been continuously recreated? Unlike the previous chapters, which focus on more visible constructions, the closing segment examines subtler dimensions. Time is the very scaffold of African diasporic philosophies:

their inner structure, their most intimate, sacred, and protected articulation. Time is the connecting energy, the imagined distance between god(s) and human generations (past, present, and future). It is not only human timing but also tempo, beat, and rhythm; it is how we organize our life and existence; it is how we position ourselves in space and history.

To build something new, to imagine a different present and future, one must be able to remember—to return to the past and learn as we retrieve what was left behind—just as the Akan people of Ghana teach us through the figure of Sankofa, the mythical bird with feet planted forward and head turned backward. While *Imagining the Past and Remembering the Future* focuses on realms and heroes that illuminate African Brazil, it also serves as a model for research on and deep appreciation for intrinsically interconnected Black Atlantic worlds.

PART I
The Euro-Afro-Brazilian Archive

European Civilization in Brazil

Brazilian Cosmology: Kingdoms and Heroes We Were Trained to See (Featuring Caravels, Oxen, Giants, Curses, a Bonfire, and a Trial)

I
Visual Art Images

"I See ... I Narrate.
But What Is It That I Am Seeing?"

At the turn of the twenty-first century, as Brazil prepared for the official commemoration of the five hundredth anniversary of its "discovery," a notable sense of incongruity surfaced. In 2000, the Brazilian government launched a series of ceremonies and events, designed to be a feel-good patriotic festival similar to the United States Bicentennial and aimed at celebrating Brazil as a successful racial-cultural enterprise.[1] Signs of discontent emerged early on when Henrique Iabaday, chief of the Suruí Nation, breached security, took the floor of the congressional palace, drew his bow, and held an arrow inches from the Senate president's face, demanding passage of the Statute of Indigenous Societies, which had been stalled in Congress for nine years.[2] While the federal government was preparing the official celebrations, a parallel movement had been coalescing around various organized segments of society. Three thousand Indigenous representatives met at Coroa Vermelha, near Porto Seguro, for the First Indigenous Conference and issued "The Brazil We Want Is Another 500" ("O Brasil que a gente quer são outros 500"). Evoking the idiom *outros quinhentos* ("that's a whole different story") the slogan rejects the triumphalist tale of the first five centuries and calls instead for a different Brazil over the next five, grounded in Indigenous sovereignty, land rights, and shared governance. The manifesto reads:

> We arrived at the Pataxó village of Coroa Vermelha, in the municipality of Santa Cruz Cabrália, Bahia, on April 17. We fulfilled our commitment to retrace the paths of the great invasion of our territories, which has persisted for 500 years.
>
> We are more than 3,000 representatives from 140 Indigenous peoples from across the country. We traveled through lands and on paths traversing rivers,

mountains, valleys, and plains once inhabited by our ancestors. We gazed with emotion upon the regions where Indigenous peoples once thrived and built a future lasting over 40,000 years. We looked with sorrow upon regions where Indigenous peoples fell defending lands scarred by *bandeirante* fortune hunters, adventurers, prospectors, and later by roads, farms, and businessmen driven by a thirst for land, profit, and power.

We retraced this path of struggle and pain to take history back into our own hands and point again to a worthy future for all Indigenous peoples.

Here, at this conference, we analyzed Brazilian society across these 500 years of history built upon our territories. We confirmed, now more than ever, that this society—founded on invasion and the extermination of the peoples who lived here, was built on the enslavement and exploitation of Black people and marginalized communities. It is a shameful history, an unworthy history.

Therefore, we reclaim this cornerstone from our past to project it toward the future, joining forces with the Black and popular movements to build a broader alliance: The Indigenous, Black, and Popular Resistance.[3]

After articulating a list of demands—including constitutional and territorial rights, access to education and health, protection and justice against ongoing violence, historical recognition, political participation, support for infrastructure and the development of Indigenous professionals, and territorial protection—the manifesto concludes with a reflection where communal purpose and hope converge at the intersection of the present, future, and past:

> We, the Indigenous peoples of Brazil, have already traveled a long path of rebuilding our territories and communities. With this history firmly in our collective hands, we are certain that we have broken with the sad past and are confidently moving toward the future. Despite the weight of the old history ingrained in the ruling classes of this country, in its culture, its political and economic practices, and its state institutions, we have already launched our war cry and started a new story, the great story of the "Other 500."
>
> Our Indigenous struggle honors the countless heroes who have fallen in battle over five centuries. Our fight is for our children and grandchildren—to be free peoples in a free land.
>
> Coroa Vermelha, Bahia, April 21, 2000.[4]

The planned yearlong festivities included the reenactment of Cabral's arrival at Porto Seguro—the hub of the official celebrations—and the construction of a replica of the Capitânia, the caravel in which Cabral crossed the Atlantic. The plan was for it to sail from Rio de Janeiro, where it was constructed, to Bahia, where guests—including political and social elites from Portugal and Brazil, local authorities, and residents—were to celebrate its arrival with fireworks and speeches. Despite its modern engine, the vessel began taking on water, forcing an interruption of the voyage before it began to sink with the entire crew aboard. As it was towed back to its port of origin, parallel unofficial events gained momentum. Members of the Black Unified Movement (MNU), the Landless Workers' Movement (MST), and representatives of Indigenous groups gathered nearby in protest, resisting the artificial commemorations and voicing their indignation at the spectacle. The military police were summoned. They deployed tear gas, nightsticks, and rubber bullets to disperse the protesters. Reporters commented that, despite all the performances engineered by the government to celebrate what was officially styled as Brazil's discovery, the lasting images etched in collective memory would be those of hundreds of Indigenous representatives and landless workers being held by the police, and the solemn request for pardon by Catholic bishops, immediately denied by the Indigenous delegation.[5]

Fernando Henrique Cardoso, then president of Brazil, reflected on these events in a speech on April 22, 2000, before Jorge Sampaio, former president of Portugal, and other ministers and senators. Cardoso addressed his immediate audience and the wider Brazilian nation with these words:

> I came to understand what is now taught in school textbooks: that the prominent figures and extraordinary deeds of official history only told a part of the story. Beneath them flowed and continues to flow, like a vast underground river, the history of millions of anonymous men and women. The intertwined destinies of these men and women make up the living fabric of what is both the driving force and the most extraordinary product of these five hundred years: the Brazilian people.... What fascinates us and motivates us to move forward today is the living part of our historical heritage. **It is the Brazilian people, at this moment when they awaken to citizenship and discover themselves, in this fifth centenary of the Discovery of Brazil, as protagonists of history**. To celebrate a historical heritage does not mean idealizing the past. Today in Brazil, we have a keen awareness of the social wounds that are part of the legacy of these five hundred years. The expansion of the borders of what would become Brazilian territory came at the cost of the extinction of Indigenous peoples, as their representatives here in Porto Seguro remind us today.... This represents a belated reparation for this painful mark of the nation's birth. It also represents a pledge of recognition of the rights of Indigenous people as full citizens and the incalculable value of the cultural diversity they bring to our civilization.... Other voices of protest and demands are heard in this celebration. They are echoes of the slaveholding, oligarchic, and patriarchal past

that still weighs on Brazilian society today, making it one of the most unjust societies in the world.[6]

In conclusion, Cardoso emphasized his pride in Brazil's multicultural society, celebrating its capacity to assimilate foreign influences seamlessly and its enduring gift for appreciating and reinventing a wide range of styles within its unique culture.[7] In a blend of lucidity and radical contradictions, one significant image from Cardoso's presidential speech that I will revisit is that of a nation **awakening** to its citizenship.

I saved a newspaper clipping from those revealing days. It is an article by art historian Jorge Coli discussing an 1888 painting by Pedro Américo titled *Independência ou morte* (*Independence or Death*), but commonly referred to by the informal name *O grito do Ipiranga* (*The Cry of Ipiranga*). The artwork imagines a pivotal historical moment—Brazil's independence from Portugal. It depicts a previous perplexing scene where Dom Pedro I (1798–1834) has just visited his lover, the Marquise of Santos, and is en route to São Paulo with his imperial entourage. At that time, São Paulo was actively seeking to become an independent province. Faced with this challenge, Dom Pedro I appointed his wife, Princess Leopoldina, as interim head of state and Princess Regent, entrusting her with national affairs while he ventured south to address the upheavals in São Paulo. Born in Portugal in 1798, Dom Pedro I moved to Brazil in 1808 during the period when his father, Dom João VI (1767–1826), king of Portugal, and his court sought refuge in Brazil from Napoleon's invasion. Once the threat subsided, the Portuguese nobles returned to Lisbon, but Dom Pedro I—though Portuguese by birth—was raised within Brazilian plantation culture, and the idea of returning to Portugal seemed to hold little appeal for him. Dom João VI allowed Dom Pedro to remain in Brazil for a time, albeit under certain conditions; he thus was able to maintain his status as Prince despite restricted administrative powers. During Dom Pedro's absence from Rio de Janeiro, Princess Leopoldina (1797–1826) received a letter from her father-in-law, Dom João VI, outlining demands for his kingdom. The letter was the final trigger that led her to sign the Declaration of Independence and inform her husband that Brazil was now independent from Portugal. It was on the banks of the Ipiranga River that Dom Pedro received this message from his wife. Likely infused with a newfound sense of determination and passion, he is said to have exclaimed the words that would become the title of the iconic painting: *Independence or Death*. On that momentous day, September 7, 1822, Brazil declares itself—at least in theory—an independent nation.

Pedro Américo's famous representation of Brazilian independence was created in 1888: sixty-six years after the event itself, and the same year that Princess

Isabel (1846–1921) signed the concise, eighteen-word Imperial Law, known as the Golden Law, marking the abolition of slavery. Observing the painting in 2000, Jorge Coli comments:

> On the canvas, an oxcart driver gazes in astonishment at an elegant group on horseback, their gestures vibrant. The artist captures the essence well: high-society figures contrasted with oxcart drivers. The former project an image of nobility, patriotism, and power, expecting the rest of us to accept it. **We, the oxcart drivers, watch the spectacle in bewilderment.** In those days, such fervent sentiments were at least taken seriously; today, nobody believes in them. This skepticism renders the current celebration of the discoveries an empty, shameless façade.[8]

Pedro Américo's painting *Independence or Death*, which became the fabricated visual narrative of Brazil's independence, features a solitary oxcart driver. This character is isolated from the other figures, positioned at the margins of the dirt paths leading to the Ipiranga River. There is a clear absence of a collective "we" for the oxcart driver. While most figures in the painting are depicted on horseback—an inconsistency given the terrain, where donkeys would have been more typical—this lone cart driver is on foot, guiding four oxen pulling a lumber-laden cart. The brown-skinned cart driver is larger in perspective than the other figures; he is also barefoot, dressed in torn clothes and wearing a straw hat. He looks toward the central scene of the painting: Dom Pedro I, positioned at the highest point and leading an imperial entourage, brandishes his sword and proclaims independence. He remains focused on a royal guardsman and does not acknowledge the cart driver—no glance is directed back at him. This oxcart driver, carrying the extracted lumber of a country named after a tree, simultaneously symbolizes the material foundation of an empire and the exclusion of Brazilian slaves, servants, and outcasts whose labor makes the foundation. This façade, depicted in 1888 and then reinterpreted in 2000 as a continuation of the same theme of "we Brazilians," remains almost unaltered.

Jorge Coli titled his article "E la nave va" ("And the Ship Sails On"), evoking Foucault's image of the ship of the insane—the peculiar, inebriated vessel—to symbolize the Brazilian oxcart driver paradigm. In this ship, "delivered to the river of a thousand arms, the sea with its thousand roads, to that great uncertainty external to everything," the nation becomes "the passenger *par excellence*, the prisoners of the passage."[9] Federico Fellini brought to life an allegorical representation of this ship of the insane in his 1983 film by the same name.[10] The crew aboard Fellini's luxurious steam liner included European socialites, aristocrats, politicians, shipwrecked Serbians, and a rhinoceros. The film begins with the sound of a projector, signaling that someone is documenting and attempting to make sense of a history that commences as a funeral procession at sea. A journalist addresses the camera, adjusting his tie and straightening his hat to look the part, while a title card reads: "I write... I narrate. But what is it that I am narrating?"[11] Like Fellini's journalist, Pedro Américo also makes an effort to appear the part. He paints... he narrates. But what is it that he is supposed to narrate? Américo's heroic depiction of national independence fulfills its intended role and conforms to the conventions of similar portrayals of national heroic independence. It also raises questions about the incongruities between the narrator and his visual narration.

In another painting created ten years later, a similar interplay of gazes and narratives unfolds. *Ham's Redemption* (*A redenção de Cam*), painted in 1895 by Spanish artist Modesto Brocos, portrays three generations of Brazilians embodying the era's ideology of *branqueamento* (whitening). At the center of the composition sits a mother with light brown skin. The rosy-cheeked infant sitting on her lap offers a symbolic vision of a future Brazil. To the right stands the father, likely Portuguese or of Portuguese descent; he is rendered in white-gray urban tones. To the left, the grandmother, likely African or of African descent, is portrayed in rural-coded tones of green, red, and brown. She gazes upwards, as if bestowing grace—or seeking it. Pedro Américo and Modesto Brocos appear to be fully aware that despite their position at the margins of the composition (and the societies they occupy), both the oxcart driver and the grandmother play crucial roles in their painting's narrative. Excluding them from the composition was not an option. There is also an almost palpable sense that the painters cannot fathom who these characters are and what their narratives may be. Their narratives are reduced to apparent expected interjections, conveying either surprise or relief, and nothing more. Nevertheless, the painters allude to echoes of the present or the present finding meaning within its past and projected future (especially in Pedro Américo's case, where the future is known). In *Ham's Redemption*, the mother points in a direction beyond the grandmother, while the infant is entirely focused on the grandmother, who, in turn, gazes upwards, beyond the borders of the image. Similarly, the image of oxcart driver is depicted reflected on a distant horizon. At the farthest point in the painting stands his counterpart—a younger female with two baskets on the back of an ox. These paintings echo Fellini's journalist: "I paint... I narrate. But what is it that I am narrating?" The more apparently uncertain and subtle the images become, the more deeply ingrained the roots of their narratives and imaginaries were, are, and will be.

The art historian Lorraine Pinheiro Mendes analyzes the contemporary artistic movement aimed at uprooting these images. She explores the supposed irrepresentability—or the aesthetic-political refusal—to depict Black Brazilians within the history of white-Brazilian art. Mendes argues that, consistent with the logic of coloniality, the white-Brazilian art system exploits and appropriates "Black bodies, histories, lives, and futures."[12] In her discussion of the colonization of the imagination, she observes how this art produces and reproduces "an imaginary that confines Black existences to precarity."[13] Beyond becoming "a repository for the denial of self to the subject-self," the Black-Other is constructed as "manipulable and controllable, hence, malleable and classifiable":

> Its identity, history, and existence are elaborated from its relationship with the self-subject, in a logic that serves coloniality and an imaginary that treats whiteness as universal, civilized, and the holder of the world, while Blackness is constituted as its opposite in a relationship of superiority and inferiority. This imaginary affects the subjectivity of Black women in particularly cruel ways. Visual creation, criticism, and the entire institutionalized art system in Brazil historically reaffirm this imaginary in a sophisticated and dynamic way—whether through narratives that sugarcoat the barbarities of slavery, such as Debret's well-nourished enslaved figures; through narratives that present the ideal of whitening in *A redenção de Cam* (*Ham's Redemption*), an 1895 painting by Modesto Brocos, still honored today at the National Museum of Fine Arts; or through the affectionate image of a Black woman, whose name we do not know, painted in 1923 by Tarsila do Amaral.[14]

"The way out to a present-future is the stone sung in the past-present," states Mendes, evoking the Orisha Elegba's philosophical concept of time.[15] She explains that "the way out" is the *rasteira* Capoeira movement—one that, when applied collectively, can cause the (art) system to stumble and fall. Mendes investigates models of this practice within the current Black Brazilian artistic movement, which has been re-signifying official, constraining images. She focuses on the 2017 performance by artist Renata Felinto in which she buries a reproduction of Tarsila do Amaral's celebrated abstract grotesque depiction of a Black woman in an invented ritual of collective cleansing and liberation.[16] Felinto performs, she narrates, and she knows exactly what she is narrating and claiming.

2
History

A Gold Medal for the Best Story

From the cry of "Independence or death!" onwards, the Portuguese heir princes and their cohorts were in charge of creating a narrative, inventing a political unity, establishing a national identity, and shaping a socioeconomic structure for Brazil as a nation-state. Dom Pedro I would return to Europe in 1831, a decade after Brazil's independence, leaving behind his five-year-old son, Dom Pedro II (1825–1891), who would be crowned in 1841. The Portuguese heirs' approach to reinventing Brazil was not particularly innovative. Their idea was to preserve the existing colonial socioeconomic system—characterized by extensive land ownership, slave labor, and production of goods for the European market—while implementing a constitutional monarchy.

As the sociologist José Antônio Segatto and the literary critic Maria Célia Leonel point out, in the process of creating and imposing an idea of national unity, the only element of consensus among the dominant groups in different regions was the preservation of slavery and the slave trade.[1] From 1822 to 1848, resistance against the centralized authority in Rio de Janeiro erupted in various regions of the country, some of which took on a separatist character. Diverse regional identities shared limited common elements that could help maintain the territorial-political framework of the former Portuguese colony.[2] Those born in Brazil—excluding those who were part of the metropolitan administrative apparatus—would identify themselves as Mineiros, Paulistas, Pernambucanos, Bahians, or even as Americans or Portuguese. It was not until 1850 that the process of creating a centralized, monarchic national state was finalized. The historian José Murilo de Carvalho (1939–2023) noted that up to that point the country consisted of loosely connected regions, lacking the cohesion of a unified nation: "a nation had yet to be built."[3] While the crown fought to suppress regional uprisings, in 1838 Dom Pedro II supported the establishment of the Instituto Geográfico e Histórico Brasileiro (IHGB), known in English as the Brazilian Geographical and Historical Institute.

The institute was founded during the era of the Empire of Brazil (1822–1889), a period characterized by political instability and internal conflicts. As Brazil sought to establish itself as a nation, it faced the challenge of legitimizing its territorial integrity and sovereignty.[4] To forge an official national identity, Brazil needed to unify a vast territory marked by conflicting political ideologies. This endeavor involved the creation of a national narrative aimed at strengthening social cohesion through the manipulation of history and the construction of shared memories. The approach centered on promoting a specific historical consciousness aligned with contemporary scientific narratives and supported by state institutions. Aiming to position Brazil alongside established nations, within the framework of ideals of civilization and progress, the IHGB faced significant contradictions. Januário da Cunha Barbosa, its inaugural secretary, reassured its members that they could demonstrate to "cultured nations" Brazil's valuation of its homeland's glory. Their goal, as stated in the Institute's mission, was to compile historical facts and geographical information about the country and rectify errors and inaccuracies found in both national and foreign publications.[5]

In its inaugural journal publication, IHGB outlined its mission: "to collect, systematize, publish, or archive the necessary documents for the history and geography of the Empire of Brazil, and also to promote the knowledge of these two philological fields through public education, as soon as its funds allow for this expense."[6] In the context of the early consolidation of a Brazilian nation, articulating the identity of a society marked by slave labor and Indigenous populations would have been particularly challenging.[7] In an 1839 speech, Barbosa emphasized the difficulty of "gathering and organizing the elements for the history and geography of Brazil, scattered throughout its provinces, necessary for any patriot desiring to accurately write this much-desired history."[8]

In 1840, the institute launched two inaugural competitions. Contestants were invited to submit treatises providing a comprehensive narrative of Brazil's historical and literary evolution:

> For the year 1841: A gold medal worth 200,000 (Rs) to the person who writes the best memoir on the History of Brazil's peculiar Legislation during the dominion of the Motherland (*Mãe-Pátria*).

For the year 1842: A gold medal worth 200,000 (Rs) to the one who presents the most accurate plan for writing the ancient and modern History of Brazil, organized in such a way that its political, civil, ecclesiastical, and literary aspects are comprehended.[9]

In addition to the gold medal, the award included the publication of the texts: "the awarded essay will become the property of the Institute, which will have it printed and published in the collection of its Memoirs."[10] The winning essay for the 1842 award was *How the History of Brazil Should Be Written* by the Bavarian botanist Karl Friedrich Philipp von Martius (1794–1868). Von Martius's treatise laid the foundation for a historical narrative model that characterized Brazil through the interaction of three main racial groups, the influence of Portuguese ideals of civilization, the foundational establishment of Brazil's constitutional monarchy, and the belief in a prosperous and promising future.

In his essay, von Martius links the writing of Brazilian history to the monarchy's agenda of reshaping the past to support its authority. In opining that the documenting of Brazil's history should illustrate the pivotal role played by the unique physical and moral attributes of each of the three races, he envisions Brazil's providential destiny as one in which "Portuguese blood, like a mighty river, will absorb the smaller streams of the Indian and African races." According to von Martius, it was the duty of the Brazilian historian to acknowledge "the physical and moral peculiarities that distinguish the various races" that constitute Brazil as unique driving forces. And while "the energy, number, and dignity of the society of each of these races" influence the national common development, the place of "the Portuguese, as discoverer, conqueror, and master" had to be highlighted. Von Martius further argues that due to their influence, the Portuguese were the providers of "moral and physical conditions" guaranteeing Brazilian independence. In summary: according to the winning thesis on how to conceptualize Brazil, the Portuguese emerge as the most powerful and essential "driving force" behind the formation of the Brazilian nation.[11]

To counteract the prevailing anti-Lusitanian sentiments in literary circles, von Martius portrayed the maritime, commercial, and military endeavors of Portuguese colonization as artistic achievements. In his chronicling of Brazilian history, he lauded the Jesuits and emphasized the importance of highlighting the heroic deeds of the *bandeirante* colonial militias in Brazil's interior. He interpreted the expansionist mission of the *bandeirantes* as aligned with the principle of nationality, suggesting that a nation is defined not only by its current territory but also by its capacity for expansion, conquest, and unification of new territories.[12] Von Martius further distinguished between the settlers of the sixteenth century and those of the nineteenth, noting that the initial wave—including princes and nobles—arrived with the intention of enriching and fortifying the Portuguese nation. In contrast, the nineteenth-century colonists were primarily driven by the pursuit of fortune and opportunism.[13]

The foundational national myth of Brazil, as articulated by the philosopher Marilena Chauí, encompasses three interconnected concepts: the belief in a redemptive paradise, the notion of history guided by divine providence, and governance determined by the divine. This worldview first emerged in the sixteenth and seventeenth centuries and outlined three divine operations for Brazil's foundation: the work of God (nature), the word of God (history), and the will of God (the state).[14] In the nineteenth century, this foundational myth evolved further, shaping a historiographical tradition that would merge naturalistic evolutionism and positivist scientism with the empirical research methods of the German Historical School—an approach exemplified by the work of the IHGB.[15] The concept of a Brazilian nation did not develop in opposition to the former Portuguese metropole. On the contrary, the emerging Brazilian nation imagined itself as the heir to Portuguese civilization, committed to carrying forward the objectives set by Portuguese colonization.[16] In this context, the concepts of nation, state, and crown were interconnected within the historiographical discourse.

3
Literature

Heroes, Monsters, Giants, and the Canon

Nation-building processes typically involve the establishment of fundamental elements that foster national unity and identity. Such elements often include the development of an internal market; the creation of civil society; the structuring of military and law enforcement institutions; the institution of currency, taxation, and legal systems; and the adoption of a national anthem, flag, revered figures, and cultural narratives. Literary and socio-historical narratives play key roles in the formulation of a distinct national culture.[1] In Brazil's nation-building efforts, the dominant elite, supported by the imperial government, pursued an ambitious cultural policy to legitimize the newly formed nation. The foundation of Brazil's cultural identity was constructed on literary and historical narratives that celebrated its present, glorified its past, and articulated its sense of purpose for the future.

The literary critic Roberto Ventura (1957–2002) argued that during the Romantic era, the nascent stages of Brazilian literary history witnessed the creation of an abstract entity, personified in literary works, that began to represent the collective spirit or character of a national essence.[2] This entity served as a somewhat vague synonym for literary history itself, contributing to the formation of a collective Brazilian identity deeply tied to the almost mythical genesis of the nation's traditions.[3] The preeminent literary scholar Regina Zilberman has noted that this movement, integral to the nation-building efforts from the 1830s to the 1870s, viewed literature as an essential tool in structuring the nation-state. Brazil affirmed its nationhood through literature, positioning itself among the ranks of civilized and progressive territories.[4] A similar movement, which employed literature as a means to shape national consciousness, was later incorporated into state policy during Vargas's government in the 1930s, further defining the key role of narrative in Brazil's nation-defining project.

Throughout various historical periods, the definition of the nation-state and its literature has continuously evolved to address shifting concerns and objectives. As explored by Segatto and Leonel, during the Estado Novo dictatorship (1937–1945), the state—as during the Empire era—played a central role in reshaping Brazil's national identity.[5] Efforts to recover the imperial vision of the country's historical continuity were spearheaded by state institutions such as the Department of Press and Propaganda and the Historical and Artistic Heritage Service. This update involved a reevaluation of aspects of a cultural Portuguese inheritance with a particular emphasis on Catholic religiosity and the notion of racial tolerance. In this context, literature was expected to authentically reflect Brazilian reality, serving as the mirror of the nation.[6]

Acclaimed literary scholars, including Antonio Candido (1918–2017), trace the origins of Brazilian literature to the eighteenth century. Following Sílvio Romero's (1851–1914) publication of the five-volume *History of Brazilian Literature* (*História da literatura brasileira*) in 1888, Candido published *The Formation of Brazilian Literature: Decisive Moments* (*Formação da literatura brasileira: momentos decisivos*) in 1959.[7] Candido's work proposed an examination of the historical and cultural landmarks—the "decisive moments"—that shaped the emergence of Brazilian literature, from eighteenth-century Arcadism to nineteenth-century Romanticism. These periods contributed to the establishment of a "literary system" characterized by a synthesis of universalist and specific trends, a dialectical movement of continuity and rupture that played a key role in the construction of the Brazilian nation and its literary development.[8] Forty years after the publication of *Formação*, Candido revisited his thesis, emphasizing that what mattered most was not determining when Brazilian literature became distinctly Brazilian, but when it became literature in the true sense, a collection of works with a unified purpose.[9] From his perspective, this moment came in the mid-eighteenth century when a system that interconnected works, authors, and readers emerged, forming a "literary tradition."[10] In a 1966 lecture in the United States, Candido candidly remarked that the literatures of the American nations "are essentially European, continuing the investigation of soul and society which arose in the literary tradition of the mother countries."[11] He argued that Brazilian literature was fundamentally an expression of the colonizer's culture and later the Europeanized colonists, adapting European aesthetics and worldviews to the unique conditions of the Americas.

In *Formação*, Candido aimed to define Brazilian literary manifestations as a system connected by common denominators.[12] As Brazil transitioned from colonial status to a national state, there was a need to develop a literary historiography that could outline the trajectory and distinctive characteristics of its national literature. Candido examined internal aspects like language, themes, and imagery, as well as "social and psychological elements" that were historically manifested within a literary framework, in order to establish literature as "an organic aspect of civilization." This approach to a literary system was meant to establish a tradition and "the formation of literary continuity."[13] In fact, one of Candido's critics, Haroldo de Campos (1929–2003), challenged Candido's approach precisely for its linear and evolutionary methodology.[14]

The chroniclers, historians, orators, and poets from Brazil's earliest centuries were typically, as Candido pointed out, priests, lawyers, officials, soldiers, and landowners. As a result, their works closely aligned with the values of European civilization, often reinforcing imposed religion on the Indigenous populations and upholding the political norms of the monarchy. In this context, Candido argued that "even when lacking any ostensible ideological content, the practice of literature constituted a European form of mental discipline which had to be imposed upon the rustic milieu, as a form of instruction for the defense of civilization."[15] Candido's examination of early Luso-Brazilian literary production focused exclusively on works that were European or Europeanized. He critiqued the romanticized notion that Brazilian literature emerged from a confluence of Portuguese, Indigenous, and African cultural traditions. While the influences of Indigenous and African traditions were profoundly felt in folklore, their impact on written literature was indirect. These influences led to a transformation of Portuguese tastes which, in turn, influenced literary creation: "What occurred, then, was not an initial confluence to create a new literature, but rather a widening of the universe of a pre-existent literature, imported so to speak with the conquest and undergoing during the colonial period a general process of adjustment to the New World."[16]

In Candido's analysis, early Brazilian literary production is viewed as both an extension and adaptation of the existing European literary tradition. He specifically excludes African and Indigenous artistic expressions, classifying them as non-artistic and nonliterary forms with little or no significance within the official literary historiography.

EURO-BRAZILIAN COSMOLOGY: FOUNDING MYTHS OF THE KINGDOMS OF THE FATHER AND THE SON

Published in 1572, four decades before *Shakespeare's The Tempest* (1611), Luís de Camões's epic *The Lusiads* had already begun to mythologize European imperial expansion. Its title, which can be read as "the Portuguese," referring to the

Portuguese nation and its people, is a neoclassical coinage along the lines of the *Iliad* or the *Aeneid*.[17] The term "lusiads" comes from the mythical figure of Lusus, son or companion of Bacchus, and founder of ancient Lusitania. The Roman province of Lusitania, established in the first century BCE in what is now Portugal, appears in *The Lusiads* as the crown of Europe. The glorified Kingdom of Lusitania is described by Camões as the highest, most prominent region of Europe. Lusus, the courageous and virtuous shepherd, is the mythic progenitor of the Lusitanians and of a kingdom as mighty as Rome:

> And here, as if crowning Europe's
> Head, is the little kingdom of Portugal,
> Where the continent ends and the sea begins,
> And where Phoebus reclines in the ocean.
> By Heaven's will she prospered
> Against the unworthy Mauritanians,
> Driving them out; and in their hot garrison
> In Africa has not ceased to harass them.
>
> This is my blessed home, my earliest love,
> Where, if Heaven allows my safe return
> With this task at last accomplished,
> I will be content to breath my last.
> She was named Lusitania, so it's said
> From Lusus or Lysa, thought to be
> Bacchus' sons, or members of his band,
> The very first to cultivate this land.
>
> Here the shepherd was born whose very name,
> Viriatus, bears witness to his manhood,
> Whose fame none could overcome,
> Nor even Rome's power undo him.[18]

The Lusiads narrates Vasco da Gama's maritime expeditions in pursuit of a sea route to Asia spanning the late fifteenth and early sixteenth centuries. The historical backdrop of this epic includes da Gama's voyages around the Cape of Good Hope and his sojourns in Mozambique (Sofala), Kenya (Melinde/Malinde, Mombasa), Tanzania (Kilwa), Goa, and various locales in India (Cannanore, Calicut). Composed during a period marked by the Portuguese empire's decline, Camões (c. 1524–1580), a soldier with extensive experience in naval expeditions along the African coast, leverages his firsthand encounters to craft this epic that celebrates and glorifies Portuguese accomplishments.

The epic opens with an assembly of gods, an invocation to the muses of the Tagus River. Drawing on the tradition of Greek classics, the gods' alliances in *The Lusiads* are split. Venus champions the Portuguese cause, foreseeing and celebrating Portugal's future triumphs, while Bacchus, protective of his Eastern territories, views the Portuguese as rivals. Venus not only shields da Gama and his crew but also grants them a heavenly respite in a *locus amoenus* after their grueling journey. Assisted by Venus, Mars, Jupiter, and Mercury, da Gama's fleet successfully reaches Calicut in southwestern India. Bacchus, on the other hand, concerned that the Portuguese might overshadow his glory in the conquest of India, conspires against da Gama and his crew. Disguised as a Moor and supported by Neptune, he plots obstacles and shipwrecks for the Portuguese fleet.

The motif of a son who becomes mightier than his father recurs throughout *The Lusiads*, and in multiple narratives. Lusus, the mythical founder of Lusitania, is portrayed as the son of Bacchus. Bacchus, who fears being eclipsed by his progeny, attempts to thwart Lusus's rise. The main treacherous scheme orchestrated by Bacchus unfolds in the shape of Adamastor, an anthropomorphic giant symbolizing the Cape of Good Hope. Adamastor can be seen, in some respects, as a forefather to Lusus—the ancestor or forerunner of European kingdoms that were once mightier than Lusitania. Adamastor serves as a primordial force, embodying those ancient realms. Vasco da Gama, the epic's heroic figure, both reflects and is mirrored by Adamastor. In a pivotal turn of events, da Gama engages in a symbolic union with Thetis, the sea goddess once loved by Adamastor. Thetis, daughter of the sea god Nereus, was destined to give birth to a son more formidable than his father. This prophecy was realized through her union with Peleus, King of Thessaly, resulting in Achilles, a figure who epitomizes the theme of surpassing paternal legacy.

The Lusiads begins with Bacchus casting a curse upon da Gama and his crew, and it concludes with the prophecy of Thetis, foreshadowing the continuation of the Portuguese explorers' legacy through future heroic figures. Thetis's encounter with the mortal da Gama is another prophecy, foretelling the emergence of a new hero or a new era for an already mighty kingdom. The initial lines of the epic extol the remarkable feats of warriors and heroes from the age of Portuguese maritime exploration. Navigating uncharted seas that extended beyond Ceylon, with prowess exceeding human limits, these heroes reach the kingdoms of the East:

> Arms are my theme, and those matchless heroes
> Who from Portugal's far western shores
> By oceans where none had ventured

> Voyaged to Taprobana and beyond,
> Enduring hazards and assaults
> Such as drew on more than human prowess
> Among far distant peoples, to proclaim
> A New Age and win undying fame[19]

In the epic's linear sequence of events, the voyage to India is already underway, following the epic convention of *in medias res*. The literary scholar Josiah Blackmore points out that the image of ships in Camões represents the principal means through which worlds come into contact and through which knowledge of those worlds is acquired and exchanged.[20]

Bernhard Klein, a scholar of early modern literature, interprets *The Lusiads* as a narrative framing imperial ideology within a broader maritime context. He emphasizes that common seamen, often overlooked, played dual roles as both participants in Portugal's imperial ventures and as cultural mediators in sixteenth-century oceanic encounters.[21] While *The Lusiads* extols sixteenth-century advancements in maritime technology and their role in expanding global trade networks, Klein argues that the epic's true focus is on the seafarers, whose experiences symbolize the emergence of a newly globalized world. He suggests that the real heroes of the epic might not be Vasco da Gama and his nobles (*os barões assinalados*), but the anonymous crew without whom the voyage would not be possible. Like the sailors in the opening scene of Shakespeare's *The Tempest*, these mariners are indispensable, yet underrecognized, contributors to the journey's progress.[22]

PROSPERO AND OTHER KINGS WHO SAILED AWAY

As in *The Tempest*, the sea in *The Lusiads* is not only "a poetic but also a historical and social space."[23] In Shakespeare's *The Tempest*, the drama unfolds against the backdrop of thunder and lightning with a ship battling the tumultuous sea. Amidst this high tension and chaotic environment, the shipmaster summons a boatswain, instructing him to direct the mariners to take immediate action to prevent the ship from running aground.[24] *The Tempest* opens and closes with images of the seamen. After regaining his nobility title, Prospero breaks his spell over the master and the boatswain. To their amazement, they find the ship at the harbor in perfect condition, as if no wreck had occurred.

Similarly, both *The Tempest* and *The Lusiads* open with the image of ships braving the ocean. In *The Lusiads*, the caravels and their crew are portrayed as masters of the high seas, nature seemingly under their command: "They were midway on the wide ocean / Cleaving the ever-restless waves; / The billowing wind blew gently, / The sails of the ships were concave; / White spume was whipped backwards."[25] In *The Tempest*, the storm that led to the shipwreck is conjured by Prospero, the deposed Duke of Milan exiled to an island, to lure his usurpers who banished him twelve years earlier. The shipwreck draws Prospero's enemies and fellow castaways to the island. By contrast, in *The Lusiads*, a storm conjured by Bacchus presents da Gama and his crew with other existential challenges.

The resolution of *The Tempest* unfolds in the final act when Prospero's assistant, Ariel, brings the entranced royal party to the magical circle Prospero had drawn to perform a ritual that will break the spell he cast on them. Prospero regains his dukedom and commands Ariel to summon the master and the boatswain. All prepare to leave the island, except Caliban and Ariel. The play concludes with Prospero bidding farewell to the island and addressing the audience directly:

> PROSPERO: I'll deliver all,
> And promise you calm seas, auspicious gales,
> And sail so expeditious that shall catch
> Your royal fleet far off. Aside to Ariel. My Ariel, chick,
> That is thy charge. Then to the elements
> Be free, and fare thou well.—Please you, draw near.[26]

Alone on stage, Prospero delivers his final soliloquy. While asserting that he has renounced the magical arts that once allowed him to hold others in captivity, he paradoxically maintains a grip on the audience's attention as he seeks forgiveness for any possible wrongs, saying, "As you from crimes would be pardoned, / Let your indulgence set me free."[27] Prospero's royal persona—seemingly relinquishing authority over an overseas realm while, in reality, maintaining control—serves as an archetype for other monarchic figures.

Stepping away from Camões's and Shakespeare's fictional universes to the trajectory of Brazilian history, we can find echoes of Prospero's unrelinquished farewell in the historical images of two Luso-Brazilian kings during the transitional era of Brazilian independence: King João VI and Dom Pedro I. Between 1808 and 1821, as the Portuguese royal family fled the Napoleonic French invasions, Brazil emerged as the epicenter of the Portuguese Empire. In 1816, it became part of a monarchy consisting of three kingdoms under a single ruler: the United Kingdom of Portugal, Brazil, and the Algarves. In 1821, King João VI bid farewell to Brazil and returned to Portugal, leaving his son Pedro de Alcântara as the prince-regent. In 1822, Prince Pedro I declared Brazil's independence and became the nation's first emperor. As mentioned earlier, Dom Pedro I abdicated and returned to Portugal in 1831, leaving his youngest son, Dom Pedro II, as the second and final emperor of Brazil. The reign of Emperor Pedro II came to an end in 1889 when the constitutional monarchy was overthrown by Marshal Deodoro da Fonseca's military coup d'état, establishing the First Brazilian Republic.

Shakespeare and Camões belonged to a literary tradition rooted in the era of maritime expansion and exploration. The characterization of figures like Shakespeare's Prospero and Camões' Vasco da Gama relied on the contrasting portrayals of those they were not—namely, and to varying degrees, Caliban and Adamastor. These contrasting characters represent those who exist outside the European realms of power, knowledge, and established organization, and who are to be subdued, tamed, conquered, and discarded as needed.

As we shall see, the images crafted by Camões will resonate (with twists and turns) in the shaping of the Brazilian nation, especially during the reign of Emperor Pedro II. That will be a story, as once explained by the Mozambican writer and poet Mia Couto, about a child who became greater than its own father.[28]

THE RIGHTEOUS CURSES OF CALIBAN AND ADAMASTOR

In *The Tempest*, Caliban's initial appearance is marked by an invocation of nature to curse Prospero and his daughter Miranda: "As wicked dew as e'er my mother brushed / With raven's feather from unwholesome fen / Drop on you both. A southwest blow on you / And blister you all o'er." This curse serves as a defiant response to Prospero's scornful threat: "Thou poisonous slave, got by the devil himself / Upon thy wicked dam, come forth!"[29] During this interaction, Prospero hurls additional curses upon Caliban. It is after this exchange of spells that Caliban defines not only himself but also his reality, his history, and the history of the land where they all stand, as well as the dynamics of subjugation and resistance that shape their relationship:

> CALIBAN: I must eat my dinner.
> This island's mine, by Sycorax my mother,
> Which thou takest from me. When thou camest first,
> Thou strokedst me, and madest much of me; wouldst give me
> Water with berries in't; and teach me how
> To name the bigger light, and how the less,

> That burn by day and night: and then I loved thee,
> And show'd thee all the qualities o' th' isle,
> The fresh springs, brine-pits, barren place and fertile:
> Curs'd be I that did so! All the charms
> Of Sycorax, toads, beetles, bats, light on you!
> For I am all the subjects that you have,
> Which first was mine own king: and here you sty me
> In this hard rock, whiles you do keep from me
> The rest o' th' island.
>
> ...
>
> You taught me language, and my profit on't
> Is, I know how to curse. The red plague rid you
> For learning me your language!"[30]

In *The Lusiads*, as the Portuguese fleet navigated near the southernmost tip of the African continent—around the Cape of Good Hope, known for its stormy weather and rough currents—an enormous and deformed (*disforme*) creature appears in the darkened skies (5.39). Since the Portuguese had ventured further than the Greeks and Romans had ever gone, it follows that they would come across a titan unknown to ancient civilizations. Departing from existing mythologies, Camões created the titan Adamastor, who had been transformed into a massive mountain and obstructed da Gama's path to India. The encounter between da Gama's fleet and the giant Adamastor marks a pivotal moment in the narrative and challenges da Gama's authority "as a reliable seer and interpreter of the world."[31] As a mosaic of European tales concerning monsters in uncharted lands, Adamastor embodies, as argued by John Laurence Hilton, "a new paradigm of the unknown."[32]

In exploring the trajectory of the images of giants and monsters, three central aspects call my attention: their prophecies or curses, the depictions of Africa and Africans in foundational European classical texts, and the transformation of these images in early formulations of Brazil as an independent nation. The historian Natalie Lawrence summarizes the characterization of monsters as follows:

> The word "monster" derives from the Latin, *monstrare*, to demonstrate, or *monere*, to warn. The *Oxford English Dictionary* defines a "monster" as "something extraordinary, a prodigy, a marvel," and "monstrous" as "deviating from the natural order." In the early modern period, monsters were seen as deviations from "normal" nature that could reveal God's plan and nature's inner workings, or singular instances that acted as omens. Monsters could take many forms.

They were commonly hybrids with characteristics that crossed accepted natural boundaries. This involved exaggeration, proliferation, or absences of normal body parts, such as deformed births with excess limbs or multiple heads, races of one-footed sciapodes and dramatically undersized pygmies.[33]

Tracing the evolution of the concept of monsters from those documented in the Roman Empire by Pliny the Elder to those conceived during the era of European expansion, Lawrence adds:

> Pliny's *Natural History* described whole populations of deviant human forms such as dog-headed *cynocephali* or headless *blemmys*. **These Plinian races and other monsters were often placed at the shifting margins of the known world**, or *ecumene*, on maps, from medieval *mappaemundi* to early modern charts. As geographical knowledge developed with exploration and colonial activity in the early modern period, the medieval *ecumene*, previously bounded by impassable ocean and an uninhabitable "torrid zone," was rapidly expanded. **The locations of these monstrous races shifted also, retreating out of reach to the edges of maps or to the unknown centers of continents.** Monsters almost always originated *elsewhere*, either from distant places or local but inaccessible locations.[34]

Camões's titan Adamastor, "placed at the shifting margins of the known world," embodies the barriers and hazards of the unfeasible.[35] Similar to Plinian monsters situated at the borders of the familiar world, Adamastor embodies the geographic frontier, and, in his extraordinary form, represents not only a geographic boundary but also an epistemological one, marking the limits of contemporary understanding and knowledge.[36] Blackmore notes that Adamastor introduces a temporary disruption in the narrative's flow, challenging the authority and certainty that usually accompanies the story of da Gama's expedition and his "privileged position as explorer and knower of the world *além mar* (overseas)."[37] The literary critic Lawrence Lipking elaborates on this by pointing out that Adamastor symbolizes the point where conventional maps lose their relevance, where historical records blur into legend, and where the bounds of human understanding are tested.[38] This figure thus stands as a threshold between the familiar and the unknown, highlighting the transition from known realities to new possibilities of knowledge and exploration.

While in East Africa, Vasco da Gama narrates to the King of Melinde (Mombasa) the history of Portugal, starting from its origins and leading up to his present expedition and their encounter with Adamastor. He recalls how, as they approach the Cape of Good Hope at the southern tip of Africa, the aligned powers of Bacchus and Neptune obscured the sky and made the sea roar. In the sky a gigantic form appeared, huge and terrifying:

> Even as I spoke, an immense shape
> Materialized in the night air,
> Grotesque and of enormous stature,
> With heavy jowls, and an unkempt beard,
> Scowling from shrunken, hollow eyes,
> Its complexion earthy and pale,
> Its hair grizzled and matted with clay,
> Its mouth coal black, teeth yellow with decay.
>
> So towered its thick limbs, I swear
> You could believe it a second
> Colossus of Rhodes, that giant
> Of the ancient world's seven wonders.
> It spoke with a coarse, gravelly voice
> Booming from the ocean's depths;
> Our hair was on end, our flesh shuddering,
> Mine and everyone's, to hear and behold the thing.[39]

In the narrative, da Gama's account takes place after they rounded the Cape, after they conquered the geographic danger and fear the anthropomorphic Cape embodies.[40] Da Gama recounts the curses cast by Adamastor and his prophecies of forthcoming tragedies. Adamastor addresses the fleet that arrogantly attempts to break the forbidden bounds:

> It addressed us: 'O reckless people,
> Bolder than any the world has known,
> As stubborn in your countless,
> Cruel wars as in vainglorious quests;
> Because you have breached what is forbidden,
> Daring to cross such remote seas,
> Where I alone for so long have prevailed
> And no ship, large or small, has ever sailed,
>
> 'Because you have desecrated nature's
> Secrets and the mysteries of the deep,
> Where no human, however noble

> Or immortal his worth, should trespass,
> Hear from me now what retribution
> Fate prescribes for your insolence,
> Whether ocean-borne, or along the shores
> You will subjugate with your dreadful wars.[41]

Adamastor, who had not yet disclosed his name, appears as the mythical guardian of the Cape. Unlike Caliban, who inherited the island Prospero would claim, Adamastor's domain over this region was the result of a punishment. Caliban was the rightful ruler of the island—"This island's mine, by Sycorax my mother"—and accuses Prospero of imprisoning him in a restricted area of the island—"In this hard rock, whiles you do keep from me / The rest o' th' island."[42] Adamastor charges da Gama with transgressing sacred boundaries of the lands he oversees. As Klein points out, "these are serious charges in the context of early modern voyaging" and in this context, it is worth underscoring Adamastor's role as "a guardian not only of geographical but also moral boundaries."[43] It is then that da Gama interrupts the giant to ask him not "what" but "who" he is: "The fearsome creature was in full spate / Chanting our destiny when, rising / I demanded: 'Who are you, whose / Outlandish shape utterly dumbfounds me?'"[44]

From this moment on, Adamastor reluctantly begins to disclose his history of defeat and the curse that transformed him. Revealing his name diminishes his power over the explorers. He starts by stating, "I am" the secret powerful Cape, before finally disclosing his name—Adamastor—once a mortal sea captain:

> His mouth and black eyes grimaced
> Giving vent to an awesome roar,
> Then answered bitterly, with the heavy voice
> Of one who speaks compelled and not by choice:
>
> —'I am that vast, secret promontory
> You Portuguese call the Cape of Storms,
> Which neither Ptolemy, Pompey, Strabo, Pliny, nor any authors knew of.
> Here Africa ends. Here its coast
> Concludes in this, my vast inviolate
> Plateau, extending southwards to the Pole
> And, by your daring, struck to my very soul.
>
> 'I was one of those rugged Titans
> With Enceladus, Aegeon, and Briareus;

> I am called Adamastor, and we fought
> With the Shaker of Vulcan's thunderbolts.
> No, I could not hurl mountain on mountain
> But choosing to fight on the waters,
> I was Lord of the sea. Whatever tactic
> Neptune attempted, I was on his track.[45]

Adamastor's initial simple response adds a dramatic layer to the encounter. This is one of only instances in Camões's poem in which the verb "to be" (*ser*) is conjugated in the first-person singular.[46] This element highlights the mirrored relationship between the defeated captain Adamastor and da Gama. Adamastor recounts his love for the goddess Thetis, wife of Peleus. He also explains how, because of his disobedience to Neptune and his pursuit of Thetis, he was punished and transformed into the rocky cape, condemned to eternally contemplate the visible yet unattainable oceanic Thetis:

> 'My flesh was molded to hard clay;
> My bones compressed to rock;
> These limbs you see, and this trunk
> Were stretched out over the waters;
> The gods molded my great bulk
> Into this remote promontory;
> And of all tortures, the most agonizing
> Is that Thetis surrounds me, tantalizing.'
>
> So he finished, and sighing dreadfully
> Vanished suddenly from our sight;
> The black clouds dispersed and a resonant
> Moaning echoed over the sea.
> Raising my hands to the sacred chorus
> Of angels, who had long watched over us,
> I prayed to God that He should turn aside
> The evils Adamastor prophesied.[47]

The boundary between da Gama, "as the representative of an itinerant Portuguese culture," and Adamastor, the menacing African figure, blurs.[48] As examined by Blackmore, Adamastor's narrative of his unsuccessful pursuit of Thetis "functions as an imperialist parable," one woven into the fabric of *The Lusiads* portraying the captain of the sea's tale of conquest and subsequent failure.[49]

On the surface, Adamastor initially inspires fear; he casts curses and prophecies and tells his tale of imprisonment. Then, in a blink, the dark clouds melt and vanish. The explorers continue their journey, sailing past the Cape with ease and leaving behind Adamastor's rage and shipwreck predictions.

BEYOND THE EDGES OF THE MAP

According to one interpretation of the erotic symbolism of navigation, da Gama's fleet exerts dominance over Adamastor, symbolically reducing him—and, by extension, Africans—to impotence in the face of Portuguese maritime prowess.[50] Despite the successful navigation around the Cape, the scene reveals a European preoccupation with the potent African male body, perceived as a potential threat to imperial ambitions. Camões emphasizes Adamastor's formidable physique with a quasi-fetishistic intensity before addressing the giant's potential to hinder their voyage.[51] In contrast, Adamastor's curse, interpreted as an expression of African rebellion fused with natural forces, suggests an inversion.[52] Initially a potent symbol of resistance, the curse shifts focus, losing its direct confrontational impact against the Portuguese. Instead, it is absorbed into the narrative, serving Portuguese interests.[53] This co-opting of African resistance is subtly transformed within the epic, overshadowed by the portrayal of Portuguese triumphs.

In his analysis of texts spanning from the mid-fifteenth century to Camões's 1572 epic, Blackmore introduces the term "mooring" to describe the textual depiction of Africa and Africans within the context of the Portuguese expansionist mindset. He highlights that it is in the interruptions, in the pauses of the journeys accounted in these oceanic narratives, where the interactions between Africans and Europeans are elaborated.[54] Camões's characters embody and convey historical dimensions that contribute to the creation of a collective historical memory of Portugal as the head of Europe.[55] The encounter between da Gama's fleet and Adamastor marks a critical juncture where European epistemological authority is challenged. Although the Portuguese momentarily overcome Adamastor's threat through navigational technology, as analyzed by Klein, it is merely a symbolic, transient conquest over African resistance. Africans do not remain overshadowed by Adamastor; rather, they assume a prominent role in subsequent interactions along the East African coast, underscoring their pivotal contribution to the Portuguese explorers' journey.[56]

Soon after the sailors' encounter with Adamastor, the text presents yet another critical moment of encounter as da Gama's fleet approaches Mozambique. Seeing small local boats, they ask: "Who are these people?" Since exploratory navigation required not only maritime skills but also "refined ethnographic skills," the interest in—or curiosity about—the unknown Other becomes, as Klein notes, a recurring theme in *The Lusiads*.⁵⁷ From historical documentation, we know that da Gama's fleet—at least the first one—included three interpreters: two who spoke Arabic, and one who spoke different Bantu languages. In the encounter of the first chant of *The Lusiads*, the people of Mozambique introduce themselves:

> —'This insignificant island we inhabit
> Happens to have the safest harbour
> Of the whole coast, wherever waves break
> From Kilwa to Mombasa or Sofala.
> We seized it only for this, living
> Here as though we were the natives;
> So, to round off all of which you speak,
> This tiny isle is known as Mozambique.'⁵⁸

In a "feasting cheery," they reciprocate interest "in Arab language," asking who the members of the Portuguese fleet were, where they came from: "The powerful Lusitanians replied, / Conscious of the need for diplomacy: /—"We are Portuguese from the Occident; / We seek the passage to the Orient."⁵⁹

In a further encounter, Camões describes "a stranger with a black skin" (*pele preta*) captured by da Gama's crew. As noted by Klein, it is important to note that this character is not described as a "Moor" (*mouro*).⁶⁰ The captured man, a honey gatherer, was probably Khoisan (a "Bushman"); he is represented as a brutish, wild creature who speaks no intelligible language:

> At this, my companions returning,
> I saw a stranger with a black skin
> They had captured, making his sweet harvest
> Of honey from the wild bees in the forest.
>
> He looked thunderstruck, like a man
> Never placed in such an extreme;
> He could not understand us, nor we him
> Who seemed wilder than Polyphemus.
> I began by showing him pure gold
> The supreme metal of civilization,
> Then fine silverware and hot condiment:
> Nothing stirred in the brute the least excitement.⁶¹

The comparison of the honey gatherer to a Polypheme, the one-eyed giant of Greek mythology, is "an imaginative stretch," as Klein comments, "since the man is described in the sources as small in stature."[62] Camões's Polypheme can see, but when exposed to da Gama's trading goods, is not able to recognize—to "see," as it were—"the signifiers of culture and civilization."[63] The parallel between a Khoisan and a gigantic character from Greek mythology leads us back to the portrayal of Adamastor as an immense, enigmatic entity.

After meeting the Khoisan, the Portuguese fleet will find itself face-to-face with subsequent unfamiliar, unintelligible worlds. They encounter two Bantu lands on the eastern coast, one by the Inharrime River (5.69) and another by the Zambezi River (5.77). They cannot communicate with the first group but are offered food and fresh water. The group farther north speaks some Arabic, demonstrates navigational skills, and provides Da Gama with helpful information to reach India:

> In the little Arabic they could manage
> And which Fernão Martins spoke fluently,
> They said their sea was crossed and recrossed
> By ships equaling ours in size;
> They appeared from where the sun rises,
> Sailing south to where the coast bulges,
> Then back towards the sun where (as they say)
> Live people like us 'the color of the day.'[64]

Consecutive encounters with African coastal societies highlight the Portuguese dependence on their African counterparts for local information and material support. During these interactions, the Portuguese ships are restocked, trades are made, and information is shared. As the crew makes its way along the east coast, they perceive the groups they encounter as increasingly sophisticated regardless of whether their interactions are friendly or hostile. They note, for instance, that the people of Mozambique Island and Mombasa demonstrate the ability to communicate in Arabic and exhibit signs of wealth and advanced weaponry—readily identifiable to the Portuguese. As the fleet progresses toward the southern boundaries of the Indian Ocean, the societies they encounter are mostly Muslim. Despite historical tensions, there are instances of mutually deferential interactions, such as the encounter between da Gama and the Sultan of Malindi. This encounter is described in detail, depicting the two leaders and their respective entourages:

> A large and lavish dhow, with awnings
> Draped with multicolored silks,

> Conveyed the Sultan of Malindi, along
> With the nobles and lords of his kingdom;
> He came gorgeously attired,
> After their fashion and style of beauty;
> On his head was a turban finely rolled,
> Embroidered splendidly with silk and gold.⁶⁵

As documented in historical records and Camões's narrative, the Sultan of Malindi provides da Gama with an adept pilot skilled at navigating through monsoons, which enables them to successfully reach Calicut.⁶⁶ During the final stage of their journey, as they are sailing back home, the mariners arrive at the Isle of Love, a place created by Venus expressly for their pleasure. Within this paradisiacal realm, the crew is rewarded with a sumptuous feast of pleasures. During the banquet, a nymph sings prophecies about future Portuguese conquests, foretelling their glory. Nereid Thetis, the goddess loved by Adamastor, receives da Gama in a chamber adorned with crystal and gold:

> Taking his hand, she guided him
> To the summit of a holy mountain,
> The setting of a magnificent palace
> Of clear crystal and finest gold.
> There they passed the long day
> In sweet games and continuous pleasure.⁶⁷

From Bacchus's curse upon da Gama and his crew to Thetis's prophetic vision of a heroic legacy, Lusitania stands at the crossroads of curses and blessings. In Camões's epic, da Gama derives all pleasure and knowledge from Thetis, while Adamastor remains imprisoned, forever yearning for his love. Da Gama is led to a summit where Thetis unveils the "World-Machine," providing him with a detailed description of the cosmic system and the universe. At the core of Thetis's revelation lies the concept of the Earth coming together as one "united sphere" ("unida Esfera" 9.86):

> Uniform, perfect, and self-sustained
> As the very Creator who fashioned it.
> Da Gama, seeing it, stood transfixed,
> Torn between fear and eagerness.
> Then the goddess spoke: 'This sphere I set before you, represents
> The whole created world, so you may see

Where you have been, and are, and wish to be.
'This is the great machine of the universe.'⁶⁸

In the tenth concluding canto of *The Lusiads*, Camões emphasizes a concept of global connection stressing the pivotal role of mariners in all culturally significant global encounters:

'This is the hostel of humanity,
Who, too ambitious to be content
With the afflictions of solid land,
Have launched out on the restless oceans.
Look at the various regions, divided
By turbulent seas, where there are lodged
Nations and tribes with various kings and chiefs,
Contrasting customs, various beliefs.'⁶⁹

Following Thetis's prophecies and revelations, the sailors, infused with renewed determination, and da Gama, now possessing supernatural knowledge of the world, embark on their journey back to their kingdom in Europe.

Within its cosmological narrative of a heroic nation, and its assertion of identity and pride, the Portuguese crafted an unparalleled titan, unknown to Greeks and Romans, a monstrous entity awaiting conquest. In a mosaic of European mythologies set in the age of maritime exploration, the figure of Adamastor assumes a protagonist role in Camões's foundational classical work. In a similar vein, Euro-Brazil drew inspiration from the mythos of its progenitor nation, fashioning an equivalent symbol to represent its own identity or reflection. This towering image of a colossal being and its interpretations of the future (as prophecies), of the present (as curses), and of the past (as a tale of transformation) would inform the imaginative construction of Brazil as a sovereign and independent nation.

THE REBIRTH OF ADAMASTOR AS BRAZIL

Some of the most recognizable lines of the Brazilian national anthem—often considered cryptic by many—evoke the image of a giant. According to these memorable lines, Brazil is addressed as a giant by its very nature: beautiful and strong, a fearless colossus whose future is mirrored in its own greatness.⁷⁰ The grand prophecies of a victorious future are echoed in Brazil's nature and its character, that of a fearless "colossus," the same term Camões uses to describe the giant at the Cape of Good Hope. Camões depicts Adamastor as larger than the Colossus of Rhodes, one of the seven wonders of the ancient world. The Greek statue, once erected on Rhodes, celebrated a military victory and paid homage to the patron god of the island, Helios, the sun god married to Perse, an Oceanid and daughter of the Titans Tethys and Oceanus. Helios was known for his daily journeys in a chariot across the sky from east to west by day and, by night, around the ocean, the outermost boundary of the ancient Greek world. The Brazilian Colossus, in the national anthem, appears as an infant—a giant infant, eternally rocking in a splendid cradle to the sound of the sea and under the deep light of the sky.[71] The giant, perhaps a son of Tethys or of Lusus, is also the shining crown jewel of America, illuminated by the sun of the New World.[72] While *The Lusiads* exalt Portugal as "the head-crowning coronet of general Europe," which is to say, the crown jewel of all Europe, Brazil is depicted as following the Portuguese crown-bearing legacy of another continent.[73]

Once the epicenter of the Portuguese colonial enterprise, Brazil embodied the concept of a global connection, of the encounter between the various realms and monarchs that Thetis once prophesied. Luso-African-Brazilian mariners and traders converged at the triangular European-African-American proto-capitalist crossroads. The trope of the giant, deeply familiar to Brazilians, became one of the symbolic keys to an emerging idea of nationhood—an ideal or dream of a future nation. The trajectory of the giant's image can be traced back to the first two chronicles of foreign sailors who described the silhouette of a sleeping giant in the neighboring mountains upon approaching Guanabara Bay from the Atlantic. "Although these reports clearly increased after 1808, when the Portuguese court fled to Brazil," notes the classics scholar Beethoven Alvarez, "similar reports have regularly occurred since at least 1663."[74] Toward the end of the eighteenth century, the image had already gained prominence and became a literary topos among neoclassical poets. In 1816, Dom João VI invited the French painter Jean-Baptiste Debret (1768–1848) to join the French Artistic Mission (Missão Artística Francesa) to Brazil. Debret published three illustrated volumes titled *Picturesque and Historical Voyage to Brazil* (*Voyage pittoresque et historique au Brésil, ou séjour d'un artiste français au Brésil*). In the second volume, Debret includes an illustration with the caption "The Reclining Giant" ("Le géant couché") and reports that this is how the sailors referred to the Guanabara Bay.[75]

As put forth by the English scholar Igor Cusack, national anthems or hymns are songs of praise not to God, but to nations, which are often treated as some kind of lesser god.[76] These anthems serve as crucial instruments of national indoctrination, articulating specific national narratives.[77] Singing one's anthem aloud in a group powerfully reinforces the sense of distinction among those who identify with a supposedly unique nation, differentiated from all others.[78] The chorus of the Brazilian national anthem is a clear example of this operation. Brazil is praised as the "adored land" who "amongst a thousand others" is the one and only "beloved homeland."[79] Anthems project distinct images of nations, often portraying them as divinely favored, uniquely situated, abundant in resources, and the homeland of heroic ancestors. These songs typically extol the virtues of an already established nation—its land, geography, and imagined past. Emerging nations are compelled to craft a shared historical narrative that encompasses both a collective memory and a vision for their future.[80] Following the work of the political scientist Benedict Anderson (1936–2015), if nation-states are to be regarded as a concept of modernity, if they are to be imagined as new, the realms they represent will, regardless, "loom out of an immemorial past" and "glide into a limitless future."[81] Cusack contends that national anthems possess this twofold character, much like the mythical Janus who gazes simultaneously back to the past and into the future. They instill in people a quasi-religious faith in the nation's glorious evolution, encompassing the present generation, their heirs, and generations yet to come.[82]

In Brazil, the establishment of a shared glorious history and the projection of an envisioned national future became an official undertaking during Emperor Pedro II's reign. Unlike his father and grandfather who—like Prospero—bid farewell to a received land, Pedro II founded a significant institution in Brazil. This institute united a select elite responsible for shaping the narratives of Brazil's past, present, and future, as well as determining the epistemologies and cosmologies that would be officially sanctioned. This deliberate crafting of national identity is also reflected in the evolution of the Brazilian National Anthem, which underwent over a century of lyrical adjustments, mirroring the shifting currents of nationalist political ideologies.

A PRAISE SONG FOR BRAZIL

From the year of Brazil's quasi-independence in 1822 until Emperor Pedro I's abdication in 1831, Brazil had a national Independence Anthem, composed by Pedro I himself. In 1831, on the very day Pedro I left for Portugal, a new anthem composed by Francisco Manuel da Silva with lyrics by Ovídio Saraiva was introduced. It was styled after early Romantic Italian opera.[83] The hymn, played as a farewell song, commemorated the abdication of Pedro I and the accession of

Pedro II to the throne. Manuel da Silva's music continued to be played as the Brazilian National Anthem in public ceremonies, but Ovídio Saraiva's lyrics were omitted.[84] In 1841, when Pedro II turned sixteen, new lyrics for the anthem were proposed for his coronation ceremony. The new lyrics were not well received, and an official decree was passed that the national anthem should be played without its lyrics.[85]

Curiously, during the era of the Brazilian Empire, the U.S. composer Louis Moreau Gottschalk (1829–1869)—originally from New Orleans but residing in Rio de Janeiro—composed two musical adaptations of the Brazilian National Anthem. This occurred toward the end of the Paraguayan War (1864–1870), also known as the War of the Triple Alliance, one of the deadliest in South American history, which had devastating consequences for Paraguay. For Brazil, the war marked a paradigm shift somewhat akin to the transformative impact of the Civil War in the United States. Gottschalk's celebratory compositions—variations on the Brazilian National Anthem—were the "Brazilian Solemn March" ("Marcha solene brasileira")—dedicated to Emperor Pedro II,—and the "Great Triumphal Fantasy on the Brazilian National Anthem" ("Grande fantasia triunfal sobre o hino nacional brasileiro")—dedicated to Pedro II's successor, Princess Isabel.[86] In 1985, during Brazil's process of democratization following the military dictatorship (1964–1985), Gottschalk's "Great Triumphal Fantasy" resurfaced and was performed at the funeral of President-elect Tancredo Neves.

In the early days of the new Federal Republic of Brazil, while the National Anthem continued without official lyrics, several versions were proposed and even adopted by different Brazilian states. The historian Avelino Romero Simões Pereira notes that, driven by the ideological aims of the republican regime, there was a concerted effort to reshape Brazil's political narrative to match the patriotic aspirations of early republican intellectuals.[87] The first contest for new lyrics was launched in 1889, following the deposition of Pedro II and the proclamation of the United States of Brazil. The eventual winner was Leopoldo Miguez, who composed what became known as the "Anthem of Brazil's Proclamation of the Republic."[88] The absence of uniform, official lyrics persisted until the centennial celebrations of Brazil's independence in 1922. At that time, an adapted version of the lyrics by poet Joaquim Osório Duque Estrada's—first proposed in 1909— was officially adopted.[89] The musical arrangement by Alberto Nepomuceno for Duque Estrada's lyrics was formally recognized in 1971, when national symbols were codified by a legal statute following the 1967 Constitution, a document that also curtailed freedom of speech and stifled political dissent.

From 1822 to 1971, the Brazilian National Anthem underwent a continuous process of revision and adaptation, reflecting the shifting "limitless glide" of political regimes and nationalistic ideologies. Fast forward two centuries to 2022: a video featuring supporters of former far-right president Jair Bolsonaro went viral. During a protest against the electoral victory of President Luiz Inácio Lula da Silva's, Bolsonaro's supporters were captured on video singing the national anthem with their right arms outstretched in a gesture disturbingly reminiscent of the Nazi salute.

Throughout these changing adaptations and performances, Duque Estrada's lyrics and the imagery of the Brazilian national anthem gradually solidified. Over the course of the nineteenth century, both national and foreign poets and intellectuals contributed to the cultivation of the imagery of the Brazilian giant.[90] From the Proclamation of the Republic in 1889 through the 1930 coup d'état ushering in the Getúlio Vargas dictatorship, this imagery gained increasing prominence in literature and became deeply embedded in politics and the national collective imagination. During the Romantic period, the giant's depiction evolved, losing some of its original traits and shifting toward a more generalized concept of natural greatness, a transformation mirrored in Duque Estrada's lyrics.[91] The Brazilian scholar Beethoven Alvarez notes how the image of the Brazilian giant evolved: from a symbol of Brazilian conservatism in the early nineteenth century, it would later come to represent economic growth during dictatorship eras, and then would finally transform into an "awakened giant" emblematic of Brazilian protests in the early twenty-first century.[92]

4
Poetics

Two Giants and Two Prophecies

The Brazilian Federal Government's webpage archives a diverse collection of legislative and governmental documents, including various national anthems.[1] The official document that regulates the lyrics of the Brazilian National Anthem features excerpts of the poem by Gonçalves Dias (1823–1864), which were incorporated by Duque Estrada. These lines, which describe the Brazilian forests as teeming with life and Brazilians as filled with love and embraced by their nation, are properly enclosed in quotation marks to denote their origin. They come from the second stanza of Dias's "Song of Exile" ("Canção do exílio"), written in 1843 during his time studying law at Coimbra.[2] Published in 1846, shortly after the crowning of Dom Pedro II (1841), this poem would eventually become one of the most renowned poems in all of Brazilian literature.

Scholar Joshua Alma Enslen has studied how "Song of Exile" became a palimpsest on which successive generations have written and rewritten the nation's history and culture in the context of their own times.[3] In his analysis, Enslen highlights that, despite its seemingly straightforward theme, the poem intricately weaves together threads of identity formation and national destiny. Composed shortly after Brazil's independence, the poem portrays the country in an idealized light, abundant in flora and fauna. While it reveals underlying Eurocentric biases, it nonetheless still resonates with Brazilians today.[4] Enslen contends that "Song of Exile" does not grapple with its complex legacy of European colonization; rather, it portrays the country as an idyllic land—unnamed, uncomplicated, and magnificent—ripe for reinvention.[5] The Eurocentric rewriting of Brazil's history and the romanticization of its precolonial past exalt Brazil's flora and fauna, often to the detriment of other nations, particularly Portugal.

Enslen describes "Song of Exile" as a late manifestation of nationalistic tendencies in Brazil that have developed since Cabral's arrival, with precedents rooted in Portuguese tradition.[6] It embodies an idealistic national spirit defined by an enduring Cabralian quest to rediscover and reenact his arrival, with the ultimate hope of "re-inventing Brazil."[7] Enslen points out that the significant elements of the poem trace back to earlier texts. Like Gonçalves de Magalhães, José de Santa Rita Durão, and Manuel Botelho de Oliveira, Gonçalves Dias aimed to craft a Brazilian nationalist epic, "a would-be response" to Camões's *The Lusiads*.[8] Literary depictions of joyous reunions, marking the culmination of a hero's journey, belong to a tradition extending from Camões to Dias. As Enslen discusses, Camões's adaptation of the biblical Jewish exile has influenced centuries of Portuguese literature and similarly made its mark on Brazilian literary tradition.[9]

As observed by Candido in a lecture tracing the European genealogy of Luso-Brazilian belles-lettres: "at the end of the nineteenth century, the poem chosen by the Republic to accompany the old tune of our national anthem has, as one of its central images, the country reclining by the shore of the sea, a giant ready to leap into action through its sons."[10] In this lecture, Candido references Luso-Brazilian epics influenced by Camões and analyzes the inherited and adapted characteristics found in early Luso-Brazilian literature. He mentions writers who, through their poetry and prose, brought nature to life, effectively transforming the entire country into an expansive, living entity. Among these, he highlights Cláudio Manuel da Costa's *Obras poéticas de Glauceste Satúrnio* (1768) and *Vila Rica* (1773), in which the landscape of the Minas Gerais region springs to life as cyclopes transform into mountains and nymphs into rivers laden with gold.[11] Other poems that mythically transform elements of the Brazilian landscape include António Diniz da Cruz e Silva's *The Hyssop* (1768), and Januário da Cunha Barbosa's *Niterói or the Metamorphosis of Rio de Janeiro* (1822).

THE SLEEPING STONE GIANT OF GONÇALVES DIAS

Gonçalves Dias's "The Stone Giant" ("O gigante de pedra," 1850) and Januário da Cunha Barbosa's earlier work, *Niterói* (1822) are two poetic texts that reimagine the preexisting European depiction of Brazil as a colossal entity.[12] Curiously overlooked, Dias's "The Stone Giant" was published six decades before Duque Estrada's poem for the national anthem and four years after Dias's "Song of Exile." Though their influence can be traced in the national anthem, Dias's "The Stone Giant" and Barbosa's *Niterói* remain relatively unfamiliar to many.

Dias portrays the giant as a proud, imposing figure with a fierce expression, peacefully sleeping on a stone bed. From the watchtower atop a hill, the giant, tasked with vigilance, was struck down by lightning and has since remained in perpetual slumber. His body extends across the visible horizon and dominates the landscape: "Higher than the clouds, facing the skies, / His body stretches over rugged mountains, / His towering feet rise above the sea!"[13]

As night falls, the stars emerge as guiding torches: "the shining stars are sails [or candles] and torches." The clouds are likened to the linen shroud that enveloped the body of Christ when he was taken down from the Cross: "the white shroud are silvery mists." Surrounded by the fragrant scent of flowers, the giant remains in a deep slumber, unable to awaken. He is lulled by a hymn of love that reaches all beings and forces of nature. Emerging from his feet is the Southern Cross constellation, its starry form positioned over his chest like folded arms, described as "crossed arms of molten iron" or "the arms of the eternal Moses."

Soon after the publication of this poem, both the giant and the Southern Cross assumed official roles in the imagery of the Brazilian nation. The constellation, composed of four stars forming a cross shape, holds cultural significance for various peoples and nations. In Brazil, it has become a national icon, prominently featured on the national flag, on the flags of several Brazilian states, and in the national anthem. Due to its distinctiveness and its constant visibility in the skies of the Southern Hemisphere, the Southern Cross has long served as a vital reference point for navigation. One of the earliest Europeans to document the appearance of a cross in the southern sky was the astronomer accompanying Pedro Álvares Cabral's 1500 expedition, which landed in Porto Seguro, Brazil.[14]

THE HURLING STONE GIANT OF JANUÁRIO DA CUNHA BARBOSA

An earlier example of a nationalistic poetic depiction of the giant can be traced back to 1822 when Januário da Cunha Barbosa (1780–1846) composed *Niterói, or the Metamorphosis of Rio de Janeiro*. Within this epic poem celebrating Brazil's accomplishments and its royal heroes, Cunha Barbosa elaborates a mythic cosmology for Brazil and the Bay of Rio de Janeiro. *Niterói* opens with the following argument:

> Niterói, son of the Giant Minas and Atlantis, was a newborn when his father was killed by Mars in the War of the Giants. Neptune, moved by the tears of Atlantis,

took charge of his upbringing in distant lands that would later become known as Brazil. As Niterói grew up, he harbored a desire to reignite the war, to take vengeance against those responsible for his father's death. For this purpose, he prepared for war well in advance by stacking rocks upon rocks in secret. These rocks eventually gave rise to the mountain range known as the Serra dos Órgãos [the Organs Mountain Range]. Jupiter, aware of Niterói's intentions, intervened and struck him down with a lightning bolt while he meditated atop those rocks. Niterói's body tumbled into a valley, shaping the bay that now carries his name. This transformation transpired because Neptune, moved by Atlantis's pleas, changed Niteroi into the sea, marking the sea's division from the ocean with the colossal rock that Niterói had intended to hurl at Mars but that tumbled down with him from the mountains. To console Atlantis, Glauco prophesied the future glory of Brazil, particularly the place where her son had been transformed into the sea.[15]

In Cunha Barbosa's poem, Neptune transforms Niterói into Guanabara Bay, formerly known as Niterói Bay. The rock Niterói clutched in his hand becomes the iconic Sugarloaf Mountain (Pão de Açúcar). The narrative then transitions to the perspective of Glauco, the prophetic sea deity who, gazing into the future, envisions a magnificent destiny for Brazil. Simultaneously, as Glauco envisions the future, he reflects on the past and recounts Brazil's history, spanning from the arrival of Pedro Álvares Cabral in 1500 to Brazil's elevation to a kingdom in 1815.

Cunha Barbosa's depiction of Niterói has been analyzed as a departure from traditional Greco-Roman epic transformations, adapting classical mythology to align with the conservative moral and political atmosphere of early nineteenth-century Brazil. While giants in mythology do not typically convey conservative or nationalistic ideals, in Brazil, the image of the nation as a giant emerges from a conservative and populist collective imagination that overlooks diversity and inequality.[16]

Ordained in 1803, Cunha Barbosa rose to prominence with the arrival of the royal family in Brazil in 1808 and was eventually appointed canon of the Royal Chapel. Enjoying direct access to the upper tiers of Brazilian politics and intellectual circles as a royal preacher, his roles expanded to include journalist, politician, professor of philosophy, historian, and chronicler of the Empire. He also served as the librarian of the Public Library of the Court.[17] A founding member of the Brazilian Historical and Geographic Institute, Cunha Barbosa navigated a complex relationship with the Portuguese Crown and the emerging Brazilian independence movement.[18]

Niterói both defends Portugal and lauds Pedro I, the future and first emperor of an independent Brazil. This dual stance reflects the period's characteristic ambivalence.[19] By blending Greco-Roman and Indigenous elements, the portrayal of a giant Indigenous Brazilian figure in the literature of the time had the potential to create an imagined geographical landscape that symbolically bridged past and present.[20]

BENTO TEIXEIRA'S PROPHECY OF A VEILED SANCTUARY

When discussing the European heritage of Luso-Brazilian belles lettres, Candido identified common characteristics and stylistic devices supposedly inherited by Luso-Brazilian writers. He focused on the use of prosopopoeia—specifically, the anthropomorphism of nature—as a prominent stylistic device and suggested that this literary technique played a role in shaping the vast and "inhospitable land" to "accommodate the colonizers' desires and imaginary."[21] Candido referred to Bento Teixeira's epic poem *Prosopopoeia*, posthumously published in 1601, as an early precursor of this tradition.[22] In Teixeira's poem, the Ocean, personified as Proteus, makes his prophecies heard. During a historical period when literature was expected to reinforce political norms symbolized by the monarchy, Bento Teixeira challenged some of these foundational principles.[23]

Bento Teixeira (1560–1600), a Portuguese descendant of New Christians, sought refuge in Brazil in 1567 to escape the Inquisition.[24] Lúcia Helena Costigan—scholar of early modern Iberian and colonial Latin American literature—has argued that although European stylistic devices were employed in *Prosopopoeia*, their purpose was not to convey the political norms symbolized by the monarchy; rather, they served the opposite function. While Teixeira's epic adheres to the meter and poetic devices of Camões's *The Lusiads*, it functioned as a tool for asserting the cultural supremacy of New Christians of Jewish ancestry.[25]

According to Costigan, Teixeira's poem protested the exploitative policies of Philip II of Spain, which from 1580 onward worsened conditions for New Christians in Portugal. When Philip II declared himself king of the Lusitanian nation and its overseas territories—effectively folding them into the Spanish Empire—the situation for New Christians deteriorated further, and many were forced to flee to Brazil. Although *Prosopopoeia* may at first seem to praise the donatary captain of Pernambuco in Northern Brazil, it subtly conveys a different narrative—one highlighting the resilience of New Christians persecuted by the Holy Office.[26]

Costigan's analysis explores how Teixeira, a convert from Judaism, uses personification in his epic to navigate his complex identity. Unable to openly acknowledge his Jewish heritage or fully assimilate as a Christian, the poet employs prosopopoeia—a figure of speech that gives voice to the unseen—to articulate his message.²⁷ Concealed within the enigmatic persona of Proteus, the sea god known for his gift of prophecy and metamorphosis to evade the questions of inquirers, the poetic voice subtly calls for justice: "In speaking the truth, I will be shallow, / For thus it is fitting for he who writes, / If he wants to provide what is due to justice."²⁸

As both Proteus and Moses, the "convert poet-shepherd" positions himself as a guide leading the descendants of Moses toward the southern seas—the region of New Lusitania (Nova Lusitânia) or what is now known as Pernambuco—portrayed as a safe haven for captives (New Christians) fleeing the tyranny of the new pharaoh, Philip II.²⁹ One of the chants from Teixeira's epic, "Description of the Recife of Pernambuco" ("Descrição do Recife de Pernambuco"), begins with the lines:

> On the southern side,
> Where the Little Bear stands surrounded by guards,
> where the luminous sky serenely spreads its tranquil influence,
> Nova Lusitânia orders nature,
> like a watchful mother,
> such a quiet, secure haven
> that serves as a wall for the curved vessels.³⁰

Recife, the main harbor of the Captaincy of Pernambuco, or Nova Lusitânia, is portrayed as a sanctuary where Portuguese New Christians could find prosperity and security.³¹ In the guise of Proteus, the poet foretells the future of this haven and its inhabitants:

> In my vision, the wise elder proclaims,
> I behold the renewal of Saturn's age,
> and opulent Olinda thrives,
> ascending to the peak of its supreme state.
> Its vast territory will be inhabited
> by fierce, warlike peoples;
> it shall be named New Lusitania;
> exempt from the fatal madness of laws.³²

Through this nuanced dialogue with Portuguese classical literature, Teixeira, embodying a complex morality that involves the denial of Christianity as the affirmation of Judaism, creates a platform that departs from Camões to serve as a cultural affirmation for New Christians.³³

GONÇALVES DIAS'S PROPHECY OF A CURSED LEGACY: THE KING SLEEPS

The genre of poetic prose offers the freedom to break away from stylistic constraints, enabling the creation of texts with a more pronounced critical stance toward the establishment. The Symbolist poet Cruz e Sousa (1861–1898) serves as a prime example of this: his narrative prose, which directly addresses the racial issues of his time and his identity as a Black man, differs markedly from his sonnets. I return to Gonçalves Dias to explore a final prophetic poetic text that interlaces the foundational texts discussed so far, shedding light on the paradoxical position held by artists commissioned by the monarchical and imperial states of Brazil.

Dias, born to a Portuguese father and a mother with African and Amerindian ancestry, was a member of the lettered elite. He actively participated in initiatives of the Brazilian Geographical and Historical Institute organized by its patron, Emperor Dom Pedro II. Writers like Januário da Cunha Barbosa and Gonçalves Dias, working within the imperial bureaucratic system, were tasked with shaping the collective imagination while facing the challenge of expressing their criticisms with intellectual autonomy.[34] Dias's prose poem "Meditation" ("Meditação"), part of the Brazilian Romanticist movement, is another text that exists on the fringes of the established literary canon. Dias published "Meditation" in the early 1850s, in three separate early issues of *O Guanabara* (*The Guanabara [Bay]*), a journal funded by Emperor Dom Pedro II.[35]

The Royal Press (Imprensa Régia) in Brazil was established through a decree signed by Dom João VI in 1808. Journals dedicated to science, literature, and the arts laid the foundation for an official literary tradition. *O Guanabara* survived for a relatively long period, with thirty-six issues published between 1849 and 1856, thanks to the financial support it received from the emperor. In 1854, the editors expressed their gratitude to His Imperial Majesty for the "boundless magnificence" that revitalized the publication with such "high and formidable protection."[36] However, epidemics like yellow fever in 1850 and cholera morbus in 1855 led to publication delays due to a shortage of contributors.[37] In the journal's final issue, the literary critic Cônego Fernandes Pinheiro (1825–1876) observed that the journal struggled, as it was "finding no one willing to write, when nothing was heard except talk of medical stations and ambulances."[38]

Dias, a member of the Brazilian Geographical and Historical Institute since 1847, was one of the founders and directors of *O Guanabara*. Despite his position within the state's patronage system, Dias criticized the Brazilian elite and challenged the foundations of the existing regime, including slavery, social exclusion, and the exploitation of public resources by the political classes for personal gain. Contrary to the perspective of José de Alencar (1829–1877) and most writers and intellectuals of the period, "Meditation" has been perceived as a pioneering critique of prevailing ideologies and established norms.[39] It is important to emphasize, however, that Dias's view on slavery—as with many of his contemporaries—was that it hindered the adoption of a capitalist model.

The literary critic Wilton Marques's study on Dias, titled "The Poet Against the Flow: Literature and Slavery in Brazilian Romanticism" ("O poeta na contramão: literatura e escravidão no Romantismo brasileiro") raises the question of whether a poet like Dias could openly criticize slavery in Brazilian society. Marques argues that for Romantic intellectuals like Dias, state employment was one of the few means of subsistence available.[40] The same applies to artists from other eras who were employed as public servants in a system marked by patronage and favoritism. The literary critic Diego Molina interprets "Meditation" as a diagnostic tool, an x-ray, revealing the deep-seated issues of the young Brazilian nation: enduring colonial ties to Portugal, the ongoing institution of slavery, the stereotyped lethargy attributed to Indigenous peoples, and the historical shackles preventing progress.[41] It depicts a society on the brink of ruin, undermined by flaws inherited from its colonizers, reflecting Brazil's troubled past, uncertain present, and ominous future.[42]

Dias's prose poem starts with a prolonged series of ellipses, spanning four lines at the start of chapter 1, signaling an interrupted or ongoing thought. The narrative action then begins abruptly with the temporal adverb "then," leading to the image of an elderly man reaching out with frail hands to touch the narrator's eyes.[43] The plot unfolds through a dialogue between a skeptical older man representing the colonial past and an idealistic young man symbolizing an aspirational, independent Brazil.[44] The in medias res narrative technique immerses the reader mid-scene, suggesting a history that is either suppressed, ineffable, or unknown, one that invites discovery or explanation—a history with a past that paradoxically behaves as a future. *Mediatation* proceeds with the interaction between the elderly seer—an "elder of white complexion, who, far from the world's bustle, had meditated for many years"—and the poetic voice of the younger interlocutor:[45]

> And the Elder then spoke, saying, 'Look from north to south—from sunset to sunrise—as far as the light of your eyes can reach, and tell me what you see.'
> And his gesture bore the weight of sovereignty, commanding and awe-inspiring, like that of an angered monarch.
> And his voice, solemn and grave, echoed the intonation of a priest chanting a somber funeral prayer on a moonlit burial night.

> And I directed my eyes from north to south, from sunset to sunrise, as far as they could reach, and replied:
>
> "My father, I see before my eyes a prodigious expanse of land: is it perhaps a great empire—so vast an empire it seems to encompass."[46]

The text's rhythm is punctuated by the conjunction *and*, connecting a series of revealing actions and infusing the narrative with a sense of hesitation as if struggling to recollect and convey the tangible realities of Brazilian life.

The poet's references to the natural landscape—the land, trees, flowers, birds, and the starry sky—evoke the image of nature crafted by a benevolent and joyful Christ. This series of interconnected visions culminates in a pause at the final image: a society under a slave system depicted as interlinked iron rings of a chain, concentric circles of subjugation.[47]

> And upon this fair land, beneath these colossal trees—I see thousands of men—with discordant countenances, of various colors and different characters.
>
> And these men form concentric circles, like those created by a stone falling into the calm waters of a lake.
>
> And those forming the outer circles have submissive and respectful manners; they are black—while the others, who are like a handful of men, forming the center of all circles, have lordly and arrogant manners—they are of white.
>
> And the men of black color have their hands bound in long iron chains, whose rings extend from one to another— as eternal as the curse that passes from fathers to sons![48]

The following chapter begins with an even longer series of ellipses, stretching across five lines and making up the entire first part of the chapter. While it is conceivable that the missing sections of the first two chapters, as well the last line of the final chapter, were deliberately employed as a Romantic device, the literary critic Lúcia Miguel Pereira (1901–1959) proposed a more compelling theory: that these sections were intentionally excluded from the text.[49] A significant portion of chapter 3—eight paragraphs—was indeed omitted in the 1850 edition of *O Guanabara* and later resurfaced in a subsequent 1868 release. In a letter to a friend, Dias, referring to the forthcoming issue that contained the final chapter of the poem, expressed his frustration: "I am extremely upset with *O Guanabara*, and since I don't want to deal with hassles, I will likely disassociate myself from it by the end of the semester."[50] After the censored publication of the last chapter of

"Meditation," Dias broke ties with *O Guanabara*. Marques argues that it is plausible to think that publishing the text, even in its altered state, served as a means for the poet to assert his literary independence in the face of institutionalized power.[51]

The final chapter of the poem delineates two distinct periods in Brazilian history, pre- and post-Portuguese invasion, culminating in an assessment of Brazil as an independent nation.

> A resounding and thunderous voice sprang from Ipiranga and reached the sea, the Andes, and from the Plata to the banks of the Amazon.
> And all rose up violently and instantaneously, like a corpse animated by galvanism.
> They released the same cry, with enthusiastic and strong voices, and they grasped their weapons with the fearlessness of a warrior and the hope of a man fighting for justice.
> And the chain that bound one Empire to another Empire, weakened by its length, violently shattered into a thousand pieces. . . .
> And Europe from the other end of the Atlantic applauded the audacity of the nascent people.[52]

The passage that was censored in *O Guanabara* depicts a nocturnal dialogue alluding to the early stages of Brazilian independence, a time when the country was moving toward solidifying its monarchical political structure. A council of five men—another version of the idealist younger character and four older politicians—deliberate on the optimal political system for post-independence Brazil. In this debate about the fate of Brazil, the elderly councilors decide to sow division between the vanquished and the victors and incite war: "and the elders rose from their ivory seats and cried out: / Let us preach revolutions as the principle of progress and kindle the torch of discord. And the fire will ignite from all corners of the vast empire."[53] Sinister laughter fades to silence, and conversation ceases as someone asks about the king's opinion.

> And one among them raised his voice in the midst of this silence and asked, "What does the King do?"
> And all repeated with the same visible anxiety, "What does the King do?"
> And beyond the chamber, the King was seen peacefully resting on a magnificently adorned bed.
> And the one who had raised the chant of the elders said in a cavernous voice, "The King sleeps!"

> And the elders descended slowly like a parchment leaf, which unfolds with difficulty, and they came to rest without echo on the plush carpets of the room.
> And the same laughter burst forth even louder.[54]

It is important to note the parallel imagery of the sleeping king in "Meditation" and the sleeping giant in the Brazilian national anthem. While in "Meditation," the king sleeps on a "magnificently adorned bed" ("um leito magnificamente adornado"), in the anthem, anthropomorphic Brazil is described as "eternally lying in a splendid cradle" ("deitado eternamente em berço esplêndido").[55] The sleeping king of "Meditation" can allude to the interregnum between Dom Pedro I's abdication in 1831 and the crowning of his son, Dom Pedro II in 1841 when he turned sixteen years old. The period's portrayal fictionalizes the conflicts of the Brazilian Regency, illustrating how monarchist reactionaries capitalized on political unrest to suppress insurrections and regain dominance through coercion and corruption.

In the final scene of "Meditation," the old politicians burn in the very fire they ignited. The poet appears to interpret their self-inflicted downfall as a form of divine punishment—an implicit condemnation of the preservation of slavery.[56] "Meditation" alludes to a cursed destiny inherited by Brazil, one that deviates from the virtuous path supposedly ordained by divine will. Divine intervention appears sporadically, attempting to redirect the nation's self-destructive course and dispense celestial justice: "And God saw that the conquering nation had become corrupt and marked the final chapter of its greatness. / And He granted it a long succession of years in which to lament its decline and recognize the inexorable justice of the Almighty."[57]

In a chain reaction of divine wrath, if the domination of Indigenous peoples and Africans marked the beginning of the Portuguese Empire's decline, similar political missteps following Brazil's independence could foreshadow a parallel decline of the Brazilian nation.[58] Molina interprets "Meditation" as a prophecy of Brazil's conditional future glory, one that draws parallels to the biblical story of Isaac.[59] By reframing the narrative of Isaac from the Book of Genesis through the figure of the elderly character, the fate of the Brazilian Empire is foretold. In the biblical account, Isaac—born to a couple long past childbearing age—serves as a test of his father's faith, as he is commanded to sacrifice his son. Drawing on the Romantic concept of the nation as a living being, Dias envisions the nature of sacrifice necessary for Brazil's progress. In contrast to other Brazilian authors of his time, Dias envisions a sacrifice not of Indigenous offspring but rather of enslaved Africans.[60] "Meditation" overlooks the contributions of African descendants in Brazil, mentioning them only in passing as part of the country's population. Similarly, in Dias's poem "The Slave Woman" ("A escrava," 1846), the character Alsgá's intense longing for Africa eclipses her response to enslavement and challenges the notion of Afro-Brazilians' societal incorporation and eventual right to citizenship.[61] The poem suggests that Alsgá's inner conflict could only be resolved by returning to her native Congo.

Like *The Lusiads*, "Meditation" ends with a scene of a feast, yet it frames a stark contrast: "And the blood flowed more and more abundantly, like wine at the end of a banquet, when merriment turns into drunkenness. / It was then that my strength failed me, and I fell lifeless, striking the earth beneath me under the weight of my body."[62] Dias's "Meditation" echoes von Martius's depiction of "Portuguese blood, as a mighty river," which would "absorb the smaller streams of the Indian and African races." This image of the supremacy of colossal nature over local lesser cultures aligns with arguments over the meaning of Brazilian history as it revolves around the interplay between Portuguese, Indigenous, and African "races."[63]

The motif of Brazil as a giant has been a recurring theme in Brazilian literature, culture, and politics. While Dias's "The Sleeping Giant" and Cunha Barbosa's *Niterói, or the Metamorphosis of Rio de Janeiro* represent early developments of this national personification, Teixeira's *Prosopopoeia* and Dias's "Meditation" explore the cosmological shaping of a new kingdom or state. These literary works forge images reflecting different aspects of Brazilian history and society, including the impacts of colonialism, slavery, and national emancipation. A mosaic of these literary images, encompassing both the imagined past (history) and future (prophecy and affirmation), has been perpetuated as myth within the verses of the Brazilian national anthem. While the evolution of this symbolic configuration may not be consciously acknowledged, it can be traced back to European colonial travel reports and Euro-Afro-Brazilian fabulations. In contrast to Adamastor— transformed into stone as divine punishment and rendered powerless against maritime conquest—Brazil, as a mythic nation, emerges as a resurgent stone giant, empowered through colonial conquest. Literary fabulations are just one branch of the broader Eurocentric lore.

5
Social Sciences

Three Founding Moments of Euro-Afro-Brazilian Studies (Separating the Wheat from the Chaff)

FIRST MOMENT: GERMAN TRAVEL INSIGHTS AND SOUVENIRS: WILD HUNTS, ROYAL DANCES, AND CACHAÇA

Euro-Afro-Brazilian studies trace their historical lineage back to sixteenth-century travel accounts. A significant early ethnographic study emerged in 1823 when, a decade before receiving recognition from the Brazilian Historical and Geographic Institute, the Bavarian botanist Karl Friedrich von Martius co-published the final volume of one of the earliest comprehensive proto-ethnographic studies on colonial Brazil. Von Martius and his collaborator, the Bavarian zoologist Johann Baptist von Spix (1781–1826), undertook a major expedition to Brazil from 1817 to 1820. During their extensive travels, they visited the captaincies of São Paulo, Minas Gerais, Goiás, and Bahia. After returning to Bavaria, they published a three-volume account of their travels titled *An Account of Travels in Brazil at the Command of His Majesty, Maximilian Joseph I, King of Bavaria, in the Years 1817 to 1820*. While the primary focus of their study was the *Flora Brasiliensis*, they also observed, sketched, and described the Brazilian sociogeographic landscape. Their illustrations depict Africans, Indigenous groups, Europeans, and *cafuzos*, or mestizos living in Brazil. Some years later, French painter Jean-Baptiste Debret depicted the "semi-African Indigenous" mestizos as "the most capable social agents" in Brazil, portrayed as living in "a state of perfect civilization" and enjoying the "general esteem earned through their achievements in various fields."[1]

Other Europeans visited Brazil before and after von Martius, von Spix, and Debret, and participated in the creation of the official visual and narrative archive of colonial life in Brazil. From 1711 to 1887, some of the most recognized visitors included Italian priest André João Antonil; British travelers like John Mawe,

John Luccock, Maria Graham, and Robert Walsh; German illustrator Johann-Moritz Rugendas; and North American, Swiss, and German explorers, including Daniel Parish Kidder, Johann Jakob von Tschudi, Louis Agassiz, and Ina von Binzer. Von Martius and von Spix left comprehensive resources to future travelers and their successors, providing documentation that helped lay the foundation for the creation of a nation that was foreign to them. Some of their accounts read like practical travel tips—similar to modern advice on traveling light, selecting transportation, and finding affordable lodging. In their early nineteenth-century Brazilian context, one of their most salient pieces of advice was how to acquire the "most important provisions" for an expedition: mules and Africans:

> We first took care of obtaining a mule troop, [mules being] the most important provisions and necessary tools for a journey in this country. . . . The last primary task remained: finding a muleteer to whom we would entrust the handling of the animals and the care of the baggage. We soon realized how difficult it is to find a competent man for the job, and even more challenging to interest him in our enterprise. After several unsuccessful attempts to find someone with the necessary qualifications, we were forced, as the appointed day of departure approached, to entrust the troop to a mulatto who, though lacking formal credentials, claimed experience in the profession. We also provided him with assistance, not only from our Black slave, but also from another freed slave.[2]

The authors provide a detailed account of their journey, including various social relations with enslaved Africans, *capitães-do-mato* bounty hunters, and farm masters. In one passage, they lament some of the inconveniences they have encountered:

> These inconveniences increased when, in the morning, we noticed the absence of the Black slave. The arduous journey, mostly through flooded terrain, had caused discontent in the young black, who could not appreciate our humane treatment and took advantage of the first favorable night to escape, a common occurrence among new slaves. Since there were no traces of him, we continued the journey to the Santa Bárbara Farm, where we should have arrived the day before and where we would make arrangements to find the runaway slave. We were received with true hospitality of bygone times, and the farmer José Antônio de Almeida, sergeant-major, and administrator of the Royal Farm, who . . . reassured us about the fugitive. In all of Minas Gerais, as well as in several other provinces where the quantity of Black slaves requires increased vigilance, there is a special force, the *capitães-do-mato*, generally mulattos or other mixed-race

individuals, who pursue every runaway slave and deliver them to their owner or the competent authority. Only the runaway who knows the terrain perfectly well and can withdraw to a distant spot can, at times, escape from these *capitães-do-mato*. So they comforted us by promising that the return of our slave would not be delayed, as he was still a New Black [*Negro Bruto*]. He was indeed restored to us from a nearby farm on the third day. Upon receiving him, we followed the advice of our host and instead of uttering insulting words to him, we treated him, according to the local custom, with kindness, and had a full glass of *cachaça* given to him. Long experience has taught Brazilians that the grant of a broad amnesty, accompanied by a glass of liqueur, has a better effect on the character of the New Black than strict punishment.[3]

Viewed from the perspective of individuals who were beneficiaries of the plantation system, these European travelers noted the disparity in power dynamics between Africans and African descendants in Brazil who were familiar with the local terrain and those who had not yet mapped it out. This is also an early perception and register of the supposedly lenient behavior of Luso-Brazilian slave owners.

Von Martius and von Spix described cultural expressions such as the Batuque (the proto-Samba), perceived by them as a dance of obscene nature widespread throughout Brazil and so favored among the people that not even the Church would succeed in prohibiting it. "The main appeal of this dance," according to them, "lies in the artificial rotations and contortions of the pelvis, which almost rival those of the fakirs of the East Indies."[4] From them, we have the earliest documented record of Congada performances. They provide a detailed description and contemplation of the festivities and ceremonies as follows:

> They seized the opportunity to choose a king of the Negroes, a tradition followed annually. It is worth noting that this title held no political or civil authority over their community, similar to the role of the Fava King during the Day of the Magi in Europe. The Luso-Brazilian government did not object to this symbolic tradition. The process involved a general vote to appoint the Congo king, Queen Xinga, the various princes, and princesses, and six *mafuca* attendants.
>
> They then held a solemn procession to the Negro church. The procession was led by Negro individuals carrying flags, followed by others carrying black-painted images of the Savior, St. Francis, and the Mother of God. A music band, dressed in torn red and purple capes adorned with large ostrich feathers, played tambourines, rattles, the noisy *canzá* [scraper] and the mournful *marimba*

[xylophone]. The procession continued with a Negro individual wearing a black mask and acting as a butler, followed by the princes and princesses, whose tails were carried by pages of both genders. Next were the kings and queens of the previous year, still holding scepters and crowns, and the newly chosen royal couple, adorned with borrowed diamonds, pearls, coins, and treasures for the celebration. The procession concluded with Negro people carrying lit candles or sticks covered with silver paper.

Upon arriving at the Negro Mother of God church, which belonged to the negroes, the outgoing king handed over the scepter and crown to the newly elected king. The new king then made a ceremonial visit to the superintendent of the Diamantino District, accompanied by the entire court. The superintendent, aware of the visit, warmly welcomed the new king. However, the newly elected king, a freed Negro cobbler, became so timid when invited to sit on the sofa, that he dropped the scepter. The superintendent, in good humor, picked it up and returned it, jokingly saying, "Your Majesty dropped the scepter!"

The musical choir expressed respect for the superintendent with a lively tune, and the entire crowd left, following the tradition of bowing with their right knee before the people of the house upon departure. Walking solemnly through the streets, the king and queen returned to their huts. The same spectacle was repeated the next day, but with some variations. The new king of the Negroes received an official visit from an envoy of the court of Congo, known as the Congada. The royal family and court, dressed in grand attire, walked in a procession to the Market Square. The king and queen sat in chairs, while the ministers, attendants, and other dignitaries sat on low benches to their right and to their left.

In front of them, in a double row, stood the musicians from the band, wearing yellow and red shoes, black and white stockings, red and yellow pants with perforated silk capes. They made a hellish racket with drums, fifes, tambourines, rattles, and the mournful *marimba*. The dancers announced the envoy with jumps and somersaults, unique facial expressions, and peculiar poses. They brought their gifts, presenting such a bizarre spectacle that one might imagine a troop of monkeys. The Negro monarchs initially declined the envoy's visit but eventually welcomed him, saying, "The port and heart of the king are open to you." The King of Congo invited the envoy to sit on his left, and amidst lively music, distributed decorations, and reeds. The festivities concluded with the king of the Negroes shouting, "Long live King D. João VI!" His entire people repeated it.

How interesting are the reflections of the thinker who, in retrospect and foresight, participated in such a strange celebration![5]

The observations documented by von Martius and von Spix conclude with a statement characterized by both hindsight and anticipation ("in retrospect and foresight"). This posture would resurface in von Martius's later award-winning essay. It reflects an effort to depict something unfamiliar and peculiar by contemplating both present and past contexts while envisioning the future of the foreign peoples and spaces under examination.

SECOND MOMENT: EARLY INSIGHTS OF EUROPEAN ACADEMIC DISCIPLINES AND PATHOLOGIZING SCIENCES

In the late nineteenth century, following the abolition of slavery, a cadre of national scholars emerged to form the bedrock of what might be considered the prehistory of Afro-Brazilian anthropology. Central figures in this development included Nina Rodrigues, Sílvio Romero, Manuel Querino, and Braz do Amaral. Influenced by the evolutionist ideas of his era, Nina Rodrigues (1862–1906) undertook forensic studies of Africans and mestizos in Brazil. His work, *Os africanos no Brasil* (*Africans in Brazil*), later vilified for its racist rhetoric, reflects the anachronistic views of its time.[6] While Rodrigues's studies have faced significant scrutiny, with some calling for their retraction, it is crucial to recognize that during this period, myths shaping the Brazilian ethos were being "scientifically documented." Rodrigues employed the cranioscopy method, developed by Italian eugenicist Cesare Lombroso (1835–1909), to support his determinist studies of Afro-Brazilian descendants. Alongside Manuel Querino (1851–1923) and Sílvio Romero (1851–1914), Rodrigues was a pivotal figure in this second proto-anthropological phase.

In his 1882 landmark study of Brazilian literature, Romero drew on von Martius's work, albeit with significant revisions. He argued for a perception of Africans in Brazil not merely as "economic machines" but as "objects of science," portraying Brazil as a cultural amalgamation of "Africa in our kitchens, America in our jungles, and Europe in our halls."[7] Despite his contextually conditioned racist views, Romero was a visionary scholar who dedicated himself to chronicling Brazilian literature, notably in his comprehensive three-volume *História da literatura brasileira* (*History of Brazilian Literature*) published in 1888. According to him:

> Intelligent, honest, and courageous individuals have extensively studied Indigenous peoples from various angles. However, nobody wants to bother with the

negroes, and this is the most objectionable ingratitude. What did the map of Africa look like when Brazil was discovered, and Africans began to be imported as slaves? And in the eighteenth century, which continued with massive numbers? And in the nineteenth century until 1850, a period during which this terrible trade extended itself? From which nations were these Africans taken, and in what numbers? What do we owe them in terms of social, political, and economic systems? Until now, nobody knows! ... Nobody ever wanted to know! It's primarily due to the deeply ingrained color prejudices that persist to this day. People fear that showing empathy for this significant segment of our population might lead others to perceive them as descendants of the African race or mestizos. This is the unvarnished reality we face. It's high time we put an end to this foolishness. We must confront our biases and fears and stop with the lies. ... God! When will the blindness finally be lifted? When will we acknowledge our true origins without illusions or biases and move forward with unwavering determination?[8]

Romero's direct address of the neglect and lack of knowledge regarding the history and contributions of Africans in Brazil, along with his attribution of this gap to deep-rooted prejudices, remains relevant. His 1888 call for a change in attitude, made nearly 150 years ago, still resonates today. What may seem outdated is his fear—rather than the hope that was ideologically being formulated—that Africans might perish before receiving recognition and study. He pleads with Brazilian scholars: "Specialists should hurry, the poor Mozambicans, Benguelas, Monjolos, Congos, Cabindas, Caçangas are dying."[9] The urgency of Romero's plea must be understood within the context of his era. One prevalent myth then was that the "whitening" of Brazilians would solve "the mestizo problem." African cultures were perceived as having their days numbered. Rodrigues also addressed this anticipated reality with concern. He expressed his fear that the Yoruba-Ewe religion, as an organized religion, would gradually fade away, citing examples of it as already happening in Maranhão. However, he also acknowledged the remarkable resistance and vitality of the beliefs of Africans in Brazil, asserting that all attempts to eradicate them would ultimately prove futile.[10]

Rodrigues took up the mantle to continue the work initiated by von Martius, aiming to document the African culture he perceived as vanishing. While he followed the proto-anthropological path blazed by von Martius, Rodrigues diverged by emphasizing that despite the greater prevalence of Congo-Bantu people in Brazil, it was the Yoruba-Sudanese people who had the most profound influence on Brazilian culture.[11] He marked the inception of what is often referred to in Brazil as Yoruba-centrism. Rodrigues exhibited a fascination with Yoruba culture in Brazil, conducting interviews and taking photographs of elderly individuals. Regardless of what he may have suspected, Rodrigues framed his studies within the French evolutionist idea that Africans were neither superior nor inferior to Europeans but represented "a different stage of intellectual and moral human development."[12] Within this framework, he viewed Africans as part of the "weak race," contributing to Brazil's perceived national inferiority despite any contributions they may have made to civilization.[13] Rodrigues opened his research by stating: "for some my book will be a fantasy or an imaginary exploration of an ethnic problem that was not supposed to exist in Brazil," and he goes further remarking: "the Portuguese blood that runs in our veins is heavy and shameful. Those of Portuguese descent often lacked basic civility."[14] Rodrigues appears as a melancholic figure constrained by science and scorned for focusing too much on what was considered an inferior subject. He transitioned from being viewed as a despondent, erratic scientist to being associated with the racism from which modern anthropology sprouted. Despite this, he also advocated for the defense of Afro-Brazilian religions, opposing their criminalization and condemning police brutality against their adherents.[15]

Rodrigues's seminal work, *Os africanos no Brasil*, wasn't published in its entirety until nearly thirty years after his death, despite earlier excerpts being published in France. It wasn't until 1932 that the full volume became available to the Brazilian public, marking a significant development in the history of Euro-Afro-Brazilian anthropology. By the 1930s, the prevailing anthropological frameworks had shifted from evolutionism to psychology and North American anthropology, particularly influenced by Franz Boas (1858–1942). Grappling with the nation's perceived ailments, Brazilian scholars moved away from brain measurements. In their efforts to diagnose and heal the "underdeveloped sick giant" plagued by anguish and an inferiority complex, they introduced updated sociopsychological tools.

THIRD MOMENT: DIAGNOSIS AND CLINICAL TRIALS

As we have seen, the official proposal for a history of Brazil originated in the empire during a time of slavery. The Brazilian sociologist Clóvis Moura (1925–2003) points out that studies about Blacks in Brazilian society were strongly influenced by academic biases. These biases include a supposed scientific impartiality on one hand and a rationalized racist ideology on the other, which portrays the remnants of the slave-based superstructure and its continuation.[16] This ideology does not represent a break but rather a dual continuation: on the one hand, with the historiography created to justify the Emperor's power and the maintenance of a slave society; and on the other, with the racist ideologies formulated by scientificism, particularly theories on the "whitening" of the Brazilian population.[17]

The third phase of Afro-Brazilian studies was initiated by another doctor, Arthur Ramos (1903–1949). The 1920s and 1930s marked not only the consolidation of Afro-Brazilian anthropology but also the emergence of a more defined formulation of Brazil as an idea and nation. Scholars of this period established the more mature rhetorical foundations of the various myths that constitute the Brazilian national ethos. Ramos continued the work initiated by Rodrigues, giving due acknowledgment to his predecessor. Ramos brought a new perspective to his research, moving away from forensic evolutionist medicine and adopting a sociopsychological approach influenced by both Jung and Freud. The significant shift in his argument was to distinguish between Africans and enslaved Africans and to explore how the latter group adapted to their new environment. In the introduction to *O negro brasileiro: etnografia religiosa e psicanálise* (*The Black Brazilian: Religious Ethnology and Psychoanalysis*) published in 1934, Ramos posed the following question:

> The American Blackman! How did he respond to his new environment? How did his psyche evolve when exposed to different races and surroundings? Conversely, how did he impact the neo-continental communities with which he assimilated? What is his status in Brazil in comparison to his counterparts in other nations across the American continent?[18]

Ramos's study focuses on Black Brazilians within a hemispheric or even diasporic framework. What distinguishes his rhetoric is its dual focus on the psyche and the environment. Rather than addressing the superiority or inferiority of races directly, miscegenation is now understood as an adaptation to the tropical climate, a consequence of cultural interactions and exchanges. It is no longer regarded as the cause of degeneration among the Brazilian population but rather as an "internal psychic constraint."[19] In 1947, prior to his passing, Ramos released a substantial three-volume work titled *Introdução à antropologia Brasileira* (*Introduction to Brazilian Anthropology*). It marked the culmination of a lineage of studies that sought to explore the African ethnic groups that arrived in Brazil, a research endeavor that ended prematurely. Following in Ramos's footsteps were scholars like Edison Carneiro (1912–1972) and Luís da Câmara Cascudo

(1898–1986), who primarily gained recognition as researchers dedicated to Brazilian Folklore.

However, in this third moment of Afro-Brazilian studies, it is not Ramos who is primarily remembered, but Gilberto Freyre (1900–1987). Freyre's classic *Casa-grande e senzala: Formação da família brasileira sob o regime da economia patriarcal (The Master's House and the Slave Quarters: The Formation of the Brazilian Family Under the Patriarchal Economic Regime)* published in 1933, laid the foundation for the official national and international discourse on Brazilian race relations. While Ramos approached his subject from an anthropological perspective, Freyre introduced a sociological viewpoint. The distinguishing characteristic of Ramos's work was the term "deculturation," specifically focusing on the deculturation of Africans and Native Brazilians. Freyre followed up with a discourse that referred to the deculturation of Europeans, as well as the acculturation or transculturation of Brazilian culture. In summary, while Ramos argued that Blacks in Brazil were not foreigners but Brazilians, Freyre contended that everybody, regardless of origin, became a foreigner in Brazil, and through cultural creolization and naturalization, all these foreigners eventually became, in principle, creolized, transformed, and equalized into Brazilians.

Freyre followed a line of research that had been introduced by Paulo Prado (1868–1943). In 1928, Prado published *Retrato do Brasil: ensaio sobre a tristeza brasileira (Portrait of Brazil: An Essay on Brazilian Sadness)*, in which he portrayed Brazil as the result of "unions of an animal character" and the "mixing of three sad races."[20] Freyre chose brighter colors to paint his vision or tale of Brazil. Up until the time I was in school in Brazil (in the 70s and 80s), our history and social science books included the view of Paulo Prado and not Freyre. Freyre can perhaps be understood as a Brazilian version of Mark Twain; or *Casa-grande e senzala* could be conceived of as a sociological version of *The Adventures of Huckleberry Finn* (1885). Freyre and Twain were the very embodiments of men descended from plantation masters—down to the white suits, Panama hats, and cigars—and their writings reflected this: coarse language, vulgarity, and problematic racial depictions. Freyre would have read *Huckleberry Finn*. We know for a fact, that he visited the North American deep South, and compared it to the Brazilian deep North.

As the literary critic Heloisa Toller Gomes points out, Freyre's discourse "serves to mitigate the social tensions inherent in the system by focusing exclusively on tradition and cultural continuity"; the tradition "is consistently described from the perspective of the master."[21] According to the Africanist Gerald Bender (1941–2017), a scholar on Portuguese-speaking African cultures, Freyre argued that "the significant impact of African civilizations on the Brazilian national character demonstrates the advancement of these civilizations," and "provided the rationale for a multiracial society in which the component races could be considered equally valuable and important."[22] Yet, as Bender perceives "many Brazilians, including Freyre himself on occasion, ignored the full ramifications of their conclusions on the importance of race in society."[23] Rather than ignoring it, it would have provided a soothing sense to the elites. As the anthropologist Hermano Vianna points out, "Freyre's book could be looked at, with better pertinence, as a project synchronized to the new revolutionary times of the 1930s."[24]

Foundational Myths: Martyrs, Tricksters, and Invitation-only Celebrations

Freyre's publication emerged a decade after the 1922 Modern Art Week, an event organized in São Paulo by Modernist artists during the celebration of 100 years of Brazilian independence. Many of these participating artists were descendants of former masters, representing the oligarchic elite and emerging urban bourgeoisie. Most of them had returned from studying in Europe. Their project of a multi-artistic manifesto centered around the concept of a truly Brazilian culture, even if seemingly unorthodox, aligned with those in power at that time. While avant-garde movements in Europe during the early twentieth century sought inspiration from a "primitive" aesthetic, Brazilians, as noted by Antonio Risério, did not need to venture far. Instead of travelling to Africa or seeking inspiration in vanished civilizations, they just needed to adapt an ethnographic approach in their quest for a modern exoticism.[25] "It is worth noting that Oswald and Mário were readers of Rodrigues and Arthur Ramos," comments Risério in reference to some of the key figures of the Modernist movement.[26] In the 1920s, São Paulo was hosting the Semana de Arte Moderna (Modern Art week) while during the same period, New York—a city with a comparable history—was experiencing the Harlem Renaissance, which laid the groundwork for what would later become known as Negritude. The Semana de Arte Moderna, on the other hand, could be seen as the emergence of a creolized art form, reaching its epitome in artists like Jorge Amado (1912–2001).

The Modernists drew inspiration from ethnographic studies to craft a new literary myth and hero that would embody the distinct characteristics of Brazilian civilization. These myths serve as artistic representations of Brazilian identity, offering justification for the organization of society and legitimizing the participation of its members. The literary critic Regina Zilbermann highlights that the pursuit of decolonization has been intertwined with the recovery of the local voice and the strengthening of national identity since the Romantic period.[27] The hero that emerged during the Romantic period (which followed the consolidation of Brazilian independence) was a noble savage character created by José de Alencar in his 1865 novel *Iracema: lenda do Ceará* (*A Tale from Ceará*). The hero Iracema, whose name is an anagram for America, is an Indigenous priestess who falls in love with a Portuguese soldier. Her love drives her to make a fateful decision—to leave her people and forsake her religious obligations. Together, the couple flees and establishes a home on the shores of the state of Ceará. Iracema gives birth in isolation and dies in childbirth. Their son, Moacir, a Tupi name that means "regret," becomes the mythical mestizo character that symbolized the origin of Brazilians.

By the time the Modernists emerged, earlier anthropological and ethnographic studies provided the support for them to introduce a more complex hero capable of embodying (perceived) African attributes. The Modernist icon Mário de Andrade (1893–1945) introduced the anti-hero Macunaíma in his 1928 novel *Macunaíma: o herói sem nenhum caráter* (*The Hero Without a Character*). In this narrative, Macunaíma and his brothers compose a racialized mosaic of ethnic images spanning diverse Brazilian cultural regions. This period marked a transformative phase in the Modernist movement, characterized by an evolving focus on folklore and nationalism. This shift, as analyzed by Zilbermann, was also mirrored in Raul Bopp's 1931 poem *Cobra Norato* and the 1928–1929 Anthropophagic Movement, led by Oswald de Andrade (1890–1954). These works drew heavily on African and Indigenous myths, employing "primitive" cultural motifs and worldviews as the cornerstone for their artistic expressions, which aimed to forge a nationalistic representation of Brazilian identity.[28] By 1928, this conceptualization of a creolized Brazilian identity was a fundamental element that permeated all facets of artistic and cultural expressions, representing a shift in perspective and a pervasive ideology.

The sociologist Renato Ortiz characterizes the myth of the three races as a cosmological narrative that emerged during a critical transformative period when Brazil transitioned from mercantilism to capitalism, monarchy to republic, and an economy based on slavery to one shaped by European migration.[29] The concept of a myth, as explained by Ortiz, usually implies a central point of origin—an axis from which all related mythic narratives emanate. While the melting pot ideology that narrates the genesis of the modern Brazilian mirrors the structure of cosmological myths found in ancient societies, it fails to ritualize itself in anthropological terms, since the concrete conditions necessary for its enactment remain purely symbolic.[30]

Futebol, Samba, and Carnaval:
Creolized Multimodal Narratives of All Things Brazilian

The 1930s were pivotal for Brazil, as the government sought to foster a cohesive sense of national identity amid regional discord and rising social disparities. This era was marked by civil rights struggles, labor uprisings, and conflicts between the agricultural elite and emerging industrialists, leading to isolated civil wars with different states or state coalitions fighting for political independence. During this period, Getúlio Vargas (1882–1954), backed by the bourgeoisie and military, seized power and launched a U.S.-backed industrialization policy that shifted economic dominance from plantation to factory owners, shaping a new ethnic-cultural national identity within a society divided between bosses and workers.[31]

Vargas ruled from 1930 to 1945 under the Estado Novo, an authoritarian regime characterized by populist policies. He crafted an image of a benevolent liberator, despite his numerous human rights violations. His administration sought to suppress regional and ethnic divisions by implementing strict immigration laws aimed at fostering "ethnic integration," a euphemism for miscegenation according to the 1934 Constitution.[32] This period saw legislative efforts to limit foreign workers in businesses and to promote European heritage within Brazil's demographic makeup, reflecting a phase of national redefinition and identity consolidation. In 1945, a decree stressed the "importance of preserving and promoting the most desirable characteristics of its European ancestors within the ethnic composition of the population."[33]

Throughout Brazilian republican history, the notion of "racial democracy" has existed alongside political authoritarianism, contributing to widespread political engagement. The sociologist Octávio Ianni (1926–2004) aptly summarized this maneuver, noting that while the ideology of racial democracy purported to "explain society," political authoritarianism was invoked to "explain the State."[34] The defense of the oligarchies, which shaped the modernized state, aligns with the role played by the patriarchal masters serving as justifications for a society of privilege, whether in the empire or the republic.[35] The authorized discourse on Brazil and its racial relations revolves around the interplay between social exclusion perpetuated by slavery (as reflected in the historiography of the Brazilian Empire) and the promotion of non-citizenship for Blacks during the abolition period and the formation of the Republic, all rooted in racist scientism.[36]

In the re-elaboration of Creole culture as the official national norm, regional cultural elements were extracted to compose the idea of a homogenized whole.[37] Creolization, a notion previously entangled with racist theories, underwent a transformation. In its new conception, it was promoted as a reason to take pride in everyday life and celebrate major events like Carnaval and soccer matches.[38] Candido perceived the 1930s as a time of burgeoning national consciousness marked by an "atmosphere of enthusiasm" for reinterpreting the national.[39] Initially emerging as isolated instances in the 1920s, these cultural shifts—which, according to Candido, seemed arbitrary and faced skepticism and resistance—became not only accepted but often appreciated by the 1930s.[40]

The ideologies and constructs of that era have undergone scrutiny and reassessment over the past few decades. As we near 2030, the ongoing disarticulation and rearticulation from the bottom up becomes increasingly visible. The steady reclamation of Afro-Brazilian cultural expressions—whether recognized as "national" by the dominant powers of the 1930s or remaining less visible and acknowledged—has laid the philosophical groundwork for African descendants in Brazil to validate their heritage and define how it should be acknowledged and treated.

During the 1930s, Capoeira, a longstanding practice of African-Brazilian civilization, went from being associated with criminal loitering to receiving official recognition as a national sport. In 1932, the first Capoeira academy was established by Manuel dos Reis Machado, known as Mestre Bimba (1899–1974). He introduced a set of rules and procedures that aligned Capoeira with practices of recognized martial arts. The government permitted its practice in enclosed areas that were registered with the police.[41] This transition culminated in 1953 when Vargas congratulated Mestre Bimba for transforming Capoeira into Brazil's "national fight."[42]

In 1933, soccer underwent a significant transformation as it became professionalized, and Black soccer players began representing Brazil on the international stage.[43] This era witnessed the emergence of soccer player Leônidas da Silva (1913–2004), fondly known as the "Black Diamond" or the "Rubber Man," who rose to become one of Brazil's most celebrated figures. One of his legacies was the introduction of a stylized signature move called the "bicycle goal," an acrobatic maneuver that involved leaping into the air, executing a reverse spin to catch a high ball, and then delivering a powerful kick towards the goal. Journalist Ruy Castro highlights that by 1937, Leônidas da Silva had achieved remarkable fame, ranking alongside "abominable dictator Getúlio Vargas" and the highly acclaimed singer Orlando Silva as one of the three most renowned individuals in Brazil.[44]

This era also marked the acknowledgement of Afro-Brazilian Umbanda as "a legitimate Brazilian" religious expression. In 1939, the first Umbanda federation, the União Espírita de Umbanda do Brasil (Spiritist Union of Umbanda in Brazil), was established, and in 1941, the first Umbanda congress was convened.[45] Umbanda, as a significant manifestation of the Kongo-Angola cultural matrix, was often diminished in importance and relevance by scholars and authorities who could only perceive it as a mere extension of African-Catholic traditions, failing to recognize the distinct elements of its cosmology. If, at the turn of the twentieth century, Umbanda practitioners struggled for more positive recognition within Brazilian society, their primary challenge since the 1990s has come from Evangelical groups, which have been steadily gaining influence. These groups, to varying degrees, have organized and adapted their doctrines in simultaneous opposition to and assimilation of Umbanda's concepts. They are defined as an imaginary opposite to demonized Umbanda, leading to violent rejection and brutal attacks on African-Brazilian religious centers and their members. Between 1990 and 2019, the number of Evangelical temples has increased by 543 percent, and the percentage of the population identifying as Evangelical has risen from 9 percent in 1990 to 31 percent in 2020.[46] This radical sociocultural change has brought about unexpected transformations, and extensive research has been conducted on this phenomenon. One clear consequence is that, among various political factions, the Evangelical group has been the only entity consistently growing in both numbers and political representation.

By far, the most unifying element of the populist ideology was Samba and Carnaval. In 1928, the first Carnaval Samba school, Deixa Falar ("Let them say whatever they want"), was founded in Rio de Janeiro, and in 1932, the first organized Carnaval parade took to the streets of the city.[47] The rise of commercial radio during the 1930s and 1940s played a pivotal role in popularizing Samba and Marcha "which were originally associated with the slums and suburbs of Rio, across the entire country and among people of all social classes."[48] Radio, as a mass medium broadcasting content over great distances, transformed these musical forms into a nationwide form of daily cultural consumption.[49] In 1935, the oldest radio program in South America—originally named "A Hora do Brasil" ("The Time of Brazil") and rebranded in 1971 as "A Voz do Brasil" ("The Voice of Brazil")—was established primarily to broadcast and promote the actions of the executive branch during Vargas's government.[50] Since then, this official news program has been delivering news Monday through Friday at 7 PM on radio stations across the country.

Popular music broadcast by radio also played a pivotal role in the process of national cultural creolization. As noted by Risério, what might once have been perceived as an exotic curiosity in the 1920s or 1930s, such as a Bahian poem about the Orisha Yemaya, today enjoys widespread recognition, with Brazilians participating in festivities and offerings to Yemaya on beaches nationwide.[51] This affirmation of non-European cultural practices has catalyzed significant shifts within Brazilian culture, making regional forms and practices of popular culture comprehensible on a national scale. Risério emphasizes the contributions of popular Brazilian "Poemusic" in providing national social projection and visibility to Brazilian cultural forms rooted in Black-African traditions.[52] Samba, in particular, has been instrumental in amalgamating diverse regional cultures into a cohesive national identity and was used by populist governments as a unifying cultural force. Samba composers assumed the role of popular philosophers who, "unburdened by elitist inhibitions, could decipher the intricate and complex socio-cultural tapestry of Brazil."[53] Risério's assertions about Samba composers underscores the distinct roles of literary and musical (or popular) genres in Brazilian culture. Music afforded a freedom to non-European expressions and their composers, a liberty that writers, expressing themselves through the most Eurocentric of all arts, could not directly access.

The White Problem: Baptism, Confirmation, and Communion

As Samba composers were shaping interpretations of a creole Brazil, scholarly analyses of the era were also being formulated. When Pedro Álvares Cabral first arrived in Brazil, he was accompanied by Pero Vaz de Caminha, an embedded reporter or scribe working for King Dom Manuel I. Caminha's report described his observations on the Island of the True Cross (Ilha de Vera Cruz). Despite the fact that Vera Cruz was neither an island nor was it India, it held a valuable resource: the Pau-Brasil, a wood with a color resembling burning coal (*brasa*).[54] As the Portuguese established their extraction and exportation of Brazilwood, the name of the island and its Indigenous people gradually gave way to the name of this valuable resource.[55] Caminha's letter is considered by some the first literary work composed in Brazil, akin to Brazil's official birth certificate in the European context. Similarly, Gilberto Freyre's 1933 *Casa-grande e Senzala* can be seen as serving as a rite of passage—an off-key coming-of-age ceremonial ode. Through this mystifying creole narrative, Brazil introduces itself to the Western world.

Freyre began writing *Casa-grande* on a snowy day in New York. Startled by the unexpected sight of Brazilian men appearing amid the snow, he may have felt compelled to unravel the enigma of Brazil. In describing his experience, he recounts this moment when, after being away from Brazil for three years, he witnessed a group of Brazilian marines disembarking and "stepping onto the soft snow of Brooklyn."[56] These "mulattos and *cafuzos*" who emerged as if in a mirage appeared to him as "caricatures of men." He relates that the image made him recall a line from an American travel report that referred to "the fearfully mongrel aspect of most" Brazilians. It was that moment that spurred Freyre into action, prompting him to take up the challenge of addressing what was perhaps for him Brazil's most pressing issue: "there was none that disturbed" him "as much as that of miscegenation."[57] With a sense of revelation and mission, he states that "it was as if everything depended on me and on those of my generation, on our way of sorting those secular issues."[58]

It has been argued that the concept of racial democracy originated from the insecurities experienced by Brazilian scholars of predominantly white heritage.[59] Facing feelings of inferiority—perceived as less cultured, capable, and developed compared to their American and European counterparts—these intellectuals crafted an ideology that posited the contrary.[60] As noted by Vianna, Freyre attributed positive traits to the mestizo population, thereby transforming Brazilian culture from perceived backwardness to a celebrated, diverse identity foundational to its unique and evolving national character.[61] Freyre's luso-tropicologist principles included reconciling Brazilian cultural contradictions through "African mediation."[62]

Moving away from earlier Romantic narratives that emphasized Indigenous contributions, Freyre positioned Africans as pivotal in bridging various colonial divides. He describes these as a series of antagonisms: between Catholics and heretics, landowners and pariahs, university graduates and the illiterate, masters and slaves.[63] Continuing the discourse established by von Martius, Freyre listed factors contributing to societal balance, including miscegenation, professional and residential mobility, accessible public office, the lyricism of Portuguese Christianity, and the absence of geographical barriers.[64] Vianna summarized the reception of *Casa-grande e Senzala*, noting its departure from prior cultural discourses and its role in redefining national identity around "constructive creolization."[65]

Emília Viotti da Costa, one of the Brazilian scholars who has examined the reasons behind the enduring acceptance of Freyre's narrative, questioned the preference of Brazil's social scientists for European and American ideologies emphasizing white superiority, given that, in 1870, only about 40 percent of Brazil's population was categorized as white.[66] According to Viotti da Costa, in the face theories promoting the inferiority of Blacks, the Brazilian elite would have found no better solution than to embrace assimilationist and whitening ideologies as an alternative to North American segregationist practices. Unlike the U.S. segregationist ideology, which emphasized origin-based prejudices, Brazil adopted a color-based system, determining race by appearance.[67]

Hiatus: Another Story, or, It Is Not What You Believe It Is

The Brazilian Luso-tropical myth, characterized by its multimodal narratives and pervasive ideological reach, has continuously evolved. Undergoing constant updates, it has replicated itself through overarching mutations. In the first decades of the twenty-first century, this ideology was legally challenged in the Supreme Court. Before moving on to the recent movements that have been dismantling Brazil's mainstream racial ideologies from multiple angles, I will first outline some of the key counter-narratives.

African diasporic cosmologies are inclusive epistemologies that have, for centuries, consistently interpreted foreign concepts and recreated them across various languages, both sacred and secular. The more visible expressions of African diasporic cultures have navigated a complex history of negotiations and mediations, with exemplary references dating back to heroic figures like Queen Nzinga of Ndongo (1582–1663).

Unlike rural African-Brazilian communities, urban communities have interacted with Luso-Brazilian hegemonic forces through negotiations with government agencies, law enforcement, and regulators. This dynamic is clearly seen, for instance, in the advancements in social rights facilitated by Candomblé *terreiro* communities and their leaders.

Historically, African-Catholic fraternities and Congada communities have sustained a centuries-long relationship with the Catholic Church, reminiscent of an era of ancient Catholicism with medieval overtones. Rural communities could, at times and to a certain extent, function akin to Maroon communities. Often less visible and unintelligible to outsiders, these communities have managed to interpret and integrate external cultures while often remaining detached from a mutual broader societal engagement.

The seemingly recognizable Catholic framework and language, deeply rooted in Kongo-Angola cosmologies, have often been misunderstood and overlooked by outsiders, who lack, among others, a comprehensive understanding of Central African Catholicism from the fifteenth to eighteenth centuries. In fact, we do not yet have a true grasp of how Catholicism was perceived and transformed from a Central African perspective during this period.

This ancient African-Catholicism has translated cosmologies into forms and terms that convey one hegemonic meaning when used outside their communities—"da porteira para fora" ("from the gate out"). When used within the community—"da porteira para dentro" ("from the gate in")—these apparently legible concepts and aesthetics take on entirely different meanings and a unique set of references, comprehensible only to those fluent in this specific cultural language, a framing I owe to ethnomusicologist Rafael Galante.[68]

From the Appendix to the Cover Page: Mãe Aninha, Iyá Obá Biyi (1869–1938), Tata Bate Folha (1881–1946), and Manuel Falefá (1900–1980)

The third founding moment of Euro-Afro-Brazilian studies is marked by two memorable conventions held in 1934 and 1937, one in Recife and the other in Salvador. The first convention, organized by Freyre, primarily consisted of scholars who aimed to demonstrate that miscegenation did not lead to genetic deterioration. In contrast, the second convention, organized by Carneiro and supported by Ramos, provided a platform for philosophers, intellectuals, and leaders, including those who may not have had formal education. Besides traditional scholars, Carneiro also invited representatives from Candomblé houses, among others, to share their testimonies.

The transcripts of these congresses offer insights into the relationships that developed between the researchers and those being studied. In the transcripts of the first congress, one scholar noted that some of the Candomblé high priests, the Babalorixás, "are so proud of their knowledge and powers that they converse with us as equals, while others cannot help but display an air of superiority." [69] In the publication of transcripts from the second congress, the testimonies of the non-traditional scholars and representatives of Candomblé communities who attended the conference appear in a 20-page appendix rather than the main 360-page compendium—and are not listed in the index.[70] The short appendix features texts by three authors and representatives of the three major Candomblé philosophical schools: Jeje (Ewe-Fon), Congo (Kongo-Angola), and Ketu (Nago). One of the authors included in the appendix, Manuel Falefá, also known as Manuel da Formiga (Manoel Vitorino da Costa, 1900–1980), was devoted to the Creator Vodun of the primeval swamps, Nana Buluku.[71] Falefá contributed an article titled "The Religious World of Blacks in Bahia."[72] The other two authors are founders of some of the most distinguished Candomblé communities in Bahia: Mãe Aninha of Ilê Axé Opó Afonjá and Tata Bernardino Bate Folha of Terreiro do Bate Folha or Mansu Banduquenqué. Both of these *terreiro* communities were designated National Historic Landmarks at the turn of the twenty-first century. In addition to these three published community scholars, Carneiro mentions in the introduction, without context, two other conference participants: Vavá Pau Brasil and Maria Bada, described as "the most knowledgeable of all 'Negras Velhas' of Brazilian Candomblés" ("a mais sabida de todas as negras velhas").[73]

Tata Bernardino Bate Folha, also known as Tata Ampumandezu (Manoel Bernardino da Paixão, 1881–1946), presented a paper titled "Ligeira explicação sobre a nação Congo" ("Brief Explanation of the Congo Nation").[74] Mãe Aninha, also known as Iyá Obá Biyi (Eugênia Anna dos Santos, 1869–1938"), contributed with a compendium titled *Notas sobre os comestíveis africanos: receitas e quitutes afro-brasileiros* (*Notes on African Edibles: Afro-Brazilian Recipes and Delicacies*), which Carneiro reports having prepared just for this occasion.[75] Only one page of the compendium is published in the appendix. Although Mãe Aninha was not acknowledged as one of the co-organizers of the Congress, Carneiro did indicate her importance to the Congress. He writes that during the Congress, "Aninha opened her home to host a beautiful African party for the congressmen, whom she had especially invited."[76] Carneiro also refers to a document signed on that occasion which reflected the high regard in which she was held by the scholars and politicians who gathered at her *terreiro* community.[77] Mãe Aninha actively participated in various movements alongside intellectuals, and with the support of politicians, she successfully persuaded Vargas to promulgate the Presidential Decree of 1934. This decree lifted the ban on Afro-Brazilian religious practices that had been in place since 1890.[78] As anthropologist Mariana Morais pointed out, by aligning themselves with the scholarly community, these religious leaders recognized an opportunity to secure protection for their practices and shield themselves from the prejudice and police violence they often faced as victims.[79] Mãe Aninha's achievements as a leader and as a Black woman were of immense significance, and she remains a powerful reference point for Afro-Brazilian communities.

Truth be told, one of the community leaders, Babalawo Martiniano Eliseu do Bomfim Ajimúdà (1859–1943), also known as Ojé L'adê, held dual roles as an official member of the Congress's executive committee and as an honorary president. Proficient in both Yoruba and English, Eliseu do Bomfim translated the presentation of Nigerian activist Ladipo Solanke (1886–1958) into Portuguese and was referred to in the anthology as a "professor."[80] His knowledge of the Ifa Oracle, his linguistic proficiency, as well as his pan-African connections, put him on an equal footing with the academic scholars (significant enough to warrant official acknowledgment). At the conclusion of the Congress, it was decided to create the Afro-Brazilian Institute of Bahia to monitor police repression and advocate for religious freedom for Afro-Brazilian *terreiros*. The board was comprised of Carneiro as the general secretary, Ramos serving as the benefactor, and Eliseu do Bomfim in the role of president.[81]

After these initial Afro-Brazilian congresses, there was a 45-year gap before another congress took place. It wasn't until 1982 in Recife that anthropologist Roberto Mauro Motta organized the Third Afro-Brazilian Congress, with Freyre chosen as the honorary president.[82] In 1949, Ramos took on the role of director of the Department of Social Sciences at UNESCO and played a pivotal role in further promoting, both nationally and internationally, the image of Brazil as "racial laboratory" or a "laboratory of civilization."[83] During the gap period between the second and the third congresses, foreign scholars like the U.S. sociologist Donald Pierson (1900–1995) and Melville Herskovits (1895–1963), visited Brazil and further influenced the discourse on African-Brazilian studies. The congresses held in Recife and Salvador—as Mariana Morais points out—played a role in the larger sphere of research being conducted at the time, specifically, African American studies.[84]

6

Law

Peace Without a Voice Is Not Harmony

My soul is armed *A minha alma 'tá armada*
And aimed at the face of harmony *E apontada para a cara do sossego*
Because peace without a voice, *Pois paz sem voz paz sem voz*
peace without a voice
Is not peace, it's fear *Não é paz é medo*

Marcelo Yuka (1969–2019)

DISARMING OFFICIAL CREOLE NARRATIVES: AFFIRMATIVE ACTION IN BRAZIL

As a result of decades of social protest by Black Brazilians, in the early years of the twenty-first century, Brazil witnessed the emergence of affirmative action policies. Government agencies and universities began implementing quotas for employees and students, which gradually gained acceptance, particularly in educational institutions. At the turn of the twenty-first century, Black students made up about 2 percent of the student body in most Brazilian universities.[1] Initially, the adoption of affirmative action policies met significant resistance. Critics argued that the government was complicating an already complex issue by importing a solution from the United States, a country with different racial definitions and dynamics. One of the most emblematic studies from the opposition was titled *We Are Not Racists: A Reaction to Those Who Want to Turn Us Into a Two-Color Nation*.[2]

The sociologist Vânia Penha-Lopes highlighted that one argument against quotas was their perceived irrelevance to Brazil's reputedly egalitarian racial nature. Yet opponents of affirmative action did not see racial democracy as a myth but as an anthropological ideal yet to be achieved.[3] Contrary to the United States, where the dream is that anyone can achieve wealth and influence, the anthropologist Jan Hoffman French notes that Brazil has promoted a notion "in which the whitening principle—an almost mirror image of the United States—would permit advancement."[4] As Penha-Lopes summarizes, unlike in the United States, where a single drop of Black blood may classify someone as Black, in Brazil, a drop of White blood might classify someone as non-Black. Her research on the first cohort admitted under the quota system at the State University of Rio de Janeiro (UERJ) in 2003 and 2004 found that most quota students she interviewed conceived of race "as a fluid and malleable system," influenced more by personal interpretations of their ancestries and life stories than by genetics.[5] The fundamental challenge with affirmative action was its emergence in a society in denial about its own racism. The feminist and philosopher Sueli Carneiro emphasized that the effects of prejudice and discrimination cannot be undone by universal policies alone; a progressive and inclusive approach is required.[6] Carneiro argued that any questioning of affirmative action and quotas likely stems from the inherent cynicism and hypocrisy of Brazilian racism.[7]

Until 1991, the Brazilian Institute for Geography and Statistics (IBGE) recognized four racial categories: White, Black, *Pardo* (Brown/Mestizo), and Yellow. In 1991, Indigenous was added as a fifth option. *Pardo* was a category introduced in 1976 following a study that prompted Brazilians to use 135 different colors to describe themselves. The term became the Brazilian equivalent of non-white and supported the perpetuation of the image of Brazil as a predominantly white country.[8] *Pardo* suggests a "shifting color continuum"—as described by the sociologist Carlos Hasenbalg (1942–2014)—offering a fantasy of multiple identities accessible only to a few.[9] Based on field research with quota students, Penha-Lopes noted that "several interviewees were clearly turned off" by the Black and white binary.[10] When asked about their loyalties, they would likely respond, "I'm Brazilian." As Penha-Lopes realized, "despite all that malleability, *pardo* is not the same as Black for many of the students"; it appeared "even as a synonym of *Brazilian*."[11] She suggested that quota policies at universities can contribute to the reformulation of the idea of nation in Brazil allowing for social mobility and fostering new individual and group identities: as "plurifunctional," such policies not only allow "the growth of opportunities for the social mobility of those who have so far been largely excluded," but also "promote the emergence of new individual and group identities."[12]

Affirmative action has had a significant impact on both society and politics, revolutionizing how administrators, academics, and the general population perceive racial issues, injustices, and their potential solutions.[13] In the first decades of the twenty-first century, the once-dominant myth of racial democracy gave way to a growing awareness of entrenched racial disadvantage and structural racism. The effects of structural racism became more pronounced and evident with the onset of the COVID-19 pandemic, highlighting significant social disparities and fueling the Vidas Negras Importam (Black Lives Matter) protests in Brazil. In 2020, the Coalizão Negra Por Direitos (Black Coalition for Rights), a coalition representing various sectors of the Black movement, was established.[14] In June of that year, they released a manifesto signed by activists, intellectuals, and artists, urging individuals, organizations, and the public sector to take a stand in the fight against racism. The manifesto opens with the phrase "Estamos por nossa própria conta" (We are on our own), a tribute to South African activist Steve Biko (1947–1977), the founder of the Black Consciousness Movement and philosophy.[15]

Biko's philosophy, which focused on decolonizing and liberating the minds of Africans, was articulated through the South African Students' Organization (SASO), a caucus formed in 1968 by Black South African students. Biko's motto, "Black man, you are on your own!" became a pan-African reference for rejecting tactics of appeasement.[16] Biko's influence extended to Brazil, where in 1992 activists and educators inaugurated the Biko Cultural Institute in Salvador, Bahia. This institute aims to facilitate the inclusion of Black students in academic spaces. Its headquarters stands in the center of Salvador in an area where slave auctions were once held.[17] The 2020 Brazilian Coalizão manifesto states:

> We are on our own. We have always fought, and we will prevail.
> We, organizations, entities, groups, and collectives of the Brazilian Black movement, reaffirm our legacy of resistance, struggle, generation of knowledge, and life. Historically, we continue to confront racism, which structures this society and produces inequalities that predominantly affect our existence. During nearly four hundred years of enslavement and since the beginning of the Republic, we have been subjected to rights violations, anti-Black racism, racial discrimination, violence, and genocide. Nevertheless, in our individual and collective journeys, we have contributed to the wealth of this country. The Brazilian state, aligned with a worldwide trend, blatantly reveals its horrifying face. A significant portion of society no longer upholds the mask of hypocrisy and openly embraces its racist, prejudiced, and intolerant nature. Its policy of death—necropolitics—and the narrative of hatred are currently in full alignment. We are dealing with a concept of the nation that manifests itself in the daily practice of young Blacks being murdered every 23 minutes, daily massacres, an increasing rate of incarceration, and severe violence against the incarcerated

population and those in socioeducational facilities. It includes the murder of Black LGBTTQI+ individuals, increasing cases of femicide of Black women, rape and murder of Black children, persecution of Black immigrants and refugees, criminalization of and violence against the homeless population, escalating conflicts in the territories of traditional *quilombola* communities, and systematic acts of terror against African-derived religions.[18]

Encompassing a wide range of issues, the manifesto denounces systemic racial inequalities and advocates for social justice for the Black population in Brazil. Among its demands are eradicating underemployment and precarious work; guaranteeing labor and social rights; protecting Quilombola (Maroon) territories, ancestral communities, and sacred sites of African-derived religions; combating religious intolerance; promoting inclusive education policies; collecting reliable statistical data on the Black population; reforming drug policies; ending the militarization of public security; reforming the prison system; enhancing Black representation in politics and the justice system; and protecting human rights defenders and social movements.

Twenty-five years before the publication of this manifesto, as the military regime came to an end, a revised Federal Constitution began to acknowledge the rights of Afro-descendants, signifying the start of a shift in the narrative on race in Brazil. A crucial milestone, described by the sociologist Sales Augusto dos Santos as a "parting of the waters in the fight against racism," was the Zumbi March in 1995, commemorating the 300th anniversary of Maroon leader Zumbi's death.[19] In 2003, November 20 was officially recognized as National Black Consciousness Day. In academia, we are currently witnessing significant emerging transformations in student and faculty demographics. The rise of new African-Brazilian generations assuming roles as university professors represents a paradigm shift pursued since at least the era of the Frente Negra Brasileira (the Black Brazilian Front) movement in the 1930s. Despite national political challenges and setbacks, we are witnessing the unfolding of a transformative period in Brazil's racial history and the establishment of a new era.

THE TRUTH COMMISSION AND THE BURNING OF ARCHIVES

In 2014, a collective of Black Brazilian lawyers took the initiative to propose a project to the Brazilian Bar Association aimed at extending the work begun by the Brazilian National Truth Commission (Comissão Nacional da Verdade), which had been established in 2011 to investigate human rights abuses during the military dictatorship (1964–1985) and to reconstruct the *truth* about the longer period stretching from 1946 to 1988.[20] This new commission, named the Truth Commission on Black Slavery in Brazil (Comissão Nacional da Verdade da Escravidão Negra), was established in 2015 with the support of the Bar.[21]

In a study on the creation and methodology of the Truth Commission on Black Slavery in Brazil, the Brazilian anthropologist Márcia Leitão Pinheiro discusses how the commission's interpretation of multiculturalism challenges the official narrative of the nation—one that has long been criticized by the Black Movement.[22] The prevalent myths of cordial slavery and racial democracy are interpreted by the commission as concealments or falsifications of historical violence. In 2017, in Rio de Janeiro, a group of Black lawyers and activists from Black Movement organizations established the Commission for Historical Reparations for Black People (Comissão de Reparações Históricas da População Negra). Both commissions aim to spark societal discussions about the excessive force directed against Brazil's Black population, with the goal of enabling change and fostering accountability in state institutions.[23]

Committees have been established in various Brazilian states and municipalities, following the methodology approved by the Federal Council of the Brazilian Bar Association.[24] These truth committees have worked to expose the crime of Black slavery, highlight its continuing effects, and hold the Brazilian state accountable.[25] They have relied on cooperation agreements and partnerships with various institutes and organizations, including universities, to extend their investigations and recover the memory of significant events from the slavery period. The coordinated efforts of knowledge production, practical engagement, and mobilization of social actors have made it possible to confront state policies that have historically normalized the marginalization of Black lives.[26]

In 2015, Humberto Adami, the president of the National Truth Commission on Black Slavery in Brazil, stated that the commission's initial goal was not to seek financial reparations but to start a process aimed at reconstructing a new nation.[27] Adami, referring to the ongoing investigations, stated that they would bring to public knowledge:

> A Brazil that is unknown to many Brazilians. A Brazil that has been hidden in the dungeons of slave quarters. A Brazil that does not recognize the value of those who came from Africa and their descendants, whose lives still bear the remnants of slavery. It is the hope of one day achieving the same standard of citizenship that non-Black Brazilians enjoy.[28]

Since the creation of the National Truth Commission on Black Slavery in Brazil, debates on constitutive violence and the nationalist imaginary from a legal perspective have intensified, aiming to dismantle the complex layers of institutionalized historical myths. A group of three constitutional law lawyers—Evandro Piza Duarte, Guilherme Scotti, and Menelick de Carvalho Netto—has conducted a legal analysis of the narrative surrounding the burning of slavery archives by Ruy Barbosa, a landmark event in Brazilian national mythology.[29] They argue that this incident is part of a broader process of erasing historical records in the construction of the nation's history. The group emphasizes that the acknowledgment initiatives started by the Truth Commission on Black Slavery in Brazil, together with the 2015 decision by the Brazilian Supreme Court to remove time limits for prosecuting racist offenses, require a comprehensive reexamination of historical *facts*, encompassing both past and present contexts. This reexamination involves empirical presentation, sociological interpretation, historiography, and analysis of the development of race relations.[30]

According to Duarte, Scotti, and Netto, the discourse surrounding the burning of the archives is part of a knowledge management system in which Black voices have historically been deemed inadequate for describing Black lives, while descendants of the elite have been presumed responsible for crafting an official narrative of slavery. Over time, this authorized voice has consolidated its dominance, particularly within academic fields such as anthropology, history, and sociology.[31]

THE TRIAL

The Brazilian Supreme Court has played a critical role in highlighting how official historiography shapes national identity and contributes to the systematic erasure of Black Brazilian memory. The first significant case occurred in 2004 and involved a Supreme Court ruling that affected the statute of limitations for racist offenses as defined by the 1988 Constitution.[32] This case centered on a habeas corpus petition filed against a Superior Court of Justice decision upholding the conviction of a writer and publisher of anti-Semitic materials. During the trial, the Supreme Court debated the limits of freedom of expression, including the publication of anti-Semitic books, the definition of "crime of racism," and the application of constitutional exceptions to the statute of limitations based on racial classification. The Court also debated whether Jews should be considered a race, thus falling under the constitutional exception to the statute of limitations established in 1988.[33]

Minister Marco Aurélio granted the habeas corpus petition, dissenting from the majority, with a rationale rooted in an interpretation of Brazilian history and the shaping of national identity. He emphasized the importance of preserving freedom of expression as a cornerstone of democracy, especially in public discourse. In support of his ruling, he referenced Ruy Barbosa's controversial decision to burn slavery archives, arguing that such actions—purportedly intended to prevent compensation claims by plantation owners—ultimately deprived future generations of a comprehensive understanding of Brazil's historical narrative. He cited Barbosa's act to contend that ignorance about the past was not inherent, but rather a result of restricted freedom of expression. This event, he argued, hindered the development of a collective consciousness informed by historical perspectives, perpetuating "the transmitted legacy" of ignorance.[34]

As part of his argument, the minister connected this historical narrative to broader discussions of national identity and miscegenation, citing criticisms faced by the sociologist Gilberto Freyre for suggesting that racial mixing has fortified the Brazilian populace. He also referenced excerpts from classic works such as Nina Rodrigues's *Os africanos no Brasil* (*Africans in Brazil*) and *Projetos para o Brasil* (*Projects for Brazil*) by José Bonifácio de Andrada e Silva (1763–1838). To justify the application of the statute of non-prescription, Minister Aurélio concluded that judgments should take into account Brazil's unique social reality rather than relying on European cultural assumptions or historical paradigms foreign to the Brazilian context—assumptions that could potentially restrict Brazilians' freedom of expression.[35]

The legal and historical discourse of the Supreme Court's deliberation has broader constitutional and societal implications, as analyzed by lawyers Evandro Piza Duarte, Guilherme Scotti, and Menelick de Carvalho Netto. It intersects with Brazilian constitutionalism and the potential legal recognition of a history rooted in colonialism and slavery. The authors raise fundamental questions about how society addresses the past to understand the present and challenge the normalization of violations against Black and Indigenous peoples' rights: "What is the significance of this past in the present?"[36] They proposed examining the contradictory aspects of the "Burning of Archives" narrative from five critical angles:

(1) The Burning of Archives, traditionally seen simply as a measure to prevent compensation to slave owners, established a framework that benefited slave owners and continues to benefit their descendants. This includes property rights

policies and fiscal support that enhanced slave-owner profits, as well as labor policies that delayed abolition and perpetuated illegal enslavement. Such policies enabled the state to favor certain rural producers and maintain a system of racialized private property. Consequently, this framework has legitimized white landowners employing rudimentary farming techniques—such as monocrop plantations—while marginalizing smallholders, traditional communities, Indigenous peoples, and Maroon lands by labeling them as underdeveloped (in terms of agricultural techniques), thereby hindering their property rights.

(2) The narrative of the burning of slave archives in Brazil conceals ongoing racial discrimination within the legal system and legitimizes unauthorized slave ownership through archival voids. It inaccurately suggests that slavery became irrelevant after abolition and portrays the transition from monarchy to republic as a major shift in social dynamics, promoting an illusory image of a racially integrated society. Black communities' struggles for recognition and opposition to racialization are often overlooked, eclipsed by the enduring legacy of Brazil's slaveholding past.[37]

(3) The belief that the burning of archives served solely to prevent compensation to slave owners oversimplifies the complex political dynamics involved. It ignores how this action benefited slave owners, enabled illicit labor exploitation under the Republican regime, and disregarded the moral and material debts owed to the enslaved. Abolitionists such as Joaquim Nabuco (1849–1910) and José do Patrocínio (1854–1905) recognized slavery as a crime against humanity and advocated for compensation to the formerly enslaved.[38] Patrocínio's calculations of the estimated debt underscored the extent of the exploitation endured by Africans and their descendants.[39] The demands for reparations came not only from property owners with illegitimate claims but also from those treated as property. Despite the visibility of these demands, key figures of both the abolitionist movement and the Republic chose to ignore them, resulting in deliberate political decisions that further perpetuated racial divisions and inequality.

(4) The claim that the burning of the archives made the study of slavery in Brazil practically impossible suggests a deliberate erasure of verifiable sources. Historians have long debunked this myth, affirming the existence of abundant documentary sources on slavery within Brazil.[40] Nevertheless, the persistence of this misconception has not only hindered scholarly research but also led to the further loss of archives through public neglect.[41] Duarte, Scotti, and Netto examine the role of archives and historical records, critiquing the belief that "no truth is truer than that legitimized by bureaucracy."[42] Official Brazilian history, tracing back to the imperial era, has mainly relied on accounts from literate

elites, government officials, clergy, and travelers, frequently overlooking the perspectives of Africans and their descendants. The act of burning the archives thus masks how the preservation of slavery's memory was undermined by widespread disregard for the perspectives of African-Brazilians who lived through it.

The authors probe the significance of archival documentation for African-Brazilians in the post-abolition context, asking why the destruction of documents affirming their enslaved status should matter. They consider whether there were unresolved labor disputes with former masters, a need to assert civil rights, a disinterest in documenting origins, or whether official registration might have served as a tool to formalize the legal status of those previously undocumented or without surnames. They also contemplate whether the absence of such records, coupled with repressive policing tactics, was strategically used to deny full citizenship to this population. This inquiry highlights the potential use of archival erasure as a deliberate strategy to undermine the citizenship of African-Brazilians.[43] Reconstructing this history requires a critical evaluation of the rhetoric surrounding documentary sources, especially the underrepresented narratives of former enslaved Africans, which have been largely omitted from official historical accounts.

(5) Duarte, Scotti, and Netto's fifth perspective on the narrative of the Burning of Archives considers its framing as a response to "historical trauma," reflecting a social construct through which the past is reinterpreted for symbolic processing. In this context, whether Ruy Barbosa ordered the burning or not is less important than what the idea of the burning represents in the struggle for institutional recognition by those who have been denied access to their historical past. This perceived disconnection from the archival record stems not only from restricted freedom of expression but, more critically, from the monopolization of historical narratives. This monopoly has fostered a myth centered around loss or the impossibility of memory. While acknowledged as a myth, it continues to resonate with the lived experiences of those affected by historical erasure.

In Brazilian historiography, the representation of Black Brazilians is restricted by a "structure of truth" that dictates a specific narrative and discourages alternative ones.[44] This historiographical approach, deeply rooted in the legacy of slavery, consistently sidelines and marginalizes African-Brazilians and their continuous struggle for freedom. The denial of Black agency is reinforced by sustained institutional efforts to shape collective memory—efforts perpetuated across diverse sectors including state institutions, museums, universities, research institutes, and the educational system—all working to obscure Black contributions to the historical narrative.[45]

THAT WHICH COULD NEVER BE BURNED

> *legacy is image* *legado é imagem*
> *a field not mist* *campo em vez de névoa*
> *a sponge (its tree)* *esponja (sua árvore)*
> *eternal is the horse* *perene o cavalo*
> *that at night, in the stirrups,* *a noite no estribo*
> *it travels raveling* *que viaja*
>
> Edimilson de Almeida Pereira

The development of a Brazilian sense of conceivable identities and the establishment of a nation above all nations within Brazilian territory have drawn extensively from African paradigms. While pan-African-Brazilian epistemologies have incorporated European paradigms deemed useful, worthwhile, or necessary, this historical reciprocity has been far from symmetrical. The first part of this book has examined how Africans have been imagined, narrated, and portrayed, from the time of Camões's *The Lusiads* right up to the first decades of the twenty-first century and the rearticulations and reconfigurations achieved by African Brazilians through their social rights conquests. We have journeyed past Adamastor and Niterói, titans crafted by Camões and Januário da Cunha Barbosa, who confronted the fury of the Sea and Water Gods only to be transmuted into stone; Bento Teixeira's Proteus, who witnessed the triumphant return of Saturn and heralded the zenith of a mighty New Lusitania; Dias's petrified giant and his Nero-like king, sleeping blissfully on a lavishly adorned bed as his kingdom succumbs to flames; Duque Estrada's Brazilian giant, eternally cradled in splendor and now reawakening in the twenty-first century—a trajectory that may well signal the breaking of a 450-year spell, a turning that clears the path for what has long been deferred, and gestures toward possible new futures.

From the aspects and imagery associated with the processes of Euro-Afro-Brazilian national and cultural formation, I shift the focus in the second half to the Afro-(Euro)-Brazilian dimension of this civilizational development. The use of parentheses in the latter term is deliberate: it emphasizes the enduring and predominant role of pan-African articulations that predate the European era of maritime expansion, as well as the limited role played by Europeans in these co-creations (despite the imposition of widely intelligible Eurocentric cultural concepts and languages that shape the lives of most of us). While **Euro-Afro-Brazil** refers to the official cultural configuration of Brazil as a nation that has drawn extensively from African mythological, musical, performance, medical, scientific, philosophical, and religious frameworks, **Afro-(Euro)-Brazil** refers to the African-Brazilian civilization that has incorporated and reimagined European arts and sciences while maintaining a predominantly pan-African orientation. Euro-Afro-Brazil adheres primarily to a Eurocentric paradigm, relying on decontextualized African cultural elements. Afro-(Euro)-Brazil, on the other hand, has an Afrocentric orientation and is grounded in recontextualized African epistemologies.

The backbone of Euro-Brazil is Afro-Brazilian. It does not stand on its own; it can only exist as Euro-Afro-Brazil. Its relationship to Afro-Brazil is both intrinsically vital and systematically exploitative, predatory, and abusive. Afro-Brazil supports itself on its own vertebrae. Its relation to Euro-Brazil, whether by force or by choice, is largely extraneous. While Afro-Brazil disavows and resists Euro-Brazilian pathologizing narratives and ideologies, it cannot fully ignore them; rather, it must grapple with them. Afro-Brazil responds to Euro-Brazil by selectively incorporating aspects and constructions deemed worthy, relevant, or pragmatically necessary. It also responds—with varying levels of acceptance, rejection, re-elaboration, or even complete disarticulation—to the constrictive and conditional place it has been assigned within the official Euro-Afro-Brazil framework.

Because African-Brazilian philosophies actively address and reinterpret national Euro-Afro discourse and ideologies, this book begins by presenting the official archive and examining it through a series of disciplinary frames. With this contextualization now introduced, other, more relevant and less familiar paradigms can take center stage—Euro and Afro configurations placed on equal footing, each with its respective mythologies and narratives. Each is as exotic and primitive, as scientific and modern, as the other. The initial segment of part 1 is subtitled "Featuring Caravels, Oxen, Giants, Curses, a Bonfire, and a Trial." The opening segment of part 2 is subtitled "Featuring Aruanda, Malungos, Bilongo, Opón Ifá, and Dikenga." The symbols and representations alluded to in the first subtitle are emblematic of the "Western" world, and widely comprehensible. Conversely, the references in the second subtitle remain unknown to most non-Africans and non-African descendants. It is only when basic references such as these—and geo-historical references such as Mbanza Kongo and Pungo-a-Ndongo—attain the same level of recognition as Lisbon and London that we can begin to envision an Afro-Euro-Hemispheric world characterized by some degree of equity.

PART II

The Kongo-Angola-Yoruba-Ewe-Brazilian Archive

African Civilizations in Brazil

Pan-African Cosmologies: Kingdoms and Heroes Never Unheard or Unseen (Featuring Ngomas, Nzimbus, Gungas, Bambas, Milonga, and Orikis)

How beautiful it is	Como é lindo, ó gente
to miss them so	A gente sentir saudades
And that everything we miss	E de tudo o que a gente sente
is already in eternity.	Já está lá na eternidade.
I miss the ox driver	Sinto saudades do boiadeiro
from the countryside of Minas Gerais	do sertão de Minas Gerais
And the old sorcerers	E dos velhos feiticeiros
who will not come back	que não voltam mais
Who, in the time of captivity,	Que no tempo do cativeiro
would always sing in the *terreiro*	no terreiro eles viviam a cantar
Diongo, mundiongo,	*Diongo, mundiongo,*
mundiongo, mundiongo	*mundiongo, mundiongo*
Over there in the sea	Lá no meio do mar
Over there in the sea, oh, *mundiongo*	Lá no meio do mar, *ó mundiongo*
Over there in the sea.	Lá no meio do mar.
And today in the present,	E hoje no presente
I miss and recollect the past	Recordo passado saudade
The histories of absent people	Histórias de gente ausente
that are called truth.	que se chama verdade.
I miss the ancestors	Sinto saudades dos antepassados
of this Brazilian land	Deste solo brasileiro
Of heroes, sacred giants,	Dos heróis, monstros sagrados
Adventurers and pioneers	Aventureiros e pioneiros
who, in the time of captivity,	Que no tempo do cativeiro
were always singing in the *terreiro*	No terreiro eles viviam a cantar
Diongo, mundiongo,	*Diongo, mundiongo,*
mundiongo, mundiongo	*mundiongo, mundiongo*
Over there in the sea	Lá no meio do mar
Over there in the sea, oh, *mundiongo*	Lá no meio do mar, *ó mundiongo*
Over there in the sea.	Lá no meio do mar.

Maria Aparecida Martins (1939–1985)

7
Mundiongo

Ancestral Languages: Entering Other Forests

The second part of this book can be compared to a river running parallel to the first: an Afro-Brazilian watershed, fed by countless tributaries. At times, these appear as deceptively narrow surface streams; at others, they take the form of mighty underground grottoes or powerful cascades flowing from towering mountains into a far-reaching system of both subterranean and aboveground channels. Its rivers intersect and collide with others controlled by Euro-Afro-Brazilian mechanisms and devices. They converge, diverge, carve different paths, shape alternate courses, and frequently reemerge as immense waves where the past, future, and present merge in a single breath, a unified tempo. Ancestral river basins and aqueducts, serving as metaphors for different civilizations, do not exist, in the form in which we know them, independently from each other. Engineered aqueducts have played a crucial role in the development of civilizations worldwide. The ancient Roman aqueduct system stands out as an early example of urban engineering, using stone and terracotta pipes to transport water across great distances. Key mechanisms—sluice gates, valves, and weirs—control the flow, direction, and distribution of water, ultimately determining who benefits from this infrastructure and how much surplus water is stored in reservoirs. This human-made civilizational structure dictates the distribution of water and power, controlling their flow, allocation, and the scope of rights and authority granted to different societal groups.

Within the framework of Euro-Afro-Brazilian civilization, the Brazilian Historical and Geographic Institute, with its contests and award-winning narratives, has played a central role in the hegemonic network of the articulation and circulation of historical and political power. This institution was explicitly designed to create a framework that upholds and legitimizes a power structure rooted in

European dominance and African slavery. The narratives, sciences, arts, imagery, and lore recognized and concocted by members of this institution were considered sovereign and absolute. Instrumental devices—such as legal certificates, constitutional bills, property deeds, maps, and historical, literary, and artistic narratives, as well as their artifacts— govern the flow and direction of social rights, determining and justifying their distribution and allocation. Despite its claims of sovereignty, alternative centers, institutions, sciences, and mechanisms—other *Mundiongo*— have envisioned different truths, narratives, and ethical perspectives.

In the epigraph for this segment, Maria Aparecida Martins (1939–1985) sings, recalls, names, and documents *Mundiongo* knowledge centers connected to ancestral lands that lie halfway between Africa and the American continent. What might appear absent is, in fact, present—hence the subtitles for the second part of this book: "those or that which were never unheard or unseen." While a lack of recognition by official canons and state policies translates into a denial of basic social rights and exposes individuals to life-threatening conditions, lack of acknowledgment does not equate to nonexistence or invisibility.[1]

The commonly articulated academic discourse of bringing authors and cultures to visibility, of making them heard, may come across as naïve—unintentionally, perhaps—and dangerously presumptuous. Who hasn't heard, seen, or read whom? Not existing within the hegemony does not mean being forgotten or deficient. One cannot forget what one was never able to see. They/That have always been very much present, in forms and languages different from those recognized and legalized in modern Eurocentric civilizations. What becomes incorporated into academic, governmental, and national canons is what can be understood and recognized by the establishment at specific historical junctures. Cultural and artistic expressions that become visible are typically those championed by insiders who invest in translating their work and addressing the establishment to demand sociopolitical change. As Afro-Indigenous-Euro-Brazilian communities and individuals assert their presence and status within Euro-Afro-Brazilian institutions through recognition of cultural forms and communities as national intangible heritage— by artists breaking their way into the national and international art circuits and displaying their art and curating exhibits; by writers achieving the placement of their work in bookstore window displays; by scholars taking the lead in classrooms and the organization of conferences; by lawyers and politicians attaining individual and group power as legislators and policymakers—they reshape the totality of the previously existing order. That is the true measure of acknowledgment.

Maria Aparecida Martins's song "Diongo, Mundiongo" rekindles images of the ocean, the land, heroes, kings, and history in a language that may appear familiar, comprehensible, and undoubtedly appealing, as evidenced by its success in the 1970s. The song appears on Aparecida Martins's 1976 LP, *Foram 17 anos* (It Has Been 17 Years), released during Brazil's military dictatorship.[2] Although a series of institutional acts enforced since the 1964 coup suspended most civil rights and imposed heavy, arbitrary censorship on all forms of media, arts, and journalism, there was nothing in her song that government agents could detect as subversive or contrary to the brutally controlled narrative of national pride during that time. Her song articulates resistance in ways that the government's apparatus of monitoring and surveillance could neither control nor fully suppress. Unlike the visual artistic portrayals of Pedro Américo and Modesto Brocos examined by Lorraine Pinheiro Mendes in the first part of this book, we are now engaging with representations that, rather than confining Black histories, lives, and futures, affirm them.[3] The song represents a *rasteira* Capoeira movement that destabilizes the oppressive system; even if the system does not tumble down, it is disempowered.[4] Artistic expressions like those exemplified in Aparecida Martins's song cannot be easily manipulated or controlled, largely because they are often neither seen nor understood. The more incomprehensible and dismissible these expressions are to the dominant system, the deeper the epistemological transformation they have undergone—and continue to carry within them. Aparecida Martins's music confronts Euro-Brazilian culture and its probationary impositions, while simultaneously shielding itself with a fierce yet unassuming form of protection. Other clear examples of this maneuver include *vissungos*, African-Brazilian work songs that conveyed coded messages and a poetics decipherable only to those who participated in singing them.

Aparecida's song reintroduces the image of the oxcart driver, a figure also featured in Pedro Américo's painting *Independence or Death*. However, while Américo portrays the driver according to Euro-Brazilian ideological perspectives on how beings and realities are structured and defined—flattening him into a background figure that is overexposed and divorced from the context he represents—Aparecida Martins restores the driver's stature. In her lyrics, he is elevated, standing alongside the *velhos feiticeiros*, the "old sorcerers": the distinguished experts and philosophers of African Brazil. In African-Brazilian cosmologies, the ox driver holds a sacred role as an embodiment of the circulation of ideas. Américo's character therefore represents a fictional figure who would have witnessed, interpreted, and conveyed what he saw to others. Américo sees and represents him pulling a loaded cart, but he cannot suspect that this cart, in African-Brazilian epistemology, is an earthly vessel, a different kind of caravel, a *ndongo* of knowledge that exists to be transported and shared.

Diongo (also referred to as *Ndiongo*, *Njongo*, or *Jongo*) derives from the Kimbundu *Ndóngo*, meaning "the word," or "knowledge." *Mundiongo* (*Umndiongo*,

Umndóngo, Umnjongo), by extension, means "the house of the word"; "the space for words," for knowledge, education, initiation, and assembly.[5] The priests and priestesses, philosophers, scientists, and healers that Aparecida Martins refers to have long pointed—and continue to point—to the assembly of philosophers, the *Diongo Mundiongo*, the erudite source of knowledge, always visible and present, right there where the ocean meets the sky. Aparecida Martins sings and narrates a history, complete with its heroes and sacred prophetic giants, that conveys a truth and reality distinct from the one proclaimed in the Brazilian National Anthem or outlined in von Martius's prizewinning essay on how the history of Brazil should be written. The heroic ancestors Aparecida Martins sings about, the adventurers and pioneers, were those who, from the sacred ground of the *terreiros*, could sing: "Diongo, mundiongo, mundiongo, mundiongo."

It is through the process of decoding—happening as your eyes now move across these printed words—that my thoughts are conveyed. The medium is a book, a space of communication. Upon entering this space, readers bring with them assumptions about what academic narratives consist of, shaped by their past experiences with books published by this press or others like it. Meaning also begins to form through peripheral or paratextual elements, such as the cover image (which, as I write this, holds the unknown future of this book), as well as the "name" of this text and its author (reflecting its past and present). Regardless of how the author acquired this knowledge, regardless of the sources consulted, there is a ritual followed in conveying ideas and sensations through silent, asynchronous words. If, instead, we could sing these thoughts or express them through performance, construction, or painting, the content would be experienced, encoded, and decoded through different senses. It is in a foreign European language, through European disciplines and their academic systematization, and within the monodimensional, sequential logic and format of a codex that we think, remember, represent, and share. In just a few lines or minutes of auditory experience, Maria Aparecida Martins imparts knowledge that exists in only a very small fraction of my personal library within my field.

ANOTHER ALPHABET FOR OTHER HYPOTHESES: DIFFERENT WAYS OF WRITING, READING, TEACHING, AND LEARNING

Siblings Isabel and Antônio Casimira—community leaders of the Guarda de Moçambique e Congo Treze de Maio (literally "The May Thirteenth Moçambique and Congo Guard") in Belo Horizonte, Minas Gerais—recently illustrated the process and nature of literacy within certain genres of African diasporic textualities during a livestream event.[6] The occasion marked the launch of the documentary *A Rainha Nzinha chegou* (*Queen Nzinga Arrived*) codirected by Isabel Casimira, acknowledged as the queen of the Guarda Treze de Maio, and filmmaker Júnia Torres.[7] The film documents the lives of three generations of Reinado queens, as well as the journey of the current queen and her brother and captain (Rainha Isabel and Capitão Antônio) to Pungo-a-Ndongo (capital of the former Kingdom of Ndongo, in present-day Angola) and Mbanza Kongo (historic capital of the former Kingdom of Kongo, near the present border between Angola and the Democratic Republic of Congo). The Guardas or Reinados are performative traditions that predate colonization and have continuously evolved as reenactments of the founding of symbolic empires in the Americas. These diasporic traditions involve a complex network of social and political praxis that reinterprets history, nations, family, and community relations.

During the livestream, a member of the audience who identified himself as a "professor" posted a question to Rainha Isabel and Capitão Antônio asking how the chants of the Reinados are "learned or taught."[8] Capitão Antônio Casimira responded:

> Our Reinado tradition is an oral tradition, right? The type in which we did not have books or anything like it. So it has to come from someone older—someone who already has the knowledge and can pass it on to the younger ones, to the newcomers entering our circle, our Reinado world. . . . The thing is, we don't take someone, sit them down on a little bench, and say, "I'm going to teach you about the Reinado. Today! You're going to leave here knowing everything." That's not how it works. Not with us."[9]

Queen Isabel Casimira continued and further elaborated the circular concept of stages of learning and the practice of seeing the world with closed (or inner) eyes:

> As we keep talking, the kids start learning, and the people around us start learning too. And sometimes you can only answer questions superficially, because the person just won't be able to understand unless they walk with us for a while. So when people come, ask questions, and follow us in our daily lives, in our religious practices, they start to understand the meaning of each thing, each word. That's how we pass it on to our kids. . . . When something appears, I pay attention to it—whether my eyes are open or not. Because if I see it with my eyes open and then close them, I still see the same thing. . . . The knowledge of the Rosário [Our Lady of the Rosary] is like this: you stick around, keep learning little by

little. Then you get to a certain point and realize that everything you thought was real, actually isn't real at all. And you go, "Holy Mother! I'm back to square one." That's why learning happens day by day.[10]

These explanations about teaching and learning point to radical differences between the Western concept of cumulative knowledge and a form of knowledge understood dialogically as an ongoing unfolding of social praxes. Because of its nature, this knowledge is transmitted within the initiatic domain, where learning is deeply tied to lived experience and its application and development in service of the community.

To explain his ongoing apprenticeship, Capitão Antônio relates another aspect of the oral canon. He explains that he does not compose chants for the community, but that he knows how to feel in his mind when the tune is coming: "I do not create a tune; a tune comes to me, already complete. The song is not new. It existed a hundred years ago, two hundred years ago, three hundred years ago. We, the younger ones, are just bringing it back."[11] Similarly, Isabel Casimira describes what we can refer to as a different way of perceiving and "reading" the world as she recalls her flight to Angola and what she decoded out of the corner of her eye. In the midst of turbulence, she recounts that she looked at the rain hitting the window and perceived "in my eye's mind" ("na mente do olho") that the rain was not falling straight down; it was falling sideways ("a chuva não caía em pé, caía deitada"). With her hands, Rainha Isabel draws in the air the waves that she saw carrying the plane and the counterclockwise Kongo cosmogram of the four moments of the sun (see Final Considerations). The airplane was a "flying ship" ("uma nave aérea"), Isabel Casimira explains, flying against ocean waves ("o avião nas ondas do mar"), symbolizing a journey that reversed the path of those who crossed the Middle Passage.[12]

One of the most prolific and in-depth contemporary researchers of Reinados and other Bantu-Brazilian textualities, Edimilson de Almeida Pereira, similarly explains in a poem entitled "Beads" ("Contas"), the development of "the eye's mind" as a reeducation of the eyes:

> The handbook for the forest asks one not to look at it
> nor what in it becomes insect smoke water.
> It asks without asking reeducation for the eyes
> other hypotheses
> on an understanding of facts.
> It is not in codex the transitive world
> of rivers and priests.

Of people so people that it hurts to think them
in our words.
The handbook for the forest follows another alphabet.
To read its text, experts are of little use.
Its language is calculus
a knowledge in number-metaphors.[13]

Western languages, in their prosaic ordinary use, fall short of adequately communicating or reflecting the forest world Pereira refers to—its inhabitants, whether winged or legged; its phenomena, such as the language of smoke, or the ebb and flow of time. To access its knowledge, our literacy skills "are of little use." Even when we believe we have decoded the characters and formed sentences, the meanings will escape us. These textualities follow another calculation, a different reasoning in which truths and realities are expressed in relational modes (imagery, analogies, tropes, allegories, figurative expressions) imbued with references and processes that are, by default, foreign to most of us. These epistemological studies are not necessarily recorded in the pages of codices; rather, they are encoded within the intricate network of forest leaves, conveying information in complex and profound ways.

TWO PARTIES ON PARALLEL WATER BANKS

At the turn of the century, the historian Manolo Garcia Florentino (1958–2021) observed that the greatest gap in Brazilian historiography lies in understanding enslaved Africans solely from the moment they arrived on Brazilian shores.[14] This gap, rooted in a historical narrative that artificially severs continents—even as tectonic plate movements reveal environmental intersections—has been actively challenged by grassroots intellectuals, academic researchers, and artists. Particularly in recent decades, driven by civil rights advancements, implementation of empowering educational policies, increased access to new archives, and enhanced circulation of ideas and materials, there has been a collaborative shift in scholarship and artistic production. This shift is breaking paradigms, reconstructing, representing, and reflecting on a history that is finally being reassembled and challenging the status quo. While this collaborative, multi-positioned movement may appear nascent, its roots extend far back, stretching back to the establishment of spatiotemporal boundaries proclaimed by Europeans during the colonization of Africa and the Americas. What the current moment offers is the opportunity to recognize narratives that have long been disregarded. The present movement is driven by the effort to learn from and validate epistemic narratives that have been discarded, discredited, and held in contempt. However, acknowledging these narratives within institutional, political, and legal spheres involves (im)possible efforts, courage, and patience. Take, for example, the insightful account of the organization of various African cultural groups or matrices in Brazil, as related by the succinct narrative of João Lopes (1930–2004), member of the Jatobá Brotherhood of Our Lady of the Rosary in Minas Gerais. From the death of his father, Virgulino Motta, in 1974, to the end of his life, João Lopes, a grassroots intellectual, served as "General Captain," a position of high-level expertise in his community. His discourse stands in sharp contrast to the historiographical perceptions of Raul Bopp's poetic voice in the 1930s (see segment "Talking Harps" in this chapter). In an interview with Leda Maria Martins, João Lopes explains in a language that can be perceived as cryptic or hermetic due to the lack of knowledge most of us have in this school of thought, the celebrations performed in homage to Our Lady of the Rosary (Nossa Senhora do Rosário) and his nuanced perspective on *where history begins*:

> So this legend is the legend of the appearance of the image of the saint and her removal from the waters. At the beginning of her second party—because the first one was not on earth, the first was in heaven—**there were people from the Kongo, people from Mozambique, people from Coast** [Western Africa], **people from Cabinda** [in present-day Angola], **people from Guinea, there were people from all nations except the Nago** [Yoruba people]. When they gathered this group of Black people to remove Our Lady from the waters, they formed a single guard, it was called the Candombe Guard of Our Lady of the Rosary. Only the Candombe could bring Our Lady from the waters, so it was then decided that the Candombe was the father of all Reinados here on earth. The Congo and Moçambique people also decided among themselves that the Candombe would bring the crowns. The Candombe is a very difficult instrument, and the only ones who had adopted it and were able to play it more or less similarly to the way Candombes are to be played were the people of Moçambique. They made their group, they formed their group, and with their drums they formed the Guard of Moçambique. This is what was decided between them . . . that the Moçambique would bring the throne and that the Congo would guide the Moçambique clearing the way, opening the roads with their high and low-pitched singing, clearing the paths and asking for protection so as to bring forth the throne of the crowns that symbolize the crown of Our Lady of the Rosary.[15]

Though João Lopes's account may seem enigmatic, and despite a common tendency to dismiss such texts as nonsensical or ahistorical, what we have here is in fact a highly condensed relational-historic account. For scholars and outsiders to the Reinado communities to read and start understanding this passage, they must step beyond their comfort zones and acknowledge the legitimacy of alternative epistemes. Even without full fluency or cultural competency, there are elements in this account that we can recognize and value. João Lopes simultaneously explains and references the history of his Brotherhood and the Jatobá community, his own role within it, the community's membership in a larger network, the African and Afro-diasporic tradition of the Reinado festivals, and the legend or myth of Our Lady of the Rosary (Nossa Senhora do Rosário). He also explores the layered meanings of "*candombe*," a term that encompasses drums, including a certain type used in Minas Gerais; a sacred yet secular performance; a specific way of dancing, chanting, and drumming; a particular group of performers within the Reinado performance; and even a designation for people in general or specifically for Blacks in Brazil.[16] Most importantly, perhaps, João Lopes's account locates the history of Africans in Brazil as starting not with the Middle Passage, but on the African continent itself.

João Lopes frames the organization of Africans of different nationalities in Brazil without any reference to the concept of Africa, instead emphasizing the coming together of Bantu nationals in Brazil. According to him, the "second party" in homage of Our Lady of the Rosary included people from Kongo, Angola, Mozambique, as well as from the Gulf of Guinea and the Western Coast. João Lopes highlights that the Nago (Yoruba) people were not part of this assembly. With just a few words, he points to a historical moment that preceded the last waves of enslaved immigration that brought massive Yoruba populations to Brazil. While the "second party"—which celebrated the reunion of the saint that emerged in the ocean with African people—took place on the shore or on the earth, the preceding celebration happened across the shores, in an indefinite beyond. João Lopes's narrative not only illustrates an epistemology based on crossroads of intersecting past and present spaces and beings but also reveals that the praxes performed in Brazil were a development and a continuation of what had already happened on the African continent. This narrative also points to different levels of interactions and exchange between African nationals in Brazil. In establishing symbolic kingdoms—territories or realms ruled by individuals selected both spiritually and collectively as authorities capable of leading and promoting rights—two major cultural groups of Bantu civilization became embodiments of values and roles.

While the descendants—spiritually and philosophically—of the smaller immigration group from the Mozambique area were entrusted with bringing the "crown and throne," the descendants of the larger group from the Kingdom of Kongo took on the role of opening paths and clearing the road for the transit of these royal insignia from the ocean to the shore. The crown (the highest point of a body, mountain, or tree; the head; the mind; the circular emblem of supreme power over a community) and the throne (the circumscribed space or center of political and divine power) are metonyms for a full spectrum of civilizational foundation, the candombe drums come to represent not only the vehicle for the transference and the medium through which to perform the reestablishment of autonomous realms, but also the peoples (from both sides of the Atlantic) who can operate this technology. The candombe drums, played according to the knowledge of those who embody Mozambique, reestablish and restore spatio-temporal boundaries. It is only through the advocacy and protection of those who came before them, of the representatives of the Kongo kingdom, that a royal African lineage, the "throne of the crowns" (embodied in the image of Our Lady of the Rosary) can make its way across the ocean.

João Lopes, one of the most knowledgeable spokespersons of Brazilian-Kongo cosmology, remains an unknown source to most scholars in the diaspora. He became a reference outside his circle's network through the fieldwork of Leda Maria Martins, a major theorist of Afro-Brazilian religious performance and an acclaimed "Congo Queen" of the same community João Lopes once led. Current shifts in artistic, historiographical, and philosophical perception became emblematic through the indirect recognition and celebration of João Lopes in highly visible and prestigious arts circles. The curatorial project of the 2023 edition of the São Paulo Art Biennial, titled "Choreographies of the Impossible," is being informed explicitly by the scholarship of Leda Maria Martins, and implicitly by masters such as João Lopes. The curatorial council of "Choreographies of the Impossible" expressed its desire "to build spaces and times of perception that challenge the rigidity of western time linearity" as well as to discern strategies that "imagine worlds that confront the ideas of freedom, justice, and equality as impossible achievements."[17] Their idea of "impossible achievements"—echoing Denise Ferreira da Silva's arguments in *Unpayable Debt* and *Toward a Global Idea of Race*—actually points to the search for possibilities like those in praxis by the Reinado communities led by João Lopes and Leda Maria Martins.[18] The 2023 São Paulo Art Biennial curatorial council further explains that the notion of "impossible" refers not only "to the political, legal, economic and social realities in which these artistic and social practices are set, but also to the way in which these practices find alternatives to circumvent the effects of these same contexts."[19]

Following a similar desire to envision alternative spaces and times of perception that challenge the rigidity of disciplines that do not account for the values of African civilizations, I propose to acknowledge and "see" those who attended the "first party." Who were the people from the Kongo, Mozambique, Cabinda, and Guinea? Which peoples from Western Africa and Central Africa "came to the party"? How did this gathering become registered in unofficial archives? How did these various people reorganize themselves in Brazil prior to or alongside the arrival of the Yoruba people?

NEO-AFRICAN-BRAZILIAN CIVILIZATION: AFRO-BRAZILIAN CIVILIZATION MATRICES AND M(O)TRICES

In comparing the development of the blues in the United States to that of samba in Brazil, the music ethnologist Gerhard Kubik emphasizes that neither of these musical genres has a direct, linear descent from a specific African genre.[20] Kubik often refers to the concept of "extensions of regional African cultures in the New World" or "Neo-African cultural zones" when considering the ever-fluid processes of change and innovation that African-derived traditions have undergone in the Americas.[21] He defines Neo-African as cultural expressions primarily influenced by African cultures in terms of their structure and content which, from an African perspective, constitute "a new regional African culture outside the African mainstream."[22] In his studies on memory and the "unconscious transmission of culture traits," Kubik explores questions such as: "What kind of music did the Africans bring with them when they first arrived on the North American mainland? How long did that music persist in its new environment, and how was it transformed into something we now call Afro-American?"[23] He sees Brazil as a significant example to illustrate the complexities of cultural superpositions over time and their mutual adaptations in different geographical spaces.[24]

One particularly important process Kubik outlines is how African diasporic cultures maintain an uninterrupted continuum across time and space through the potential to switch fluidly between different channels of expression.[25] He refers to historical periods when drums were banned in some New World cultures due to concerns that they could be used to send coded messages to incite rebellions. However, unlike electronic data storage, drum rhythms are not easily eradicated; they can be silently reproduced on any surface once they are culturally ingrained in an individual's memory.[26] Kubik argues that these rhythmic patterns not only exist in sound but can also manifest visually, such as in the abstract designs displayed in African-American quilts. Cultural transmission is not limited to one medium; it can switch between auditory, physical, and visual channels. The process of decoding these patterns is largely unconscious and, depending on stimuli and variables in place and time, "the individual's unconscious can reassemble the missing patterns."[27] The understanding that rhythmic patterns can extend beyond the realms of sound and motion to include visual forms of expression is a central tenet of the cultural transmission of African diasporic philosophies.

Kubik comments that when the African diaspora is examined only through the lens of acculturation and evolutionary frameworks, it is not recognized as having its own independent history but rather is perceived as beginning only with interactions on American soil.[28] Earlier theories suggested that African New World culture formed from interactions between a relatively uniform African cultural background and various European "master-cultures" such as Portuguese, Spanish, French, or English influences.[29] Kubik, however, emphasizes that diverse African ethnic traditions in the Americas underwent centuries of "internal selection" and competition among themselves, leading to the survival and adoption of the most adaptable cultural elements.[30] Historical interactions that took place in Brazil and along the African coast were marked by numerous encounters and conflicts, producing both cultural continuities and discontinuities of varying degrees.

One specific example Kubik gives is the formation of Afro-Brazilian Candomblé and the Yoruba cultural history that informs its religious practices. Understanding Candomblé's nature and evolution requires looking beyond a generalized view of Yoruba culture to examine specific Yoruba-speaking regions such as Ọ̀yọ́, Ọ̀ndó, Ijẹ̀sà, Ẹ̀gbá, Ẹ̀gbádò, Ìjẹ̀bú, and Èkìtì, as well as their historical contexts during the seventeenth to nineteenth centuries.[31] Referring to individuals from these regions simply as "Yoruba" during the late nineteenth century is an anachronism that imposes a late twentieth-century understanding onto a period when such identities were still forming.[32] Similarly, research shows that Central Africans labeled "Congo" by Europeans adapted various elements of their cultural heritage in the Americas, motivated by the need to create a restorative sense of community among themselves in new and often shifting circumstances.[33]

When addressing the African geographic origins of the Afro-Brazilian population, Kubik hesitates, as most of us do, to oversimplify these into broad regions. An initial oversimplification of cultural-geographic references is, however, a helpful entry point. Kubik outlines two major cultural regions: the area of southwestern Nigeria including Dahomey (Benin), Togo, eastern Ghana, and adjacent regions; and the area commonly referred to as Kongo-Angola (encompassing most of Angola, southwestern Congo, Cabinda, and parts of Congo-Brazzaville) as well as regions of the interior of Central Africa.[34] Two other significant additional areas to be taken into consideration are the hinterland of the stretch of coastal West Africa beginning in Senegal all the way to Nigeria, and regions in Mozambique.[35]

Despite its generalizations and plantation-era etymological baggage, the concept of "matrices" as fluid, evolving umbrella groups remains relevant for understanding the formation of African community identities in Brazil. Euro-Afro-Brazilian scholarship, as discussed in the chapter "Social Sciences: Founding Moments of Euro-Afro-Brazilian Studies," has classified African ancestry in Brazil into three primary cultural or civilization matrices: 1) the Nago-Ketu, which encompasses present-day Benin and Nigeria, home to speakers of Yoruba; 2) the Jeje-Mina, covering present-day Togo and Benin, inhabited by speakers of Ewe, Fon, Gun, and Mahi; and 3) the Angola-Kongo group, consisting of Central Africans who speak Kikongo and Kimbundu.

These three matrices can be metonymically represented by their respective religious or philosophical conductors for social exchange, namely: the Nago-Ketu's Orishas (*Orixás*), the Jeje-Mina's Vodouns (*Voduns*) or Loas (Lwa), and the Angola-Congo's Minkisi (*Inquices*).[36] The sociologist Muniz Sodré highlights that the religious cosmological sustainers of these matrices—the Orishas, Vodouns, and Minkisi—served as the symbolic sustainers from which African-Brazilian civilizations developed.[37] Cultural matrices provided frameworks for processing cultural and identity rearticulations, countering the ethnic divisions that colonial administrators attempted to impose in their efforts to curb their fears of insurrections, as seen in events like the Haitian Revolution (1791–1804) or national projects such as the African-Brazilian Republic of Palmares (c. 1605–1695).

Africans from the Nago-Ketu and Jeje-Mina cultural groups include, among others, the Yoruba, Igbo, Fon, Ewe, and Nupe people. From the hinterland of West Africa also came the Hausa and Malinke people. The term "Nago" derives from "anago" (*ànàgó*), a term used by speakers of Éwé of Dahomey to refer to those who spoke Yoruba, whether in Nigeria, Dahomey, Togo, or neighboring areas of the Abeokuta province (in present southwest Nigeria).[38] *Ànàgó* also refers to the Kingdom of Ketu in present-day southeastern Benin, one of the sixteen original kingdoms of the Oyo Empire during the seventeenth and eighteenth centuries. The Yorubas, in turn, referred to neighboring Ewe-speaking people as "Jeje or Gege," from the term *àjèjì*, meaning "foreigner, stranger, peculiar."[39] These Dahomeans also became known as Mina, referring to a major center of the transatlantic slave trade, the slave emporium El Mina or São Jorge da Mina in Ghana, with its fort built in 1482 by the Portuguese. Over time, the Nago-Ketu and Jeje-Mina matrices, due to their intrinsic affinities and history in Africa, merged into one compound matrix and became known in Brazil as a

Yoruba-Ewe cultural matrix (also identified as the Jeje-Nago syncretism). The Yoruba-Ewe—as will be explored in chapter 9—became a major organizational structural matrix for most Afro-Brazilian religious cosmological traditions.

In African-Brazilian literature and oral traditions, references to the Nago-Jeje matrix are found through historical and geographical terms such as Egbá, Fanti, Fon, Ibadan, Ibeju or Ijebu, Ijesha, Jeje or Gege, Ketu, Mahi, Nago, Oyo, and Popo. Other groups associated with the Nago-Jeje matrix included Muslim Africans known in Brazil as Malês, Muçumis (or Muçumurin) and Alufás; or more specifically as: Hauçás (Hausas), Fulanis (Fulás), Mandingas (Mandês), Gurunsis, Tapas (Nupês), and Bornus (Kanuris). Furthermore, some African Northern groups, referred to in Brazil as the Adras, Bambaras, Jalofos, and Papéis, were partially absorbed into the Nago-Jeje matrix. These nations or groups were often identified according to the harbors from which Africans were shipped to Brazil. Designations from harbors in the regions of Senegambia, Sierra Leone, Windward Coast, Ivory Coast, Gold Coast and Slave Coast (Bight of Benin or Bight of Biafra) include Gore, Bissau, Gallina, Axim, Mina (El Mina), Accra, Keta (Coto, Quittah), Agoué, Popo, Ajudá (Whydah), Cotonu, Porto Novo, Appa, Badagri, Lagos (Onim), and Calabar.

The second major civilizational African matrix is the Angola-Kongo group, which comprises the revered realm of Mozambique, historically referred to as Portuguese East Africa. "Kongo" refers to the Bakongo people, while "Angola" refers to the kingdom of Ndongo, ruled by a N'gola leader. Similarly, "Mozambique" traces its roots to Musa Bin Bique (Muça Al Bique, also known as Musa Malik or Ali Musa Mbiki), the Muslim sultan who governed the island of Mozambique when Vasco da Gama, en route to India, landed there at the end of the fifteenth century. This matrix of unparalleled importance to the Americas encompasses groups originating from Western Central Africa (including the Bakongo, Bateke, Mbundu, and Ovimbundu peoples) and various interior regions of Central Africa (comprising the Baluba, Bayaka, Baunda, Chokwe, Nganguela, Humbi-Handa, and Herero peoples). It also includes people from Mozambique originating from three different regions: 1) the Ruvuma Basin and Lake Nyasa area in northern Mozambique and Malawi, which were home to the Makonde, Makhuwa, Yao, and Nyanja peoples; 2) the Zambezi Valley region in central Mozambique near Quelimane, inhabited by the Chuwabu, Shona, Sena, and Nyungwe peoples; 3) and the southern region around Inhambane Bay in Mozambique, home of the Shangaan, Tsonga, Chopi, Nguni, and Batonga peoples.

The contemporary usage of the term "nation" refers to various African cultural and cosmological traditions and affiliations. When individuals claim to be of the "Angola nation" ("da nação Angola"), or of the Ketu (Queto) or Ijesha (Ijexá) nations, they assert bonds and identity relationships to groups informed by the philosophies of these matrices. This is evident in cultural expressions such as Capoeira Angola, Candomblé Ketu, or Ijexá Carnaval. Ancestry derived from these geographical or national concepts typically revolves around questions of family or individual adopted lineage. Through conscious ideological choices, individuals and communities designate one or more Afro-Brazilian traditions as their chosen school(s) of thought.

The ethnologist Yeda Pessoa de Castro emphasizes that while the establishment of Afro-Brazilian "nations" was initially a political endeavor of lay organizations, today they should be understood primarily as theological formations.[40] Makota Zimewaanga Valdina Pinto (1943–2019), a priestess and scholar of Kongo-Brazilian philosophy, elucidates this process. According to Valdina:

> Considering that traditional African religions are closely intertwined with the way of life, behavior, and thinking of traditional Africans, I believe that since their arrival here—even while living in the conditions of slavery in slave quarters—Africans found ways to maintain their religiosity. They continued to recreate and reconstruct it in their new environment, in their new reality, until it took the form we practice and live today, which we call Candomblé.[41]

The philosopher Marco Aurélio Luz adds to this perspective by regarding African diasporic religions as pivotal hubs for the reassembly of Africans and their descendants. Luz emphasizes that it is never enough to highlight the value and significance of religion in the formation and evolution of Black civilizations.[42] According to him, these meticulously organized religious communities played a crucial role in reinstating the diverse social hierarchies and relationships within Black cultures and civilizations.[43] Associations of different Candomblé practices (such as Ketu, Jeje, Angola, or Caboclo modalities) serve as religious, educational, medicinal, and political nuclei. Together with various other practices, Candomblés form confederations comprised of organized centers of higher learning in schools of thought encompassing the philosophy, culture, and cosmology of African-Brazilian civilizations. Among these diverse philosophical and religious practices, alongside the more prominent forms of Candomblé, are other schools or associations such as Umbanda (Quimbanda, Embanda, Banda, or Macumba) in Rio de Janeiro and São Paulo; Batuque (or Culto de Nação) in Rio Grande do Sul; Tambor de Mina and Terecô in Maranhão; Pajelança in the Amazon region; Cabula in Espírito Santo; Xambá in Alagoas, Paraíba, and

Pernambuco; Catimbó in Pernambuco and Paraíba; Babassuê in Pará; Xangô in Pernambuco; and Toré in Alagoas and Sergipe.

Just as we discuss Greco-Roman civilizations, we can also speak of a Bantu-Yoruba civilization that incorporated cosmologies of Indigenous groups and radically reconfigured European Judeo-Christian traditions. The parallels between Greco-Bantu (for the Kongo-Angola matrix) and Roman-Yoruba (for the Nago-Jeje matrix) are particularly apt in illustrating how these cultural relationships unfolded on Brazilian soil. The performance studies scholar Zeca Ligiéro questions the usefulness and limitations of the term "matrix."[44] Derived from the Latin *matrice*, "matrix" refers to the uterus, an origin, a source, or a fountain, as well as a mold that, once imprinted with a specific design, allows for the replication of that same design on various objects. As argued by Ligiéro, in the context of African-Brazilian cultural and artistic performances, the term "matrix" takes on a different dimension, representing a dynamic framework where diverse elements come together to shape a new context, be it for entertainment, religious rituals, or a fusion of both.[45] African-Brazilian cultural expressions have been studied as creations that, drawing upon common references from African matrices, seek to preserve an African past. Ligiéro argues that the concept of matrices—"a kind of legitimizing origin of African identity in the diaspora, that does not take into account neither its multiplicity nor cultural diversity"—falls short in conceptualizing "the complexity of interethnic and transitional processes observed in performative practices or cultural performances."[46] In its place, Ligiéro coins the term "motrizes," which encompasses both matrices and the idea of motion and motive power or energy. "Motriz," a force that induces movement, derives from the Latin word *motrice*, which means "that which causes movement" or "that which sets in motion." Ligiéro's African "motrizes" or driving forces do not merely refer to a force that triggers action, but also to an inherent quality related to what moves and the individuals or collectives involved in that movement. In sacred and secular performances, culture manifests itself not solely through symbols and forms (matrices), but also through the knowledge embedded in the performers' bodies and their coordinated movements in time and space.[47]

For the full realization of performative practices rooted in African origin, the presence of *mestres* (masters) is essential. *Mestres* are custodians of philosophies and exceptional cosmological understanding, and serve as the guardians of the liturgical knowledge that has been passed down orally. The novice becomes initiated and learns both through interaction with their master and through active participation. Initiates and performers make their own unique contributions and develop their distinct style when putting into practice what they have learned from their mentors.[48] They rearrange the materials and techniques acquired from tradition into fresh "strips of behavior," akin to segments of a film, as the performance studies scholar Richard Schechner explores with his concept of restored behavior.[49]

Ligiéro's concept of cultural driving forces is understood as a series of procedures that are part of the inseparable quartet "sing-dance-drum-tell." These Afro-Brazilian performances, marked by the convergence of philosophical concepts and beliefs embedded within shared cultural elements, "can occur both in the field of religion and in performative practices where devotion is not directly involved."[50] The classic separation between religion and entertainment does not apply to African performances; they are often complementary forms within the same rituals.[51] "Cultural matrices" speak their own lexicon in body movements articulated with rhythms and chants that are emblematic of the mythology of the group or nation in question.[52] The performative techniques of singing, dancing, drumming, and storytelling are seamlessly integrated within the performer's body, contrary to the Western paradigm of segregating music, dance, and theater as independent arts. The singing-dancing-drumming-storytelling quartet transcends linear time, immersing itself in a mythical cycle forged by the performer in the presence of the audience, often invoking or embodying natural forces. Depending on the context of the performance, new elements are incorporated and creatively adapted without compromising their original identity. These performed narratives encompass a reverence for nature in its physical and symbolic dimensions and interweave ethical principles passed down through the wisdom of elders, masters, performers, and priests.[53] The rituals, dances, rhythms, and myths of African and Indigenous cultures are a source of inspiration for artists who, even though they may not necessarily belong to the communities or have undergone initiation into their rites, still incorporate elements of tradition and its cultural dynamics into their work.[54]

As the Congolese philosopher Bunseki Fu-Kiau (1934–2013) explains, when someone plays a drum—or any musical instrument, for that matter—a spiritual language is being articulated.[55] Singing is perceived as the interpretation of these languages for the community present in the here and now. Dancing is the "acceptance of the spiritual messages propagated" through bodies, as well as the gathering of community members in joint celebrations, under the perfect balance (*Kinenga*) of life.[56] Drumming-singing-dancing, as well as storytelling and the interpretative praxis of divination, allow the broken social circle to be reconnected, enabling the flow of energy between the living and the dead to be restored.[57]

TALKING HARPS: URUCONGOS, LUNGUNGUS, AND GUNGAS

>*The* berimbau *is the ancestral Master.*
>Mestre Pastinha (1889–1981)

If this book were focused on the cultural production of Brazilian descendants of European immigrants—Italian Brazilians, for instance, with their strong regional identities, culinary traditions, and religious festivals—it would typically be expected of me to provide a concise overview of European immigration to Brazil: which nationalities arrived, when, and which subgroups within these populations settled where. Much of the introduction to Euro-Brazilian cultural histories could remain unstated or taken for granted. In stark contrast, our understanding of Africa and its diasporas, shaped within societies structured and dominated by Western philosophies and cosmologies, is often woefully inadequate and reductive. Africa is routinely portrayed as a monolith, and enslaved Africans are frequently depicted as having landed in the diaspora stripped of memory, as if by a form of irreversible historical amnesia. One example of this reductive perception appears in the work of the Brazilian Modernist poet Raul Bopp (1898–1984), who published a poem in the 1930s encapsulating this view. In his poetic voice, Bopp conveys:

>In your blood weighs the voice of unknown origins.
>The forests kept in shadow the secret of your history.
>Your first bas-relief inscription
>was a lash on your back.
>
>One day,
>they threw you into the hold of a slave ship.
>And for long nights and nights
>you came listening to the roar of the sea
>like a sob in the gloomy hold.
>
>The sea was a brother of your race.
>
>One dawn
>they lowered the sails on the deck.
>There was a strip of land and a port.
>Warehouses with slave depots
>and the grumble of your brothers tied in iron collars.

That's where your history began.

The rest,
what was left behind,
the Congo, the forests, and the sea
continue to hurt on the string of the *urucongo*'s bow.[58]

If "the rest"—call it the past, or History—was left behind in the shadows of distant, forgotten forests, the Middle Passage would have had effectively erased millennia of histories. Instead of African history, the ground zero of Afro-diasporic civilizations would be portrayed as the nearest comprehensible image that the Eurocentric mechanisms of the post-slavery-plantation era could conceive: the vast, undecipherable ocean. Odes from poets like Camões to Shakespeare celebrated the relentless maritime trade circuit, crafting images that included the Luso-Brazilian landscape and its oceanic routes. Images of sails bearing red Portuguese crosses, harnessing the wind's power to propel caravels and slave ships—known as *tumbeiros* ("floating tombs or sailing dungeons")—across the Atlantic, became deeply ingrained in the collective consciousness. Not much more beyond this archive would have been known to Bopp and those he represents. Still, he is able to notice that the "rest" is sung and played with the *urucongo*. This instrument—already part of the Brazilian soundscape—enters the realm of what can be recognized and imagined. Bopp alludes to the Kongo not as a kingdom, federation, or civilization, but simply as a forest. What he is able to recognize is imbued with a history that is unfamiliar to him. The instrument and its music are part of another ode, a different collective consciousness. Within the space-time coordinates of his context, Bopp can discern the *urucongo* as a vessel for expressing the enduring, heartfelt yearning of a "race" with ancestral ties to the ocean.

The *urucongo* one-string harp and resonating gourd is a precursor to the *berimbau*, an instrument widely recognized today due to its integral role in Brazilian Capoeira. To trace the history of the *berimbau* is to follow the creation of a pan-African harp, its translation not only into the musical instrument it materializes, but also into the role and language this instrument had/has in Kongo-Angola societies and how these emerged in Brazilian Kongo-Angola civilization. The word *berimbau* contains in it the Kimbundu words *mbimbi* and *rimba*. The former means "timbre, vocal tone, speech, way of expressing oneself, language, way of speaking"; the latter translates as "function, ratchet, the musical instrument, its sound."[59] Similar to a talking drum, the *berimbau* is a talking harp.

The manifold origins of the *berimbau* include the Angolan *hungu* bows and the *umgunga* mouthbow, as well as the *lungungu* (or *lungulungo*) harp from

Madimba (a territory located in what is now the Democratic Republic of the Congo) and possibly Mbala (a district in present-day Zambia).[60] Central African harps like the *lungungo* have served as instruments for spiritual meditation and prayer and funeral ceremonies, as well as storytelling by griots. Jean-Baptiste Debret painted an image of a griot master in Brazil and entitled it *The Old African and His Instrument, the Oricongo*.[61] Harp bows have also been depicted in Brazil in the callings of street vendors, such as in the 1814 painting by Portuguese architect Joaquim Cândido Guillobel (1787–1859) and the 1822 painting by British Army officer Henry Chamberlain (1796–1843).[62] Chamberlain adds information in his text explaining that these harps "are generally accompanied by the performer with the voice and consist of ditties of his native country sung in his native language."[63] One of the earliest depictions of such harps in the context of dancing and fighting in an early form of Capoeira can be found in the c. 1840 painting *Dance of Black Musicians Playing the Instruments of Their Country* by Danish artist Harro Paul Harring (1798–1870).[64] Harring's image shows the musical bow being played in a manner similar to a violin, rather than the typical position known for contemporary *berimbaus*.

Harring's painting captures the development of Brazilian Capoeira and the ongoing transformation of harps and fighting techniques. Friar Cavazzi, who depicted gourd-resonated harps in Nzinga's kingdom in 1670, used the term "*sangamentos*" as a synonym for public military reviews, showcasing troops' physical agility and prowess.[65] The Africanist historian John Thornton highlights the prominence of mock combats in military training in Kongo/Angola.[66] During a visit to Brazil in the 1960s, Angolan artist Albano de Neves e Souza was struck by the similarities he observed between the movements of Brazilian Capoeira and Southern Angolan combat N'golo. Upon returning to Angola, Neves e Souza published a series of drawings depicting both N'golo and Capoeira. One of the captions summarizes his hypothesis:

> N'golo, the Zebra Dance, is possibly the origin of the Capoeira, the fighting dance of Brazil. It is danced at the time of the "Mufico," a puberty rite for the girls of the Mucope and Mulondo regions. The object of the dance is to hit your opponent's face with your foot. A rhythm for the dance is beaten by clapping hands, and anyone who attempts a blow while outside the marked arena is disqualified. The "Angolan Capoeira" in Brazil also has its special rhythm, which is one more reason to believe that it originates with the N'golo. N'golo means "zebra," and to a certain extent the dance originates from the leaps and battles of the zebra; the blow with the feet while the hands are touching the ground is certainly reminiscent of the zebra's kick.[67]

Câmara Cascudo endorsed the hypothesis of N'golo as the ancestor of capoeira and T. J. Desch-Obi further developed this hypothesis, defining N'golo as the great "Bantu pugilistic tradition."[68]

Mestre Pastinha (Vicente Ferreira Pastinha, 1889–1981) published a short book about capoeira Angola and left several manuscripts, the most substantial one subtitled "Metaphysics and Practice of Capoeira."[69] Pastinha became the first Capoeirista to analyze Capoeira as an Angolan philosophy and to concern himself with the ethical and educational aspects of its practice. As Röhrig Assunção pointed out, "claiming Angola as a marker of traditionalism represented a challenge even within the Afro-Brazilian community."[70] Since Nina Rodrigues, the Yoruba (Nago) held a dominant position in Afro-Bahian culture and religion, which became firmly established in the 1930s. Among academics and Afro-Bahians alike, the Bantus were viewed as inferior and not adhering to "traditional" practices. Advocating for a revival rooted in Angolan traditions represented a twofold challenge and a bold endeavor.[71] Mestre Pastinha standardized the instruments that would form the capoeira Angola orchestra; three *berimbaus*, two *pandeiro* tambourines, one *agogô* bell, one *reco-reco* scraper, and one *atabaque* drum. Röhrig Assunção comments that the combination of these instruments represented an innovation that was not tied to any specific Capoeira tradition, although one could argue that Pastinha innovated within a broader Afro-Bahian tradition.[72] The inclusion of three *berimbaus* allowed for the development of complementary rhythms and aligned with Pastinha's vision. Being a skilled musician, he aimed to emphasize the musical aspects of the Angola style, believing that the *berimbau* should preside over Capoeira. In his book, Pastinha states that while "the musical or rhythmic ensemble is not indispensable for Capoeira, the rhythm is the "mysticism that stirs the soul."[73]

The *berimbau* rules absolute in Capoeira, a pan-African art form that encompasses cultural rituals, dance, musical, philosophic, and martial systems including not only the N'golo, but also the Ninja, Basula, and Gabetula.[74] During the 1930s, the Brazilian Capoeira tradition was codified based on the philosophies of both Mestres Pastinha and Bimba and their negotiations with the establishment.[75] Elements that became part of this tradition include the orchestra comprising three *berimbaus*: the larger *gunga* played by the Capoeira Mestre, the *berimbau médio* (also known as *berimbau de centro* or simply *berimbau*), and the *viola* (or *violinha*). These *berimbaus* symbolize lineages of ancestors, and therefore, those who practice Capoeira salute them as one would salute an elder. The trio of musical instruments plays an intrinsic role in maintaining the flow and balance of Capoeira and other circular performances of African diasporic civilizations. A trio of instruments with rising sizes and tones is a recurring pattern in sacred music and can be found in, among others, the Kongo-Angola Candombe and the Yoruba-Ewe *rum-rumpi-lé* drum trio of Candomblé. This tripod metaphor, as explored in the next chapter, holds significant cosmological symbolism within Bakongo culture.

Between 2006 and 2007, an inventory report for Capoeira was presented to the National Institute of Historic and Artistic Heritage in Brazil (IPHAN). Popular art curator Wallace de Deus Barbosa led the effort to compile a dossier aimed at officially promoting Capoeira as a significant cultural and historical heritage of Brazil. Barbosa described the challenge of succinctly tracing Capoeira's three centuries of history and establishing a dialogue between the past and the present.[76] One of the bases for Barbosa's argument lies precisely in the comparison of the three *berimbaus* of Capoeira and the three Atabaques of Candomblé. The larger *gunga berimbau* emits a deeper and more resonant sound, serving as the guiding force for the rhythm in a Capoeira. Its position holds a prominent role in the hierarchy of instruments, since it is responsible for activating the musical codes that commence and conclude the performance. Similarly, the larger *rum atabaque*, the lower-pitched drum in Candomblé, is typically positioned to the right of the other two drums. Unlike the Capoeira *gunga*, the Candomblé *rum* does not mark the rhythm but instead introduces variation and improvisation. Despite this distinction, both the *rum* and the *gunga* embody leadership and command roles in the musical actions of the ritual performance. The *viola berimbau* corresponds, in the same analogy, to the smaller drum in Candomblé known as the *lé atabaque*. While the Capoeira *viola* introduces variations and improvisations, the Candomblé *lé atabaque* drum is responsible for maintaining the rhythm's structure. The high-pitched sounds of these two instruments fill the space of their secular and sacred ritual performances. Finally, the *médio berimbau* finds its counterpart in the *rumpi atabaque* drum, both acting as a bridge between the two sound poles. They harmonize the dialogue between the lower- and higher-pitched sounds produced by the other two *berimbaus* and *atabaques* in Capoeira and Candomblé.[77]

TALKING BELLS: NGUNGAS, NZIMBUS, AND SEASHELLS THAT GROW IN THE SOIL

The word *gunga*, originating from the Kimbundu and Kikongo word *ngunga*, holds a range of interconnected meanings. Primarily, it refers to any instrument capable of producing sound, with its most common association being bells and the sounds these emit when struck or chimed.[78] Additionally, *ngunga* encompasses the concept of flowing streams and the currents that propel them, as well as the movement of air or fluid in a specific direction. It also refers to two large animals, one aquatic, a sizeable sea fish known for its resonant, prolonged sounds; the other terrestrial, a large jungle ruminant bigger than a cow.[79] In Western understanding, the Kimbundu and Kikongo *ngunga* would encompass at least three separate concepts: a bell or other bell-like musical instruments, a movement of nature, and a cosmological model and metaphor that refer to the worlds of the living and the dead.

The concept of the *ngunga* as a bell that acts as spiritual communicative vehicle and bears symbolic significance as an embodiment of power resonates across both African and European cultures. In Catholicism, bells are rung three times during mass to signal the Canon or the communion prayer and the presentation of bread and wine, which undergo transubstantiation into the blood and body of Christ. The communion prayer evokes God and the Holy Spirit through his Son: "to you, most merciful Father, with reverence we pray through Jesus Christ, your Son, our Lord." One of the Kimbundu meanings of *ngunga* is "only son." Assis Júnior refers to the Apostles' Creed prayer in Kimbundu—"I believe in God, the Father Almighty, the Creator of heaven and earth, and in Jesus Christ, His only Son, our Lord"—where "only Son" is translated as *wongunga*.[80] The Kimbundu term, an epithet for an only son who parents a global community, is likely a combination of *wô*, meaning "all," and *ngunga*.[81]

In African-Brazilian Candomblé rituals, handbells also play intrinsic ritual roles. The bitonal *agogô* (derived from Yoruba *agogo*) and the *gã* (derived from the Ewe and Fon terms *gankogui*, *gakpavi*, or *gakpevi*) are double-handed iron cowbells with two different sized metal bells without a clapper, played with striking sticks. As a central part of the sacred orchestra, these bells serve several functions: they guide the flow and transitions in the music performed by the three main drums, and they also signal the beginning and end of the ritual. Another bell, the *adjá* (from Yoruba *àjà*), a metallic bell made up of two to four connected cups, holds a central position in summoning the presence of the Orishas. These African-Brazilian sacred bells which activate, articulate, and maintain the tempo of rituals, embody the power of spiritual transubstantiation and offer a different measure and experience of time. While *àája* also refers to a powerful wind manifested as a whirlwind (metaphorically representing another model of spiritual transubstantiation), the Yoruba term *agogo* also denotes a clock or watch, measuring human rather than divine time).[82]

The ethnomusicologist Rafael Galante, who has researched the history of bells in Africa and Europe, identifies the metal bell as a sonic representation of political and spiritual power across Africa and its diaspora.[83] In examining the cultural exchanges initiated by the arrival of Europeans in Central and broader Atlantic Africa, Galante analyzes the deep cultural impact—particularly in

Central Africa—and the resulting processes of mutual recognition. The encounter between African and European civilizations is often framed, as Galante points out, by an emphasis on their profound cultural differences.[84] Yet the specific case of bell cultures offers a compelling counterpoint: there exists "a shared material culture between the Mediterranean and Atlantic African worlds, characterized by more similarities than differences."[85] When the Europeans arrived with their bells, African communities were already familiar with similar technologies and traditions; as a result, they appropriated Western bells as new communication tools into their preexisting traditions.[86] Galante explains that, in the Catholic tradition, bells function as a kind of code—where the number and sequence signify: "A sequence of tolls indicates a specific occurrence: someone has passed away, a mass is to be held, the hour. African bells, on the other hand, exhibit a higher level of sophistication." Given that many African languages are tonal, bells speak: "when utilized by a priest-healer in an act of healing, these frequencies assume a sacred textual dimension. They effectively and literally articulate an ancestral vocalization."[87]

As Africans assumed the physically demanding and often perilous role of bellringers in Brazilian Catholic churches, they were able to create a form of communication that was both public and coded. The tolling of bells could notify African-Brazilian communities about events taking place within Black Catholicism. This practice evolved into a more sophisticated form of communication, particularly in the church towers of Bahia and Minas Gerais, where bellringers began to play rhythms rooted in African traditions. Sacred rhythms from Candomblé and Congada, such as "Toque de Barravento" and "Samba de Caboclo," were (and still are) performed with the tolling of church bells—the very bells meant to serve colonial religious authority.[88]

The church tower and the role of the bellringer served as parallel sacred spaces and roles within early forms of Capoeira. Holding the post of bellringer carried profound spiritual significance. As researched by Galante, during the eighteenth and nineteenth centuries, church towers served as sites for initiation into the Capoeira tradition.[89] Unlike modern Capoeira, which is often viewed as a sport, a dance, or a secular cultural expression, early forms of Capoeira were closely intertwined with the spiritual beliefs of Africans and Afro-Brazilians. To become a Capoeirista, individuals underwent a spiritual initiation process, part of which occurred within the church towers. Galante highlights that many of Brazil's prominent bell ringers were also Capoeiristas. The memory of these revered masters is preserved in both sacred and secular Afro-Brazilian traditions, symbolizing the crossroads of Orisha Eshu-Elegba. Galante further explores the association, stating:

> the connection to Eshus, entities associated with paths, with time, is precisely what is activated within African and Afro-Brazilian cosmology through the

ringing of bells. Through the tolling of bells, I control time. Through the tolling of bells, I open paths. These bell masters are also the masters of roads, paths, and urban territory. Like Eshu, they oversee communication.[90]

These early Capoeira players played a pivotal role in the development of other Afro-Brazilian genres, such as Samba in Rio de Janeiro and Carnaval Frevo in Recife. Connected to the same civilizational African matrix, they were the masters of urban communication and connection, carried out through the ringing of bells.[91]

The Kimbundu and Kikongo *ngunga* as well as the African-Brazilian *gunga* as adjectives or nouns signify superiority, leadership, or command. *Ngunga Mukisi* or *Gunga Mukixi* refer to a *nkisi* high priest.[92] In Portuguese, *ngunga* became the verb, *gungunar* (or *gogonhar*), which in liturgical language means "to communicate" or "to talk with high spirits" ("conversar com o santo").[93] The association of *ngunga* with both a large singing fish and a large wild ruminant underscores the spiritual and philosophical dimension of this term. Among the diverse spirits that emerged from and governed waters and lands, aquatic and terrestrial beings reign as rulers of their respective realms and their relationships with humanity. Africanist Ras Michael Brown, referring to the Kongo proverb "Where your ancestors do not live, you cannot build your house," investigates how cosmological concepts and the relationship to the environment could have been reestablished in the New World:

> The Kongo proverb reflects another aspect of the interdependence of both worlds. It expresses a vital concern for those who arrived in lands where they had no blood ties to the inhabitants and no established connections to the spiritual world. No ancestors in the new land meant no graves, and no graves meant no access to the land of the dead. So, how did the Kongo people taken to new lands during the era of the trade in captive Africans cope with this crisis? Their ancestors had remedied that problem already, as they too had been strangers in new lands long before. They called upon the most distant ancestors imaginable, so ancient in many cases that these spirits remained immobile, although exceptionally powerful, in the waters and remarkable features of the landscape. These spirits were not the ancestors of particular lineages linked by shared blood. Instead, these spirits acted as the surrogate ancestors of every person who entered their territories, and they governed their domains with the proper amount of rain and a suitable supply of animals and fish so that the living could obtain sustenance. People in West-Central Africa knew them by many names, such as the *nkisi*, *nkita*, and *simbi*. While people applied specific names to these spirits in familiar domains, they knew that the spirits existed in all territories regardless of what

inhabitants already occupied those lands and waters and what these indigenes called the spirits found there. They also knew that as long as newcomers established relationships with the spirits of any domain, they could find a place in the land of the living and maintain their ties to the land of the dead.[94]

Since the Kongo had no blood ties or established connections in these new lands, they called upon ancient spirits known to act as surrogate ancestors for all newcomers. By establishing relationships with these spirits, newcomers could find their place in the land of the living and maintain ties to the land of the dead, ensuring their survival and spiritual continuity. Brown observes the continuity of key cosmological terms such as *Kalunga* and *Finda* in the Lowcountry of South Carolina.[95] Like in other regions of the African diaspora, these terms retain their significance, echoing their usage in the Kongo to denote not only "ocean" and "forest" but also the spiritual realms of the deceased and the living.

Central African nature spirits embrace several entities that share fundamental traits yet also display unique attributes specific to their manifestations in different regions. These spirits were perceived and named individually, but also understood as members of broader regional categories, such as "the *nkisi* of the Loango Coast and Lower Nzadi, the *nkita* of Kongo, and the *kilundu* of Angola."[96] These and other more general designations, like *simbi*, were often used interchangeably, particularly in regions where spiritual traditions intersected along migration paths and trade routes. As stated by Brown, not only were there no "absolute boundaries between the spiritual cultures of West-Central Africa," but "extensive exchanges and mutual influences" created "a diverse sacred landscape inhabited by various nature spirits that bears witness to the many overlapping patterns of cultural interaction over long periods of time."[97] The diverse range of nature spirits, including *nkisi*, *nkita*, and *simbi*, originates from ancient Niger-Congo cultural traditions, deeply ingrained in early Bantu languages and cultures. These spirits, alongside creator deities and ancestors, played crucial roles in early Bantu civilizations: they were channeled through rituals and tools to provide spiritual protection for individuals and safeguard villages.[98]

Musical instruments serve as crucial tools for spiritual protection and connection, encompassing not only the physical objects and their symbolic representations, but also those who wield them—players, singers, and dancers—whose embodied knowledge activates and sustains their force. The music produced constitutes narratives conveyed through coded language, demanding skill and proficiency for effective production (coding) and interpretation (decoding). In Capoeira, *gungas* refer to the larger *berimbau* musical bows that lead. In Congadas, *gungas* are smaller gourd or metallic rattles fastened to the ankles of dancers within the Guarda de Moçambique. These rattles are commonly fashioned from small tin cans filled with lead pellets or seeds known in Brazil as Tears of Our Lady (Lágrimas de Nossa Senhora) or rosary seeds, and in the United States as Job's tears or Chinese pearl barley. Other musical instruments played in the Congadas include the *caixa* drums as well as the *campana* shakers, which refer both to *gungas* and *patangomes*. The *caixa* drums have skins on both sides, are suspended by neck straps, and played with drumsticks. While the Portuguese term *caixa* refers broadly to drums, *campana* generally refers to hanging bells found in churches or public squares. The *patangome* (also called *patangoma* or *patangonga*) are shakers larger than the *gungas*, often made from repurposed cookie tins or welded automobile hubcaps filled with rosary seeds. They are hand-played with a shaking motion that evokes the use of sieves by miners during the gold rush. This historical memory, evoked through gesture and the sound of rattling seeds—which also carry devotional significance in Rosary prayers—prompts us to consider the engagement of sensory faculties that blend cognition with emotion, incorporating music, dance, and visual representations.

The Tears of Our Lady (Lágrimas de Nossa Senhora) or rosary seeds serve as metonyms for the concept of *gunga*, embodying the symbolism of both fish and ruminant animals, as well as the Brazilian Kongo-Angola cosmology surrounding the apparition of Our Lady of the Ocean. These seeds, resembling small, hard oval fruits that grow on millet stalks, are akin to terrestrial shells. Their whitish to greyish hue gives them the appearance of pearls or tiny sea snails found along the ocean shore. For African descendants residing inland in Brazil, far from the coast, these botanical "snails" take on the role of other significant symbols from Kongo-Angola culture and history, such as the *nzimbus*. The name "Tears of Our Lady" evokes the Virgin Mary's narrative from European medieval and Renaissance traditions. The etymology of her title "Stella Maris," meaning "star of the sea," is a variation of the earlier "Stilla Maris," signifying a drop of the sea.[99] Each seed is a tear of Mary, a drop of the ocean. These enclosed vessels, filled with many seeds, are like encapsulated micro-oceans when played as musical instruments. When played together by hand and foot, they become an ocean-like orchestra—an ocean that references not only a topography and its history, but also the realm of supreme deities and ancestral voices.

If we trace the migration paths of rosary seeds, which are native to the countries of Southeast Asia, to the African continent and Brazil, we locate their significance in the trajectory of civilizations spanning from Miyako Island in Okinawa to Kongo-Angola and beyond, to Minas Gerais. This offers us a framework within which historical narratives can be radically reshaped by bypassing and displacing Europe.[100]

MILONGA: THE CAPOEIRA'S WHEEL, THE SUN'S PATH, THE NGOMA CANOE, AND THE MUNDIONGO IN KALUNGA

> *The Bantu believes that our world is an egg. An egg that can expand.*
> *We believe that in this expansion, many worlds are being created.*
>
> Fu-Kiau (1934–2013)

Capoeira is performed within a circle or semi-circle formed by the singing, playing, and dancing bodies of its participants. The *roda* (literally "circle" or "wheel") symbolizes learning and meditating in a microcosm. It is regarded as a semisacred space, one "that is not to be entered without spiritual preparation."[101] Before stepping into the center of the *roda*, the players perform the *preceito*, also known as "prayer" (*reza*) or "waiting for the divine ancestral presence" ("esperar o santo").[102] The *preceito* involves both silent contemplation and verbal and visual prayers, such as the drawing of cosmograms on the floor, often followed by both adepts making the sign of the cross.[103] Two players squat before the three *berimbau* players as the *mestre* at the larger *gunga berimbau* begins singing a litany (*ladainha*), songs of praise that metaphorically convey a historical tribute to the elders, as well as Capoeira worldviews and life philosophies.[104] The *ladainha* is accompanied by the call-and-response *chula* salutations, reverences to God and ancestors that are repeated by the chorus. From the moment the fighters enter the arena and crouch in front of the orchestra, they are not allowed to speak, only after the *ladainha* verses may the game or fight begin.[105] The beginning of the game, or entering the *roda*, is referred to as departure (*saída*), signifying not only that the players are "leaving the foot of the *berimbau*," but also that they are leaving the "mundane world and entering the spiritual world of the *roda*."[106] The salutation line "Iê, volta do mundo" (meaning, "you or yours" and "the circle of the world," or "the turn that the world makes") tells players to start the game, to travel around the world, a Kongo-Angolan concept of the smaller-scale cosmic circle mirroring the cosmos.[107] This transition is possible through a "circling" headstand movement, an upside-down inversion, that as Farris Thompson has observed, represents walking in the spirit world.[108] The singing then changes to *corridos*, which also follow chorus responses.[109]

The objective of a Capoeira game, as outlined by Kenneth Dossar, is for the Capoeiristas to employ "finesse, guile, and technique" to maneuver their opponent into a vulnerable position, making them susceptible to a blow, kick, or sweep.[110] Typically, there is minimal physical contact during strikes, and an implied strike—especially when the opponent has been clearly outmaneuvered into an indefensible stance—is esteemed more than a direct one. Unnecessary aggression or bravado in the game is looked down upon.[111] Engaged in a full performative dialogue within the *roda* space, Capoeira practitioners seek answers to questions regarding the significance of the past, the present, and the delicate equilibrium between continuity and change.[112] As a discourse concerning fundamental philosophical matters, a Capoeira *roda* "allows one to log into the homepage of an epic past and a glorious present."[113] Historians T. J. Desch-Obi and Matthias Röhrig Assunção are some of the prominent figures within a broad community of pan-African scholars dedicated to researching Capoeira and interpreting its *jogo* (*game*) performance, oral literature, philosophies, and rituals.

The first detailed description of the Capoeira *roda* was provided by Edison Carneiro in 1936.[114] A decade later, the Argentine-Brazilian artist Carybé (1911–1997) depicted various Capoeira strikes, movements, and codes, including the *ladainha* opening, the *berimbau* orchestra, and the *aú* handstand.[115] French photographer and Yoruba Ifa diviner Pierre Fatumbi Verger also documented Capoeira through photographs, which were included alongside Carybé's storyboard images in the 1954 documentary titled *Vadiação* (literally meaning "vagrancy," "loafing," or "loitering").[116] The records of Carneiro, Carybé and Verger further contributed to Pastinha's codification of the Capoeira tradition.

Malícia and *milonga* are intertwined Kongo-Angola philosophical concepts and praxis at the core of Capoeira. Coming from the same root as the English word "malice," the *malícia* of Capoeira—as well as in Jongo, Congada and other related expressions—has "a set of related, but generally more benign, meanings."[117] *Malícia* is disguising one's intentions and abilities, strategically awaiting the opportune moment to express them with full impact. In the dialogue established through body movements in a *jogo* of *Capoeira*, *malícia* can be a sudden unexpected interruption of the conversation, or a moment in which a player, instead of waiting, takes two turns, "usually by faking one attack and making another, or by attacking twice in a row."[118] In these maneuvers, there is a deliberate shift in directional focus, characterized by a skillful alternation between direct and indirect approaches. This means that practitioners can create the illusion of having no specific intentions, appearing as if their attention is wandering, all to lure their adversary into making a move.[119] Eye contact serves as an example of this indirect spatial mode; many masters intentionally avoid direct eye contact and instead rely on peripheral vision to give the impression that they are not closely observing and predicting their opponent's move.[120] As pointed out by Charles Daniel Dawson, *malícia* in Capoeira is the gracefulness and effectiveness of stylized personal moves. Dawson defines the practice of *malícia* as deflection, improvisation, beautiful movement, and grace: a concept related to the Kongo philosophy that believes that direct confrontation of "force against force is stupid."[121] He further observes that in the United States, this concept can be found in the names chosen by boxers (such as "Sugar") and in practices such as the basketball "shake-and-bake."[122]

In his considerations on the use of the word *milonga* in Brazil, Câmara Cascudo lists four possible meanings: 1) meaningless conversation, swindling, bad excuse; 2) noise, argument; 3) cunningness, slyness (and here the *milongueiro* is the professional of this art, the one who knows how to use his arguments well, the one with a "well-oiled tongue"); and 4) medicine, hex, or talisman. In Kimbundu, the word *milonga* is the plural for *mulonga* and means "words." According to Cascudo, in Angola, the main square used for judging crimes or determining legal decisions was known as the *Di-kanga dia milonga*, the yard of arguments. He adds that since "every African is born a natural public speaker," it is understood that *milonga* refers to both the introduction and deduction of formal law: encompassing both the content and the form.[123] Capoeiristas, Candomberos, Jongueiros, Mandingueiros—as well as boxers, soccer, and basketball players—who possess *malícia* become acclaimed winners. Whether verbally, physically, or mystically, they have the gift of performing the unexpected in a beautiful manner, of seeing beyond the reality of what is in plain sight. They are philosophers and practitioners who can read the world inside out and upside down, and devise unexpected, unforeseen, and alternative moves, words, or paths.[124]

The historical and philosophical aspects of Capoeira were compellingly explored by Bunseki Fu-Kiau during a presentation in Bahia in 1997. He traced the origins of Capoeira back to the Kongo and Angola region. Possibly beginning with ancient contact between the Kongo and Phoenician Westerners, continuing with the rise of the Kongo-Angola kingdom around the late thirteenth century, and the subsequent gap in historical records, he proceeded to examine key historical junctures. Fu-Kiau highlighted the contributions of European figures such as Portuguese trader Duarte Lopes, whose report on the Kongo was first published in 1591, and French anthropologist Georges Balandier, known for his 1965 publication on the four primary Kongo philosophical schools of thought.[125] Balandier's research, in particular, shed light on the kingdom's importance, documenting institutions like the Lemba, Kimpassi, Kikumbi, and Welo. Fu-Kiau's lecture illuminated the history and influence of the Kongo kingdom on the development of Capoeira.[126]

Fu-Kiau talked about the abduction and fate of accomplished masters and younger generations from the Kingdom of Kongo and how their presence and articulation in the Americas spurred the development of both sacred and secular cultural and philosophical expressions intertwined with Capoeira. He highlighted Kongo's fragmentation by Western powers seeking to exploit its strategic significance. Divided into southern Angola under Portuguese control, central Zaire (or the Republic of Congo) under Belgian rule, and northern Congo under French authority, this once-mighty kingdom served as a major source of enslaved Africans, with over 40 percent of those trafficked to the Americas originating from this region. Slave trade dealt a severe blow to the Kongo kingdom, depriving it of its greatest masters and vital youth. Those who resisted the Atlantic crossing and slave work faced a formidable challenge without the weaponry of their oppressors. Yet, through clandestine organization, they tapped into and adapted the powers acquired in Africa, birthing Capoeira in Brazil and reclaiming an identity rooted in the beliefs and worldview of their people.[127]

Fu-Kiau further explored how the epistemological journey revealed through Capoeira serves as a conduit to cosmological principles, illuminating the dynamics of life, death, and the intricate connection between the living and their ancestors. Unlike other cultural forms of the New World, such as Tango, Capoeira encompasses a comprehensive Bakongo epistemological archive.[128] During his lecture, attended by prominent scholars such as Makota Valdina, Charles Daniel Dawson, and Mestre Cobrinha, Fu-Kiau outlined fundamental facets of the Kongo-Angola civilization in Brazil. He explored concepts that included the perspective on death held by the Kongo people, who perceive it not as an end but as a process akin to music: "Just as we're born with music in our hearts, we depart with it." He emphasized that this understanding is essential for those involved in Capoeira, who "must realize that music is inherent in their very biology, resonating from their hearts."[129] Living, for the Kongo, is an emotional and perpetual journey synonymous with learning and movement in all directions—forward, backward, left, right, upward, and downward. Fu-Kiau underscored the importance of discovering the seventh direction, a concept which holds significant importance outside the realm of Capoeira. He likened the movements of Capoeira to dancing inside of and breaking free from an egg. While the movements of a Capoeirista encompass striking in all directions, the most crucial is the inward strike. This seventh movement pertains to encountering, recognizing, and engaging with both the living and the deceased, an aspect often overlooked in the West, yet central to African culture According to Fu-Kiau, "that's why the West hasn't understood African culture very well."[130]

Fu-Kiau shared a Bantu proverb that advises "to listen more to the dead than the living, for while the dead have become stones, the living are grass." Despite the evolution of Capoeira over time, he sees its essence remaining rooted in a foundational seed, akin to immutable stones. He illustrated this point by referencing the Tango, a dance with African origins reflected in its name, derived from the term *tanga* or *matanga*, a communal gathering held upon the passing of a chief, symbolizing a second funeral. Fu-Kiau emphasized that while the Kongo cannot claim ownership of the Tango in its current form, they acknowledge their influence on its origins. He stressed the importance of understanding the cultural roots of words like Tango for the Western world to truly appreciate their heritage.[131]

The basic translation of the Kikongo term *n'tângu* is "time." Expanding on Fu-Kiau's insights regarding Argentine Tango, Farris Thompson explored the historical underpinnings of this cultural phenomenon.[132] According to him, *tango* is not merely a word, but encompasses a multifaceted semantic spectrum of meanings.[133] On both sides of the Atlantic, *tango* signifies, among other things, a dance, a venue for dancing, the people who dance it, and the rhythmic essence of the dance itself.[134] Thompson elucidates that on the African side of the Atlantic, there are the related concepts of *tanga* and *matanga* that encompass the funeral, the dance, and the drum.[135] In the Bakongo culture, funerals involve bidding farewell to the departed with music, ensuring they transition to the afterlife without sorrow. Thompson draws parallels to similar practices, like the jazz funerals of New Orleans and the Candombe funerals of Montevideo and Buenos Aires.[136] He contemplates the intricate relationship between *tanga* and its creolized form, *tango*, as more intricate than a simple correlation. The word *ntangu* means "sun," and time; *ntanguzazo*, meaning "forever and ever," is an eternity akin to multiple suns. Thompson poses the rhetorical question: "Now what in the hell does the sun have to do with a dance?" In Kongo culture, he states, the answer is everything: "The sun's path—*'nzila ya ntangu'*—is a counterclockwise circle, danced in—they're trying to tell us something—conga lines."[137]

Fu-Kiau and Thompson, directly and indirectly addressing the "wheel" of Capoeira, prompt us to seek out the archives of alternative forms of linguistic, epistemological, and performative creolization. While official narratives of Euro-African creolization dominate the physical spaces of libraries, universities, courts, and governmental offices, where do we uncover the archives of the Pan-African creolization described by Thompson? Where can we find *ntanguzazo* documentation of the creolized cosmology of planets and humanity in space and time? Within the ever-turning world and the *rodas* that continue to revolve, both in the visible and unseen realms, where are the archives of 500 years of the perpetual sun trajectories of African civilizations in Brazil?

One Capoeira chant (among many) invokes specific spaces and concepts tied to circular dances and circulation of goods. In one particular instance, it references goods produced and acquired in the Brazilian state of Maranhão and traded in the legendary, affluent, eastward-extending realm of King Solomon, the biblical emperor and sage who conducted trade in the Mediterranean Sea, lost his opulent empire, and saw his homeland divided into two often-hostile kingdoms.[138] Maranhão, from 1641 to 1644, was under Dutch control. During this period, the Dutch were fighting against the Portuguese both in Brazil and in Central Africa, where they forged a triple alliance with the Kongo and Ndongo kingdoms. The chant begins weaving this context:

Girl, what do you sell there?	Sinhazinha o que vende aí?
I sell rice from Maranhão	Vendo arroz do Maranhão
My master ordered me to sell	Meu sinhô mandou vendê
In the land of Solomon, Aruandê	Na terra de Salomão Aruandê
(The chorus responds:)	(O coro responde:)
Ye ye, Aruandê, comrade	ê, ê, Aruandê, camarado
The rooster crowed	Galo canto
Ye ye, the rooster crowed, comrade	ê, ê, galo canto, camarado
Cock-a-doodle-doo	Cocôrocô
Ye ye, cock-a-doodle-doo, comrade	ê, ê, galo canto, camarado
Starch for ironing	Goma de engomá
Ye ye, starch for ironing, comrade	Ê, ê, goma de engomá, camarado
Iron for killing	Ferro de matá
Ye ye, iron for killing, comrade	Ê, ê, ferro de matá, camarado
Sharp knife	Ê faca de ponta
Ye ye, sharp knife, comrade	Ê, ê, faca de ponta, camarado
Let's go	Vamos embora
Ye ye, let's go, comrade	Ê, ê, vamos embora, camarado
Around the world	Pro mundo afora
Ye ye, to around the world, comrade	Ê, ê, pro mundo afora, camarado
Encircle the world	Dá volta ao mundo
Ye ye, encircle the world, comrade	Ê, ê, dá volta ao mundo, camarado[139]

In this Capoeira chant, Kongo-Angola (Kongo-Ndongo) is further referenced with the term Aruandê, which appears as an equivalent to the lands of Solomon. These geographic coordinates—both literal and symbolic—make reference to the east where, in the Kongo cosmology, the sun (*ntangu*) emerges to start its cycle, its counterclockwise "nzila ya ntangu" path.

The chant tells us that a rooster crowed to announce the rise of the *ntangu* sun. One of the animals that serves as a spiritual, imagistic metaphor for the priest-doctor in Central Africa is the rooster. Its placement and call in this chant trigger the emergence of the *ngoma* drum (in the homophone *engoma*, "ironing with starch"); as well as the sharp "faca de ponta" knife, the weapon of choice of Capoeiristas; the "volta ao mundo" circle of the world as the cosmological journey of all beings; and the companions in this journey referenced here as *camarado* (comrade). The images and concepts, from rooster to *ngoma*, trace us back to Maria Aparecida Martins's song "Diongo, Mundiongo" and her images of the old sorcerers, ocean, the land, heroes, kings, and history. *Diongo* (*Ndóngo*) comes from Kimbundu, meaning "the word," or "knowledge."[140] *Mundiongo* (*Umndóngo*), by extension, means "the house of the word"; "the space for words"—for knowledge, education, initiation, and assembly.[141]

Diongo is a reference to another circular dance performance, the Jongo. Similar to Capoeira, Jongo typically involves two performers at the center of the circle, and the ritual begins with the act of paying respect to the elders, in this case known as "saravar a ngoma" ("to praise the *ngoma*"). The *ngoma* drum, like the Capoeira *gunga* is an embodiment of the elders. The eldest Jongueiro, the Cumba (from *ngunga*) seeks blessings from the ancestors and permission from the present audience.[142] Like in Congada, the bonfire holds fundamental significance, not only for tuning the drums but also for maintaining communication between the past and present, the deceased and the living.[143] Jongo songs are often categorized into *visaria*, aiming to energize the circle, and *engoromenta*, featuring challenges between the Jongueiros.[144] These challenges are infused with various *mandinga* and *milonga* "spells," including the verbal "tying up" maneuver, which silences and defeats the opponent.[145]

The Jongo *ngoma* drum is sometimes referred to as *calunga*, a key term in Bakongo cosmology that signifies, among other meanings, a superlative—in this context, denoting the larger drum. In Kimbundu, Kalunga refers to graveyards, the realm of the dead, the ocean, and the permeable boundary that divides the worlds of the living and the dead. It also marks the northern and southern hemispheres of the Bakongo cosmogram, which together encapsulate various forms of totality. Kalunga represents the ancestral realm, the home of Nzambi, God, and the afterlife. The term Nzambi is a compound word consisting of *nza* (world) and -*mbi* ("extremely wonderful").[146] According to Fu-Kiau, Nzambi literally translates to "the one who is complete within the all-in-all," while Kalunga is "the invisible boundary or barrier between the physical and spiritual realms," serving as "the balancing line of all energies."[147] The historian Robert Slenes highlights that Kalunga signifies not only the ocean but also the boat used to navigate it.[148] In Kimbundu, *ngoma* refers to a drum "made of long hollow wood," and by extension, it also signifies a canoe constructed in a similar manner, as well as the sound produced by drumming. *Ngoma* is also synonymous with "dawn" or "time to wake up," linking sound, movement, and awakening.[149]

A Jongo performer uses chants to seek permission to enter the circle. As documented by the folklore scholar Maria de Lourdes Ribeiro (1912–1983), one traditional song foregrounds this: "The white-tailed deer [*Ngulungu*] is at the border of the ocean, asking for permission to approach."[150] The ocean's edge, or seashore symbolizes the boundary of the Jongo circle. To join the circle is to metaphorically enter the sea. As psychologist Ricardo Mattos observes, the *terreiro* ground is likened to the shifting surface of the ocean; the Jongo circle ritualizes a vessel adrift at sea; the main Jongo *ntambu* drum symbolizes a canoe; the dancer or player is referred to as the sailor (*marinheiro*); and the swaying movement of the dance embodies the act of canoeing.[151] In Jongo ritual, the physical shores of Brazil merge with the mythical Africa, symbolized as Aruanda. The chant uses variations such as *Aruandê* and *Aruandá*. Similarly, *Calunga* may appear as *Calungaê* or *Calungá*. In addition to their rhythmic functions, these variations carry distinct meanings. They signify belonging either to Aruanda or to Calunga and are associated with verbs or actions related to them, such as entering, walking on, or dreaming of these realms.

In a process of geographic synthesis, as analyzed by Mattos, a historical continuum links Aruanda to Brazil. The immanent present merges the realms of the deceased and the living, ancestry and reality. This reconciliation of opposites finds expression in the fluid currents of a moving sea, where spaces and times ebb and flow in enchanted tides. The Jongo circle, ceremonially adrift in the grand Calunga of the *terreiro* sea, gathers the *malungos*—comrades of a continuous journey— in the *mundiongo* assembly that bridges here and there, then and now.[152]

8
Aruanda

Ancestral Geographies:
A Map to Aruanda and Other Realms

I watched the bright, burning sunrise in my homeland, and bursting with pleasure at that morning hour, when everything there exhales, love, I'd run to the wide, sandy beaches.

Maria Firmina dos Reis (1822–1917)
Translation by Cristina Pinto-Bailey

The epigraph of this chapter consists of recollections from an elderly enslaved character named Mother Susana who fondly recalls her childhood spent by an ocean adorned with thousands of tiny shells "embroidering the sand."[1] In the 1859 novel *Úrsula*, Susana serves as an alter ego of the author Maria Firmina dos Reis (1822–1917) and embodies a narrative oracle that weaves together the past, present, and future through announcements and predictions that drive the story's pace and incite reflection.[2] Both character and creator emerge from the margins of the narrative and of Brazilian literature, paving new paths.[3] Considered the first abolitionist novel in Portuguese and the first novel published by an African-Brazilian woman, *Úrsula* represents the emergence of literary narratives of the Black diaspora in the Americas.[4] By collecting stories from her enslaved acquaintances and integrating them into her narrative, Firmina dos Reis carved out a distinctive place for herself, surpassing any existing literary conventions and contributing a unique voice to Brazilian abolitionism and literature.[5]

Firmina dos Reis's portrayal of girls playing at the shore, surrounded by thousands of tiny shells, transports us to the island of Luanda in the grand southern province of Mbamba. The island of Luanda, once the largest and wealthiest among the twelve provinces that formed the Kongo Kingdom, played a crucial economic role, controlling the vital route from its shell-rich fisheries to Mbanza-Kongo, the capital. Luanda was a veritable treasure trove, with its sandy shores yielding the currency of the kingdom and its surrounding regions—the *nzimbu*, small and spiraled sea snails adorned with vibrant hues. These shells were harvested by the island's women, who waded into the sea, filled their baskets with sand from the seabed, and carefully sifted them out. Sorted by size and brilliance, these shells were then sent off to Mbanza-Kongo.[6] Throughout much of West Africa, *nzimbu* served as the standard currency in the market, occasionally facing devaluation due to the influx of thousands of tons of cheaper counterfeit shells imported from Zanzibar and Bahia.[7] As the source of supply of *nzimbu*, Luanda was the analogue of the U.S. Federal Reserve.

The Bay of Luanda is referred to as Kalunga Kofele, meaning "the little ocean," as opposed to Kalunga Konene, "the great ocean."[8] A cosmological reference in the Kongo foundation myth, Luanda refers to "beginning," "origin" and, "the east." The Angolan social anthropologist Patrício Batsîkama highlights that its first meaning, before that of a geographic region, is a direction, a cardinal point.[9] In a literal translation of the traditional adage, "ku Ngangela tangwa cicamene; ku Luanda cangoloshi," it is understood that while Ngangela is where the sun rises, Luanda is where the sun "goes to sleep."[10] If the sun (as we know) rises in the east, how could Luanda refer to both east and sunset? Batsîkama explores the interrelated meanings of Luanda and Ngangela, focusing on their opposition as cardinal points, geographic regions, and other layers of semantic reference. In the etymology of Ngangela, there is the verb *ganga*, which means "to shine," "to sparkle," "to transmit fire from the eyes." It is connected to the suffix *la* (or *hala*), which marks its action.[11] Ngangela refers to a place where the sun burns or where the sun is fire. In the adage, the sun referred to in Ngangela designates the region of the rising sun, where east is only one of its meanings.[12] The question then becomes how to locate the lands from which the Ngangela sun rises—the place of the Kongo's origin—which leads Batsîkama to the Kalahari's southern desert, its springs, and the primordial source of water: the point of original migration.[13]

In Brazil, along its eastern coast where major cities are located, the sun rises over the Atlantic Ocean and sets toward the land. In Africa, along its western coast, the sun rises over the land and sets over the Atlantic Ocean. The Bakongo cosmology is centered around the sun's coordinates in relation to the ocean and the ground and its mountains. A journey across the Atlantic—from Luanda to Recife, for instance—can be depicted as folding the world like a piece of paper, with the Kalunga line serving as the crease. This dislocation signifies that from one shore to the other, the sun no longer rises over the land, as it does at the Mountain of the Living, but over the ocean, as it does in the Realm of the Ancestors.

GINGA'S GINGA: IN THE FOOTSTEPS OF QUEEN NZINGA

Queen Nzinga is a warrior woman, she has two hips surrounded by blades!

Rainha Jinga é mulher de batalha, Tem duas cadeiras arredor de navalha!

Congada chant

Snail shells are representations of the creator god Mbumba-Lowa, who is also symbolized by the python and the rainbow, indicating dominion over both land and water. Theologist Kiatezua Lubanzadio Luyaluka explains that the Kikongo verb *bûmba*, also found in Mbumba, means "to give a shape" while the title Lowa denotes "solar," conveying the idea of enlightenment in creation.[14] For the Bakongo, creation implies the act of illuminating and enabling originally formless entities to take a form.[15] One of the representations of the Kingdom of Kongo and its rulers is the Nkodia shell.[16] The spirals of these shells are visual blueprints of time, development, and ruling power. The anthropologist José Carlos de Oliveira argues that, metaphorically, the Nkodia spirals can be understood as the original diaspora of the Kongo—that is, its *nzinga*, which translates as "to coil."[17] Oliveira adds that Nzinga is a reference to the oldest of the peoples in the Congo Basin and is also used as a nickname attributed to children born with an umbilical cord wrapped around their necks (as was the case with Queen Nzinga Mbandi). Nkita-Nzinga is the greatest of all midwives, the first grandmother, and the eldest daughter of the three siblings who were the first ancestors of all Kongo.[18] The term Nkita, literally meaning "a person who has returned from the world of the ancestors," serves as a title denoting initiates or scholars within Kimpasi societies, one of the four primary Kongo philosophical schools of thought.[19]

The historian Mariana Bracks Fonseca, who studies Queen Nzinga Mbandi (1582–1663)—spelled "Ginga" or "Jinga" in Portuguese—notes that the name Nzinga denotes both a specific lineage and an ancestral political principle ingrained in Kongo tradition.[20] She notes that the first king of Kongo baptized by the Portuguese was named Nzinga-a-Nkuwu (1470–1509), and that several other rulers in the sixteenth century bore Nzinga in their names, including Mvemba-a-Nzinga Afonso I (1509–1540), Nkumbi Mpudi-a-Nzinga Diogo (1546–1561), and Mvemba-a-Nzinga Afonso II (1561).[21] Fonseca explores how Queen Nzinga Mbandi's name took on new dimensions after her death in 1663, coming to signify not only a political title but also an ethnic group.[22] Several Nzinga queens reigned over the region in the eighteenth century, reinforced the legacy of the first queen by affirming the immortality of her name and maintaining continuity with Nzinga Mbandi's legendary resistance in defense of her territories.[23] Fonseca explores how the disintegration and reconfiguration of various peoples during the slave trade era led to the emergence of an ethnogenesis and the development of the Jinga ethnic identity—a group primarily shaped by the strategies and tactics of its queen.[24]

One of Fonseca's noteworthy contributions lies in her pivotal analysis of the term-title-concept *ginga*. She questions whether the essential body movement of Capoeira and the queen known in Brazil as Ginga could be mere homonyms. She relates how her research was sparked by a footnote she encountered in a publication by the historian Luiz Felipe de Alencastro. The note makes reference to an observation he heard from a colleague at a colloquium in São Paulo who suggested that the Capoeira *ginga* movement might have been invented by Queen Nzinga or served as a tribute to her. Alencastro himself firmly denied any connection, stating: "The term ginga, used by Capoeiristas, comes from seamanship and refers to the 'stern oar' and its pivoting movement. Its origin can be traced back to the Old High German verb gingen, meaning 'to sway.'"[25] Fonseca expresses bewilderment at this assertion. She examines the semantic evolution of this term across Portuguese dictionaries to track its lexical entry and historical variations in meaning within Luso-Brazilian contexts. Rather than claiming a direct link between the historical figure of the queen and the Capoeira body movement, Fonseca shows how, within the cultural grammar of Angola and Brazil, behaviors associated with Nzinga share cultural patterns and meanings adapted to new contexts.[26] She characterizes *ginga* as a system of knowledge that integrates wisdom and warfare strategies, showcasing Queen Nzinga's martial and diplomatic prowess.[27] Queen Nzinga became a transdiasporic myth embodying a model and narrative of creation that reaches back to a primordial era predating Portuguese dominance in Angola.[28] Her legacy became embedded in the *ginga* of Capoeira, both in its practice and historical narrative. History, in this context, has been imprinted and conveyed through corporeal movements and rhythmic expressions.[29]

Another contemporary Capoeirista and scholar who has focused her research on the concept of *ginga*, though from a performance rather than historical perspective, is Cristina Rosa. Referring to historic-anthropological studies, Rosa explores Nzinga's unconventional diplomacy and the various meanings of her name: from a Portuguese reference to Nzinga's soldiers to a Mbundu concept that refers to ceaseless movement and unending articulation.[30] She portrays Capoeira as a process—a means of expressing ideas through the body—rather than a product—a strictly regulated technique with established rules.[31] Within its lexicon of movements, as well as its array of rhythms, lyrics, stories, symbols, and actions, Rosa traces the historical association of Capoeira to African political resistance in Brazil, from Maroon communities to activist movements combating racial discrimination, which gained momentum following Brazil's redemocratization in the 1980s.[32] According to Rosa, the basic Capoeira movement, *ginga*, represents "a slippery concept" that resists an easy definition; "its undulating ebb-and-flow conveys the swaying motion of the sea, the riff of waves, the dynamic balance of tides and, by extension, the sensation of standing in a small boat on the water."[33] She draws a comparison between the kinesthetic experience of "restful awareness" that characterizes the *ginga* movement and the sensation of standing on a sail raft or a small riverboat moving through water.[34] This swaying action of *ginga* is also central to other Afro-Brazilian circular and ambulatory sacred and secular dances, such as Candomblé, Umbanda, Jongo, Folia de Reis, and Samba, as well as the dribbling strategy of Brazilian soccer.[35] Rosa proposes an outline of *ginga*'s aesthetic principles and its connection to other West African dance forms in the Americas, ranging from social dance and team sports to concert dance.[36]

Ginga is an integral component of the inseparable and often simultaneous techniques of the "motrix" sing-dance-drum-tell quartet, as codified by Zeca Ligiéro as the common denominator of several African performance traditions.[37] Capoeira involves body movements that simulate combat within its *ginga* technique, wherein the body continually transfers weight between arms and legs, creating a bridge between the vertical and horizontal, as well as between past and present. Masters transmit the ritualization of their relationship with a long genealogy of previous masters, sages, and chiefs, who are evoked and made present through the activation of the "motrix" quartet. *Ginga* serves as a mnemonic trigger, facilitating the recreation of new repertoires based on ancient themes learned from the masters. These themes are articulated through the musical composition of the berimbau orchestra, along with the clapping and call-and-response singing of all participants.

Capoeira movements both reveal and conceal. Capoeiristas who are adept in the *mandinga* spiritual wisdom and techniques can honor a memory by embodying it fully, while simultaneously "closing their bodies," shielding themselves from both visible and invisible destructive forces.[38] One of its chants references the technique and the attributed spiritual geographic origin of the practice: "Ye, Aruandê / Ye, Aruandê, comrade (chorus) / It's the game of *mandinga* / It's the game of *mandinga*, comrade (chorus) / Ah, knows how to play, / Ah, knows how to play, comrade (chorus) / Ay-ay-ah, Capoeira, / Ay-ay-ah, Capoeira, comrade (chorus)."[39] The circular dance of Capoeira, with players converging to the center only to be successively replaced by different pairs, embodies a secular organic prayer.[40] Like the orbital dance of planets, Capoeira invites and represents, both directly and indirectly, historical realms, sovereigns, principles, and ethics. It evokes and embodies, whether explicitly named or not, the solar creations of Mbumba-Lowa, the founding siblings Nsaku-Mpanzu-Nzinga, the lineages of queens and kings, and the sacred and historical realms of Kongo-Angola-Mozambique, epitomized as Aruanda.

Capoeira movements and chants invoke the motion of celestial bodies: "in the turns the world made, in the turn the world makes" ("na volta que o mundo deu, na volta que o mundo dá"). The *roda* of Capoeira, often translated as "the Capoeira circle," is more accurately and literally a "wheel." Unlike a circle, which may suggest a static and two-dimensional shape, a wheel implies dynamism—a structure that revolves and spins either autonomously or with assistance. According to a well-known Congada chant: "the wheel of the world is large, but Nzambi's wheel is larger" ("a roda do mundo é grande, mas a de Nzambi é maior"). One of Capoeira's core movements—"to circle the world" or "to go around the wheel of the world" ("dar a volta ao mundo")—involves walking around the wheel's circumference or the ring of the performance, usually in a counterclockwise movement performed at the game's inception or during intervals and transitional moments. The Capoeira scholar Maya Talmon-Chvaicer observes that this is not merely circling the field of play or the Capoeira wheel but an embodiment of a universal orbit.[41] To traverse the Capoeira wheel—a microcosm of the universe or a world within a world—is to navigate within the cosmos's safe and sheltered confines, echoing the protection sought for one's personal sphere.[42] Africanist Alan Santos de Oliveira views this counterclockwise progression as a means of starting over, setting a return in motion to resume the present and project the future, aligning with the Sankofa principle.[43] The Capoeira wheel turns in an ascending direction, but always circumnavigates the present and transports to an ancestral future.[44]

FROM PUNGO-A-NDONGO TO ARUANDA

> *Teensy-weensy pebble* *Pedrinha miudinha*
> *In Aruanda, my friend* *Na Aruanda, auê*
> *A large bedrock, so large* *Lajeiro tão grande, tão grande*
> *In Aruanda, my friend.* *Na Aruanda, auê.*
>
> Capoeira chant

In Brazil, the significance of Luanda as a slave port has evolved into a mythic geographical icon, a sacred realm that exists "all by itself, as an independent cell and as a magical abstraction or dream."[45] The Portuguese dictionary defines Aruanda, with roots in the toponym Luanda, as the "heaven or celestial abode for Orishas and associated deities."[46] In Afro-Brazilian philosophy, Aruanda—also known as Aluanda, Aluangüe, Aruandê, Aruenda, and Zaluanda—holds a revered status as a magical and curative realm. It symbolizes Luanda beyond its physical location as São Paulo de Luanda, representing the homeland of supreme Kongo-Angola spirits, a mythological ancestral Africa, and an ideal of achievable freedom, health, and joy. Aruanda serves as the earliest reference in Brazil to a concept akin to mother-Africa.

In an effort to map the imagery of Aruanda, I came to recognize the importance of revisiting the apparently straightforward verses of the poem-chant in the epigraph of this chapter and rectifying previous translation oversights.[47] Each process has its own rhythm and should adhere to its natural pace; the unknown demands time, patience, and the development of new frameworks and lexicons. In seeking an entry point to access a neglected philosophical corpus, I revisit this symbolic text and its possible translations as a covert gateway leading to a vantage point from which one can behold the intertwined ancient and ever-evolving pathways within the corpus of Afro-Brazilian epistemology. As a conduit of knowledge, the poem-chant about Aruanda's pebble is emblematic of a broader poetic tradition. While it may initially seem simple and straightforward, closer examination reveals its complexity: it encodes allusions to profound cultural and sophisticated concepts; it conveys knowledge in a veiled language accessible only to erudite intellectuals and grassroots scholars, whose contributions have often gone unrecognized as scholarship. Within this metonymic chant lies an exemplary, condensed compendium of literary, historical, and philosophical wisdom. Structured similarly to Japanese haiku in its depth, brevity, and apparent simplicity, the verses about Aruanda diverge from the Japanese minimalist tradition through repetitive and melodic cadences that allude to an epic spanning over five centuries. Embedded within are Bantu-Brazilian epistemological motifs, often overlooked for their presumed lack of sociohistorical, cultural, or ethical substance and frequently misunderstood through Catholic reinterpretations. These subtle yet complex textualities harbor multiple levels of significance.

Africanist translator Raquel de Souza argues that translation within the Black Atlantic scope goes beyond mere dictionary consultation and grammatical proficiency. It requires a profound understanding of the diverse ethnicities, intricate cultural networks of the African continent, and the specialized lexicon of knowledge that has emerged within the African diaspora.[48] De Souza is critical of translations conducted by scholars lacking this essential insight, which often reveal underlying neglect and ignorance.[49] The poet Guellwar Adún emphasizes the urgent necessity of "the translation of languages, cultures, semiosis and epistemes across diverse locales of the Afrodiaspora," underscoring the critical and complex task facing translators in this specialized field.[50] Building upon the insights shared by de Souza and Adún, it is important to keep in mind that grasping diasporic philosophies often involves immersing oneself in practices and traditions that are inherently ritualistic and initiatory, where knowledge transmission is viable only through communal practice rather than an individualistic or accumulative research approach.

In reviewing my previous translation of the poem-chant about Aruanda, I still stand by the translation of the phrase "na Aruanda, auê" as "in Aruanda, my friend." To most Portuguese speakers, *auê* might seem like a nonsensical onomatopoeic interjection—a rhythmic exclamation devoid of specific meaning. However, this term implies an address to an unspecified entity or person. In Yoruba, *àwé* serves as a salutation for someone not personally known, translating as "my friend, sir/madam," or "excuse me."[51] In Afro-Brazilian ceremonies influenced by Yoruba-Ewe-Fon traditions, the term is akin to "my friend" ("meu camarada").[52] It is also prevalent in the liturgical language of various Kongo-Angola-oriented rituals in Brazil. Yeda Pessoa de Castro cites the phrase "cum licença de Zambiapongo, auê," translating to "with the permission of the supreme god, my friend," or "may you, supreme god, grant me permission, sir."[53] "Zambiapongo," derived from "Nzambi ampungo," is a Kikongo salutation to an entity roughly equivalent to God. Nzambi is a compound of *nza* (world) and *mbi* ("extremely wonderful").[54] Fu-Kiau clarifies that Nzambi is "a synonym and epithet for God," signifying "the one-who-is-complete-by-self in the all-in-all."[55] The musician and researcher Tiganá Santana suggests translating Nzambi as the "Always-Present-Ancestral-Whole" (*Totalidade-Ancestral-Sempre-Presente*).[56]

A seemingly minor adjustment I made in my earlier translation concerns the phrase now rendered as "a large, so large bedrock" ("lajeiro tão grande, tão grande"), which I had first translated as "a rock, such a big rock" in Aruanda. At the time, my frame of reference did not include the image of the rocky outcrops in the former capital of Ndongo. I was not yet acquainted with the dark stones of Pungo-a-Ndongo, the towering monoliths that emerge from the savanna, overlooking the Kwanza River on the distant horizon. The image of queen Nzinga's mythic domains, the historical heart of Ndongo in present-day Angola, had yet to be formed in my imagination. At that time, I could recognize the rock's surface—the ground—but not the unconsolidated materials that underpin and characterize bedrock. I could grasp the connection between the "pebble" ("pedrinha miudinha") and the "big rock" ("lajeiro tão grande") mentioned in the lyrics. I perceived them as the vehicles and foundation of past, present, and future—a "teensy-weensy pebble" linking the singer in the present to a vast, ancestral rock in Africa, a place to which one can ritually return and toward which one moves over the course of life and death. However, at that time, I simplified the meaning of the Portuguese word *lajeiro* (bedrock) to merely "rock." *Lajeiro* denotes an immense, expansive rock formation—an ancient, stratified geological structure. It is the visible and walkable flat sheets that, like the visible part of an iceberg, emerge at the earth's surface. The bedrock of Pungo-a-Ndongo, also known as Pungo Andongo, Mpungo-a-Ndongo, or Maupungo-a-Ndongo, holds spiritual, geographical, and historical significance as a portal to an ancestral domain.

From the lowland plains of Luanda Island to Pungo-a-Ndongo, there spans an approximately 250-mile stretch of land showcasing varied topography and ecosystems. As one moves inland, the terrain transitions to rugged landscapes, featuring stepped mountainous escarpments rising to heights of up to 3,300 feet.[57] These escarpment formations, dating back to the Gondwanan era when Africa separated from other continents, mark the rifted continental margin. Angola boasts some of the most prominent escarpments in Southern Africa.[58] Beyond these escarpments, further inland, lies an extensive interior plateau, constituting about 65 percent of the country's landscape. This area is characterized by plateaus and valleys, with coastal scrub and savanna giving way to more diverse woodland along river valleys. It is in the Malange Province that the massive granite bedrock of Pungo-a-Ndongo, known in Portuguese as Pedras Negras (Black Rocks), rises abruptly from the surrounding savanna.[59] Located approximately ten miles away from the Kwanza River, Pungo-a-Ndongo is characterized by massive conglomerate boulders, pillars, and whalebacks, some towering over 656 feet high.[60] Standing out from its surrounding topography, the mysterious allure of Pungo-a-Ndongo is enhanced by its ever-changing colors, ranging from gray and brown to pink, red, or black, with occasional patches of green, yellow, or orange. This phenomenon arises from a complex interplay of geological elements (including minerals like quartz, feldspar, and mica), chemical processes (such as weathering and oxidation), biological influences (such as the growth of lichens and algae on the rock surface), and environmental factors.[61] Among the rock formations of Pungo-a-Ndongo lies a rock floor adjacent to a perennial stream. A few meters from the stream is a smooth patch bearing about ten engravings of human footprints, ranging in length from six to ten inches.[62]

Legend has it that these are the footprints of King Ngola-Kiluanji and Queen Nzinga Mbandi. The mystique of Pungo-a-Ndongo and Nzinga's prowess are intricately linked. According to oral tradition, Nzinga was bathing in a stream at the base of the rocks when she was spotted by Portuguese soldiers.[63] As she fled, the sheer force of pressing her foot onto the rock left her footprints imprinted. These tales evoke the image of Nzinga as a mythical figure endowed with political and spiritual powers. The ancestral footprint forms part of a visual narrative that carries movement within itself. By observing it, one can envision Nzinga in motion, gathering momentum to ascend into the air, leaving behind a mark of her connection with the rocks that propelled her into other realms or dimensions where no force could hinder her complete mastery over her body and surroundings.

In Eurocentric narratives, Pungo often refers either to the Pedras Negras jail founded in the area in 1597 or to the throne of the kings of Ndongo, which was seized by the Portuguese from Ngola-a-Hari II (Dom João de Sousa) in 1671.[64] Geologically, the imposing black stones of Pungo-a-Ndongo's bedrock tell an ancient tale of magma surging upward millions of years ago. The seafloor tore open, allowing lava to erupt, and subsequent energy releases propelled the formation of sediments, with layers settling atop each other, gradually shaping a new world. A team of geologists presents the following imagery for bedrock formation: "outcrops of rocks show evidence of more than one 'story' of formation. The successive chapters of its history are superimposed on its features, like a warrior accruing scars through a long and glorious career."[65] This striking geological metaphor mirrors the Bakongo cosmological philosophy regarding the formation of planets, the cycles of life, and the dimensions of space and time. The exposed subterranean rock formations, protruding through the earth's surface, evoke the Bakongo worldview of the earth as dual peaks in reflection. Makota Valdina elucidates this perspective:

> The Bakongo imagine the world as two opposing mountains that are mirrored at their bases, divided by a body of water along the unseen boundary of the Kalunga line. They perceive themselves on the mountain of the living—a place from where they can see the sun emerging, rising, and growing, expanding through their heads, and then disappearing, dying on the other side, to rise on the other mountain, in the world of Mpémba—the world of the ancestors and the unseen. The sun rises every day not just to usher in daylight but to renew life within humanity.[66]

The scientific metaphor likening Earth's geological formations to battle-scarred warriors, with their bodies etched by the struggles and triumphs of life, aligns with the Dikenga, the cyclical cosmogram of the Bakongo. In Bakongo belief, everything—humans, planets, civilizations—follows a broad, cyclical path known as Dingo-Dingo, a circular formation process. All entities—from life cycles to civilizations, flora to fauna—adhere to this circular journey marked by the passage of four cardinal suns in the Dikenga cosmogram. In Bakongo ideography, the sun's circuit around the earth holds paramount importance. The act of "tracing God" ("zanga Nzambi") is manifested in the traditional representation of the Dikenga cross, an emblem symbolizing life and cosmic transformation.[67] While condensed pictographs (or encoded philosophical and sacred texts) of the Four Moments of the Sun cosmogram are primarily observed as ritual ground drawings in the African diaspora, in Central Africa these motifs appear in rock art and carvings on objects associated with political and spiritual authority. These ancient philosophical notations address "fundamental issues of the land, cosmos, medicine, law, authority, and the power of the dead."[68] As described by Fu-Kiau, in Bakongo iconography, "dots or small circles on the intersecting arms of the Kongo cross" represent men or women as secondary suns, journeying through time and space.[69]

As Yeda Pessoa de Castro has documented, the entity Zambiapongo in Brazilian Kongo-Angola cosmology is Nzambi-a-Mpungu, the "Always-Present-Ancestral-Whole" force.[70] This primal energy unites all of existence, serving as the foremost progenitor who initiated and set in motion the wheel of the universe. The term Mpungu simultaneously evokes the primal ancestral entity and the foundational realm for the Bakongo. According to Assis Júnior's Kimbundu dictionary, *pungo* can also be translated as *mocho*, the Portuguese word for "owl," metaphorically indicating "hornless," or in botanical terms, "branchless."[71] This image circles back to the concept of an entity devoid of divisions, singular and complete. Assis Júnior further clarifies that *pungo* can also refer to a large sea fish, to the high and rugged mountain chain, and to the Almighty Nzambi, "the one without parallel," "the large," or "the greatest." Pungo-a-Ndongo thus emerges as a locale that embodies Nzambi-a-Mpungu and epitomizes the foundational cycle of the Kongo Dikenga cosmology based on the four cardinal suns.

In sacred Kongo-Angola geography, Pungo-a-Ndongo is one of the representations of the epicenter of the world's creation and the foundational land for all living beings. Similarly, in the Yoruba-Ewe-Fon sacred cosmological geography, the town of Ilè Ífé serves as the epicenter. The pebble mentioned in the poem-chant about Aruanda can symbolize the genesis of the bedrock of Pungo-a-Ndongo, its foundational layer. While a pebble fits snugly within the grasp of a hand, a bedrock beneath the feet reveals its expansive nature. Aruanda's journey extends from *Ku nseke*, the realm of the living, to *Ku mpemba*, the domain of the ancestors. It shuttles from Africa to Brazil and back again, in a continuous cycle maintained by the rhythms of music, dance, and the heartbeat. From the hush of midnight to the peak of noon, from the southern origins to the northern pinnacle of life's trajectory, the poem-chant illustrates in successive lines the presence of both the diminutive pebble and the expansive bedrock within Aruanda. Through this transition from pebble to bedrock, one can discern the initial revolution of the Eastern Sun, orchestrating the "turning of the world's wheel" ("dando a volta do mundo").

Pungo-a-Ndongo can be poetically and spiritually understood as the southern setting sun of a civilization that would later be recreated and recognized in Brazil as Kongo-Angola. Over millennia, it gradually emerged from the Kalunga Ocean along the Eastern Sun of Luanda. Advancing toward the Northern Sun, it rose majestically above the African Savanna until it reached its zenith as Queen Nzinga's kingdom. Its Dikenga Sun began moving westward, to sunset, during the nine-month encirclement when the Portuguese attacked and plundered Ndongo, culminating in the Battle of 1671 in which they besieged the kingdom. According to the victorious Portuguese narrative, they scaled the rocky outcrops, encircled the fortified settlement, and seized the kingdom. This narrative resembles the Portuguese depiction of the destruction of the African-Brazilian republic of Quilombo dos Palmares (c. 1605–1695) in Alagoas, where the soldiers, like those of Ndongo, are said to have perished by leaping from high cliffs to evade capture.[72] While these narratives unconvincingly proclaim overwhelming victories, they nevertheless point to the waning of an era. As the Dikenga Sun of Ndongo sets in the ocean to the west and crosses the Kalunga line, Time turns its wheels until the kingdom rises again in the east—from the Atlantic, in Brazil—where it assumes a different identity, hidden from plain view: the Kingdom of Aruanda.

FROM PUNGO-A-NDONGO TO BAHIA: ROYAL PERFORMANCES AND THE EXILE OF NDONGO ROYALTY IN BRAZIL

In his investigation into the conceptualization of African-Brazilian "nations" (nações) as cultural identity affiliations embraced and reshaped by African descendants, Gerhard Kubik highlights the cohesive function of parade performances such as Congada, Capoeira, Maracatu, Marujada, and Bumba-meu-Boi. Building on earlier observations by Brazilian scholars, Kubik notes that these

African-Brazilian dramatic performances—reenactments of distant historical events—serve as a means to transmit elements of political structures from the African homeland of their ancestors.[73] He emphasizes that, while these cultural expressions are rooted in dominant Bantu-African traditions, they cannot be directly traced back to any specific African expressions; stylistically, they represent what he terms "Bantu-African extensions."[74]

As part of a performative tradition found across the diaspora, the Brazilian Congada features the symbolic coronation of a King of Congo. Rooted in references to the political structure of the former Kingdom of Kongo, Congadas incorporate ceremonial rituals that represent a governmental system including envoys (*embaixadores*), secretaries of war (*secretários de guerra*), ministers (*ministros*), and others. Originally performed in northern Angola and southwestern Congo, these coronation festivals gradually assumed a pivotal role in fostering solidarity among those within the Angola-Kongo cultural matrix in Brazil. They evolved into symbols of political significance, becoming deeply interwoven with Afro-Brazilian political consciousness and cultural identity as "a sort of fictional Kingdom of Kongo took hold in the imagination of enslaved Africans on Brazilian soil."[75]

The historian Marina de Mello e Souza, who studied the establishment of social ties through Congadas, clarifies that elections and celebrations of the Congo kings took place primarily, though not exclusively, within Bantu-speaking communities.[76] Congo kings represented ethnic identities or "nations" that held authority over groups organized around identities built with elements drawn from a number of African cultures. Although different ethnic groups often lived in close proximity, people tended to establish ties with others from neighboring regions who shared similar cultural backgrounds.[77] Catholic lay brotherhoods, known as Irmandades—the first reportedly formed in Recife in 1552—played a significant role in the forging of new identities among enslaved Africans and their descendants.[78] The Irmandades were endorsed by slave masters and government authorities, with parish priests overseeing their activities. Some of the festivities organized by these brotherhoods were (and continue to be) held publicly during Catholic festivals dedicated to saints such as Our Lady of the Rosary and Saint Benedict. During these events, royal figures and their entourages parade through the streets, accompanied by musicians and dancers enacting a variety of choreographed performances.[79] As Mello e Souza points out, Angola-Kongo cultural expressions, and especially celebrations related to the election of a king, have remained largely incomprehensible to those outside the community.[80] Within the Congada lexicon, references to Kongo, Angola, and Mozambique do not denote specific historical events but rather signify an entire epistemic framework. To describe Congadas as mere symbolic or performative acts, rather than acknowledging them as the effective coronations of "real kings," reflects a fundamental misunderstanding of what these events truly embody.

One way to grasp the power of the coronation festivals is by examining historical documents from periods when authorities sought to prohibit these events. The Guinean historian José Lingna Nafafé studied the life trajectory of Ndongo Prince Lourenço da Silva Mendonça (1620–1698) and the connections he forged in exile, tracing his travels from Angola through Brazil, Portugal, Spain, and the Vatican. It was during his time in Brazil, from 1672 to 1673, that colonial authorities attempted to suppress popular festivities—an effort that clearly acknowledged the political influence and power of such events.[81] Prince Mendonça was the grandson of former king Ngola-a-Hari I (Felipe I de Sousa) and the nephew of Hari's successor, Ngola-a-Hari II (João de Sousa), who, after nearly forty years of an exploitative alliance between Ndongo and Portugal, severed all ties of dependence with the country after his ascension to the throne. Ngola-a-Hari II revitalized traditional Mbundu political structures and reinstated the Makota council to support the government.[82] Portugal retaliated by waging war against Ndongo. Although Ngola-a-Hari II rallied support from various constituencies across the region, including Matamba, Kansanje, Mbangala, and Ndongo, Pungo-a-Ndongo was besieged in 1671. The destruction of Pungo-a-Ndongo and the death of the last king are attributed to the *guerra preta* ("Black War") army. Equipped with intimate knowledge of local customs, language, and internal political dynamics, the soldiers infiltrated and betrayed Ndongo.[83] The war resulted in 2,000 fatalities, and the army took numerous captives. Ndongo royals were either murdered or sent into exile. Adopting Mbundu military customs, the Portuguese decapitated Ngola-a-Hari II and the queen using iron weapons—considered an especially egregious act, particularly when committed against royalty. In Mbundu tradition, decapitation alone wasn't sufficient to prevent a powerful adversary from returning to life; to ensure this, the body parts had to be scattered and buried in distant locations that were separated by natural barriers like seas or rivers.[84] Following this ritual, the Portuguese sent the head of Ngola-a-Hari II to Lisbon.

After Ngola-a-Hari II's death, Prince Mendonça, along with several other exiled members of the Royal House of Ndongo (including Mendonça's three brothers, ten cousins, and various aunts and uncles), were sent to Brazil. Because of Ngola-a-Hari I's loyalty to Portugal, their status differed from that of war captives sold into slavery, and they were treated as "special prisoners" by the Portuguese.[85] Their exile in Brazil also aimed to quell their influence and render them politically impotent. Yet, Brazil afforded a new arena for political engagement, enabling the younger Ndongo royals to broaden their sphere of influence.[86]

Mendonça initially resided in Salvador for eighteen months before being sent to Rio de Janeiro in 1673, where he stayed for approximately six months.[87]

Focusing on the connections Mendonça established with converted Jews, enslaved Africans, and Indigenous Americans—and how these connections posed a threat to the Portuguese Crown—Nafafé's study sheds new light on the seventeenth century Black Atlantic abolitionist movement. Portuguese colonials became aware that Ndongo political exiles could not only forge networks with enslaved Africans but also potentially integrate into the maroon community at Quilombo dos Palmares. Portuguese authorities were increasingly apprehensive that "the presence of Angolan royals in Brazil might lead to the formation of an African state."[88]

In the region of Palmares, white settlers, known as *colonos*, paid taxes to the Palmarists in exchange for the use of land for cattle ranching or plantation farming. Among these *colonos*, Cristovão de Burgos de Contreiras, an affluent octogenarian Brazilian-born judge serving in the high court of Salvador, was accused of being an enemy to the people.[89] He faced allegations of obstructing the conquest of Palmares for personal gain and conspiring to prevent its annexation. In 1675, he was charged with tax evasion. His refusal to pay taxes could be interpreted as a rejection of the Portuguese Crown's authority over Brazil, suggesting his allegiance lay elsewhere—possibly with the Palmarists' ambition for independence as an African republic.[90] While there is no direct evidence of the royals' presence in Palmares or of any meeting with Burgos, correspondence between overseas councils in Lisbon, Angola, Bahia, and Rio de Janeiro suggests it is plausible the royals explored the option of joining Palmares. This could have occurred through contact either with enslaved Africans in Salvador or with dissatisfied Brazilians such as Burgos.[91]

The existence of Palmares represented a significant threat to the Portuguese: it served not just as a haven for maroons but also as an alternative power structure—a formidable sociopolitical and economic entity that directly challenged the Portuguese colonial model. African-Brazilian festivities such as the Congadas could have served as a conduit between urban and rural areas, potentially facilitating contact between the royals and Palmares.[92] Direct contact between the Palmarists and recognized political figures was a concern for Portuguese authorities, as it could have led to the establishment of a parallel empire, uniting Indigenous peoples and creating a semblance of an African state within Brazil.[93]

Prince Mendonça's interactions with Africans and New Christians in Brazil and later Portugal enabled him to connect his anti-slavery advocacy with a critique of the Inquisition's persecution of Jews and New Christians. His argument for the emancipation of enslaved Africans, which he presented to the Vatican in 1684,[94] included an elucidation of the various forms of servitude prevalent in

Africa and the factors distinguishing them from chattel slavery. In West Central Africa, distinct models allowed for the integration of war captives into society, offering avenues for social mobility.[95] Thornton's research on the *Kijiko* warrior captive social group of Ndongo illuminates this aspect. Under the protective umbrella of seventeenth-century Mbundu legislation, these captives were granted amnesty upon escape and return to their original homeland or upon finding sanctuary under the patronage of a ruler elsewhere.[96] The laws governing captive mobility, which were based on the principles of return, safe haven, and asylum, facilitated status changes that enabled former captives to be recognized as free individuals.[97]

New Christians in Portugal supported Mendonça's court case for the abolition of the Atlantic slave trade.[98] While in Lisbon, Mendonça forged a strong bond with Gaspar da Costa Mesquita, a New Christian and prominent figure in the city. Mesquita, who served as an apostolic notary, recommended Mendonça to the Vatican in 1681. His extensive travels across the Atlantic—to places such as Rio de Janeiro, Bahia, India, and Rome—enabled him to recognize the parallels between the struggles faced by Africans and New Christians and to support Mendonça's efforts in advocating for the liberation of Africans.[99] These views appear to resonate throughout Mendonça's case, which sought to persuade the Vatican that enslaving Africans in the Americas was a crime against humanity because, according to human, natural, divine, and civil law, their right to freedom was inherent.[100]

THE CORONATION OF KINGS ON BOTH BANKS OF THE ATLANTIC

In 1662, the Capuchin friar Cavazzi (1621–1692) witnessed the coronation of the King of Kongo in Mbanza-Kongo, the kingdom's capital.[101] According to his account, the gathering took place in the town square, while the election occurred inside a church. Only three individuals cast votes: the Mani-Efunda (or Mani-Cabunda, the religious chief), the Mani-Mbata (the chief of Mbata), and the Mani-Sonho (the chief of Sonyo). After pledging to live in accordance with Catholicism and to protect his people, the elected king was crowned.[102] Friar Cavazzi also documented other ceremonies related to the Congadas in Brazil. Every three years, people from the provinces would converge on Kongo to honor the king and pay their tributes in festive gatherings—a concept distorted by Portuguese colonialism.[103] Cavazzi reported that some of these Kongo celebrations were known as *Sangamento* or *Sagaras* (derived from the Kikongo *cu-sanga*, meaning "to have or show faith").[104] During these events, warriors would appear in attire adorned with animal skins and feathers, brandishing weapons and engaging in simulated combat. The king would inspect the soldiers, offering praise or reproach, and the grand occasion would culminate in a lavish feast.[105] Cavazzi also referrred to "obscene diabolic dances around fire"—such as the *mampombo, mpambuatadi, quitombe, quixia,* and *quingadia*—each named "according to the places or the people who danced it."[106] He documented dances known as *quissanji*, which incorporated poetry and were linked to those who lived in Quissanji in the Province of Malanje, and *maquina-ma-fuete*, performed in the presence of royalty and high-ranking officials.[107]

In Brazil, the earliest recorded Reisado festivity dates back to 1674 in Recife, Pernambuco. Reisado, literally meaning the actions performed by or related to kings (*reis*), refers to celebrations surrounding the crowning of monarchs. It typically takes place on January 6th, the day of the Epiphany, and is either an alternative name for or part of the larger Congada tradition. The Congada, literally meaning the action performed by or related to the Kongo kingdom or its people, is also known by various other designations, including the Feast of the Children of the Rosary. The songs and narratives of the Congadas serve as a performative record of the histories of kingdoms or states of western and eastern Central Africa, chronicling their struggles and negotiations. Various elements of this performance—from the lyrics of chants to dramatic enactments, dance movements, and symbology—reflect aspects of Angola-Kongo aesthetic, ethical, and philosophical values. The narratives primarily focus on struggles and negotiations between kingdoms, featuring protagonists such as Rei Cariongo, or Nerika-a-Mpudi (Henrique I), ruler of the Kingdom of Kongo in the mid-sixteenth century, and Rainha Ginga or Queen Nzinga, ruler of the Kingdoms of Ndongo and Matamba in the seventeenth century.

During colonial times, Congada performers required official authorization to hold Congadas.[108] Since their inception, Congadas have been organized by African descendants associated with the Irmandades lay societies, which have served as corporate spaces advocating for civil and human rights, funding manumissions, and providing funerary services for their members.[109] As African-Catholic associations, they coalesced around chosen Black patron saint, such as Saints Benedito, Gonçalo, Onofre, Efigênia, Rosário, and Aparecida.[110] Arthur Ramos interpreted these associations as collective efforts aimed at structuring community life in terms of spirituality, economics, and cultural entertainment.[111] Members of the Irmandades raised funds to purchase the freedom of Africans, participated in abolitionist campaigns alongside figures like Luiz Gama, and consistently addressed the needs and demands of their urban communities. According to the anthropologist Júlio Braga, the Irmandades played a crucial role in fostering a Black consciousness and sense of identity, effectively serving as a form of counter-acculturation to the prevailing social structures of the time.[112] The Irmandades have always functioned as nuclei of cultural resistance, aligning with Beatriz Nascimento's concept of a cultural Quilombo. To this day, they continue grassroots work and uphold their tradition of organizing events such as the Congada, Moçambique, and other performative celebrations.

Cascudo divided Congada performances into three main segments: the crowning of the king and queen, followed by the visit and performance of diplomatic envoys, which then transitioned into a display of mock combats between kingdoms.[113] The crowning ceremony, or Reisados, has been studied by musicologist Oneyda Alvarenga (1911–1984) as a celebration paralleling Kongo traditions related to the election of a new king.[114] The crowning of kings and queens was often officiated by a priest at the entrance of a consecrated church. During these ceremonies, the Congadeiros pay homage to Our Lady of the Rosary, alongside other Black saints recast as Kongo ancestors.[115] Alvarenga identified three distinct types of Congadas in her analysis. All three types involve the crowning of the king and queen, followed by a royal court procession featuring dances and chants. While some performances include representations of mock combats, others replace these combats with the performance of an *Embaixada* (a diplomatic delegation).[116]

The performative Embaixada consists of "an envoy either on a peace mission or to declare war."[117] These envoys embody the collective memory of the power struggles and negotiations that characterized interactions among the West Central African kingdoms and their dealings with the Portuguese and other European kingdoms.[118] Each envoy, representing the warrior strength of their people, approaches the enemy with either an intimation or a resolution. Often, these encounters culminate in a sword fight, with victory signifying the group that, on a mythical level, enjoys the protection of Our Lady of the Rosary or other Black saints.[119] Originally, the Embaixadas featured dialogues, either chanted or narrated. Over time, these evolved into monologues carrying the *recado*, meaning the "reminder" of the performance.[120] The *recado* serves as either the opening or central part of the Congada; it announces the event, invites community members to attend, and pays respects to the person and saint sponsoring the celebration.[121] Von Martius and Spix's description of a Congada in Minas Gerais in 1818 identified both Queen Nzinga (spelled as Xinga) and the King of the Congo (see chapter 5). The performances they observed may refer to a historic moment when the kingdoms of Ndongo and Matamba, both ruled by Queen Nzinga, were in peaceful collaboration with the Kongo. Interestingly, von Martius and Spix describe the diplomatic envoys as what is now generally known as Congada.

According to them: "The new king officially received a visit from an envoy to the court of Congo (known as the so-called Congada)."[122]

In mock combats within Congada performances, variations in plot and characters abound, but the fundamental structure involves the staged interaction of two or more dancing groups arranged in rows. One configuration depicts the soldiers of the King of Congo confronting the soldiers of Queen Nzinga; another presents the Congo guard facing off against the Angola or Moçambique guards; a third dramatizes the maroons pitted against colonial bounty hunters known as *bandeirantes*. Each variation carries a distinct designation: in the first configuration, the performance is referred to as Congada proper; in the second, it can be called either Congada or Filhos do Rosário (Children of Our Lady of the Rosary); and in the third, it is referred to as Quilombo. According to Mário de Andrade's research from the 1960s, one group of performers was comprised of the King of the Congo, two nobles from the Congo court, a secretary, and a minister, while the other group was formed by Queen Nzinga, her envoy, and the general of her army.[123] The plot revolved around the struggles between Queen Nzinga and the King of the Congo, with Nzinga ultimately emerging victorious. An excerpt of the chants from the performance reads: "She gave orders to have you killed, King, my Lord! / And the one who ordered this was Queen Nzinga!" which is followed by the chorus: "Queen Nzinga is a warrior woman / She has two hips encircled by blades."[124] In some other versions of the Congada, known as Cucumbi, the plot depicts the King of Congo engaged in battles against Prince Suena or King Bamba (referring to the Kongo provinces of Soyo and Mbamba).[125] Additional characters may include Quimboto (the witch doctor), Capataz (the overseer who can serve as a singer, dancer, and master of ceremonies), Prince Mameto, Caboclo, and Língua—literally meaning "tongue," referring to the interpreters who played a crucial role in envoys and dealings between Africans and the Portuguese.[126] In versions featuring Prince Mameto, the plot unfolds around his murder. The witch doctor Quimboto intervenes, using chanting and magic to resurrect Mameto. In most of these versions, the King of Congo ends up either arrested or defeated.[127]

FROM THE MIDDLE OF THE OCEAN TO THE SHORE: THE POETICS OF CONGADAS

In the 1990s, Núbia Pereira Magalhães Gomes (1940–1994) and Edimilson de Almeida Pereira co-authored groundbreaking research on the Congada and its cosmology, with a focus on the Arturos community in Contagem, Minas

Gerais.[128] In 2014, some years after their trailblazing research, the Feast of Our Lady of the Rosary of the Arturos Community was declared an intangible cultural heritage of Minas Gerais. The Arturo community is named after their common ancestor, Arthur Camilo Silvério da Silva (1885–1956), the son of Arthur Camilo Silvério, who arrived in Brazil from Angola in the mid-nineteenth century. Upon arriving in Rio de Janeiro, Camilo was sent to Minas Gerais to work in a settlement located in the mines of Mata do Macuco (now Esmeraldas, in Greater Belo Horizonte). He married Felisbina (also spelled Felismina) Rita Cândida, and from this union, six children were born, including Arthur Camilo Silvério da Silva. In 1912, Arthur married Carmelinda Maria da Silva, and together they acquired the property where the descendants of their ten children still reside.[129] In 2021, following the passing of the Congada leader Captain Mário Braz da Luz, the last direct child of Arthur and Camelinda, the Arturo community comprised approximately 80 families, or about 500 members.[130]

As narrated by Captain João Lopes of the Jatobá community, the tradition of Congadas traces back to the sighting of the image of Our Lady of the Rosary in the sea. The Arturo community, along with other Congada communities, celebrates this shared memory. According to this account, a group of Congo gathered on the beach drumming and singing and calling out to Our Lady of the Rosary. Although the saint noticed them and approached, she did not come all the way to the shore. A group of Moçambique then stepped forward. They brought drums covered in yam leaves and began to play and sing gently, inviting the saint to draw closer. Slowly, carried by the waves, the image of the saint moved toward those gathered at the beach.[131] Captain Mário Braz da Luz conveyed this foundational myth to Núbia Gomes and Edimilson Pereira as follows: "Didn't I tell you how Our Lady came from the ocean? We too came from the ocean, from far away. All these things, these secrets, they all came from the ocean. We are sailors. That's why we sing that we want to die drowning in the rosary of Maria. We even call Maria, *Mareia* [tide movement], as if she was a mermaid."[132]

Gomes and Pereira's rich documentation and careful analysis of the poetics of Congada performance vividly portray the symbolism embedded in the specific choreography, chants, colors, attire, and instruments presented by the dancers and musicians of the Congo and Moçambique guards. Leading the procession are the Congo guards, dressed in pink and green attire symbolizing leaves and flowers, and wielding swords. Some Congo carry large drums known as *tamboril*, which are secured over the shoulders by a strap and positioned transversely in front of the player's torso. Two thick drumsticks are used, one for each drumhead, so that both sides of the instrument are played alternately. The Congo guard initiates the procession, opening the roads with a fast-paced dance that announces the arrival of the Children of Our Lady of the Rosary. In contrast, the Moçambique guard wears blue and white, representing the ocean and waves and implying a vertical, north-south directional movement, unlike the east-west motion of the Congo. While the pink and green attire of the Congo sways from side to side, the Moçambique's blue and white attire complement a dancer whose movements are forceful, pounding the ground.[133] During the parade, the Moçambique carry the image of Our Lady of the Rosary on a processional bier. They proceed at a slow pace behind the Congo, bearing a wooden staff that serves as a source of support, a spiritual weapon, and a symbol of "the axis of the world."[134] The sacred handling of the staff is a lesson passed down from the elders. Skilled in the art of improvisation, the Moçambique captains possess the ability to sing for hours. Their guards can make the floor "open up" to the sound of the *gungas* tied around their ankles. Each Moçambique wears four *gungas* on the right ankle and three on the left. As Gomes and Pereira explain, the right foot serves as the leader, "calling" (*puxando*) the other foot.[135] The movement of the right foot toward the left is akin to pulling or summoning. The Portuguese verb *puxar* encompasses more than the exertion of physical force; it also conveys a sense of achievement or enactment, similar to the English word "to pull off." In Afro-Brazilian contexts, *puxar* is commonly associated with prayers, chants, and music, signifying the act of drawing sacred and secular narratives from memory or another realm. Others subsequently join in, engaging with and activating the performance.

The Moçambique guard advances, rhythmically pounding their staffs and feet against the ground, the sound of their *gungas* echoing as if to awaken the earth or break through earthly boundaries.[136] They maintain a deliberate pace, aligned with the narrative of drawing the image of Our Lady from the ocean—moving slowly, with unhurried steps, accompanied by gentle drumming and singing. If the rhythm of the *gungas* quickens, the captain of the guard issues a cautionary chant-reminder: "Hey, let's proceed slowly, çambiqueiro, / She cannot run, çambiqueiro."[137] The term *çambiqueiro*, derived from *caçambeiro*, is one of several diasporic terms akin to "brother" or "traveling companion." It originates from the Kimbundu *kisambu*, meaning a "big basket" or a container for water, and is also associated with those who draw water from a well (in this context, a communal well).[138] The *gunga* embodies ancestral sacred rhythms that illuminate, clarify, and energize, carrying profound significance. Certain chants explicitly underscore this importance: "This *ngunga* is playing, / This *ngunga* is from my dad, / This *ngunga* is from my mom, / This *ngunga* is from the Lady of Rosary. / Clear up, my father! / Clear up, my mother!"[139] The *gunga* opens up the pathway to

Nzambi, the force of the "Always-Present-Ancestral-Whole," and to Our Lady of the Rosary. Another chant tells us: "Aruera, aruera / We can hear the *ngunga*, / Let's wage war / Nzambi's crown / Let's go greet it, of course!"[140] *Aruera*, another key concept in the Congada lexicon, literally refers to the Aroeira tree, known as the California Pepper tree in the United States.[141] The Aroeira is a medicinal tree extensively used across Brazil and throughout the Amazon. In Brazilian-Yoruba-Ewe-Fon cosmology, this tree is associated with the blacksmith Orisha Ogun. For Brazilian-Kongo-Angola Candomberos (practitioners of Candombe), this sturdy-barked tree represents a "powerful Black man, a knower of mysteries."[142] As one chant expresses, "Oh, hey, Candombe / It is of *aroeira* man! / Oh, Candombe."[143] Gomes and Pereira explain that Candombe signifies people as strong as the Aroeira tree: "Black men who are as sturdy as the tree trunk, possess healing properties like its bark, and are adaptable like the tree sapling that undergoes changes in appearance."[144]

As explained by Captain João Lopes of Jatobá, Candombes were the drums with the power to summon Our Lady of the Rosary from the sea. They served as the (musical) instruments initiating the articulation of Africans who, in Brazil, were part of the broad Kongo-Angola-Mozambique cultural group. The Candombe is considered the most sacred aspect of Congada. In some communities, private Candombe rituals in honor of the ancestors are performed at the onset of each feast cycle, prior to the public parades, as well as on special occasions. The term Candombe encompasses not only ritual practices and cosmological beliefs but also the physical space—often a designated room or chapel—that houses sacred regalia and tools, including crowns, swords, and drums. Candombe rituals typically involve dances, chants, and praises directed to the ancestors and may also feature *desafios* (challenges), which are lyrical and choreographic dialogues expressed through chants and movements.[145]

Similar to Candomblé and other sacred or secular traditions, Candombe features three primary drums. In Minas Gerais, these are known as Santana, Santaninha, and Jeremia—or Sant'Ana, Crivo, and Requinta.[146] According to Yeda Pessoa de Castro, Candomblé is derived from the Kimbundu, Kikongo, and Umbundu terms *kandombele, kulombela,* and *kulomba*, which mean "to pray," "to evoke," or "to ask for the intervention of the gods," as well as the space where a ritual takes place.[147] Similarly, *candombelê*, a term found in Congada rhymes and other Kongo-Angola practices, originates from the Kimbundu and Kikongo *kalombé*, meaning "let's offer praise" or "let's perform the eulogy" ("vamos à louvação").[148] Olga Gudolle Cacciatore suggests that Candomblé may have originated from the combination of *kandombe* with *ile* (meaning "house" in

Yoruba).[149] Both Cacciatore and Nei Lopes also agree that it is possible the terms derive from the Kimbundu and Kikongo words *ka* (behavior, usage) and *ndômbe* (Black people). Essentially, the terms Candomblé and Candombe are rooted in the concepts of "the house of drumming and worship" and a spiritual practice focused on chanting and dancing.[150]

Captain Geraldo Camilo, the formerly elected King of the Congo of the Arturos, further relates the term Candombe to a particular moment or action: "Candombe is when Our Lady appeared on the sea. She was brought to the shore from the sea with the Candombe, because no other drum could have done it."[151] In this analogy, Candombe becomes nearly synonymous with Our Lady of the Rosary and represents the moment of convergence and articulation of the Kongo-Angola-Mozambique matrix. Because the Moçambique were the ones who succeeded in bringing the saint from the ocean, they are considered the "strong ones," holders of wisdom and deep knowledge.[152] They are the owners of the crown worn by Our Lady of the Rosary: "Eh, Moçambique is great / Moçambique is of Blacks and crowns."[153] The second line of the chant can be translated as Moçambique is, belongs to, or is made of crowned Blacks. According to another chant: "These people know mysteries, aye / The more you *ask* (*puxa*) from it, the more it gives, aye!"[154] The more you ask, or the more you "pull," the more it gives, following the same concept as the right foot pulling the left, or the "pulling" of chants, prayers, or memories from another realm. It also adds the image of "pulling" from the ocean, as if fishing for nourishment, or for Our Lady—the divine representation and connection to home, both physical and ethereal. Another chant confirms this concept: "Eh, let's draw the gold / From the bottom of the ocean / Let's draw gold."[155]

In the procession, as the Moçambique pound the ground, seemingly breaking through the earthly boundary, their chants echo this movement: "Hey, Kalunga, take me away / to my home country," and referring to their guard, "I've already sent for it / I've already sent someone to pick it up / I've already sent this world / I've already sent someone to fetch it." [156] In a cyclical motion, the Moçambique are coming from and returning to a realm beyond the Kalunga line, which marks the boundary between the worlds of the living and the ancestors. They traverse the Atlantic Ocean, moving back and forth between Brazil and Angola-Kongo-Mozambique. Some Moçambique chants, as previously explained by Captain Mário Braz da Luz, identify them as sailors: "Hey, the sailor came from far away, / he came from Angola, / *saravando* the *rigunga* so as to fetch Our Lady."[157] *Rigunga* (short for *zirigunga* or *ziriganga*) refers to those with advanced knowledge, those who possess mastery over all the mysteries of the Congada.[158] *Saravando*, loosely translated as "greeting" or "hail," is a Bantu-ization of the

Portuguese infinitive *salvar*. It is both an exclamation of praise and a ritualistic gesture aimed at harmonizing or balancing the energy polarities of beings or spaces.[159] In the Congada lexicon, *saravar* also denotes the greeting exchanged when captains, queens, and kings meet.[160]

In Afro-Brazilian oral traditions, Angola, Mozambique, and Kongo may appear as interchangeable realms with intertwined languages. While some Congada chants contain multiple geographic references, they often indicate the mastery of one common language understood only by those within their extended families. One example refers to an elder from Lugamba who speaks in the "language of Angola": "*Calundunga*, old black man / Old Black man came from *candonga*, / Old Black man came from Lugamba. / It is in the Black man's language, / It is in the language of Angola. / See what I am saying? Nobody understands me. / See? The language of Angola. / See? Nobody comprehends me."[161] *Calundunga*, derived from the Kimbundu terms *kilundu* and *ndunga*, refers to an ancestor or a chief priest. The term *dunga*, from the Kikongo *ndunga*, denotes an important or brave person.[162] In Brazil, Calundu became a reference to Afro-Brazilian religious ceremonies and the place where they were performed; *calunduzeiro*, by extension, was the chief priest of the Calundu.[163] The Moçambique performer embodies Calundu and *calundunga*—an ancestor who was a high priest, an ancient master of souls. Yet, the line "Old Black man came from *candonga*" suggests that the Moçambique simultaneously embodies youthful zest, sly resourcefulness, and charm. Nei Lopes translates *candonga* as "sweet talk, caresses, pampering" as well as "cheeky, crafty."[164] He also highlights the controversial origin of the term and cites Jacques Raimundo Ferreira da Silva, one of the earliest scholars to explore the relationship between African languages and Brazilian Portuguese in the early twentieth century: "The etymology, if accurate, reveals an intriguing semantic evolution. We suggest it may originate from *ka-ndonga*, a diminutive of *ndonga*, referring to a native of Angola, specifically the *pretinho* [a young Black boy] skilled in sweet talk."[165] Lopes further suggests that the etymology could derive from the Kikongo *nkua-ndunge*, meaning "clever, astute" (related to the Kimbundu *múkua-ndunge*), or possibly from the Kikongo *ki-ndonga*, meaning beginner, novice, student, or apprentice.[166] The elder Black man—symbol of wisdom, leadership, and spiritual authority—is also depicted as an endearing, astute boy who comes from Angola, just beginning his schooling. This duality represents the "turning of the wheel," where endings and beginnings converge. At the same time, the chant gestures beyond Angola, invoking references to other parts of Africa, such as Mozambique (the performer's identity) and Lugamba (a central region in present-day Uganda).

The reference to *candonga*—a possible place of origin for the elder mentioned in the chant ("Old Black man came from *candonga*")—merits further exploration through the scholarship of Robert Slenes and Wyatt MacGaffey.[167] In Jongo challenge-song performances, three drums are employed: the smallest is the *candongueiro*, followed by the medium-sized *caxambu* and the largest, *tambu*. The term *candongueiro* fuses the diminutive Kimbundu prefix *ka-*, the noun *Ndongo* (which can refer to either a large dugout canoe or a hollowed-out log), and the Portuguese suffix *-eiro*, indicating agency. Slenes suggests that this suffix represents the sound produced by drumming a hollowed-out log—or more aptly put, the "voice" of the drum itself: "the hollowed-out drum serves as a conduit for messages from the spirit world."[168] Slenes investigates this term within the framework of Central African canoe-kinship metaphors, tracing their symbolic resonance across diverse cultural contexts.[169]

Slenes posits that in West Central Africa, the dugout canoe served as a central metaphorical vehicle through which individuals and communities navigated the full spectrum of life experiences—including migration driven by adversity, healing from personal or societal afflictions, marriage, the forging of alliances, death, and the founding of political institutions.[170] Drawing on MacGaffey's analysis of Kongo praise names, Slenes underscores how clan narratives often begin with accounts of canoe migrations, which symbolically mark the passage from a state of social disorder to one of ideal governance and stability.[171] These canoe metaphors, deeply ingrained in rituals, social customs, and public discourse, weave together key facets of historical experience and offer a distinct cultural reframing of the conceptual metaphor "life is a journey" as "life is a canoe path." Slenes highlights the Kikongo expression "dīa lúngu nzíla," translating to "to take the circular canoe path," which suggests navigating in an opposite direction to circumvent obstacles or reconnect.[172]

Similar to Yoruba Oriki (Òríkì), Congada poems and chants adhere to a standardized structure that allows for variation and improvisation. Moçambique chants often explore philosophical and spiritual themes that reference ancestral Africa and Our Lady of the Rosary, while Congo chants playfully tease fellow performers, share community histories, and comment on contemporary events. The Congo dance style blends Capoeira and Samba, featuring *ginga* movements, hip swings, leaps, rapid footwork, and intricate crisscross steps. Dancers expertly navigate ring-round movements, seamlessly interweaving and disentangling dance lines with joyful enthusiasm.[173] During the parade, which starts at the community chapel and ends at the town's main church, the Congo follow a counterclockwise route. At crossroads, a shift occurs: one guard or line of dancers moves clockwise, while the other simultaneously begins moving counterclockwise.[174]

In these movements, the dancers inscribe variations of Bakongo cosmograms into space and time, choreographing cosmological meaning through their bodies, surroundings, and interactions.

A noteworthy aspect of this performance is the potential inclusion of Congo performers representing the Caboclos.[175] While in some performative expressions the Caboclo is portrayed as an adversary, in this context he is depicted as an ally. These seemingly opposite portrayals do not constitute a historical contradiction. During the colonial period, some Indigenous peoples were conscripted into *bandeirante* militias and fought alongside Portuguese forces, while others aligned themselves with, or lived among, *quilombola* communities. As Captain Mário Braz da Luz explains, "Our songs reflect this duality, inspired by the Quilombos, the ancient ones, and the Caboclos in the bushes."[176]

The symbolism embodied by the Congo and Moçambique resonates deeply with Yoruba-Ewe-Fon imagery, particularly that of Orishas Ogun and Oshosi. Ogun, often depicted with his knife and machete, is renowned for his role in clearing paths through the forest. Oshosi, though not physically as strong, follows Ogun into the wilderness. Together they hunt and provide sustenance to the community. Oshosi, reminiscent of the Moçambique, is described as "wearing bells on his left leg, the leg of power, as he traverses the forest."[177] His deep connection to the forest, his use of a bow and arrow, and his symbolic association with birds (indicated by his feathers) also parallel the imagery of Brazilian Caboclos as ancestral deities. It is noteworthy that Congada cosmology depicts the right foot as the commanding one, whereas in Yoruba cosmology the left foot is the strong, magic one. This distinction may point to the different kinds of "magic" or spiritual interventions that are achievable by humans as opposed to divine beings— whether gods, Orishas, or Inkices. If humans are seen as mirrors of the gods, as is often the case in African cosmologies, the right foot of humans could correspond to the left foot of the gods. In representations of Oshosi across Brazil and the African diaspora, as New York Babalawo John Mason points out, Oshosi is regarded as the ultimate magician and embodiment of magic and potions: "Oshosi, the left-handed one. When the word Oshosi is punned, it means he is a wizard."[178] Oshosi may walk more slowly than Ogun; he may appear smaller and less powerful. Yet once he shoots his arrow, he accomplishes everything he intends with a single, swift motion. He is described as "a reserved Orisha who sits back and watches until called upon to act."[179] Ogun represents boundless energy; he is the force of nature responsible for keeping matter in motion. According to numerous chants and narratives, Oshosi and Ogun are portrayed as blood brothers who share a deep friendship and hunt together. As John Mason explains, "in the New World, it is said that Ogun baptized Oshosi and Oshosi baptized Ogun."[180]

The depiction of Indigenous Caboclos by Congo guards alludes to a range of symbolic references but is also susceptible to misinterpretation. One significant source of these misinterpretations appears to stem from the rigid association of feathered headgear with Indigenous peoples, overlooking its use and significance among Central African cultures. The figure of the Caboclo, often interpreted through the Yoruba concept of Onilé—the original owner of the lands—establishes a historical link between the Kingdom (or Federation) of Kongo and its neighboring polity, Ndongo. Muniz Sodré has observed that some of the earliest Brazilian-Yoruba *terreiro* communities featured a designated space to honor the Caboclo as a spiritual ancestral entity embodying the Indigenous peoples of Brazil. Sodré also notes that Black communities in the United States similarly honor Indigenous peoples of North America as the original inhabitants of the land. Within Brazilian-Yoruba-Ewe-Fon cosmologies, the homage paid to Caboclos grants them a spiritual ancestral status akin to that of the Eguns, or revered ancestors.[181]

The Congada performance of the Filhos do Rosário begins with the captains of the guards calling upon the performers. The Congo captain rallies his men: "Come out everybody, Kalunga / Come to the window / Come see the Congos, Kalunga / Who are going to war."[182] In this context, Kalunga refers to Black men and women.[183] The Moçambique captain sings his call: "Hey, it was not even midnight / When the first rooster crowed / It was not even midnight / But the children of the Rosary arrived," to which the performers reply: "Hey, oy lele oy / eh oy eh / Ayo lele oy / Oy the wheel of the world is big / The wheel of Nzambi is even bigger."[184] Throughout the procession, the Moçambique sing to the Lady of Rosary as a Nzambi-Kalunga Queen: "Hail Queen / Over there, in the middle of the ocean"; "Help us, Queen of the ocean / For us to get to the gate / Queen who rules over the earth / Who rules over the ocean"; "Aye if I were a little fish / That knew how to swim / I would take Our Lady / From the bottom of the ocean."[185] Many songs from these performances have become ingrained in other communal chants and songs, such as the children's game of Ring Around the Rosie. One popular song goes: "The canoe tumbled / They let it tumble / It was because of (so-and-so) / Who didn't know how to row."[186] The child named then has to let go of the hands of the other children, turn around, and hold hands again, facing the outside of the circle. The child to the left of the first one who turned away from the center of the ring will be the next one responsible for having let the canoe tumble. The game continues until all children are facing the outside. It is at this point that the chant switches to "If I were a little fish / And knew how to swim / I would take (so-and-so) from the depths of the ocean," and one by one, the children turn back to face the inside of the circle.[187] The spiral-like movement observed in these children's games resonates with the Dikenga cosmogram and its visual rendition of life processes, relationships, and history.

As the Congada procession arrives at the church in town, the performers sing, asking for permission to enter: "Lady, grant us permission, aye / Lady of the Rosary / Mister Saint Benedict, aye, aye / I came to ask your permission"; "To enter the holy house / Which God chose as his home / Home of the blessed chalice / And the holy bread / Cry, *ngoma*."[188] There, the elected king and queen are crowned, and the priest, either a performer or an actual priest, blesses them. At the end of the crowning, all dancers walk around the church three times and ask to be illuminated: "Yes, it is as it should be Master King, aye, aye / Your crown brings me light / Hey, Queen's crown, oh my God / Give light to the whole world."[189] The Moçambique leave the church walking backwards, facing the altar.[190] As the procession resumes its journey back to its community, the Congo continue to lead the Moçambique, who follow slowly behind singing chants with lines such as: "This *ngoma*, my God, of grandpa / Left the world, left the ocean / And traveled to these lands"; "Come, my father / Come to protect me / On this day of Congada / Don't let your children suffer."[191] When walking through the town, they greet people with the chant: "The parrot sang / Over there in the cliffs / He sent a hug / To the people of these lands!"[192] While parrots are associated with royalty in Kongo culture, in Brazil they share traits with the Caribbean trickster character Ananse and have come to symbolize a joyful and creative Brazilian identity.[193] Along their walk, the Congo may sing: "I am not from here / I come from out there / I came to bring my people / And Our Lady" while asking for something to drink or eat with lines such as "Oh, let's *curiá*! / Oh let's *curiá*!" (from the Kimbundu *kûria*, meaning to eat).[194]

Núbia Gomes and Edimilson Pereira, through their unique and comprehensive research on the Arturos community, have provided us with an unparalleled record of a living cultural archive. With a deep understanding of the metaphysical complexities, poetics, and symbology of the Congada, they approached its members and spaces with respect and humility. They refrained from attempting to fix or hypercorrect the transcripts of spoken Portuguese, a common practice in anthropological studies. Instead, when encountering expressions or words of African origin they could not immediately recognize, they preserved them in their original form. Their approach reflects a sensitivity toward poets and a reverence for the traditions they documented. In doing so, they have not only offered invaluable insights but also provided a blueprint for how to perceive, hear, describe, transcribe, and contemplate African-Brazilian textualities.

DANCING AGAINST:
OWNING SPACES, TIMES, BONDS, AND HISTORY

for we who have achieved "nothing"
work
who have not built
dream
who have forgotten all
dance
and dare to remember
Kamau Brathwaite (1930–2020)

African diasporic celebrations and performances are dynamic, ongoing engagements in asserting and transforming ancestral cosmologies and traditions. When a beloved person passes, a Bakongo proverb—"Wele kuna nkembo, nkinu, you nkiya"—is invoked to indicate that the deceased has transitioned to "glory, dancing, and travel," an ideal realm where there are no physical constraints.[195] Congadas serve as vehicles through which the living community connects with its history, the realm of the ancestors, and the larger cosmos. Through dance, individuals can transcend the limitations of the physical body and material spaces, journeying to alternate realms. Gomes and Pereira eloquently describe this journey: "Processional celebrations signify a return to the Sacred and the recreation of the divine. Walking the paths of ancestors is to relive the connection with the unseen, participating in the enigma of those departed. Spaces visited and times experienced become sources of renewal, guiding a return to Unity through ancestral wisdom. Revisiting and reliving connect descendants with their primal forebears, fostering communion with their ancestral lineage."[196]

In a similar vein, Muniz Sodré has analyzed the potency of these performances as acts of reterritorialization and assertions of the community's centrality. They not only sustain communities but also imbue the dancers with energy, enhancing their embodiment of radiant human values and rights:

> When I dance, shifting my position from here to there, I transcend my reliance on temporal and spatial distinctions. In essence, my movements liberate me from the mundane differences in height, weight, and length. Put differently, dances create their own spatial dimensions, temporarily erasing temporal disparities. This occurs because they are not guided by space but rather serve as space generators. They eagerly invite appropriation by the world, expanding human

presence and disrupting the structured framework of space-time established to confine free movement. Similarly, the void between objects offers a platform for altering situations or expressing sentiments. . . . Dance serves as a decentralization mechanism, symbolically reshaping space. Consider slave dances: by moving within the master's domain, the slave momentarily transcends his status and redefines his surroundings from an alternative perspective. This references a symbolic system distinct from that controlled by the master, capable of dismantling previously imposed territorial boundaries.[197]

Sodré further elaborates on the concept of altering space and time, explaining that through the practice of repetition—both in performance and within the musical form itself—and improvisation, understood as individual will or personal stamp, spirit, or creative insignia, performers connect themselves to a matrix that provides cosmological orientation while retaining the freedom to generate alternative moves or lines responsive to the immediate context. According to Sodré, to repeat is to incite the manifestation of the creative force:

> There is no way to avoid repetition: it exists in natural phenomena, in the changing seasons, in days, in language. To emphasize the repetitive character of existence is also a way of being driven by the dynamics of enchantment or myth (that which resists the ephemeral, the transitory). Myth implies the eternal reiteration of the same form, of a destiny, but giving way to variations. Improvisation is precisely the activation of this mythical margin, enabling the confrontation of a real, private moment (originating from a matrix) with the temporality instituted by social productive life.[198]

During colonial times, Congadas and similar performances represented transient opportunities for collective penetration into forbidden territories.[199] Over time, these transient moments of reterritorialization paved the way for more permanent territorialization through which African descendants could own and control their counter-space:

> The spaces shaped by rhythm were typically small and served as arenas for various exchanges or transactions, where lower social classes and ethnic groups not only sought to claim a share of the social product, such as jobs or small business opportunities, but also sought to assert their presence within the social fabric through an array of tactics by exploiting the loopholes inherent in capitalist social relationships. In essence, they aimed to carve out their own niche or establish a distinct identity. Carnaval, soccer, and religious celebrations were among

the cultural performances that Blacks appropriated from the Portuguese to construct spaces of identity and social interaction. It was from these encounters that the unique urban landscape of Rio emerged. . . . Additionally, there emerged the phenomenon of a "Black counter-space," a symbolic territory where former slaves and their descendants could convene without fear of repression, recrimination, or unwelcome scrutiny.[200]

Brazilian activists and intellectuals, particularly during the 1970s and 1980s, struggled to recognize the significance of these performances and the organizations that orchestrated them. Irmandades, Congadas, and similar expressions and networks were often interpreted as forms of accommodation within an oppressive system, rather than as deliberate acts of open resistance. Globally, intellectuals and activists tended to view diasporic dance performances as counterrevolutionary: a mystical return to origins or a depoliticized, ahistorical form of escapism that offered no potential for "victory" or "success."

Scholars like the Martinican philosopher Frantz Fanon (1925–1961) have emphasized the alien nature of the power inherent in traditional practices. In his seminal work *The Wretched of the Earth* (1961), Fanon notes that "the phenomena of dance and possession" are crucial for understanding how native communities cope with the pressures of colonialism.[201] He perceives these traditional practices as outlets in an oppressive world for releasing "accumulated libido" and "hampered aggressivity," which dissipate "as in a volcanic eruption." However, during liberation struggles, he argues, there is a critical need to move beyond these practices: "after centuries of unreality, after having wallowed in the most outlandish phantoms, at long last the native, gun in hand, stands face to face" with the colonizer.[202] The French philosopher Jean-Paul Sartre (1905–1980), in the preface to Fanon's *The Wretched of the Earth*, adds that formerly, "possession by spirits" was "a religious experience in all its simplicity, a certain communion of the faithful with sacred things."[203] Over time, this evolved into "a weapon against humiliation and despair; Mumbo-Jumbo and all the idols of the tribe descend among them, rule over their violence, and dissipate it in trances until it is exhausted." As a defense mechanism, the colonized resort to what Sartre terms "religious estrangement." Sartre concludes that this estrangement acts as "a form of defense, but it also signifies the end of the story; the self is dissociated, and the individual heads for madness."[204]

Fanon discusses the dissolution or splitting of personality into an unfamiliar realm, while Sartre interprets it as religious estrangement. However, the true significance of these performative dances lies in their capacity to integrate and invigorate rather than disintegrate or deplete. What Fanon and Sartre failed to recognize is that these dances are not mere forms of alienation or wasteful expressions of aggressive energy directed toward warfare. Instead, they serve as vital conduits connecting individuals to sacredness, completeness, and a history characterized by elements outside Western disciplinary norms. Far from being pointless or apolitical, these dances are deeply imbued with political significance. As Muniz Sodré aptly states, dance is also political resistance: "It's a well-established fact that in ancient Africa, warrior armies would be invigorated by dance. Since the 1980s, when television broadcasts worldwide depicted racial conflicts in South Africa, footage often showed Black crowds dancing in protest against racial oppression, even amidst violent police attacks. This serves as evidence that it is indeed possible to 'dance against' oppression."[205]

ARUANDA FROM THE INSIDE OUT

Go, go, go to Aruanda *Vai, vai, vai pra Aruanda*
Come, come, come from Luanda *Vem, vem, vem de Luanda*
Dorival Caymmi (1914–2008)

The sacred geography of major religions often centers on specific locations, commonly referred to as "source areas" or "cradle lands," as well as particular directions and orientations—such as sun-worshipping traditions that venerate the east.[206] As we shall see, in Kongo cosmology, foundational provinces and migration routes both hold deep significance. In the ancient Egyptian worldview, the land inhabited by the Egyptians was not merely a physical territory but the very site of creation and divine habitation.[207] Geographer Chris Park highlights how sacred Egyptian architectural structures were carefully aligned toward the presumed location of the original primal hill, believed to be the source and nucleus of the entire cosmos. Moreover, the Egyptian practice of map-making served a dual purpose: fulfilling secular functions and also guiding souls through the complexities of the afterlife.[208]

Geographic references tied to the Atlantic slave trade, such as Luanda and Porto Novo, have become enduring symbols that resonate with profound ancestral and cultural significance. Aruanda, a mythical or spiritualized vision of Africa, represents a foundational ancestral realm, a site of origin, and a repository of divine energy. Along with other sub-telluric sacred realms of the African diaspora—such as Mayombe and Vilokan, allegorical references to Kongo and

Guinea for Cuban and Haitians respectively—Aruanda constitutes a myth of origin and defines a cardinal point of sacred geography for the diaspora. Images of Aruanda appear throughout various archives of Afro-Brazilian philosophy and cosmology, including praise or invocation chants of Afro-Brazilian religions, and performative retellings of foundation myths that preserve continuities with the royal traditions of Central African kingdoms. Less commonly explored are literary expressions—including novels and treatises—that, in keeping with Spiritist (or Spiritualist) doctrine, were reportedly dictated to their authors by spirits.

Proposed by French philosopher Allan Kardec (Hippolyte Léon Denizard Rivail, 1804–1869), Spiritualist doctrine (often termed Kardecist Spiritualism) revolves around the concept of reincarnation, whereby spirits undergo a series of successive incarnations until they attain perfection as "higher spirits," exemplified by figures such as Jesus Christ and Leonardo da Vinci, at which point their cycle of reincarnation ends.[209] Spiritual progression is achieved through the consistent practice of Spiritism's cardinal virtues, especially study and charity, across multiple lifetimes. The anthropologist Marion Aubrée emphasizes the pivotal role of mediums—individuals trained to communicate with spirits—in facilitating this process of spiritual evolution.[210] Introduced to Brazil in the 1850s, Kardecist Spiritism initially appealed to the urban elite in cities like Rio de Janeiro and Salvador (Bahia). Notions of human and spiritual evolutionary hierarchies—along with the scientific racism inherent in the French doctrine—were transposed to the Brazilian context, where they were variously integrated, reinterpreted, or contested to differing degrees.

Considered Brazil's foremost psychographic medium, Chico Xavier (Francisco Cândido Xavier, 1910–2002) played a pivotal role in shaping the Catholic-inflected dimension of Brazilian Spiritism, juxtaposing it with the perception of Umbanda as a more "primitive" and syncretic tradition, as opposed to the supposedly "scientifically advanced" character of Kardecist Spiritualism. Xavier's mediumistic career began in the 1930s, marked by the psychographic publication of *Parnaso de além-túmulo* (translated as *Parnassus from Beyond the Grave*), a "collaborative effort" purportedly authored by the spirits of renowned deceased poets, including Augusto dos Anjos, Castro Alves, Casemiro de Abreu, Olavo Bilac, Guerra Junqueiro, and Gonçalves Dias.[211] The title references French Parnassianism—a literary movement characterized by aesthetic rigor, formal precision, and emotional restraint—which had taken root in Brazil during the late nineteenth century through poets such as Raimundo Correia, Alberto de Oliveira, and Olavo Bilac. Among Xavier's extensive corpus of psychographed novels and treatises, *Nosso lar* (*Our Home*), purportedly dictated by a spirit and published in 1943, serves as a cornerstone of Brazilian Spiritism. Combining elements of a coming-of-age narrative and doctrinal exposition, the novel recounts the afterlife experiences of its disincarnate narrator in a sacred colony located above Rio de Janeiro, allegedly founded in the sixteenth century by Portuguese spirits.[212]

A bestselling genre in Brazil, Spiritist literature comprises thousands of works purportedly dictated by "disembodied spirits" and transcribed by various mediums. As scholars have observed, the emphasis on books and reading within Brazilian Spiritism reflects not only a pursuit of social legitimacy but also delineates the boundaries of its practice in relation to Umbanda and Candomblé.[213] In noting that "Spiritism, to a large extent, is a religion of the book and reading," the anthropologist Bernardo Lewgoy also pinpoints various ways in which Spiritist practitioners cultivate a deep engagement with a literature regarded as having authoritative significance.[214] The act of Spiritist mediumistic writing serves a doctrinal purpose within a highly ritualized experience known as psychography. In their study of Spiritualist novels, the anthropologists Maria Helena Concone and Eliane Rezende point out that references to Umbanda are largely absent, highlighting a discursive and symbolic distancing between the two traditions.[215]

Novels published in the twenty-first century increasingly reimagine Aruanda through a science-fiction lens, reconfiguring traditional cosmological concepts. In these narratives, Aruanda is portrayed simultaneously as a vibrant metropolis and a tranquil sanctuary—a space for the convergence and exchange of beings and crafts from diverse eras and realms, ranging from the medieval to the futuristic. It emerges as a hub of sophisticated medical, scientific, and philosophical knowledge and practice, fostering the continuous transformation of beings and cosmic processes. *Vozes de Aruanda* (*Voices from Aruanda*) exemplifies this genre. Presented as a psychographed work by Norberto Peixoto, the novel is attributed to the spirit Ramatis, described as the bearer of ancient esoteric teachings called the Secret Knowledge. In the narrative, Ramatis—revealed as the true author—uses Peixoto as his living vessel. According to the narrative, Ramatis died in the tenth century in China, and his spiritual journey spans incarnations across ancient civilizations—beginning in Atlantis; serving as an interlocutor to Allan Kardec in ancient Egypt; advising King Solomon's court; incarnating as a son of Moses; and acting as a bodyguard to Jesus.[216] Now a denizen of the afterlife, Ramatis offers detailed observations of his visit to Aruanda, a constellation of spiritual colonies established by the "High Cosmic Brotherhood under the guidance of Christ-Jesus, Earth's spiritual guardian." Within these celestial territories are "vast spiritual metropolises reminiscent of ancient Egypt." These celestial centers possess technologies that surpass human understanding and are "supported by interplanetary, extraterrestrial stations that facilitate the regular movement of spaceships from distant civilizations, aiding in the development of our small blue planet."²¹⁷ The cosmically advanced society chronicled by Ramatis is led by a planetary commander-in-chief. It is home to the descendants of Afro-Brazilian and Indigenous Brazilian peoples, as well as extraterrestrial beings from space outposts, all united in their commitment to the welfare of the living and the departed.

A similar portrayal of Aruanda appears in the 2004 treatise *Aruanda: magia negra, elementais, Preto-Velhos e Caboclos sob a ótica espírita* (*Aruanda: Black Magic, Entities of the Four Elements, Preto-Velhos and Caboclos According to Spiritist Perspective*), the fourth publication channeled by Robson Pinheiro from the spirit of Ângelo Inácio.²¹⁸ Concone and Rezende recognize Robson Pinheiro as a pioneering figure in the depiction of Umbanda in Spiritist literature.²¹⁹ Despite facing prejudice from Spiritism adherents who perceive Umbanda as inferior, Pinheiro's 1998 work *Tambores de Angola* (*Drums from Angola*) achieved considerable success.²²⁰ On his YouTube channel, Pinheiro identifies himself as a "medium, writer, therapist, and founder of the 'Guardians of Humanity' project."²²¹ In the preface to the 2004 novel/treatise *Aruanda*, the spirit Angelo Inácio, channeled by Pinheiro, introduces himself as a journalist and a writer and articulates the book's objective: to combat religious, racial, and spiritual prejudice against Umbanda.²²² Inácio candidly reveals his past indulgence in carnal pleasures and substance abuse during his earthly existence, expressing a desire for redemption through the publication of his books. He describes his arrival in Aruanda and encounter with a Preto-Velho spirit as follows:

> We encountered an imposing edifice. Massive bulwarks reminiscent of ancient medieval castle constructions stood before us. Within those grand walls, one could see soaring towers and buildings emitting light, piercing the surrounding darkness. These structures appeared to be made from a substance akin to solidified astral light.... The ramparts, echoing the medieval architecture of Earth, serve as an energy shield: they not only protect and secure the first aid facility but also shield its inner sanctum from negative mental emanations.²²³

Robson Pinheiro/Ângelo Inácio present Aruanda as a hybrid establishment blending aspects of both a hospital and an educational institution, catering specifically to newly arrived spirits. It is likened to a medieval village, characterized by castles constructed from cosmic solidified light and enclosed by walls designed to repel malevolent energies. This imagery evokes the concept of solidified light, symbolizing a frozen force, a celestial sanctuary, and a center for healing and education. The architecturally enclosed Aruanda mirrors Central African concepts of *n'kisi-bilôngo* and *futu*, sacred medicine and healing energy safeguarded within a pouch or enclosed space activated when bound or sealed—here depicted by the enclosing medieval ramparts that both preserve and unleash the positive energy within. A ceremonial chant from the Kongo-Angolan Candomblé emphasizes this symbolism, stating: "when I arrived from Aruanda I brought medicine in my pouch."[224] Within this cosmology, "medicine" refers to *n'kisi-bilôngo*, denoting sacred medicine or energy, while the "pouch" signifies a *futu*, "a container of something secret and of great value to its owner," usually made "of soft material inside which the owner carries protective or curative medicine."[225]

In the context of Spiritualist literature, Daniel Soares Filho's 2017 publication, *Aruanda: a morada dos orixás* (*Aruanda: The Dwelling of the Orixás*), stands out.[226] The author's aim, as outlined in the preface, is to provide readers with "the key to the front door of Aruanda, its mythical origins, its etymology, its various spiritual and cultural representations, its meanings, and its inspirations (narratives)."[227] He defines his work as a research treatise on the concept of Aruanda, resulting from research on the realm of the living and that of the deceased: "this is the result of research conducted by the author, both through existing literature and interviews with 'entities' of the Pretos Velhos [Black Elders]."[228] Furthermore, he specifies that despite the "spiritualistic tone" of the text, his intended audience is Umbanda practitioners. To depict Aruanda, the author draws on the Spiritist notion of spiritual colonies, as depicted in Chico Xavier's *Nosso lar*, yet emphasizes the concept is distinct.[229]

Soares Filho quotes from an Umbanda chant to demonstrate the interconnectedness embodied by the Caboclo as a spiritual entity: "When the Caboclo comes from Aruanda / Hey, in Umbanda, he steps slowly. / Step, Caboclo, I want to see you step. / Step, Caboclo / Hey, step over there that I will step over here."[230] These lines, appearing in multiple variations across sacred and secular chants, evoke the sacredness of the ground—how one should interact with or step upon it—and how this sacredness reverberates beyond the individual scale. Against this textual backdrop, the author introduces a romanticist portrayal of the Indigenous character, highlighting the emergence of the Caboclo as a literary national hero. "If we consider the idea of true Brazilians," he points out, or, "the men of our homeland," then, he argues, there are other national heroes also worthy of praise.[231] He names other spirits who, like the Caboclo, embody the healing practices of Umbanda: the *boiadeiros* (cattle drovers), *sertanejos* (individuals from the arid Northeastern *sertões* hinterlands), *cangaceiros* (paramilitary forces of the *sertões*), and *baianos* (referring both to natives of Bahia and to migrants from the *sertões* following the late nineteenth-century exodus). Within a rhetoric that can be perceived as nationalistic, Soares Filho evokes literary images elaborated by authors such as Gonçalves Dias and Januário da Cunha (see chapter 4), alongside Pedro Américo's marginal ox cart drivers (see chapter 1). In Soares Filho's text, as well as in narratives oriented around Brazilian-Bantu culture, these figures are portrayed not only as embodiments of sacredness but also as representations of what the realm of Aruanda signifies.

Soares Filho describes the class sessions he attended with Pai João da Aruanda (Father Joaquim from Aruanda) as taking place within the forest of Aruanda. Seated in a circle of *tocos* ("tree stump" or "stubs"), a council of Black Elders deliberated on matters brought before them and contemplated how best to prepare mediums in Umbanda temples to assist those seeking help.[232] In Kikongo, *Mfinda* (forest), like *Kalunga* (ocean), is the dwelling place of the dead. In Umbanda, *toco* signifies a spiritual presence and is considered a channel of communication between the spiritual and physical worlds. The term can also refer to a short stick or staff, or to a medicinal plant—the Tamboril (which shares its name with the larger drum used in Congada), also known as Orelha-de-negro (literally "Black man's ear"), or Timbaúva.[233] With its long, thick roots, this tree is used to construct rafts, serving as another significant symbol in Brazilian-Bantu semantics. Soares Filho's narrative underscores a moment of convergence in which Aruanda merges with the imagery of *Quilombos* (maroon societies): Aruanda is envisioned as the vast forest that encompasses the Quilombo, whose inhabitants are portrayed as a wise council—resembling a Supreme Court, guiding the spiritual and social order.

Representations of Aruanda are woven into the fabric of various cultural expressions of the Kongo-Angola matrix, resonating in the rhythms of Samba, the movements of Capoeira, the beats of Maracatu, the poetry of Jongo, the ritual dances of Congada, and the sacred chants and stories of Afro-Brazilian religions. The sacred narratives of the Orishas, Voduns, and Inquices within the Patakis storytelling prose tradition are predominantly conveyed in Portuguese. However, the names of ancestral deities, mythical locales, and philosophical concepts retain their original or adapted African terms. In the sung poetic genres of Oriki and Mlenmlen from the Yoruba and Ewe-Fon traditions, as well as the Ingorôssi or Ponto from Kongo-Angola traditions, the virtues of deities and ancestral spirits are celebrated and invoked. This genre, commonly known as "praise poetry," is typically performed in sacred contexts using African or African-based languages. Exceptions to this include chants primarily in Portuguese, such as the *pontos* of Umbanda and chants honoring the Indigenous Caboclo in certain Candomblé communities. Aruanda appears most frequently in Umbanda chants, where it occupies a central place in its sacred narratives.

The etymology of Umbanda can be traced back to the Bantu word *mbanda*, which signifies the act, space, or person that calls upon ancestral spirits. In Assis

Júnior's Kimbundu dictionary, the entry for *mbanda* includes meanings such as "precept, commandment, prescription, indication, permission, acts prescribed by religion against supposed evil spirits, rules."[234] Gerhard Kubik points out that the concept of Umbanda originated in Angola, where it denotes the knowledge and practice of the art of healing. Kimbanda, Ocimbanda, and Cimbanda (in Kimbundu, Umbundu, and Ngangela, respectively) refer to practitioners of this indigenous medicine.[235] Kubik emphasizes the shared elements between Umbanda in Brazil and Angola: the focus on healing and alleviating psychological suffering; the establishment of harmony with transcendental beings; communication with beings from the transcendental realm through mediums; initiation rituals for those aspiring to become mediums; and the use of common terms in Angolan languages, such as *pemba*, a limestone powder used for sacred writing, among other purposes.[236]

Brazilian Umbanda, as a modern and inclusive religious system formulated in the early twentieth century, integrates diverse traditions—bringing together Kongo-Angola and Yoruba-Ewe-Fon philosophies, Amerindian cosmological concepts, elements of Catholicism, Spiritism, and the Hindu cyclical concept of Karma. Umbanda has evolved into an urbanized religion, constantly transforming and redefining itself, while remaining firmly rooted in the spiritual heritage of Central Africa. In contrast to the more exclusivist-driven African identity of Candomblé's Yoruba-Ewe-Fon cosmologies, Umbanda outlines a Pan-Brazilian religious and philosophical framework that continuously interprets and integrates the myriad cultures found in contemporary Brazil.

Within Umbanda's cosmology, two principal groups of ancestral spirits are venerated through mystical trance possessions: the Caboclos, Indigenous ancestors acting as protectors and messengers of the Yoruba-Ewe-Fon deities; and the Preto-Velhos, wise African elders. These spirits are systematically organized into lines, kingdoms, and phalanxes—formations evocative of ancient Greek warfare. This classification not only organizes the spirits by their attributes and evolutionary progress (similar to Karma), but also allows for the inclusion of new entities into its adaptable hierarchy. This hierarchy is structured as seven primary lines or kingdoms, with each further divided into seven phalanxes. As elucidated by Lourenço Braga (1900–1963), one of the pioneering authors on Umbanda:

> Line formation, in this context, denotes a large army of spirits aligned under the command of a chief or Orisha, with spirits tasked with specific missions or duties within the cosmos. Each line formation is further divided into seven legions, with each legion under the guidance of its own commander. Furthermore, each legion is composed of seven substantial infantries, each with its own designated

leader. This hierarchical pattern extends further, with each large infantry being subdivided into seven smaller infantries, each following a descending hierarchical order.[237]

The representation of ancestors and deities in Umbanda through militaristic concepts holds particular significance. It is noteworthy how the syntax, imagery, and intricate command structure symbolically parallel the political organization of the Federation of Kongo (often, though inaccurately, as a kingdom—as will be explained later). The mythical forces, celestial entities, or spirits of Umbanda are conceptualized as forming armies within the Kingdom of Light. These armies are comprised of the noble spirits of Aruanda, who "ride" mediums during trance possession. Mediums are metaphorically referred to as horses, symbolizing their role as earthly vessels for the divine cavalry of Aruanda's transcendent realm.[238] According to an Umbanda chant: "Reflecting divine light / In all its splendor. / From Oshala's realm / Where there is peace and love, / What reflects on earth, / What reflects in air, / What comes from Aruanda, / Illuminating everything."[239] The "divine light from Aruanda" can be brought forth by ancestral African or Indigenous spirits. The Preto-Velhos and Caboclos act as mediators between the higher ancestors (or Orishas) and humanity. When they "mount" their mediums during mystic trance, they bring light and healing energy to the community.

In Afro-Brazilian imagery, Aruanda transcends all geographical borders. According to one chant: "In the North Pole / Where everything is frozen, / There are Eskimo people, / Who come from Aruanda. / Far away in Greenland, / Where everything is snow-covered, / There are Eskimo people, / Who know the Law of Umbanda."[240] The divinized force emanating from the mythical Aruanda is felt not only across the Americas and Africa but also at the North Pole and in Greenland, among the Inuit and the frozen realms. This may reflect a poetic fascination with light sparkling off ice, or perhaps symbolize a preserved force, an energy frozen in time. What we can observe, without needing to speculate, is that Aruanda has journeyed vast distances—both geographically and poetically—from the colonial port city of Luanda. This compression of temporal and spatial dimensions, weaving human and spiritual interactions on a planetary scale, stands as a profoundly creative phenomenon. While open to diverse adaptations and interpretations worldwide, Aruanda remains solidly grounded in very specific Kongo-Angola cosmological principles.

One Umbanda chant states: "A little chick chirped over there in Angola, / The rooster crowed in the Kalunga, / Hail Congo who comes from Aruanda, / Bringing gifts in his pouch."[241] In Kongo cosmology, Kalunga represents Nzambi's home, the ancestral realm, God, the ocean, the afterlife. Kalunga is the "invisible line or wall between the physical and spiritual worlds" and "the balancing plane-line of all energies."²⁴² The realm of Kalunga is linked to *Musoni*, the Southern Sun of the Kongo, and to *Ku mpèmba*, the world of the dead. A rooster crowing in Kalunga heralds the dawn of a new day, a new cycle, or the beginning of a new transformative process. Similarly, the chirping of a chick in Angola symbolizes *Butuka*, representing birth and the emergence of a vibrant Sun from the depths of the spiritual realm of the ancestors. This Sun brings with it light, joy, hope, and creative energy into *Ku nseke*, the realm of the living. The all-powerful Sun of Kalunga is carried in the pouch of a Kongo spirit from Luanda, echoing the concept of *n'kisi / bilôngo* in a *futu*, where sacred medicine is safeguarded within a pouch.

Another aspect that merits attention in this chant is the parallel notion of Angola-Luanda and Kongo. The memories of the kingdoms of Angola, Kongo, and Mozambique are constantly referenced in Afro-Brazilian cultural manifestations. Although they exist together as a triad, they are not always conflated. Another chant tells us: "Three stones. / Three stones within this village [*aldeia*]. / One is larger, another is smaller, / The smallest one is what lights our way."²⁴³ Three stones are in this Amerindian village. The smallest one is the one which brings light. In the Kongo tradition, a cooking pot representing the kingdom of Kongo or the Big Bang era of Kongo cosmology, "Makukwa matatu malâmb'e Kôngo," balances upon "three stones."²⁴⁴ In Brazil, the three cooking stones symbolize the tripod formed by the mythic kingdoms of Kongo, Mozambique, and Angola. On these stones rests a pot containing *bilôngo* medicine which, when "cooked up" in Kalunga, brings health and joy to the living. Which is the smallest stone? "Teensy-weensy pebble / In Aruanda, my friend / A large bedrock, so large / In Aruanda, my friend."²⁴⁵ A small pebble from Aruanda, separated from a larger rock, becomes a cosmological metaphor: the individual as a fragment of the greater bedrock, which represents God—or Nzambi—in Aruanda or Luanda. In Africa, Capuchin missionaries introduced the practice of using pebbles to count Rosary prayers. Each pebble, already regarded by Central Africans as a vessel of divine energy, came to symbolize sacred words—links in a chain connecting humanity to the divine.

In Brazil, Luanda, symbolized as a vast, omnipotent bedrock, became an emblematic icon representing the entirety of the African continent. Aruanda, a small yet potent pebble that drifted from Luanda, evolved into a poetic and philosophical allusion to a cosmological essence. Aruanda serves as a quintessential connection between Africa and Brazil, functioning as a satellite receiving signals from the frozen station of colonial Luanda. These signals can be transmitted through mediumistic or telepathic communication, collective memory, or in the kinesis of sacred and secular Afro-Brazilian performances and oral literature. Luanda, once the primary hub of the largest slave trade network in Central Africa, took root in Brazilian soil and in the collective memory of Afro-Brazilians as a source of divinized power. Through time and remembrance, it metamorphosed into Aruanda—forming part of a triad of interconnected sacred forces that communicate through mediumship and mystical trance. Aruanda became both a metaphysical geographical reference and a mediator of peace, invoked and envisioned in Brazil and beyond. Its island-rock essence, a component of the broader African continental bedrock, was poetically conceived as drifting into the heart of Brazil. As a cosmology born of the diaspora, Aruanda both encapsulates and is encapsulated by the memory of the kingdoms of Angola, Kongo, and Mozambique. This triad of realms functions as mnemonic anchors and navigational beacons, charting the evolving map of Afro-Brazilian history and cosmology.

THE THREE ROCKS THAT HOLD THE POT: A BRIEF CONTEXTUALIZATION OF KONGO AND NDONGO

It was then decided that the Congo would guide the Moçambique clearing the way, opening the roads with their high-and low-pitched singing, clearing the paths and asking for protection so as to bring forth the throne of the crowns.

Mr. João Lopes, Captain-General of the Jatobá Brotherhood (1930–2004)

The original realm, now remembered in Brazil as Kongo-Angola, undoubtedly grounds the fabric of Brazil's formulation as a collective cultural imagination and a national project. Situated in the tropical central part of the African continent, it extended out from the basins of the Kongo and Kwanza Rivers and their interconnected network of tributaries. The origins of the Kongo Federation or Kingdom date back to the fourteenth century when provinces, typically remembered in multiples of three, merged.[246] Some sources suggest that the Kongo resulted from the alliance of twelve *makanda* clans—the plural form of *kanda*, a term that can be broadly defined as clans or lineages.[247] According to oral traditions, around 1390, Lukeni-lua-Nimi—the son of the sovereigns of merging states—declared Mbanza-Kongo, located in present-day northern Angola, the capital of a new state. The son of Nimi-a-Nzima, King of Mpemba, and Lukeni-Luansanze, Queen of Mbata, became the first king of the Kongo.[248]

From the fourteenth to the eighteenth centuries, the kingdom expanded. At the height of its power, it stretched from the Atlantic Ocean to the Kwango River in the east, encompassing what is now the Democratic Republic of Congo and the northern region of present-day Angola, extending as far south as the latitude of Luanda.[249] This expansion was facilitated through mutual agreements and protection treaties among various self-governing states or commonwealths. By the late fifteenth century, Kongo had developed a vast commercial network and boasted an estimated population of three million subjects.[250] During this period, territories such as Mbamba, Soyo, Nsundi, Mpangu, Mbata, and Mpemba were integrated into the kingdom as royal provinces.[251] These provinces became regional hubs, gradually absorbing smaller districts as subprovinces. Meanwhile, the kingdom's original realms remained relatively compact and under the direct administration of the royal court.[252]

In the sixteenth century, the kingdom expanded further to encompass regions on its eastern and southern flanks, including Ndongo, Matamba, and other Kimbundu-speaking territories. These territories were either annexed as royal provinces or incorporated into preexisting ones, often retaining some degree of autonomy rather than falling under direct royal control.[253] This administrative pattern was characterized by "a voluntary league of equals" rather than subjugation through coercion.[254] Formerly sovereign provinces maintained distinct ties with Kongo, suggesting a federative model or "an inherently democratic character" compared to a centralized empire.[255]

Patrício Batsîkama, in his insightful exploration of Kongo culture that draws on linguistics, oral traditions, and historiography, grounds his analysis in "what can be scientifically explained through language and in accordance with the collective thought of the Kôngo."[256] He explains that it is widely believed that the Kingdom of Kongo started in the South, in present-day southern Angola—specifically, the region spanning the lower basin of the Kunene River near the borders of present-day Angola, Namibia, and Zambia. Batsîkama refers to the Kikongo proverb "Nsûndi tuila ntu, Mbâmba tulambudila malu," which conveys that while the province of Mbamba (in the south) indicates a point of departure, the province of Nsundi (in the north) refers to the destination—a place to be reached, a goal to be achieved, or a conclusion. In its ritualistic usage, the proverb invokes the original ancestors and is a plea for reorganization and order.[257] Batsîkama alludes to contemporary variations of this maxim, which unveil the ancestral "master-movement" (*movimento-mestre*) that led to the expansion and establishment of the kingdom.[258] To clarify, the Bakongo perspective appears to be centered not so much on the concept of originary spaces but rather on the notion of a foundational direction or pathway between established coordinates.

These coordinates include the provinces of Mbamba (South), Mbata (East), Nsundi (North), and Soyo (West). The province of Mpangu lies between Mbata and Nsundi, while at the heart of the five provinces stands the sixth province of Mpemba and the ancient capital of Mbanza-Kongo in present-day Angola.[259] Fu-Kiau, on the other hand, locates the deeper ancestral origin of the Kongo people in the once-fertile Sahara, in a place known as Kayinga. As climatic changes and desertification took hold, the people migrated southward.[260] It is possible that Fu-Kiau's concept of Kayinga predates the departure from Mbamba referenced by Batsîkama. Despite the different geographical emphases, both concur that the foundational "master-movement" of the Kongo people came from the South.

In explaining the Kikongo proverb "makukwa matatu malâmb'e Kôngo," Batsîkama elucidates that *makukwa*—the plural form of *kukwa*—holds layered meanings. It refers not only to the traditional method of cooking with a pot resting on three stones but also to the agricultural act of shaping mounds of earth before planting, as well as to great mountains or even elevated beings. Across these varied domains, *makukwa* symbolizes completeness, unity, gathering, fullness, perfection, and readiness.[261] The foundation of the Kongo is metaphorically attributed to these three pot-supporting stones or mountains. This concept is reinforced by other proverbs such as "enanthiya kalinthiki mbiya," which emphasizes that one stone (mound, hill, or mountain) alone cannot support the pot—and by extension, one family alone cannot build a country.[262] *Enanthiya*, akin to *makukwa*, connotes family and mountain-stone support, and each stone represents one of the three families in the Kongo.[263] Regarding the concept of *matatu*, as in "makukwa matatu," Batsîkama highlights the singular form *tatu*, which signifies not only the number three but also peace, friendship, beginning, morning, connection, radiance, resonance, and kindling fire.[264]

BENEATH THE NSANDA TREE: A KINGDOM IS NOT BUILT BY A SINGLE FAMILY

The Bakongo had long structured their society and public administration around a tripartite system before Portuguese contact altered these institutions. Three families—the Kinsaku, Kimpanzu, and Kinzinga—each held distinct roles. The Kinsaku were responsible for judicial and legislative powers, serving as clergy, healers, diplomats, delegates, and ambassadors.[265] They interpreted and enforced laws related to people's rights and duties, oversaw the appointment of authorities, and upheld religious and philosophical principles underpinning this hierarchical power. The Kimpanzu oversaw national security, including military defense, safeguarding resources and the economy, and supervising voting rights. Meanwhile, the Kinzinga held executive power, overseeing administration and limited ruling rights related to the state and territorial matters such as migration and annexation.[266]

The first two families, Kinsaku and Kimpanzu, were responsible for voting on members of the executive power drawn from the Kinzinga family. The verbs *sâka* and *vânzu*, found in Kinsaku and Kimpanzu, mean to choose, separate, sift, set aside, and elect.[267] The name Kinsaku derives from *kie sâku*, signifying the act of separating wheat from chaff, while Kimpanzu derives from *ki pânzu*, referring to those capable of making wise choices.[268] Together, the Kinsaku and Kimpanzu formed the Yala Nkuwu council, which can be likened to a national congress. The Makota elders of the Yala Nkuwu convened in Mbazi'a Nkanu—the town or court of legal litigations—beneath the Nsanda tree, a Mulemba tree of the mulberry family, adjacent to the king's residence.[269] Across the centuries, from before the establishment of the Kongo Kingdom to the present day, the Nsanda tree has remained standing at the center of Mbanza Kongo.

While the Kinsaku and Kimpanzu served as voters, the Kinzinga were those elected to office. As Batsîkama explains, within the spiritual and governmental structure of the Bakongo, the King of Kongo fulfilled various roles. He was a Ntotila, a title specifically reserved for the chief of the capital city Mbanza-Kongo; a Mani, a chief elected by a council of elders known as the Makota; and a Mwene, the one responsible for managerial oversight of the region's economic resources.[270] While there was only one Ntotila, there were various Mani and Mwene. The extent of their authority was determined by the geographical scope of their domain: a ruler of a province was a Nsundi, a ruler of a smaller territory within the province was a Mpumbu, and a ruler of an even smaller village was a Mpangu. Europeans often misconstrued these distinctions and tended to label each one as "kings."[271]

In an etymological analysis of Mbanza-Kongo, Batsîkama reveals that the word Mbanza derives from *bânzama*, which as a noun denotes a city, the main village, the chief's residence, and even the graveyard; as a verb, it conveys the idea of being visible, extended, or unfolded.[272] The earliest known inhabitants of the Kongo capital named the hill on which the town sits Nkumb'a Wungudi, meaning both "hill" and the "navel" of the kingdom.[273] It is located in a part of the state once known as Kongo-dya-Kati (or Zita-dya-Nza), meaning the "knot of the world."[274] The name Kongo itself stems from the verb *kônga*, meaning to join, unite, mix, or form a circle, as well as *kôngola*, which refers to the act of bringing people together and uniting them in institutionalized friendship.[275]

The Knot of the World: Kongo's Makanda and Zimvila

The original realms that formed the Kongo were structured around matrilineal clans known as *mvila* or *kanda*.[276] While *mvila* were determined at birth, life achievements—including the ability to navigate internal clan conflicts—depended on one's spiritual connection to the paternal clan.[277] *Mvila* denotes the bond shared among individuals of common lineage.[278] The *kanda* ideology has been described as the foundational organizing principle of historical kinship relations, regulating and legitimizing claims to land ownership.[279] Each *kanda* bore its own name, ancestral lineage, and traditions, and could establish land designations and alliances through marriage. Prior to the centralization of the Kongo Kingdom, *makanda* (plural of *kanda*) functioned as smaller autonomous units organized as extended families, allowing members a degree of flexibility in their affiliations.

Some studies of the *mvila* clans indicate that an unnamed king established the Kongo Kingdom by dispatching the founders of the nine clans from its capital, Mbanza-Kongo.[280] These original founders—often cited in multiples of three, most likely six—departed after participating in festive rituals and reciting their *zimvila* (plural of *mvila*), which are clan mottoes or ancestral affirmations.[281] The *zimvila* are concise poetic or proverbial texts committed to memory to affirm identity and lineage. A compilation of five hundred such mottoes was published in 1934 by the Belgian missionary Jean Cuvelier (1882–1962). Copies of this publication were stored in family safes alongside documents and other objects of sacred significance to the clans, such as *malungu* (bracelets) and *nkangi kiditu* (images of Jesus). These safes, kept by *mfumu za makanda* (clan heads), are passed down through successive generations.[282]

The Kongo was initially ruled by a council formed by the leaders of the six founding provinces involved in the ancestral "master-movement" described by Batsîkama: Mbamba, Mbata, Nsundi, Soyo, Mpangu, and Mpemba. Historically, these leaders were recognized as kings.[283] Initially, the power of the king was largely limited and mainly symbolic.[284] Over time, however, a movement toward centralization gradually eclipsed the local claims of the *makanda* over their lands and extended family units. Membership in the Kongo became increasingly organized according to the Mani Kongo rather than the *makanda*, which traditionally had been governed by one male and one female chief.[285]

The Mani Kongo council, known as the Mwissi Kongo, came to consist of representatives from twelve founding *kanda*, divided into three groups. Of these, four positions were reserved for women—former *makanda* chiefs within the Mani Kongo lineage—with one designated as the Mother of the Mani

Kongo.[286] The formation of the Mwissi Kongo council reinforced patrilineal bonds among the ruling elite, while kinship relationships underwent profound transformations through sustained interactions with Europeans. Beginning in the early sixteenth century, baptized Mwissi Kongo members adopted Christian names alongside their patrilineal ones. These names signified wealth, power, and prestige associated with new trading relationships.[287] New lines of power were established based on these evolving titles and names, reshaping the ruling elite over the *makanda* while simultaneously weakening their traditional authority and control over lands and resources. The disruption of *makanda* structures during the sixteenth and seventeenth centuries was partially rectified with the decline of the Kongo Kingdom. From the nineteenth century onward, a new interpretation of the kingdom's foundational myth emerged, suggesting that all *makanda* had once coexisted at the core represented by Mbanza-Kongo. According to one rendition, while in pursuit of prey, a hunter paused to appreciate the beauty around him. Enchanted by what he saw, he decided to establish a settlement in that very place.[288]

Kongo's origin story has undergone multiple reinterpretations over time, shaped by shifting political agendas. Following the civil war that erupted after the Battle of Ulanga (Mbwila) in 1665, the narrative transformed significantly.[289] Initially, the kingdom's founding was attributed to a skilled blacksmith who served as a mediator and negotiator in disputes. By 1710, this image coexisted with an earlier version centered on a conquering hero. After 1850, yet another narrative gained prominence—one emphasizing Kongo's origin as a series of migrations from the ancient capital. This version aligned with a political landscape increasingly influenced by trading clans, rather than the centralized power of a king. In each iteration, the origin story mirrored the evolving constitution of the country, tracing Kongo's trajectory from an emerging polity to a consolidated monarchy; through periods of fragmentation, civil strife, and attempted reconciliation; and eventually toward a reimagined identity aligned with the interests of a rising commercial elite.[290]

Nzinga-a-Nkuwu Welcomes the Portuguese

The relationship between the Kongo Kingdom and Portugal began in 1483, when explorers landed at the port of Mpinda, near the mouth of the Congo River, and dispatched messengers to Mbanza-Kongo to meet with King Nzinga-a-Nkuwu (1440–1509), the kingdom's fifth ruler.[291] In mainstream European accounts, when Captain Diogo Cão (c. 1450–1486) discovered that his messengers had not returned from Mbanza-Kongo, he seized four Bakongo and took them to Lisbon as hostages.[292] However, Capuchin friar Cavazzi gives a different version: he claims this was an agreement reached by both parties, wherein Cão promised to return with the Kongo ambassadors by the fifteenth moon, leaving four of his men behind as proof of his word.[293] King Dom João II of Portugal (1455–1495) seized this diplomatic opening to impress King Nzinga-a-Nkuwu, welcoming his Kongo guests with royal hospitality, providing them with the finest meals, attire, housing, and access to education and Christian instruction. Likewise, the Portuguese visitors were warmly received during their two-year stay in Mbanza-Kongo. This initial exchange allowed both Portugal and Kongo to closely observe and assess one another from the heart of their respective kingdoms.[294] Initially characterized by cultural and economic exchange—most notably Nzinga-a-Nkuwu's conversion to Catholicism—the relationship between Kongo and Portugal shifted dramatically. By 1576, the Portuguese had established a colony in present-day Angola, renaming Mbanza-Kongo as São Salvador and progressively transforming the region into a hub for the transatlantic slave trade.

In the early sixteenth century, Nzinga-a-Nkuwu was baptized and bestowed with the same name as the king of Portugal, João I. This practice extended to other members of the Kongo court, who were baptized with names from the Portuguese king's household. In both Kongo and Portugal, the king, queen, and prince were baptized as João, Eleanor, and Álvaro, respectively. The same pattern of mirroring occurred in other parts of Africa, as seen in the Monomotapa Empire of Mozambique, where the king and queen were baptized as Sebastião and Maria in 1560. Families in Kongo adopted surnames such as Castros, Meneses, Silvas, and Vieiras not only as markers of their Catholic affiliation, but also to signify the wealth and influence derived from their growing participation in burgeoning Atlantic trade networks.[295] The British historian Anne Hilton emphasizes how Mvemba-a-Nzinga João I institutionalized Christianity as a royal cult directly under his authority to enhance his political influence. This move legitimized his own position and raised the status of the kingship above that of rival factions.[296] Initially, he sought exclusive rights to "Christian power" for himself and his closest allies. Following the recommendations of Portugal, Kongo chiefs and members of the elite were granted noble titles and baptized with Portuguese names.[297]

Nzinga-a-Nkuwu's collaboration with Portugal, supported by military aid, facilitated Kongo's territorial expansion.[298] His death sparked a succession conflict, igniting a civil war that concluded in triumph for the pro-Portuguese faction.[299] Mvemba-a-Nzinga Afonso I (1456–1542) assumed the throne of Kongo in 1509, becoming a Christian ruler with strong connections to the Portuguese crown. In 1512, King Manuel I of Portugal (1469–1521) and King Mvemba-a-Nzinga signed the Regimento, a treaty drafted by the Portuguese that outlined the terms of the alliance between the kingdoms. The agreement tasked the Portuguese with assisting the Kongo in multiple domains, including the introduction of European legal and military concepts, the construction of churches, and the teaching of courtly etiquette. The document also stressed the importance of diplomatic conduct, aiming to establish an African society modeled—where feasible—on Portuguese norms. In return, Kongo was expected to provide cargoes of copper, ivory, and captives.[300] Gerald Bender highlights certain ostensibly egalitarian principles within the *Regimento*, which were unique in early European-African relations but ultimately unrealized in practice. While these decrees from Lisbon may have reflected the ideals of sixteenth-century Portuguese society, their implementation did not necessarily align with the sociopolitical realities of Kongo.[301]

Mvemba-a-Nzinga Afonso I initially prospered through the trade of copper with Portuguese merchants. The early years of his reign symbolize a rare period in Angolan history marked by optimism regarding Afro-European cooperation.[302] During this period, the monarchs of Kongo and Portugal cultivated a diplomatic relationship, addressing each other as "royal brothers" and exchanging letters as equals. Emissaries traveled between Mbanza-Kongo and Lisbon, and Kongo established diplomatic relations with the Vatican. Mvemba-a-Nzinga Afonso's son, Henrique, underwent 13 years of clerical study in Lisbon and returned to Kongo as the first appointed bishop of Kongo ordained within the Roman Catholic Church.[303] However, as Portugal expanded its sugar plantations in São Tomé and Príncipe—and later in Brazil—it increasingly relied on enslaved captives to perform forced labor. This shift profoundly altered the nature of the Kongo-Portuguese relationship. Mvemba-a-Nzinga began to lose control of the situation as new traders began arriving on the shores and engaging directly with Portuguese counterparts in violation of existing agreements. In 1526, in an attempt to reassert authority, he issued a royal decree banning all trade and ordering the expulsion of all Portuguese except teachers and missionaries. Yet mounting external pressures forced him to revoke this order only a few months later.[304] Mvemba-a-Nzinga's continued appeals to the Portuguese crown for technical assistance, including doctors, artisans and educators, were largely ignored. Portugal's interest had shifted decisively to acquiring captives, a demand that intensified over time and soon eclipsed all other priorities.[305] Early exchanges had included efforts to introduce European technical know-how to the Kongolese, but those ambitions were quickly abandoned. Despite Mvemba-a-Nzinga's persistent requests for doctors, teachers, ships, and technological resources, what Portugal provided instead were firearms, alcohol, and mounting pressure to provide captives as human cargo.[306] In an effort to regain control, Mvemba-a-Nzinga wrote to his "Royal Brother," King João III (1502–1557), stating:

> We cannot reckon how great that damage is, since the above-mentioned merchants daily seize our subjects, sons of the land and sons of our noblemen and vassals and our relatives.... Thieves and men of evil conscience take them because they wish to possess the things and wares of this kingdom.... They grab them and cause them to be sold: and so great, Sir, is their corruption and licentiousness that our country is being utterly depopulated. The king of Portugal should not countenance such practices. And to avoid them we need from your Kingdoms no other than priests and people to teach in schools, and no other goods but wine and flour for the holy sacrament: this is why we beg of Your Highness to help and assist us in this matter, commanding your factors that they should send neither merchants nor wares, because it is our will that in these kingdoms there should not be any trade in slaves nor market for slaves.[307]

In 1540, Mvemba-a-Nzinga wrote to Portugal again, this time to negotiate the acquisition of war captives from the Anziku Kingdom.[308] According to one account, in that same year, a friar hired eight men to assassinate Mvemba-a-Nzinga during an Easter service. Although a cannonball fired into the church missed the king, it wounded others. He passed away shortly thereafter.[309] The death of Mvemba-a-Nzinga signaled the beginning of the end for the unified Kingdom of Kongo.

By the late sixteenth century, Portuguese efforts toward further colonial expansion and the pursuit of exclusive dominance in coastal trade, coupled with their increasingly aggressive capture of war captives, further strained the alliance between Portugal and Kongo.[310] The administrative structure of Kongo began to erode. With the loss of fiscal and tribute revenue, the economic and political foundations of Kongo power disintegrated.[311] During the seventeenth century, particularly in the final decades of the Iberian Union (1580–1640), when Portugal was a vassal of the Spanish Empire, diplomacy gave way to coercion and control. Initially, like other European nations, Portugal confined itself to purchasing captives obtained from wars waged by others. However, with limited industrial capacity compared to England and the Netherlands, it eventually resorted to conducting its own military campaigns.[312]

From the sixteenth to the eighteenth centuries, the relationship between the Kongo and Portuguese kingdoms—characterized by fluctuating power dynamics—had a profound impact on the political structure and stability of the

Kongo Kingdom. Initially, Kongo supported Portugal's endeavors in Angola. Despite changing circumstances, Kongo's kings sought to leverage Portuguese expertise, permitting missionaries to operate among their people and employing Portuguese craftsmen and educators to train local subjects. Meanwhile Portuguese expansion primarily targeted the Mbundu region. The period from 1605 to 1641 proved catastrophic for the Mbundu people of Ndongo, turning the area into the largest slave emporium in Central Africa and leading to the obliteration of entire communities.[313] The English historian David Birmingham identifies three principal methods by which the Portuguese enslaved people in Angola during the first half of the seventeenth century:[314]

(1) The feudal arrangement, introduced and ritualized by the Portuguese, involving the imposition of a feudal-like structure in the Mbundu territories. This entailed the ritualized demotion of Mbundu chiefs—whom the Portuguese would generically refer to as *soba*—to the status of vassals. In return for land and protection, these vassals and their descendants were obliged to render annual tribute, facilitate trade, provide military support, and supervise tribute payments from sub-chiefs.[315] In Kongo, as well as in other parts of Africa, systems of contribution bearing superficial resemblance to European-style taxation were already in place. Provinces within the Kongo, including the Mbundu of Ndongo before their separation, paid a tribute known as *kabakula*.[316] Through etymological examination of *kabakula*, we find a possible combination of *kabaku* and *kula*. *Kabaku*, the diminutive form of *kibaku*, refers to various objects: footstool, platform, pedestal, podium, support, stool, domestic animal, or captive.[317] Meanwhile, *kula* translates to "to grow."[318] Wooden footstools and stools, as significant as thrones, symbolize the ruling status of a king or chief. Thus, *kabakula* seems to encompass the notions of chiefdoms and the dynamic expansion of political influence (or more literally, platform). This expansion was not merely territorial but also accomplished through tribute payments in kind and coalition-building among allied parties. *Kabakula* signifies more than a mere contract; it embodies alliance, acknowledgment, and a tradition of paying respect to elders. Once emblematic of provincial cohesion, *kabakula* evolved into a Portuguese taxation system for rulers and citizens.[319] The aggressive Portuguese tax policy, characterized by intimidation, aggression, and coercion, sharply contrasts with the traditional principles of mutual respect and consent.[320]

(2) Direct warfare and raids through the creation of the *guerra preta* ("Black War") troops. With Spain focusing its imperial resources on Spanish America during the Iberian Union (1580–1640), there was limited support for Portuguese endeavors in Kongo-Angola. Between 1575 and 1594, approximately

two thousand Portuguese soldiers were deployed to Ndongo; by 1594, disease, desertion, and attrition had reduced their numbers by approximately two-thirds, leaving about three hundred survivors.[321] Portugal's solution to this deficit was to enlist Brazilian mestizos, Indigenous peoples, and African soldiers. It was not uncommon for these *guerra preta* units to have a ratio of one Portuguese soldier for every one hundred non-European slave-soldiers. These ethnically diverse, largely coerced forces played a central role in large-scale raids that supplied captives to the transatlantic slave trade.[322]

(3) The third Portuguese enslaving method identified by Birmingham involved the use of intermediary commerce, in which Portuguese agents negotiated with itinerant African traders who traveled between inland markets and the coast, purchasing captives from local chiefs and transporting them back to Luanda. One of the most notable slave markets was situated among the Mpumbu people near Stanley Pool.[323] These inland markets became trading hubs known to the Portuguese as *pombos*; the traders operating them were *pombeiros*. European traders often remained on the coast, sending their mestizo offspring or servants to conduct transactions at the *pombos*.[324] *Pombeiros* would embark on journeys from Luanda with trade goods—such as palm textiles, cowrie shells, and alcohol—which they would barter during their travels in exchange for captives. They typically spent one to two years away, returning with hundreds of individual captives.[325] Their merchandise was often acquired through credit from Portuguese merchants and dealers in Luanda.[326]

Independent *pombeiros* who had been in Africa since the fifteenth century—known as *lançados* or *funantes*—established their own trafficking networks with the Mbundu people and in the interior regions. Neither the *pombeiros* nor the Mbundu people saw the arrival of new Portuguese traders as reliable or desirable.[327] While the Portuguese crown established itself in Luanda, *pombeiros* maintained independent connections with local chiefs. They had long before formed alliances through marriage with ruling families and brokered deals with them, either independently or on behalf of European merchants.[328] Most had likely been established in Central Africa for generations, a legacy of Portugal's longstanding practice, dating back to the early fifteenth century, of sending convicts (*degredados*) from metropolitan prisons to its overseas colonies.[329]

The first groups of exiled *degredados* sent to Central Africa were mainly composed of individuals persecuted for their religious beliefs. These early settlers competed with subsequent waves of traders who arrived as official representatives of the Portuguese crown. A similar dynamic unfolded in Brazil, where emissaries of the Portuguese crown found that these early *degredados* and their descendants had no desire to share their business connections overseas. In Central Africa,

Portuguese Jews found success as entrepreneurs in the slave trade, while in Brazil they emerged as major investors in sugar cane plantations and the sugar industry during the sixteenth and seventeenth centuries.[330] By the late seventeenth and early eighteenth centuries, the Portuguese slave trade was predominantly controlled by Brazilian interests, with a significant presence of a strong Jewish business network operating on both sides of the Atlantic.

The Merchants of the Portuguese Nation and the Ha-goyim

New Christians established alliances with the elites of the Kongo, often through marriages. In Africa, the Americas, and Portugal, churches served as meeting grounds for New Christians and free or enslaved Africans, facilitating their connections through shared religious, cultural, and economic experiences. New Christians were frequently accused of favoring Kongo over Portuguese interests and of providing legal assistance to local elites in disputes against the Church.[331]

Toward the end of the fifteenth century, as Portugal embarked on its overseas expansion, thousands of Sephardic Jews comprised a large part of the population. Father António Vieira noted that in Europe, the terms "Jews" and "Portuguese" became nearly interchangeable, though initially, the term "people of the Portuguese nation" was used in 1511 to denote Portuguese merchants residing in the municipality of Antwerp (modern-day Belgium).[332] The term *nação* (nation), later used to denote the generic origins of African captives, had previously been utilized among Iberian Jewish communities. *Nações*, the plural form of *nação*, corresponds to the Hebrew *goy* and *ha-goyim* ("nation" and "nations"), signifying non-Jewish individuals, pagans, gentiles, or those outside the cosmology of the twelve tribes constituting the Israelite nation.[333] Portuguese Jews referred to themselves using variants like "os da nação" (those of the nation), "homens de nação" (men of the nation), "nação judaica portuguesa" (Portuguese Jewish nation), or "mercadores de nação portuguesa" (merchants of the Portuguese nation). The "Portuguese people of the nation" took care to distinguish themselves from Jews originating outside the Iberian Peninsula.[334]

In Portugal, prior to the Inquisition, non-Christians were required to live in segregated quarters, separated from the Christian population by walls. They were subjected to heavy taxation, and were prohibited from holding public office, practicing certain professions, and owning land.[335] The high concentration of non-Christians in Portugal can be attributed to the country's relatively stable political conditions, especially when compared to other European regions where intolerance frequently gave rise to anti-Judaic violence and persecution.

This scenario shifted during the reign of King Manuel who, following the example of his Spanish counterparts, prohibited Jewish religious practices in 1496 and subsequently issued an Edict of Expulsion.[336] The Spanish and Portuguese edicts of 1492 and 1497 mandated Catholic conversion within one year or expulsion from their respective territories.[337] Portuguese New Christians were encouraged to settle in Angola, Cape Verde, São Tomé, and Príncipe through Manueline ordinances as early as 1502, predating the formal establishment of the Portuguese Inquisition in 1536.[338]

Forced conversions led to the emergence of New Christians, who were distinct from families with longstanding Catholic roots, known as Old Christians. The Inquisition's jurisdiction extended to baptized individuals practicing religions other than Catholicism. Merely belonging to a "caste of Jews," "caste of converts," or "people of the nation" constituted a grave accusation under the Inquisition.[339] Migration waves of New Christians to Brazil intensified toward the end of the sixteenth century and the beginning of the seventeenth century. While there are no precise quantitative statistics to specify the New Christian presence in Brazil, they are understood to have constituted a significant contingent among the freemen in major colonial cities.[340] Unlike in Portugal—where they faced legal impediments, especially in mercantile business during the seventeenth century—in Brazil, New Christians could more easily acquire land and engage in sugarcane cultivation.[341] The period of the Inquisition in Brazil, spanning from 1570 to 1630, marked a turning point in relations between Old Christian and New Christian populations. Visits from the Holy Office occurred in Bahia and Pernambuco (1591–1595), Olinda (1599), and Salvador (1610), prompting the Old Christian population to scrutinize the *ajudengados* (those following Jewish practices) with denunciatory intent.[342] The historian Maria Luiza Tucci Carneiro notes that the seventeenth century marked the beginning of a significant spread of "blood prejudice" in Portugal, which also extended to Brazil. She emphasizes a legacy that encompassed not only legislative measures but also a social structure organized around discriminatory groups.[343] Due to New Christians' vulnerability to discriminatory laws, they often concealed their identities and posed as Old Christians as a survival strategy. This allowed them to gain access to positions and opportunities that were otherwise prohibited to them.[344]

A brief respite occurred during the Dutch occupation of Pernambuco (1630–1654), when Jews in Brazil experienced religious and civil freedoms, including the ability to hold public administrative positions—rights that were otherwise restricted under Portuguese blood purity laws.[345] It was during this period that the first two synagogues in the Americas were founded in Recife: Kahal Tzur Yisrael (the Rock of Israel) and Magen Avraham (the Shield of Abraham).[346]

THE VICTORIES OF THE MBUNDU AND THE ROSE OF ARUANDA

The arrival of the Portuguese at Luanda is remembered in the oral traditions of the peoples whom they met there. These say that the white men arrived in ships with wings which shone in the sun like knives.

David Birmingham

In 1622, Portugal launched a military invasion, the Battle of Mbumbi, of southern Kongo. Traditionally perceived as a defeat for Kongo, a document unearthed by John Thornton reveals a second battle in which Kongo achieved a decisive victory.[347] Most historical accounts emphasize the Dutch role in invading Angola in 1641, often seen as an extension of their activities in Brazil since 1630 and aimed at disrupting Angola's slave trade to redirect it to Pernambuco. As Thornton's research unveils, the Dutch invasion was only possible through an alliance with the Kingdom of Kongo. This alliance, initiated by King Nkanga-a-Mvika Pedro II of Kongo (reigning from 1622 to 1624), proposed a coordinated land and sea invasion of Angola. The joint Kongo-Dutch campaign to seize Luanda and expel the Portuguese from Angola proved victorious, enabling Kongo to gradually reclaim territories previously under Portuguese rule.[348]

Although officially allied with Portugal, the Kongo had maintained ties with the Dutch for some years, finding favor in their presence in Luanda and the commercial advantages it brought. Similarly, the Ndongo and Matamba welcomed the arrival of the Dutch, motivated both by commercial interests and political considerations.[349] In 1647, a triple alliance was formed uniting the Dutch, Kongo, and Ndongo, with the shared objective of eradicating Portuguese military influence in the region.[350]

While Kongo held sway as the dominant power in West Central Africa during the fifteenth century, by the sixteenth century the Mbundu State of Ndongo (later known as Angola) began to ascend, supplanting Kongo's position and later ceding prominence to the Kingdom of Kasanje.[351] In a 1521 letter from Mvemba-a-Nzinga to King João III of Portugal, Ndongo—inhabited by the Mbundu people—was identified as part of the Kongo Federation.[352] The Mbundu, primarily Kimbudu speakers, were composed of various ethnic groups, integrated through shared cultural similarities. They lived in decentralized provinces or clans organized matrilineally. Following invasions, they migrated from Matamba, their historical homeland, westward toward Luanda, forming what some historians distinguish as Eastern (Matamba) and Western Ndongo (Ndongo proper).³⁵³ Those who lived in the western region of the province, close to the shore in Luanda, had access to *nzimbu* currency shells.³⁵⁴ This facilitated direct trade with independent Portuguese traders. As trade flourished, by the late fifteenth or early sixteenth century, the Mbundus of Eastern and Western Ndongo became part of a more centralized state.³⁵⁵

According to one of the foundation myths, a hunter named Ngola led the emergence of the Ndongo kingdom.³⁵⁶ In Cavazzi's register, the first Ngola-Mussuri, the "Smith King," was purportedly named Zimbo, a protégé of the gods who was said to have been taught to forge iron using fire and stone hammers.³⁵⁷ Zimbo's subjects, the *Muzimbo*, expanded their lands, conquered provinces, and eventually invaded the Kongo where they established an alliance with "the Mbundu rural peasants."³⁵⁸ Historians identify Zimbo as the Jaga King of Matamba who conquered Ndongo.³⁵⁹ While Zimbo remained the ruler of the Matamba lands, his nephew Ngola-Kiluanji-Kia-Samba became the ruler of the Ndongo lands.³⁶⁰

The Ndongo kingdom had a hierarchical political structure consisting of 736 provinces, each governed by soba chiefs. These chiefs reported to the Ngola, or king, who held authority over the entire region.³⁶¹ The Ndongo's political system was rooted in the governance model of Old Kongo, maintaining its structure even after its separation from Kongo in the seventeenth century. This system featured a centralized hierarchy with the king at the apex and *soba* chiefs enjoying a measure of autonomy in their local administration.³⁶² Sobas acted as intermediaries between the king and their communities, implementing local decisions on his behalf.³⁶³ The Ngola's authority was supported by the Angolambole (army general), the Camaristas (council overseeing matters of peace and war), and the Makota, an elder council composed of selected sobas who provided counsel to the king.³⁶⁴ Ambassadors known as Makunji were also appointed from among the sobas. Smiths held a prominent economic and cultural role in Ndongo, revered both as the kingdom's founders and custodians of its myths. Other societal groups, including the Murinda (farmers and commoners) and Kijikos (pl. Mijiko, war prisoners), enjoyed equal social status alongside the smiths.³⁶⁵

With the upheaval in ties with the Kongo, Portuguese interests sought to recalibrate trade routes and establish new footholds. In 1559, a diplomatic envoy was dispatched to Ndongo. Upon their arrival, they encountered Portuguese *lançado* merchants already engaged in trade with the Ngola, who were resistant to the expansion of Portuguese authority.³⁶⁶ Since its earliest commercial ventures, Portugal had favored granting licenses to private traders for a fee.³⁶⁷ Early settlers often evaded taxes and duties. As Portugal sought to reassert control over trade, many local traders, recognizing their continued disadvantage within the regulated system, shifted their alliance to African partners in pursuit of greater opportunities than those offered by Portugal.[368] Father Diogo Gomez, a Jesuit, cautioned against abruptly shifting trade from Kongo to Ndongo and urged caution. Despite his advice, a fleet of three ships arrived at the mouth of the Kwanza River in 1560.[369]

Against protocol, and ignoring warnings from local clergy, the diplomatic mission led by Paulo Dias Novais proceeded to dispatch an embassy group inland to establish direct contact with Ngola-Kiluanji-Kia-Ndambi (1556–1561). The group returned with the Ngola, who gave them a cold reception—likely due to breaches in protocol and because the invitation had been issued by the previous king (Ngola-Kiluanji-Kia-Samba, 1515–1556), who was already deceased.[370] Kiluanji-Kia-Ndambi had been cautioned by the Kongo about the Portuguese, having been told that the Jesuits had arrived to assess the presence of silver or gold—resources that could prompt the Portuguese to attempt a conquest of his lands.[371] Kiluanji-Kia-Ndambi ordered the detention and seizure of belongings of the Portuguese mission. Although a group was eventually released after several months, Novais, and Friar Mendes remained imprisoned.[372]

Novais remained a prisoner of Ndongo for five years. Upon his release, he advocated for, and subsequently led, a second expedition. In 1575, rather than sending a diplomatic mission, the Portuguese dispatched a military expedition to Ndongo, marking a decisive shift away from diplomacy and toward overt aggression.[373] The expedition—comprising seven hundred soldiers and farmhands, accompanied by four Jesuit priests and two secular clergy—arrived at Luanda, then part of Kongo. This violated a treaty signed with the Kongo during the reign of Nimi-a-Lukeni-lua-Mvemba Álvaro I (1568–1587), which restricted Portuguese activities to the island of Luanda and safeguarded the area between the island and the mainland—then the primary source of *nzimbu* shells. In 1576, Novais founded São Paulo de Luanda, the first European city in Southern Africa, and became its first administrator. Portuguese ambitions soon extended eastward in pursuit of silver mines, but these efforts were hampered by internal strife within the ranks and fierce opposition from the Mbundu people. Tensions persisted and intensified, leading to a pivotal event in 1622, when the daughter of Kiluanji-Kia-Ndambi and Kangela visited Luanda as an ambassador of Ndongo.[374] Shortly after her visit, Nzinga-Mbandi-Ngola-Kiluanji (1582–1663) became the Queen of Ndongo and Matamba, emerging as a dynamic and pivotal figure in the resistance against Portuguese rule.

Nzinga, the Queen

Queen Nzinga Mbandi Ngola Kiluanji, who ruled Ndongo from 1624 to 1626 and 1657 to 1663 and is remembered in Brazil as Rainha Ginga, remains a central figure in the historical narratives of Angola and Brazil, serving as a catalyst of resistance during and after her lifetime. The Island of Luanda, revered as Aruanda, also has major importance for African-Brazilian civilization. Both Queen Nzinga and Luanda have ascended to mythical status, embodying ideals of resilience and empowerment. Novais, other than as a generic reference to Portuguese colonizers, is entirely absent from this memory. The African American historian John Henrik Clarke (1915–1998) describes Queen Nzinga as the "quintessence of early Mbundu resistance." He argues that although she did not succeed in expelling the Portuguese, "her historic importance transcends this failure as she awakened and encouraged the first known stirring of nationalism in West Central Africa by organizing both national and international (the Mani-Kongo) assistance in her total opposition to European domination."[375]

The idea of failure, which appears in Clarke's quote, reverberates in historical accounts. However, in African Brazil's noncanonical registers, her memory is exclusively associated with victory. Consider this Maracatu Carnaval chant from Recife: "Rose from Aluanda that *tenda, tenda* / that *tenda, tenda* / that has *tororo*!"[376] The word *tenda*, from the Kimbundu *kútenda*, signifies remembrance and longing, while *tororo*, from *kutolola*, represents victory.[377] Luanda's *tororo*, the victorious forces of Luanda, are embodied by the historical figure of Queen Nzinga.

From the sixteenth to the seventeenth centuries, the Mbangala entered Ndongo along the Kwanza River, coinciding with the arrival of the Portuguese. Around 1560, under the leadership of Kinguri-kya-Bangela, the Mbangalas settled in Matamba, encountering Ndongo people who were trading with independent Portuguese merchants.[378] Kinguri-kya-Bangela attacked Ndongo but faced resistance from the Ngola and died in battle in 1563, leading to the fragmentation of the Mbangala into various autonomous groups. This event marked the beginning of the Mbangala's expansion through new organizational forms that united multiple microstates. Around 1620, a military raiding band of Mbangala organized as the Kasanje state (c. 1620–1910), moving toward Luanda and driving out Mbundu traders allied with the Portuguese.[379] The Kasanje shared a common ancestry with the Ndongo through the founding figure Zimbo. While Ndongo recognized Zimbo as their first Ngola (king), the Kasanje traced their lineage through Temba-Ndumba, a key successor in their historical and spiritual genealogy.

The Kasanje formed a society that grouped its members not by lineage or origin but through initiation into Kilombo rituals and lifestyle. Temba-Ndumba, one of the first Mbangala leaders remembered in oral traditions, is a legendary female leader and one of the successors of the founding smith-king, Zimbo. She is credited with organizing both the spiritual and political foundations of the Kilombo, establishing its administration pattern through what became known as "the Laws of Temba-Ndumba" or "the Quijila Laws." Derived from the Kimbundu *kiîla*, meaning traditional taboo, the Quijila laws encompassed a range of domestic, religious, and civic prohibitions.[380] Through the Kilombo initiation ritual, members of the Kasanje severed ties with their original matrilineal clans to join a new lineage.[381] This model proved instrumental in creating a transethnic, international military force—a strategy later adopted with great skill by Queen Nzinga.

Nzinga was raised in the tradition of a Kilombo warrior, following a lineage in which her father and previous Ndongo chiefs had already adopted Jaga traditions. Drawing on her personal background, warrior training, and an alliance with the Kasanje, Queen Nzinga adapted the Laws of Temba-Ndumba to a new context. From the 1620s to the 1660s, after ascending to power over Ndongo and Matamba, she implemented the Kilombo structure into Matamba's governance. Around 1630, she established the capital of Matamba as the Kilombo and City of Saint Mary of Matamba. Nzinga achieved the highest rank in the Kilombo hierarchy: Tembanza, the leader responsible for invincibility rituals.[382] From then on, she organized her territories according to a revised version of Temba-Ndumba's military and spiritual structure. What set Nzinga's Kilombos apart was her decision to fully embrace and maximize their military potential. Leveraging her military prowess, she rallied a multiethnic army and promoted united resistance against Portuguese domination.[383] In addition to training war captives and selected youth, Nzinga boldly liberated captives and raised political awareness to recruit more members. She strategically targeted areas under Portuguese authority, leading her army westward to liberate captives held by the Europeans.[384] People from various ethnic backgrounds began to rally around her. Her Kilombos became havens for those unwilling to compromise with the Portuguese.

Ngangas and Kilombos:
The Science and Politics of Queen Nzinga's Realm

Nzinga's strategic adoption of Temba-Ndumba's laws and rituals bolstered her reputation as a formidable leader. She gained renown as a powerful witch, reputed for her ability to predict events and transform into various "monstrous forms."[385]

From friar Cavazzi's sensationalist descriptions during his visit to Central Africa from 1654 to 1667, we can gather valuable information, though it requires a measure of skepticism and critical scrutiny. According to Cavazzi, Nzinga employed five Xinguila priests, each channeling the spirits of different ancestors for consultation. Moreover, Nzinga herself was recognized as a Xinguila priestess, serving as a vessel for the protective spirits of different provinces as well as the spirit of her predecessor, Ngola Mbandi.[386] Cavazzi distinguished a wide variety of Ngangas, broadly defined as doctors, scientists, priests, philosophers and counsellors, each with specialized roles: those who controlled the weather, elements, animals or plants; healers who made diagnoses or specialized in auditory, dermatological or emotional disorders; sculptors who worked to prevent illness; specialists who attended exclusively to warriors and chiefs; and those who walked on their hands to perceive what others could not.[387]

According to Cavazzi, the Kasanje believed that the souls of the dead would occasionally visit the world of the living to "eat." They would, on these occasions, disguise themselves as serpents or insects.[388] This concept of souls, or the dead, returning to the world of the living to eat is connected to the Kongo spiritual force known as *kindoki*. Buakasa Tulu Kia Mpansu (1937–2004) explains *kindoki* as a force that can be used for good or evil, to protect or to destroy. He explains the distinction between *kindoki kia dia* (literally, "eating kindoki") and *kindoki kia lunda* ("protecting kindoki").[389] The verb *dia*, "to eat," describes the destructive force of the *ndoki* spirits that destroy their victims by consuming them—drawing invisibly upon their psyche, their inner source of life and vitality.[390] Beyond "eating," *dia* has related meanings that imply collecting a debt, assessing a fine, or possessing. In his study of Kongo cosmology, Simon Bockie (1944–1993) distinguishes between the Nganga and Ndoki: the Nganga priest practices *kinganga*, while the Ndoki priest practices *kindoki*.[391] Though most Nganga possess knowledge of both *ndoki* (negative) and *nkisi* (benevolent) spirits, Ndoki primarily engage with destructive or "eating" spirits.[392] The British travel writer Cyril Claridge (c. 1885–?) notes that a *ndoki* targets a person's soul for three main reasons: causing illness, death, or enslavement. Such souls could be sold to Europeans, who were said to hide them in luggage, water containers, or tin cans to transport them back to Europe.[393] A person whose soul has been stolen is no longer considered truly alive, but is instead described as *kafi* or *evuvu*—"a shell without a kernel, a body without a spirit."[394] Their involuntary movements before ceasing to exist resemble the reflex of a chicken after its head has been severed. Unlike the Ndoki, the Nganga—a physician, pharmacist, prophet, seer, visionary, fortune-teller, priest—is capable of *kindoki* if necessary and provides assistance and protection rather than harm.[395]

The term "Xinguila," as mentioned by Cavazzi, corresponds to the designation of Queen Nzinga as "Xinga" in von Martius and Spix's 1818 account of a Congada performance in Minas Gerais. "Xinguila" is derived from the Kimbundu terms *muxingiri* and *muxinguidi*, which mean "diviners" who engage in *xingila* or the evocation of the dead.[396] In both Kimbundu and Kikongo languages, *muxínga* can denote "whip or discipline," as well as "rope, tie, or knot."[397] The latter set of definitions is particularly insightful, as it relates to the use of knots in the concepts of encoding and decoding within incantation and medicine, and further extends to interpretations of time, history, and the cosmos. Another figure skilled in handling *muxínga* is the *muxinganeke*, defined in dictionaries as "philosopher."[398] Accordingly, in Western academic frameworks, Ngangas and Xinguilas can be understood as the philosophers, scholars, and intellectuals who possess profound analytical capabilities that surpass the ordinary.

Additionally, Cavazzi's accounts provide insights into various aspects of the Kilombos. He described the Laws of Temba-Ndumba as food prohibitions, as well as prescriptions for health and endurance, and the continuation of the group through the continuous introduction of male children in the Kilombo. Power was to be ritualistically transmitted. The energy of younger beings would be symbolically kept in the *maji-a-samba* ointment with which converted members were anointed.[399] Cavazzi's descriptions of Kilombo rituals include explorations of the practices of Xinguila healers, reverence for ancestors, rituals surrounding funerary ceremonies, and the celebrations of victory involving rituals with defeated enemies (the origin of the cannibalistic image of the group).[400] According to Cavazzi, parents eagerly sought acceptance for their sons to participate in the Kilombo initiation ceremonies. The ceremony featured music, dancing, and the presentation of safes containing ancestral bones. These safes were placed on earth mounds and guarded by the commander and the Tembanza, the chief of the Kilombo, who would sit next to them while overseeing the mock combats and proceedings. A key part of the ritual was the symbolic, performative transition of boys from familial ties to adherence to new lineage laws.[401]

Structurally Kilombo are described as fortified settlements, strategically located, often close to cliffs. The selection of the settlement site was a task entrusted to the general and religious leaders, who ensured its security by surrounding its circular construction with twelve sturdy poles, each guarded by a captain.[402] Cavazzi refers to the consistent structural plan and military structure of the Kilombo.[403] At the heart of the Kilombos stood the king's residence, enclosed by a strong square fence, where servants and key figures protected and served the king. The second nucleus housed the Ngola-Mbole—the army's commanding general, responsible for strategic decisions and overseeing military operations—who was referred to as either Mutue-a-ita ("war chief") or Mutue-a-ulungo, ("captain of the ship"). The third nucleus was governed by Tandala, the backup commander who assumed leadership in the king's absence. The fourth, known as Mutunda, accommodated the Mani-lumbu, responsible for building and maintaining the fences and trenches around the Kilombos and around the home of the king. Positioned on the eastern side was the fifth nucleus, home to a minister responsible for clandestine missions carried out discreetly. The sixth housed the Ilunda, or baggage commander, tasked with storing weapons under the direction of the Ngola Mbole, and the seventh was occupied by another Iluanda, responsible for safeguarding the king's garments and accessories.[404]

Nzinga's Kilombos adhered to a uniform town plan, primarily focused on military defense.[405] Advanced military tactics and expertise in guerrilla surprise attacks shaped the structure of both Nzinga's army and the maroons of Palmares in Brazil. Nzinga adapted Kilombo cosmology to her context, establishing alliances and forging a vast, multiethnic army. This principle also guided those who were captured and sent from Angola to Brazil, where they further adapted Kilombos to a different context across the Atlantic.

Queen Nzinga's Attempts to Negotiate with the Unreliable Portuguese

When Queen Nzinga arrived in Luanda as an ambassador in 1622, she was greeted by a gathering of prominent figures from various sectors, including judges, merchants, senior civilian officials, clergy, and military personnel. Cannon salutes echoed through the air as Portuguese soldiers lined the streets leading to her residence, where she would stay during her visit.[406] Nzinga was impressed by the grandeur of the reception ceremony, especially by the military prowess displayed by the Portuguese troops. Recognizing the strategic importance of Ndongo, the Portuguese did their best to lure Nzinga into becoming a subject.[407] They were impressed by her eloquence and fluency in their language as she advocated for her brother's sovereignty and equal relations with Portugal. Nzinga negotiated for the release of Mbundu captives, taken in previous conflicts, and advocated a mutual defense against common enemies.[408] Intrigued by life in Luanda, she received permission to stay temporarily, and in 1622, was baptized as Ana de Sousa. Nzinga returned to her brother's court adorned with gifts and newfound European-influenced changes, arousing both admiration and jealousy. Her half-brother's death in 1623 paved the way for her rise to power, and at forty-one, she became Queen of Ndongo and Matamba, though she preferred the title of King, so as to signify her status as ruler..[409]

The peace treaty signed with the Portuguese in Luanda in 1622 marked Nzinga's first victory. She sought to engage in trade with the Portuguese on her own terms, asserting her sovereignty as the leader of her nation, a goal she ostensibly achieved. But the Portuguese consistently failed to honor the treaty.[410] While they sought to avoid direct conflict with Nzinga's kingdom, they continued to subject an increasing number of Mbundu chiefs to feudal agreements, disregarding Nzinga's authority over those provinces. Unable to meet Portuguese demands, many chiefs allied with Nzinga, seeking refuge in her lands.[411]

In early 1645, the Dutch began providing military support to Nzinga in exchange for access to commercial trade. During this time, Nzinga was conducting military campaigns in Wambu territory, where many chiefs had been subjected to Portuguese rule.[412] She used Wambu captives as commodities in trade with the Dutch, with estimates suggesting she traded between 12,000 and 13,000 captives annually.[413] From 1641 to 1683, Portugal faced opposition from the Dutch, the Kingdom of Kongo, and Ndongo. At first, the Dutch did not share Nzinga's ambition to expel the Portuguese, as they regarded them as convenient trading partners in the slave trade. The Portuguese were relegated to the role of mere "middlemen," sharing the same dependence on the slave trade as any African state. They had transitioned from being the masters of the slave trade to becoming its most subservient participants.[414] During this period, the Kingdom of Kasanje assumed a pivotal role. By the late seventeenth century, Kasanje had emerged as the leading slave-trading kingdom in West Central Africa. Bolstered by strong military capabilities and armed with weapons acquired from the Portuguese, Kasanje had a history of navigating shifting alliances, aligning either with Nzinga or the governors in Luanda. In 1647, the Portuguese sought Kasanje's support, offering military assistance in exchange for siding against their common adversary. Tempted by the promise of vindication against Matamba, Kasanje was enticed further by the title of Captain General in the army of "His Faithful Majesty, the King of Portugal."[415]

The alliance dealt a significant blow to the African resistance movement. With the backing of Kasanje's Jaga warriors, the Portuguese managed to defeat the Mbundu-Kongo-Dutch coalition, assembling an army consisting of 140 Portuguese soldiers and 10,000 African soldiers, predominantly from Kasanje.[416] By 1648, Portugal had successfully driven the Dutch from both Angola and Brazil. In 1671, they reclaimed control of Luanda, establishing authority over the "Portuguese Kingdom of Angola." In the aftermath of the conflict, the Dutch were expelled, prompting the Portuguese to once again attempt negotiations with Nzinga.

Although Nzinga received letters from the king of Portugal and the governor of Luanda urging her to negotiate a peace agreement, she was deeply distrustful of the Europeans due to their failure to honor the 1622 treaty regarding Mbundu territorial and political sovereignty.[417] During diplomatic discussions, Queen Nzinga demanded the retreat of the Portuguese army from Mbaka and a formal apology for the violations committed by previous governors.[418] Additionally, she called for the return of Matamba lands invaded by the Kasanje. In exchange, she agreed to open the port to commerce, cease attacks against the Portuguese, and convert to Christianity. She refused to accept a clause in the peace treaty stipulating that she pay an annual tribute to the Portuguese Crown, which would nullify the entire treaty if not fulfilled.[419] Despite being seventy-five years old, Nzinga remained steadfast in her refusal to become a subject of Portugal, a stance she had maintained since her initial negotiations with the Portuguese. In her reply, she stated: "If your sovereign, the king of Portugal, wishes to return the portion of my kingdom of Ndongo that he seized by force, he should do so with integrity without resorting to deceit. If his intentions are sincere, negotiation should be conducted with honesty and in accordance with Christian principles. . . . I have the right to govern this land and do not answer to anyone. I am the undisputed ruler of this country and will never submit to servitude."[420] The Portuguese accepted Nzinga's terms, and the clause was removed, rendering the documents official in 1657.

Following her meeting with the Portuguese ambassadors, Nzinga proceeded to a chapel where she performed an act of great significance for her country. Standing before the altar, she retrieved the silver box containing her ancestors' bones and placed it in a dark corner. Then she knelt before the cross and kissed it.[421] Nzinga enacted a law imposing the death penalty for making offerings to or invoking non-Christian deities. All "idols" were ordered to be burned, and any remnants surrendered to the clergy. However, it seems that these rules and prohibitions were not strictly observed.[422] It is said that Nzinga no longer sought guidance from the Mussete ancestor safe, but she hadn't yet burned it either. Despite publicly embracing Christianity, she kept the silver box containing her brother's ashes nearby. Under pressure from the priests, she arranged a bonfire and burned all her jewelry, which the friars regarded as linked with non-Christian practices. She then entrusted the silver safe to a priest, requesting that it be transformed into a silver chandelier. In late 1662, the box was sent to a renowned goldsmith in Luanda for this purpose.[423] The silver from the Mussete ancestor box was melted down to create a chandelier, which Nzinga offered to the Church. Cavazzi recounts that when the chandelier was first used in the church, it began to oscillate violently, swinging from side to side. He believed this was because he had failed to bless the silver.[424] The swaying chandelier must have been an alarming omen for Nzinga and her subjects.

As the resistance movement weakened, Nzinga attempted to leverage Catholicism as a unifying factor in the national reconstruction effort. Despite successfully persuading Portuguese authorities to acknowledge Ndongo's independence and to assist in expelling the Kasanje from her territory, the treaty ultimately paved the way for Ndongo's downfall. Glasgow notes that the peace treaty neutralized the resistance movement led by Nzinga, making it legally impossible for her to attack the Europeans and their allies.[425] This limited maneuverability contributed to the eventual destruction of the Mbundu monarchy after Nzinga's death.

In 1661, Nzinga initiated the construction of a new capital, Uamba, situated two miles from the old one. Named after the river that flowed nearby, the new capital revolved around Nzinga's grand palace and a magnificent cathedral dedicated to Saint Anne. Nzinga had the streets adorned with crosses, inviting people to bow in reverence as they passed.[426] The layout and design of Uamba reflected Nzinga's aspiration to create a majestic city admired by both Africans and Europeans. The imperial palace and cathedral were prominently placed in the main square, with the palace featuring a complex labyrinth of corridors, all leading to the throne room.[427] When Queen Nzinga passed away in 1663, Cavazzi honored her request to have a Christian funeral. He dressed her in her chosen attire, placing a rosary and cross in her hands. Her grave was dug in the Church of Saint Anne, where her tomb, adorned with golden fabric, held treasures such as jewelry, cloth, and her bow and arrows. Following the ceremony, the chiefs of Nzinga's Kilombos were allowed to hold a Tambo funeral, with the condition set by Cavazzi that no humans or animals were to be sacrificed. The eight-day event was marked by music, lavish feasts, mock combats, and women reenacting scenes from Nzinga's life.[428]

Nzinga's sister, Mukambu-Mbandi Bárbara, received the royal arrow and bow and succeeded Nzinga as the Ngola of Ndongo and Matamba.[429] However, following Nzinga's death, the empire she had maintained began to disintegrate, much like the Kongo kingdom after Mvemba-a-Nzinga's reign. To thwart her Mbangala war general, Njinga-Mona, from grabbing power, Nzinga had arranged her sister's marriage to Ngola-Kanini João Guterres.[430] Mukambu-Mbandi Bárbara's death in 1666 sparked a succession conflict between Ngola-Kanini and Njinga-Mona. By 1671, the Portuguese governor of Angola, Francisco de Távora, had taken control. That same year, Ngola-a-Hari II, who had severed all ties of dependence with Portugal, was decapitated and his nephew Lourenço Mendonça was exiled to Brazil.

Pungo-a-Ndongo, the former capital of the Ndongo, was destroyed and fell under Portuguese control. Through Pungo-a-Ndongo the Portuguese could connect the trade routes leading to Mozambique. In the nineteenth century, the Portuguese plan to establish an inland fortress there led to tensions with Great Britain, sparking the "rose-colored map" dispute.

UNDER THE COMPASS AND THE RULER: THE LEGACY OF COLONIAL CARTOGRAPHY

A deep lash in the map's flesh:
American and African coastlines
sea of salt, blood, and tears:
A slave ship as knife.

Um talho fundo na carne do mapa:
Américas e Áfricas margeiam
mar de sal, sangue e lágrimas no meio:
Um navio negreiro como faca:

Oliveira Silveira (1941–2009)

The European delineation of African geographical boundaries initially centered on establishing sites for human resource extraction in so-called unexplored territories. Fifteenth-century European spatial concepts of Africa laid the groundwork for the colonizing project, which was later formalized during the Scramble for Africa (1884–1914), resulting in the division of the continent into artificial states shaped by European political and economic interests. These states, characterized by geographic borders that frequently diverged from how local populations organized their ethnic affiliations, served as the spatial framework upon which Western enterprise was built.[431] Just as we tend to assume that basic cultural concepts—such as towns, kings, families, cultures, and wealth—remain relatively consistent across civilizations and time periods, we also tend to view the formation of national borders as the result of similar historical processes. Even with contemporary critical perspectives, such as the growing recognition and acknowledgment of Indigenous lands in the Americas, the foundational paradigms that define the idea of the nation-state are rarely questioned.[432]

We generally envision the world—its continents and countries—as a cohesive whole. Within this framework, portrayals of the African continent—its countries, the formation and history of their borders, and the states they contain—often betray a profound collective obliviousness. The boundaries of African states were drawn by Europeans with little regard for Africa or its inhabitants, and they failed to align with historic, ethnic, or political boundaries established by Africans themselves.[433] In the modern "anomalous and anachronistic geographical framework" that continues to define most African political borders, African countries remain, as the geographer Ieuan Griffiths notes, "territorially identical to the European colonies they replaced."[434]

At the dawn of industrial-scale production, Africa's value surged, not only for its abundant resources and strategic trade routes but also as an expanding market for European goods.[435] European powers and the United States convened at the Berlin Conference of 1884–1885 to settle their own rivalries and power struggles without input from African rulers or representatives. Some of the conference's early deliberations addressed issues such as freedom of commerce in the Congo Basin and neighboring regions, as well as the abolition of the slave trade and related operations.[436] The Berlin Conference concluded with the signing of the General Act, which stipulated that the ratified agreements—signed by representatives of all participating powers—would be drawn up as a protocol and deposited in the archives of the German Empire.[437] The Protocol, which set forth directives for abolishing slavery, protecting free trade, and demarcating new African borders, became known as the Scramble for Africa. It was signed "in the name of Almighty God" by the presidents of the United States and the French Republic; the kings of Portugal and the Algarves, Spain, Italy, the Netherlands, Prussia, Hungary, and Denmark; the queen of the United Kingdom of Great Britain and Ireland; the duke of Luxembourg; the empress of the Indies; and the emperors of Germany, Austria, Russia, Sweden, and Norway.[438] By 1914, 90 percent of Africa would be under European occupation, with only Liberia and Ethiopia remaining independent.

The arbitrary partition and occupation of Africa followed artificial spatial concepts seen in other colonial settings: the 1494 Treaty of Tordesillas, which divided South America into eastern Portuguese and western Spanish colonial possessions; the fifteen proprietorships (or donatory captaincies) established in sixteenth-century Brazil; and the thirteen colonies founded in seventeenth- and eighteenth-century British North America. Administrative territories took the form of long, narrow strips stretching from the Atlantic coast inland—often with no clear inland boundaries, as the interior remained uncharted—and were demarcated by royal decree (Portuguese in Brazil; British in North America). Private entrepreneurs—merchants, colonial military men, and petty nobility—were awarded governing privileges over these land grants. The territories demarcated in the Land of the Holy Cross (Terra de Santa Cruz), later called Brazil, were granted to individually selected beneficiaries who received the title of captain-general. Portugal had already experimented with the captaincy system in other territories it occupied, such as the islands of Azores and Madeira. While the British Colonies and the Portuguese Captaincies were not the first colonial settlements on the American continent, they served as prototypes for modern states.

Following the Berlin Conference and the subsequent European occupation of Africa, coupled with the shift from monarchy to republic and the abolition of slavery in Brazil in 1888–1889, a noticeable rupture emerged in the historical trajectory of transatlantic nations. This disruption, despite periodic interactions and varying degrees of direct contact, led to a gradual distancing from the unfolding histories of African states and their counterparts in Brazil. Until more recent twenty-first-century migration movements, such as the influx of Angolans to Brazil, African states had, in part, become increasingly abstract and mythologized in the collective memory.[439]

QUEEN NZINGA'S KILOMBO AND ZUMBI DOS PALMARES' QUILOMBO

Zumbi dos Palmares and Queen Nzinga personified resistance; their stories intertwined across time. Both led multiethnic states and commanded guerrilla forces that directly challenged Portuguese colonial rule in Angola and Brazil. The historian Carlos Serrano, emphasizing Nzinga's enduring legacy in the collective memory of the Brazilian diaspora, points out that both she and Zumbi were united by the ethos of Quilombo resistance.[440] While the concept of Aruanda emerged as the first Afro-Brazilian symbol akin to Mother Africa, Queen Nzinga was among the earliest figures of colonial resistance. Over time, the idea of Aruanda eclipsed that of the maroon community of Palmares. Zumbi dos Palmares, for his part, would come to embody Nzinga's legacy of military and political defiance, ultimately becoming its most visible symbol.[441]

In 2002, on the twenty-seventh anniversary of Angola's independence, a statue of Queen Nzinga was erected in Luanda's commercial district. The inscription reads: "Mwene Njinga Mbandi, Sovereign of Ndongo and Matamba (1562–1663)." Among the monuments to Nzinga, her footprint carved into the rocks of Pungo-a-Ndongo remains the most emblematic of her presence. The site has evolved into a bustling hub for tourism and pilgrimage, drawing visitors who celebrate her legacy. In Brazilian Congada performances, Queen Nzinga is portrayed alongside the King of Kongo as an icon of a unified, mythical Africa.[442] One Congada chant narrates, "Here comes the King of Congo with his infantry Crown upon his head, / and Mary's rosary / (Chorus) / Hey, it is time to depart / and no one shall be left behind / The Virgin of the Rosary / will accompany us too / (Master) Oh, my Queen Nzinga / Tread lightly, / So the pebbles / won't shift from their resting place."[443]

Queen Nzinga's portrayal in Brazilian Congadas presents her as a formidable woman of unwavering conviction, known for dispatching skilled emissaries who embody her commitment to the dual pillars of effective resistance and diplomatic negotiation. She is represented as a fearless warrior who boldly confronts and overcomes her adversaries. Accompanied by her entourage, which includes ambassadors, *mocambas*, and *mufukas*, she appears in regal processions adorned with crowns, capes, emblems, and swords. These elements not only narrate her story but also articulate and summarize the hierarchies and political structures of the Central African states. Her symbols and regalia display the political and military organization of her realm and reflect the philosophical and spiritual tenets of her time.[444] The Congada thus serves as a distinctive medium for conveying and perpetuating history, infused with religious rites and myths that reinforce underlying beliefs and conduct. This celebration serves as a cultural vessel, conveying history in a manner distinctive to the memory construction of the society.[445] Historically in Africa, identities were defined by groups such as the Mbundu, Mbaka, Kasanje, Libolo, and Lunda, among others. The construct of a national identity known as Angola emerged during the slave trade and its expansion in the Americas. Diverse peoples gradually embraced this identity and organized themselves accordingly.[446]

Today's widespread celebration of Quilombos and their leaders, such as Zumbi, stands in stark contrast to an era when these potent symbols of historical leadership were largely muted. Reflecting on his treks to Serra da Barriga, the former capital of Palmares in Alagoas, the historian Joel Rufino dos Santos (1941–2015) described a time in the 1980s when such symbols of resistance were scarcely acknowledged in Brazil's national consciousness. He and his peers were among the few who ventured to this sacred place with a vision of its future significance, which seemed almost whimsical to the modest group accompanying him: "my colleague Willie from Brasília foresaw the site becoming a pilgrimage destination for Black Brazilians. The only reason the laughter wasn't resounding was the small audience. We were less than fifty people trekking in a north-south direction, along that kind of Chinese wall that, 290 years ago, was the capital of Palmares."[447] Rufino dos Santos describes the transformation of the Serra da Barriga from a forgotten landscape to a vibrant hub of cultural and spiritual pilgrimage, drawing thousands of visitors annually: "Fast forward six years, and we recalled Willie's prophecy. With each passing year, the visitors to Serra da Barriga increased: 50; 1,500; 5,000; again 5,000; 7,000, and by 1985, around 10,000."[448]

People from various faiths gathered there, creating a tapestry of cultural expressions that Rufino dos Santos likened to a religious experience, paralleling the rebirth of Zumbi's memory after centuries of obscurity. Indeed, just fifteen years prior, Zumbi dos Palmares was a figure shrouded in mystery: "Zumbi was nearly unknown, with all information about him fitting on a single book page. Some even questioned whether he was in fact a single historical figure."[449] Today, the reality could not be more different. Zumbi dos Palmares stands as one of the most venerated historical figures in Brazil and the African diaspora. The Brazilian national celebration on November 20 is a dynamic remembrance of life's victory over death and has taken on an almost mystical resonance within Brazilian culture.[450]

As Kamau Brathwaite articulates, "wherever there has been slavery, there has been maroonage."[451] The earliest known Brazilian quilombo dates to 1575, at the dawn of the transatlantic slave trade.[452] Defined by Portuguese colonial authorities "as settlements of five or more fugitive slaves," these communities often flourished through agriculture, trade, and a form of economic democracy—posing a stark contrast, and indeed a threat, to Portuguese colonial rule.[453] During the Dutch presence in Brazil, many enslaved Africans took advantage of the upheaval caused by the conflict between the two European empires and escaped to quilombos. The population of Palmares grew considerably during that period (from 6,000 to 20,000) and more quilombo towns were established around it. Palmares became a conglomeration of settlements, including Zumbi, Acotirene, Tabocas, Dambranganga, Subupira, Osenga, and Macaco.

The Republic of Palmares stood as a beacon of African resistance in Brazil for nearly a century (c. 1605–1695). It was also known as Angola Janga, deriving from *Ngola Rianga*, meaning "the first Ngola chief" or "the first area ruled by a Ngola in Brazil."[454] Palmares served as an open sanctuary for all those persecuted and marginalized by colonial society.[455] The maroon population may have reached nearly 30,000, and their lingua franca was a blend of Kimbundu, Portuguese, and various Tupi languages.[456] The quilombo towns of Palmares evolved from the seven nuclei that formed the Kasanje Kilombo. The first settlement, Serra do Macaco (also called Serra da Barriga, "Monkey" or "Belly" Mountains), was dubbed the "Royal City" by the Portuguese.[457] It was the capital of Palmares and home to its principal leaders: Ganga-Zumba and, later, Zumbi, the last king of Palmares. Subupira, the second city, served as the headquarters for military instruction.[458] All towns were protected by fences made of stone and wood. In the capital, this fortification was "triple-layered" and measured approximately 34 miles in circumference. Surrounding the perimeter were ditches covered by leaves, and beyond that, a large area where pointed stakes, tall enough to reach a man's throat or groin, were embedded in the ground in a circular formation. Nearby lands were leased to ranchers in exchange for intelligence about imminent attacks. Palmares's governance featured a council of chiefs, presided over by the principal leader. The government hierarchy operated through symbolic kinship: ministers were the leaders' "sons"; military leaders their "brothers"; quilombo leaders their "nephews"; other officers their "grandchildren"; and older women their "mothers."[459] As in the Kasanje Kilombo, Palmares created its own ancestral lineage, those who came to Palmares of their own free will became free citizens and referred to one another as *malungo*, akin to "comrade," from the Kikongo "mu alungo," meaning "in the ship."

The military campaign against Palmares, led by Domingos Jorge Velho (c. 1641–1705), was notable for both its scale and the tactics employed. A mestizo, Velho commanded a *bandeirante* army that essentially followed the same formation as the *guerra preta* ("Black War") in west-central Africa—the colonial police force that, since the writings of von Spix, has often been characterized as heroic. The historian Décio Freitas (1922–2004), however, in the early 1970s, more aptly described the *bandeirantes* as "nothing more than shock troops at the service of Portuguese colonials."[460] Velho led an army of nine thousand men to defeat Palmares—more than the seven thousand needed to defeat the Dutch. In one of the final confrontations, the maroons of Palmares were compelled to adopt an unfamiliar tactic: frontal assault. They fought at the cliff edges, resulting in the deaths of approximately 500 maroons who fell—a tragic event that contributed to the enduring narrative of collective suicide.[461] Although Palmares was proclaimed fallen in 1695, reports persisted into December that Zumbi remained alive. It is believed that, under torture, a maroon from Palmares disclosed Zumbi's hiding place; Zumbi and six companions were found there and killed on November 20, 1695. In the wake of Palmares's fall, surviving maroons formed new quilombos that evolved into guerrilla groups across the northeast.[462] By 1730, around one thousand maroons were still living in Serra da Barriga, the original heartland of Palmares. Some survivors established the Quilombo do Cumbe in Paraíba, which persisted until its destruction in 1731.[463]

The Bissau-Guinean historian José Lingna Nafafé posits that Palmares could not have sustained itself for almost a century without partnering with Indigenous peoples and achieving some level of legal recognition within its territory.[464] He examines the dynamics of Brazilian maroons through the lens of seventeenth-century Mbundu legal principles regarding captives. According to Nafafé, the amnesty laws of the Mbundu of Angola were founded on three principles: the Principle of Return, the Principle of Safe Haven, and the Principle of Asylum.[465] The Principle of Return, or *Mucuâ*—meaning "home"—pertains to one's origins and citizenship. It is anchored in the broader concept of *nbata rinène*, "a great house" or "a great community" to which, under proper procedures, one almost always has the option to return.[466] *Mucuâ* embodies not only the right to seek freedom but also a legitimate route through which to achieve it. The Principle of Safe Haven offers amnesty to those in search of refuge from a despotic patron or chief. This principle can be invoked by individuals questioning the legality of their capture or its process, provided they secure sponsorship from an alternate patron.[467] The Principle of Asylum allows an individual, whether convicted or simply accused without sufficient evidence, to relocate to a different province to evade punishment. This principle stipulates that one must not return to the place where they faced allegations, especially for serious offenses such as murder or witchcraft.[468] For these fugitives, escaping was not merely a choice but a necessity, supported by a legal framework, the assistance of a sponsor, and a safe destination. Palmares was a recognized sanctuary that enjoyed legal autonomy and collaboration with Indigenous Brazilians.

Zumbi emerged as a prominent symbol of resistance, his legacy interwoven with the influences of African figures, especially Queen Nzinga. The quilombola resistance, as highlighted by the historian Rufino dos Santos, challenges reductive views of the master-slave relationship, revealing a complex interplay of active defiance and the creation of alternative societies.[469] Ganga Zumba sought a precarious balance with colonizers, a strategy that Zumbi would later repudiate as he ascended from the role of leader of a mocambo to that of military chief. Zumbi's rise is marked by strategic cunning and mirrors the unyielding determination of African monarchs, including the formidable Queen Nzinga of Ndongo and Matamba. Detailed historical records reveal Zumbi's strategic acumen as he fortified the quilombo's capital, the Cerca Real do Macaco, and repositioned his forces for a decisive battle against colonial powers, seeking not mere skirmishes but an all-encompassing victory.[470]

In Brazil, Palmares and Zumbi have become symbols and catalysts for imagining a different future. Alongside Haiti—the other major autonomous state organized by the Black diaspora—Palmares exemplifies not only the vision of an alternative nation but its actual establishment. Kamau Brathwaite captures this potency:

> In 1790, the slaves of Saint-Domingue successfully revolted against Napoleon Bonaparte and the French Empire. Under the leadership of Toussaint Louverture, they conducted the first successful slave rebellion in history. That is an event of tremendous importance. That is a victory for the underclass which is stupendous. And still no one in the Caribbean has any knowledge of it, no one in the Caribbean has internalized it . . . People do not even understand very much about Toussaint Louverture. Again, he has been demonized and distorted. Therefore, it does not allow us that trigger into the future which we would normally have had or that we should have had. Here is a victory that we should understand and use. **We should fly that flag.**[471]

This flag, symbolizing the achievements of maroons and the establishment of autonomous republics, has flown in Brazil since time immemorial. In modern times, the legacy of Palmares has been commemorated and reimagined, particularly by the Brazil's Black Movement. The Black Unified Movement (Movimento Negro Unificado, or MNU), founded in the late 1970s, played a pivotal role in challenging the myth of racial democracy and recovering and honoring the history and values of Afro-Brazilian culture. The quilombo-maroon ethos continues to inspire a vision for a more inclusive and democratic society, rooted in the spirit of Palmares. In 1978, a MNU National Assembly held in Salvador announced:

> We, Black Brazilians, proud descendants of Zumbi, the leader of the Black Republic of Palmares, stand together today to proclaim to all Brazilians our true and significant day: November 20, the National Day of Black Consciousness. This day honors the memory of Zumbi, the great Black national leader who pioneered the first and only Brazilian attempt to establish a free, democratic society inclusive of Blacks, Indigenous peoples, and Whites, and who achieved significant economic and political progress. The fruits of this endeavor were evident across all quilombos.[472]

In 2002, Sueli Carneiro, the driving force behind Geledés—a key non-profit organization in Brazil—reflected on the evolution of the Black Movement, and particularly the MNU, as it stood at the dawn of the new millennium.[473] The MNU, which emerged in São Paulo in 1978, marked a bold shift from the cultural focus of the 1960s and 1970s toward a more politicized agenda. According to Carneiro, drawing from leftist ideologies, the MNU adopted a definitive stance on racial issues, signifying a pivotal moment in its political development.[474] It was a dynamic Black movement and a long-awaited cohesive political force, propelled by influential figures such as Abdias do Nascimento (1914–2011), whose reputation extended beyond São Paulo to national prominence.[475] One of the MNU's notable victories was its confrontation with the pervasive myth of Brazil's racial democracy. However, "despite the groundbreaking nature of this challenge, the movement's achievements were frequently overlooked, and its activism was systematically obscured."[476] Nonetheless, the MNU succeeded in sparking new research and engaging with non-Black entities in the conversation. This feat was all the more remarkable given the daunting task of dismantling the myth of racial democracy, an idea deeply ingrained in the national consciousness and endorsed by official state policy.[477]

In 1980, the Zumbi Memorial was inaugurated in Volta Redonda, Rio de Janeiro. According to Abdias do Nascimento, this was a memorial built by and for the Black community in order to recover the memory of the first Black republic in Brazil.[478] In 1988 the Fundação Cultural Palmares (Palmares Cultural Foundation), connected to the Ministry of Culture, was established with the legal mandate to "promote the preservation of cultural, social and economic values which resulted from Black influence in the formation of Brazilian society," as well as to "work to identify the remaining quilombo communities, proceed with their official recognition and boundary demarcation, and grant them proper titles of land ownership."[479]

In 1989, the documentary *Órí*, named after the Yoruba concept of destiny, was released. Directed by the Jewish historian Raquel Gerber, the film was scripted and narrated by Beatriz Nascimento (1942–1995), an activist, historian, poet, and seminal figure in the Afro-Brazilian cultural movement.[480] Presenting a woven filmic narrative in the form of a poetic collage, the film showcases the Black Movement in Brazil during the 1970s and 1980s, placing it within the broader context of Black movements across the diaspora. It starts with the narration of a statement that poignantly encapsulates the disconnect between Africa and Brazil: "To us, in the Western Hemisphere, Africa is a buried continent. It's a continent we don't know much about. It's a frozen knowledge. Its people are frozen—in our relationships, our communications, our subconscious, and in who they are."[481] After a pause, the narrator posits:

> This raises the question posed by Black thinkers shaping the concept of maroonage: Who is the maroon? What does maroonage mean today? It is a quest to unearth a concept, a historical fact, a memory, an ideology, a legend—personified by a man, Zumbi dos Palmares. Maroonage engenders a sense of nationality rooted in African and Bantu identity, a nation woven into a Bantu tapestry—a network of relationships among various African ethnic groups. This sense is grounded in the very root of the word "Bantu," from "untu," denoting communal bonds. It is through this root that communication unfolds. It is through this root that Africans come to know one another.[482]

After a cut, the documentary transitions to a scene showcasing a parade by Vai-Vai, one of São Paulo's premier Carnaval groups, with narration provided by the Black rights activist Ciro Nascimento:

> In Brazil, African kingdoms have been recreated in Umbanda and Candomblé, samba schools, in Maracatu, Ranchos, and Frevo Carnaval ensembles. These cultural forms are continually recreated and thrive in an antagonistic environment. Vai-Vai [a prominent samba school] exemplifies Bantu civilization in São Paulo—its structure, the traditional cordão, symbolizes a kingdom complete

with king, queen, page, and courtiers.... You can see how Bantu influence permeates the drums' rhythms, the collective spirit of participants and even their physical presence.[483]

While the camera presents an aerial view of the *quadra da escola de samba*, the headquarters of the Vai-Vai Carnaval organization, Beatriz Nascimento resumes narrating and concludes:

> Quilombo is a history. The word itself also has a history. It possesses a typology that varies according to geographic region, across time, and in relation to its territory. Quilombo, for us, is not merely a geographical space; it is a space that exists within a symbology. I have the right to be in the space I occupy, within this system, this nation, within this geographical myth that is the Capitania of Pernambuco. The Earth is my Quilombo. My space is my Quilombo. Wherever I am is my place. My place is wherever I am.[484]

The documentary *Ôrí* follows Beatriz Nascimento's cadence, perspective, and journey as she explores quilombos across the Americas and Africa. This quest was not hers alone, but part of a collective pursuit—an entire movement that would gain increasing visibility and force. Beatriz Nascimento was murdered at the height of her creative, spiritual, and intellectual journey. Her groundbreaking conceptualization of quilombos as a contemporary ideology—and her recognition of maroon societies as the earliest, and perhaps only, proposal for a Brazilian nation since Portuguese colonization—remained, up until very recently, largely uncredited as part of her radical historical intervention.

Abdias do Nascimento, who would sometimes sign his name as "um Quilombola dos Palmares," or "a maroon from Palmares," became the main leader of the modern maroonage movement in Brazil. It was his belief that in contemporary Brazil, a vast network of associations constitutes contemporary quilombos: fraternities, clubs, corporations, centers, samba groups, *gafieira* dance halls, and *terreiro* grounds for Candomblé and Umbanda.[485] For Nascimento, "either the legal or illegal quilombos were and are a unity, a human ethnic and cultural affirmation, which integrates a practice of liberation and assumes the power of its own history."[486] Abdias do Nascimento—who, to my knowledge, quoted Beatriz Nascimento on this point only once—referred to this "Afro-Brazilian praxis" as *quilombismo* (maroonage). In contemporary Brazil, *quilombismo* is the belief in the possibility of creating of a society grounded in true social and economic democracy, modeled on the structure that existed in the quilombos, particularly Palmares.

THREE ROCKS ACROSS THE ATLANTIC: FOUNDATION MYTHS OF AFRICAN-BRAZILIAN CIVILIZATION

Throughout history, foundation myths have continuously evolved, shifting like colored pieces in a kaleidoscope in response to migrations, encounters, mergers, conflicts, and alliances. These myths have existed both independently and in relation to one another, with varying degrees of fusion and prominence. Some have ascended to hegemonic status, while others have lapsed or faded from view—though they may still underlie prevailing structural concepts. Embedded within our deepest reservoir of existential paradigms and enshrined in our collective treasury of myths and archetypes, foundation myths play a pivotal role in meaning-making and existential cognition. They form the bedrock of our relationship to the land, shape our identities within communities, and delineate boundaries that either conform to or deviate from our concepts of who and what we believe ourselves to be a part of (or apart from). They inform our understanding of power dynamics, hierarchies, and the spectrum of possibilities and impossibilities in forging connections and negotiating cultural similarities and differences. Across different times and spaces, the layering and sedimentation of these foundational myths continually shape our lives and our perception of the world around us.

For those of us raised within Western cultural paradigms, the foundation myths of ancient Rome and Greece have monopolized our education, dictating what should be recognized as legitimate knowledge and determining acceptable disciplines and perspectives. Indigenous foundation myths, when mentioned at all, often appeared as mere footnotes, relegated to the status of anecdotal folklore. African foundation myths were largely absent from consideration, except when selectively appropriated by nationalistic regimes, as occurred in 1930s Brazil. During that period, glorified narratives of African origin were curated to highlight cultural expressions deemed uniquely Brazilian. These narratives served as the framework for constructing the image of an independent, modern Brazil and continue to be adapted as patriotic tropes. While they uphold Brazil as a sovereign nation, they largely disregard the contributions of foundational African civilization mythologies, particularly those originating beyond Brazil's immediate scope of influence.

In recent years, various African-Brazilian cultural expressions have garnered recognition and been officially acknowledged as part of the national cultural heritage. A crucial milestone occurred at the turn of the twenty-first century with the passage of a Brazilian bill mandating the inclusion of African and Indigenous history and culture in national education programs. This legislative accomplishment reflects ongoing efforts to reform the education system and expand historical perspectives, archetypes, imagery, and cultural references beyond the confines of the Greco-Roman canon.

To move beyond the conventional starting point anchored in the iconic imagery of fifteenth-century Portuguese caravels crossing the Atlantic and venturing into the Indian Ocean, we must reposition ourselves, adjust our lens, and seek out less familiar landscapes and historical actors. By exploring potential African perspectives, we open the door to studying other ancient civilizations and alternative mythic frameworks, and visualizing landscapes, individuals, interactions, and epochs that remain largely unexplored. To grasp the evolution of African civilizations in Brazil and honor their historical narratives and foundation myths, we must examine the influence and significance of these myths across diverse chronological and geographical eras and contexts. This entails considering the interplay among various migration routes and geographical features that have shaped cultural values and points of reference.

Informed by European languages, our terms for designating spaces, entities, and concepts inevitably carry specific conceptualizations and paradigms that are often foreign to non-European cultures. As we approach the original foundational realms that shaped the birth and development of African-Brazilian civilization, it is crucial to highlight a key *caveat*: translations are, at best, rough approximations. We have limited and inadequate tools at our disposal. Our understandings of concepts such as towns, realms, families, cultures, wealth, and ethics will often differ across civilizations, places, and historical periods. Due to lack of proficiency in the languages central to the multiethnic and multilingual dynamics of the colonization of the Americas—coupled with a persistent tendency to prioritize European languages, structures, and disciplines—it is easy to unintentionally oversimplify and homogenize differences. For example, when referring to Portuguese, Yoruba, or Kongo kingdoms or empires, we must consistently remind ourselves that these terms do not align precisely with notions of governance or sociopolitical organization, or the intricate relationships that characterize them. The concepts and attributes of "king" or "emperor," for instance, fall short of capturing the historically rooted, culturally specific meanings that have evolved over centuries for a Yoruba *oba*, a Kongo *mani* or a Ndongo *ngola*.

To conceptualize African-Brazilian foundation myths within the framework of contemporary African cosmological values and references, I propose mapping the contours of their fundamental structure. Through a conceptual representation of its multiple narratives, I suggest imagining African-Brazilian civilization as primarily rooted in two major African states and centers of ancient civilization. By considering foundation myths in their sacred and secular roles, we can situate the historical and mythological origins of African-Brazilian civilization at the capitals of two ancient kingdoms or empires: Ile-Ife (Ilé-Ifẹ̀) and Mbanza-Kongo. Although African-Brazilian civilization emerged from the convergence of extensive lineages across various realms, for the sake of epistemological orientation, we can identify these two principal lineages symbolized by the towns of Ile-Ife and Kongo. In Brazil, the realms of Ile-Ife (the center of the Oyo empire and the Dahomey kingdom) and Mbanza-Kongo (the center of the united federation of the Kongo), are juxtaposed with at least one other realm: the center of the Ndongo Kingdom. While Ndongo's capital was Pungo-a-Ndongo in Malange, present-day north-central Angola, the realm that emerged more prominently in African-Brazilian collective memory—and attained a spiritual status parallel to Ile-Ife—was Luanda.

The Kikongo proverb cited at the beginning of this section reverberates throughout Brazil in both direct and indirect forms. The concept and image of three rocks supporting a pot, where a civilization is metaphorically "cooked," provide an ancestral framework for envisioning the three "mountains" that act as the cradle for African-Brazilian civilization. Inspired by the teachings of Queen Isabel Casimira of the Guarda Treze de Maio teachings, I tried reading from the corner of my eye, in the eye's mind ("na mente do olho") (see chapter 7). From the corner of my eye, I imagined a nonexistent landscape and drafted its chart. I share this visual concept, best described as an ever-shifting cosmos balanced on three stones. I propose imagining three sustaining stones, or mountains of an Africa-in-Brazil: two mountains represent parallel political, economic, and administrative structures (homes to monarchs, governors, and councils), while the third symbolizes overlapping spiritual and ethical values (homes to gods, ancestors, and deities): (1) **Mountain One—Kongo and Ndongo Kingdoms or Federations**—Capitals: Mbanza-Kongo, Kabasa, and Matamba; Rulers: the Ntotila of Mbanza-Kongo, the Mani of other Kongo provinces, and the Ngola who ruled Ndongo; (2) **Mountain Two—Ọ̀yọ́ Empire and the Dahomey Kingdom**—Capitals: Ọ̀yọ́-Ilé and Abomey; Rulers: the Ọ̀yọ́'s Aláàfin, the Fon Fiaŋutsu (or its shortened form, Fia), and the Dahomean king, along with the co-king known as the "king-as-prince" (see chapter 8); (3) **Mountain Three—Pungo-a-Ndongo, Ilé-Ifẹ̀, Cana, and Luanda/Aruanda**—Rulers: Nzambi (Zambi) and Lemba; Obàtálá, Onilé, and Mawu-Lisa; and Rainha Ginga, Rei Congo, Caboclos, and Orixás.

The image of these three mountains represents a generalization that spans space and time, from disparate to analogous contexts. The relationship between spirituality and political power varied markedly by region. In Dahomey and Ọ̀yọ́, political power and authority were closely intertwined with the sacred. By contrast, West Central African regions lacked a unified governance model and some states had no kings. There was never, for example, a Benguela kingdom. Centralized states like Kongo and Ndongo existed, but the Ovimbundu developed a model of decentralized power. Even in regions where monarchs ruled, there was no state religion in the formal sense. Power was not deified in West Central Africa as it was in Dahomey–Ọ̀yọ́, and religion did not serve as the primary vehicle for constructing political authority, unlike in Europe.

The West Central African concept of the sacred is, first and foremost, connected to healing. Disease is understood not as an individual affliction but as a collective phenomenon—an expression of humanity's disruption of the world's harmony. The role of the *nganga* is to restore order. In Western frameworks, the *nganga* is called a "priest doctor" or healer practicing "traditional medicine." However, the Western bifurcation of medicine and religion does not apply within African cosmologies. Equating terms across these systems can lead to significant misunderstandings and misinterpretations. By outlining key elements of an Afro spiritual grammar, we can reflect cautiously on how Western concepts, especially beyond Africa, have historically flattened these differences. Though less stark today, these divergences still retain their specificities.

At **Mountain One**, the numbering is used purely for differentiation, with no implication of chronological sequence or hierarchical importance, I positioned the Kongo and Ndongo kingdoms, collectively known in Brazil as Kongo-Angola. This cultural group established a sacred realm in Luanda, which came to be known in Afro-Brazilian cosmology as Aruanda. Ntotila, Mani, and Ngola, the original titles for monarchs in these regions are rarely referenced in Brazil today. Instead, the monarchs preserved in Afro-Brazilian oral literature include Rainha Ginga or Jinga (Queen Nzinga Mbandi) and Rei do Congo or Caricongo (Curiboca, Cabouco)—a more generic reference to the *Ntotila* or *Mani* of Kongo. These refer, in particular, to the elected king of the Kongo federation and its capital, though it is important to recall that the Kongo polity included various Bamani, or regional rulers.

Cosmologically, Zambi (Nzambi-a-Mpungu) is the God of Creation, while Lemba (Lembarenganga, Lemba Nganga)—venerated as the Supreme God and sharing attributes with the Orisha Obatala (Oxalá)—is prominently acknowledged in Brazil through various spiritual entities known as Caboclos. The term Caboclo has historically referred broadly to Indigenous peoples and, in religious contexts, to deified Indigenous ancestors. It aligns with the Yoruba concept of Onilé, the deified original owner of the land, who, under different epithets, is honored throughout Afro-Brazilian cosmologies. In Yorubaland, Onilé is worshipped by Ogboni societies—sociocultural institutions that function as initiatic councils of elders, a town council, and an electoral body responsible for selecting and, if necessary, deposing kings.[487] The Yoruba terms Onilé and Onilẹ́ can be translated as the "owner of the house" and "owner of the land" respectively.[488] In Brazilian-Yoruba Candomblé, Onilẹ, as the owner of the land, was a concept adapted to a new context.[489]

In his 1889 Brazilian Portuguese dictionary, the lexicographer Macedo Soares (1838–1905) investigated possible etymologies for the Brazilian Portuguese term *caboclo*.[490] Drawing on dictionaries published in 1779 and 1889, Soares suggests two underexplored possibilities: *caboco* and *curiboca*.[491] In Kikongo, these terms would translate as *káboco* and *kuriboca*. Assis Júnior defines *káboco* as a "speaker, lecturer, preacher; someone who is eloquent in their speeches" and *kuriboca* as "to preach, to lecture, to pray in public."[492] These definitions are intrinsically related to the ancestral Caboclo spirits, who in ritual contexts, communicate with the living through visual cosmograms, chants, proverbs, lectures, and intimate spiritual consultations and advice. Soares also links Caboclo with the term *cabouco*, which was documented by Portuguese colonial writer Alfredo de Sarmento in 1889. Sarmento referred to "Dembo Cabouco" as someone who he encountered in Angola. While *dembo* derives from the Kikongo title Ndémbu, meaning "an authority figure superior to that of a 'soba' or who has 'sobas' under their jurisdiction," *Cabouco*, in this context, designates a specific geographic area.[493] Macedo Soares adds that it would not be unlikely for the word *caboclo* to have originated in Angola.[494] *Soba*, a Kimbundu title for a community leader with political authority, was adopted by the Portuguese across Central Africa as a generic term for "chief," even in regions where neither "chief" nor "soba" were relevant concepts.[495] Dembo Cabouco, the chief of sobas who Sarmento met in Angola in 1889, either held authority over "all provinces" (as per Soares's dictionary entry) or, most likely (according to Assis Júnior's entry), over Káboco only.[496]

Caboclo thus also becomes associated with Caboco, which evokes a paramount geographic point of passage and remembrance in Kongo-Angola cosmology. In the dictionary entry for *káboco*, Assis Júnior defines the term not only as a "lecturer" or "preacher," but also attributes to it this secondary geographic resonance. Caboco today designates a small hamlet in Kwanza Norte province, a settlement of likely precolonial origin and absent from colonial cartography.[497]

At **Mountain Two**, I position Oyo (Ọ̀yọ́) and Dahomey, known in Brazil as Nago-Jeje-Ketu. This cultural group preserved the geographic term referring to their original sacred center: Ile-Ife. In Yorubaland, the current ruler of Ile-Ife is the Óòni, Oba Adeyeye Enitan Ogunwusi, Ọjájá II, who ascended to the throne in 2015. In Brazil, the rulers of a parallel, conceptual Ile-Ife are envisioned as *Orixá* (Orisha) gods. While all *Orixás* are depicted as queens and kings, some possess distinct regal attributes, notably Xangô (Shango), lord of thunder and the *oxê* (ọ̀ṣẹ̀), the double-edged axe. As the political sovereign of the Yoruba people and the third king of Ọ̀yọ́, Xangô holds the title of Aláàfìn, signifying ownership of all palaces. In Africa and its diaspora, he is addressed with reverence as Kabeisilê (Kábiyèsi), meaning "His Majesty."[498]

At **Mountain Three**, we stand where space and time converge. From its peak, gazing at the water below and the sky above, we see a sunlit, glittering cross, shaped by flickering reflections across two axes: the Ndongo–Kongo axis, stretching from east to west, and the Dahomey–Ọ̀yọ́ axis, stretching from south to north. As these axes accelerate and spiral in unison, we catch glimpses and notes of the Children of the Rosary, the Children of Gandhy, and other Children, countless extended lineages.

The last chapter and the final considerations will explore the living sanctuaries of wisdom, innovation, and resistance on Mountains Two and Three.

9
Ìtàn

Ancestral Genealogies: Oshala Came Before Us

OYO AND ILE-IFE: MIND, HEART, AND SOUL

There were people from all nations except the Nago.
Mr. João Lopes (1930–2004)

Having circled around Mountain One, envisioning some of its layers of Brazilian Kongo, Angola, and Mozambique cultures, we now ascend Mountain Two, home to Brazilian Yoruba and Ewe communities. Initially, we encountered the fragmentation, conflicts, and interactions of the Kongo Federation and the kingdoms of Ndongo and Matamba. Now we shift our focus to two other major African states, the Oyo (Ọ̀yọ́) Empire and the proto-kingdom of Dahomey, and explore their conflicts and alliances. At Mountain Three, ancestral memories of realms and beings will converge. Here, ancient capitals, rulers, and heroes gather as ancestors, drawn together by shared traits, complementarities, and the needs and capabilities of the living. The African-Brazilian civilization is "cooked" on the balance provided by this mountain tripod: two standing parallel like ridges, and a third concentric, lying subterranean. The future of these intersecting, intertwined pasts is at the crossroads of contemporary diasporic fabulation and the immemorial ebb and flow of sacred and secular exchanges from Africa to Brazil, back to Africa and then back, again and again.

Starting in Yorubaland (modern-day Nigeria, Togo, and Benin), we encounter the ancient realm of Ile-Ife (Ilé-Ifẹ̀), which has long served as both a geographic and spiritual nexus for Africans and their descendants. Since the seventh century

BCE, well before the concept of "Yoruba" emerged, Ile-Ife had evolved into one of the earliest kingdoms in sub-Saharan Africa, growing increasingly powerful. By the twelfth century CE, Ife was an urban center and the sacred and secular homeland for all future Yoruba states. In the ancestral dynasties of Yorubaland, Oduduwa is revered as the first Oòni, or divine king of Ile-Ife, and the ancestor of all future Yoruba kings. Oranyan, heir to Oduduwa, the Oòni, or king of Ile-Ife, founded Oyo and served as its first Alaafin.

Between the fifteenth and eighteenth centuries, organized kingdoms dominated the Guinea coast, including the Edo kingdom of Benin, the Fon kingdom of Dahomey, and several Yoruba kingdoms, with Oyo being the most prominent.[1] In Brazil, mythical geographic references such as Ife and Benin were complemented by the original kingdoms of Kétou (Ketu/Keto) and Ìjèṣà (Ijesha/Ijexá). Over time, the origin stories of these former kingdoms and their capitals became intertwined and condensed with that of Ile-Ife.[2] John Thornton, in his analysis of the formation of the Oyo Empire and other kingdoms like Igala, Dahomey, Allada, Whydah, and Olukumi, explores how various states developed traditions that traced their roots to Yoruba mythology. He notes that while these narratives generally maintained a consistent structure, the specific names of the countries of origin evolved in response to changing circumstances. For example, Thornton points out how the creator god of the Igala kingdom, Oghene, came to be associated with the Yoruba city of Ife.[3]

European historiography indicates that around 1485, a Portuguese expedition led by a certain João Afonso de Aveiro reached Edo in the Benin kingdom. Despite Aveiro's inability to differentiate the Igala Kingdom (where he had actually arrived) from the Benin kingdom, it is generally accepted that this was when the Portuguese entered Yorubaland.[4] During this period, from 1483 to 1504, Oba Ozolua ruled the Benin kingdom. According to the Yoruba scholar Jacob Egharevba, King Ozolua "fought and won no less than two hundred battles, earning him the epithet Ozolua n' Ibaromi, Ozolua the conqueror."[5]

The Earth Is Spreading!

The Yoruba narrative of their civilization's origins revolves around the creation gods Oduduwa and Obatala. According to various accounts, including one recorded by Pierre Fatumbi Verger in "Olofin-Oduduwa cria o mundo em lugar de Oxalá" (Olofin-Oduduwa Creates the World in Place of Obatala), published in *Lendas africanas dos orixás* (*African Tales of the Orishas*), the story unfolds as follows:[6]

In the realm of the Beyond, beyond a world which didn't yet exist, lived Olodumare, the Almighty God. He didn't reside alone but in the company of four hundred and one *imole* Orishas, beings he had created himself.[7] Initially, he created six hundred *imole* Orishas, keeping two hundred to his right and four hundred to his left. Discord plagued the two hundred on his right, who lived in constant arguments and disputes. Soon enough, Olodumare lost patience and sent one hundred and ninety-nine of them back to the Nothingness. Only one among these remained—the enchanted ironsmith Ogun, who was appointed leader of the remaining four hundred *imole*. From then on, four hundred and one Orishas lived with Olodumare in the ethereal realm of Ile Orun.

When Olodumare decided it was time to create Ile Aiye, the world of the living, he summoned the four hundred and one Orishas and shared his vision with them. In the new space, each Orisha would be given a realm to rule. Guided by Orunmila, the Witness of Fate, each of them would receive all the tools and power necessary for the development of their realms. Olodumare called upon his main assistant, Obatala, the Owner of the White Cloth, and entrusted him with the most crucial mission in the creation of Aiye: "While all Orishas have important roles in this project, you will lead and advise them," he instructed Obatala, presenting him with the *apo iwa*, the bag of life, emphasizing that all instructions should be followed very closely.

Before leading the journey to the place where Ile Aiye would take shape, Obatala, following Olodumare's directions, consulted the diviner Orunmila. All Orishas, including Ogun and the *imole*, were to receive guidance from the Ifa oracle before departing. When Orunmila advised Obatala to make an offering to Eshu, the Trickster, Obatala took offense. How could he who was so powerful, who had the control of the *apo iwa*, the bag of life, be asked to make sacrifices to a younger and lesser *imole* like Eshu? Obatala understandably failed to grasp Eshu's importance as Onibode, the Guardian of All Borders. Until that moment in History, no border had yet been crossed.

Ignoring Orunmila's advice, Obatala led the four hundred *imole* through the desert. The journey proved longer than expected, and they had not taken enough water. Obatala felt parched when he spotted a palm tree. Unaware that the trickster Eshu could have put that palm tree on his path. Obatala made a hole in the trunk of the tree and the juice of the plant started to pour out. Obatala drank the palm wine until he passed out drunk. He fell unconscious by the road. The *imole* sat around Obatala, waiting for him to recover consciousness. All of them waited, except one. Olofin Oduduwa, who had performed all the offerings exactly as Orunmila's had advised, witnessed Obatala's debacle with dismay. Observing Obatala's unconscious state and the dropped *apo iwa*, Oduduwa seized the bag and retraced his steps to Olodumare.

Olodumare, who was already aware of Obatala's negligence, bestowed upon Oduduwa the authority to lead all the *imole*, tasking him with completing the mission. Returning to find Obatala still sound asleep, Oduduwa informed the *imole* of his new role and outlined his project to accomplish such a difficult mission. Oduduwa then secured his four hundred thousand chains to a stake in the beyond realm of Ile Orun. He climbed down the chain rope, until he got to the last chain. It was then that he saw an enormous body of water. He untied the *apo iwa* and released its brown powder into the water. The powder quickly turned into a mountain above the water's surface. He then released a five-legged hen he had with him. The hen landed on the mountain and started to scratch the earth and spread it around. The Earth started taking shape, stretching itself more and more. In joy, Oduduwa shouted: "Ilè nfè!" meaning "the Earth is spreading!" Unintentionally, he had named the land which would eventually be known to all as Ile-Ife.

Once the hen completed its mission of spreading and shaping the ground of the new world of Ile Aiye, Oduduwa sent down a chameleon to check if the earth was firm enough. When assured that the land was ready, he invited all the Orishas to descend with him. Most of them did, but some stayed behind with Obatala waiting for him to wake up. Eventually, Obatala regained consciousness and sought forgiveness from Olodumare, who granted him the task of creating life on Earth: "You didn't create the earth, but I'll give you a second chance," said Olodumare. "You are now in charge of the creation of human beings, the animals, the birds, and the plants."[8]

The relationship between Oduduwa and Obatala in the Yoruba creation narrative suggests a potential chronology of migration and shifts in political power. According to Ulli Beier (1922–2011), the German literary scholar and promoter of Nigerian literature, this foundational myth holds both mythological and political significance.[9] Beier explains that the myth of the creation of Ile-Ife aims to establish Oduduwa as the senior leader of all Orishas, as he assumes the role originally attributed to Obatala, his older brother.[10] While Obatala can be viewed as "a representative of the aboriginal inhabitants of the area," Oduduwa may represent "a specific wave of immigration."[11] Politically, attributing the foundation of Ile-Ife to Oduduwa asserts the city of Ife's seniority over other Yoruba towns, a claim that was later contested by the Oyo empire.[12]

Following Beier's interpretation, the Nigerian historian Babatunde Aremu Agiri argues that while the Oduduwa myth of Yoruba and Oyo origins establishes Oduduwa's cosmological status among the other Orishas, politically it contains a historical reference to a migration wave from the east.[13] Cosmologically, Oduduwa "descended from heaven and created the earth at Ife," which has since been regarded by most Yoruba as the center of the world and their civilization. Politically, Oduduwa was a leader who originated from the east and "fought and conquered the earlier inhabitants of Ife, represented by the term 'Igbo.'"[14] Agiri suggests the existence of a pre-Oduduwa group in Ife and its subsequent conquest.[15] He speculates that the earlier center of this civilization may have been the town of Oba. Drawing from oral traditions of Orikis of the Oba people found near the city of Akure, it is possible to glean the following information: there was an earlier agricultural center in Ife; the Oba worshipped a sky-god associated with making rain and creating the day; the name of this god may have been Obatala; and there was a taboo against drinking palm wine.[16]

The conquest of this civilization by the Oduduwa group is commemorated in the annual Itapa festival in Ife, which reenacts Oduduwa's victory over Obatala in battle. Initially exiled, Obatala was later readmitted to the town and into the pantheon. The festival's performance, as described by Babatunde Agiri, attempts to encapsulate what likely was a lengthy process of conquest, reconciliation, and assimilation.[17] Before the Oduduwa group's migration, a network of towns, each connected to their own indigenous gods, had already established a Yoruba civilization. Upon their arrival, the Oduduwa group faced the challenge of legitimizing themselves within some of the existing religious and political practices.[18] According to Agiri, the Oduduwa episode likely represented a significant, albeit not necessarily brief, moment in the political development of some Yoruba-speaking communities. It appears that a reinvigorated Ife state was established, which gradually subdued the remaining pre-Oduduwa towns in the vicinity. Following the consolidation of power in Ife, a process that might have unfolded over several generations, subsequent expeditions were launched to conquer neighboring towns or states.[19]

Obatala is celebrated in Yoruba mythology as the King of the White Cloth, a symbol of purity and clear thinking. Renowned for his calm demeanor and profound wisdom, he is often regarded as the elder among the Orishas. John Mason emphasizes that Obatala's leadership derives not merely from his age but from his virtues—his humility, aesthetic appreciation, and keen intellect—which have earned him a revered position to lead the Orishas.[20] Ulli Beier describes how, in Yoruba belief, Obatala, the God of creation, molded humanity from clay, creating men and women and soliciting the divine breath from Olodumare to bring them to life. There is an *itan* tale that recounts how Obatala became inebriated with palm wine and crafted people with differences such as albinism and other special physical traits. According to this narrative, such individuals are considered sacred to Obatala and are often found in his sanctuary, illustrating the Yoruba value that all beings enjoy divine protection. This perspective contrasts with the stricter views of perfection found in Christian and Islamic traditions. The *itan* underscores the Yoruba's inclusive approach to humanity, where individuals with physical differences play a respected role in society and are integral to Obatala's worship, fulfilling unique duties in his shrines.[21] Beier notes that Obatala's act of creation is an ongoing process, continually shaping new life in the womb, unlike the biblical portrayal of God's creation as a finite event.[22]

SEVEN YEARS OF DEATH AND INFERTILITY: A PARABLE FOR THE ATLANTIC SLAVE TRADE

Every year, a series of processional ceremonial feasts known as "Águas de Oxalá" (Obatala's Waters) marks the opening of the Candomblé liturgical calendar. Devotees set out at dawn in search of the closest source of water to "cool" the sacred *quartinhas*, that is, to refresh the water in the vessels containing the sacred rocks and symbols of the Orishas. This procession with its chants and narratives evokes the mythological journey of Obatala and the conflicts between Oyo and Ile-Ife. The ceremony historically references the *itan* tale of an unjust imprisonment that led to seven symbolic years of drought, unhappiness, and sterility.[23]

One of the *itan*, or oral texts, used to reflect on the history of transatlantic slavery in Brazil and Cuba originates from the 256 Odu, or sacred texts, of the Yoruba Ifa oracle. The Odu verse Okànrànméjì, known as Ocanran (or Ocarã) in Brazil and Ocana in Cuba, embodies transformation through tragedy and crisis. It emphasizes that fruitful transformation requires negotiation and collaboration. A verse from this Odu illustrates the principle: "One hand cannot lift a calabash onto the head; one foot cannot walk on the path and wear the path smooth; one foot is not safe on the bridge."[24] Associated with Okanran is the tragic *itan* of the kingdom of Ejigbo. This tale gained widespread recognition across Brazil and transcended the sacred confines of Candomblé *terreiros* in 1987 when the singer Margareth Menezes and the Bahian Carnaval group Araketu (literally "people from Ketu") released the Carnaval hit "Uma História de Ifá: Elegibo" ("The Ruler of Ejigbo: An Ifa Story"), composed by Ythamar Tropicália (Itamar Ferreira da Silva) and Rey Zulu (Reinivaldo Silva). The song celebrates Ejigbo, a vibrant and radiant city, and pays tribute to the historic cities of Ketu (Kétou, Keto) and Sabe (Savè). Its lyrics recount a time of great hardship when humanity endured immense suffering. Scarred by their own actions, they faced years of adversity—pastures lay barren, nature ceased to thrive, and women could no longer bear children. Despite these struggles, the city's spirit remained unbroken. Warriors engaged in ritual battles, embodying the eternal struggle between good and evil. Eventually, peace was restored, and the people returned to the sacred forest with the king. There, they shared a communal meal of pounded *iyán*, a dish symbolizing unity, resilience, and communion with the divine. The song connects this sacred act to the enduring strength and solidarity of the Black community, both in the past and present.[25]

This Carnaval hit draws inspiration from and adapts an oracular story involving Obatala, known as Oshagiyan (Òṣàgìyán), and the diviner Awolede (Awọlẹdẹ). Oshagiyan, an Oriki or praise name for Obatala, emphasizes his love for yams, which symbolize both physical and spiritual sustenance in Yoruba culture. Awolede, a praise name for the diviner, embodies the phrase "Awo ni èdè," which translates to "wisdom dwells in language and communication." Here is how the *itan* tale unfolds:

The king of Ife, Oshalufan, had a son who was affectionately known as Oshagiyan. The young prince's favorite dish was iyán, made from pounded yam, and he adored it so much that he earned the nickname Oshagiyan, the "yam-starch-eater." As Oshagiyan matured, he embarked on a quest to establish his own kingdom, accompanied by his trusted friend, the diviner Awolede. Upon their arrival in the lands of Ejigbo, they instantly knew they had found their new dominion. Oshagiyan was declared king and henceforth known as Elejibo, "owner of Ejigbo," or Kabiyesi, "Your Majesty." Only the Orishas and his closest friends continued to address him as Oshagiyan. When the time came for Awolede to depart, Oshagiyan consulted his wise friend on how to ensure the flourishing of his kingdom. Heeding Awolede's advice on the necessary offerings, Ejigbo thrived and prospered.

Years later, Awolede returned to Ejigbo and was delighted to find his visions for the kingdom fulfilled. Ejigbo had evolved into a formidable realm, safeguarded by tall walls and guards, with a vibrant market in front of the palace drawing people from afar to exchange a variety of goods and captives. Overjoyed, he inquired of a guard, "Where is my friend Oshagiyan? How is he faring?" The guards were appalled by such disrespect. How dare this outsider refer to their king as the "yam-starch-eater"? Without hesitation, they beat him and threw him into prison. Awolede remained imprisoned for seven years. For seven years, no rain fell, the king's horses starved, and the women ceased to bear children.[26]

In another rendition of this *itan*, Obatala is presented as the king of Ejigbo. He plans a visit to his friend Shango, the king of Oyo.[27] Before embarking, he consults an Ifa diviner, who reveals the *itan*, or history, Èjìogbè, the first Odu verse of Ifa. Despite the auspicious and transformative aspects of this forecast, it warns of complex situations requiring disciplined composure to avoid "losing one's head." Historically, individuals associated with this Odu verse risked decapitation; today, it symbolizes the severe consequences of losing self-control, understood in Yoruba philosophy as "coolness."[28] Obatala was informed that he would face extraordinary difficulties on his journey, yet he remained resolute in proceeding with his plans. Heeding the diviner's advice, he prepared for challenges by taking three white cloths and black soap to maintain his composure and purity.

On his journey, he met Eshu Legba, the Orisha of the crossroads, who feigned needing help to carry palm oil. Eshu stained Obatala's white garments—symbols of his serenity and balance. Although Obatala washed his clothes in the river, he soon faced further incidents with kola nuts and charcoal that stained his garments again. Nevertheless, he followed the Ifa's advice and continued undeterred. Approaching Oyo, Obatala found one of Shango's horses running loose. As he was leading the horse back to his friend, he was detained by soldiers, beaten, and imprisoned. After seven years of turmoil and destruction in Oyo, Shango consulted Ifa, which unveiled that the cause of the calamities was Obatala's wrongful imprisonment.[29] Upon discovering his friend detained, Shango prostrated himself before Obatala, seeking forgiveness, and ordered silence throughout Oyo. Obatala was bathed and redressed in pristine white. The friends reflected on their trials, contemplating the deep lessons learned.[30]

The *itan* of Obatala's imprisonment and the subsequent reconciliation with Shango has been interpreted as a representation of the historic tensions between Oyo and Ile-Ife, Oyo's rise through military force, and the enduring recognition of Ife as the spiritual heartland of the Yoruba people.[31] In Nigeria, in the town of Ejigbo, Osun State, an annual five-day festival is held for Orisha Ogiyan at the onset of the new yam harvest in September. The highlight of the festival is the Ewo, a ritual in which the townspeople split into two groups, the Isale Osolo and the Oke Mapo, and engage in daylong mock combats with sticks.[32] The festival's narrative traces back to a past offense: Sawoleje, an Ifa diviner without whom the town of Ejigbo would not have prospered, was accused of adultery and beaten nearly to death. To avoid Sawoleje's curse, the mock combat represents the physical pain endured by the diviner, now endured by the townspeople. The German ethnologist Leo Frobenius (1873–1938) detailed that during each morning of the festival, women selected by the Orishas were tasked with fetching water. They were to approach the stream without uttering a word, avoid speaking or acknowledging anyone along the way, and then proceed back equally silently, ignoring anyone they encountered. Upon reaching the temple, the water was then poured into Obatala's vessel.[33]

During the Obatala's Waters festival in Brazil, a similar moment of attunement is observed. Silence is upheld, and the use of palm oil in cooking is prohibited. Processions carry vessels of fresh water to the *terreiro*, to a space designated for Obatala's shrine. Initiates cleanse themselves with black soap and leaves, while the community honors and celebrates its ancestors. Meals are shared between the living and the dead, fostering communion and reinforcing solidarity and unity within the community and with the ancestral world. These festivals celebrate the future through the reenactment of past tragedies, interpreted and attuned in the present.

The variations of this tradition in the feasts of Obatala's Waters in Brazil and the Ogiyan festival in Nigeria represent atonement for the ancestors' mistakes and a commitment to ensuring the ongoing peace and prosperity of the communities. The diviner Awolede, whose praise name suggests that the wise approach to destruction caused by misunderstanding lies in effective communication and collaboration, embodies this *itan* tale across different interpretations. While the Ifa oracle refers to Oyo, Ile-Ife, and Ejigbo, the narrative also covers the impacts of Oyo's military expansions into regions such as Dahomey. Further explorations, underscore guidance from maintaining composure and consulting the Ifa oracle before acting, to reflecting on the consequences of ruptures—whether personal or political, as in civil wars—and the paths to reconciliations.

The construction of Yoruba identity has centered around Ile-Ife as its religious center and Oyo as its political capital. From the consolidation to the decline of Oyo, various Orishas have been pivotal in valorizing Yoruba indigenous traditions. Central to this process, Olodumare and Ifa have facilitated both intra- and interreligious dialogues, engaging with Islamic and Judeo-Christian paradigms.³⁴ Thomas Mákanjúọlá Ilésanmí, an expert in Yoruba oral traditions, notes how diverse Yoruba linguistic groups, despite their heterogeneity, viewed themselves as interconnected identities.³⁵ The Ifa oracle played a key role in unifying these groups through its philosophical and religious system, encapsulated within a mythological corpus. Recognized as an UNESCO heritage site in 2005, Ifa epitomizes Yorubanity. It emerged from a continuous recombination of experiences across space and time, forming a coherent theological, ethical, and philosophical whole.

Similarly, Brazilian Candomblé Jeje-Nago, which originated during the eighteenth and nineteenth centuries amid the slave trade and was consolidated by the early twentieth century, has evolved through inter and intra-African hybridization. It unified various Orishas under one roof, establishing different worship modalities that incorporate elements from proto-Yoruba, Fon, and Bantu cultures, alongside influences from Indigenous and popular Catholic traditions. This blend has led to the reconfiguration of ethnic identities into distinct meta-ethnic identities, known as *nações* (nations). These identity groupings have gradually shifted from direct political-ethnic connotations to encompass stronger theological references.³⁶ The first world conference on Orisha religions in Ile-Ife in 1981 marked a significant re-Africanization of Brazilian Candomblé, introducing Yoruba language courses in *terreiros* and reintroducing the Ifá system, building on initiatives from the 1930s led by Mãe Aninha and Martiniano Eliseu do Bonfim.³⁷ This re-Africanization process observed in Candomblé is also evident in Carnaval. While Kongo-Angola processional parades have continued evolving their interpretations of Catholic aesthetics, other musical parade performances, influenced by both Kongo-Angola and Yoruba-Ewe cultures, have increasingly retranslated themselves into Carnaval formats. They have distanced themselves from peripheral connections to the Catholic Church and engaged with other spheres of power (from parallel to official) to negotiate their place within multiple cultural, religious, and institutional frameworks.

Among the various Carnaval expressions, the Afoxés reveal a specific deep-level continuity with the Congadas. In the sense of entourage, Carnaval procession, or "street Candomblé," the Afoxés trace their origins to Afro-Brazilian performative festivals such as the processions of the Congadas.³⁸ The term *Afoxé* has been defined as "divination," "a plague or curse," "the enunciation that makes (something) happen," a "royal entourage in the representation of a group of noble hunters originally from Africa who carry as a symbol a black doll (the *babalotim*)," and "semireligious Carnaval groups composed of Candomblé devotees wearing white tunics of West African style and singing songs in Yoruba."³⁹

Founded in 1948 and revitalized in the 1970s, the Filhos de Gandhy, an Afoxé group, is inspired by the Obatala's Waters feasts and recasts Obatala, reinterpreted through the figure of Mahatma Gandhi, not in Ile-Ife but in Salvador. Through their attire, aesthetics, dance movements, chants, symbolism, and representations, the performers have also come to embody, to a large extent, a reimagined version of the Moçambique guards from the Congadas.

THE SONS OF OBATALA AND GANDHI: AFRICAN-BRAZILIAN COSMOLOGIES AS EXPLAINED BY CARNAVAL GRIOTS

A large group of men have donned long white tunics; they have decorated themselves with white terry cloth turbans, each with a large plastic sapphire-blue gem sewn on the front.

Pravina Shukla

The figure of Mahatma Gandhi fascinated me as a preteen living in São Paulo. I remember the enthusiasm with which I watched Richard Attenborough's movie *Gandhi* in the early 1980s.[40] At the time, I had not yet seen images of the Bahian Carnaval group Filhos de Gandhy (Sons of Gandhi), but I was already quite familiar with Gilberto Gil's musical homage to them.[41] Gil's lyrics introduced me to these male performers who honored both the Orishas and Gandhi, presenting the latter as a cherished descendant and protégé of Obatala, the deity of creation and lord of white cloth. Like other Brazilians, I must have "Brazilianized" Gandhi in my imagination, and because of that, I must have felt a sense of kinship with the historical figure portrayed in Attenborough's film. I remember how, when I later came across images of this "semireligious Carnaval group," or Afoxé, I found myself enchanted by what I perceived as beautiful, poetic, political, and "carnavalistically" sacred. Nothing in my state of enchantment was threatened by a critical stance or by uncomfortable perceptions of corruption, contradiction, or exotification. Years went by. I continued to follow the group's development, its portrayal by the media, and its analysis by scholars. Even if my enchantment remained unbroken, as I zoomed in on the group's symbolism, layers of metaphorical puzzles increasingly intrigued me.

In his 1973 song "Filhos de Gandhi," Gilberto Gil invokes various Orishas (Omolu, Ogun, Oshun, Oshumare, Yansan, Yemaya, and Shango), as well as different Afoxé Carnaval groups and Christ as the Lord of the Good End (Nosso Senhor do Bonfim), inviting them all to gather and witness the procession of the Filhos de Gandhi. The translated lyrics are as follows:

> Omolu, Ogun, Oshun, Oshumare,
> Everyone,
> Come down to see
> the Filhos de Gandhi.
>
> Yansan, Yemaya, call upon Shango
> And Oshosi too,
> Come down to see
> the Filhos de Gandhi.
>
> Mercador, Cavaleiro de Bagdá,
> Oh, Filhos de Obá,
> Come down to see
> the Filhos de Gandhi.
>
> Our Lord of Bonfim,
> please do me a favor,
> Call everyone,
> Come down to see
> the Filhos de Gandhi.
>
> Oh my God up in heaven,
> It's Carnaval down on earth.
> Call everyone,
> Come down to see
> the Filhos de Gandhi.[42]

Gilberto Gil composed the song "Filhos de Gandhi" upon his return from exile in London, imposed by the Brazilian military dictatorship (1964–1985). Gil has remarked that the group represented one of the "strongest emblems" of his childhood and that his post-1972 participation served as a stimulus to "thicken the stew."[43] While Gil retained the original spelling of the Mahatma's name for the title of his 1970s song, the Carnaval group had altered it to Gandhy in the 1940s. This precaution was taken by the group's founders: dockworkers frequently labeled as communists by authorities during a previous period of Brazilian army intervention. To preemptively thwart Bahian officials from banning their parade on grounds of "offense" to the United Kingdom or alleged communist advocacy, the altered spelling served as a strategic defense.

The Healing Chant of a Griot: Grace and Serenity Amidst Brutality and Terror

Gilberto Gil's song was nationally launched in 1973 at the Polytechnic School of the University of São Paulo during the "Years of Lead" (1968–1978), the most oppressive and violent phase of Brazil's military dictatorship.[44] Amid this perilous climate, Gil's performance emerged as a landmark event, conveying a powerful political message. The show culminated in the presentation of "Filhos de Gandhi," which featured Gil's griot-style narrative about the origins and significance of the group. During his performance, Gil transformed audience members into active participants, inviting them to sing along and engage with rhythmic applause.[45] Two hours into the show, he unveiled a twenty-three-minute rendition of "Filhos de Gandhi." Strumming his guitar to mirror the Ijexá sacred rhythm, Gil unfolded the piece over a hypnotic musical phrase, backed by two simple, looping chords and layered Yoruba verses offered as salutations.[46] Channeling the persona of an elder ancestor from Umbanda tradition, he drew the crowd into a collective trancelike state.[47] His intimate melodic storytelling built a connection with his listeners as he recounted the tale leading up to the formation of the Afoxé Filhos de Gandhy. He began by explaining the term "Afoxé" in both Yoruba and Bahian contexts:

> Afoxé, in Yoruba Nago, means the blowing of powder—
> powder blown by the mouth, forming the sound, the verb.
> In Bahia, Afoxé is something else.
> In Bahia, Afoxé is a Carnaval *bloco*.
> It's a Carnaval street parade group.
> Something special, something original
> that happens *in* Carnaval, but it is not *of* Carnaval.
> Afoxé is not a samba school.
> It is not a Trio Elétrico. It is not Frevo. It is not Marcha.
> It is Afoxé,
> Afoxé, Afoxé.

> It is born from Candomblé,
> Candomblé, Candomblé, Candomblé, Candomblé.
> A bunch of Blacks, all dressed in white,
> singing some invocations, some melodies,
> with their own rhythm.
> The atabaque drums beating, the agogô bells singing,
> and they call upon the Orishas.
> So, it is a religious thing in Carnaval.
> This is why I say that it is *in* Carnaval, but it is not *of* Carnaval.
> The Afoxé comes to Carnaval to sing
> the religious traditions of Blacks in Bahia.[48]

Gil's introduction to the song was uniquely tailored to that historic performance. After delivering the lyrics, he orchestrated a call-and-response with the audience, creating a powerful, interactive, and communal experience.[49] Gil's griot narrative continued as he recounted a day when he ran into the multifaceted artist Mestre Didi (1917–2013)—one of Brazil's most prolific researchers and philosophers—who also served in various religious roles, including as Alapini, a high priest of the ancestral Egungun tradition:

> So, Didi was telling me about the first Afoxé—
> it was he who brought it to the streets, he and some of his friends,
> and they called it Sons of Gandhi.
>
> I asked: "Didi, why this story of Gandhi, this oriental thing?"
> He said: "I don't know. It was just a whim of the people."
>
> The Afoxé is like this: the women in Baiana costumes, right? All in white,
> and the men with turbans, tunics, carrying some *alegorias*—
> some elephants, some camels, all sorts of oriental things. . . .
>
> Then I said: "But, Sons of Gandhi!?"
> He nodded and said: "Yeah."
>
> Later, after talking with Didi,
> I got some information—you know how it is.
> We always manage to dig up something.

We read some books, we talk to some people,
and somehow, we end up knowing a few things.

So, I found out that in Bahia, near the end of the last century,
just before Abolition, some Blacks arrived,
Blacks from North Africa, from the Malê nation—
the Indigenous Malês.
They believed in Allah and spoke Arabic.

And I thought to myself: "Maybe the Afoxé has something to do with that."
Didi told me how Gandhi came out the first year,
then it came out again the second year,
and by the third year, it was catching on.
People liked seeing it out there on the streets, that thing on the streets,
that playful Carnaval vibe, but focused, peaceful.
It was like a procession. Joyful.
A procession in the name of joy, in the name of euphoria, in the name of playfulness,
and connected to the Orishas,
to the saints of the Black religion
that had been preserved there in Bahia, thank God.

And so it is that now, well, now the Afoxé is about to end,
it's about to end....

After Gandhi, a bunch of others showed up, and they became important too:
Deixa a Vida de Kelé, Mercadores de Bagdá, Filhos de Obá,
and a whole lot more—even some smaller ones.
Those smaller ones are even cooler,
with Caboclos dressed as Indigenous people,
dancing alongside the Baianas.
It's a wild mix, it's everything, all at once—a pure pandemonium.

And now, it's all about to disappear, it's under threat.

The other day, during the last Carnaval, I went to play in Praça da Sé.
I was there playing, and suddenly, I remembered the Afoxé.

There was this guy standing next to me, so I asked him:
"My brother, where's the Afoxé? Tell me, have you seen the Afoxé?"

He said: "Afoxé? Oh yeah, there was one here earlier. It passed by already.
It's probably over there somewhere."

I said: "Over there where?"
He said: "Over there."
I said: "Where?"
He said: "Go."

So, I went.

But then I found it strange. Because back in the day, when the Afoxé was in the square,
there was no need to look for it. The sound filled everything. . . .

I said: "But strange, it wasn't like this before. The Afoxé didn't need to be searched for.
Afoxé was there in the square—the atabaque drums beating, the agogô bells singing,
people getting goosebumps with that mystical energy in Carnaval."
I mean, Carnaval is already mystical, of course,
but I'm talking about that other, explicit, specific, religious side,
brought straight from the *terreiros*.
That was powerful, magnetic stuff, really.
It's the thing I love most about Carnaval in Bahia.

So, I went over there.

"Excuse me, excuse me."
I made my way to a corner of the square and saw a small group—the boys in white turbans, white tunics, blue pants.

I said: "It's the Sons of Gandhi!"
Sons of Gandhi are blue and white.

I walked up to one of them and said: "My brother, come here. How's the Afoxé? Is it lively?"

He said: "The Afoxé is about to end!"
I said: "End?"
He said: "Yes, it's no longer possible. Afoxé is barely hanging on.
This year it almost didn't happen, and next year, I don't think it will."

I said: "But why? What's going on?"

And he said: "The directors—they're all fighting.
The vice-president wants one thing; the president wants another.
And then there's this guy who says he's in public relations—
I don't even know what the hell he does.
And then there's this other director who said this year we needed to buy that fabric that doesn't wrinkle or lose its crease.
Because, well, you know, it might rain, and if it rains, the fabric won't shrink, and everything stays pretty. That kind of stuff.
And it all looks like the deputies and councilmen, you know?
Those clothes with those shiny fabrics, blah blah blah."

I said: "Yeah."

And he went on: "And tourism—the tourism department doesn't want to help.
It's all falling apart; everything's bad. This year, look, there are only about 20 or 30 of us who made it. Next year, I don't even think it will happen."

And I stayed there thinking.
That whole thing shocked me, you know?
All that talk when I was so excited.
So, I went home, feeling kind of sad. . . .

The other day, I was home in Rio, thinking about Afoxé again. . . .
And suddenly, I said: "Ah, maybe. Who knows?
We know how to sing, right? At least a little bit, we know how to.
If we sing, maybe God will hear us."

Of course, since He's right here inside of us, He hears everything, right?
I mean, there are also the Orishas—who are up there, right?
People think They're up there.
They are the ones, the Gods.

Because God, himself, right? He's in everything.
But then there are the Gods.
Blacks have their own:
The Orishas.
Ogun, Oshun, Oshumare, Yansan, Yemaya, and so on.
So, I said: "Maybe if we sing, They'll come together up there, right?
And decide to help us.
And the Afoxé won't end."[50]

Gil's choice to infuse Eastern cultural elements into his music not only echoed the countercultural sentiments of the era but also challenged the Eurocentric perspective of modernity, proposing an alternative vision for society's future.[51] During a performance in São Paulo in the 1970s, before a predominantly white audience largely unfamiliar with the intricacies of Bahian Candomblé, its intelligentsia, or the history of Afoxé Carnaval groups, the cohesive power of communal empowerment and celebrative defiance transcended the need for a deep understanding of African-Brazilian cosmologies. Gil tapped into the *encantamento* (enchantment) movement, where humans are transformed into *encantado* (enchanted) spirits—a metaphysical phenomenon interweaving the afterlife, music, environment, and our shared interconnectedness. In sum, by employing the tools of Candomblé epistemology, Gil evoked in his audience—gathered at an event organized by student movements denouncing the repression of the military dictatorship—a restorative effect akin to that generated by the Filhos de Gandhy during Bahian Carnaval. He invited those present to "sing against" the system.

Gil's song and its national debut in São Paulo became part of the various aspects that contributed to the ongoing national popularity of the Filhos de Gandhy.[52] Other significant contributors included two principal government tourist agencies—Bahiatursa (State of Bahia) and Emtursa (City of Salvador)— which began to sponsor the Filhos de Gandhy toward the late 1970s. By the 1980s, the *bloco* was able to field 10,000 "sons" on the streets and had become an international emblem for Bahia and Salvador. As Gil noted in his narration, the Filhos de Gandhy have occasionally faced accusations of being coopted by government bureaucracies.[53] The trajectory of the Filhos de Gandhy from the 1970s onward was inevitably conditioned by the consolidation of the cultural and telecommunications industries that took place during that period, leading to the transformation of Carnaval into a mega-event in which each Carnaval group functions as an industry within itself (and as such, deals with other private and state industries, including those that promote sexual and Afrocentric tourism).[54]

Mahatma Gandhi (1869–1948), the pioneer of *satyagraha*—the principle of nonviolence as a form of protest and revolution—inspired generations of activists. In Brazil, Gandhi was transformed into a sacredly profane Carnaval icon. The Hindu anthropologist Pravina Shukla pertinently questioned, "How did Gandhi shift from South Africa to India and end up in the heart of the African Diaspora in the sweltering heat of Salvador?"[55] In light of Shukla's awe and bewilderment, I reflected on the development and aesthetics of the Filhos de Gandhy within the performatic tradition of Afro-Brazilian Carnaval, as well as on questions of gender in the group, its cosmology according to its founders' narratives, and the process of a Hindu-Muslim-Bahian aesthetic enunciation. The enigmatic and contradictory paradigms of this interpretive community pose an analytic challenge, best approached with an open and metaphorically plausible reading.

In a recent study on the Gandhys, the historian Marc Hertzman references an article I authored and the conversation I initiated with Shukla about her reactions to the Filhos de Gandhy.[56] Hertzman argues that to grasp why the Gandhys incite such disparate reactions—one scholar finding them "jarring" (Shukla) and another "alluring" (myself)—it is essential to explore the historical backdrop of the group's creation.[57] Although my original presentation positioned Shukla's perspective and mine as complementary, Hertzman portrays them as polar opposites. He contributes valuable historical insights, yet interestingly claims that while my analysis offers a "more thoughtful consideration" compared to that of Shukla's, I "confess enchantment" with the group's "incongruent metaphors and symbolism."[58] Contrary to Hertzman's depiction, however, my professed "enchantment" with the group does not stem from incongruities but rather from the profound, resonant layers of poetry, politics, philosophy, aesthetics, and history that it embodies. The "enchantment" I profess toward the epistemological realms the group enacts and represents is informed by my recognition and appreciation for the cosmological legacy that shapes the group. After presenting what he perceives as a compelling contrast, Hertzman, adopting the guise of an unbiased historian, advances his analysis by treading the paths laid out by his predecessors. In the epigraph of the article Hertzman references, I state:

> This article has been propelled by a silent dialogue with Pravina Shukla's *avatāra*. I dedicate it to Ana Maria Gonçalves who, on August 3rd, 2006, in Rio de Janeiro, wrote and signed a message on the opening page of her Kehinde's saga informing me: "The history of what may have been if time preserved certainties."
>
> Brave breeze of these *iyás*. May it guide us. Much love, respect, and gratitude.[59]

Making reference to the 2006 launch event of Ana Maria Gonçalves' re-fabulated novel *Um defeito de cor* (*A Color Defect*), now widely recognized as a milestone, and invoking Shukla's ancestors, I simultaneously praised fictional and poetic (both literary and "popular") historical reconstructions of the Black diaspora, paid homage to the contributions of Gonçalves and Shukla, and invoked their extraordinary insights and boldness.[60]

There are different ways to enter a debate or join an existing movement. There are recommendations and common knowledge on how to engage in cycles of *encantamento* (enchantment), on how to enter Capoeira, Candomblé, or Samba circles. It is of utmost importance to be conscious of and discerning in our praxes both inside and outside academia, especially when exploring epistemologies that have yet to receive proper acknowledgment.

The Contextualization of the Gandhys Within the Performatic Tradition of Afro-Brazilian Carnaval

The first significant "Afro-Carnavalesque tide" of Bahia occurred toward the end of the nineteenth century and was recorded by Rodrigues, who described groups such as the Embaixada Africana (African Embassy), Filhos da África (Children of Africa), A Chegada Africana (African Arrival), and Pândegos da África (African Merrymakers).[61] Muniz Sodré analyzed a major aspect of these groups—especially in the pre- and post-abolitionist periods—as a "tactic of collective penetration (with regard to time and space) in urban territory," that is, a "reterritorialization (the breaking of topographical limits imposed by urban social division on the Blacks)."[62] Two highly visible groups towards the end of the nineteenth century were especially paradigmatic: the Embaixada Africana and Pândegos da África, making their debut in 1895 and 1896 respectively. According to Nina Rodrigues, while Embaixada and Pândegos were the most influential clubs, other smaller groups emerged, such as A Chegada Africana and Os Filhos da África.[63] Rodrigues distinguishes between the Embaixada and the Pândegos by asserting that while the former celebrated the endurance of a tradition among "the most intelligent or most adapted Blacks" and among "the educated people of Africa, the Egyptians, the Abyssinians, and the like," the latter focused on "the uncultured Africa that arrived enslaved in Brazil."[64]

The different tendencies of early Bahian Carnaval performances registered by Rodrigues suggest varying levels of participation and acceptance of Afro-Brazilians in the Carnavais of the 1890s. As observed by the historian Kim Butler, when Embaixada Africana organized processions within the formats established by white clubs and presented an image of a "civilized" Africa, the white elite was more accepting than the Black masses of Bahia.⁶⁵ Yet despite adhering to the format of the white Carnaval clubs, Pândegos da África introduced the aesthetics and rhythms of Candomblé. Finally, those currently known as *pipocas* (popcorns), "the anonymous African groups and isolated African revelers" cited by Rodrigues, were perceived as the subversive elements of Carnaval, terrifying the white population.⁶⁶ The urban penetration tactic of these revelers did not seek to follow the aesthetic or conduct of a "civilized Africa" or of an "enslaved Africa," but of a "Maroon Africa." These were "guerrilla" performers interested in giving free expression to their emotions, critiques, and desires. Antonio Risério's study concurs with Butler that the "Afro-Carnavalesque" displays at the end of the nineteenth century were hierarchized by the spokespersons of the dominant culture: the *clubes uniformizados* (organized clubs) who imposed the theme of the "cultured people" of Africa, while the Afoxés or *Candomblés de rua* ("street Candomblés") were cast as "expressions of primitiveness and barbarism that were an embarrassment to Bahia."⁶⁷

Some changes occurred from 1905 to 1914, when "the Black-mestizo Carnaval" was prohibited, but as Peter Fryer points out, "It was not so easy to take the streets away from Black people in Brazil. And one of their responses was the creation of Afoxés which took shape in Salvador in the 1920s."⁶⁸ The influence and visibility of the Afro-mestizo-organized Carnaval groups declined. They became smaller Afoxés (such as Filhos d'Oxum, Lordes Africanos, and Filhos de Obá), until 1949, with the birth of the Filhos de Gandhy, the Trio Elétrico of Dodô and Osmar, and the landmark first performance of Ilê Aiyê in the 1970s. This was a period Risério calls the "re-africanization" of the Bahia Carnaval. One could point to the Embaixada Africana as one of the matrices for the formation of Rio de Janeiro's *escolas de samba* and to Pândegos da África as the matrix for the creation of the *blocos* of Bahian Carnaval.⁶⁹

Raul Lody describes Pândegos as an Afoxé whose performance included a central group of revelers adorned in the clothing and symbols of the Orishas, and musicians dressed in Moorish-style turbans, tunics with puffed-out sleeves, and *bombacha*-style pants. They carried the *babalotim*, a wooden totem with magical properties that only a male child could carry during the procession. Lody explains that the mystery surrounding the totem restricted its handling to boys only.⁷⁰ Encased within the *babalotim* were sacred implements consecrated in Candomblé temples, embodying its *ashe*—"the magic energy or object that contains it." Once "fed" and activated, the *babalotim* symbolized the community's protection and empowerment. Positioned at the forefront of the formation, the *babalotim* served as an effective magical *abre-alas*, or lead-off contingent, believed by the participants to emit positive influences and ward off negative ones.[71] The connection between the *babalotim* of the Afoxé and the *calunga* doll, which remains present in Maracatu performances of Recife and Olinda, is evident. The crucial difference is that the *calunga* must be carried by a woman, the *Dama do Paço* (Lady of the Palace), who marches in front.

One of the founding members of the Filhos de Gandhy relates that the first group of Gandhys set out with "a black-clothed doll," a *calunga*.[72] The initial *calunga* has disappeared. Curiously, the figure of the *babalotim*, literally "the owner of the cachaza," was substituted in the Filhos de Gandhy, first by a figure known as Cândido Elefante, "a gentleman weighing over 200 kilos who could dance to the Ijexá rhythm beautifully."[73] A second substitution of the *babalotim* involved the incorporation into the parade of a portrait of Mahatma Gandhi, introducing a quasi-processional element or aspect of an almost profane pilgrimage.[74] The third and definitive substitution was the "materialization" and embodiment of the image portrayed by Raimundo Queiróz Lima, "Raimundo Gandhy" (1925–2006), a reveler who recalls being informed one day, "You are going to represent the portrait."[75]

Edison Carneiro explains that in the standard formation of an Afoxé, the participants would line up in the following order: "the *arauto* [announcer]; the *guarda branca* [white guard]; *rei* and *rainha* [king and queen]; Babá l'ôtin; Papai Cachaça [Daddy Cachaza], the masculine equivalent of the Maracatu doll; the *estandarte* [flag-bearer]; the *guarda de honra* [guard of honor]; and the *charanga de ilús* [*atabaques*], *agogôs* and *cabaças* Ijexás [the band of *ilú* drummers, cow bells, and shakers]."[76] According to Lody, the *ilús* are small, two-headed *atabaque* drums that are used in the ceremonies to Oshun, "a riverine deity," in the temples of Ijesha.[77] In the Afoxés, the *atabaque* are not taken to the streets "dressed" or decorated as they would appear inside Candomblé temples. There are no *ojá* straps in the colors of the celebrated Orishas tied around them. The call-and-response melodies of Afoxés sung by a soloist and repeated by a chorus are practically the same as the ones sung in Afro-Brazilian temples that follow the Ijexá cosmology, while the choreography simplifies the traditional steps and gesticulations of sacred Candomblé evocation dances. According to Lody, "What really matters when the Gexá (Ijexá) is danced—and this is what is danced in the Afoxé—is the characteristic *ginga* swing, the movement of the shoulders and arms and the quick, short, cadenced steps."[78] But what constitutes the Candomblé Ijexá performative repertoire? Is there, in fact, a clear distinction between the sacred drumming and dancing of Candomblé Ketu and Ijexá (Yoruba cosmologies respectively originating from present-day Benin and Nigeria)? Risério is right when he affirms that "the term 'Ijexá' acquired a generic meaning from the fact that the majority of new Afro-Carnavalesque groups do not use *aguidavis*, that is, drumsticks, when playing the *atabaque* drums."[79] The followers of Candomblé Ijexá play the *atabaque* drums with their hands. Yet the generic meaning of *Ijexá* as a secular musical and dance style has transcended its association with a particular type of percussion, extending to choreography and song not strictly tied to any specific Yoruba-Brazilian cosmology.

Descend Into the Realm of the Living to Watch Your Beloved Sons

Aside from the symbolic conversion of sacred Candomblé into secular Candomblé, and the influence of other secular performances such as the Maracatus and Congadas, less explicit influences may help illuminate not only the figure of the *babalotim* but also the question of male exclusivity within the Filhos de Gandhy Afoxé. The Beninese Africanist scholar Olabiyi Yai (1938–2020) had already pointed to the influence of the Geledé societies in the formation of Brazilian Carnaval.[80] In the Yoruba tradition, female ancestors are referred to as Ìyámi Agbà ("my ancient mother"). These ancestral spirits are worshipped in Nigeria by the Geledé (Gẹ̀lẹ̀dẹ́) societies, which consist exclusively of women. Oro (Òrò) societies also exist in Nigeria. Oro is considered the general representative of male ancestors and can be worshipped only by men. The Egungun (Egúngún) societies carry out another form of male-ancestor worship. Only the spirits of deceased men can manifest themselves as apparitions, as it is believed that only men possess or maintain individuality after death; women are denied this privilege as well as the right to participate directly in worship. In Brazil, there are two Egungun societies, both located on the island of Itaparica in Bahia: Ilê Agboulá and Ilê Oyá. Although the Geledé and Oro societies did not maintain a "literal" continuity in Brazil, the Geledé society did, in fact, exist in Brazil for some time and had as its last high priestess Omonikê, Maria Júlia Figueiredo (1890–1994), "major purveyor of the devotion to Nossa Senhora da Boa Morte (Our Lady of Good Death), which was established in the 1820s by women who were members of the Irmandade dos Martírios (Confraternity Martyrs)."[81] The Irmandade da Boa Morte ("Sisterhood or Sorority of Good Death") continued the Geledé ceremonial worship of female ancestors through a women-only group while absorbing and adapting Catholic referents. The Oro societies, by contrast, appear to have been transformed into the Filhos de Gandhy Afoxé, or perhaps even earlier into the exclusively male Afoxé, or Folia de Reis (Revelry of the Kings), which likewise excluded women from their processional performances.

According to Yoruba cosmological principles, every person has his or her own Orisha. The archetypical personality characteristics shared by Orishas and their human protégés are maintained after death by the spirits, or *eguns*. Mahatma Gandhi, both physically and ideologically, evokes aspects of the archetype of Obatala. As in the Egungun societies, Gandhi is praised by the Filhos de Gandhy for his essential individuality—a privilege reserved for male spirits. As in the Oro societies, he transcends this individuality to represent the power of a male collective ancestry.

Former president of the Filhos de Gandhy, Agnaldo Silva (1949–2021), offers a more pragmatic explanation for the non-participation of women in this Afoxé. According to him, since the group was originally formed by stevedores—men who unloaded the ships—women could only provide "logistical support" by taking care of the costumes and "beautifying the turbans."[82] Such a clear division of roles in this dockworker-based Afoxé has not been typical in the formation and development of other groups. The Caribbeanist scholar Carole Boyce Davies observes, "The group remains all male exclusively. Thus, the question of gender in Afoxé becomes important. While some of the Afoxés tend to incorporate both men and women, Filhos de Gandhy is principally a brotherhood."[83] Davies's analysis of the question of male exclusivity of Filhos de Gandhy points to an apparent reversal of roles when she states: "The masculinist orientation of Afoxé as represented in Filhos de Gandhy tended to relocate women to the periphery which they are not in Candomblé ritual."[84]

Indeed, far from occupying a peripheral position, women in Candomblé have traditionally held central roles of authority and influence, both in practice and perception. This status quo invites reflection on the historical process that shifted the position of men from more centralized roles in original Yoruba cosmologies to more peripheral ones in the New World, particularly in Brazil. The anthropologist Lorand Matory analyzes both the evolution of Candomblé's current characterization as a matriarchy, and the role intellectuals—such as Arthur Ramos, Gilberto Freyre, and the New York cultural anthropologist Ruth Landes (1908–1991)—have played in the repositioning of men within it.[85] Landes, author of *The City of Women* (1947), played a crucial yet often overlooked role in this process, as evidenced by an article from 1940 in which she makes a surprising and unprecedented statement that subsequently sheds light on her intentions and purpose: "A mother of a Nago cult tries to avoid making 'sons.' She prefers instead an inconclusive ritual or cure."[86] She further notes that male leadership in Candomblé was only present "in very rare instances in the past."[87] Most significantly, while a temple might have few "sons," there were many "daughters"—initiated women priestesses. The male *sacerdotes* would have been forbidden "to dance with the women or to dance publicly when possessed and debarred male novices from certain female mysteries. In comparison with the women, they were only partially initiated and tolerated in view of certain anomalies."[88]

As Matory observes, the figure of the gay man in Candomblé, the *adé*, was transformed into the antihero of the matriarchal nation as defined by Landes. "From the 1930s onward," states Matory, "the priestess became an object of public talk to the same degree that her *adé* antitype became an object of silencing."[89] The silence surrounding the *adés* promoted both a series of negative stereotypes—some of which are reflected in the practice of Candomblé—and the marginalization of heterosexual men, who feel compelled to "prove" their heterosexuality by adopting patterns of behavior in opposition to the *adés*. One of the stereotypes of the *adés* is to simulate possession, or "dar ekê" ("to give ekê"). *Èké* in Yoruba means "lie."[90] As Patrícia Birman, Brazilian religious studies specialist, explains: "To give *ekê* means a paroxysmal exhibition of competence in this obscurely sexualized and feminine realm." Although this is not exclusively "a practice of the *adés*, it is, at the very least, a recurrent charge made against them."[91]

The terms *egun* (ancestral spirit) and *elegun* (one who has the power to receive and materialize the ancestral energy) are concepts offering us other interpretative channels into the social paradigms reflected in the Filhos de Gandhy. In Yoruba, the meanings of the radical *gùn* involve references to mounting, saddling, and riding, and to spiritual or sexual possession. *Gùn* means to mount—as a horseman mounts his horse, or as an Orisha mounts and "rides" a human. It also refers to the sexual act of a man "mounting" a woman or another man from behind. As Matory observes, "Since a physically mountable man seems highly qualified, in a symbolic sense, to be mounted spiritually," there is "a reluctance of 'real men' to be possessed in the Brazilian Candomblé."[92] This notion of "real man" resonates in the definition of the Filhos de Gandhy by one of the founders—curiously nicknamed Quadrado (square or straight)—as a "*bloco* of respectable men."[93]

The development of a group of men that gradually incorporated Candomblé referents into their Afoxé—a male group that uses the music and dance of the Orishas without being "mounted"—reveals an affirmation of ultra-masculinity. This dynamic is observable even in the song by Gilberto Gil that became a national hit, and which reveals an inversion of roles between humans and Orishas. In the lyrics, Gil—as a participant of the Filhos de Gandhy—evokes the Orishas, the ancient Afoxés, and Nosso Senhor do Bonfim (Our Lord of the Good End), to summon one another, to command each other to "come down" to the world of the living to witness the parade of the Filhos de Gandhy. Thus, the role of the gods and the ancestors becomes that of a voyeuristic audience: the Filhos de Gandhy are not invoking the gods in order to be mounted, but rather to be seen and admired.

During the parade of the Filhos de Gandhy parade, the performance is used to seduce the onlookers, who are cordoned off from the group. Shukla notes in detail:

> Over 5,000 men in one place for the days of carnival. This fact, inevitably, is appealing to young women interested in boyfriends for the duration of the carnival festivities. Gay men of Salvador, likewise, scope out the parading route of Filhos de Gandhy for precisely the same reason, to have a quick pick at the turbaned, majestic men of the carnival ... Just as [their] perfume should be shared with others in an act of good faith and symbolic blessing from Oxalá, members of Filhos de Gandhy have customarily carried a small stash of beaded necklaces to give out on the streets. Although many members of the *bloco* still give out beads, an increasing number of young men use the beads and a dab of perfume as barter for a can of cold beer or a kiss ... During the quest by many members of Filhos de Gandhy to look attractive in order to appeal to the young men and women of Salvador, the connection with the Mahatma's humble appearance and years of celibacy becomes ironic. Another strong incongruity between the Mahatma and the carnival revelers who impersonate him has to do, again ironically, with what Gandhi is most associated with: peace. The *bloco* Filhos de Gandhy attracts many young men who exhibit violent behavior, and in fact, see membership in the group as an opportunity to enable aggressive tendencies while hiding behind the guise of a peaceful group of marchers.[94]

The original fame of the Filhos de Gandhy as seducers and tough guys persists. Today they are called by the press "the *bloco* of smoochers," and fights between them and other, smaller *blocos* frequently break out in the various circuits in Praça da Sé, the heart of the city of Salvador. Current members of the group cultivate images of courage, virility, and irresistible allure. An example of the consciously crafted image of brave, desirable men are today's widely-accepted narratives of police aggression faced by the Filhos de Gandhy during their first participation in Carnaval, as well as their courage in confronting the police.[95] Interestingly, these accounts are not corroborated by any of the interviews that the Brazilian historian Anísio Félix (1936–2007) conducted with the group's founding members.

Beneath a Mango Tree: The Cosmology of the Filhos de Gandhy

Gandhi was assassinated in New Delhi in 1948. The following year, a group of stevedores—a unionized labor elite—took to the streets of Salvador with a Carnaval *bloco* paying tribute to the Mahatma. As the anthropologist Anamaria Morales explains, identification with India's struggle for independence, after enduring economic and cultural oppression under British colonization, imbued the Filhos de Gandhy's debut with "an (un)disguised political character."[96] The group's foundational narratives, like those of all oral traditions, are multiple and poetic.

Founding member Manoel dos Santos, known as "Guarda Sol" (Parasol), recalls that "'Vavá Madeira' [Durival Marques da Silva] would have been inspired by the newspaper headlines about the death of Gandhi."[97] Eduarlino de Souza, known as "Dudu," adds, "We were sitting there under a mango tree, drinking and chatting away when the wind blew a magazine our way; Antonio and Vavá looked at it, and there he was: Gandhi. Right then they got the idea to start a Carnaval group named after him."[98] Djalma Conceição, the former president of the Filhos de Gandhy, adds another element to the story: "One of them had seen a movie called *Gunga Din*. They thought it was a nice name (the stevedores mixed up Gunga Din with Gandhi), and then a few of the guys suggested the name 'Sons of Gandhi' because Gandhi was a man who had fought for peace."[99] Other participants and founders conferred a politico-religious meaning on the group. Humberto Café, a member of the board of directors of the Filhos de Gandhy, confirmed that "Gandhy was founded with the objective of bringing Candomblé to the streets. The offerings performed today by the members were the same as those originally performed by the founders when it started."[100] Nelson dos Santos (1925–2009), known as "Lobisomem" (Wolfman), had a different understanding: "The fellows who inspired the creation of the group were more into booze than into religion."[101] Arivaldo Fagundes Pereira, known as "Carequinha" (Little Baldy) and the composer of the hit song "Patuscada de Gandhi" ("Gandhi's Revelry"), is the founder who provides the most detailed version of the evolution of the group's performance:

Gandhy was formed as a *bloco*. Its music was percussion, just *batucada* drumming. In the second year, we were singing Afro chants, and by the third year it was transformed into an Afoxé. As time passed there were a number of modifications in the costumes... In the second year, we had the goat and a small camel as *alegoria* floats. In the fourth and fifth years, we had the lancer, the gunner, and for the big *alegoria* floats we had an elephant and a big camel. In the third year, the number of participants increased to about two hundred men... Only after the third year, when the Candomblé people started showing up, did Gandhy begin leaning toward this syncretic side. From then on, we always did the *padê* [propitiatory Candomblé offering] before we started... The idea for starting the Filhos de Gandhy didn't come from *Gunga Din*, as some people claim, but there was a connection, because the film had to do with India and their struggle against England.[102]

The association of the Filhos de Gandhy with the film *Gunga Din* (directed by George Stevens and released in 1939)—even if perceived as peripheral by the most founders, current members of the group, and researchers—still presents itself as yet another contradictory and revealing influence.[103] The protagonists of the film are three British sergeants (one played by Cary Grant) and the Hindu water bearer Gunga Din (played by the New York Jewish actor Sam Jaffe).[104] The plot centers on the struggle between the British Army and the Thugees, a Hindu group that worships the goddess Kali and seeks the extermination of the British colonizers. The group's war cry is "Kill for the love of Kali!" The destroyer/builder archetype embodied by Kali in Hindu cosmology resembles that of Orisha Ogun, "the violent warrior who, having water in the house, bathes in blood."[105] Ogun also represents, among many other aspects and through his connection to other Orishas: metamorphosis and "the primordial abyss"; he is associated "with brotherhood guilds, fraternal organizations and friendships."[106] The Hollywood Thugees, as one would expect, are portrayed in the film as fanatical terrorists. Their revolutionary struggle fails due to the actions of the water bearer Gunga Din, who, by sounding a bugle, warns the British Army that they are walking into an ambush set up by the Thugees. Gunga Din, previously treated with irony and condescension, is transformed into a hero worthy of official burial; a stanza from the Rudyard Kipling homonymous poem is read in eulogy: "You Lazarushian-leather Gunga Din! / Tho' I've belted you an' flayed you, / By the livin' Gawd that made you, / You're a better man than I am, Gunga Din!"[107]

One of the founding members of the Filhos de Gandhy states, "Gandhy was not inspired by the movie *Gunga Din*, as many people think, just the outfits."[108]

Another adds, with respect to the figures, "There was a lancer and a water bearer," but "the water bearer isn't used anymore."[109] The lancer's role was to prevent people—"mainly women," noted another founder—from breaking past the security cordon that protected the group during the parade.[110] Today it is primarily women who patrol this cordon, and the lancer has become more of a supervisor. It is known that in the beginning there was a certain degree of concern about respectability and preventing confrontations with the police. As a result, alcoholic beverages were prohibited during the parade—a rule still officially in place. Originally there were revelers who performed the role of water bearers in Filhos de Gandhy, and one can no longer ascertain the ethylic properties of the liquid they were then bearing. Nowadays it is primarily the women accompanying the parade who offer the "logistical support" in this arena, exchanging drinks for kisses and bead necklaces. The original figure of the water bearers appears to be a direct reference to the figure of Gunga Din. If in fact the costumes worn by the first Filhos de Gandhy had some connection to the film, the source of inspiration was not the film's heroes, but the "bloodthirsty" Hindu Thugees.[111] Gunga Din could never be viewed as a pacifist or as a revolutionary; indeed, his association with Gandhi is nonexistent. But as a "water bearer" he shares, along with Gandhi, the archetype of Obatala. (As previously mentioned, Gandhi represents, both physically and ideologically, aspects of the archetype of Obatala.) This aesthetic and cosmological similarity points us toward another reference point that will help us decipher the representation of the water bearer Gunga Din within the Bahian context.

The Bahian Águas de Oxalá (Obatala's Waters) ceremonial feasts introduce two key aspects that are important for understanding the Filhos de Gandhy: the metaphor of water and water bearers in the sacred universe of Candomblé, and the symbolic "colonization" of Obatala by a despotic power. The connection between the water bearer Gunga Din and the Filhos de Gandhy supports these metaphoric constructs in multiple ways. Perhaps the major contradiction is that Gunga Din betrayed the Thugees. However, considering that the Thugees—rather than the British Army—inspired the lancers' costumes, and that the iconic Gunga Din inspired the Filhos de Gandhy, we are directed toward representations rooted in the Bahian imaginary from a somewhat different historic moment, when men dressed in white filled Salvador's streets: the Afro-Muslim-Brazilian Malê Rebellion. This revolt relied on the crucial support of the water bearers, and was also defeated because of informers. In this sense, *Gunga Din*, as interpreted in Bahia in 1949, would simultaneously represent the desire for liberation from colonial domination—which in Brazil prevented Bahia's separation and the establishment of an independent Muslim state—and concomitant efforts to uphold the ruling powers.

The Malês Rebellion ("Malês" refers to African Muslims in Bahia) was the organized culmination of a series of insurrections that occurred between 1807 and 1835. As explored further in this chapter, African Muslims—including notably the Hausas, Fulanis, and Nupes—were brought to Brazil in the final decades of the eighteenth century, following the civil wars in the Oyo Empire. As Décio Freitas describes, the rebels prepared for the uprising by manufacturing uniforms six months in advance, consisting of "berets or hoods made of white and blue cloth" and "large camisoles or *roupetas* [tunics] worn over pants and fastened at the waist with white cotton belts."[112] According to Risério, the revolt of 1835 resulted in a "frantic race against time—uncontrolled and bloody—through the rugged landscape of the city of Bahia."[113] The dream of "the establishment of a caliphate in Bahia died that night," the dream of "an all-Black Bahia where the whites would be exterminated ... and the mulattos turned into slaves."[114] The saga of the Malês—despite being somewhat "nebulous"—has endured in Brazil as a powerful source of mythic pan-African inspiration.[115] Raphael Vieira Filho recalls that as early as 1897, the Carnaval group Embaixada presented a manifesto demanding reparations for the Africans killed during the Malês Rebellion. References to the Malês are common in the theme songs and plots of *escolas de samba* and in a Filhos de Gandhy offshoot, the Afoxé Malê Debalê (founded in 1979).

The testimonies of the Gandhy founders mention three tunes originally sung by the group: the "Entra em Beco, Sai em Beco" ("Go In Through an Alley, Come Out Through an Alley"), a reference to the meandering route of the group through the city, through the "rugged landscape of the city of Bahia"; a melody from Candomblé "Êfila-la-e-ô de Balalaêôaa," a reference to the *filá*, a hat used by Orisha Obatala, and to the somewhat conical cap worn by Black Muslims; and "Alá-lá-ô," a tune composed by Haroldo Lobo and Nássara for the Rio de Janeiro Carnaval group Bloco da Bicharada (Bloco of a Herd of Animals) in 1940, which refers to the Sahara Desert and to the beneficent Allah (recall that *alá*, in the Afro-Bahian context, is also a reference to the white shawl that envelops and protects Obatala).[116] The fact that the Filhos de Gandhy reference Candomblé and Islam merely reflects the religious syncretism or resignification that was already well underway in Africa long before Europeans arrived.

A Hindu-Muslim-Bahian Fantasia

Abadá, a Yoruba word referring to the white tunic of Arabic origin worn by the Malês, is currently used to refer to the uniforms that participants wear in Afro-Bahian Carnaval associations.[117] The members of Filhos de Gandhy wear a costume that consists of *abadás* and turbans. As we know, Gandhi did not wear a turban. Careful analysis reveals that the turbans the Filhos de Gandhy wear do not derive from a Hindu aesthetic but more closely resemble the headdresses of the Sikhs, the inhabitants of Punjab—a border region between India and Pakistan that was divided into Indian Punjab and Pakistani Punjab in 1947. This aspect seems remarkable. Far from suggesting that the founders or current participants in the Filhos de Gandhy intentionally constructed a metaphor based on this referent, what emerges instead is a conscious and unconscious collage of signifiers and signifieds—an inclusive performative discourse open to continuous interpretation. Gandhi opposed any plan to divide India into two states; yet the Afoxé Filhos de Gandhy developed into a quasi-processional spectacle in which men wear Sikh turbans and Muslim *abadás* while following the mythical figure of a Hindu leader. The division of Punjab occurred a few years before Gandhi's death, and it was, in fact, his support of Pakistan that led to his assassination. Punjab, a historic borderland between Hindus and Muslims, and in the Indian section, largely populated by Sikhs—emerges as a powerful metaphor. This border area, a contested space of conflict and negotiation, is reflected in the layered aesthetic of the Filhos de Gandhy.

Around sixty years after Gandhi's death, Pravina Shukla, visiting Salvador during Carnaval, observed:

> The parade float, white with sapphire-blue painting, features what are considered to be symbols of India—a camel, elephants, and a goat—yet these are relegated to secondary place in the iconography when compared with the implements of the *orixás*, mainly the sword of Ogun, the crown of Oxalá, and the bow and arrow of Oxóssi, the *orixá* of the hunt. The carnival processions and any other important presence of Filhos de Gandhy also feature the Gandhi "look-alike," a slender older Black man with an uncanny resemblance to Gandhi himself. This Brazilian Gandhi sits atop a white elephant effigy ... The costume, said to emulate that of the Mahatma, consists of a long tunic, in the Brazilian carnival tradition of the requisite African *abadá*. The turban, as used in caricatures, conjures up images of majestic "Oriental" kings, surrounded by incense, rich foods, and harem beauties, straight from a fantasy inspired by *One Thousand and One Nights*. ... It is not the dress of the simply clad, threadbare Mahatama, but rather the display of a kingly African man in cool and flowing garments, adorned with the requisite turban that is worn because, as one informant told me, "everybody looks better in a turban." The turban not only frames the face; it adds a few inches to the height of the wearer, an important reason why many men opt to join the group, the choice reflecting not political and musical affiliation, but pure vanity.[118]

Yet the turbans were already part of the Afro-Brazilian reality well before India-via-Hollywood. As observed by Lody, the white turban worn by a Bahiana is traditionally styled in such a way that it resembles a regal crown.[119] In Brazilian culture, turbans are emblematic of the historical influences of Islamic traditions and double as protective carriers. They discreetly hold herbs such as rue, guinea, or saint-basil, which are believed to provide spiritual protection.[120] The connection between turbans and Islam is multifaceted. As the head is the seat of our cognitive choices, discerning between reality and illusion, or right and wrong, the turban acts as a symbol and amplification of our spiritual awareness. Within the Islamic tradition, the turban is seen as a barrier against the secular world; it safeguards one's thoughts, which are naturally prone to wandering and lapses of memory.[121] According to early descriptions, the turbans that the Filhos de Gandhy initially used were garlands tied with ribbons and garlic, much like the *selis* of the Sikh gurus, which are tied with strings.[122] The contemporary turbans follow the configuration of the Sikh turbans, the *dastaars*, which are decorated with a *khanda* (a brooch) and which the Filhos de Gandhy replaced with a circle containing a synthetic blue stone. The Sikhs decorate the *dastaars* with *khandas* in weddings during the Anand Karaj, or "blessing ceremony" representing the union of the individual soul with the universal soul. The *khanda* is therefore a metonymy of a ceremony that seeks the individual's fusion with the universe.[123]

A decade after her initial publication on the Gandhys, Shukla published a comparative study across the United States, Brazil, and Sweden, focusing specifically on the role of costume in celebrating and reenacting ancestral legacies and historical events. She offers a succinct and precise definition: "costume is to daily dress as ritual is to daily life—heightened in beauty, power, and meaning."[124] One of her insightful observations is that the Gandhys—in their white turbans, clothes, and beads—can be seen as male versions of the Baianas. Supporting this image is the fact that they are the only Carnaval group that parades in all public sacred events and processions in Salvador.[125]

The mixture of geographical, rhythmic, and thematic references of the Bahia Carnaval can be read, according to Araújo Moura, as the expression of a conscience that perceives the multiplicity of the world and attempts to position itself within it in order to elaborate its identity.[126] A cosmologically fertile and protean foundation allied to the political and poetic consciousness of the organizers and participants of the Bahian Carnaval allows for the inclusion of foreign icons and elements. And these—especially when they serve as metonymies of other cosmologies—often produce performative creations of a metaphorical value that not even the creators could anticipate.

Fantasia (the Brazilian-Portuguese term for "costume") contrasted with the Portuguese *disfarce*, which translates literally as "disguise"—beautifully encapsulates the various processes of re-membering and re-imagining the present, past, and future. This word seems to wear its meaning; it is as if the word "costume" would dress up as "fantasy," embodying all its beauty and potential. Shukla notes that *fantasias* are not replicas of historical garments; rather, "they are exaggerated" elaborations, "expressed through material and trim, cut and silhouette, color, glitter, and shine."[127] Instead of adding fictional aspects to the wearer's identity, they amplify or "add imaginary facets" to the wearer's performative self.[128] *Fantasias* are designed not to conceal or change, but to enhance aspects of the wearer's identity.[129] Shukla identifies several roles of costumes, including fostering community bonds, communicating with and informing a broader audience, expressing cultural heritage, and celebrating and affirming self-identities.[130]

Shukla once argued that any observation of the Filhos de Gandhy would immediately reveal fundamental contradictions between the group and Gandhi: "The Mahatma was simple; his 'sons' are extremely vain, bejeweled, perfumed and beautiful. The Mahatma was celibate; his 'sons' swap beads for kisses and hope for more. The Mahatma was a vegetarian; his sons eat the flesh of animals cooked and sold on the streets. The Mahatma was a pacifist; his 'sons' are aggressive and unduly violent."[131] But who is this Gandhi whom the revelers of yesterday and today celebrate? Agnaldo Silva defines the group as a "Hindu-African entity," and adds that "Ijexá fits right into the philosophy of Gandhi."[132] A member of Gandhy stressed the importance of learning Yoruba, "the language of the secret," since according to him, "Gandhi also works his magic in Yoruba."[133] The group known as "the sorcerers of Candomblé" has interpreted Gandhi as the greatest sorcerer.[134] However, the lure of Carnaval is sexual and carefree, the exact opposite of the self-control and self-discipline preached by Gandhi as the paths to divine truth. This apparent contradiction can also be explained according to an African diasporic logic, for a reading of Gandhi from within the cosmology of the Orishas immediately invests him with sexuality—so much so that the *avatār* of Obatala portrayed in the Filhos de Gandhy is Oshaguian (a younger warrior Obatala) and not Oshalufan (an older Obatala). The sexuality of the Orishas and their "children"—of the gods and human beings—resonates with Hindu traditions, where deities likewise embody sexuality openly. The sexual potency of certain Orishas is celebrated precisely as aspects of their divinity.

Shukla offers pertinent observations regarding the constructed caricature of an exoticized India as seen through the filter of secondhand Hollywood orientalisms.[135] The mass media of popular culture plays an undeniable role in the construction of Carnaval performances. The old Afoxé Mercadores de Bagdá

(Merchants of Baghdad) emerged in the same era as the Filhos de Gandhy and "promoted re-creations from movies with storylines from the East of the *One Thousand and One Nights* in their elaborate parades."[136] The Caboclo Afoxés presented "costumes and plots inspired by the North American Indians of John Ford and other directors of Western films."[137] What initially escaped Shukla's perception is that these recreations or idealizations occur not only in the "profane" realm of Carnaval, but also in the sacred realm of Candomblé and Umbanda, in religions and philosophies that have an inclusive, interpretive character. As previously analyzed, the Indigenous Caboclo in Umbanda and Candomblé refer primarily to Afrocentric Bantu and Yoruba concepts rather than cosmological principles of the Indigenous peoples of Brazil. Although Gandhi has not yet—as far as I know—been included in the sacred repertoire of Umbanda, the secular reverence with which Carnaval revelers receive him follows a similar process of interpretation and inclusion.

In 1999, the Afoxé Filhos de Gandhy marked its fiftieth year. Lula Buarque de Hollanda filmed a documentary with scenes in which some members of the group parade through the streets of the city of Udaipur in India.[138] If, for Shukla, the group was a source of awe, how might the figure of Raimundo Gandhy and his "sons" be perceived by the people of Udaipur? The documentary presents images of Sikhs and Hindus greeting Raimundo Gandhy and reverently touching the ground, but we do not know what they are thinking or how they interpret this unexpected figure. According to one of the Filhos de Gandhy founders, the group is "almost a sect" nowadays.[139] The people of Udaipur seem to have recognized this essential element—between devout and festive, between sacred and profane. Mestre Moa do Catendê (1954–2018), the founder of Afoxé Badauê in 1979, who was later fatally stabbed by supporters of Bolsonaro, spoke of the significant expectations that leaders of Afoxés and Afro-Carnaval groups must fulfill:

> High expectations are placed upon us as sources of spiritual sustenance. We have, in various ways, awakened the community from a dreadful sleep plagued by recurring nightmares. Each step we take, be it during Carnaval rehearsals or performances, showcases the profound strength of our culture. This empowers those within the Black community who are perceptive to realize that our struggle is singular: a struggle for the social integrity of Blacks.[140]

In his analysis of the Carnaval ensemble Olodum, Brazilianist Piers Armstrong characterizes their approach as a dynamic bricolage that weaves together narratives of resistance and liberation alongside essentialisms, utopias, modernities, para-religiosities, and vanities.[141] This observation resonates with the multifaceted identity of Filhos de Gandhy, which acts as a nexus for diverse communities including Hindus, Sikhs, Indian Muslims, Yorubas, Hausas, Fulanis, and Nupes. Serving as a transdiasporic paradigm or archetype, Filhos de Gandhy continuously recreates itself at the intersection of intricate African diasporic cosmologies and modernity. It interprets the past through the lens of the future while remaining anchored in the present.

The metaphors of the ocean, canoes, journeys, and crossing boundaries—geographic, mythic, and spiritual—observed in the Central-African-Brazilian poem-chants and performances of Capoeiristas, Candomberos, and Jongueiros in chapters 7 and 8 also carry over into Carnaval chants and performances. This will be further explored in the section of this chapter entitled "Agontimé and Chacha Ajinacu as Sung by Carnaval Griots." Shukla analyzes the "mysterious journey" experienced by the Filhos de Gandhy and Carnaval revelers from all over Brazil, a journey that is also undertaken by participants in many other sacred and secular performances:

> By traveling through space or time, the magical trip of Carnaval reveals the mundane and the local. Ultimately the social commentary is not about Egyptian pharaohs and "tribal mythology," but about the race and class struggles in the metropolis of Rio de Janeiro or Salvador. Celebrants travel far, metaphorically, to see the near clearly. Filhos de Gandhy takes its members and spectators on a voyage to India, to Africa, in order to expose the reality of Salvador.[142]

TRADE WINDS AND TRADE HUBS ALONG THE GULF OF GUINEA: FROM LUANDA TO OUIDAH

> *It was easy to set sail from Pernambuco, Bahia, and Rio de Janeiro to Luanda or the Gold Coast, and vice versa, [since] the Portuguese-Brazilian [system of] navigation . . . utilized the counterflow of what the Anglo-Saxons would later term "trade winds."*
>
> Luiz Felipe de Alencastro

Prior to the arrival of European traders, West African commerce was predominantly oriented northward, across the Sahara toward influential savannah states such as Ghana, Mali, Songhai, Kanem, and the Hausa city-states. These states were culturally and commercially connected to the Arab and Berber nations of North Africa. However, as European influence expanded, the savannah empires began to decline, and the once-remote West African seaboard was transformed into a crucial hub, creating a new frontier for unprecedented global interactions. Within a century, the sparsely populated Niger Delta was transformed into a bustling nexus of trading states, altering the continent's historical trajectory.[143] Further east from the coastal zones of West Africa, powerful kingdoms such as Benin, Oyo, and Asante rose as strategic negotiators with European powers. The emergence of the Atlantic trade created a new market for African products, including gold, ivory, cloth, and malagueta pepper—and eventually, also, for those who were enslaved through judicial decisions or warfare.[144]

Regions such as the Kongo and the Guinea Coast in West Africa had markedly different experiences with Europe. The Kongo primarily came under the influence of a single European power, while the Guinea Coast emerged as a competitive arena where multiple European nations vied for control. This dynamic was aptly characterized by the British Africanist Basil Davidson (1914–2010) as "an international partnership in risk and profit."[145] While the Portuguese enjoyed immense trading privileges in Kongo, along the Guinea Coast they faced stronger competition from the English, Dutch, and French, all of whom had the political stability and capital to pursue trade without haste. The Portuguese dealings with the Guinea Coast kingdoms were initially diplomatic and amicable, much like their earlier approach in Kongo. They began by opening negotiation channels and eventually established strategic outposts along the coast. What was the nature of the Portuguese presence on the Slave Coast? Who were its emissaries? In Kongo, a mixed Afro-Brazilian-Portuguese community facilitated direct trade with Brazil. Porto Novo, now part of modern Benin, along with other port towns such as Ouidah and El Mina, evolved into an enclave economy. These areas became hubs of economic and demographic expansion, partially insulated from the destabilizing impact of trade on the surrounding hinterlands.[146]

After establishing agreements and negotiating trading rights with local authorities, the Portuguese began to construct forts along the West African coast. In 1482, they secured a commercial trading agreement with the Akan people of the Gold Coast, leading to the construction of São Jorge da Mina, later known as Elmina Castle. Further west in what is now Ghana, they built several more forts: Fort Santo Antônio, established in 1515 in Axim; Fort São Francisco Xavier, established in 1557 in Accra; and Fort São Sebastião, built in 1558 in Shama. However, Portugal lost its leases to these trading posts to the Dutch in 1637. The Portuguese only managed to establish a new fort in 1721 in present-day Ouidah,

Benin, named São João Baptista de Ajudá.[147] After Luanda, Ouidah became the most prominent African slave port.[148]

The year 1721 marked the period when Brazilian residents began to assert control over Ouidah.[149] According to the Africanist historian Robin Law, the "fort's connections were primarily with Brazil, rather than directly with Portugal or the local West African administrative centers of Portuguese rule, such as the island of São Tomé."[150] The last director sent from Brazil to the fort, arriving in 1804 from Bahia, died shortly after his arrival. Despite a disruption in official communication between Bahia and Ouidah, the fort's personnel remained in residence.[151] The 1815 ban on the slave trade north of the Equator and the British-Portuguese anti-slave treaty of 1817 did not lead Portuguese authorities in Brazil to abandon or evacuate the fort.[152]

A substantial part of the Brazilian-African community in Ouidah consisted of former slaves, especially those deported following the Muslim insurrections in Bahia, which culminated in the 1835 rebellion. This community was organized and financially supported by Francisco Félix de Souza, a Brazilian trader born in Bahia around 1754. Initially arriving in Ouidah as a subordinate Portuguese official, de Souza served as the fort's director before the ban on the slave trade.[153] During a dispute over the Dahomey throne, de Souza supported King Adandozan's younger brother, Gezó, who successfully staged a coup d'état in 1818. In return, Gezó appointed Félix de Souza as the administrator of the port of Ouidah, which flourished during the period following the United Kingdom's prohibition of the Atlantic slave trade.[154]

Although commonly referred to as a harbor, Ouidah is more accurately described as a strategically positioned small market situated within the interior lagoons, with connections extending as far east as Lagos.[155] Ouidah's significance grew as a major trading center for the export of enslaved captives under the governance of the Dahomey kingdom. Robin Law identifies two significant periods in the history of Ouidah prior to French rule: the period of Dahomean control, following its conquest in 1727; and, in the early nineteenth-century, the era dominated by de Souza's influence, marked by the economic ascendancy of an elite composed of African-Brazilian returnees.[156]

In the Belly of the Beast: Oyo, Ouidah, and Dahomey

The Oyo Empire, which emerged in the thirteenth century, spanned present-day southern Benin and western Nigeria and eventually became the largest

Yoruba state. According to its cosmology, it was founded by Oranyan, a king from Ile-Ife and son of Oduduwa. *Itan* legends hold that Oranyan followed a charmed snake to the spot where the city of Oyo was to be established. He became the first "Alaafin of Oyo"—meaning "owner of the palace" in Yoruba—and appointed a separate ruler to govern Ife. By the sixteenth century, Oyo had evolved into a formidable inland power. During the seventeenth century, it experienced a phase of expansion and consolidation, establishing itself as the most populous Yoruba kingdom. The empire was underpinned by its powerful military and centralized governance. In the latter half of the eighteenth century, the Oyo Empire began to falter with internal dynastic conflicts, coups, and military setbacks.

At the beginning of the eighteenth century, Yorubaland was divided into fourteen major and many minor kingdoms in the east, including Benin (or Ibini), Ekiti (or Efon), Egba, Egbado (or Awori), Ife, Igbomina, Ijamo, Ijebu, Ijesa, Kétou, Owu, Ondo, Oyo, and Sabe. The Fon Aja people resided in the western region known as the Yoruba-Aja area. Prior to establishing Dahomey (Danxomê) in what is now Benin, the Aja lived in autonomous villages.[157] Dahomey, commonly regarded as a kingdom, was established in the early seventeenth century on the Abomey Plateau. Its residents, initially called the Foy (Fon), later became known as the Dahomeans. The name "Dahomey," or "Da-Homey," is derived from the Fon (Fongbe) language, often rendered as "Dan's Belly."[158]

Oral traditions recount an early seventeenth-century succession dispute in the kingdom of Allada between two rival princes, Teagbanlin and Dogbari. They resolved their conflict by parting ways: Teagbanlin moved south to establish Porto Novo, while Dogbari settled north on the Abomey Plateau near Cana (Kana).[159] Dogbari's son, Dakodonu (or Tacoodonou c. 1620–1645), later settled in Huawe (Hwawè) with the permission of local Guedevi chiefs. Seeking further expansion, he asked for more land near a local Guedevi chief named Dan. The chief replied with a question: "Have I given you so much land and yet you want more? Must I open my belly for you to build your house upon?"[160] It was then that Dakodonu seized a *kpatinpole*—a stake typically used by Dahomeans to mark new housing boundaries—as a weapon.[161] He skewered Dan with it, built a palace over his entrails and proclaimed that his kingdom would forever lie "in the belly of Dan."[162] The name "Dahomey" embodies its founding myth: "Dan" (the victim), "xo" (stomach), and "me" (inside).[163] It serves as a lasting reminder of the Fon's overthrow of the indigenous Guedevi claims to the land.[164]

This *itan* narrative refers to the chief Dan as the Vodun deity Danh (or Dañh), the rainbow snake that drinks from pools when touching the earth. Known properly as Anyi-e'wo (Ayidohwédo, "Great Snake of the Underneath"),

Danh usually resides beneath or at the edge of the world, emerging into the sky only when thirsty.[165] The Haitian anthropologist Leslie Desmangles defines Da-Homey as "the womb of Dahn." As such, Dahomey can be seen as the offspring of Dahn.[166] The fate of Dahomey would then be in the transformative hands of the creating androgynous deity Mawu-Lisa and also of Dahn, who together embody the ongoing cycle of movement and renewal continuously reshaping and regenerating life.[167]

In the Dahomean sacred geography, Cana—the place where Dakodonu's father settled—parallels Ile-Ife as a holy center, while Abomey parallels Oyo as a locus of political decision-making. The Beninese historian Jérôme Alladayê explains that "the buried dead, the protective gods for which sanctuaries have been built" lend deep significance to Cana, "a place where the founders of Danxomê and their descendants are mindful of the need and duty to come and periodically immerse [themselves] in the regenerative grace of the protective spirits."[168]

The development of Dahomey mirrors that of Ndongo in the sense that this was another state that rose during the era of the slave trade. As argued by the anthropologist Stanley Diamond (1922–1991), Dahomey was an emerging expansionist state that never firmly established itself.[169] Terms such as "monarchy" and "kingdom" do not quite describe the intricate social dynamics of Dahomey, which functioned more as a proto-state undergoing significant internal conflict and a complex transition from a kin-based to a civil power structure.[170] Before the French occupation, the kinship foundations of Dahomean society effectively preserved their cohesion, which prevented Dahomey from becoming the "absolutist" monarchy it is often perceived to be.[171]

By the eighteenth century, Dahomey had expanded into a significant political and economic regional power.[172] This included the conquest of key coastal cities such as Ouidah, which enabled extensive participation in the triangular trade across three continents, eliminated intermediaries, and established a direct tributary connection to Abomey.[173] The port, known to the Portuguese as São João Baptista de Ajudá, drew its name from the kingdom of Whydah (known as Ouidah in French and Fon). The former kingdom of Whydah had gained dominance over the Ardras but was conquered by Dahomey in 1727. Ouidah, crucial for its access to the sea, became instrumental in Dahomey's rise, initially through the slave trade and later through the palm oil trade.[174] A critical hub in the global slave trade from the seventeenth through the nineteenth centuries, Ouidah established itself as a major competitor among the ports along the Bight of Benin.

Under the rule of Agaja (r. 1718–1740), the fourth Dahomean chief enstooled in 1718, the regime shifted the region's dynamics with expansionist pursuits that led to the conquest of surrounding Aja territories. The Aja states at the time followed a governance model resembling a family hierarchy, where the ruler of Allada acted as the "father" and the rulers of Whydah and Abomey as "elder" and "younger" brothers, respectively.[175] This mirrored the familial structure of the Yoruba, where the Ooni king was considered the "father," and the ruler of Oyo was a prominent "son." King Agaja's invasion of Allada, the "father" realm, disrupted not only the traditional but also the constitutional order of Aja and its neighbors.[176] As Allada was a tributary to Oyo, its conquest directly threatened Oyo's national interests, compelling them to defend both the defeated and their own interests. Bolstered by his victory at Allada and access to firearms, King Agaja underestimated Oyo's military capabilities. In 1726, a brief yet intense conflict inflicted severe losses on Dahomey and resulted in many being enslaved. Despite this defeat, Agaja's continued defiance forced Oyo's Alaafin Ojigi (r. 1724–1735) to choose between accepting the Dahomean victories or defending the established order. Oyo chose the latter, seeing the preservation of the traditional way of life as crucial for maintaining regional stability.[177]

From that moment on, Oyo continuously invaded Dahomey, and after three years, Dahomey found itself impoverished.[178] In 1730, Dahomean refugees fled from European forts to Abomey. Although Oyo had agreed to withdraw, the refugees found Oyo's forces still nearby and were forced to retreat. Agaja moved his capital from Abomey to Allada, informed European directors of his decision, and sought their support.[179] In 1730, a peace treaty was signed, and Oyo could no longer invade Dahomey at the behest of the defeated rulers of Allada and Whydah. This allowed King Agaja to consolidate his territories.[180] Key provisions of the treaty included Agaja retaining control over the entire Kingdom of Whydah and a substantial part of Allada, while remaining a tributary state to Oyo, thereby solidifying Oyo's dominance over the region. Areas outside Dahomey's eastern boundary came under Oyo's protection, and some of the Aja people resettled in an area of Ajase, which in the nineteenth century became the Kingdom of Porto Novo.[181] Nine years after the 1730 peace treaty—further solidified through royal marriages—Oyo resumed its invasions of Dahomey. Dahomey continued paying annual tribute to Oyo for seventy years, until King Gezó declared independence in 1818.[182] Throughout its peak, Dahomey was subjugated by the Oyo Empire, which itself was under pressure from the Hausa and subsequently the Fulani, illustrating a complex hierarchy of regional dominance.[183]

The establishment of a slave market near Cotonou and the designation of Porto Novo as Oyo's main port deprived Dahomey of its primary sources for enslaved captives. Dahomey's attempts to compensate through increased local raiding were thwarted by King Tegbesu's (r. 1740–1774) prevailing policy of prioritizing trade over warfare.[184] The economic foundation of Dahomey, heavily reliant on the slave trade, made the kingdom vulnerable to shifts in international trade dynamics. This vulnerability was exacerbated when, in 1774, Oyo's Alaafin Abiodun (r. 1770–1789) established new economic policies that monopolized the market trade. King Tegbesu's son and successor, Kpengla (r. 1774–1789), realized that as long as Dahomey remained under Oyo's control, achieving an effective independent policy, especially over strategic locations such as Porto Novo, would be unattainable.[185] At one point, Dahomey refused to pay the corals owed to Oyo, claiming a shortage. However, Alaafin Abiodun contested this claim after discovering that Oyo merchants could still obtain the corals from Whydah. Kpengla was forced to appease Abiodun with significant gifts to maintain Dahomey's autonomy.[186] Growing antagonism toward Oyo led to escalating challenges for Dahomean rulers seeking full independence. King Agonglo (r. 1789–1797) was murdered in a coup by King Adandozan (r. 1797–1818). Adandozan's reign, beginning in 1797, was marred by his reputation as a despotic ruler, infamously selling his own kin into slavery—a heinous act in Dahomean society.[187] He was deposed in 1818 by King Gezó (r. 1818–1858). Meanwhile, in Oyo, Alaafin Awole (r. 1789–1796), Abiodun's successor, worsened the problems he inherited by attacking inviolable towns—actions that violated his oath of office—leading to an army revolt and his eventual suicide.[188]

In 1804, King Adandozan of Dahomey reached out to the Regent Prince of Portugal, Dom João Carlos de Bragança, seeking a commercial alliance. The king's communication, transcribed by a captive Portuguese sailor, opened with a deferential tone: "My Beloved Brother, much time has elapsed since I beseeched our esteemed God, Legba, to look favorably upon my aspiration to ally with the Portuguese, and to consider the proposition and terms I am eager to set forth."[189] Adandozan expressed his desire to align with the Portuguese under favorable terms, including access to fabled gold mines in exchange for an exclusive partnership through the trading post of Ouidah, trade rights, and goods such as silver shotguns, ornate hats, and silk.[190] Despite his diplomatic efforts, the Portuguese Crown dismissed the king's overtures.

Dahomey's struggle for autonomy concluded with its annexation by the French in 1892 and the downfall of Dahomean King Behanzin (r. c. 1890–c. 1894), despite his armed resistance with German weaponry.[191] Prior to French conquest,

Dahomey thrived through wars of expansion and trading captives, predominantly with Brazil, Cuba, and Haiti, under a centralized system akin to that of Kongo and Loango. Despite the British ban on the Atlantic slave trade in 1807 and Portugal's subsequent prohibition in 1815, the trade persisted illegally—even after Brazil's formal abolition in 1850—and its eventual decline precipitated economic challenges that undermined Adandozan's rule. Notorious for his ruthless decision to enslave his half-brother Gezó's mother and her relatives, Adandozan struggled to maintain power by attempting to secure an exclusive trading agreement with Portugal. Further complicating his rule, João de Oliveira established competing ports to the east of Ouidah, such as Porto Novo and Onim (present-day Lagos). By offering more favorable conditions, Oliveira attracted European traders and weakened Adandozan's grip on the lucrative Atlantic trade routes. Ultimately, in 1818, Gezó ousted Adandozan, fulfilling the Fa oracle's prophecy.[192]

In 1823, Dahomey raided villages under Oyo's protection. King Gezó appointed the Brazilian Francisco Félix de Sousa as his envoy to negotiate with the Alaafin of Oyo, but the peace talks failed, leading to another attack by Oyo. It was then that Dahomey finally defeated the Oyo forces. Throughout the mid-nineteenth century, after ceasing to be a tributary state to the Oyo Empire, Dahomey emerged as a crucial regional state. Its political and economic strategies included forging international relationships, exemplified by diplomatic missions sent to Brazil from the early eighteenth century onward. In 1823, Dahomey was among the first states to formally recognize Brazil's independence. Despite international pressures, Dahomey's involvement in the transatlantic slave trade with Brazil remained intense.

The fall of the Oyo Empire was hastened by a confluence of internal strife and civil unrest, along with concerted military campaigns by both the Dahomeans and the Fulanis, which, having subdued the Tapas around 1820, were later overcome by the Hausa. This tumultuous period marked a significant reshuffling of power dynamics in the region and epitomizes, as Davidson notes, the devastating ripple effects of the slave trade.[193] Kingdoms jostled for survival by negotiating with European traders and forming precarious alliances. Through its intertwined history with Oyo and Brazil, Dahomey not only witnessed the deification of a Brazilian slave trader but also the transformation of its kings, or Fia (short for *Fiaŋutsu* in Fon), into a reinvented cultural phenomenon and strategic construction, analogous to Nzinga's refashioning and updating of the Kilombos. This Dahomean reimagining of kings alongside their doppelgängers, as we will explore, represents one of the most enigmatic phenomena; it also challenges cultural translations long taken for granted, and presumed understandings by outsiders.

Sanctified Slave Traders: Power and Anachronistic Legacies

Born around 1700 in Yorubaland, João de Oliveira was captured as a child and sold to Portuguese slave traders who transported him to Recife. Noted for his trustworthiness, industriousness, and intelligence, Oliveira gained favor with his master and was entrusted with managing the transport of enslaved captives from Benin to Recife. While still enslaved, he secured his emancipation through his work as a slave trader.[194] Oliveira challenged the Dahomean monopoly in the region by establishing competitive trading ports at Porto Novo and Onim. This move disrupted the established dominance of Ouidah and El Mina and altered the dynamics of the transatlantic trade. Pierre Verger refers to Oliveira as the first unofficial Portuguese Ambassador to the region. However, upon his return to Bahia in 1770, near the end of his life, Oliveira was imprisoned instead of commended.[195] Oliveira's establishment of Porto Novo and Onim marked a significant chapter in transatlantic trade, laying the groundwork for an Afro-Brazilian-Portuguese trade network.

Oliveira's contemporary, Francisco Félix de Souza (c. 1754–1849), was born a free Indigenous-Portuguese mestizo in Bahia and forged a similar yet distinct path by forming an alliance with the monarch who succeeded Dahomean King Adandozan.[196] While de Souza's name is still revered, the contributions of Oliveira and many other traders like Joaquim Teles de Menezes, Juan José Zangronis, Joaquim de Almeida, and Domingos José Martins have largely been forgotten.[197] According to the transnational historian Ana Lucia Araujo, "even if historical new evidence shows that there were other more prosperous traders, Francisco Félix de Souza continues to occupy a central place in the memory of the slave trade, not only in Bahia but across the whole South Atlantic region."[198]

In the 1830s and 1840s, Dahomey was deeply involved in trade negotiations with Brazil, primarily through the port of Ouidah. The Brazilian slave trader overseeing this harbor was Francisco Félix de Souza. De Souza began his trading career in Ouidah around 1810..[199] He traded not only with the Portuguese and Brazilians, but also with the English and French.[200] King Gezó of Dahomey gave de Souza authority to act on his behalf along the coast and bestowed upon him the honorific title of Chacha, often understood as "Royal Brother" and likened to that of a viceroy. "Chacha" seems to be a nickname that originated during de Souza's escape from prison with the aid of his allies. In Fon, "chacha" (spelled "cacà") translates to "quickly done." This term likely evolved from "já já," a Portuguese expression meaning "quick, quick," or "hurry, hurry," an expression de Souza himself may have used. Over time, "Chacha" became a hereditary title within the Souza family, denoting its highest-ranking representative.[201]

De Souza rose to become arguably the most renowned slave trader in Brazilian history. For approximately thirty years, as "Chacha Ajinacu," he dominated all commerce between Dahomey, Europe, and the Americas.[202] The Fon title "Ajinacu" can be dissected into components from Fon and Yoruba languages. *Aji* may derive from *jí*, meaning "to wake" or "awaken"; *na* is a contraction for *naa*, a term that suggests continuity or persistence; and *ku* means "to die." Thus, the title "Ajinacu" can perhaps be translated as "one who wakes and does not die," or "one who has the power to wake and defy death."

Throughout his rule, King Gezó initiated expeditions to locate his mother, Queen Agontimé, who was sold into slavery by his predecessor Adandozan. De Souza participated in organizing these searches, which spanned from Havana to Bahia, but despite their efforts, they could not find her. It was only recently that Pierre Verger may have succeeded in uncovering, or in fabulating, the narrative of Gezó's mother.

From the Nineteenth Century Brazilian Jihad to UNESCO's Contemporary Slave Route Project: Tracing the Legacy from Chacha I (c. 1754–1849) to Chacha IX (1958–)

In the latter stages of the Portuguese-Brazilian Atlantic trade, the Dahomeans overpowered the Oyo Empire, which was simultaneously besieged by the Fulanis. The Fulanis had previously conquered the Tapas (Nupe), a predominantly Islamic community, and sold their war captives to the Portuguese, many of whom ended up in Salvador, Bahia. The Oyo Empire was also unraveling from within due to a series of civil wars beginning in 1796. The historian João José Reis documents that these civil conflicts were instigated by Afonjá, a non-Muslim general of Oyo's Imperial Army, who defied the Alaafin's royal command and invaded the sacred city of Ife.[203] During this uprising, Afonjá was supported by numerous Muslim Yoruba and Hausa captives who were experts in various fields ranging from agriculture to medicine and typically worked within the Yoruba community rather than being traded with Europeans. His attempt to forge an alliance with the Fulanis in Sokoto backfired disastrously, leading to his betrayal and death, and his forces were subsequently deployed to initiate a jihad against Oyo.[204] The vanquished forces, including many Muslim soldiers, were then captured and transported as slaves to Bahia.

Bahia experienced an influx of Muslim Africans, including Hausas and Tapas, who, along with other African Muslim groups, such as Kanuris and Fulanis, were collectively referred to in Brazil as Malês (from the Yoruba *Ìmàle*, or the Fon *Malé* meaning Muslims). In Salvador, Bahia's cosmopolitan hub, these groups mingled with other ethnic Africans who had embraced Islam. Reis highlights Islam's unique position as a cross-ethnic unifier, transcending individual ethnicities to bring together diverse groups.[205] This unity empowered Islam to mobilize Africans in Bahia. Islam played a dual role in the sociopolitical dynamics of West Africa in the early nineteenth century: it was both the ideology of expansionist states, aligning with rulers to support slave traders and masters; and a source of solace and strength for the oppressed, fostering community among impoverished free men who lived under the rule of the elite and adhered to traditional religions.[206] For the many enslaved Muslims, Islam fostered hope for freedom and sparked rebellion.

From 1807 to 1835, Bahia witnessed a series of insurrections spearheaded by Muslims, initially by the Hausas and later by the Tapas. In 1807, a Hausa group plotted to seize the Portuguese weapons warehouse. Concurrently, other insurgents planned to create distractions by setting fires at the customs office and a nearby church, facilitating a coordinated multidirectional assault on the town. Their objective was to subjugate Portuguese inhabitants and commandeer ships in Salvador's harbor to sail back to Africa.[207] The leaders of this initial revolt—Antônio, a manumitted slave, and Baltazar, still enslaved—were captured and executed.[208] A subsequent uprising in 1808 erupted in Salvador's rural outskirts, where slaves set fire to plantations and converged at a predetermined location near the city. Meanwhile, over four hundred Africans left Salvador to join the assembled forces, aiming to take control of the city center.[209]

By 1810, a fully articulated rebellion was orchestrated by a maroon community near Salvador.[210] Armed and resolute, they marched from plantation to plantation, rallying the enslaved who often set fire to the properties, killed their overseers, and joined the burgeoning insurrection.[211] These Muslim insurgents repeatedly struck Bahia, setting plantation fires, tainting public water sources, and liberating fellow Africans from confinement. In 1835, they launched a meticulously planned insurrection known as the Revolta dos Malês.[212] On January 25, 1835, the streets of Salvador were filled with hundreds of African rebels dressed in traditional white Muslim attire. The uprising coincided with Ramadan, shortly before Lailat al-Qadr, the revered "Night of Power," when it is believed that Allah restrains all evil spirits to reorder the world. Had the Malês' revolt succeeded, this night would have marked their victory celebration. The insurgents' intention, as gleaned from testimonies made by arrested rebels, was to eliminate "all the people of the land of the Whites," with Blacks and Mestizos native to Brazil either to be killed or enslaved.[213] Although these revolts did not achieve their literal goals, they instilled terror within the ruling class and continue to be a potent symbol of Afro-Brazilian resistance.

The Malê Rebellions have been romanticized as a Pan-African movement. Figures such as Abdias do Nascimento read into this uprising two idealized traits: first, that the Brazilian Muslims, unlike their African counterparts, did not wage jihad to spread Islam but instead fought for the freedom of all Africans in Bahia, irrespective of faith; and second, that the rebellions were inherently Pan-African, uniting Africans across all statuses and ethnicities. While the desire to view these rebellions as an inclusive Pan-African struggle is appealing, it oversimplifies the complexities involved. The organization of the Malê Rebellions was distinctly Muslim, though it occasionally included some non-Muslim participants. However, there was limited involvement from Fon Dahomeans, and no recorded participation by Kongos.[214] A significant Kongo population, present in Bahia even before the Muslims, had by then largely assimilated into the colonial way of life. Moreover, back in Africa, the Fon Dahomeans were historically adversaries of the Muslims. To dismiss the insurrections as non-jihadist seems to ignore the evidence that, had they succeeded, Bahia might well have transformed into a Muslim state.

The Malê Rebellions were a stand against the enslavement of African Muslims by Catholic Portuguese, Brazilian Portuguese, or Afro-Brazilians. Despite their scale and impact—arguably constituting the most significant urban slave revolts in the American diaspora—the Malê Rebellions mirrored the complexities and contradictions of their era. In his research, the poet and historian, Nei Lopes observes that, while the legacy of Muslims in Brazil looms large, its details remain elusive.[215] As noted by Lopes, in the late twentieth century, a widespread tendency emerged among Afro-Brazilians to identify with the Malês. While the Hausas, Tapas, Kanuris, and Fulanis were celebrated for establishing a heritage of resistance, the historical significance of Palmares was downplayed until the late 1970s, when it began to gain broader recognition. In Salvador, during the early 1980s, a fascination with Malê heritage surged among the Black community. Without evidence, many began claiming "noble" Malê lineage.[216] This sense of identity persists in the arts and discourse, a phenomenon Antonio Risério terms "an understandable but reproachable arrogance."[217] The pride associated with a Yoruba-centric line of thought manifests as a dismissive view of Central Africa, its movements for freedom, and its cosmologies, suggesting a form of intellectual elitism and a claim to an "authentic," non-creolized African identity. Academia, in part, has endorsed this narrative, proposing cultural superiority among the peoples of the Guinea Coast.

The African Returnees and the Chachas

During the thirty-year period of Muslim urban guerrilla warfare in Salvador, those apprehended faced execution, incarceration, or deportation. The overcrowded jails led to the deportation of many arrested Africans. In 1841, a decree mandated the deportation of all freed Africans imprisoned in Bahia.[218] This scattering of Africans and their descendants dispersed them to various regions and many deportees had to part from their spouses and children. The return journey to Africa often followed routes different from those that had initially brought them or their ancestors to Brazil. Some Africans, perceived as threats by the colonial powers, were sent to Ouidah (Ajudá) and became known as Agudas or Brazilians, receiving support from Brazilian traders already established there.[219] Francisco Félix de Souza wielded significant influence in Ouidah, both politically and financially, and he utilized a subordinate workforce for both legal and illegal trade with the Americas and Europe.

The Agudas gradually transformed the Benin landscape with Brazilian colonial architecture. When constructing a mosque, they adopted the Brazilian Baroque style typical of a Catholic church, replacing the cross with a minaret.[220] They introduced Brazilian clothing, furniture, utensils, and Afro-Brazilian cuisine, along with associated religious and cultural practices. These traditions persist today, with the Agudas still identifying as Brazilians. During festivities, women don traditional Brazilian colonial attire from the nineteenth century, perform samba, and sing songs in Portuguese, which had become forgotten in Bahia. Upon settling in the Bight of Benin, the Aguda repatriated slaves sought to emulate the structure of Brazilian slave society not only in their customs and culture but also in commerce; many became slave traders themselves. While not all amassed vast fortunes, a number achieved prosperity. By 1850, a group of these former slaves were actively engaged in the slave trade in Ouidah, Agoué, and Porto Novo.[221]

Being an Aguda meant belonging to a modern bourgeoisie in which many collaborated with the French regime and received favors that cemented their privileged status within colonial society.[222] However, following the independence of Dahomey in August 1960, the Agudas' influence markedly declined. The end of the dictatorship ushered in a new era characterized by efforts to promote Vodun cultures and religions and to memorialize slavery, leading to a resurgence in prestige and visibility for some members of the Aguda community on the political scene.[223] In the early 1990s, the memorialization of slavery and the transatlantic slave trade grew into a transnational movement that extended beyond the Americas and Europe. In Benin, during the commemoration of the five hundredth anniversary of Columbus's arrival in the Americas, a debate emerged on the memory of slavery. The underrepresentation of the contributions of Africans to the Americas sparked the emergence of two distinct initiatives: the transnational "The Slave Route," and "Ouidah 92," a festival rooted in Vodun religion and partly aimed at boosting tourism. Both projects, while initially separate, eventually merged and received support from UNESCO and Benin's newly democratic government.[224] While these projects have facilitated open discussions about the slave past in Benin, slavery within Africa and the Muslim slave trade remain taboo topics in many contexts. [225]

Unlike other African nations, Benin has acknowledged its role in the slave trade. Journalist Kevin Sieff notes that while Americans are reexamining the ways in which slavery and the Civil War are memorialized, Benin, along with other West African nations, is confronting its own complex legacy of involvement in the trade.[226] In collaboration with the Smithsonian Institution, the government of Benin plans to construct two museums dedicated to the slave trade, emphasizing its complex and contentious aspects. This subject, often a central issue in political debates, tends to be downplayed by descendants of those who profited from the trade and strongly criticized by descendants of those who were enslaved. It remains particularly controversial in Benin, where the kingdoms that historically captured and sold slaves still exist as "tribal networks," as do the communities they once preyed upon.[227] With the construction of the new museums, Benin faces a crucial decision on how to articulate its role in the slave trade.

In Benin, UNESCO projects have paradoxically commemorated both the victims of the slave trade and the enslavers. According to Ana Lucia Araujo, while the idea of celebrating a slave trader may be inconceivable from a Western perspective, it is more acceptable within the African context. This is because the Atlantic slave trade and slavery in the Americas are not viewed solely as African issues.[228] Benin has struggled to acknowledge the victims' stories, often commemorating instead those who enslaved them.[229] The country remains divided between the descendants of the enslaved and those of slave traders, with the elite showing reluctance to confront this divisive past.[230] Olabiyi Yai highlights that families such as the de Souza, descendants of slave merchants, continue to wield significant influence over national narratives, controlling how Benin's history is portrayed.

The biography of Francisco Félix de Souza illuminates the varied and conflicting memories surrounding slavery, highlighting the disparities between descendants of former slaves and slave traders.[231] Robin Law challenges the portrayal of de Souza as a viceroy-like figure, suggesting instead that he was a *caboceer*, or local chief.[232] His descendants try to recast his historical image, portraying him not as a slave trader but as an entrepreneur. This reimagining has transformed de Souza's legacy from that of a slave trading tycoon into the myth of "a benevolent patron" who helped a community of Brazilian returnees reconnect with Africa.[233] This narrative of benevolence also stems from accounts in which he reportedly found the king's mother, turning a traumatic historical rupture caused by the transatlantic slave trade into a meaningful connection with Brazil.[234] While there is no solid evidence that de Souza traveled to Brazil to find Na Agontimé, it is suggested that Gezó sent one of de Souza's employees—possibly one who aided his escape from Abomey's prison—to do so.[235] De Souza thus embodies the bond between Brazil and Dahomey, with modern narratives emphasizing the region's renewed ties with Brazil and depicting him as a figure of blended identity associated with "an imaginary or imagined Brazil."[236] Although he was not the only prominent merchant in the region—as documented by Robin Law and others—it is a romanticized, fabulated memory, rather than historical "facts," that has elevated Francisco Félix de Souza, despite his Brazilian ancestry, to the status of an idealized African chief.

When King Gezó invited de Souza to settle in Ouidah, he granted him two Voduns to protect the city—one at its entrance and another at its exit—and later, a third for his personal protection: Dagoun.[237] Despite being Catholic, de Souza was the only Aguda to have his own Vodun.[238] Vodun divinities are believed to inhabit specific physical spaces. Approximately one hundred meters from the de Souza family compound in Singbomey, on the road towards the beach, lies the temple of Dagoun, the Vodun of de Souza. De Souza's tomb in his former bedroom became a major symbol of an ancient bond with Brazil.[239] Water from an earthenware jar by his grave is believed to have healing properties. Less than a mile from what was once West Africa's largest slave port stands a statue of Francisco Félix de Souza, revered as the father of Ouidah. There is a museum dedicated to his family and a plaza, a former auction site for slaves, bearing his name.[240] Recently, there has been talk of renaming the "Place de Chacha," though a new name has yet to be selected.

The rehabilitation of Francisco Félix de Souza's memory gained momentum at the turn of the twenty-first century, notably under Chacha VIII Honoré Feliciano de Souza, who held the title from 1990 to 2014. Currently, de Souza's descendants maintain that past actions should be assessed within their historical context and not by today's standards.[241] The lineage is now led by Chacha IX Roger Moise de Souza, a construction engineer who was officially appointed in 2017 after consultations with elders and senior figures within the House of de Souza. He was formally invested by the King of Abomey, Dadah Dedjalagni Agoli-Agbo (1934–2018), under the regnal name Mito, continuing the lineage that started with Chacha I.²⁴² Chacha IX's light brown skin is a point of pride for a family that often boasts about its ties to colonialists.²⁴³ During an interview, he acknowledged the burdensome legacy of his ancestors' role in the slave trade: "It is something that makes me feel bad. We know it's painful, and all I can do is apologize." He has also expressed opposition to portraying de Souza as a slave merchant in the new Ouidah Museum, claiming that his family's reputation should be protected.²⁴⁴

In January 2018, Chacha IX and other de Souza descendants made their annual pilgrimage to Abomey, the former capital of the Kingdom of Dahomey. They met with the former ceremonial King Agoli-Agbo and other descendants of Gezó. This annual gathering celebrates the enduring ties between the two families; bonds originally forged through the slave trade.²⁴⁵

RETRACING THE FOOTSTEPS IN DAHOMEY AND OYO OF THOSE WHO STAND BEHIND: QUEEN NA AGONTIMÉ AND ÌYÁ NÀSÓ

In a quiet provincial city in northeastern Brazil there stands a white stucco house where an aggressive water spirit and certain deified kings of a remarkable West African dynasty continue to dance in company with less particularized forces of nature and the human mind.

Judith Gleason (1929–2012)

Until the mid-nineteenth century, following a king's death, princes vying for the royal stool had to physically take control of the palace in Abomey. These princes and their supporters frequently engaged in civil wars until one faction achieved dominance. The defeated parties faced one of three grim options: execution, imprisonment, or being sold into slavery.²⁴⁶ Among those who lost in these political struggles were some deemed too dangerous or powerful to be killed—they were often believed to possess supernatural abilities, and sometimes commanded large followings. A notable example is King Adandozan, who was overthrown in 1818 but lived in a royal residence in Abomey until the 1860s. Despite being depicted as a tyrant in oral traditions, Adandozan reportedly played advisory roles to his successors. Evidence from documents and oral traditions indicates that the Dahomean elite considered selling political rivals into slavery as a form of political exile for those opposed to the ruling powers.

Selling rivals into slavery carried the paradoxical risk that, should they find a way to return, they would become even more powerful.[247]

The option of selling political rivals into slavery was not only a source of income but also a means to remove potential threats without direct violence, thus avoiding accusations of murder. The anthropologist Melville Herskovits documented instances of families sold because they were considered too magically powerful.[248] In tracing back through the origins of the Dahomean state, the term Ghede emerges—a name that has also carried over into Haitian Vodou. Originating from Ghedevi, which means "children of Ghede," this group is believed to have been the original inhabitants of the Abomey plateau. They reportedly resisted the founders of Dahomey and, as a result, were displaced and likely sold into slavery.[249] Although the identities of the individuals on slave ships were often unknown to the captains, some people in Dahomey managed to track the whereabouts of exiled persons. This suggests that some traders knew they were dealing with prominent individuals and reported on their status. Herskovits documented a ritual prayer in Dahomey that called for news of family members who had been sold into slavery in Brazil, highlighting a connection maintained even across the Atlantic.[250]

The return of exiled individuals was not unheard of; the African-Brazilian community on the coast proves that it was possible to come back after being sold overseas. This resilience and eventual return occasionally boosted the stature of those who had been exiled.[251] Notably, a prince who had been sold to Brazil and returned was among the contenders for the royal stool after King Kpengla's death in 1789. Known as Don Jeronimo in Brazil, Prince Fruku had spent twenty-four years abroad before being redeemed by Kpengla and returning to contest the royal succession. These complex dynamics of exile and return in the Dahomean understanding of the slave trade suggest that survival and return could significantly enhance the status of returnees and their political influence.[252]

Queen Mother, Kpojito Na Agontimé

Queen Agontimé, sold into slavery amid the political turmoil following King Agonglo's assassination in 1797 and during the rise to power of King Adandozan, stands out as one of the most renowned returnees from the Western Hemisphere.[253] Following King Agonglo's death, there were at least two significant battles before Adandozan could establish control. After these conflicts, several members of the royal family and opposition were either killed or imprisoned, and a total of 900 opposition members were captured. Three hundred of these captives were enslaved and distributed among the new king's followers, while another 600, including Queen Agontimé, were sent to Ouidah to be sold into the overseas slave trade.[254]

While Queen Agontimé is frequently depicted as the wife of King Agonglo and referred to as "the mother" of King Gezó, this latter designation does not necessarily denote a biological relationship with Gezó. In the eighteenth century, the *kpojito*, or "Queen Mother," served as the reign-mate or ally of the new king, sometimes drawn from the household of his predecessor. Those holding the highest female rank in the kingdom were politically and spiritually powerful women, "often reputed to be skilled in the use of supernatural powers," who forged alliances with princes before transitions of the royal stool occurred.[255]

Following his coup in 1818, King Gezó dispatched delegations to locate Agontimé, leading to diverse narratives about their journey and its outcomes. While some traditions and historians contend that she was never found, others—including Pierre Verger and Nicolau Parés—believe she established a significant religious community in Brazil.[256] The Africanist Edna Bay notes that, despite uncertainties regarding the historical accuracy of her return, Agontimé is reputed to have returned to Dahomey from Brazil more than two decades after her enslavement and to have ascended to the position of *kpojito* alongside King Gezó.[257] The timing of her enstoolment and her supposed twenty-four-year absence in the Americas hint at her return to Dahomey around 1821, which would coincide with a Dahomean victory over Oyo in 1823.[258] Her praise name, Agontimé, which translates as "the monkey has come from the country of the whites and is now in a field of pineapples," symbolically contrasts the harsh realities of her past with the opulence of her present life, illustrating how her return from exile led to renewed prestige within the royal court.[259]

If Queen Na Agontimé had been exiled in Brazil, it is conceivable that traces of her presence would surface within the Brazilian-Fon orature. Given the interaction between the Fon (Jeje) and Yoruba (Nago) cultures, scholars for a long time doubted the existence of an exclusive Fon (Jeje) cosmology in Brazil. Arthur Ramos corroborated Nina Rodrigues's observation that Fon rites were subsumed by the Yoruba and that even subtle Dahomean elements had merged into the Jeje-Nago syncretism.[260] A different perception emerged with the research of the anthropologist Manoel Nunes Pereira (1893–1985) on an established form of Vodun rituals with clear Dahomean roots in Maranhão.[261]

Two centuries after the efforts of Gezó and Francisco Félix de Souza to locate Queen Agontimé, Pierre Verger pieced together historical clues over decades, ultimately formulating a compelling hypothesis about her fate. According to Verger, King Adandozan's decision to sell Queen Na Agontimé was likely motivated by a desire to remove any claims to the throne by Gezó.[262] Maria Jesuína, known as Na Agontimé, was not in Havana or Bahia as previously suspected but rather in the northern Brazilian region of São Luís de Maranhão. Following Agonglo's death in 1797, Agontimé appears to have founded a pivotal African-Brazilian religious center known as the Querebentã de Zomadônu or Casa Grande das Minas.[263]

Verger's claims were supported by popular knowledge collected by Melville Herskovits during his fieldwork in Dahomey.[264] Moreover, Octavio da Costa Eduardo, who was mentored by Herskovits, studied how several Dahomean kings were worshipped as Voduns in the Casa das Minas.[265] Verger's further research in 1948 in Benin with the Nesuhué royal cult corroborated that the Voduns worshipped at Casa das Minas were deified ancestors from the royal family of Abomey. This supports Verger's theory that only someone very close to the royal family could have established such a cult in Brazil, likely Na Agontimé herself.[266] Verger's conclusions were based on comparing the names of the Dahomey kings known in Brazil with the dynasty's historical lineage, identifying Agonglo as the last king known in Brazil. Thus, he posited that the establishment of the Casa das Minas occurred after the end of Agonglo's reign, and that Na Agontimé, sold as a slave during that tumultuous period, could have been the one who founded the center. Parés later supported Verger's hypothesis that the religious figures who established the Casa das Minas were likely from Abomey or its vicinity, given the cult's deep connections to the Nesuhué royal traditions. The prominence of Vodun Zomadonu and other deities associated with the Abomey royal family within Casa das Minas underscores the significant influence of Dahomean religious practices on its formation.[267]

Succession disputes in Dahomey following King Agonglo's death created unique circumstances under which royal religious figures such as Na Agontimé might have been sold into slavery. In eighteenth-century Dahomey, while priesthood roles in the royal Vodun cults were assigned to *anato* (non-royal) families, exceptions existed allowing members of *ahovi* (royal) families such as Na Agontimé to engage in religious activities, potentially due to her status as a "queen mother" or *kpojito*.[268]

The 1998 controversial documentary *Black Atlantic: The Route of the Orishas*, directed by Renato Barbieri, featured Adjahô Houmasse, the High Priest from Abomey, watching a video recording from Casa Grande das Minas.[269] This footage, which captured the Afro-Fon-Brazilian community's homage to their ancestors, provoked a profound reaction from the elderly priest. Well into his eighties, he expressed his amazement, shaking his head in disbelief and awe, and with palms turned upwards, remarked:

> I pray for the coming together of these two nations, because we grind the same spices in the same mortar. I believe this is the tale of two siblings separated in childhood who never reunited. Yet, imagine if one day, their children were to meet. Such an encounter would defy any explanation. The joy from this reunion would be immeasurable, beyond any description. It would be something truly extraordinary.[270]

The Great-Great-Great-Grandson of Ìyá Nàsó: Mestre Didi

> *The son asked his father, "Where is my grandpa?*
> *My grandpa? Where is he?"*
> *The father asked his grandfather, "Where is my great-grandpa?*
> *My great-grandpa? Where is he?*
> *The grandfather asked his great-grandfather, "Where is my*
> *great-great-grandpa?*
> *My great-great-grandpa? Where is he?"*
> *Great-great-grandfather! Great-grandfather! Grandfather!*
> *Aganju! Father Shango!*
> *Hail Egun! Baba Alapala!*
> Gilberto Gil

Another powerful act of re-membering of the past—this time focused on Oyo instead of Dahomey—is that registered by Mestre Didi, Deoscóredes Maximiliano dos Santos, high priest of the Axé Opô Afonjá Candomblé house, sculptor, and scholar.

Mestre Didi (1917–2013), a member of the Asipà lineage traditionally associated with the former Oyo Empire, was the son of Maria Bibiana do Espírito Santo (also known as Mãe Senhora or Oxum Muiuá, 1890–1967), the grandson of Claudiana do Espírito Santo, the great-grandson of Maria Madalena da Silva (c. 1829–1892), the great-great-grandson of Marcelina da Silva and Obá Tossi (c. 1812–1885), and the great-great-great-grandson of Ìyá Nàsó (Francisca da Silva, c. 1780–1859).

Originally from Yorubaland, Ìyá Nàsó was enslaved during the conflicts that precipitated the fall of the Oyo Empire. The title Ìyá Nàsó is one of the highest-ranking titles for a high priestess dedicated to the Orisha Shango in the royal palace of Oyo.[271] Known only by her title, Ìyá Nàsó arrived in Bahia around 1810 alongside one of her sons, and they were baptized as Francisca and Domingos. After securing her freedom around 1820, Ìyá Nàsó took the surname da Silva. In Bahia, she became one of three founding priestesses of the first Kétou (or "Nago") Candomblé *terreiro*, Ilê Axé Airá Intilê, in the early nineteenth century. Ìyá Nàsó returned to Africa later in life and passed away in Ouidah.[272]

In an interview with actor and director Haroldo Costa, Mestre Didi recounted how he used to shrug off stories from his mother and the elders who claimed they came from a royal bloodline in Kétou.[273] His perspective on what he once somewhat dismissed as fanciful shifted after he received a UNESCO scholarship through the Afro-Oriental Center of Studies at the University of Bahia. This opportunity enabled him to conduct comparative research in Nigeria and Dahomey on the influence of West African art in Brazil. Mestre Didi's research took him into the heart of his ancestral heritage—to the kingdom of Kétou itself.

In the company of his wife, the Argentine anthropologist Juana Elbein dos Santos, and Pierre Verger, Didi first stopped in Cotonou, where the group stocked up on fine French wine to offer the king. Verger, known locally as Babalawô Fatumbi, was well acquainted with the monarch and made the introductions as Didi presented their gifts. The king thanked him and immediately served the wine to everyone present, making sure he was the last to sip, following tradition. As they chatted, Mestre Didi casually mentioned his Kétou ancestry. Surprised by how well Didi spoke Yoruba, the king put him on the spot to prove his heritage. In response, Didi recited songs of praise for the land, the king, and the people's prosperity. The king, his ministers, and all those present were moved and surprised, as they had not expected someone from across the sea to know their ancestral songs.[274]

Juana Elbein dos Santos spoke of Didi's family's saga and urged him to recite his family's Oriki, an oral emblem akin to a coat of arms. He shied away from the request, but Verger and Santos insisted, especially since the king's curiosity had been piqued. So, Didi complied, and out came "Asipá Borogun Elesé Kan Gongóò." The king's face lit up, and he jumped out of his chair, pointing right to a corner of the palace. "That's where your folks live!" he exclaimed. The revelation left everyone in awe. The king then called one of the elders, Iya Naná, and asked her to take Mestre Didi to the Asipá's house—an entire community. Most of the men were out working the family fields of Kosiku (literally meaning "no death"). Didi recounts that those who were not working gathered around him, and when he pronounced his Orilé, emotions ran high as they applauded and greeted him. An overwhelming surge of joy—"pure, undiluted happiness"—left him speechless. The group was later escorted to the Ojubó Odé, the sacred space honoring Orisha Oshosi, and informed about Didi's family's spiritual foundation. The borough's elders and family members convened. They filled in the gaps, confirming everything Mestre Didi's mother and the old-timers had been telling him all along in Bahia. The profound connection prompted repeated invitations for him to build a home in Kétou and reunite with his ancestral kin.[275]

The oral traditions surrounding the founding of Casa Branca (or Ilê Axé Iyá Nassô Oká), one of Brazil's oldest and most significant *terreiros*, trace back to the voyage of Mestre Didi's great-great-great-grandmother, Iyá Nassô, and of his great-great-grandmother Marcelina da Silva (or Obá Tossi).[276] Evidence supporting these narratives, beyond Marcelina da Silva's will and oral accounts, was lacking until Nicolau Parés and Lisa Castillo unearthed documents such as emancipation letters, court records, and property deeds. These documents not only corroborate the oral tradition, but also unveil new details, such as Marcelina's ownership of enslaved people and more intricate details about Iyá Nassô.[277] This research counters prior skepticism from scholars who viewed these narratives as mere fabrications to legitimize ritual purity. Parés and Castillo's research provides substantial backing for the remarkable histories of priestess Iyá Nassô, Marcelina, and her daughter, Maria Magdalena, founders of "one of the most well-known dynasties in the history of Afro-Brazilian religion."[278]

In her will, Marcelina requested Catholic masses for her former master and mistress, José Pedro Autran and Francisca da Silva, and their son Domingos, highlighting the complex social relationships of the time, including the common practice among freed Africans of owning enslaved people.[279] Like José Pedro and Francisca, Marcelina was part of a small but significant group of freed African elites in Bahia. Parés and Castillo note that the "institution of slavery was a pervasive and fundamental part of Bahian social structure at that time."[280] Previous research shows that from the late eighteenth to the mid-nineteenth century, 75 percent of freedmen in Bahia owned at least one slave.[281] Those who had the means to do so invested in slaves as they did in real estate.[282]

According to one version of the story, Marcelina and Iyá Nassô spent seven years in Ketu, returning with Marcelina's daughter, Magdalena, born in West Africa, and the Ifá diviner, Bamboxê Obitikó. Another version claims Iyá Nassô never returned from West Africa, and after her death, Marcelina returned to Brazil and assumed leadership of her mother's *terreiro*.[283] This narrative needs to be understood within the context of the Malê insurrections, which led to widespread persecution of Africans in Bahia, influencing many to return to West Africa.

Following the Malê Rebellion, the African community in Bahia faced severe persecution, including frequent police raids on homes. Any Arabic documents discovered were interpreted as evidence of involvement in the uprising. As a result, many Africans either fled Bahia or were deported, driven away by newly imposed restrictive laws concerning employment and housing. Francisca and José Pedro lived in a neighborhood of Salvador that was particularly targeted by the police. While their departure from Brazil might be seen as a direct response to widespread repression, Castillo and Parés reveal that other specific reasons and direct threats to their safety also influenced their decision. Police records from 1835 show that Domingos da Silva and Thomé José Alves (sons of Francisca and José Pedro, either by blood or through religious ties) were arrested on suspicion of participating in the Malê Rebellion.[284] Neighbors accused them of hosting suspicious gatherings of Africans, during which the brothers and others wore beaded necklaces and white clothes adorned with red. At that time, white clothing was strongly associated with the white outfits worn by the Malês on the day of their insurrection. While their participation in the rebellion is plausible, the documents also attest to the existence of an early Candomblé house dedicated to Orisha Shango.[285]

This Candomblé temple dedicated to Shango, located in downtown Salvador and likely overseen by Iyá Nassô (also known as Francisca da Silva), was probably closed following the repression but later revived under the leadership of Marcelina da Silva.[286] Parés and Castillo's research demonstrates that Iyá Nassô, the founder of the Casa Branca *terreiro*, and Francisca da Silva, Marcelina's former mistress, were the same person. Francisca da Silva would have been Marcelina's mother in the sense of a spiritual mother: "the African freedwoman whose memory Marcelina would still cherish when she made her will half a century later, in addition to having been her slave mistress, was also her *ialorixá* (high priestess)."[287]

In 1836, the sentences of Domingos da Silva and Thomé José Alves were changed from prison to deportation. In the following year, while the brothers were sent back to Africa by order of the imperial government, the group with Francisca da Silva and José Pedro Autran was recorded in the passport records. In 1837, Francisca and José Pedro issued manumission letters to around ten of their enslaved people, including Marcelina and Maria Magdalena, who later received passports for West Africa.[288] In a letter to the authorities, Francisca declared that her decision to leave Bahia for West Africa was voluntary and at her own expense, emphasizing that it was not motivated by the prejudice she endured following a local rebellion.[289] Francisca stated she would never return to Brazil, underlining her commitment with the threat of severe penalties should she break her promise. Post-1837, no records of Francisca or José Pedro appear, suggesting they remained in Africa as they had sworn to do.[290]

The exact destination of the group remains uncertain. While Marcelina's great-granddaughter told Verger they settled in Ketu, this seems improbable given that Francisca was originally from Oyo, which by 1837 was a war-torn state under Fulani control and an unlikely refuge.[291] The anthropologist Renato da Silveira proposes that either Ketu (still relatively stable politically) or Onim (Lagos), a common arrival point for those returning from Brazil, could have been their destination.[292] How Marcelina managed to return to Bahia is still also uncertain; her reentry would have faced significant legal obstacles since, after the Malê uprising, laws were enacted in 1831 and 1835 that explicitly prohibited African freedmen from entering Bahian ports.[293] What is known is that Marcelina did return, and upon her return, she engaged in economic activities, following the example of her former religious godmother and mistress. She quickly accumulated wealth through investments—first in enslaved people and then in real estate—circumventing laws that prohibited freed Africans from owning property by registering her assets under her daughter's name.[294] She primarily owned enslaved women of Nago origin and their children, born into captivity, favoring those who, like herself, spoke Yoruba.[295] Given Marcelina's dual role as both a religious leader and someone who had previously been enslaved to her religious mentor, it is probable that the enslaved in her household served not only in conventional roles such as domestic workers or street vendors but also participated as initiates within her religious community.[296]

The 1837 voyage of Francisca da Silva marked the beginning of the migration wave that followed the Malê uprising. This migration continued throughout the latter half of the nineteenth century and included a reverse migration from Africa back to Bahia, exemplified by Marcelina da Silva's return in 1839.[297] While the white elite of Bahia sent their children to Paris for education, the African elite sent theirs to West Africa, especially Lagos.[298] This is illustrated by the case of Martiniano Eliseu do Bonfim (1859–1943), who studied in Lagos from 1875 to 1886. During this time, he became fluent in English and Yoruba and was trained as an Ifá diviner and scholar.[299] The affluent African freed community played a crucial role in this transatlantic movement. Supported by a network of kinship and trade that spanned the Atlantic, this movement facilitated the exchange of children between continents for education, as well as cultural and religious exchanges that influenced the development of Candomblé in Brazil.[300] Within the broader social and historical context of post-abolition Brazil, African freedpeople faced growing racialization and mounting challenges to the economic and social gains they had previously achieved. Despite these challenges, figures like Marcelina da Silva, Eliseu do Bonfim, his son Martiniano, and other transatlantic priests, scholars, and philosophers continued to exert significant influence within African-Brazilian communities.[301]

From Dahomey-Oyo Conflicts to Jeje-Nago Collaborations

Approximately three miles separate the city of Ouidah from its port. Men and women captured from various kingdoms under Dahomey's control were held in Ouidah. Oral tradition holds that, as the time for their departure to the New World approached, they would march from the city to the port, passing through the Door of No Return. Along the way, they would encounter the Tree of Forgetfulness. Before continuing to the port, men were required to circle this tree nine times and women seven times. This Dahomean ritual was believed to erase the captives' memories and quell their longing for freedom.[302] "Yet," as the Benin historian Emmanuel Karl-August explains, "they remembered everything. Upon arrival, they recreated their deities. Our metaphysical beliefs posited that forgetfulness should afflict them; without it, they might bring a curse upon Dahomey. It was crucial for the king to avoid being cursed by the enslaved captives; hence ceremonies were performed to ward off such maledictions. In our religious context, a curse from one who is either at the brink of death or leaving forever is profoundly terrifying."[303]

As the Dahomean captives trekked the three miles to the sea, they paused to encircle the Tree, meant to transform them into someone—something—else. Handed over to traders and packed tightly, they awaited departure until the ships were filled to capacity. Those who retained enough sodium—and the will to survive dehydration and terror—would cross the Atlantic. Following the Atlantic crossing, euphemistically referred to as the Middle Passage, there was another lengthy wait on the shore until they were selected as commodities and then transported to their new lives in Brazil.[304] There, Dahomeans, along with Nagos, Ketus, Egbas, Ijeshas, Ifes, and others, became collectively known as Nagos. The Oyo Yoruba referred to the Dahomean people as *àjèjì*, meaning stranger or foreigner. In Brazil, they generally became known as the Jejes. The Jeje originated from the Gbe-speaking region of West Africa; a region that is home to linguistically related groups such as the Fon and Gun, among others.[305] In Haiti, Cuba, and Trinidad, the "Jeje" became known as "Alada" (Lada, Arada, Rada, Ardra) or "Mahi" (Mai).

While the Malê uprisings did not achieve the establishment of a Muslim state in Brazil, the Nagos and Jejes succeeded in founding an Orisha-Vodun state that extended beyond Bahia. Although their cosmological framework did not initially integrate the Bakongo, the Brazilian-Kongo themselves absorbed and then reinterpreted aspects of Jeje-Nago cosmology. Despite being former political foes, the Jejes and Nagos formed deep bonds in the New World. The interwoven nature of Dahomean and Oyo cosmologies led early researchers of Bahia's Orisha tradition, starting with Nina Rodrigues, to initially describe the practice as a Jeje-Nago religion or mythology.[306] To this day, the Yoruba-modelled Brazilian Candomblé encompasses not only Dahomean practices but also Vodun deities.

The coming together of formerly rival nations marked the genesis of the Orisha tradition, now evident in Brazilian Candomblé and Cuban Santería. Brazilian Candomblé evolved into a robust Pan-African cosmology that both integrated and was influenced by other African belief systems.[307] This Orisha tradition has illuminated and bestowed recognition upon a variety of African philosophies, aesthetics, and cosmologies. The Jeje-Nago cosmological framework has evolved into what has been described as a defining cultural matrix, or the "central code" of Afro-Brazil. Risério posits that this cultural matrix serves as a "meta-language, a foundational ideology, and a geometric framework." Within this structure, the diverse African cultural expressions "converge, resonate, and become legible, translating into each other, transfixed."[308]

Throughout the twentieth century, Afro-Brazilian cultures and religions served as arenas for scholarly debates on race, culture, and history—debates that emphasized African origins, validated Bahian Candomblé, and often distanced themselves from syncretic expressions. During the 1970s and 1980s, significant political and cultural shifts within Brazil spurred a reaction against the prevailing cultural purist perspective, prompting a critical reevaluation of Afro-Brazilian identities and religious expressions. By the end of the twentieth century, scholars increasingly focused their analysis on Afro-Brazilian religions, exploring the broader ideological implications through the lens of social construction of identity, power dynamics, and the invention of traditions.[309] Beginning in the 1990s, a new generation of initiated devotees and scholars began writing from within the tradition.[310]

The anthropologists Nicolau Parés and Roger Sansi have outlined four principal areas of sociological research in Afro-Brazilian religious studies: the paradigm shifts emphasizing African origins and transatlantic networks; the interactions between Afro-Brazilian religions and the rise of Pentecostalism; the embedding of religious practices within the broader social and cultural fabric of Brazil; and explorations into the ontological and cosmological aspects of former taboo subjects like trance.³¹¹ This contemporary research builds on the foundational work of historians such as Verger, Manuela Carneiro da Cunha, and Jerry Turner, who explored the nineteenth-century movement of formerly enslaved Africans returning to Africa.³¹² Other prominent scholars like Robert Slenes, James Sweet, and Elizabeth Kiddy have focused on Central African cultural expressions in southern Brazil; Parés has explored the Ewe contributions to Bahian Candomblé, while Walter Hawthorne has explored the impact of Africans from Upper Guinea in Maranhão and Pará.³¹³ Together with Farris Thompson's concept of the Black Atlantic, revisited partially by Paul Gilroy, and the broader frameworks of diaspora studies and Atlantic history, this body of work has prompted a reassessment of historical movements from Africa to Brazil, emphasizing the interconnectedness of Africa, Europe, and the Americas. This research challenges the linear narrative of the transatlantic slave trade, advocating for a more nuanced understanding of cultural exchanges.³¹⁴

Parés has conducted groundbreaking research on the origins and impact of Vodun traditions in Brazil, particularly their central role in shaping contemporary Candomblé. Captives of various origins traded in Porto Novo became collectively known as "Jeje." Over time, Jeje came to signify not only generalized ethnic origins but also a shared spiritual orthodoxy that is distinct from other African "nations" such as Nago or Angola.³¹⁵ The Jeje (Ewe-Fon) Vodun tradition manifests itself across a range of Afro-Brazilian religious practices, including specific Candomblé systems, as well as in Xangô, Batuque, and Tambor de Mina.³¹⁶ The oldest Jeje religious communities, established by the mid-nineteenth century, are predominantly found in Bahia and Maranhão. The term "Jeje," documented in Bahia since 1739, has given rise to various etymological theories.³¹⁷ In Porto Novo, *djédji* primarily referred to the Fon people or their language by the latter half of the nineteenth century.³¹⁸ Most scholars believe the term derives from the Yoruba word *àjèji*, meaning stranger or foreigner; some suggest that Brazilian returnees in the nineteenth century might have introduced the term to Benin.³¹⁹

Although scholars since the early twentieth century tended to identify Jeje Voduns alongside Nago Orishas, assumptions about the absence of a distinct Jeje identity within Brazilian religious practices have been challenged since the 1940s, particularly following the studies of Nunes Pereira.³²⁰ Some of the distinctive ritual practices associated with Jeje traditions center around tree shrines (known as Atinsa) and tree Voduns such as Loko, who is represented by the *gameleira* fig tree.³²¹ Parés clarifies that the number of Jeje communities in Brazil has proportionally decreased due in part to an inherited or constructed tradition that only one *terreiro* should exist per town. This suggests a strategy employed by established religious centers to legitimize their authority, particularly during transitions of power. Other factors include urban expansion and the fact that

Jeje rituals are intrinsically linked to nature, particularly trees. Nevertheless, the Jeje maintain prestige and influence within the broader Candomblé community alongside other major "nations" such as Nago-Ketu and Congo-Angola. Some *terreiros*, such as the Alaketu (or Ilé Axé Mariolajé), identify as Nago-Vodun, integrating the worship of both Orishas and Voduns.[322] In Bahia, prominent Jeje Voduns include Bessen, a snake deity from the Dan family; Sogbo, associated with thunder from the Hevioso or Kaviono family; and Azonzu, linked to smallpox from the Sakpata family. Other well-known Voduns—such as Nana-Buruku, the eldest female Vodun; Loko, associated with the *gameleira* tree; and Lisa, Aizan, and Elegbara—are also revered, but the first three Voduns form the core of the contemporary Brazilian Jeje pantheon.

The most significant presence of the Jeje tradition in Brazil is found in São Luís, within the religious community that descends from Na Agontimé's legacy. Casa das Minas, also known as Querebentã de Zomadonu, organizes its Voduns into four distinct linhas (lines) or families—Kevioso, Dambirá, Savaluno, and Davice—corresponding to royal worship practices from Benin.[323]

DAHOMEAN DIVINE AND ROYAL TWINS: MAWÚ-LISÀ AND GEZÓ-GAAKPÉ

At the dawn of creation, Mawu-Lisa (Mawú-Lisà), traveling in the mouth of her serpent, Dan Ayido Hwedo, embarked on a cosmic journey to the four corners of the universe. Wherever Mawu-Lisa traveled, mountains sprang forth from Dã's excrement. At each cardinal point, she gathered elements to shape into the two halves of a cosmic gourd.[324] Over the four days of a traditional Fon week, Mawu-Lisa, with Dã's assistance and using the resources of the preexisting universe, crafted the universe. Their journey traced a cross-shaped pattern in the sky, spanning from west to east and from north to south.[325] Before welding the gourd's halves, Mawu-Lisa noticed that the weight of the mountains threatened to sink the universe into the primordial waters.[326] To prevent this, she defined the water's boundaries and instructed Dã to coil beneath the world. As Dã coiled to support the weight of the world, he also erected four iron pillars at the cardinal points of the universe, anchoring them within the cosmic waters to stabilize the earth.[327]

In Haitian Vodun, a *terreiro* is referred to as the *ounfò*: a designation that encompasses a temple, a patio, yards, and the rooms or homes of different Orishas or Lwa, as well as priests and members of the community. The Vodun temple, or *peristil*, is composed of a roof structure supported by four poles. The central pole, known as the *potomitan*, serves as the primary conduit to the world of the

Lwa, the Vodou deities.[328] The structure of the *peristil* follows the Fon image of Mawu-Lisa's universe as two halves of a gourd seamlessly welded into a sphere intersected by two perpendicular planes that form a cross-section resembling the arms of a cross.[329] The horizontal line symbolizes the earthly plane, intersected by a vertical line representing Vilokan, the spiritual realm and home of the Lwa. This vertical axis extends into the cosmic abyss.[330] The cosmic mirror and its mundane representation form a cosmographic structure shaped like a cross. The intersection of these two lines marks a crucial "zero-point," where the spiritual and temporal worlds converge. At this juncture, ordinary existence and time are suspended, allowing sacred beings from Vilokan to manifest within the *peristil* through their *Vodouisant* initiates.[331]

Mawu-Lisa is imagined as a singular androgynous entity with two faces. One face is feminine, with the Moon serving as its eyes, and is known as Mawu. The other face is masculine, with the Sun as its eyes, and is called Lisa. Mawu governs the night, while Lisa oversees the day. Lisa, bearing attributes of Obatala, is a Vodun whose emblem is a red clay pot with a white-striped cover and topped by a chameleon figure, symbolizing his messenger.[332] Mawu-Lisa, more commonly portrayed as one androgynous complete Vodun, is also depicted either as twins or as partners and parents of the world.[333] According to Leslie Desmangles, Mawu-Lisa is referred to by the Fon by her female designation and as the Godhead.[334] Being both male and female, Mawu-Lisa conceived and gave birth to other deities.[335] Aligned with its social structure, the Fon's worldview is governed by a hierarchy of deities who are the offspring of Mawu-Lisa and organized into pantheons associated with natural elements. Legba, the youngest child of Mawu-Lisa, does not preside over any pantheon. Mawu-Lisa endowed each of her children with a unique language. Legba stands out as her youngest and her messenger, being the only one besides her who comprehends the languages across all domains.[336]

In Fon cosmology, the notion of doubling or duality is essential; complementary forces fundamental to the universe's structure predate human society.[337] This concept of doubling extends beyond religious practices to encompass military and political structures. Within the Fon ideology of doubling, every significant role, force, element, or being has an equivalent: state ministers worked in pairs, roles within the king's palace had equivalents outside, members of the royal family had their counterparts known as *tohossu*, and the structure of living families is reflected in *kutome*—the land of the dead.[338] *Kutome* derives from the words *ku* (dead), *to* (land), and *me* (place of or interior). The afterlife mirrors the earthly world, embodying the "continuance theory" where individuals maintain their earthly roles, abilities, and tastes.[339]

A refashioned Dahomean governance model, aligning with the Fon ideology of doubling, began to incorporate a double or doppelgänger of the king. This system, known as "the Bush King" or more aptly "the King-as-Prince," mirrored the organizational framework that Nzinga adapted into her Kilombos, symbolizing the complex interplay of power and social dynamics during the transatlantic slave trade. This arrangement was essentially a reinterpretation of a recognizable institution from the past, creatively modified to meet the challenges of the era, with the goal of ensuring survival and maintaining continuity into the future.

As explained by Stanley Diamond, Dahomey was structured as a military state led by royal lineages, supported by an emerging bureaucracy. This hierarchical arrangement disrupted traditional lineage dynamics, transitioning from a kin-based societal framework to a more autocratic system centered around the royal Aladaxonou clan—whose name in Fon translates to "people of Allada." The Dahomean rulers aimed to create a class system to shift loyalties from kinship to the monarchy and dismantle extended family structures.[340] Herskovits highlighted the enduring significance of kin loyalty in Dahomean society, noting the severe consequences of being expelled from the kin group, including exclusion from ancestral ceremonies and inheritances.[341] The breakdown of these joint family systems would lead to individuals becoming disconnected and rootless, essentially becoming subjects wholly owned by the king.[342]

The supreme military and civil command belonged to the Aladaxonou, the lineage of which Kings Tacoodonou and Agaja were members. Their primary challenge was maintaining dominance within the royal clan. The secondary challenge was to develop an effective bureaucracy to administer the newly conquered territories and manage tribute collection. This bureaucracy, intentionally kept separate from the royal clan, served as a buffer and control mechanism over the local kin units. The Aladaxonou's strategies included restricting royal lineage members from holding state offices and prohibiting princes from ascendant maternal lines from becoming king. These rules were designed to prevent power dilution and ensure that control remained tightly within its lineage.[343]

In the dynamics of Dahomey's governance, the census was a closely guarded state secret crucial for maintaining control. The power of Dahomey lay in the number of its inhabitants. The population was counted through a symbolic representation of pebbles in sacks. During the enstoolment ceremony, new kings were solemnly shown the pebbles, each signifying a citizen of Dahomey, and were instructed never to let these numbers dwindle.[344] The Aladaxonou used both traditional and new methods to assert their authority, including itinerant criers to proclaim the praises of the king, and symbolic fetishes placed strategically to remind everyone of the king's omnipresence and power—among these a "proto-passport," a token resembling the king's stick that served as proof that the bearer was traveling with the king's permission.[345]

King Gezó (r. 1818–1858), the eighth king of the Aladaxonou lineage, recognized the difficulty of maintaining traditional patriarchal roles amid changing societal dynamics and sought to revive a past tradition. The presence of a dual monarchy dates back to the eighteenth century when King Akaba (or Adahunzo, r. 1685–1716) ruled alongside his twin sister Hangbe (or Na Hangbe). Later, King Gezó revitalized the tradition of twin rulers to secure his claim to the royal stool. Gezó's revival was crucial because honoring his predecessor, King Adandozan—from whom he had seized power—posed a significant challenge: Adandozan was still alive and secluded in one of Gezó's palaces. Unable to perform the traditional funerary rites to honor his predecessor, Gezó devised a solution: the creation of his doppelgänger, the King-as-Prince Gaakpé.[346] Through this persona, Gezó could annually demonstrate his reverence for his father while bolstering his own legitimacy as monarch.[347] King-as-Prince Gaakpé's role extended beyond mere legitimacy; it also embodied Gezó's former status as prince during King Adandozan's reign. This ceremonial role ensured that duties to ancestors and the kingdom continued to be fulfilled, maintaining continuity with past traditions and symbolizing stability amidst political turbulence. The concept was multifaceted, serving not only symbolic but also the practical purpose of adapting strategies and ideologies to the economic and political changes of the time. It underscored the complex interplay among history, mythology, and governance in Dahomean society, highlighting how the kingdom adapted its traditions to meet contemporary economic and political challenges.

As a fictional character, King-as-Prince Gaakpé embodied the ideal of the dutiful prince, loyally conducting ceremonies that underscored his commitment to his father, dynasty, and nation, even amid potential coups. This portrayal of Gaakpé helped dissociate Gezó from any direct involvement in the overthrow of his predecessor, painting him instead as a peaceful, pastoral figure forced into leadership.[348] The Dahomeans recount that Gaakpé was a farmer residing in a palace named Akpueho, located southwest of Abomey. In ceremonies, an announcer would proclaim Gaakpé's arrival from the farm. The Gaakpé-Gezó duality is significantly underscored by their association with the countryside versus the urban center of Abomey. In Dahomey, the countryside symbolized a lack of power, whereas Abomey represented the seat of royal authority. Historically, Dahomean princes who did not ascend to the throne were relegated to the countryside, managing estates and embodying a figurative lack of royal power, similar to the narrative surrounding Gaakpé.[349]

Edna Bay explored how the construction of the term "Bush King," which is absent from the cultural consciousness of the Fon people, was created and developed by nineteenth- and twentieth-century European scholars who adopted and adapted it for their own analyses.[350] European visitors were often hosted by Fon monarchs in Xwetanu—annual events honoring the king's father and other royal ancestors. These weekslong ceremonies included two rituals, held in alternate years: the Attoh (meaning "platform," the ceremony for the king), and the So-sin (meaning "horse-tie," the ceremony for the king's double). Xwetanu showcased the monarch's wealth and generosity through lavish displays, gifts of food and drink, marriage arrangements, and the conferral of ranks. The king's subjects reciprocated with gifts, effectively paying their annual taxes. These ceremonies allowed the commoners to feel involved in policymaking discussions crucial to the kingdom's governance, covering economic, political, military, and religious aspects.[351]

It was the British explorer Richard Burton (1821–1890), during his 1861 visit to the court of King Glele (r. 1858–1889), who coined the term "Bush King." Burton described the term as a role encompassing the rural and agricultural domains, contrasted with the city's governance by the official king. In his two-volume work of 1864, Burton noted that this rural king had his own court, including a chief executioner and a master of ceremonies, and his palace was a hub for economic activities.[352] Josiah Skertchly (1850–1926), an English entomologist who spent five months in the Abomey region in 1871, later expanded on Burton's observations by describing the role of the "Bush King" in economic terms. He portrayed the figure as essential for conducting trade without diminishing the royal stature, managing transactions in captives and palm oil that were crucial to the kingdom's economy. This setup allowed the actual king to maintain a regal and generous image, buying goods with the profits made by his rural counterpart.[353]

Twins were to be treated with absolute equity in Fon societies. In the same manner, the king and his counterpart divided two parts of their rule. Bay explains that each controlled a portion of the kingdom, maintaining their own palace, court, queen mother, ministers, wives, and slaves. Both performed ancestral ceremonies and utilized the primary symbols of royalty, such as stools and umbrellas.[354] Skertchly observed that when King-as-Prince Addokpon (the double of King Glele) took part in the Attoh ceremony for the king, he did not use his umbrella—the traditional symbol of the highest station in Dahomey.[355]

King Gezó's invention of the king-as-prince was perpetuated by successive kings, including King Glele. Gaakpe and Addokpon were, respectively, symbolic representations of Kings Gezó and Glele as princes. Contemplating the significance of the names Gaakpe and Addokpon, Skertchly notes how the doubles handled the responsibilities of the "ignoble trade," enabling the true monarchs—Gezó and Glele—to focus on ruling their subjects and overseeing their revenues:

> Gezó's "double" was called Gah-qpweh, the first two words of a short proverb, as most of the Dahomean names, or rather titles, are viz., *Gah*, market day, *qpweh*, coming; "plenty of things will be there," being understood as completing the sentence. Addokpon, the alter ego of Gelele, is an egotistical strong name. *Addo*, a yellow popo bead, imperishable by fire, *kpon*, look at it, i.e. behold the eternal. All the oil and palm kernels sold at Whydah are the produce of Addokpon's plantations, but Gelele buys the rum, powder, and cloth; a very convenient arrangement for getting a good name for spending money, since Addokpon sells only, whereas the generous Gelele does nothing but buy. Nevertheless, at Customs Gelele has by far the largest share of tribute, Addokpon being put off with a very meagre allowance.[356]

These practices showcased the delicate balance that Dahomean rulers strived to maintain between portraying themselves as timeless, patriarchal figures while evolving their authority to meet the needs of a centralized state.[357]

Gezó's governance system facilitated the kin society's transition to a more civil structure without eliciting resistance through overt alterations of traditional roles. The King-as-Prince symbolized continuity amidst change, acting as a buffer to obscure the growing secular power of the king, aligning with the people's reluctance toward drastic change and helped maintain a façade of traditional governance. It served primarily as a symbolic figure to mask the Aladaxonou's direct involvement in state-building and to maintain the illusion of a benign patriarchal rule amid their actual secular and militaristic governance.[358] Residing on the outskirts of Abomey, the King-as-Prince managed exploitative economic activities such as the slave trade and palm oil production, which were crucial for supporting the state's bureaucracy and controlling the royal clan.

The secrecy surrounding the roles and lives of kings, such as concealing their deaths to prevent instability and propagating myths like not being seen eating to elevate their status above mere mortality, supported the performance of the kings and their doubles. The introduction of other institutions such as the "best friend" reflected this blend of tradition and adaptation.[359] Each Dahomean was required to have three "best friends," chosen from clans other than their own and ranked by their level of intimacy and trust. This hierarchy of friendship ensured that if the closest friend passed away, the others would rise in rank, maintaining a social support system that reinforced community ties while operating within the broader context of the state's governance framework.³⁶⁰

The leadership of the Aladaxonou in Dahomey was a sophisticated blend of traditional kinship structures, strategically crafted to ensure compliance and support for their reign, while covertly consolidating power and adapting to the demands of statecraft as the society shifted from kinship-based to civil administration.³⁶¹ The concept exemplified by Gaakpé became a defining element of the Dahomean monarchy in the nineteenth century. Although not as directly relevant to Gezó's successors, they continued to engage with the tradition, performing ceremonies for their own figures.³⁶² Bay observes that while there is no clear explanation for the continuation of the King-as-Prince tradition, two fundamental elements of the Fon cultural ethos likely influenced its continuation: "the need for constant expansion and aggrandizement, and the importance of change and innovation in the kingdom."³⁶³ The symbolic duality is enshrined in the unique tomb of King Gezó, located in the central palace at Abomey. Unlike the typical Dahomean royal tombs, which are modest structures, Gezó's tomb is a distinctive double structure composed of two conjoined circular houses—one for Gezó and the other for Gaakpé.³⁶⁴ This architectural expression stands as a lasting tribute to Gezó's strategic and dualistic approach to kingship.³⁶⁵

AGONTIMÉ AND CHACHA AJINACU AS SUNG BY CARNAVAL GRIOTS

Carnaval, with its diverse forms of expression—from the Afoxés of Bahia to the vibrant parades in the Sambadromes of Rio de Janeiro, São Paulo, and other Brazilian metropolises—embodies an artistic genre that restores, updates, and fabulates African-Brazilian history. As Ana Lucia Araujo notes, religious processions and festivals have been "privileged occasions to reinforce or reinvent connections" between Africa and Brazil.³⁶⁶

In 1961, the public in Rio de Janeiro began paying to attend the Carnaval samba parades. While Afro-Brazilian communities remained central to organizing the Escolas de Samba, over time, the elite also began to participate in the festivities.³⁶⁷ One such group, Acadêmicos do Salgueiro, founded in 1953, emerged as a leader in highlighting the history of slavery and Afro-Brazilian heritage. In 1957, their themed performance, "The Slave Ship," featured lyrics by Armando Régis and Djalma Sabiá that did not focus on the Middle Passage itself but instead paid homage to the abolitionist poet Castro Alves (1847–1871), author of the poem

"Navio negreiro" ("Slave Ship").[368] The performance conveyed a mainstream narrative of abolition as a benevolent gift, achieved through a series of laws and culminating with Princess Isabel's (1846–1921) signing of the Golden Law in 1888.[369] In subsequent years, Acadêmicos do Salgueiro continued to explore themes related to Africa, enslaved Africans, and Afro-Brazilian historical figures—compensating for their exclusion from Brazilian textbooks at the time.[370]

During the 1960s, Salgueiro shifted its focus from Princess Isabel to the maroon history of Zumbi and the Quilombo dos Palmares. Other Afro-Brazilian icons they honored included Chica da Silva (c. 1732–1796), a formerly enslaved woman from Minas Gerais who gained her freedom and rose to prominence, and Chico Rei, another legendary figure from the region. Believed to have been born in the early eighteenth century in the Kingdom of Kongo, Chico Rei was taken to the gold mining region of Minas Gerais, where he amassed wealth and established the Church of Saint Iphigenia, home to the Brotherhood of Our Lady of the Rosary.

In the 1970s, Salgueiro paid homage to Afro-Brazilian samba composers, enslaved Africans who arrived in Rio de Janeiro at the Valongo Wharf, the cosmology of Candomblé Orishas, and ancestral enslaved Africans as kings and heroes. As Araujo highlights, beginning in the 1980s, Carnaval parades began expressing "new aspects of Afro-Brazilian civil rights movements," challenging official narratives and promoting Afro-Brazilian mythical figures who bridge the African past and the present.[371]

In 2007, Rio de Janeiro's samba group Beija-Flor presented the samba plot "Africas: From the Royal Cradle to the Brazilian Court," which simultaneously paid tribute to Queen Na Agontimé, Queen Nzinga, Zumbi dos Palmares, Chico Rei, Tia Ciata (1854–1924), and the Orishas Obatala, Shango, and Ogun.[372] Through these performances, Carnaval not only re-members ties with an idealized Africa but also amplifies the visibility of Afro-Brazilian heroes. By identifying with these restored historical figures, Afro-Brazilians reshape memories of slavery and redefine its narratives.[373]

During the twentieth century, various Carnaval associations paid tribute to Na Agontimé and Félix de Souza. Among them were the Rio de Janeiro groups Grêmio Recreativo de Arte Negra Escola de Samba Quilombo (which, in 1984, presented "The Chacha of Ouidah and Queen Mina of Maranhão") and Grêmio Recreativo da Beija-Flor de Nilópolis (with the 2001 and 2007 samba plots "The Saga of Agontimé, Maria Mineira Naé" and "Africas: From the Royal Cradle to the Brazilian Court").[374] Verger, in his analysis of the 1984 samba lyrics, noted that "both King Gezó, supplier of slaves, and Chacha de Souza, who sold them to Brazil, curiously became, in the eyes of descendants of Africans, symbols of Afro-Brazilian identity."[375] Verger sees the mythification of Na Agontimé as involving negotiation processes that symbolically redeemed her son, King Gezó, and Francisco Félix de Souza. In Beija-Flor's 2007 plot, Na Agontimé is the sole focus of historical reconstruction, with no mention of Gezó or Félix de Souza. According to Araujo, while reciprocal exchanges in Benin highlight the political importance of Dahomean royal families who perpetuated the Atlantic slave trade, for millions of Afro-Brazilians—whose ancestors lived under slavery—Agontimé represents agency, pride, and self-esteem.[376]

Most recently, in 2020, during the COVID-19 pandemic, the Grêmio Recreativo Império do Rio Belo, a samba school from Belo Horizonte, Minas Gerais, presented the samba plot "The Great Empire of Dahomey-Maranhão and the Boundless Borders of the Spiritual Enchantment of Querebentã of Zomadônu."[377] Created by Victor Nowosh, Eduardo Tannus, Isac Ferreira, and Victor Fernandes, the composition portrays a Candomblé Jeje (Ewe-Fon) ceremony. In this ceremony, Vodunsi channels various Lwa Vodun spirits, including those of sweet water, the ancestral Queen Na Agontimé, and a lion transformed into a panther.[378] In Savalou, Benin, the entrance to the royal palace leading to its sacred courtyard is shaped like a lion's head—a potent symbol echoed in Vodun ceremonies across the Americas. During these rituals, the hands of Vodunsi initiates—channeling the energy of the Lwa Agassou, associated with volcanoes by the Yoruba and a panther by the Fon—curl into clawlike shapes, embodying their connection to the spirit. The Rio Belo Carnaval chant brings this imagery to life, portraying a lion transforming into a panther and reigning over the parade street, its roar both saluting and embodying Queen Agontimé: "My queen, do not weep. Your panther roar shall forever echo."[379] The song concludes by invoking an eternal Ewe/Fon-Brazilian realm: the empire of Dahomey-Maranhão.[380]

In 2003, the Unidos da Tijuca samba school in Rio de Janeiro chose the theme "Agudas: Those Who Carried Africa in Their Hearts and Brought Brazil Back to the Heart of Africa."[381] Composed by Rono Maia, Jorge Melodia, and Alexandre Alegria, the song weaves a narrative that begins with a reference to Obatala, the Orisha of Creation, and Orunmila, the Ifa oracle Orisha known for his foresight of human destiny.[382] The narrative unfolds as Obatala summons his children. Guided by Orunmila, they fulfill their destiny by breaking the bonds of captivity and returning to Africa. The song transitions from a future foretold by Orunmila to a past scarred by captivity, and finally to a present that flows back to reconnect with Africa: "Mother Africa, gather your lions, as the foam drifts back to shore."[383] This journey reflects ongoing Atlantic crossings—"in drum roll, crossing Yemaya's ocean"—and culminates in Porto Novo, the capital of Benin and home to the Yoruba-Brazilian returnee Aguda community, described as "brave people who blend together in resilience."[384]

The Unidos da Tijuca song unites diverse African cultures, linking the Kongo and Angola peoples—tracing the roots of Brazilian Carnaval and Samba—with the Yoruba and Ewe peoples, emphasizing reverence for the Dilogun oracle and the ring of Dagoun's dragon. Dilogun, derived from Merindilogun, refers to the Yoruba oracle performed with sixteen cowrie shells (èrindínlógún, meaning "four minus twenty"). The protective ring symbolizes the ancestral Ewe spirit of Dagoun. This cultural and spiritual union is brought to life through a Candomblé ceremony, rich with the scent of benzoin incense, the rhythms of chief drummer Alabê, and *acarajé*, a sacred food offering to Oya Yansan, the Orisha of wind and transformation: "When we dance for the Orishas, it smells of benzoin, Alabê! Fry acarajé in palm oil."[385] The song concludes with a tribute to Francisco Félix de Souza, celebrated as a symbol of Negritude: "Long live the Chacha, long live all Negritude."[386]

Nearly two centuries after his time, Francisco Félix de Souza, the prominent slave trader and the first Chacha of Benin, has emerged in Brazil as a symbol of Negritude. Are there other instances in the history of the Atlantic Slave Trade where a slave trader is revered as a hero or a luminary by non-European groups? Are there any Mardi Gras or Calypso chants that exalt the deeds of a slave trader?

It is said that Francisco Félix de Souza possessed a ring featuring a dragon-serpent, symbolizing protection and linking him to the serpent energy of the Lwa Dan. Dan, also known as Danbala or Damballah, the Fon deity associated with creation, originates from the city of Ouidah. Typically depicted as either a rainbow or a large white or black serpent, Dan is a symbol of continuity and life. Stemming from Francisco Félix de Souza's spirit, Dagoun became an ancestral, deified figure, venerated by the de Souza family descendants and safeguarded by a high priest known as Dah Dagoun-non.[387]

If Nzinga can be perceived as a complex and contradictory hero, how then should we perceive Francisco Félix de Souza and the Brazilian African community of the Agudas? To the Agudas, Francisco Félix de Souza represented a chance at a new beginning in Africa. They built a thriving community in Benin with a distinct Brazilian African identity, sustained initially by the very trade that had once enslaved their ancestors. Born in Brazil and of mixed heritage, Félix de Souza embodied African roots in Brazil and a Brazilian identity in Benin. Climbing to the apex of the colonial mercantile system, he garnered respect and trust from European powers, securing open lines of credit in London, Liverpool, Bristol, and New York.[388] In Benin, he rose to become the king's right hand—a self-made man of the Afro-Brazilian colonial era, destined for the margins yet achieving a prominent destiny. In Benin, Félix de Souza is revered as an ancestor; in Brazil, he can be perceived as an emblematic yet controversial figure of Black pride. Faced with such a paradox, some might argue that, like the Malês, Francisco Félix de Souza has become a vague memory, shaped by romanticization and limited historical insight. While this critique holds some truth—and there have been agents in Benin and Brazil who, consciously or not, contribute to the mythologization of Francisco Félix de Souza—is it not presumptuous for us, centuries removed, to claim superior moral clarity over those directly impacted by his legacy? As scholars grappling with historical complexities, how do we honor ancestors whose actions conflict with our present values? Do we dare commemorate them, or do we simply bear witness to their commemoration? Alternatively, can we choose to spotlight other historical figures whose values align more closely with our own?

Shifting the focus from Chacha to Na Agontimé may mark a significant change in perspective, offering a lens of agency and empowerment. How are we to comprehend the relationship between Mestre Didi's great-great-grandmother Marcelina da Silva (or Obá Tossi) and Iyá Nassô? Is it even feasible to strip away our time-conditioned biases to try to grasp the significance of contradictory historical figures?

THE HEAD'S NAVEL AND THE FUTURE'S PAST

In Yoruba cosmology, each person, known as *ara-aiyê*, is envisioned as crafted from sacred mud, *oke ipori* (*òkè ìpòrí*). This essence is molded by *emi* (the breath of life force, encompassing the experiences and transformations we undergo in *aiyê* (*àiyé*), the realm of the living), by *iyé* (life itself), and by *ìrántí* (the memories carried from *orun*, the ancestral world). When becoming *egun*, or spirits, our flesh returns to *oke ipori*, ready to give rise to new *ara-iayê* (*ara-aiyê*). The energy of *ashe* (*àṣẹ, axé*) embodies potential, a capacity that may remain untapped, unfulfilled, or not fully fulfilled within our lifetimes. We enter this world charged with a life force, termed *ori-inu* (*orí-inú*) by the Yoruba ("the inner head," or "the head within the stomach").[389] Yet, it is not always that the stomach heeds the head, or that the head aligns with our innermost seat. Obstacles can divert us from our possible paths. Fulfillment, health, and equilibrium are states in which the *ori* (head) and *inu* (stomach) are aligned, moving in harmony towards one's purpose, regardless of moral judgements.

To shed light on the Yoruba concept of the living, or *ara-aiyê*, it is insightful to think of Ikú, the Orisha of Death. According to an *itan*, during the creation of humans, Obatala tasked the Orishas with finding the most suitable material. The Orishas unanimously settled on the *oke ipori* mud but, because it wept when touched, none could bear to scoop it. None except Orisha Ikú. He scooped it up and led the Orishas to deliver it to Obatala. It was indeed a perfect material for crafting *ara-aiyê*, but even Obatala was concerned about its cries. To resolve the matter, he entrusted Ikú with returning to the mud what would be taken from it, thus ensuring the cycle of life and death. The *oke ipori* mud resembles a river source, spawning the stream of life. The selection of *oke ipori* by an Orisha informs the new person's characteristics. Infused with the traits of their ancestors, *Egun Ipori* always reincarnates into new beings. From this sacred mud, the *ori*, or the spiritual essence, and its vessel, the *apere*, are formed, intertwining the realms of *aiyê*, the physical world, and *orun*, the spiritual plane. Since each element of a person, *ara-aiyê*, comes from an entity in the *orun*, there is a counterpart of that person in the *orun*.[390] This is how the head, *ori*, connects itself to what we can refer to as fate. Each fate is unique to each person since the parts that come from the *orun* are combined in a unique manner, according to the saying, "dide inu aiyê dogba ki i se ki ti ika owo," meaning "just as our fingers differ from one another, so do people."[391]

A person's potential, *ori-orun*, can be strengthened through *bori* ceremonies, which bolster one's life path by replenishing *ashe*, vital energy, to the *ori-orun*. In these rituals, a meal is prepared and offered to the *ori-orun* and *ori-aiyê*, as well as the community. If a participant's parents have passed away, *ashe* is also offered to the *Egun Ipori* during the *bori* (*bòrí*), placed on the corresponding big toe (right foot for the father and left foot for the mother), symbolizing their connection to the earth and the spiritual domain to which we all return. The crafting of *ori* is an art performed by Ajala and Obatala. A favorable *ori* requires a contribution from Ajala, who daily molds both auspicious and inauspicious fates, assisted by seventeen Odus—including Egi Obe (Èjì Ogbe), Iwori Meji (Ìwòrì Méjì), and Ose Meji (Òsé Méjì). This selection process underscores the importance of *ori-inu*, the inner head that is chosen before the person is born and that influences the potential trajectories of a person's life.[392]

Life is a plexus of potential destinies and agency. Everyone is born with paths and crossroads. How we thread these paths hinges, among others, on personal choices. The most immutable aspect of a person's fortune is the *ori* (or "head"). The "inner head" and the multiple paths it embodies is chosen prior to birth. Before entering the world, we choose from among endless heads the one we will live in and the nature of our demise. It is through forging connections with the past (the ancestors and the Orishas), the present (the communities we belong to and our potential), and the future (both communal and individual) that the nature of our journey along possible paths and within the plexus of a larger whole keeps on being actualized and transformed.

When we explore history and strive to comprehend the paradoxes embodied by heroes—whether celebrated nationally or remembered locally—and their actions, be they brilliant, mundane, or despotic, we can think of them beyond their tangible acts and in terms of what they came to symbolize as ancestral figures: the present of a past that remains future. Within the kaleidoscopic permutations of what we may refer to as core energies, what we know (or believe we know) about national heroes must be assessed beyond their historical achievements, beyond the past itself. What are the present-day versions or interpretations of such figures within historical and popular narratives? How do their evolving narratives and images shape our aspirations for societal change and the futures we seek to forge?

Grasping the complexities of African heroes of the diaspora, especially those from the Atlantic Slave Trade era, is inherently challenging. These figures are enshrouded in contradictions, and as Kamau Brathwaite noted, they leave little "verifiable official record" besides collective memory.[393] It is rare for a human to fully live out, express, or manifest their entire potential (*ashe*) in a lifetime. Yet, even if unfulfilled, they leave behind an essence that continues to exist and evolve. This essence, if potent and acknowledged, continues to evolve, unfolding its latent possibilities. This, I argue, is the guiding force of the Afro-Brazilian archive—a recognition and celebration of a core quality, a constructive potential that keeps nourishing and animating a poetic and cosmological ecosystem. Here, ancestral figures are not mere memories; they are dynamos propelling us toward beauty, justice, and well-being.

Are historians, novelists, poets, minstrels, and storytellers deceivers for shaping history and transforming the ignoble into the revered, recasting the fool as a hero or the drunkard as a sovereign? Or are they visionaries who discern the lasting essence of the past and reenvision it for the present? While canonical artists, historians, and scholars of other disciplines maneuver between creative liberties and constraints, they nonetheless play a crucial role in reinforcing and officially sanctioning these reinterpretations. Figures such as Na Agontimé, Francisco Félix de Souza, Nzinga, Zumbi, Obá Tossi, Iyá Nassô, and other luminaries of Afro-Brazilian cosmology have become icons within their own eras, radiating a powerful energy that surpasses the confines of their time to shed light on the greater narrative. The enduring legacy of these heroes forms the foundational bones of our communal heritage, serving as cornerstones of identity, power, and collective life force. This shared vitality, or *ashe*, is safeguarded by its custodians: poets, griots, artists, healers, scholars, and philosophers.

RELEASING CURSES, REDEEMING PROPHECIES

Three miles—approximately three miles—separate the city of Ouidah from its port. Along the path stands the *l'Arbre d'oublier*, the Tree of Forgetfulness. Before reaching the port, captives were ordered to circle the tree—men nine times, and women seven times. The purpose of the invented Dahomean ritual was to erase the memory of the future.

Moving back in space and forward in time to Ouidah in the second decade of the twenty-first century, we find the Brazilian artist Paulo Nazareth walking around the Tree of Forgetfulness quietly and slowly. Retracing the steps of the ancestral rite meant to make one forget and forgive those left on the continent, Nazareth circles the tree backward—four hundred and thirty-seven times.

Nazareth restaged and recorded this ritual performance around landmark trees in Maputo, Mozambique, and Belo Horizonte, Brazil, unwinding spells and enacting a rewinding—a *zinga*—a reconfiguration of history.

Final Considerations

Dikenga and Opón Ifa:
Ancestral Times and Technologies

*The younger woman turned her face from the path toward the first arrows
of light shooting up on the horizon. She looked for a soothing word, an
answer, an affirmation of alternatives.
She chose to remain quiet, to look into the eye of the hurricane,
breathe it in, give it time.
In the sky a small òpeèré took flight, direct as an arrow.*

The basic coordinates we rely on to orientate, situate, and define ourselves are shared concepts of time and space. "Time occupies the key position," states the English astronomer Sir Arthur Eddington (1882–1944), in "any attempt to bridge the domains of experience belonging to the spiritual and physical sides of our nature."[1] The Congolese philosopher Kia Bunseki Fu-Kiau (1934–2013) adds, "Time validates and provides truths to our existence"; it is "through time that both nature and man become comprehensible to us."[2] Cultures register the human presence in the world, as a scrolling of meaningful or symbolic events and as genetic or ancestral timelines. History may be understood as event-oriented time scales that organize the human odyssey according to numeric combinations, extraordinary historical moments, or ancestral timelines continuously rearranging themselves to organize and reorient the flow of human experience. Such generalized approaches to historical time, often combined, rely on spatial perspectives, which may refer to a distant never-before-seen past, or to planets, or to realms of the dead and the gods.

One can visualize time through water-flowing metaphors, through measuring technologies—such as astrolabes, hourglasses, optical and atomic clocks—or through our experience of it, such as the way we envision modernity via virtual time. The first major shift in the Western world of time and spatial consciousness probably came from early philosopher St. Augustine, whose writings were crucial in the foundation of Christian philosophy. Replacing the Greek time conception of Okeanos, the circular ocean of multiple crossing tides, St. Augustine introduced the notion of a one-directional tide, a river flowing from the future, through the present, to the past.[3] All epistemologies make a distinction between the time and the space of the living and the dead, of gods and humans. Time is the connecting energy, the imagined distance between god(s) and human generations (past, present, and future). Time is not only human timing but also tempo, beat, rhythm; it is how we organize our life and existence; it is how we position ourselves in space and history.

The shape in which we remember refers to our understanding of human, historical, and cosmological time. It is at once a powerful tool, offering us a code through which we can make sense of our existence, and a hindrance, preventing us from reasoning and rhyming beyond our cultural frames. Following Jan Vansina's perception that different cultures have different "mental maps" of history, *Imagining the Past and Remembering the Future* analyzes how history is coded, elaborated, and communicated in diasporic oral genres. "The semantic code," according to Vansina, "is the key to the whole operation of memory. It is a worldview, or a mental map acquired during childhood. Hence it is an acquired system, and because it is taught it is largely part of a shared collective code. Because their mental maps are different, the memories of people in different cultures vary."[4]

As Pindorama—later called the Island of Vera Cruz, then Terra de Santa Cruz—and eventually Brazil began to take shape, what concepts of time and space did Europeans, Indigenous peoples, and Africans use to define their worlds and histories? What happened when the Judeo-Christian-Muslim cosmology collided with the cosmologies of the Karaja, Xavante, Kaingang, Javae, Xambiva, and Apinaye, as well as those of the Yoruba, Kongo, Kuba, Fulani, Hausa, Khoisan, and so many others? Kayapo writer Kaká Werá Jecupé narrates that when Portuguese sailing vessels, "the Big Wind Canoes," arrived, Wahutedw'a, the Spirit of Time, had its wrists handcuffed. From then on, time began to be told in a different manner and gave birth to history, which "from then on, told only what happened to some."[5]

What are the metaphors for African concepts of time in the continent and its diaspora? How did African concepts of time reach and transform themselves in the New World, and how have they been continuously recreated? A major African representation of time is the symbol of a Mamba, the continuous-motion python biting its own tail such as a great river flowing into its own source.⁶ The Bakongo "mental map" could be drawn or performed as a Dikenga, the Kongo cosmogram of the four moments of the sun, moving in its Dingo-Dingo counterclockwise rhythmic motion. The Yoruba "mental map" could materialize itself as a detailed Opón Ifa, the circular divination board of Orunmila, "the greatest linguist" of the Yoruba pantheon.⁷

The Dikenga, also known as Yowa and the "Four Moments of the Sun," is the cyclical Kongo cosmogram, an epistemological concept that emerged from different perspectives and underlined the organization of this book. As explained by Fu-Kiau, the Dingo-Dingo cyclical movement of the Dikenga starts from the southern sun, the yellow sun of Musoni: representing midnight, the world of the dead, deepest mysteries, state of perfection, purity. From the south, it moves to the east, to the black sun of Kala, symbolizing the rising of a living sun from the depths of the spiritual world of the ancestors, as well as vitality, fertilized land, germinal state, birth stage, and cooler seasons which feed the vegetable realm. It follows up to the north, to the red sun of Tukula: the zenith of the sun, the highest possible level of any growing life, creation, activity, symbolizing passion, fire, maturity, and the season when trees lose their leaves in preparation for a new cycle. It then starts its descent in the west heading to the grayish white sun of Luvèmba: sunset, death stage, transformation, the setting of a living sun in the lower world of the ancestors, symbolizing the point of completion of the circle of cosmic time, the season in which "the vegetable realm rediscovers its green blanket, when nature's green cover or bush dries up, that is, dies to yield a new cover."⁸ Everything follows the Dingo-Dingo movement of the Dikenga: people, animals, nations, social systems, creations, days, weeks, songs, books. Everything is conceived in the south, born in the east, matures in the north, and dies in the west. From west to south, all beings, concepts, and ideas cross the Kalunga line: the invisible line between the physical and spiritual world from which all things emerge and to which all things submerge and undergo a transformation, a period of regeneration: "When events (*dunga*) take place, 'things' move and the timeline path clears itself. A new cycle of time goes in motion, and another collision stops it for a new beginning, a new motion of time to start."⁹

The Dikenga is represented particularly in chapters 7 and 8: from the rise and fall of the Ndongo and Kongo to the capital of Pungo-a-Ndongo as the geographic center that embodied the foundational cycle of the Kongo. Pungo-a-Ndongo was eventually read as the southern setting sun of a civilization that would reemerge from the Kalunga along the Eastern Sun of Aruanda in Brazil. The northern zeniths of these movements and spaces were placed at Nzinga's kingdom and Zumbi's Quilombo dos Palmares. The cyclical—progressed into spiral and coiled movements of the Dikenga—was furthered observed in the visual and musical renditions of life processes, relationships, and history, especially through the languages of Congadas and Capoeira.

The Kongo-Angola Dikenga and the created legend of Adamastor followed movements and embodiments that led to significant transatlantic transformation. Aruanda and the Stone Giant are icons that traveled from Africa to the core of Brazil. Among the differences are that while Aruanda was a mythic elaboration by African descendants about Africa, Adamastor was a European mythic elaboration of itself in relation to Africa, further reinvented by Brazilians. As I stated in the introduction, the backbone of Euro-Brazil is Afro-Brazilian. It does not stand on its own. It can only exist as Euro-Afro-Brazil. Afro-Brazil stands on its own vertebrae, but it does not exist in a vacuum.

The narratives and poetics of the Opón Ifa are at the center of chapter 9. *Itan* narratives about the creation of the world, the unjust imprisonment of Obatala, the place of the trickster Elegba, and the Babalawo diviners are seen from both sides of the Atlantic. As previously mentioned, the Ifa oracle, through its philosophical and religious system and encapsulated within a mythological corpus, played a key role in unifying diverse Yoruba linguistic groups. It emerged from a continuous recombination of experiences across space and time, forming a coherent theological, ethical, and philosophical whole. The *Opón Ifa* board embodies the Ifa oral literary corpus: a cycle structured around two-hundred and fifty-six *eses*, or life possibilities, combined into permutations of sixteen-by-sixteen signs of *odù*, or roads that symbolize historical and philosophical developments of the human experience. Orunmila, the Orisha of the Ifa, is called "òpìtàn lé-Ifẹ," meaning "he who de-riddles *itàn*, or unravels history throughout Ifè territory."[10]

The icons and case studies explored in this book shed light on interlocking forms and processes shaped by the migrations and encounters of the African diaspora. Olabiyi Yai teaches us that the noun *itàn* (History) contains in it the verb *tàn* which means "to spread, reach, open up, illuminate, shine."[11] "Pa ìtàn" refers to the practice of telling a story and disentangling or de-riddling history as one sheds light on human existence through time and space.[12] The concept of *itàn* refers to a code for interpreting History, which presumes that there are certain archetypes (personal and historical) and that these are recurrent, never precisely the same, but with essential similarities. Unlike a causal-effect chain logic, we are introduced to a spider web logic in which interpretations and comparative readings of history connect chronologically distant events and lead us to continuously different understandings of present and past events.

Similarly, according to Kongo philosophy, time is conceived as the trajectory of energy, "the moving of the conscious energy ("ngolo zasikama") within the biological matter/body (*ma/nitu*) on the path of both self and the universal cosmic wheel of life and social systems ("Dikenga dia zingu/ moyo ye fu").[13] Fu Kiau teaches us that, to understand the interrelation between the past, the present, and the future, we have to be able to "roll and unroll the scroll of time."[14] History is conceived of as scrolls which require a double action of rolling and unrolling. The past can be unrolled (*zingumuna*, or "the future comes to us") or rolled (*zinga*, the present, or "the daily processes of human life").[15] To understand the present, we have to unroll and review "the historical part of the scroll that contains the accumulated experience of learning, and to position oneself," to remember the future (the past of tomorrow), "by rolling or revealing the hidden part of the scroll on which new dams of time are to be imprinted by man or nature."[16]

Focusing on stories, poetry, and chants that stem from sacred corpus, *Imagining the Past and Remembering the Future* explores alternative understandings of time and history through epistemological representations such as the Dikenga and the Opón Ifa. Such considerations reconfigure the notions of literacy and present textualities that have been overlooked as poetic genres of the diaspora. One clear example is the Afro-Brazilian genre of *pontos-riscados* (along with the Haitian *vèvès* and the Cuban *firmas*), visual texts that, stemming mainly from the Kongo cosmology, were further developed in the diaspora and can be studied as part of a larger corpus of kindred visual poetic traditions.

PAN-AFRICAN DIKENGAS AND THE EURO-CANON

In the literary study of orature, the sung or recited word constitutes the major scaffold of meaning, the central code which leads us to a system of mutual conversions. Within that system, performance, music, gestures, and space create a complex whole of metalinguistic interdependent meanings. As I have written in the past, the *ponto-riscado* can be considered an African-Brazilian poetic genre.[17] Along lines demonstrated by Farris Thompson, who shows that these cosmograms, like the Haitian *vèvès* and the Cuban *firmas*, are ritualistic forms developed in the diaspora stemming mainly from the Kongo cosmology, I have proposed the understanding of *pontos-riscados* as a literary form, as visual poems, and as an aesthetic representation of a condensed text or a codified message.[18]

Western kindred poetic traditions include calligrams, poetic forms in which structural layout and typography offer a figurative suggestion of the messages or essence addressed. A classic example is the poem "The Altar," by seventeenth-century British metaphysical poet George Herbert.[19] His poem, alluding to

Western liturgical forms, became a reference to a specific configuration for calligrams known as altar-poems. Herbert's text follows the Western literary genetic line of poetic texts from the Greek anthology (written c. 325 BCE–200 CE and published during the Middle Ages), whose metaphysical poems appear materialized as altars, eggs, wings, and other configurations. Addressing God, Herbert opens the poem with an offering of a shattered altar. In the typographical composition and layout, the words lie upon one another like bricks, rebuilding the object and place of veneration and religious sacrifice: "each part / of my hard heart / Meets in this frame, / To praise thy name." Herbert concludes the poem with a plea directed to God: "sanctify this Altar to be thine."[20] The typographical format of "The Altar" is organic to its meaning: at once a sanctuary of Greek antiquity and the letter/word "I," defining both the local and the object of ritually symbolic self-sacrifice. "The Altar" is a poetic offering which visually establishes the space where the poetic "I" offers itself to God, beseeching redemption and wholeness.

Altar-poems are part of a Western literary genre that extends the poetic visual repertoire through the integration or juxtaposition of diverse semantic and semiotic structures. With regard to integration, we observe an expansion through which the abstract code of the text acquires a tri-dimensional body that is often the very essence or soul of the poetic work. The mystic and religious nature of altar-poems circumscribes the content and form of these poetic texts; in a liturgical universe, the poet and the reader seem to activate a ritualized process of magical evocation and metaphysical meditation. In an analogous dynamic, the *pontos-riscados* can be interpreted as a poetic tradition that situates the reader and text in a sacredly evocative aesthetic universe.

Pontos-riscados are mediums of expression whose function is essentially, and often solely, understood as ritualistic magical activators. *Pontos-riscados* and altar-poems are expressions of literary traditions that spring from distinctive genealogical trees. If we read the Kongo/Brazilian *pontos-riscados* as visual poems, the Greek/British altar-poems might be seen as unsuspected distant relatives. They offer a mystical and visual analogy and a direct suggestion to the *pontos-riscados* as a sacred poetic genre that simultaneously invests a mystic concrete anatomy in the message and in the space established by that message. According to Olga Cacciatore, *ponto-riscado* is "the picture formed by a set of cabalistic signs (magical-symbolic), which, outlined with a *pemba* (chalk) in the color associated with a specific entity, helps to invoke the entity to the earthly realm. When the picture is drawn by the incorporated medium, it identifies the entity which rides the medium."[21]

In reference to a mediumistic text, Cavalcanti Bandeira defines the *ponto-riscado* as the exteriorization of the thoughts of a spirit who presents the living with its "letter of introduction endowed with all the powers that the spirit brings forth."[5] Makota Valdina explains the importance of the *pemba*:

> *Pemba* is a substance well-known among members of Afro-Brazilian religious communities. In the Yoruba *terreiros*, it replaces the *efun*. Although the term *pemba*, like many others associated with Candomblé, is thought to be of Yoruba origin, it is actually derived from the Bantu (Kikongo) word *mpeemba*, meaning both "chalk" and, in its religious significance, "sacred powder." During various, primarily secret, rituals, *pemba*'s purifying properties are used to repel negative influences from physical surroundings and persons.[22]

Valdina adds that an annual ritual of preparation and consecration of the *pemba* is conducted in the hours between the evening of June 23 and the early morning hours of June 24, and that the elders in Candomblé Angola consider *pemba* to be "the soul of Angola."[23]

A further distinctive feature concerns the authorship of *pontos-riscados*: they are sketched or written by the Umbanda practitioner as an evocation of the ancestors or by the ancestors themselves. They are both messages sent to the ancestors and messages sent by the ancestors. As an identifying sign of an ancestral presence, the *ponto-riscado* is the Afro-Brazilian cousin of the Afro-Cuban *firma* (signature). The Cuban anthropologist Miguel Barnet, analyzing the *firma* sign of the Kongo-based cosmology of Palo Mayombe, explains that it is not only "the supernatural forces that have a range of *firmas*; every priest bears his *firma* as means of identification, regardless of the rank or prestige of any member of a *casa de palo*."[24] In Umbanda, through the kinesis of dance and chants (*pontos-cantados*), the *pontos-riscados* open themselves up, transferring the symbolic load of their geometrical visual tangibility to human beings, who as "horses" are "ridden" and lend movement and corporeal presence to perform, expand, and improvise their own versions of the mystical text.

In the same manner as the *vèvès* of Haitian Vodun and the *firmas* of Cuban Palo Mayombe, the *pontos-riscados* are not objects for static mystic or aesthetic contemplation. Rather, they are graphic commands invested with performative energy and dynamic generators of verbivocovisual transmutation. In her study of the structural analysis of the visual imagery of the *vèvès*, Karen Brown (1942–2015) observes: "Like a man adrift at sea will try to communicate his need for help in all means available to him: semaphore, shouting, smoke signals and radio message, so a culture involved in the very serious business of world construction will use all means available to it to externalize (in order to internalize) its own view of itself."[25] Voduisants Paleiros, and Umbandistas use different mediums to communicate their need for contact with their own subtelluric realms: Vilokan, Mayombe, and Aruanda (allegorical references to Guinea, Kongo, and Angola). The *pontos-riscados, vèvès,* and *firmas* are part of an extensive repertoire of the sacred languages of the African Diaspora.

Pontos-riscados, vèvès, and *firmas* are often contained in circular forms that function as placentas, fabrics, or borders whose porousness allows the essence of what is circumscribed to be transferred to those who are bound to it. Etymologically, *punctu* denotes a small orifice. In the Umbanda context, the *ponto-riscado* is metaphorically a small orifice in the Kalunga line: a polarized field of energy that dilates the pores of the fabric dividing the world of the living from the world of the dead. The concept of *ponto* (point) is also prevalent in the Haitian *vèvès*. In a *vèvè*, a *ponto* is referred to as *pwen*. *Pwen* is a line of energy or a point of contact with the world of the lowas or Vodun spirits. Haitian *pwens* exhibit such kindred characteristics to the Afro-Brazilian *pontos* that both can be either *riscados* (drawn, outlined) or *cantados* (sung). "Nô d'pwen or voye pwen," literally means to throw or to send a point.[26] The *pwen* as "thrown-point" can occur either in the sacred space of the peristil (the Vodun ceremonial ground) or in the secular spheres of daily life.[27] As proverbs, *pwens* are charged with highly metaphorical condensation, and thus render themselves open to suggestive expressions of indirect challenges and provocations. This use of *pwen* (which can occur both in sacred and secular realms) makes me question the adjective *riscado* in *ponto-riscado*.

A *ponto* is not *desenhado*, "drawn," but *riscado*—"traced," "outlined," or "scribed." The choice of the term would not be casual. While a Palo practitioner who undergoes ritual initiation is said to be *rayado* (scratched), a Cuban *firma* is *trazada* (traced, outlined, designed)—the same designation used in the creation of a *vèvè*.[28] The Kongo *zanga Nzambi* ("tracing God") presents itself in the traditional display of the Dikenga cross, which represents the processes of transformation of life and the cosmos and symbolizes a cosmogramic altar.[29] The *pontos-riscados, vèvè,* and *firmas* are also cosmogramic altars. They define the properties of a sacred microcosm and are in turn defined via their extension and reverberation, according to their related coordinates and corresponding to the cosmological signifying repertoire.

As communicative codes, abridged scripts in constant creation and interpretation, *pontos-riscados, vèvè,* and *firmas* challenge their producers and receivers to decode, narrate, and perform highly metonymic poetic texts according to human and divine semiotic interactions. Through various expressions, most tangible perhaps in the dance steps of Umbandistas, Voduisants, and Paleiros, as well as Congadeiros, Capoeiristas, and Sambistas, the ground is traced and scribed according to a fully orchestrated, integrated, and interrelated ancient and modern corpus.

DIFFERENT FAMILY TREES

Imagining the Past and Remembering the Future models the search for alternative critical paradigms to conceptualize the artistic repertoire of the great Afro-hemispheric archive. To speak of paradigms is to speak of a unifying package of practices and concepts, of a conceptual structure of beliefs and sciences that opens a community's field of vision and informs, upon being informed, its worldview.[30] It involves a pact, a social agreement that illuminates our field of vision by graying out other fields. Through paradigms, we see what we see by virtue of what we render invisible. As the French philosopher Edgar Morin explains, paradigms carry out selections and determinations of logical operations designating fundamental categories of intelligibility and control; in other words, it is according to culturally inscribed paradigms that individuals know, think, and act.[31] Paradigms are at once subterranean and sovereign in that they organize "all of man's thoughts, feelings, and desires."[32]

In his 1919 essay titled "Tradition and the Individual Talent," one of the most widely received critical essays of Western literature, T. S. Eliot suggested the image of a perpetually moving loop in which the totality of European literary production is simultaneously and productively active in the poetics of the present. In this essay, Eliot reupholsters the concept of tradition with a historical perception that involves the past as a present element.[33] Within the principle of a critical aesthetic, every new artist is situated in contrast and comparison to the past, inevitably modifying the totality of a previously existing order. The meaning and appreciation of a poet, says Eliot, need to be situated: "His significance, his appreciation is the appreciation of his relation to the dead poets and artists. You cannot value him alone; you must set him, for contrast and comparison, among the dead."[34]

Eliot affirms this process does not signify an evolution, merely an awareness that the constant flow and changing outlook of the country represented by the poet, "the mind of his own country," translates the substance of art. "Every nation, every race," says Eliot, "has not only its own creative, but its own critical turn of mind."³⁵ The historical sense leads the poet to express himself not merely within the boundaries of the generation to which he belongs, but with an attitude in which the totality of European literary production is simultaneously and productively active in the poetics of the present. Eliot's essay recalls a literary family tree, a large *padê* (an Afro-Brazilian ritual gathering) of the poet with his Western ancestors. The best part of a poetic work, says Eliot, occurs when "the dead poets, the poets' ancestors, assert their immortality most vigorously."³⁶

In his 2017 work on Brazilian-Kongo-Angola-Catholic poetics, Edimilson de Almeida Pereira intersects with Eliot in certain aspects. In *A saliva da fala* (*The Spit of Speech*), Pereira observes: "singer-poets simultaneously interpret the present as the ancestors' future and their own dynamic past."³⁷ Referring to fundamentally oral textualities that are based on non-European aesthetics, Edimilson de Almeida Pereira puts forth: "to apprehend them it is necessary to recognize another historical dynamic (that of marginalized groups during and after colonization) that rolled out parallel to the historical revisionism considered to be official."³⁸

In 1959, Antonio Candido, published the classic *Formação da literatura brasileira* (*Formation of Brazilian Literature*), in which he reworks concepts proposed by Eliot to study the formation of Brazilian literature. Rather than maintaining Eliot's metaphor of a literary circle, Candido imagines literary continuity as the passing of the torch between runners.³⁹ In this ensemble of literary producers and receptors supplied with a transmitting mechanism, Candido evokes the Olympic Games, with their history of world powers flexing their muscles. Regardless of the results of Candido's criticism, some of the most fertile elements in Eliot's matrix are lost. Candido's study reveals a supposedly Brazilian tradition (no longer Western) and its "internal causality" ("casualidade interna").⁴⁰ Whereas Eliot uses the concept of historical sense to situate English literature within the belly of the global West, Candido uses his concept of the historical point of view to withdraw Brazilian literature from the Western belly and insert it into an exclusively Brazilian "articulated system" ("sistema articulado").⁴¹ Thus, Candido abandons Eliot's transnational ancestral perspective. Within the national Brazilian literary system articulated by Candido—baggage we have long inherited—some Afro-Brazilian textualities were, as pointed out by Edimilson de Almeida Pereira, exiled.

Pereira observes that the way in which "singer-poets" (*cantopoetas*) have been treated "deprive them even of literary marginality."⁴² Those poets, representatives of oral African traditions from Minas Gerais, are, as Pereira indicates, "relegated to another space beyond the margin."⁴³ He adds: "rather than say this textuality lost its place in the field of legitimate literature, it is better to change the thickness of the analytic lens and observe that it is actually in a situation of exile."[44] Unlike the Yoruba-Ewe literary forms, oral textualities from the Kongo-Angola archive end up occupying an extraordinary situation and space. Pereira continues: "Their exclusion from the literary canon, with its forms and rules, allowed them to delineate their own field of play without dismissing the possibility of dialogue with other textualities."[45] Borrowing Antonio Riserio's terms "poemusic" and "underground literature" (*poemúsica* and "literatura subterrânea"), adding Leda Maria Martins's *oralitura*, and contributing his own "song-poem" and "silent literatures" (*cantopoema* and "literaturas silenciosas"), Pereira observes that these are textualities that, despite having been "tossed to the back of the maze of Western literary canons," demonstrate "an expressive capacity for social interference."[46]

Yoruba-Ewe textualities received more attention than those of the Kongo-Angola archive, even gaining some projection in the realm of canonical literature, despite not having the autonomy of a literary system as such. Pereira comments on the existence of particular African languages that "crossed remote lands and seas to reconstitute in a new way in the Americas ancient human hopes of maintaining a connection to the divine."[47] These life experiences generated Kongo-Angola Catholic philosophical, poetic, and cultural repertoires that present themselves as some of the most challenging.[48] The character of this particular hybrid text, perceived as enigmatic, is linked as much to its linguistic structure as it is to its cultural practices and the value systems that inform its worldview. Such a textuality, says Pereira, in this sense, "is as enigmatic and as comprehensible as the languages produced by other groups, since these notions are relativized according to the degree of the subject's immersion within a determined form of language."[49]

Which alternative paradigms, which models, could serve as supports for the reading, outlining, and comprehension of a corpus that could never simply be added to the Western canon? How can we work on overcoming graphocentrism—the discrimination based on the belief that written textualities, as modeled by Western civilizations, are superior to other fully-fledged textualities expressed not only through scrolls, pages, and screens but also through dances, sounds, and human-built constructions? How can we advocate that access to the corpus of such textualities involves the same, if not higher, level of commitment to apprenticeship to move from illiteracy to acquired fluency and knowledge?

One of the main claims of *Imagining the Past and Remembering the Future* is that in order to conceptualize the great African diasporic archive, we need to be able to recognize a different historical dynamic that leads us to multiple spheres of convergence. In delineating inclusive hermeneutics that stem from the genres and textualities that African ancestors brought to Brazil, understood within their larger context of our past and current realities, we can shed light, *tàn*, on the vastly unacknowledged African diasporic artistic sources, languages, technologies, and philosophies, and contribute to the ongoing reframing of African diaspora studies and the Western disciplines and canons as a whole.

"So as you walk on this world of the living and see what you see, and hear what you hear, beyond this àiyé, there is an òrun which is the source of the reflections of everything you may feel over here. Everything is connected like each grain of corn has a string to its husk. Each herb offers a map that directs us to one ancestral family. Their wind, their strength, are all around us. Before receiving we need to attract. Before attracting we need to be clear. In order to be clear, we need to listen to this silence and understand it."

Notes

INTRODUCTION: ENTERING OTHER FORESTS

1. Following usage in Brazilian Portuguese and U.S. English, I use the terms African-Brazilian and Afro-Brazilian with subtle distinctions. I hyphenate African-Brazilian to signal a single compound modifier conveying an inseparable cultural and historical identity. The hyphen echoes familiar diaspora terms. In Black Brazilian activism and scholarship, it serves as a political marker by joining African heritage to Brazilian social realities while avoiding hierarchical framing, and prevents confusion that might suggest Brazilians born in or living in Africa rather than descendants of the African diaspora within Brazil. In the United States, the term African American is the widely accepted term, and modern style guides prefer it to the outdated Afro-American. In Brazil, however, the historical trajectory of these terms differs. Today, *afro-brasileiro* (Afro-Brazilian) coexists mainly with *afrodescendente* (Afro-descendant) and *negro* or *preto* (Black). The term *afro-brasileiro* has been used in the Black press since the early twentieth century and gained national prominence with the First Afro-Brazilian Congress held in Recife in 1934. In the 1940s political and religious movements adopted it in their names, and from the 1960s onward it became an identity marker in newspapers, cultural groups, and academic research. In the early twenty-first century, it entered federal law: Law No. 10.639/2003 (the Afro-Brazilian and Indigenous History and Culture Law) that mandated the teaching of African-Brazilian history and culture in all schools. *Brasil africano* (African Brazil) and *brasileiro africano* (African-Brazilian) are less colloquially used expressions that make a pointed reference to spaces, histories, and cultures created by Africans and their descendants in Brazil.
2. Robert Farris Thompson, "Canons of the Cool: Interview with Robert Farris Thompson," interview by Fred Iseman, *Rolling Stone*, November 22, 1984, https://www.rollingstone.com/culture/culture-news/robert-farris-thompson-canons-of-the-cool-58823.
3. Michel Foucault, "Two Lectures: Lecture One: January 7, 1976," in *Power/Knowledge: Selected Interviews and Other Writings*, ed. and trans. Colin Gordon (Vintage Press, 1980), 83.
4. Paul Tiyambe Zeleza, "Rewriting the African Diaspora: Beyond the Black Atlantic," *African Affairs* 104, no. 414 (2005): 49.
5. UNESCO, "Declaration on Race and Racial Prejudice," adopted by the General Conference at its twentieth session, Paris, November 27, 1978, articles 27, 42, and 119, https://www.un.org/ruleoflaw/blog/document/declaration-on-race-and-racial-prejudice.
6. UNESCO, "Declaration on Race," articles 5 and 8.
7. Joseph Roach, *Cities of the Dead: Circum-Atlantic Performance* (Columbia University Press, 1996), 43.

8. Toni Morrison, "Memory, Creation, and Writing," *Thought: A Review of Culture and Idea* 59, no. 235 (December 1984): 388.
9. Saidiya Hartman, "Venus in Two Acts," *Small Axe: A Caribbean Journal of Criticism* 12, no. 2 (2008): 1–14.
10. Alexis Okeowo, "How Saidiya Hartman Retells the History of Black Life," *The New Yorker*, October 26, 2020, https://www.newyorker.com/magazine/2020/10/26/how-saidiya-hartman-retells-the-history-of-black-life.
11. Kamau Brathwaite, *Wars of Respect: Nanny, Sam Sharpe and the Struggle for People's Liberation* (API for the National Heritage Week Committee, 1977), 6.
12. Brathwaite, *Wars*, 7.
13. Marlene Nourbese Philip, "The Absence of Writing or How I Almost Became a Spy," in *Out of the Kumbla: Caribbean Women and Literature*, ed. Carole Boyce Davies and E. S. Fido (Africa World Press, 1994), 273.
14. Kamau Brathwaite, *Folk Culture of the Slaves in Jamaica* (New Beacon, 1981), 12.
15. Brathwaite, *Folk*, 13–14.
16. C. Daniel Dawson, "Treasure in the Terror: The African Cultural Legacy in the Americas," *The Freedom Chronicle* (Institute for Freedom Studies, Northern Kentucky University) 2, no. 1 (Fall 2002), n/p.
17. Edimilson de Almeida Pereira, *A saliva da fala: notas sobre a poética banto-católica no Brasil* (Azougue, 2017), 145.
18. Dawson, "Treasure."
18. Dawson, "Treasure."
20. Leda Maria Martins, *Afrografias da memória: o reinado do Rosário no Jatobá* (Editora Perspectiva; Mazza Edições, 1997), 26.
21. See Beatriz Nascimento, *The Dialectic Is in the Sea: The Black Radical Thought of Beatriz Nascimento*, ed. and trans. Christen A. Smith et al. (Princeton University Press, 2023). The 2020 Congress of the Latin American Studies Association (LASA) paid homage to Lélia Gonzalez with the theme "Améfrica Ladina: Connecting Worlds and Knowledge, Weaving Hopes" (Améfrica Ladina: vinculando mundos y saberes, tejiendo esperanzas). As LASA explained, "Améfrica Ladina aims to take a step in the same direction as the title *Nuestra América*, as opposed to *América Latina*, which emphasizes the region's Latin tradition and ties to Europe while obscuring or excluding the role of other populations, such as Amerindian and African-descended communities, in this process." See "About LASA 2020," Latin American Studies Association, accessed October 23, 2023. https://lasaweb.org/en/lasa2020/.
22. Lélia Gonzalez, "A categoria político-cultural de amefricanidade," in *Primavera para as rosas negras: Lélia Gonzalez em primeira pessoa*, ed. Raquel Barreto (Diáspora Africana, 2018), 329; originally published in *Tempo Brasileiro* 92/93 (January/June 1988): 69–82.
23. Gonzalez, "A categoria," 330.
24. Bryce Henson, "Communication Theory from Améfrica Ladina: Amefricanidade, Lélia Gonzalez, and Black Decolonial Approaches," *Review of Communication* 21, no. 4 (2021): 356.
25. Brathwaite, *Wars*, 6; Robert Farris Thompson, *The Four Moments of the Sun: Kongo Art in Two Worlds* (National Gallery of Art, 1981) and *Flash of the Spirit: African and Afro-American Art and Philosophy* (Random House, 1984); William Bascom, *African Folktales in the New World* (Indiana University Press, 1992); and William Bascom and Melville Heskovitz, *Continuity and Change in African Cultures* (University of Chicago Press, 1970).
26. Roach, *Cities*, 286.
27. Elizabeth Isichei, *Voices of the Poor in Africa: Moral Economy and the Popular Imagination* (University of Rochester Press, 2002), 32.
28. Ngũgĩ wa Thiong'o, *Decolonizing the Mind: The Politics of Language in African Literature* (J. Currey; Heinemann Kenya, 1986); Ruth Finnegan, *Oral Literature in Africa* (Clarendon Press, 1970) and *Oral Poetry: Its Nature, Significance and Social Context* (Indiana University Press, 1992); Isidore

Okpewho, *African Oral Literature: Backgrounds, Character, and Continuity* (Indiana University Press, 1992); Paul Zumthor, *Oral Poetry: An Introduction* (University of Minnesota Press, 1990).

29. T. S. Eliot, "Tradition and the Individual Talent," *Selected Essays* (Faber and Faber, 1932). For a reflection on critical paradigms and canons, see Isis Barra Costa "Other Forests: The Afro-Brazilian Literary Archive," in *Améfrica in Letters: Literary Interventions from Mexico to the Southern Cone*, ed. Jennifer Carolina Gómez Menjívar (Vanderbilt University Press, 2022), 129–49.
30. Roach, *Cities*, 77.
31. Brathwaite, *Wars*, 4.
32. Brathwaite, *Wars*, 3–4.
33. Roach, *Cities*, 26–27.
34. Brathwaite, *Folk*, 44.
35. Paul Griffith, *Afro-Caribbean Poetry and Ritual* (Palgrave Macmillan, 2010), xii.
36. Griffith, *Afro-Caribbean*, xiii.
37. J. Edward Chamberlin, *Come Back to Me My Language: Poetry and the West Indies* (University of Illinois Press, 1993), 176; Antonio Benítez-Rojo, *The Repeating Island: The Caribbean and the Postmodern Perspective* (Duke University Press, 1997), 3.
38. Griffith, *Afro-Caribbean*, xii.
39. Griffith, *Afro-Caribbean*, xiii.
40. See Robert Macfarlane, "The Secrets of the Wood Wide Web," *The New Yorker*, August 7, 2016, https://www.newyorker.com/tech/annals-of-technology/the-secrets-of-the-wood-wide-web; Lindsey Jean Schueman, "Welcome to the Wood Wide Web," One Earth, October 25, 2021, accessed September 26, 2023. https://www.oneearth.org/welcome-to-the-wood-wide-web. The term "Wood Wide Web" was coined by Suzanne Simard.
41. Ira Berlin, "Time, Space, and the Evolution of Afro-American Society on British Mainland North America," *The American Historical Review* 85, no. 1 (1980): 44.
42. Berlin, "Time," 78.
43. David Scott, "That Event, This Memory: Notes on the Anthropology of African Diasporas in the New World," *Diaspora: A Journal of Transnational Studies* 1, no. 3 (1991): 278.
44. Scott, "That Event," 278.
45. Scott, "That Event," 278–79.
46. John Thornton, *A Cultural History of the Atlantic World, 1250–1820* (Cambridge University Press, 2012), 2.
47. Thompson, "Canons."
48. Roach, *Cities*, 4–5.
49. Roach, *Cities*, xii.
50. William Shakespeare, *The Tempest*, ed. Barbara Mowat and P. Werstine (Folger Shakespeare Library, 2015), 1.2, https://folger.edu/explore/shakespeares-works/all-works.
51. Igor Cusack, "From Revolution to Reflection: The National Anthems of the New Lusophone Worlds," *Luso-Brazilian Review* 45, no. 2 (2008): 49.
52. I am using the spelling "Kongo" and "Mozambique" when referring to the former kingdom and country, respectively. "Congo" and "Moçambique" (as spelled in Portuguese) will be used for references to Congada performers.
53. Jan Vansina, *Oral Tradition as History* (University of Wisconsin Press, 1985), 22.
54. Isichei, *Voices*, 4.
55. Filhos de Gandhy (@Banda_Gandhy), "Como tudo começou," Twitter (now X), 22 July, 2016. twitter.com/banda_gandhy?lang=en.
56. Oyèrónkẹ́ Oyěwùmí, *The Invention of Women: Making an African Sense of Western Gender Discourses* (University of Minnesota Press, 1997).
57. Oyěwùmí, *Invention*, 13.

58. Oyěwùmí, *Invention*, 12–13.
59. Oyěwùmí, *Invention*, 13–17.
60. Carla Regina Diéguez, "A masculinidade do trabalhador portuário: novas questões em tempo de automação" (paper presented at the IX Seminário Fazendo Gênero: Diásporas, Diversidades, Deslocamentos, Universidade Federal de Santa Catarina, Florianópolis, August 2010).
61. Roberta Sampaio Guimarães, "Patrimônios e conflitos de um afoxé na reurbanização da região portuária carioca," *Mana* 22, no. 2, (2016): 311–40.
62. Pierre Fatumbi Verger, *Os libertos: sete caminhos na liberdade de escravos* (Corrupio, 1992), 137.
63. Luís Henrique Dias Tavares, *Comércio proibido de escravos* (Ática, 1988); Karl Polanyi, *Dahomey and the Slave Trade: An Analysis of an Archaic Economy* (University of Washington Press, 1966); Verger, *Os libertos*.
64. João José Reis, *Rebelião escrava no Brasil: a história do levante dos malês em 1835* (Companhia das Letras, 2003), 138.
65. Lisa Earl Castillo and L. N. Parés, "Marcelina da Silva: A Nineteenth-Century Candomblé Priestess in Bahia," *Slavery & Abolition* 31, no. 1 (March 2009): 18.
66. Dan Sperber, *Rethinking Symbolism*, trans. Alice L. Morton (Cambridge University Press, 1975), 43.
67. Vansina, *Oral*, 23.
68. Roach, *Cities*, 194.
69. Roach, *Cities*, 198,
70. FuKiau, quoted in Roach, *Cities*, 251.
71. John Mason, and G. Edwards, *Black Gods: Orisa Studies in the New World* (Yoruba Theological Archministry, 1985), 92–97.

1. VISUAL ART IMAGES: "I SEE . . . I NARRATE. BUT WHAT IS IT THAT I AM SEEING?"

1. Larry Rother, "500 Years Later, Brazil Looks Its Past in the Face," *New York Times*, April 25, 2000, https://www.nytimes.com/2000/04/25/world/500-years-later-brazil-looks-its-past-in-the-face.html.
2. Daniel Bramatti, "Índio aponta flecha para ACM em Brasília," *Folha de São Paulo*, April 13, 2020, https://www1.folha.uol.com.br/fol/pol/ult13042000259.htm.
3. "Documento final da conferência dos povos e organizações indígenas do Brasil," Programa de pesquisas sobre povos Indígenas do Nordeste Brasileiro, April 21, 2000, https://pineb.ffch.ufba.br/downloads/1242404195Documento%20Final_Outros%20500.pdf.
4. "Documento final," Programa de pesquisas sobre povos Indígenas do Nordeste Brasileiro.
5. Sandra Brasil and D. Camargo, "De nau a pior," *Veja*, May 3, 2000.
6. Fernando Henrique Cardoso, "O discurso de FHC que abre as comemorações em Porto Seguro," *Folha de São Paulo*, April 22, 2000 (emphasis mine).
7. Cardoso, "O discurso de FHC."
8. Jorge Coli, "E la nave va," *Folha de São Paulo*, April 30, 2000.
9. Michel Foucault, *Histoire de la folie à l'âge classique* (Gallimard, 1972), 18–22.
10. Frederico Fellini, *E la nave va* (Concorde Film, 1983), film, 135 min.
11. Fellini, *E la nave va*.
12. Lorraine Pinheiro Mendes, "Minha história é suada igual dança no ilê, ninguém vai me dizer o meu lugar." *Políticas Culturais em Revista* 14, no. 2 (July/December 2021): 124.
13. Mendes, "Minha história," 125.
14. Mendes, "Minha história," 125.

15. Original excerpt: "A saída em direção a um presente-futuro, é pedra cantada no passado-presente: a rasteira é dada pela coletividade," Mendes, "Minha história," 124.
16. Mendes, "Minha história," 124, 132–40; Renata Felinto, *Axexê da negra ou o descanso das mulheres que mereciam serem amadas*, 2017, accessed October 23, 2023. https://renatafelinto.wordpress.com/axexe-da-negra. "Axexê," from the Yoruba *ijeje*, is the funeral ritual of Candomblé.

2. HISTORY: A GOLD MEDAL FOR THE BEST STORY

1. José Antônio Segatto and Maria Célia Leonel, "Formação da literatura e constituição do estado nacional," *Itinerários* 30 (January–June 2010): 19.
2. Segatto and Leonel, "Formação," 19–20.
3. José Murilo de Carvalho, *Pontos e bordados: escritos de história e política* (Editora UFMG, 1999), 236.
4. Several insurrections erupted throughout Brazil, including the Cabanagem (1835–1840) in Pará; the Confederação do Equador (1824) in Pernambuco; the Balaiada (1838–1841) in Maranhão; the Federação dos Guanais (1832), the Revolta dos Malês (1835), and the Sabinada (1837–1838) in Bahia; and the Farroupilha (1835–1845) in Rio Grande do Sul.
5. Januário da Cunha Barbosa, "Discurso," *Revista do Instituto Histórico e Geográfico Brasileiro* 1 (1839): 9, https://ihgb.org.br/publicacoes/revista-ihgb/.
6. Instituto Histórico, "Fim e objeto do objeto do instituto," *Revista do Instituto Histórico e Geográfico Brasileiro* 1 (1839): 18.
7. Manoel Luís Lima Salgado Guimarães, "Nação e civilização nos trópicos: o Instituto Histórico Geográfico Brasileiro e o projeto de uma história nacional," *Caminhos da Historiografia* 1, no. 1 (1988): 6.
8. Barbosa, "Discurso," 9.
9. Instituto Histórico, "Prêmios popostos pelo Instituto na segunda sessão pública aniversária," *Revista do Instituto Histórico e Geográfico Brasileiro* 2 (1840): 642, https://ihgb.org.br/publicacoes/revista-ihgb/.
10. Instituto Histórico, "Prêmios popostos," 642.
11. Karl Friedrich von Martius, *Como se deve escrever a história do Brasil*, ed. Manoel Luiz Sagrado Guimarães (EdUERJ, 2010), 64–65.
12. Von Martius, *Como se deve escrever*, 64, 76, 78–79.
13. Von Martius, *Como se deve escrever*, 72–73.
14. Marilena de Sousa Chauí, *Brasil: mito fundador e sociedade autoritária* (Fundação Perseu Abramo, 2000), 8.
15. Chauí, *Brasil: mito fundador*, 49.
16. Guimarães, "Nação e civilização," 6.

3. LITERATURE: HEROES, MONSTERS, GIANTS, AND THE CANON

1. José Antônio Segatto and M. C. Leonel, "Formação da literatura e constituição do estado nacional," *Itinerários* 30 (2010): 20.
2. Roberto Ventura, *Estilo tropical: história cultural e polêmicas literárias* (Companhia das Letras, 1991), 166.

3. LITERATURE

3. Ventura, *Estilo tropical*, 166.
4. Regina Zilberman, "História da literatura e identidade nacional," in *Literatura e identidades*, ed. José Luiz Jobim (EdUERJ, 1999), 27.
5. Segatto and Leonel, "Formação," 26.
6. Segatto and Leonel, "Formação," 26–27; Monica Pimenta Velloso, "A literatura como espelho da nação," *Revista Estudos Históricos* 1, no. 2 (1988): 240.
7. Sílvio Romero, *História da literatura brasileira*, 3 vols. (Livraria Garnier: 1902), https://bibdig .biblioteca.unesp.br/items/d592b722-45a6-4cba-8a5c-baa173eeffa4. Antonio Candido, *Formação da literatura brasileira: momentos decisivos, 1750–1836* (Ouro sobre Azul, 2006); and *Formação da literatura brasileira: momentos decisivos, 1836–1880* (Martins, 1971).
8. Candido, *Formação da literatura (1750–1836)*, 23.
9. Antonio Candido, "Variações sobre temas da formação," in *Textos de intervenção*, ed. Vinício Dantas (Duas Cidades/34, 2002), 94.
10. Candido, "Variações," 95.
11. Antonio Candido, "Literature and the Rise of Brazilian National Self-Identity," *Luso-Brazilian Review* 5, no. 1 (1968): 28. His *Formação da literatura brasileira* was first published in 1959.
12. Candido, *Formação da literatura (1750–1836)*, 23.
13. Candido, *Formação da literatura (1750–1836)*, 23–24.
14. Haroldo de Campos, *O sequestro do barroco na formação da literatura brasileira: o caso Gregório de Mattos* (Fundação Casa Jorge Amado, 1989).
15. Candido, "Literature," 28–29.
16. Candido, "Literature," 28–29.
17. Bernhard Klein, "Camões and the Sea: Maritime Modernity in *The Lusiads*," *Modern Philology* 111, no. 2 (2013): 163–64.
18. Luís Vaz de Camões, *The Lusiads*, trans. Landeg White (Oxford University Press, 2008), 3.20–22, 52. Original excerpt: "Eis aqui, quase cume da cabeça / De Europa toda, o Reino Lusitano, / Onde a terra se acaba e o mar começa, / E onde Febo repousa no Oceano. / Este quis o Céu justo que floreça / Nas armas contra o torpe Mauritano, / Deitando-o de si fora; e lá na ardente / África estar quieto o não consente. // Esta foi Lusitânia, derivada / De Luso, ou Lisa, que de Baco antigo/ Filhos foram, parece, ou companheiros, / E nela então os Íncolas primeiros // Desta o pastor nasceu, que no seu nome/ Se vê que de homem forte os feitos teve; / Cuja fama ninguém virá que dome, / Pois a grande de Roma não se atreve," in Camões, *Os Lusíadas*, 4th ed., ed. Álvaro Júlio da Costa Pimpão and Aníbal Pinto de Castro (Instituto Camões, 2000), 3.20–22. Unless otherwise noted, all original quotations from *Os Lusíadas* and *The Lusiads* are taken from these two editions (printed by Oxford University Press and Instituto Camões).
19. "Taprobana: the Greek name for the eastern limit of the known world. In canto 10:51, Camões identifies it with Ceylon"; see Camões and White, *The Lusiads*, 229. Original excerpt: "As armas e os barões assinalados, / Que da ocidental praia Lusitana, / Por mares nunca de antes navegados, / Passaram ainda além da Taprobana, / Em perigos e guerras esforçados, / Mais do que prometia a força humana, / E entre gente remota edificaram / Novo Reino, que tanto sublimaram," 1.1
20. Josiah Blackmore, *Moorings: Portuguese Expansion and the Writing of Africa* (University of Minnesota Press, 2009), 145.
21. Klein, "Camões," 160.
22. Klein, "Camões," 161.
23. Klein, "Camões," 158.
24. William Shakespeare, *The Tempest*, ed. Barbara A. Mowat and Paul Werstine (Folger Shakespeare Library, 2015), https://www.folger.edu/explore/shakespeares-works/the-tempest/read/, 1.1. Unless otherwise noted, all citations from *The Tempest* are from this edition.

25. Camões, *The Lusiads*, 6. Original excerpt: "Já no largo Oceano navegavam, / As inquietas ondas apartando; / Os ventos brandamente respiravam, / Das naus as velas côncavas inchando," 1.19.
26. Shakespeare, *The Tempest*, 1.5.
27. This is the last line of the epilogue. See Shakespeare, *The Tempest*, 5.1.
28. Victor Lopes, *Língua, vidas em português* (Costa de Castelos Filmes, 2007), film. Original excerpt: "Portugal deu origem a um filho maior que o próprio pai."
29. Shakespeare, *The Tempest*, 1.2.
30. Shakespeare, *The Tempest*, 1.2.
31. Blackmore, *Moorings*, 134.
32. John L. Hilton, "Adamastor, Gigantomachies, and the Literature of Exile in Camões' Lusíads," *Journal of the Australasian Universities Language and Literature Association* 112 (2009): 2.
33. Natalie Lawrence, "Making Monsters," in *Worlds of Natural History*, ed. Helen Anne Curry et al. (Cambridge University Press, 2018), 94, doi:10.1017/9781108225229.007.
34. Emphasis added. Lawrence, "Making Monsters," 95
35. Blackmore, *Moorings*, 94.
36. Blackmore, *Moorings*, 124.
37. Blackmore, *Moorings*, 215.
38. Lawrence Lipking, "The Genius of the Shore: Lycidas, Adamastor, and the Poetics of Nationalism," *PMLA* 111.2 (1996): 215. See also Blackmore, *Moorings*, 215.
39. Camões and White, *The Lusiads*, 105–106. Original excerpt: "Não acabava, quando uma figura/ Se nos mostra no ar, robusta e válida, / De disforme e grandíssima estatura, / O rosto carregado, a barba esquálida, / Os olhos encovados, e a postura/ Medonha e má, e a cor terrena e pálida, / Cheios de terra e crespos os cabelos, / A boca negra, os dentes amarelos. // "Tão grande era de membros, que bem posso / Certificar-te, que este era o Segundo/ De Rodes estranhíssimo Colosso, / Que um dos sete milagres foi do mundo: / Com um tom de voz nos fala horrendo e grosso, / Que pareceu sair do mar profundo: / Arrepiam-se as carnes e o cabelo / A mi e a todos, só de ouvi-lo e vê-lo," 5.39–40.
40. Blackmore, *Moorings*, 106.
41. Camões and White, *The Lusiads*, 106. Original excerpt: "E disse: —"Ó gente ousada, mais que quantas / No mundo cometeram grandes cousas, / Tu, que por guerras cruas, tais e tantas, / E por trabalhos vãos nunca repousas, / Pois os vedados términos quebrantas, / E navegar meus longos mares ousas, / Que eu tanto tempo há já que guardo e tenho, / Nunca arados d'estranho ou próprio lenho: // —"Pois vens ver os segredos escondidos / Da natureza e do úmido elemento, / A nenhum grande humano concedidos / De nobre ou de imortal merecimento, / Ouve os danos de mim, que apercebidos/ Estão a teu sobejo atrevimento, / Por todo o largo mar e pela terra, / Que ainda hás de sojugar com dura guerra," 5.41–42.
42. Shakespeare, *The Tempest*, 1.2, 37.
43. Klein, "Camões," 173.
44. Original excerpt: "Mais ia por diante o monstro horrendo / Dizendo nossos fados, quando alçado / Lhe disse eu: —Quem és tu? que esse estupendo / Corpo certo me tem maravilhado," 5.49.
45. Camões and White, *The Lusiads*, 107–108. Original excerpt: "A boca e os olhos negros retorcendo, / E dando um espantoso e grande brado, / Me respondeu, com voz pesada e amara, / Como quem da pergunta lhe pesara: // —"Eu sou aquele oculto e grande Cabo, / A quem chamais vós outros Tormentório, / Que nunca a Ptolomeu, Pompónio, Estrabo, / Plínio, e quantos passaram, fui notório. / Aqui toda a Africana costa acabo/ Neste meu nunca visto Promontório / Que para o Pólo Antarctico se estende/ A quem vossa ousadia tanto ofende. // —"Fui dos filhos aspérrimos da Terra, / Qual Encélado, Egeu e o Centimano; / Chamei-me Adamastor, e fui na Guerra / Contra o que vibra os raios de Vulcano; / Não que pusesse serra sobre serra, / Mas conquistando as ondas do Oceano, / Fui capitão do mar, por onde andava / A armada de Netuno, que eu buscava," 5.49–5.51.
46. Blackmore, *Moorings*, 137.

47. Camões and White, *The Lusiads*, 109–10. Original excerpt: "Converte-se-me a carne em terra dura, / Em penedos os ossos se fizeram, / Estes membros que vês e esta figura / Por estas longas águas se estenderam; / Enfim, minha grandíssima estatura / Neste remoto cabo converteram / Os Deuses, e por mais dobradas mágoas, / Me anda Tétis cercando destas águas." // Assim contava, e com um medonho choro / Súbito diante os olhos se apartou; / Desfez-se a nuvem negra, e com um sonoro / Bramido muito longe o mar soou. / Eu, levantando as mãos ao santo coro / Dos anjos, que tão longe nos guiou, / A Deus pedi que removesse os duros Casos, que Adamastor contou futuros," 5.59–60.
48. Blackmore, *Moorings*, 133.
49. Blackmore, *Moorings*, 136.
50. Blackmore, *Moorings*, 146.
51. Blackmore, *Moorings*, 146.
52. David Quint, *Epic and Empire: Politics and Generic Form from Virgil to Milton* (Princeton University Press, 1993), 118.
53. Quint, *Epic*, 123.
54. Blackmore, *Moorings*, xvi.
55. Blackmore, *Moorings*, xvi.
56. Klein, "Camões," 174–75.
57. Klein, "Camões," 166–67.
58. Camões, *The Lusiads*, 13–14. Original excerpt: "Esta ilha pequena, que habitamos, / em toda esta terra certa escala / De todos os que as ondas navegamos / De Quíloa, de Mombaça e de Sofala; / E, por ser necessária, procuramos, / Como próprios da terra, de habitá-la; / E por que tudo enfim vos notifique, / Chama-se a pequena ilha Moçambique," 1.54.
59. Camões and White, *The Lusiads*, 13. Original excerpt: "Comendo alegremente perguntavam, / Pela Arábica língua, donde vinham, / Quem eram, de que terra, que buscavam, / Ou que partes do mar corrido tinham? / Os fortes Lusitanos lhe tornavam/ As discretas respostas, que convinham: / "Os Portugueses somos do Ocidente, / Imos buscando as terras do Oriente," 1.50.
60. Klein, "Camões,"167.
61. Camões and White, *The Lusiads*, 102–103. Original excerpt: "Eis, de meus companheiros rodeado, / Vejo um estranho vir de pele preta, / Que tomaram por força, enquanto apanha / De mel os doces favos na montanha // "Torvado vem na vista, como aquele / Que não / se vira nunca em tal extremo; / Nem ele entende a nós, nem nós a ele, / Selvagem mais que o bruto Polifemo / Começo-lhe a mostrar da rica pelo / De Colcos o gentil metal supremo, / A prata fina, a quente especiaria; / A nada disto o bruto se movia," 5.27–28.
62. Klein, "Camões,"169.
63. Klein, "Camões,"168.
64. Camões and White, *The Lusiads*, 113. Original excerpt: "Pela Arábica língua, que mal falam, / E que Fernão Martins muito bem entende. / Dizem que, por naus que em grandeza igualam / As nossas, o seu mar se corta e fende; / Mas que, lá donde sai o Sol, se abalam / Pera onde a costa ao Sul se alarga e estende, / E do Sul pera o Sol, terra onde havia / Gente, assi como nós, da cor do dia," 5.76–77.
65. Camões and White, *The Lusiads*, 43–44. Original excerpt: "Um batel grande e largo, que toldado / Vinha de sedas de diversas cores, / Traz o Rei de Melinde, acompanhado / De nobres e seu Reino e de senhores: / Vem de ricos vestidos adornado, / Segundo seus costumes e primores; / Na cabeça uma fota guarnecida / De ouro, e de seda e de algodão tecida," 2.94.
66. Klein, "Camões,"176.
67. Camões, *The Lusiads*, 194. Original excerpt: "Tomando-o pela mão, ela o conduz / Para o cume de um monte alto e divino, / Onde uma majestosa construção se ergue / Feita inteiramente de cristal, ouro puro e fino. / A maior parte das horas ali passam, / Em jogos doces e contínuo prazer," 9.87.
68. Camões and White, *The Lusiads*, 213. Original excerpt: "Uniforme, perfeito, em sisustido, / Qual, enfim, o Arquetipo que o criou. / Vendo o Gama este globo, comovido/ De espanto e de desejo ali

ficou. / Diz-lhe a Deusa: —"O transunto, reducido / Em pequeno volume, aqui te dou / Do Mundo aos olhos teus, pera que vejas / Por onde vás e irás e o que desejas. // "Vês aqui a grande máquina do Mundo," 10.79–80.

69. Camões, *The Lusiads*, 215. Original excerpt: "Neste centro, pousada dos humanos, / Que não sòmente, ousados, se contentam / De sofrerem da terra firme os danos, / Mas inda o mar instábil exprimentam, / Verás as várias partes, que os insanos / Mares dividem, onde se apousentam / Várias Nações, que mandam vários reis, / Vários costumes seus e várias leis," 10.91.

70. "Giant by thine own nature, / Thou art beautiful, strong, a fearless colossus / And thy future mirrors that greatness," my translation. Original excerpt: "Gigante pela própria natureza, / És belo, és forte, impávido colosso, / E o teu futuro espelha essa grandeza." For the full text of the anthem, see Joaquim Osório Duque Estrada and Francisco Manuel da Silva, "Hino Nacional," https://www.planalto.gov.br/ccivil_03/constituicao/hino.htm. All original anthem lyrics are taken from this source.

71. "Eternally lying on splendid cradle, / to the sound of sea and under deep sky light," my translation. Original excerpt: "Deitado eternamente em berço esplêndido, / Ao som do mar e à luz do céu profundo."

72. "Thou flashest, Brazil, jewel of America, /illuminated by the sun of the New World," my translation. Original excerpt: "Fulguras, ó Brasil, florão da América, / Iluminado ao sol do Novo Mundo!" Estrada and Silva, *"Hino Nacional."*

73. As translated by Richard Francis Burton. Luís Vaz de Camões and R. F. Burton, *The Lusiads*, vol. 1 (Bernard Quaritch, 1880), 93, https://burtoniana.org/books/1880-Os%20lusiadas/index.htm. Original excerpt: "Eis aqui, quase cume da cabeça / De Europa toda, o Reino Lusitano," 3.20.

74. Beethoven Alvarez, "The Metamorphosis of the Giant Nicteroy in Brazilian Conservatism since 1822," *Gremium: Studies in History, Culture and Politics* 15 (December, 2021): 212, https://doi.org/10.34768/ig.vi15.358.

75. Jean-Baptiste Debret, *Voyage pittoresque et historique au Brésil*, 3 vols. (Firmin-Didot Frères, 1838), 2:26, https://digital.bbm.usp.br/handle/bbm/3813.

76. Igor Cusack, "From Revolution to Reflection: The National Anthems of the New Lusophone Worlds," *Luso-Brazilian Review* 45, no. 2 (2008): 46.

77. Cusack, "From Revolution," 46.

78. Cusack, "From Revolution," 47.

79. "Beloved land, / Amongst a thousand others, / Thou art, Brazil, / O beloved homeland!" Original excerpt: "Terra adorada, / Entre outras mil, / És tu, Brasil, / Ó Pátria amada!"

80. Cusack, "From Revolution," 49–50.

81. Benedict Anderson, *Imagined Communities: Reflections on the Origin and Spread of Nationalism* (Verso, 1992) 11–12.

82. Cusack, "From Revolution," 49.

83. Cusack, "From Revolution," 52.

84. Avelino Romero Simões Pereira, "Hino nacional brasileiro: que história é esta?" *Revista do Instituto de Estudos Brasileiros* 38 (1995): 22–23.

85. Pereira, "Hino," 25.

86. "Gottschalk, Louis Moreau," *The International Music Score Library Project (IMSLP)*, https://imslp.org/wiki/Category:Gottschalk,_Louis_Moreau.

87. Pereira, "Hino," 31.

88. Pereira, "Hino," 29–30.

89. Pereira, "Hino," 34.

90. Alvarez himself mentions it, as do Gonçalves Dias, Fagundes Varella, Bernardo Guimarães, Francisco Dutra, Muniz Barreto, and the Portuguese poet J. Feliciano de Castilho. See Alvarez, "The Metamorphosis," 214.

91. Alvarez, "The Metamorphosis," 220.

92. Alvarez, "The Metamorphosis." 220.

4. POETICS: TWO GIANTS AND TWO PROPHECIES

1. Portal do Poder Executivo Federal, "Serviços e informações do Brasil: símbolos nacionais," https://www.gov.br/planalto/pt-br/conheca-a-presidencia/acervo/simbolos-nacionais.
2. Original excerpt: "Nossos bosques têm mais vida" / "Nossa vida" no teu seio "mais amores." Translated excerpt: "Our forests have more life," and in your embrace, "our lives" are filled with "more love." Joaquim Osório Duque Estrada and F. M. da Silva, "Hino Nacional," https://www.planalto.gov.br/ccivil_03/constituicao/hino.htm.
3. Joshua Alma Enslen, *Song of Exile: A Cultural History of Brazil's Most Popular Poem, 1846–2018* (Purdue University Press, 2022), 4. Translated poem: "My homeland has many palm-trees / and the thrush-song fills its air; / no bird here can sing as well / as the birds sing over there. //We have fields more full of flowers / and a starrier sky above, / we have woods more full of life / and a life more full of love. //Lonely night-time meditations / please me more when I am there; / my homeland has many palm-trees / and the thrush-song fills its air. // Such delights as my land offers / Are not found here nor elsewhere; / lonely night-time meditations / please me more when I am there; / My homeland has many palm-trees / and the thrush-song fills its air. // Don't allow me, God, to die / without getting back to where / I belong, without enjoying / the delights found only there, / without seeing all those palm-trees, / hearing thrush-songs fill the air." Gonçalves Dias and N. Ascher, "The Song of Exile," https://allpoetry.com/opoem/122918-Antonio-Goncalves-Dias-The-Song-Of-Exile.

    Original poem: "Minha terra tem palmeiras / Onde canta o sabiá. / As aves que aqui gorjeiam / Não gorjeiam como lá. // Nosso céu tem mais estrelas, / Nossas várzeas têm mais flores. / Nossos bosques têm mais vida, / Nossa vida mais amores. // Em cismar, sozinho, à noite, / Mais prazer encontro eu lá. / Minha terra tem palmeiras / Onde canta o sabiá. // Minha terra tem primores/ Que tais não encontro eu cá; / Em cismar—sozinho, à noite—/ Mais prazer encontro eu lá. / Minha terra tem palmeiras / Onde canta o sabiá. // Não permita Deus que eu morra / Sem que eu volte para lá; / Sem que desfrute os primores / Que não encontro por cá; / Sem que ainda aviste as palmeiras / Onde canta o sabiá." Gonçalves Dias, "Canção do exílio," in *Cantos: Coleções de Poesias* (F. A. Brozkhaus, 1857), 3–4, https://digital.bbm.usp.br/handle/bbm/442.
4. Joshua Alma Enslen, "Graphs, Maps and Palm Trees: Constructing an Associative Literary Network from Gonçalves Dias' 'Canção do exílio,'" paper presented at the Ninth Conference of the American Portuguese Studies Association, University of New Mexico, 2014.
5. Enslen, *Song of Exile*, 18.
6. Enslen, *Song of Exile*, 14.
7. Enslen, *Song of Exile*, 18.
8. Enslen, *Song of Exile*, 17–18.
9. Enslen, *Song of Exile*, 26.
10. Antonio Candido, "Literature and the Rise of Brazilian National Self-Identity," *Luso-Brazilian Review* 5, no. 1 (Summer 1968): 33.
11. Candido, "Literature," 33, 41.
12. Gonçalves Dias, "Gigante de pedra," in *Cantos*, 433–39; Januário da Cunha Barbosa, *Nicteroy: Metamorphose do Rio de Janeiro* (R. Greenlaw, 1822), https://digital.bbm.usp.br/handle/bbm/7704.
13. Original text: "Gigante orgulhoso, de fero semblante, / Num leito de pedra lá jaz a dormir! / Em duro granito repousa o gigante, / Que os raios somente puderam fundir. // Dormido atalaia no serro empinado / Devera cuidoso, sanhudo velar; / O raio passando o deixou fulminado, / E à aurora, que surge, não há de acordar! // Co'os braços no peito cruzados nervosos, / Mais alto que as nuvens, os céus a encarar, / Seu corpo se estende por montes fragosos, / Seus pés sobranceiros se elevam do mar! // De lavas ardentes seus membros fundidos / Avultam imensos: só Deus poderá / Rebelde lançá-lo dos montes erguidos, / Curvados ao peso, que sobre lhe 'stá. // E o céu, e as estrelas e os astros fulgentes / São velas, são tochas, são vivos brandões, / E o branco sudário são névoas algentes, / E o

crepe, que o cobre, são negros bulcões. //Da noite, que surge, no manto fagueiro / Quis Deus que se erguesse, de junto a seus pés, / A cruz sempre viva do sol no cruzeiro, / Deitada nos braços do eterno Moisés. // Perfumam-no odores que as flores exalam, / Bafejam-no carmes de um hino de amor / Dos homens, dos brutos, das nuvens que estalam, / Dos ventos que rugem, do mar em furor. // E lá na montanha, deitado dormido/ Campeia o gigante,—nem pode acordar! / Cruzados os braços de ferro fundido, / A fronte nas nuvens, os pés sobre o mar!" Dias, "Gigante," 433–34.

14. One of the earliest Europeans records of the appearance of a cross in the southern sky was a report by João de Faras, also known as Mestre João, an astronomer who accompanied Pedro Álvares Cabral's 1500 expedition. "Painel do Cruzeiro do Sul," *USP: Centro de Divulgação da Astronomia*, https://cda.jct/cruzeiro-sul/index.html.

15. Original excerpt: "Niterói, filho do Gigante Minas e de Atlântida, era nascido de poucos dias, quando seu pai foi morto por Marte a Guerra dos Gigantes. Neptuno tocado das lágrimas de Atlântida, o fez criar em terras desconhecidas, que depois se chamarão Brasil. Niterói, crescendo, tentou vingar a morte de seu Pai renovando a Guerra. Com este fim, com muita antecipação e segredo, juntou pedras sobre pedras, que ainda formam a Serra chamada dos Órgãos. Júpiter, conhecendo seus intentos, o matou com um raio, quando ele estava sobre aquele cúmulo de penedos meditando na empresa. O seu corpo tombou sobre um vale, que hoje é baía do seu nome, porque Neptuno o converteu em mar, cedendo às súplicas de Atlântida, e marcando a sua separação do Oceano com o grande rochedo, que fora arrancado por Niterói para ser arremessado à Marte, e com que ele desabará da Serra. Glauco, para consolar Atlântida, profetiza a glória do Brasil, e com especialidade a do lugar em que seu filho fora convertido em mar." Barbosa, *Nicteroy*, 3–4.

16. Beethoven Alvarez, "The Metamorphosis of the Giant Nicteroy in Brazilian Conservatism Since 1822," *Gremium: Studies in History, Culture and Politics* 15 (December, 2021): 203–04.

17. Lia Ramos Jordão, "Januário da Cunha Barbosa," https://bndigital.bn.gov.br/dossies/biblioteca-nacional-200-anos/os-personagens/januario-da-cunha-barbosa.

18. Alvarez, "The Metamorphosis," 206.

19. Alvarez, "The Metamorphosis," 218.

20. Alvarez, "The Metamorphosis," 217.

21. Candido, "Literature," 32–33.

22. Candido, "Literature," 33. Bento Teixeira, *Prosopopéia* (Typographia do Imperial Instituto Artistico, 1873), https://digital.bbm.usp.br/handle/bbm/4060.

23. Candido, "Literature," 29.

24. "Bento Teixeira," in *Enciclopédia itaú cultural de arte e cultura brasileira*, 2023, http://enciclopedia.itaucultural.org.br/pessoa21740/bento-teixeira.

25. Sílvio Romero is an early exception to the interpretation of *Prosopopeia* as a criticism of the monarchs of that era. Costigan adds that it would take nearly a century after Romero for the interpretation of literary discourses by New Christians to gain further traction. See Lúcia Helena Costigan, "A experiência do converso letrado Bento Teixeira: um 'Missing Link' na história intelectual e literária do Brasil-colônia," *Revista de Crítica Literaria Latinoamericana* 20, no. 40 (1994): 77–78, 83.

26. Costigan, "A experiência," 77, 82, 85–86.

27. Costigan, "A experiência," 86.

28. Costigan, "A experiência," 86. Original excerpt: "Em falar a verdade serei raso, / Que assim convém fazê-lo quem escreve, / Se à justiça quer dar o que se deve." Teixeira, *Prosopopéia*, "Canto do Proteu," XXIV.

29. Costigan, "A experiência," 87–88.

30. Original excerpt: "Pela a parte do Sul, / onde a pequena Ursa se vê de guardas rodeada, / onde o Céu luminoso mais serena tem sua influição, e temperada; / junto da Nova Lusitânia ordena / a natureza, mãe bem atentada, / um porto tão quieto e tão seguro, / que para as curvas Naus serve de muro." Teixeira, *Prosopopéia*, "Descrição do Recife de Pernambuco," XVII.

31. Costigan, "A experiência," 88.

32. Original excerpt: "Vejo (diz o bom velho) que, na mente, / o tempo de Saturno renovado, / e a opulenta Olinda florescente / chegar ao cume do supremo estado. / Será de fera e belicosa gente / o seu largo destrito povoado; / por nome terá Nova Lusitânia, / das Leis isenta da fatal insânia." Teixeira, *Prosopopéia*, "Canto de Proteu," XXVI.
33. Costigan, "A experiência," 84–85.
34. Diego A. Molina, "'A meditação' de Gonçalves Dias: A natureza dos males brasileiros," *Estudos Avançados* 30, no. 86 (2016): 235.
35. Molina, "A meditação," 236. The last chant is dated by Gonçalves Dias as "Maranhão, May 8, 1856." Gonçalves Dias, "Meditação," in *Gonçalves Dias: poesia completa e prosa escolhida*, ed. Manuel Bandeira, A. Houaiss, and A. Herculano (Editora José Aguilar, 1959), 741–74.
36. Plínio Doyle, "Histórias de revistas e jornais," *Revista do libro* INL/MEC, no. 32 (1968): 64. Wilton José Marques, "Revista e ruptura" *Caderno de Resumos*, 2 Congresso da História do Livro e da Leitura no Brasil de Campinas (2003): 342.
37. Marques, "Revista," 342.
38. Hélio Lopes, *A divisão das águas: contribuição ao estudo das revistas românticas Minerva Brasiliense (1843–1845) e Guanabara (1849–1856)* (Conselho Estadual de Artes e Ciências Humanas, 1978), 63, quoted in Marques, "Revista," 342.
39. Molina, "A meditação," 249.
40. Wilton José Marques, *Gonçalves Dias: o poeta na contramão: literatura e escravidão no romantismo brasileiro* (EDUFSCAR, 2010), 9.
41. Molina, "A meditação," 237.
42. Weberson Fernandes Grizoste, "Gonçalves Dias e a procura da identidade nacional, brasileira," *Brasiliana: Journal for Brazilian Studies* 2, no. 2 (Nov 2013): 372.
43. (1.2) Original excerpt: "Então o velho estendendo a mão desencarnada e macilenta tocou as minhas pálpebras," in Dias, "Meditação," 741.
44. Cilaine Alves Cunha, "A meditação bíblica de Gonçalves Dias," *Revista Limiar* 3, no. 5 (2016): 92.
45. (1.3) Original excerpt: "E o ancião de cor branca, que, longe do bulício do mundo, havia meditado longos anos," in Dias, "Meditação," 742.
46. (1.2) Original excerpt: "Então o velho estendendo a mão descarnada e macilenta tocou as minhas pálpebras. / E as minhas pálpebras cintilaram como sentindo o contacto de um corpo eletrizado. / E diante dos meus olhos se estendeu uma corrente de luz suave e colorida, como a luz de uma aurora boreal. / E o Ancião me disse: "Olha do norte ao sul—do ocaso ao nascer do sol—'té onde alcançar a luz dos teus olhos, e dize-me o que vês." / E o seu gesto era soberano e tremendo, como o gesto de um monarca irritado. / E a sua voz solene e grave, como a voz do sacerdote que salmeia uma oração fúnebre em noite de enterramento. / E eu levei os meus olhos de norte a sul, do acaso ao nascer do sol, 'té onde eles alcançavam, e respondi:/ "Meu pai, vejo diante de meus olhos uma prodigiosa extensão de terreno: é por ventura algum grande império—tão grande império me parece que encerra," in Dias, "Meditação," 741.
47. Molina, "A meditação," 238.
48. (1.2) Original text: "E sobre essa terra mimosa, por baixo dessas árvores colossais—vejo milhares de homens—de fisionomias discordes, de cor vária e de caracteres diferentes. / "E esses homens formam círculos concêntricos, como os que forma a pedra, caindo no meio das águas plácidas de um lago. / "E os que formam os círculos externos têm maneiras submissas e respeitosas, são de cor preta;—e os outros, que são como um punhado de homens, formando o centro de todos os círculos, têm maneiras senhoris e arrogantes;—são de cor branca. / "E os homens de cor preta têm as mãos presas em longas correntes de ferro, cujos anéis vão de uns a outros—eternos como a maldição que passa de pais a filhos!" in Dias, "Meditação," 742.
49. According to Lúcia Pereira, in 1846, Gonçalves Dias sent the second chapter of "Meditation" to a friend with instructions for its publication in the journal *O Arquivo*. Accompanying the chapter

was Dias's directive: "Cut without mercy, whatever you deem bad or dangerous to print." See Lúcia Miguel Pereira, *A vida de Gonçalves Dias: contendo o diário inédito da viagem do Gonçalves Dias ao Rio Negro* (José Olympio, 1943), 132.

50. 1849 letter of Gonçalves Dias to Teófilo Leal. See Marques, "Revista," 339.
51. Marques, "Revista," 348.
52. (3.4) Original excerpt: "Uma voz sonora e retumbante partiu do Ipiranga e foi ao mar aos Andes e do Prata às margens do Amazonas" / E todos se ergueram violenta e instantaneamente como um cadaver por virtude do galvanismo" / E soltaram o mesmo brado como voz entusiasta e forte, e travaram das armas com a impavidez do guerreiro e com a esperança do homem que pugna em favor da justiça / E a corrente que prendia um Império a outro Império, fraca com o seu comprimento, estalou violentamente em mil pedaços. . . . E a Europa da outra extremidade do Atlântico aplaudiu o arrojo do povo nascente," in Dias, "Meditação," 763.
53. Cunha, "A meditação bíblica," 107. (3.10) Original excerpt: "E os velhos ergueram-se dos seus assentos de marfim e clamaram: / Preguemos as revoluções como princípio de progresso, e acendamos o facho da discórdia / E o incêndio se ateará por todos os ângulos do vasto imperio," in Gonçalves Dias, "Meditação," 771.
54. (3.10) Original excerpt: "E um entre eles levantou a voz no meio deste silêncio e perguntou 'O Rei que faz?' / E todos repitiram com a mesma ansiedade visível: 'O Rei que faz?' / E viu-se além do aposento o Rei, que tranquilo repousava em um leito magnificamente adornado / E o que tinha alevantado o canto dos rases disse em voz cavernosa: 'O Rei dorme!' / E os rases desceram lentamente como uma folha de pergaminho, que a custo se dedobra, e vieram morrer sem eco nos tapetes felpudos da sala / E a mesma risada rebentou com mais força." Dias, "Meditação," 772.
55. (3.10) Original excerpt: "o Rei, que tranquilo repousava em um leito magnificamente adornado," in Dias, "Meditação," 772. See also Estrada and Silva, "*Hino*."
56. Cunha, "A meditação bíblica,"108.
57. (3.2) Original excerpt: "E viu Deus que a nação conquistadora se tinha pervertido e marcou-lhe o último período da sua grandeza / E deu-lhe uma longa série de anos para que ela lastimasse a sua decadência, e conhecesse a justiça inexorável do Todo-Poderoso," in Dias, "Meditação," 762.
58. Cunha, "A meditação bíblica," 108
59. Molina, "A meditação," 249.
60. Molina, "A meditação," 241–42.
61. Cunha, "A meditação bíblica," 103.
62. (3.13) Original excerpt: "E o sangue corria cada vez com mais abundância, como o vinho no fim de um banquete, quanto a hilaridade se converte em embriaguez. / Foi então que as forças me faltaram, e eu caí exânime, abatendo a terra como o peso do meu corpo." Dias, "Meditação," 774.
63. Cunha, "A meditação bíblica," 99.

5. SOCIAL SCIENCES: THREE FOUNDING MOMENTS OF EURO-AFRO-BRAZILIAN STUDIES (SEPARATING THE WHEAT FROM THE CHAFF)

1. Jean-Baptiste Debret, *Viagem pitoresca e histórica ao Brasil: 1816–1831* (EDUSP, 1972), 22.
2. Johann Baptist von Spix and Karl Frederich von Martius, *Viagem pelo Brasil, 1817–1820*, 3 vols. (Senado Federal; Conselho Editorial, 2017), 1:132–33.
3. Von Spix and Von Martius, *Viagem*, 1: 236–37.
4. Von Spix and Von Martius, *Viagem*, 1: 231.
5. Von Spix and Von Martius, *Viagem*, 2: 61–63.

6. Published posthumously in 1932. Other publications by Nina Rodrigues include: *Os mestiços brasileiros* (1890), *O alienado no direito civil brasileiro* (1910), *O problema negro na América do Sul* (1932), *O animismo fetichista dos negros baianos* (1935), and *As coletividades anormais* (1939).
7. Sílvio Romero, *Estudos sobre a poesia popular do Brasil* (Typographia Universal de Laemmert, 1888) 10–11.
8. Sílvio Romero, *História da literatura brasileira*, 3 vols. (José Olympio, 1943) 1:199–200.
9. Romero, *Estudos*, 11.
10. Raymundo Nina Rodrigues, *Os africanos no Brasil* (Editora Nacional, 1932).
11. Rodrigues, *Os africanos*, 58.
12. French evolutionist Abel Hovelaque, author of *Les négres de l'Afrique sus-équatoriale* (1889); Rodrigues, *Os africanos*, 14.
13. Rodrigues, *Os africanos*, 18.
14. Rodrigues, *Os africanos*, 10.
15. Rodrigues, *Os africanos*, 364.
16. Clóvis Moura, *Sociologia do negro brasileiro* (Ática, 1988), 17.
17. Clóvis Moura, *Dialética radical do Brasil negro* (Anita, 1994) 79–86. See also Júlio José Chiavenato, *O negro no Brasil: da senzala à guerra do Paraguai* (Brasiliense, 1986); and Thomas Skidmore, *Preto no branco: raça e nacionalidade no pensamento brasileiro* (Paz e Terra, 1976).
18. Arthur Ramos, *O negro brasileiro: ethnographia, religiosa e psychanalyse* (Editora Nacional, 1940), 7.
19. Edison Carneiro and Aydano do Couto Ferraz, eds., *O negro no Brasil: trabalhos apresentados ao 2º Congresso Afro-Brasileiro da Bahia, 11 a 20 de janeiro de 1937* (Civilização Brasileira, 1940), 8.
20. Paulo Prado, *Retrato do Brasil: ensaio sobre a tristeza brasileira* (Duprat-Mayença, 1928), 53.
21. Heloisa Toller Gomes, *As marcas da escravidão: o negro e o discurso oitocentista no Brasil e nos Estados Unidos* (Editora UFRJ, EdUERJ, 1994), 16.
22. Gerald J. Bender, *Angola under the Portuguese: The Myth and the Reality* (University of California Press, 1978), 207.
23. Bender, *Angola*, 207.
24. Hermano Vianna, *O mistério do samba* (Editora UFRJ, 1995), 61.
25. Antonio Risério, *Caymmi: uma utopia de lugar* (Editora Perspectiva; COPENE, 1993) 16–17.
26. Risério, *Caymmi*, 16–17.
27. Regina Zilbermann, "Mito e literatura brasileira," in *Negros e índios: história e literatura*, ed. Moacyr Flores (Editora da PUC Rio Grande do Sul, 1994), 118–19.
28. Zilbermann, "Mito," 123.
29. Renato Ortiz, *Cultura brasileira e identidade nacional* (Brasiliense, 1985), 38.
30. Ortiz, *Cultura*, 38–39.
31. Darcy Ribeiro, *O povo brasileiro: a formação e o sentido do Brasil* (Companhia das Letras, 1995), 453.
32. Vianna, *O mistério*, 73.
33. Skidmore, *Preto no branco*, 219.
34. Octávio Ianni, *A ideia de Brasil moderno* (Brasiliense, 1994), 85.
35. Clóvis Moura, *Sociologia do negro brasileiro* (Ática, 1988), 24.
36. Evandro Duarte, *Criminologia e racismo: introdução à criminologia brasileira* (Juruá, 2002), quoted in Evandro P. Duarte, G. Scotti, and M. C. Netto, "Ruy Barbosa e a queima dos arquivos: as lutas pela memória da escravidão e os discursos dos juristas," *Universitas Jus* 26 (2015): 27–28.
37. Vianna, *O mistério*, 61.
38. Ortiz, *Cultura*, 41.
39. Antonio Candido, "A revolução de 1930 e a cultura," *Novos Estudos CEBRAP* 2, no. 4 (1984): 32.
40. Candido, "A revolução," 27.
41. Nestor Capoeira and A. Ladd, *The Little Capoeira Book* (North Atlantic Books, 1995), 12.

42. Capoeira, *Little Capoeira Book*, 12.
43. Ruy Castro, *O vermelho e o negro: pequena história do Flamengo* (DBA Dórea Books & Art, 2001), 69.
44. Castro, *O vermelho*, 76.
45. Lísias Nogueira Negrão, *Entre a cruz e a encruzilhada: formação do campo umbandista em São Paulo* (EDUSP, 1996), 76.
46. Rone Carvalho, "O que explica multiplicação de templos evangélicos no Brasil," *BBC News Brasil*, July 12, 2023.
47. Monique Augras, *O Brasil do samba-enredo* (Editora Fundação Getúlio Vargas, 1998), 30.
48. Candido, "A revolução," 36; Augras, *O Brasil*, 52.
49. Risério, *Caymmi*, 29.
50. Câmara dos Deputados, "A Voz do Brasil está no ar há 80 anos," July 22, 2015, https://www.camara.leg.br/radio/programas/465232-a-voz-do-brasil-esta-no-ar-ha-80-anos.
51. Risério, *Caymmi*, 23.
52. Risério, *Caymmi*, 22–23.
53. Risério, *Caymmi*, 22.
54. Jorge Caldeira, *Viagem pela história do Brasil* (Companhia das Letras, 1997), 2.
55. In Bahia, the Portuguese initially referred to Indigenous people as "Brasis" or "Brasilienses."
56. Gilberto Freyre, *Casa-grande e senzala: formação da família brasileira sob o regime da economia patriarchal* (Fundação Gilberto Freyre, 1992), xlvii.
57. Freyre, *Casa-grande*, xlvii.
58. Freyre, *Casa-grande*, xlvii.
59. Vianna, *O mistério*, 64.
60. Vianna, *O mistério*, 64.
61. Vianna, *O mistério*, 64.
62. Gilberto Freyre and S. Putnam, *The Masters and the Slaves: A Study in the Development of Brazilian Civilization* (Alfred Knopf, 1946), 76.
63. Freyre, *The Masters*, 77.
64. Freyre, *The Masters*, 77.
65. Vianna, *O mistério*, 75–76.
66. Emília Viotti da Costa, *Da monarquia à república: momentos decisivos* (Brasiliense, 1985), 256.
67. Costa, *Da monarquia*, 254.
68. Rafael Galante pointed out these expressions as key concepts in "'Essa gunga veio de lá': filosofias espirituais centro-africanas e narrativas históricas diaspóricas nos reinados de Minas Gerais," Mukanda Cultural Course, September 11, 2023.
69. Pedro Cavalcanti, "As seitas africanas do Recife," in *Estudos Afro-brasileiros: trabalhos apresentados ao Primeiro Congresso Afro-brasileiros do Recife em 1934*, ed. Gilberto Freyre et al., 2 vols. (Fundação Joaquim Nabuco; Editora Massangana, 1988), 1:245.
70. Edison Carneiro and A. C. Ferraz, "Apêndice," in *O negro no Brasil: trabalhos apresentados ao 2º Congresso AfroBrasileiro da Bahia, 11 a 20 de janeiro de 1937*, ed. Edison Carneiro and A. C. Ferraz (Civilização Brasileira, 1940), 343–63.
71. Luis Nicolau Parés, *A formação do candomblé: história e ritual da nação jêje na Bahia* (Editora da Unicamp, 2007), 254.
72. Manoel Vitorino da Costa, "O mundo religioso do negro da Bahia," in *O negro no Brasil: trabalhos apresentados ao 2º Congresso AfroBrasileiro da Bahia, 11 a 20 de janeiro de 1937*, ed. Edison Carneiro and A. C. Ferraz (Civilização Brasileira, 1940), 343–47.
73. Edison Carneiro and A. C. Ferraz, "Congresso afro-brasileiro da Bahia," in *O negro no Brasil: trabalhos apresentados ao 2º Congresso AfroBrasileiro da Bahia, 11 a 20 de janeiro de 1937*, ed. Edison Carneiro and A. C. Ferraz (Civilização Brasileira, 1940), 7–11.

74. Manoel Bernardino da Paixão, 349–56 "Ligeira explicação sobre a nação Congo," in *O negro no Brasil: trabalhos apresentados ao 2º Congresso AfroBrasileiro da Bahia, 11 a 20 de janeiro de 1937*, ed. Edison Carneiro and A. C. Ferraz (Civilização Brasileira, 1940), 349–56.
75. Eugênia Anna dos Santos, "Notas sobre os comestíveis africanos," in *O negro no Brasil: trabalhos apresentados ao 2º Congresso AfroBrasileiro da Bahia, 11 a 20 de janeiro de 1937*, ed. Edison Carneiro and A. C. Ferraz (Civilização Brasileira, 1940), 357.
76. Edison Carneiro, "Segundo congresso afro-brasileiro: o dia de ontem—os congressistas no Ôpô Afonjá—os trabalhos de hoje," *O Estado da Bahia* (Salvador), January 14, 1937.
77. Carneiro, "Segundo congresso."
78. In accordance with the provisions of the 1890 Penal Code, practices of magic, spiritism, sorcery, and healing associated with Afro-Brazilian religious tradition were deemed illegal and criminal. See Negrão, *Entre a cruz*, 44.
79. Silene Ferreira Claro, "Eugênia Anna dos Santos, a Mãe Aninha do Ilê Axé Opô Afonjá," in *Anais do 3 Encontro Internacional História & Parcerias* ANPUHRJ 1 (2021): 7.
80. Ladipo Solanke, "A concepção de Deus entre os negros yôrubás," in *O negro no Brasil: trabalhos apresentados ao 2º Congresso AfroBrasileiro da Bahia, 11 a 20 de janeiro de 1937*, ed. Edison Carneiro and A. C. Ferraz (Civilização Brasileira, 1940), 239–43.
81. It was only in 1976, almost forty years later, that a law was enacted eliminating the requirement for police registration by Candomblés.
82. Roberto Motta, *Os afro-brasileiros: anais do III Congresso Afro-Brasileiro* (Fundação Joaquim Nabuco; Editora Massangana: 2017).
83. Ana Lucia Araujo, "Zumbi and the Voices of the Emergent Public Memory of Slavery and Resistance in Brazil," *Comparativ* 22, no. 2 (2012): 97.
84. Mariana Ramos de Morais, "Race, Culture, and Religion: The Afro-Brazilian Congresses and Anthropology in 1930s Brazil," in *Encyclopédie Bérose des histoires de l'anthropologie*, 2020, 12. https://www.berose.fr/article2170.html?lang=en.

6. LAW: PEACE WITHOUT A VOICE IS NOT HARMONY

1. Cleusa Turra and G. Venturi, ed., *Racismo cordial: a mais completa análise sobre preconceito de cor no Brasil* (Ática, 1995), 47.
2. Ali Kamel, *Não somos racistas: uma reação aos que querem nos transformar numa nação bicolor* (Nova Fronteira, 2006).
3. Vânia Penha-Lopes, "Affirmative Action and Racial Identity in Brazil: A Study of the First Quota Graduates at the State University of Rio de Janeiro," in *The Melanin Millennium: Skin Color as 21st Century International Discourse*, ed. Ronald Hall (Springer, 2013), 326.
4. Jan Hoffman French, "Race, Racism, and Affirmative Action in Brazil and the United States," *Latin American Research Review* 56, no. 4 (2021): 992.
5. Penha-Lopes, "Affirmative," 338–40.
6. Sueli Carneiro, "Entrevista," *Revista Afirma*, March 11, 2002.
7. Carneiro, "Entrevista."
8. Turra and Venturi, *Racismo cordial*, 32–35. "*Pardo*: From the Latin *pardu*, leopard. Adjective 1) Of a color between black and white; almost dark. 2) Of a dirty white, suspicious. 3) Of an opaque color, between yellow and hazel. 4) Reference to any of these colors. 5) Mulatto. 6) The color pard." Aurélio Buarque de Holanda Ferreira, *Novo aurélio século XXI: o dicionário da língua portuguesa* (Nova Fronteira, 1999), 1500.
9. Carlos Hasenbalg, *Descriminições e desigualdades raciais no Brasil* (Edições Graal, 1979), 118.

10. Penha-Lopes, "Affirmative," 340.
11. Penha-Lopes, "Affirmative," 340.
12. Penha-Lopes, "Affirmative," 340.
13. João Feres Júnior and J. Zoninsein, eds., *Ação afirmativa e universidade: experiências nacionais comparadas* (Editora Universidade de Brasília, 2006), 170.
14. Coalizão Negra Por Direitos, "Carta proposta da Coalizão Negra Por Direitos," January 2020, accessed October 23, 2023, https://coalizaonegrapordireitos.org.br/sobre.
15. Coalizão Negra.
16. Steve Biko, "Black Consciousness and the Quest for True Humanity," *SASO Newsletter* 1, no 4 (May 1971): 17–21.
17. Instituto Cultural Steve Biko, https://www.stevebiko.org.br.
18. Coalizão Negra.
19. Sales Augusto dos Santos, *O sistema de cotas para negros da UnB: um balanço da primeira geração* (Paco Editorial, 2015), 32.
20. Márcia Leitão Pinheiro, "Uma Comissão da Verdade no Brasil escravidão, multiculturalismo, história e memória," *Civitas* 18, no. 3 (Sept–Dec 2018): 686. It was only after three decades of the creation of truth commissions in neighboring countries, such as Argentina and Chile, that this process was initiated in Brazil.
21. Karine Melo, "OAB cria comissão nacional da verdade sobre a escravidão" *Agência Brasil*, June 2, 2015. Since the South African Truth and Reconciliation Commission in 1995, truth commissions have become a popular tool worldwide for nonjudicial inquiries into past abuses. Priscilla Hayner notes their widespread adoption by new governments and civil societies aiming to investigate human rights violations and recommend reforms. These commissions are shaped by their local contexts, despite international support, and strive to uncover the causes of past conflicts and abuses. Priscilla B. Hayner, "Truth Commissions: A Schematic Overview," *International Review of the Red Cross* 88, no. 862 (2006): 295–96.
22. Pinheiro, "Uma comissão," 638.
23. Márcia Leitão Pinheiro, "'The Sound of Silenced Voices': Mobilizations, Connections and Demands in the Investigation of Slavery in Brazil," *Vibrant* 15, no. 3 (2018), n.p.
24. Pinheiro, "Silenced Voices."
25. Cláudia Alexandre, "Comissão da Verdade Sobre a Escravidão Negra no Brasil: relatório parcial inédito mostrará necessidade de reparações urgentes à população Negra," *Portal Geledés*, June 23, 2015.
26. Deborah Pool, "El estado y sus márgenes: etnografias comparadas," *Cuadernos de Antropología Social*, no. 27 (2008), quoted in Pinheiro, "Uma comissão," 695.
27. Alexandre, "Comissão."
28. Alexandre, "Comissão."
29. Evandro Piza Duarte, Guilherme Scotti, and Menelick de Carvalho Netto, "Ruy Barbosa e a queima dos arquivos: as lutas pela memória da escravidão e os discursos dos juristas," *Universitas Jus* 26 (2015): 23–39.
30. Duarte, Scotti, and Netto, "Ruy Barbosa," 23.
31. Duarte, Scotti, and Netto, "Ruy Barbosa," 35.
32. Duarte, Scotti, and Netto, "Ruy Barbosa," 28.
33. Evandro Duarte and Guilherme Scotti, "História e memória nacional no discurso jurídico: o julgamento da ADPF 186," *Universitas Jus* 24, no. 3 (2013): 33–45.
34. Supremo Tribunal Federal, "Crime de racismo e antissemitismo: um julgamento histórico no STF," Habeas Corpus No. 82.424/RS (STF, 2004), quoted in Duarte, Scotti, and Netto, "Ruy Barbosa," 28.
35. Supremo Tribunal, quoted in Duarte, Scotti, and Netto, "Ruy Barbosa," 28–30.
36. Supremo Tribunal, quoted in Duarte, Scotti, and Netto, "Ruy Barbosa," 30.
37. Duarte, Scotti, and Netto, "Ruy Barbosa," 33.

38. Joaquim Nabuco, *A escravidão* (Fundação Joaquim Nabuco, 1988). José Patrocínio, "Discurso na Gazeta de Notícias de 06 setembro de 1880," in *A Campanha Abolicionista. Ministério da Cultura*, Fundação Biblioteca Nacional, http://www.dominiopublico.gov.br/download/texto/bn000110.pdf.
39. Patrocínio, "Discurso."
40. Antônio Carlos Wolkmer, "Paradigmas, historiografia, crítica e direito moderno." *Revista da Faculdade de Direito* 28, no. 28 (1994–1995): 55–67. Sidney Chalhoub, *Visões da liberdade: uma história das últimas décadas da escravidão na corte* (Companhia das Letras, 1990).
41. Robert Slenes, "Escravos, cartórios e desburocratização: o que Rui Barbosa não queimou será destruído agora?" *Revista Brasileira de História* 5, no. 10 (March/August 1985): 168.
42. Marcos Magalhães de Aguiar, "Historiadores e arquivos: testemunho de uma experiencia," *Revista Múltipla* 5, no. 7 (December 1999): 109.
43. Duarte, Scotti, and Netto, "Ruy Barbosa," 34.
44. Paolo Rossi, *O passado, a memória e o esquecimento* (Unesp, 2010), 21.
45. Rossi, *O passado*, 31–38.

7. MUNDIONGO: ANCESTRAL LANGUAGES: ENTERING OTHER FORESTS

1. The twenty-first century enactment of state policies acknowledging and safeguarding sociocultural expressions of both sacred and secular traditional knowledge is a significant achievement of social movements. These policies emerged from advocacy efforts that date back to the 1970s and 1980s, culminating in Brazil's 1988 Constitution, often referred to as the "Citizen Constitution." In 2000, Decree-Law 3551 established mechanisms for various groups to participate in cultural heritage disputes, ensuring broad protection and recognition of diverse cultural practices. However, as Henrique Antunes notes, the National Institute of Historic and Artistic Heritage (IPHAN), responsible for implementing these policies, has faced various challenges and contradictions. Livio Sansone discusses the difficulties that arise when previously unrecognized cultural forms gain significant visibility as intangible heritage. He also points to the challenge of defining Afro-Brazilian culture and identifying its particular elements. This need for definition clashes with the understanding of culture as dynamic and ever-changing. See Henrique Fernandes Antunes, "'It Is Not Solved Just by Writing It Down on Paper': Patrimonialization Policies and the Religious Use of Ayahuasca as a Brazilian Intangible Cultural Heritage," *Law and Religion in a Global Context* 4 (2023): 112–17. See also Livio Sansone, "The Dilemmas of Digital Patrimonialization: The Digital Museum of African and Afro-Brazilian Memory," *History in Africa* 40 (2013): 264.
2. Maria Aparecida Martins, *Foram 17 anos*, LP, Gravadora CID & Nas Nuvens Catalog, 1976.
3. Lorraine Pinheiro Mendes, "Minha história é suada igual dança no ilê, ninguém vai me dizer o meu lugar," *Políticas Culturais em Revista* 14, no. 2 (July/December 2021): 124.
4. Mendes, "Minha história," 124.
5. Rafael Galante, "'Essa gunga veio de lá': Filosofias espirituais centro-africanas e narrativas históricas diaspóricas nos reinados de Minas Gerais," Mukanda Cultural Course, October 4, 2023. In Assis Júnior's dictionary, *mundóngo* is defined as a meeting where opinions, views, judgments are expressed and also as a council—of family, ministers, or war. *Ndóngo* refers to ceremony, solemnity, conventional formalities for certain acts, precept, a deliberative body, and also denotes a large canoe or river vessel for transporting cargo. It can also mean church, cathedral, temple, house of prayer, or the residence of the king (Ngola, Dom João Hari). See António de Assis Júnior, *Dicionario kimbundu-português: linguístico, botânico, histórico e corográfico 1* (Santos, 1934), 32.

6. Embaúba Filmes, "Live de lançamento de *A Rainha Nzinga chegou*," YouTube, Jun 29, 2021, https://www.youtube.com/watch?v=wpV-EStqdQI.

   Reminder: I am using the spelling "**Kongo**" and "**Mozambique**" when referring to the former kingdom and country, respectively. "**Congo**" and "**Moçambique**" (as spelled in Portuguese) appear only when referencing Congada performers.
7. Embaúba Filmes, "Live."
8. Embaúba Filmes, "Live."
9. "A nossa tradição do Reinado aqui é a tradição oral, né? Aquela que a gente não tinha livro, não tinha nada. Então é uma pessoa mais velha, não naturalmente o mais velho, mas uma pessoa que já conhece, passa pro mais novo, o que está chegando novo no nosso ambiente, no nosso meio de Reinado. . . . A questão também é que a gente não pega a pessoa e senta ela assim no banquinho e diz: "Eu vou te ensinar sobre o Reinado. Hoje! Hoje você vai sair daqui aprendendo tudo." Não é assim que acontece. Não com a gente." Embaúba Filmes, "Live."
10. "Também, professor, a gente vai falando e os meninos vão aprendendo, e as pessoas que vão nos rodeando vão aprendendo também. E, às vezes, as perguntas têm que ser respondidas só superficialmente, porque a pessoa não tem como ela entender se ela não caminhar um pouco com a gente. Então quando as pessoas veem e fazem perguntas e vão nos acompanhando no nosso dia a dia, nos nossos afazeres religiosos, eles vão aprendendo o significado de cada coisa, de cada palavra, e assim que é passado para os nossos meninos. Uma outra coisa que fala que fulano viu, ciclano viu. Isso aí eu não vejo o tempo inteiro, nem vejo porque eu quero ver. Ah, meu Deus, que vontade de ver uma coisa assim. Não é assim. É uma coisa que eu não domino. É uma situação que aparece, e eu presto atenção naquela situação, independente do meu olho estar aberto ou não. Porque se eu estiver com o olho aberto e ver a situação e fechar o olho, eu continuo vendo a mesma situação. Então é só para . . . Ilustrar. Não é que eu quero ver isso, quero ver aquilo, não. Quer que aconteça ou não quer. Eu não tenho querer. Acontece. Acontece. Normalmente, do nada. . . . O saber do Rosário é assim, por exemplo. Você vai ficando, ficando, vai aprendendo, aprendendo. Quando você chega numa certa parte, você toma consciência de que nada aquilo que você pensava que era verdade é a verdade real. Você fala: "Nossa Senhora! Voltei a estaca zero." Por isso que o aprendizado é dia após dia." Embaúba Filmes, "Live."
11. "Eu não criei a toada. A toada veio pra mim. A toada já tava pronta. É o que eu entendo por isso, né? O canto não é novo. O canto existiu há 100 anos atrás, há 200 anos atrás, há 300 anos atrás. Ele só é resgatado por nós, mais novos. É o meu entendimento." Embaúba Filmes, "Live."
12. Uma hora e meia de turbulência. E aí, balançava, balançava, e não parava de balançar. Eu pensei: "Gente, mas será possível que eu vou morrer de acidente de avião?" Pensei: "Não, não tem necessidade de eu entrar no avião pra morrer de acidente de avião, não. Que bobagem, Belinha!"

    E eu olhei pro ladinho assim e vi, percebi, que a veneziana da janelinha do canto, do outro lado, tava aberta. E eu percebi a chuva caindo no vidro do avião. E ela não caia em pé. Ela caia deitada, batendo assim na janela, no vidro da janela. E eu fui olhando aquilo e percebi que aquela água batia no avião como se fosse que o avião estivesse nas ondas do mar. Com isso eu percebi que eu estava num navio aéreo.

    Aí começou o que eu não esperava de acontecer. Porque quando eu olhei pra lá, percebi na mente e no olho aquela onda batendo no vidro e percebi que aquilo era uma onda do mar, que eu estava num navio aéreo. Foi muito lindo aquilo. Falei: "Meu Deus, o que é isso?"

    Aí eles me falaram: "Rainha, nós viemos fazer a sua escolta de volta. Nós estávamos esperando para retornar com a senhora."

    "Mas . . . retornar comigo? Vocês me esperaram esse tempo todo!?"

    "Sim. Era o nosso compromisso de só retornar pra nossa terra quando a senhora retornasse."

    Falei: "Meu Deus, o que é isso? Que proteção maravilhosa!" Fiquei maravilhada com aquilo. Falei: "Gente, meu Deus do céu, mas que cuidado é esse?"

E aí ele me disse que ia fazer a escolta de volta, e aí eu percebi que a gente tava fazendo a viagem reversa. Que nós viemos pelo mar, viemos pelo Atlântico, e voltamos pelo ar. Quando cruzou o Atlântico, nos voltamos pelo ar. Embaúba Filmes, "Live."

13. Edimilson de Almeida Pereira, *Lugares ares: obra poética 2* (Mazza Edições, 2003), 190.
14. Manolo Garcia Florentino, "A heranca africana," *Folha de São Paulo* (São Paulo), April 2, 2000.
15. Mr. João Lopes, sixty-four years old, Captain-General of the Our Lady of the Rosary of the Jatobá Brotherhood. The following is an excerpt of the original interview recorded in January 1994: "Então essa lenda é a lenda do aparecimento da imagem da santa e a retirada dela da água. No início na segunda festa dela, que a primeira não foi feita na terra, a primeira foi feita no céu, tinha nego do Congo, nego do Moçambique, nego da Costa, nego Cabinda, nego da Guiné, tinha todas nações, só não tinha nagô. Quando eles ajuntaram esse grupo de negos pra tirar Nossa Senhora eles fizeram uma só guarda, chama-se guarda de Candombe de Nossa Senhora do Rosário. Porque eles que tiraram Nossa Senhora do mar junto do Candombe, ficou assim definido: o Candombe, o pai de todos os reinados aqui da terra e ficou também definido entre esse povo do Congo e de Moçambique, que o Candombe que puxaria as coroas, mas como o candombe é um instrumento muito difícil de carregar, o único pessoal que adoptou bater os instrumentos com mais ou menos a semelhança que bate o candombe, foi o povo de Moçambique; eles fizeram o seu grupo, formaram o seu grupo e com seus tambores formaram a guarda de Moçambique e ficou assim definido entre eles… que o Moçambique puxaria o trono, o Congo seria o guia de Moçambique, limpando o caminho, cantando assim a arruação, que eles canta agudo e canta grave, limpando os caminhos e pedindo as proteção pra que passasse o trono das coroa, simbolizando a coroa de Nossa Senhora do Rosário. See: Sr. João Lopes, 64 anos, Capitão-mor da Irmandade N. S. do Rosário do Jatobá, interview recorded January 12, 1994, cited in Leda Maria Martins, *Afrografias da memória: o reinado do Rosário no Jatobá* (Editora Perspectiva and Mazza Edições, 1997), 55.
16. Sônia Queiroz, *Palavra banto em Minas Gerais* (Editora UFMG, 2019) 196. Nei Lopes translates the Kimbundu word *kiandombe* as Black; see Lopes, *Novo*, 63. Perhaps *kia ndombe* refers to "that or those" who exhibit "blackness," by way of reference to Blacks. The translation for both the Portuguese *preto* and *negro* in (blackness or Blacks) appears indeed as *ndombe*; while the Kikongo *buka kia ndombe* is translated in Portuguese as *negrada* (a group of Black people). See Francisco Narciso Cobe, *Novo dicionário português-kikongo* (Mayamba, 2010), 411, 463.
17. Bienal de São Paulo, "Between Ancestralities and the Diasporas, the 35th Bienal de São Paulo Announces the First List of Artists of the *Choreographies of the Impossible*," April 26, 2023, https://35.bienal.org.br/en/primeira-lista-de-artistas-coreografias-do-impossivel.
18. See Denise Ferreira da Silva's studies *Unpayable Debt* (Sternberg Press, 2022) and *Toward a Global Idea of Race* (University of Minnesota Press, 2007).
19. Bienal de São Paulo, "Between Ancestralities."
20. Gerhard Kubik, *Africa and the Blues* (University Press of Mississippi, 1999), 4.
21. Gerhard Kubik, *Extensions of African Cultures in Brazil* (Diasporic Africa Press, 2013), xiii, xvi
22. Kubik, *Extensions*, 151.
23. Kubik, *Africa*, 5.
24. Kubik, *Africa*, 47.
25. Kubik, *Africa*, 60.
26. Kubik, *Africa*, 61.
27. Kubik, *Africa*, 61–62.
28. Kubik, *Extensions*, vi.
29. Kubik, *Africa*, 58.
30. Kubik, *Extensions*, vii; and Kubik, *Africa*, 200.
31. Kubik, *Extensions*, vii.
32. J. Lorand Matory, *Black Atlantic Religion: Tradition, Transnationalism and Matriarchy in Brazilian Candomblé* (Princeton University Press, 2005), 56–57.

33. Joseph Miller, "Central Africa During the Era of the Slave Trade, c. 1490s–1850s," in *Central Africans and Cultural Transformations in the American Diaspora*, ed. Linda Heywood (Cambridge University Press, 2002), 43.
34. Kubik, *Extensions*, 2–3.
35. Kubik suggests the grouping of six main distinct "regional neo-African cultures" that have evolved in Brazil over the course of three centuries. These summarized key cultural zones in Brazil include: 1) Bahia, characterized by a significant influence of cultural elements from southwest Nigeria and Dahomey as well as Congo-Angola elements; 2) Rio de Janeiro, influenced by Angolan-area cultural elements; 3) São Paulo State, primarily influenced by Congo-Angola region, with some contributions from Mozambique; 4) Minas Gerais, where the majority of cultural elements have their origins in the hinterland of Benguela in Angola; 5) cultural islands in Brazil's interior areas, such as Mato Grosso, with predominantly Congo influences; and 6) northern region areas, such as Maranhão, which feature Fon and Ewe influences. See Kubik, *Extensions*, 28–29
36. Muniz Sodré, *O terreiro e a cidade: a forma social negro-brasileira* (Vozes, 1988) 55.
37. Sodré, *O terreiro*, 55.
38. Olga Gudolle Cacciatore, *Dicionário de cultos afro-brasileiros* (Forense-Universitária, 1988), 178. In Cuba they were known as Lukumí.
39. José Beniste, *Dicionário português-yorùbá* (Bertrand Brasil, 2011), 79.
40. Yeda Pessoa de Castro, "Religions of African Origin in Brazil: Designation, Origins and New and Little-known Cults," *UNESCO African Culture: Proceedings of the Meeting of Experts on the Survival of African Religious Traditions in the Caribbean and in Latin America* (São Luiz do Maranhão, 1985), 138.
41. Valdina Oliveira Pinto, "Candomblé de Angola: uma recriação de tradições culturais Bantu sobreviventes entre nós," in *II Encontro de Nações de Candomblé Setembro de 1995* (Centro de Estudos Afro-Orientais da UFBa, 1997), 1.
42. Marco Aurélio Luz, *Cultura negra e ideologia do recalque* (Achiamé, 1983) 28–29.
43. Luz, *Cultura*, 28–29.
44. Zeca Ligiéro, "O conceito de 'motrizes culturais' aplicado às práticas performativas afro-brasileiras," *Revista Pós Ciências Sociais* 8, no. 16 (July/December 2011): 133.
45. Ligiéro, "O conceito," 132–33.
46. Ligiéro, "O conceito," 130.
47. Ligiéro, "O conceito," 132.
48. Ligiéro, "O conceito," 134.
49. Richard Schechner "O que é performance?" *O Percevejo: Revista de Teatro, Crítica e Estética* 12, no. 11 (2003): 34.
50. Ligiéro, "O conceito," 134.
51. Zeca Ligiéro, "Motrizes culturais: do ritual à cena contemporânea a partir do estudo de duas performances: Danbala Wedo (afro-brasileira, do Benin, Nigéria e Togo) e Sotzil Jay (Maia, da Guatemala)," *KARPA 10: Journal of Theatricalities and Visual Culture* (2017): n/p, https://www.calstatela.edu/al/karpa/karpa-10.
52. Zeca Ligiéro, *Corpo a corpo: estudo das perfomances brasileiras* (Garamond, 2012), 131–32.
53. Ligiéro, "Motrizes."
54. Ligiéro, "Motrizes."
55. Fu-Kiau, "A Powerful Trio" (unpublished), quoted in Ligiéro, "Motrizes."
56. Fu-Kiau, "Powerful" in Ligiéro, "Motrizes."
57. Fu-Kiau, "Powerful" in Ligiéro "Motrizes."
58. Emphasis added. Excerpt of Bopp's 1932 poem "Negro." Original excerpt: "Um dia / atiraram-te no bojo de um navio negreiro. / E durante longas noites e noites/ vieste escutando o rugido do mar/ como um soluço no porão soturno. / O mar era um irmão da tua raça. // Uma madrugada / baixaram

as velas do convés. / Havia uma nesga de terra e um porto. / Armazéns com depósitos de escravos / e a queixa dos teus irmãos amarrados em coleiras de ferro.// Principiou aí a sua história.// O resto, / a que ficou pra trás, / o Congo, as florestas e o mar / continuam a doer na corda do urucungo." See Raul Bopp, *Poesia completa de Raul Bopp* (José Olympio, 1998), 209.

59. Assis Júnior, *Dicionário*, 22, 346. For Yeda Pessoa de Castro it comes from the Kikongo, Kimbundu, Umbundu term "Madimbaw." Yeda Pessoa de Castro, *Falares africanos na Bahia: um vocabulário afro-brasileiro* (TopBooks, 2001), 174.

60. For "lungungu," see Castro, *Falares*, 348. See also Richard Graham, communication with Kubik and Farris Thompson, cited in "Technology and Culture Change: The Development of the 'Berimbau' in Colonial Brazil," *Latin American Music Review / Revista de Música Latinoamericana* 12, no. 1 (1991): 10. The term "lungu" in M'Bundo is defined as "rope, guide, filament," as well as "that which creates oscillation" and "boat." See Albino Alves, *Dicionário etimológico bundo-português*, 2 vols. (Tipografia Silvas, 1951), 1:592.

61. Jean Baptiste Debret, "Le viel orphée africain (Oricongo)," *Voyage pittoresque et historique au Brésil*, 3 vols. (Firmin Didot Frères, 1834–1839), 1: plate 30, https://digital.bbm.usp.br/handle/bbm/3813.

62. Joaquim Cândido Guillobel, "Vendedor ambulante tocando berimbau," in *Enciclopédia itaú cultural de arte e cultura brasileira* (Itaú Cultural, 2024), http://enciclopedia.itaucultural.org.br/obra65322/negro-vendedor-ambulante-tocando-berimbau.

63. Henry Chamberlain and Rubens Borba de Moraes, *Vistas e costumes da cidade e arredores do Rio de Janeiro em 1819–1820* (Livraria Kosmo, 1943), 105, http://www2.senado.leg.br/bdsf/handle/id/227375.

64. Harro Paul Harring, "Danse de nègres musiciens jouant les instruments de leur pays," 1840, https://www.brasilianaiconografica.art.br/obras/19278/danse-de-negres-musiciens-jouant-les-instruments-de-leur-pays.

65. Friar Cavazzi, *Descrição histórica dos três reinos Congo, Matamba, Angola*, 2 vols. (Edição da Junta de Investigações do Ultramar, 1965), 1:151.

66. John K. Thornton, "The Art of War in Angola, 1575–1680," *Comparative Studies in Society and History* 30, no. 2 (1988): 364–65.

67. Albano de Neves e Souza, *Da minha África e do Brasil que eu vi . . .* (Lello, 1974), illustrations with numbered captions 57–63.

68. Câmara Cascudo, *Folclore do Brasil: pesquisas e notas* (Fundo de Cultura, 1967), 182–87. See also T. J. Desch-Obi, "Engolo: Combat Traditions in African and African Diaspora History" (PhD diss., University of California, 2000), 203.

69. Mestre Pastinha, *Quando as pernas fazem miserê: Metafísica e prática da capoeira, Bahia, Pelourinho, 1960*, in *A herança de Pastinha*, ed. Ângelo Decânio (Salvador, 1996). This was preserved for decades by Mestre Decânio and digitized in 2003 by Hilton Bruno de Almeida Sousa, a capoeira practitioner known as Teimosia. See *Manuscritos de Mestre Pastinha*, "Caderno Albo," accessed September 26, 2023, https://www.capoeirashop.fr/en/blog/pdf-manuscritos-de-mestre-pastinha-n19.

70. Matthias Röhrig Assunção, *Capoeira: The History of an Afro-Brazilian Martial Art* (Routledge, 2005), 156.

71. Röhrig Assunção, "Capoeira,"156.

72. Röhrig Assunção, "Capoeira," 157.

73. Mestre Pastinha, *Capoeira Angola* (Escola Gráfica N. S. de Lorêto, 1964), 39. Original excerpt: "o misticismo que bole com a alma."

74. T. J. Desch-Obi "Combat and the Crossing of the Kalunga," in *Central Africans and Cultural Transformations in the American Diaspora*, ed. Linda M. Heywood (Cambridge University Press, 2002), 361. Building on the work of Câmara Cascudo, Desch-Obi has expanded upon the hypothesis that the primary ancestor of Capoeira would have been the N'golo, also known as the Zebra Dance found in the Southern Angolan Efunda rites of passage for girls transitioning into womanhood. See Luís da Câmara

Cascudo, *Folclore do Brasil*, 182–87. See Desch-Obi, "Engolo," and also Desch-Obi, *Fighting for Honor: The History of African Martial Art in the Atlantic World* (University of South Carolina Press, 2008).

75. The trajectory and shifts of Capoeira can be summarized in the following eras: from its prohibition in 1890 during the Republic period; to its legalization in 1943 during Getúlio Vargas' era; to the foundational codifications by Mestre Bimba and Mestre Pastinha; to its recognition as a national sport by the Ministry of Education and Culture in 1973 during the military dictatorship; to the establishment of the initial four capoeira schools in the United States in 1980; to its expansion across the world; and to more recent transformations (Capo-ballet, Hydro-Capoeira, Capo-therapy, and Capoeira de Cristo) and international developments, including the creation of capoeira characters in computer games.

76. Wallace de Deus Barbosa, *Dossiê: inventário para registro e salvaguarda da capoeira como patrimônio cultural do Brasil* (IPHAN, 2007), 8.

77. Barbosa, *Dossiê*, 83–84

78. Yeda Pessoa de Castro, *Camões com dendê: o português do Brasil e os falares afro-brasileiros* (Topbooks, 2022), 403.

79. Assis Júnior, *Dicionário*, 46–47.

80. Assis Júnior, *Dicionário*, 46–47.

81. Yeno Matuka and A. Mawadza, *Dictionary and Phrasebook: Kikongo-English / English-Kikongo* (Hippocrene Books, 2021), 70.

82. Beniste, *Dicionário*, 77; see also Glosbe dictionary, "Clock," acessed 23 October, 2023, https://glosbe.com/en/yo/clock.

83. Rafael Galante, "Essa gunga veio de lá!: sinos e sineiros na África Centro-Ocidental e no Brasil centro-africano" (PhD diss., Universidade de São Paulo, 2023), doi:10.11606/T.8.2023.tde-23052023-132320. See also Rafael Galante and Marcos Cardoso, *Essa gunga veio de lá: tradição africana nos sinos do Brasil*, video, Canal USP, 2023, accessed May 11, 2023, https://www.youtube.com/watch?v=TKOaAjd7bts.

84. Galante and Cardoso, *Essa gunga*.

85. Galante and Cardoso, *Essa gunga*.

86. Galante and Cardoso, *Essa gunga*.

87. Galante and Cardoso, *Essa gunga*.

88. Galante and Cardoso, *Essa gunga*.

89. Galante and Cardoso, *Essa gunga*.

90. Galante and Cardoso, *Essa gunga*.

91. Galante and Cardoso, *Essa gunga*.

92. Assis Júnior, *Dicionário*, 47. Castro, *Camões*, 403,

93. Castro, *Camões*, 403.

94. Ras Michael Brown, *African-Atlantic Cultures and the South Carolina Lowcountry* (Cambridge University Press, 2012), 90–91.

95. Brown, *African-Atlantic*, 91.

96. Brown, *African-Atlantic*, 93.

97. Brown, *African-Atlantic*, 93.

98. Brown, *African-Atlantic*, 94.

99. Marina Warner, *Alone of All Her Sex: The Myth and Cult of the Virgin Mary* (Knopf Doubleday, 1976), 262.

100. For a review of the "Ocean Road hypothesis," see Hiroto Takamiya, "Introductory Routes of Rice to Japan: An Examination of the Southern Route Hypothesis," *Asian Perspectives* 40, no. 2 (2001): 209–26.

101. T. J. Desch-Obi, "Deadly Dances: The Spiritual Dimensions of Kongo-Angolan Martial Arts raditions in the New World," in *Fragments of Bone: Neo-African Religions in a New World*, ed. Patrick Bellegarde-Smith (University of Illinois Press, 2005), 84.

102. Edison Carneiro, *Religiões negras e negros bantos* (Civilização Brasileira, 1981), 212–13.
103. Desch-Obi "Deadly," 84.
104. Desch-Obi "Deadly," 83. Assunção, "Capoeira," 364.
105. Carneiro, *Religiões negras*, 212–13.
106. Desch-Obi "Deadly," 84.
107. Desch-Obi "Deadly," 83. *Iê* can mean his, hers, or yours. According to Assis Júnior, *iê* is both an adjective and possessive pronoun, a contraction of the preposition *ia*, and the personal pronoun *muene*. *Iá* is demonstrative pronoun in the plural to designate "the people who are present, or close to the speaker, or those who were last spoken to." See Assis Júnior, *Dicionário*, 54–55.
108. Robert Farris Thompson, "Capoeira Tough Guys Do Dance," *Rolling Stone*, March 24, 1988.
109. Assunção, *Capoeira*, 365.
110. Kenneth Dossar, "Capoeira Angola: Dancing Between Two Worlds," *Afro-Hispanic Review* 6, no.1–3 (1992): 7.
111. Dossar, "Capoeira," 7.
112. Assunção, *Capoeira*, 208.
113. Assunção, *Capoeira*, 208.
114. Edison Carneiro, "Capoeira de Angola," *Religiões negras*.
115. Carybé, *O jogo da capoeira*, (Livraria Turista, 1951).
116. Macedo, Ana Paula Rezende. "A capoeira angola: história, persistências e transformações," *História e Perspectivas* 1, no. 34 (2006): 448–49. Alexandre Robatto Filho, *Vadiação*, 1954, video, accessed September 26, 2023, https://www.youtube.com/watch?v=rUO691y4F3A.
117. John Lowell Lewis, *Ring of Liberation: Deceptive Discourse in Brazilian Capoeira* (The University of Chicago Press, 1992), 32.
118. Lewis, *Ring*, 102–03.
119. Lewis, *Ring*, 102–03.
120. Lewis, *Ring*, 102–03.
121. Charles Daniel Dawson, class lecture, *African Spirituality in America*, New York University, September 16, 1997.
122. Dawson, *African Spirituality*.
123. Câmara Cascudo, *Made in Africa: pesquisas e notas* (Civilização Brasileira, 1965), 182–84.
124. "Q: Master, tells us how many strikes there are in capoeira? A: Young man, it isn't possible to say; they are without a number. For every strike which is launched, there are two defenses already prepared, and for those two defenses, four more strikes. One is always improvising and thinking while fighting." Mestre Pastinha, interviewed in 1963, quoted in Lewis, *Ring*, 105.
125. Duarte Lopes's report to Filippo Pigafetta on the twelve years he spent in the Kongo in the late sixteenth century. Filippo Pigafetta and D. Lopes, *Relação do reino do Congo e das terras circunvizinhas: uma verdadeira história de navegações e aventuras do século XVI* (Alêtheia Editores, 2015).
126. Fu-Kiau, "Kapuera e cultura ancestral Bantu," lecture, Salvador, 1997, accessed October 23, 2023, https://terreirodegrios.wordpress.com/2022/03/09/palestra-do-dr-fu-kiau-salvador-1997-kapuera-e-cultura-ancestral-bantu/.
127. Fu-Kiau, "Kapuera," n/p.
128. Fu-Kiau, "Kapuera," n/p.
129. Fu-Kiau, "Kapuera," n/p.
130. Fu-Kiau, "Kapuera," n/p.
131. Fu-Kiau, "Kapuera," n/p.
132. Robert Farris Thompson, *Tango: The Art History of Love* (Knopf Doubleday, 2010).
133. Robert Farris Thompson "A Tango with Robert Farris Thompson: Interview with Ned Sublette," *AfroPop Worldwide*, October 20, 2005, https://afropop.org/articles/robert-farris-thompson-interview-2005.

134. Thompson "Tango," n/p.
135. Thompson "Tango," n/p.
136. Thompson "Tango," n/p.
137. Thompson "Tango," n/p.
138. Cyrus Gordon and M. Stefon, "Solomon," *Encyclopedia Britannica*, https://www.britannica.com/biography/Solomon.
139. Carybé, *O jogo*, n.p.
140. Galante, "'Essa gunga."
141. Galante, "'Essa gunga."
142. Ricardo Mendes Mattos, "Jongo: travessias atlânticas e retorno ritual a Aruanda," *Letrônica* 15, no.1 (2022): 3–4, https://doi.org/10.15448/1984-4301.2022.1.40930. The association of *cumba* and *gunga* (*ngunga*) is in Queiroz, *Palavra banto*, 129, 165. It is also connected to *kumbi* meaning "the sun" or "the day", or the midday sun, which can also metaphorically represent the strength or power of a man; see Slenes, "'Malungu, ngoma vem!': África coberta e descoberta no Brasil," *Revista USP*, no. 12 (1992), 18.
143. Mattos, "Jongo," 4.
144. Mattos, "Jongo," 4.
145. Mattos, "Jongo," 4.
146. Cyril Claridge, *Wild Bush Tribes of Tropical Africa* (Negro University Press, 1969), 268.
147. Fu-Kiau, *Self-Healing Power and Therapy: Old Teachings from Africa* (Vintage Press, 1991), 114.
148. Slenes, "Malungu," 19.
149. Slenes, "Malungu," 19.
150. Original: "Veado gaieiro / tá berando o má / tá pedindo licença / prá poder chegá." Maria de Lourdes Borges Ribeiro, "O jongo," *Revista do Arquivo Municipal* 16, no. 216 (1960): 192.
151. Mattos, "Jongo," 4.
152. Mattos, "Jongo," 10.

8. ARUANDA: ANCESTRAL GEOGRAPHIES: A MAP TO ARUANDA AND OTHER REALMS

1. Original excerpt: "divagávamos em busca das mil conchinhas, que bordam as brancas areias d'aquellas vastas praias." Maria Firmina dos Reis, *Úrsula* (Editora PUC Minas, 2017), 201.
2. Eduardo de Assis Duarte, "Úrsula e a desconstrução da razão negra ocidental," in Reis, *Úrsula*, 229
3. Duarte, "Úrsula," 229
4. Eduardo de Assis Duarte, *Literatura, política, identidades* (FALE-UFMG, 2005).
5. Maria Helena Machado, "Maria Firmina dos Reis, Nineteenth-Century Maranhão (Brazil), in *If She Were Free: A Collective Biography of Women and Emancipation in the Americas*, ed. Erica L. Ball, Tatiana Seijas, and T. L. Snyder (Cambridge University Press, 2020), 345.
6. David Birmingham, "Speculations on the Kingdom of Kongo," *Transactions of the Historical Society of Ghana* 8 (1965): 3.
7. Jan Hogendorn and M. Johnson, *The Shell Money of the Slave Trade* (Cambridge University Press, 2003); Luiz Felipe de Alencastro, *O tratado dos viventes: formação do Brasil no Atlântico Sul, séculos XVI e XVII* (Companhia das Letras, 2000), 256–59.
8. Heli Chatelain, "Geographic Names of Angola, West Africa," *Journal of the American Geographical Society of New York* 25, no. 1 (1893): 308, https://doi.org/10.2307/197042.
9. Assis Júnior, *Dicionario kimbundu-português: linguístico, botânico, histórico e corográfico*, (Santos, 1934), 269; Patrício Batsîkama, *As origens do reino do Kôngo* (Mayamba Editora, 2010), 66–67.

10. Batsîkama, *As origens*, 66–67.
11. Batsîkama, *As origens*, 67.
12. Batsîkama, *As origens*, 67.
13. Batsîkama, *As origens*, 67–68.
14. Kiatezua Lubanzadio Luyaluka, "Comparative Theology: Sumer, Memphis, Kongo Religion and Natural Systematic Theology," *Journal of Religion and Theology* 2, no. 1 (2018): 36.
15. Luyaluka, "Comparative Theology," 36.
16. José Carlos de Oliveira, "Os zombo e o futuro (Nzil'a Bazombo): na tradição, na colônia e na independência" (PhD diss., Universidade de Coimbra, 2008), 132.
17. Oliveira, "Os zombo," 132.
18. Oliveira, "Os zombo," 132.
19. See "Milonga: The Capoeira's Wheel, the Sun's Path, the Ngoma Canoe, and the Mundiongo in Kalunga," in Cécile Fromont, *Art of Conversion: Christian Visual Culture in the Kingdom of Kongo* (Chapel Hill, 2014), 117.
20. Mariana Bracks Fonseca, "Ginga de Angola: memórias e representações da rainha guerreira na diáspora" (PhD diss., Universidade de São Paulo, 2018), 29–30.
21. Fonseca, "Ginga," 29–30.
22. Fonseca, "Ginga," 37.
23. Fonseca, "Ginga," 55.
24. Fonseca, "Ginga," 62.
25. Alencastro, *O tratado*, 82, quoted in Fonseca, "Ginga," 28.
26. Fonseca, "Ginga," 191.
27. Fonseca, "Ginga," 38.
28. Fonseca, "Ginga," 13.
29. Fonseca, "Ginga," 191.
30. Júlio César de Souza Tavares and J. Miller, quoted in Cristina Rosa, "Playing, Fighting, and Dancing: Unpacking the Significance of Ginga Within the Practice of Capoeira Angola" *TDR: The Drama Review* 56, no. 3 (Fall 2012): 150.
31. Rosa, "Playing," 143.
32. Rosa, "Playing," 144.
33. Rosa, "Playing," 146–47; Nei Lopes, *Novo dicionário banto do Brasil* (Pallas, 2003), 109.
34. Rosa, "Playing," 153.
35. Rosa, "Playing," 146–47; Lopes, *Novo dicionário*, 109.
36. Cristina Rosa, "Playing," 141–66.
37. Kimbwandende Kia Bunseki Fu-Kiau, "A Powerful Trio: Drumming, Singing and Dancing," unpublished, quoted in Zeca Ligiéro, *Corpo a corpo: estudos das performances brasileiras* (Garamond, 2011), 157.
38. Ligiéro, "O conceito de motrizes," 142–43.
39. "Iê aruandê / Iê aruandê camarada (coro) / I jogo de mandinga / I jogo de mandinga camarada (coro) / Ai sabe jogá / Ai sabe jogá camarada (coro) / Aiaiá a capoeira / Aiaiá a capoeira camarada (coro)." See Alexandre Robatto Filho, *Vadiação*, 1954.
40. Fu-Kiau, "A Powerful Trio," quoted in Ligiéro, *Corpo a corpo*, 157.
41. Maya Talmon-Chvaicer, *The Hidden History of Capoeira: A Collision of Cultures in the Brazilian Battle Dance* (University of Texas Press, 2008), 144–45.
42. Talmon-Chvaicer, *The Hidden History*, 144–45; Floyd Merrell, *Capoeira and Candomblé: Conformity and Resistance in Brazil* (Markus Wiener Publishers, 2005), 53.
43. Alan Santos de Oliveira, "Círculos, espirais e rodas no mundo afro-atlântico: itinerários do pensamento rodante" (PhD diss., Universidade de Brasília, 2021), 198.
44. Oliveira, "Círculos, espirais," 156.
45. Câmara Cascudo, *Made in Africa: pesquisas e notas* (Civilização Brasileira, 1965), 95.

46. Aurélio Buarque de Holanda Ferreira, *Novo Aurélio século XXI* (Nova Fronteira, 1999), 109.
47. Isis Barra Costa, "O Reino de Aruanda: de porto escravista luso-angolano a reino mítico afro-brasileiro," *Revista Scripta: Revista de Letras da Pontifícia Universidade Católica, Minas* 11, no. 20 (2007): 127–35.
48. Interview with Raquel de Souza, "Salvo-conduto," in *Traduzindo no Atlântico negro: cartas náuticas afrodiaspóricas para travessias literárias*, ed. Denise Carrascosa (Ogum's Toques Negros, 2017), 195–96.
49. Souza, "Salvo-conduto," 202.
50. Guellwar Adún, "Nota do editor" and "Rotas, bússolas, sextantes, faróis, sotaventos, porões, portos," in *Traduzindo*, ed. Carrosca, iii, 11.
51. José Beniste, *Dicionário yorubá-português* (Bertrand Brasil, 2019), 138.
52. Yeda Pessoa de Castro, *Camões com dendê: o português do Brasil e os falares afro-brasileiros* (Topbooks, 2022), 308.
53. Yeda Pessoa de Castro, *Falares africanos na Bahia: um vocabulário afro-brasileiro* (TopBooks, 2001), 106.
54. Cyril Claridge, *Wild Bush Tribes of Tropical Africa* (Negro University Press, 1969), 268.
55. Kimbwandende Kia Bunseki Fu-Kiau, *Self-Healing Power and Therapy: Old Teachings from Africa* (Vintage Press, 1991), 114.
56. Tiganá Santana, "A cosmologia africana dos bantu-kongo por Bunseki Fu-Kiau: tradução negra, reflexões e diálogos a partir do Brasil" (PhD diss., Universidade de São Paulo, 2019), 190; see also Claridge, *Wild Bush*, 270.
57. Brian Huntley, *Ecology of Angola: Terrestrial Biomes and Ecoregions* (Springer, 2023), 83, https://doi.org/10.1007/978-3-031-18923-4_4.
58. Huntley, *Ecology*, 76.
59. Huntley, *Ecology*, 85–86.
60. See "Welcome to Angola Portal, 'Black Rocks of Malanje,'" *Welcome to Angola*, https://welcometoangola.co.ao/en/directorio/black-rocks-de-malanje/; see also Jalmar Rudner, "An Archaeological Reconnaissance Tour of Angola," *The South African Archaeological Bulletin* 31, no. 123/124 (1976): 102, https://doi.org/10.2307/3887731.
61. See Luís Vítor Duarte, "De regresso à geologia de Angola: I. A zona costeira de Luanda ao Cuanza Sul," *Revista de Ciência Elementar* 7, no. 4 (2019): 1–8, http://doi.org/10.24927/rce2019.078. See also Rudner, "Archaeological Reconnaissance," 102–03.
62. Rudner, "Archaeological Reconnaissance," 103.
63. Rudner, "Archaeological Reconnaissance," 103.
64. Mariana Bracks Fonseca, *Nzinga Mbandi e as guerras de resistência em Angola, século XVII* (Mazza Edições, 2015), 147; see also Assis Júnior, *Dicionário*, 335.
65. Callan Bentley et al., "Palimpsest outcrops," *Historical Geology*, 2020, https://opengeology.org/historicalgeology/case-studies/palimpsest-outcrops.
66. Valdina Oliveira Pinto, "Candomblé de Angola: uma recriação de tradições culturais Bantu sobreviventes entre nós," *II Encontro de Nações de Candomblé setembro de 1995 anais* (Centro de Estudos Afro-Orientais da UFBa, 1997), 153.
67. Robert Farris Thompson. *Four Moments of the Sun: Kongo Art in Two Worlds* (National Gallery of Art, 1981), 151. See also Isis Costa McElroy, "Poemas-altar afro-brasileiros: o texto poético dos pontos-riscados," in *Um tigre na floresta de signos: estudos sobre poesia e demandas sociais no Brasil*, ed. Edimilson de Almeida Pereira (Mazza Edições, 2010), 669–82.
68. Thompson, *Four Moments*, 42.
69. Thompson, *Four Moments*, 43.
70. Tiganá Santana, "Tradução, interações e cosmologias africanas," *Cadernos de Tradução* 39 (2019): 67, https://doi.org/10.5007/2175-7968.2019v39nespp65.
71. Assis Júnior, *Dicionário*, 335.

72. Gastão de Sousa Dias, *Os portugueses em Angola* (Agência Geral do Ultramar, 1959), 158. In Portuguese, a maroon settlement is referred to as a Quilombo or Mocambo, and its warriors are termed Quilombolas or Mocamaus. The term Mocambo derives from the Kimbundu word *mukambo*, meaning "hideaway." See R. K. Kent, "Palmares: An African State in Brazil," in *Maroon Societies: Rebel Slave Communities in the Americas*, ed. Richard Price (The Johns Hopkins University Press, 1979). According to Décio Freitas, the term Quilombo does not appear in official documentation until the mid-eighteenth century. Before that, the term Mocambo was used. The use of Quilombo was later instituted by historians and anthropologists, with Francisco Adolfo de Varnhagen among the first to adopt it. See Décio Freitas, *O escravismo brasileiro* (Mercado Aberto, 1991), 30.
73. Gerhard Kubik, *Extensions of African Cultures in Brazil* (Diasporic Africa Press, 2013), 92. Kubik refers to Rossini Tavares de Lima, *Folguedos populares do Brasil* (Ricordi, 1962).
74. Kubik, *Extensions*, 93.
75. Kubik, *Extensions*, 97–98.
76. Marina de Mello e Souza, "Kongo King Festivals in Brazil: From Kings of Nations to Kings of Kongo" *African Studies Quarterly* 15, no. 3 (2015): 38–45.
77. Mello e Souza, "Kongo," 39.
78. Peter Fryer, *Rhythms of Resistance: African Musical Heritage in Brazil* (Wesleyan University Press, 2000), 55.
79. Mello e Souza, "Kongo," 43.
80. Mello e Souza, "Kongo," 39–40.
81. José Lingna Nafafé, *Lourenço da Silva Mendonça and the Black Atlantic Abolitionist Movement in the Seventeenth Century* (Cambridge University Press, 2022).
82. Nafafé, *Lourenço*, 177.
83. Nafafé, *Lourenço*, 189.
84. J. A. da Graça Barretto, *Monstruosidades do tempo e da fortuna: diário de factos que sucederam no reino de 1625 a 1780* (Tipografia da Viúva Sousa Neves,1888), 202; Antonio de Oliveira Cadornega, *História geral das guerras angolanas 1680*, 2 vols. (Agência Geral das Colónias, 1972), 357, quoted in Nafafé, *Lourenço*, 2:190–92.
85. Mariana Candido, *An African Slaving Port and the Atlantic World: Benguela and Its Hinterland* (Cambridge University Press, 2013), 155–56, quoted in Nafafé, *Lourenço*, 139. See also Carta de Salvador Correia de Sá, quoted in Nafafé, *Lourenço*, 206
86. Nafafé, *Lourenço*, 275–76.
87. José Lingna Nafafé, "Lourenço da Silva Mendonça: The First Anti-Slavery Activist?" *Modern Maroonage*, March 12, 2019, accessed October 23, 2023, https://mmppf.wordpress.com/2019/03/12/lourenco-da-silva-mendonca-the-first-anti-slavery-activist.
88. Nafafé, *Lourenço*, 208.
89. Nafafé, *Lourenço*, 256–57.
90. Nafafé, *Lourenço*, 256–57.
91. Nafafé, *Lourenço*, 302.
92. Nafafé, *Lourenço*, 221.
93. Nafafé, *Lourenço*, 270–71.
94. Nafafé, *Lourenço*, 329.
95. Nafafé, *Lourenço*, 154.
96. John Thornton and L. Heywood, *Central Africans and Cultural Transformations in the American Diaspora* (Cambridge University Press, 2002); see also Nafafé, *Lourenço* 155–56.
97. Nafafé, *Lourenço*, 244.
98. Nafafé, *Lourenço*, 278.
99. Nafafé, *Lourenço*, 315–16.
100. Nafafé, *Lourenço*, 153.

101. Friar Cavazzi, *Descrição histórica dos três reinos Congo, Matamba, Angola*, 2 vols. (Edição da Junta de Investigações do Ultramar, 1965), 2:286. Also known as Padre João António Cavazzi or Priest Giovanni António de Montecúccolo Cavazzi, he resided in Angola from 1654 to 1667. In 1687, he published his comprehensive work on Kongo-Angola, Cavazzi's account of Central Africa, which combined personal experience, missionary reports, and documentary research. During his time in Africa, the Kongo was in a weakened state following the 1665 battle of Mbwila. While residing primarily in Mpungo-a-Ndongo, Cavazzi was influenced by negative portrayals of Queen Nzinga. However, after a brief stay in Luanda, he went to live in the Kingdom of Matamba, where he befriended Nzinga and served as her advisor and representative on diplomatic missions. See John Thornton, "The Kingdom of Kongo, ca. 1390–1678: The Development of an African Social Formation," *Cahiers d'Études Africaines* 22, no. 87/88 (1982), 330.
102. Cavazzi, *Descrição*, 1:222–24.
103. Cavazzi, *Descrição*, 1:220.
104. Cavazzi, *Descrição*, 1:151.
105. Cavazzi, *Descrição*, 1:152–53.
106. Cavazzi, *Descrição*, 1:163.
107. Cavazzi, *Descrição*, 1:163.
108. Câmara Cascudo, *Literatura oral no Brasil* (Editora da Universidade de São Paulo, 1984), 417.
109. Roger Bastide, *As religiões africanas no Brasil* (Pioneira, 1960), 167–68.
110. Antonia Aparecida Quintão, *Irmandades negras: outro espaço de luta e resistência*, São Paulo: 1870–1890 (Annablume; Fapesp, 2002), 38.
111. Arthur Ramos, *A aculturação negra no Brasil* (Companhia Editora Nacional, 1942), 120.
112. Júlio Braga, *Sociedade protetora dos desvalidos: uma irmandade de cor* (Edições Ianamá, 1987), 20.
113. Câmara Cascudo, *Dicionário do folclore brasileiro* (Editora Itatiaia, 1993), 242.
114. Alvarenga, *Música*, 100.
115. Lélia Gonzalez, ed., *Festas Populares no Brasil/Popular Festivals in Brazil* (Editora Index, 1989), 93.
116. Oneyda Alvarenga, *Música Popular Brasileira* (Livraria Duas Cidades, 1982), 101–07.
117. Fryer, Rhythms, 67.
118. Cavazzi refers to the "ambassadors" as "secretaries carrying out messages to and from the king." See Cavazzi, *Descrição*, 1:228. Nzinga, as we know, was at one time an envoy of her brother's kingdom.
119. Núbia Pereira Magalhães Gomes and E. A. Pereira, *Negras raízes mineiras: os Arturos* (EDUFJF; MinC, 1988), 182.
120. Gomes and Pereira, *Negras*, 183; Alvarenga, *Música*, 129.
121. Cascudo, *Dicionário*, 304.
122. Von Martius and von Spix, *Viagem pelo Brasil 1817–1820*, 3 vols. (Senado Federal, Conselho Editorial, 2017), 2:61–63.
123. Andrade, "Os Congos," 298.
124. "Mandou matar Rei Meu Senhor! / E quem madou foi a Rainha Jinga!"; "Rainha Jinga é mulher de batalha, / Tem duas cadeiras arredor de navalha!" Cascudo, *Made*, 32.
125. Andrade, "Os Congos," 298.
126. Gonzalez, *Festas Populares no Brasil*, 93. Mameto is a child character symbolizing the son of the King of the Congo. The name "Mameto" originates from the Kimbundu language, specifically from the term "mama etu," which is an exclamation meaning "Oh mom!" (Lopes, *Novo dicionário*, 158).
127. Mário de Andrade, "Os congos," Câmara Cascudo ed., *Antologia do folclore brasileiro*, 2 vols. (Martins, 1965) 2:315–55.
128. Their copublications include *Negras raízes mineiras: os Arturos*, and *Arturos: olhos do rosário* (Mazza Edições, 1990).
129. Instituto Estadual do Patrimônio Histórico e Artístico de Minas Gerais, *Dossiê de Registro da Comunidade dos Arturos—Contagem / MG*, (IEPHA/MG, 2014).

130. Elian Guimarães, "Morre patriarca da Comunidade Quilombola dos Arturos," *Estado de Minas Gerais* (Belo Horizonte), May 7, 2021.
131. Gomes and Pereira, *Negras*, 240.
132. Mário Braz da Luz (Congada performer in Arturo, Minas Gerais), interview by Gomes and Pereira, *Negras*, 373.
133. Gomes and Pereira, *Negras*, 240–43.
134. Gomes and Pereira, *Negras*, 413.
135. Gomes and Pereira, *Negras*, 435–36.
136. Gomes and Pereira, *Negras*, 241.
137. "Ih, vamo divagá, çambiqueiro / Ela num pode corrê, çambiqueiro," in Gomes and Pereira, *Negras*, 231.
138. Lopes, *Novo dicionário*, 57.
139. "Esse gunga tá brincano, / Esse gunga é de papai, / Esse gunga é de mamãe, / Esse gunga é do Rosaro. Clareia, meu pai! / Clareia, minha mãe!" Gomes and Pereira, *Negras*, 366.
140. "Aruera, aruera / Aruera, aruera / A gunga bateu / Vamo guerreá / Coroa de Zambi / Vamo saravá, ué!" Gomes and Pereira, *Negras*, 370.
141. Brazilian women use the bark of the Aroeira tree to prepare an infusion following childbirth, as it promotes the health of their reproductive organs. It also helps manage bleeding, improve circulation, and treat infections. The bark is widely available at street markets across Brazil. In the United States, herbalists often recommend the use of Mulberry tree bark, which shares some of the same properties.
142. Gomes and Pereira, *Negras*, 626.
143. "Ô, ei, Candome / É de aruera sô / Ô Candome." Gomes and Pereira, *Negras*, 300.
144. Gomes and Pereira, *Negras*, 300.
145. Gomes and Pereira, *Negras*, 627.
146. Glória Moura, "A força dos tambores: a festa nos quilombos contemporâneos," in *Negras imagens: Ensaios sobre cultura e escravidão no Brasil*, ed. Lilian Moritz Schwarcz and L. V. S. Reis (EDUSP, 1996), 66. In Uruguay they are called Chico, Repique, and Piano.
147. Castro, *Camões*, 349.
148. Castro, *Camões*, 349.
149. Olga Cacciatore, *Dicionário de cultos afro-brasileiros* (Forense Universitária, 1988), 78.
150. Cacciatore, *Dicionário*, 78; and Lopes, *Novo dicionário*, 63.
151. Geraldo Camilo, interview by Gomes and Pereira, *Negras*, 219.
152. Gomes and Pereira, *Negras*, 177.
153. "Êe, maçambique é coisa boa / Maçambique é de nego e de coroa," in Gomes and Pereira, *Negras*, 178.
154. "Esse povo é de mistério, ai, ai / Quanto mais puxa mais dá, ai," in Gomes and Pereira, *Negras*, 329.
155. "Ei, vamo tirá oro / Ô no fundo do mar / Vamo tirá ôro," in Gomes and Pereira, *Negras*, 178.
156. "Ei Calunga me leva / Pra minha terra" and "Eu já mandei leva / Já mandei leva / Eu já mandei, ó no mundo / Já mandei leva," in Gomes and Pereira, *Negras*, 222–23.
157. "Ei, marinheiro vei de longe / Ele vei de Angola / Saravano na rigunga / Pra buscar Nossa Senhora," in Gomes and Pereira, *Negras*, 294.
158. Sônia Queiroz, *Palavra banto em Minas Gerais* (Editora UFMG, 2019), 159.
159. Lopes, *Novo dicionário*, 235.
160. Gomes and Pereira, *Negras*, 530.
161. "Calundunga nego véio / Nego véio de candonga / Nego véio de Lugamba / É na língua de um nego / É na língua de Angola / Olha ninguém me entende / Olha a língua de Angola / Olha ninguém compreende," in Gomes and Pereira, *Negras*, 295.
162. Lopes, *Novo dicionário*, 102.
163. Lopes, *Novo dicionário*, 64.
164. Lopes, *Novo dicionário*, 163.

8. ARUANDA

165. Patrícia Souza Borges, "O contato entre o português brasileiro e as línguas africanas na visão de Mendonça (1935[1933]) e Raimundo (1933): uma análise historiográfica," in *Cadernos de historiografia linguística do CEDOCH*, ed. Cristina Altman and O. Coelho (FFLCH/USP, 2015), 45; see also Jacques Raymundo, *O elemento afro-negro na língua portuguesa* (Renascença Editora: 1933), 117–18, quoted in Lopes, *Novo dicionário*, 163.
166. Lopes, *Novo dicionário*, 163.
167. Including, among others: Wyatt MacGaffey, *Religion and Society in Central Africa: The Bakongo of Lower Zaire* (University of Chicago Press: 1986) and *Kongo Political Culture: The Conceptual Challenge of the Particular* (Indiana University Press, 2000). See also Robert Slenes, "'Malungu, Ngoma's Coming!': Africa Hidden and Discovered in Brazil," in *Mostra do redescobrimento: Negro de corpo e alma: Black in Body and Soul. Exhibition catalog*, ed. Nelson Aguilar (Fundação Bienal de São Paulo, 2000); and *Na senzala, uma flor: esperanças e recordações na formação da família escrava: Brasil Sudeste, século XIX* (Unicamp, 2011), 221–29.
168. Thompson, *The Four Moments*, 80; Robert Slenes, "'I Come from Afar, I Come Digging': Kongo and Near-Kongo Metaphors in Jongo Lyrics," in *Cangoma Calling: Spirits and Rhythms of Freedom in Brazilian Jongo Slavery Songs*, ed. Pedro Meira Monteiro and Michael Stone (University of Massachusetts Press, 2013), 69–70.
169. Robert Slenes, "Metaphors to Live by in the Diaspora: Conceptual Tropes and Ontological Wordplay among Central Africans in the Middle Passage and Beyond," in *Tracing Language Movement in Africa*, ed. Ericka Albaugh and K. de Luna (Oxford University Press, 2016), 345.
170. Slenes, "Metaphors," 350–60.
171. MacGaffey, *Kongo*, 209, quoted in Slenes, "Metaphors," 360, 357.
172. Slenes, "Metaphors," 350–51.
173. Gomes and Pereira, *Negras*, 305.
174. Gomes and Pereira, *Negras*, 346.
175. Gomes and Pereira, *Negras*, 305.
176. Gomes and Pereira, *Negras*, 408.
177. John Mason and Gary Edwards, *Black Gods: Orisa Studies in the New World* (Yoruba Theological Archministry, 1985), 24.
178. Mason and Edwards, *Black*, 23.
179. Mason and Edwards, *Black*, 23.
180. Mason and Edwards, *Black*, 16–25.
181. Muniz Sodré, *O terreiro e a cidade: a forma social negro-brasileira* (Vozes, 1988), 138.
182. "Saia o povo todo, Calunga, / Saia na janela, / Venha ver os Congos, Calunga / Quando vão prá Guerra," in Alvarenga, *Música*, 112.
183. Lopes, *Novo dicionário*, 65.
184. "Ei, inda num era meia noite / Quando o primeiro galo canto / Inda num era meia noite / Mas o fio do Rosaro chegô," in Gomes and Pereira, *Negras*, 164. Compare this to the Capoeira song: "The rooster sang / Cocorocô / It is time to go / Let's go / Out into the world / Go around the world / Around the world, camará," in Bira Almeida and Mestre Acordeon, *Capoeira, a Brazilian Art Form: History, Philosophy, and Practice* (North Atlantic Books, 1986), 90. See also "Ei oi lelê oi ê oi ê / Aió lelê oi / Aió lelê iai / Aió ei ei ei / A roda do mundo é grande/A de Zambi inda é maió," in Gomes and Pereira, *Negras*, 164; and "Lé! Lé! Lé! exclamation used to ask for help, silence, or to call attention." Cavazzi, *Descrição*, 2:156.
185. "Salve Rainha / Lá no meio do mar"; "Para no portão chegá / Ajuda a rainha do mar / Que manda na terra / Que manda no mar" (page); "Ai seu eu fosse um peixinho / Ai seu eu fosse um peixinho / Que soubesse a nadá / Que soubesse a nadá / Tirava Nossa Senhora / Tirava Nossa Senhora / Lá no fundo, lá no mar / Lá no fundo, lá no mar." In Gomes and Pereira, *Negras*, 282.
186. "A canoa virou / Deixá-la virar / Por causa da [name inserted by singer] / Que não soube remar."

187. "Se eu fosse um peixinho / E soubesse nadar, / Tirava [name inserted by singer] / Do fundo do mar."
188. "Ih, a senhora me dá licença, ai / A Senhora do Rosário / O sinhô São Benedito, ai, ai/Vim pedi sua licença." ; "Pra entrá na casa santa / Onde Deus fez a morada / Onde mora o cális bento / E a hóstia consagrada / Chora ingoma." See Gomes and Pereira, *Negras*, 166.
189. "É devera, Sinhô Rei, ai, ai / Sua coroa me alumeia / Ei coroa de Rainha, ô meu Deus / Alumeia o mundo inteiro," in Gomes and Pereira, *Negras*, 190.
190. Gomes and Pereira, *Negras*, 169.
191. "Vem, meu pai / Vem me valê / Nesse dia de congá / Num deixa seus fio sofrê." See Gomes and Pereira, *Negras*, 158. *Congá*, from *conga*, a synonym to Congada. Gomes and Pereira, *Negras*, 528. *Congá* carries the meaning of action, to do or perform the Congada. "Essa ingoma, meu Deus de vovô / Dexô o mundo, dexô o mar / Viajano pra terra de cá," in Gomes and Pereira, *Negras*, 296.
192. "Papagaio canto / Foi lá na serra / Mandô um abraço / Pra esse povo dessa terra!" in Gomes and Pereira, *Negras*, 320.
193. According to Cascudo the parrots "were common trade merchandise of Luso-Brazilians in Angola, Cape Verde, and Guinea"; see Cascudo, *Made*, 36. Over time, the parrot became a Brazilian cultural icon, an urban trickster character akin to Anansi. This legacy is reflected in Disney's creation of Zé Carioca, the cartoon parrot who came to symbolize Brazil during the Roosevelt era. Cascudo also recorded a drinking song from Minas Gerais that says: "A true Brazilian parrot, / even in its color it is Brazilian. / How does the parrot sing? / The parrot sings like this: *gro, gro, gro*." Cascudo, *Literatura*, 365.
194. "Num sô daqui / Eu sô lá de for a / Vim trazê meu povo / E Nossa Senhora," in Gomes and Pereira, *Negras*, 321. "Ô, vamo curiá! / Ô, vamo curiá!" in Gomes and Pereira, *Negras*, 322. Queiroz, *Palavra banto*, 136–37. Assis Júnior, *Dicionário*, 222. When offered lunch they sing: "Eh praise canduru / Let's candaru / Praise canduru" ("Ê canduruê / Canduruá / Canduruê"); see Gomes and Pereira, *Negras*, 323. *Candaruá* means to perform the *Candaruê*: "*candaruê* is a word that appears in chants that praise the lunch table," Gomes and Pereira, *Negras*, 528. In addition, "*Candaru*: type of incense receptacle in which aromatic herbs are placed on burning coal; from the Kikongo *ndalu*, fire"; see Lopes, *Novo dicionário*, 69.
195. Claridge, *Wild Bush*, 292.
196. Gomes and Pereira, *Negras*, 157–59.
197. Sodré, *O terreiro*, 122–23.
198. Sodré, *O terreiro*, 131.
199. Sodré, *O terreiro*, 133.
200. Sodré, *O terreiro*, 139–41.
201. Frantz Fanon, *The Wretched of the Earth* (Grove Press, 1965), 57–58.
202. Fanon, *The Wretched*, 57–58.
203. Jean-Paul Sartre, Preface to *The Wretched of the Earth*, by Frantz Fanon, trans. Constance Farrington (Grove Press, 1965), 19.
204. Sartre, Preface, 19.
205. Emphasis added. Sodré, *O terreiro*, 125.
206. Chris Park, "Religion and Geography," in *Routledge Companion to the Study of Religion*, ed. John Hinnells (Routledge, 2004), 450, 460.
207. Park, "Religion," 460.
208. Park, "Religion," 460.
209. Marion Aubrée, "Brazil: Mental Health and the Magic-Religious Sphere", *Revue Tiers Monde* 187, no. 3, (2006): 552.
210. Aubrée, "Brazil," 552.
211. Chico Xavier, *Parnaso de além-túmulo* (Federação Espírita Brasileira, 1932).
212. Bernardo Lewgoy, "A antropologia pós-moderna e a produção literária espírita," *Horizontes Antropológicos* 4, no. 8 (1998): 103. Xavier authored over 400 titles, with total sales exceeding 25 million

8. ARUANDA

213. copies. Maria Helena Villas Boas Concone and E. G. Rezende, "Umbanda in the Kardecist spiritualist novels," *Revista Eletrônica de Comunicação, Informação e Inovação em Saúde* 4, no. 3 (2010), 49. DOI: 10.3395/reciis.v4i3.385en. 47–58.
213. Lewgoy, "A antropologia," 97.
214. Lewgoy, "A antropologia," 97.
215. Concone and Rezende, "Umbanda," 47.
216. Believers assert that the spirit of Ramatis now manifests as distinct forces within the cosmos. The name Ramatis is reminiscent of the Iraqi city of Ramadi. It also brings to mind the 5.8-million-year-old hominid fossil found in Ethiopia, dubbed Ramadis Kadaba, where "Ramadis" signifies "root" in the Afar language, native to Eritrea.
217. Norberto Peixoto, *Vozes de Aruanda: obra mediúnica*. (Editora do Conhecimento, 2005), 15.
218. Robson Pinheiro, *Aruanda: magia negra, elementais, Preto-Velhos e Caboclos sob a ótica espírita* (Casa dos Espíritos, 2004).
219. Sales surpassed 130,000 copies by April 2009. Concone and Rezende, "Umbanda," 48.
220. Concone and Rezende, "Umbanda," 49.
221. Robson Pinheiro, WEBtv, https://www.youtube.com/@RobsonPinheiroWEBtv.
222. Pinheiro, *Aruanda*, 9–11.
223. Pinheiro, *Aruanda*, 87–89.
224. Fu-Kiau, *Self-Healing*, 112.
225. Fu-Kiau, *Self-Healing*, 112.
226. Daniel Soares Filho, *Aruanda: a morada dos orixás* (Anúbis, 2017).
227. Ademir Barbosa Júnior, "Prefácio," in Soares Filho, *Aruanda*, 11–12.
228. Soares Filho, *Aruanda*, 15.
229. Soares Filho, *Aruanda*, 32–33.
230. The original reads: "Caboclo quando vem lá de Aruanda / Oi, na Umbanda, ele pisa devagar. / Pisa Caboclo, quero ver você pisar. / Olha, pisa caboclo, / Oi pisa lá que eu piso cá." See Soares Filho, *Aruanda*, 85.
231. Soares Filho, *Aruanda*, 86.
232. Soares Filho, *Aruanda*, 101–102.
233. "Enterolobium contortisiliquum," Wikipedia, last modified June 28, 2025, https://pt.wikipedia.org/wiki/Enterolobium_contortisiliquum.
234. Assis Júnior, *Dicionário*, 18.
235. Kubik, *Extensions*, 136.
236. Kubik, *Extensions*, 243.
237. Lourenço Braga, *Umbanda, magia branca, Quimbanda, magia negra* (Editora Moderna, 1946), 15.
238. Braga, *Umbanda*, 69.
239. Renato Ortiz, *A morte*, 109. "Refletiu a luz divina / Em todo seu esplendor / Vem do reino de Oxalá / Onde tem paz e amor / O que refletiu na terra / O que refletiu no ar / O que vem lá de Aruanda / Para tudo iluminar."
240. Ortiz, *A morte*, 106. "Lá no Pólo Norte / Onde tudo é gelado. / Tem povo esquimó, / Que vem de Aruanda. / Lá na Groelândia / Onde tudo é nevado, / Tem povo esquimó / Que conhece a Lei de Umbanda."
241. Ortiz, *A morte*, 31. "Pinto piou lá na Angola / Galo cantou na Calunga / Salve Congo que vem de Aruanda / Trazendo presente na sua sacola."
242. Fu-Kiau, *Self-Healing*, 114
243. Nilton Mendonça, *3000 pontos riscados e cantados na umbanda e candomblé* (Editora Eco, 1974) 154. "Três pedras. / Três pedras dentro desta aldeia, / Uma é maior, outra é menor, / A menorzinha é que nos alumeia."
244. Batsîkama, *O reino*, 202.

245. Raul Lody, *O povo do santo: religião história e cultura dos orixás, voduns, inquices e caboclos* (Editora Pallas, 1995), 137. "Pedrinha miudinha / Na Aruanda, auê / Lajeiro tão grande, tão grande / Na Aruanda, auê."
246. John Thornton, "The Origins and Early History of the Kingdom of Kongo, c. 1350–1550," *International Journal of African Historical Studies* 34, no. 1 (2001): 105, https://doi.org/10.2307/3097288.
247. Anne Hilton, "Family and Kinship among the Kongo South of the Zaïre River from the Sixteenth to the Nineteenth Centuries," *Journal of African History* 24, no. 2 (1983): 189. Wyatt MacGaffey, "The Black Loincloth and the Son of Nzambi Mpungu," *Research in African Literatures* 5, no. 1 (1974): 23.
248. Thornton, "Origins," 105.
249. John Thornton, *The Kingdom of Kongo: Civil War and Transition, 1641–1718* (University of Wisconsin Press, 1983).
250. Ch. Didier Gondola, *The History of Congo* (Greenwood Press, 2002), 28.
251. Filippo Pigafetta, *Relatione del reame di Congo e delle circovincine contrade* (Bartolomeo Grassi, 1591), 36, quoted in Thornton, "Origins," 103.
252. Thornton, "Origins," 119–20.
253. Thornton, "Origins," 119–20.
254. Thornton, "Origins," 112.
255. Patrício Batsîkama, *O reino do Kôngo e a sua origem meridional* (Universidade Editora, 2011), 353.
256. Batsîkama, *O reino*, 233.
257. Patrício Batsîkama, *As origens*, 48.
258. Batsîkama, *As origens*, 61.
259. Batsîkama, *As origens*, 61.
260. Fu-Kiau, *Self-Healing*, 126.
261. Batsîkama, *O reino*, 233–34.
262. See Batsîkama, *As origens*, 353; see also Patrício Batsîkama and R. Batsîkama, "Estruturas e instituições do Kongo," *Revista de História Comparada* 5, no. 1 (2011) 38; and Batsîkama, *O reino*, 352.
263. Patrício Batsîkama, "As origens do reino do Kôngo segundo a tradição oral," *Sankofa. Revista de História da África e de Estudos da Diáspora Africana* 5 (2010): 16.
264. Batsîkama, *O reino* 234–35
265. Batsîkama, *O reino*, 202.
266. Batsîkama, *O reino*, 201–02.
267. Batsîkama, *O reino*, 201–02.
268. Batsîkama, *O reino*, 352.
269. Batsîkama, *O reino*, 112, 202.
270. Batsîkama, *O reino*, 106–07.
271. Batsîkama, *O reino*, 106–07.
272. Batsîkama, *O reino*, 209.
273. Batsîkama, *O reino*, 109.
274. Batsîkama, *O reino*, 138.
275. Batsîkama, "As origens," 19.
276. MacGaffey, "Black Loincloth," 189.
277. MacGaffey, "Black Loincloth," 23.
278. Batsîkama, *O reino, 353*
279. Hilton, "Family," 189.
280. Mpetelo Boka, quoted in Thornton, "Origins," 93; Wyatt MacGaffey, *Kongo Political Culture*, 71.
281. Thornton, "Origins," 92.
282. Jean Cuvelier, *Nkutama a Mvila za Makanda* (Imprimerie de la Mission Catholique, 1934), quoted in Thornton, "Origins," 197–98.

283. Thornton, "Origins," 105
284. John Thornton, "Modern Oral Tradition and the Historic Kingdom of Kongo," in *The Power of Doubt: Essays in Honor of David Henige*, ed. Paul S. Landau (Parallel Press, 2011), 196.
285. Hilton, "Family," 193
286. Hilton, "Family," 195.
287. Hilton, "Family," 197
288. Simon Bockie, *Death and The Invisible Powers: The World of Kongo Belief* (Indiana University Press, 1993) 2–3.
289. Thornton, "Origins," 98.
290. Thornton, "Origins," 98–99.
291. Gondola, *The History*, 30.
292. Bender, *Angola*, 14.
293. Cavazzi, *Descrição*, 1:234.
294. Gerald J. Bender, *Angola under the Portuguese: The Myth and the Reality* (University of California Press, 1978), 14.
295. Hilton, "Family," 89.
296. Hilton, "Family," 60.
297. Hilton, "Family," 52. Cascudo mentions some of the names chosen by Kongo ministers in 1665, which, when translated, include: Calisto Sebastian White Castle Magdalena's Tears at the Feet of the Cross in the Calvary Mount; Geraldo Zilote Manuel Saint Peter's Regret in the Grotto of Earth; Cristovão de Aragão dos Vieiras of Happy Memory; and Miguel Tércio Pêlo from Three Highs for Boots that Cover the Feet of My Lord The King. See Cascudo, *Made*, 186.
298. Basil Davidson, *The African Slave Trade Pre-colonial History, 1450–1850* (Little, Brown & Company, 1961) 15.
299. David Birmingham, *The Portuguese Conquest of Angola* (Oxford University Press, 1965), 6.
300. Davidson, *The African*, 139.
301. Bender, *Angola*, 16, 18.
302. Birmingham, *Portuguese Conquest*, 6.
303. Bender, *Angola*, 18.
304. Bender, *Angola*, 16.
305. Emphasis added. Davidson, *The African*, 156.
306. John M. Lipski, "Portuguese Language in Angola: Luso-creoles' Missing Link?" (paper presented at the American Association of Teachers of Spanish and Portuguese [AATSP] Conference, San Diego, 1995), http://www.personal.psu.edu/faculty/j/m/jml34/angola.pdf.
307. Quoted in Davidson, *The African*, 159.
308. Hilton, "Family," 59.
309. Bender, *Angola*, 17–18.
310. John Thornton and A. Mosterman. "A Re-interpretation of the Kongo-Portuguese War of 1622 According to New Documentary Evidence," *Journal of African History* 51, no. 2 (2010): 237.
311. Hilton, "Family," 112.
312. Birmingham, *Portuguese Conquest*, 1–2, 24.
313. Birmingham, *Portuguese Conquest*, 27.
314. Birmingham, *Portuguese Conquest*, 25.
315. Chiefs faced coercion into submission, with choices ranging from resistance to deportation to participation in an *undar* ceremony, akin to a strategic alliance or marriage of convenience. In the ceremony of the invented Portuguese ritual, the *sobas* received Christian baptism and were declared subjects in the presence of authorities. See Roy Arthur Glasgow, *Nzinga: resistência africana à investida do colonialismo português em Angola, 1582–1663* (Editora Perspectiva, 1982), 65.

316. Linda Heywood, *Njinga of Angola: Africa's Warrior Queen* (Harvard University Press, 2017), 12.
317. Agostinho da Silva Milagres, *Dicionário Kimbundu/Português/Kimbundu*, 28, 36, https://www.academia.edu/43089182/Dicion%C3%A1rio_de_Kimbundu. See also Assis Júnior, *Dicionário*, 111.
318. Milagres, *Dicionário*, 62.
319. Nafafé, *Lourenço*, 145.
320. Nafafé, *Lourenço*, 175.
321. Glasgow, *Nzinga*, 32. Malaria was one of the reasons for high mortality rates. Cavazzi describes how European settlers, believing their blood unsuited to the local climate, often resorting to excessive bloodletting as a remedy for fevers. He concludes that African kingdoms became "an open graveyard for Europeans." Cavazzi, *Descrição*, 1:147.
322. Nei Lopes, *Bantos, malês e identidade negra* (Forense Universitária, 1988), 106.
323. Glasgow, *Nzinga*, 72.
324. Birmingham, *Portuguese Conquest*, 25.
325. Boxer, *Salvador Correa de Sá*, 1952, quoted in Glasgow, *Nzinga*, 72.
326. Glasgow, *Nzinga*, 72.
327. Birmingham, *Portuguese Conquest*, 18.
328. Glasgow, *Nzinga*, 73.
329. Bender, *Angola*, 57.
330. Gilberto Freyre, Gilberto. *O mundo que o português criou: aspectos das relações sociaes e de cultura do Brasil com Portugal e as colônias portuguesas* (José Olympio, 1940), 113.
331. Nafafé, *Lourenço*, 316–17.
332. João Henrique dos Santos, "Gente da nação: os judaizantes e a preservação do judaísmo no Brasil," in *Identidade e cidadania como se expressa o judaísmo brasileiro*, ed. Helena Lewin (Centro Edelstein de Pesquisas Sociais, 2009), 67.
333. In Latin translations of the Bible, *ha-goyim* was rendered as *gentes* (singular *gens*) or *gentiles* (an adjectival form of *gens*). See "Gentile," *Encyclopedia Britannica*, accessed June 28, 2025, https://www.britannica.com/topic/Gentile.
334. Santos, "Gente da nação," 64–67.
335. Bender, *Angola*, 11.
336. Marcos Chor Maio and C. E. Calaca, "New Christians and Jews in Brazil: Migrations and Antisemitism," *Shofar: An Interdisciplinary Journal of Jewish Studies* 19, no. 3 (2001): 73–74.
337. Santos, "Gente da nação," 67.
338. Charles Boxer, *A igreja e a expansão ibérica 1440–1770* (Edições 70, 1981), quoted in Santos, "Gente da nação," 65–66.
339. Santos, "Gente da nação," 24–25.
340. Maio and Calaca. "New Christians," 75.
341. Maio and Calaca. "New Christians," 75.
342. Santos, "Gente da nação," 67–68.
343. Maria Luiza Tucci Carneiro, *O preconceito racial no Brasil Colônia* (Brasiliense, 1983), 201.
344. Carneiro, *O preconceito*, 196–97.
345. Santos, "Gente da nação," 68.
346. Santos, "Gente da nação," 69.
347. An excerpt of a 1623 Dutch manuscript was translated by Andrea Mosterman. See Thornton and Mosterman, "A Re-interpretation," 235.
348. Thornton and Mosterman, "A Re-interpretation," 245–48.
349. Birmingham, *Portuguese Conquest*, 34.
350. Glasgow, *Nzinga*, 128.
351. Birmingham, *Trade and Conquest*, ix
352. Glasgow, *Nzinga*, 19.

8. ARUANDA

353. Glasgow, *Nzinga*, 15.
354. Birmingham, *Portuguese Conquest*, 36.
355. Edwards Adrian, *The Ovimbundu Under Two Sovereignties* (International African Institute; Oxford University Press, 1962).
356. Birmingham, "Speculations," 8.
357. Cavazzi, *Descrição*, 1:253.
358. Cavazzi, *Descrição*, 1:176.
359. Glasgow, *Nzinga*, 19.
360. Cavazzi, *Descrição*, 1:254–57.
361. Elikia M'bokolo, *África negra: história e civilizações* (EDUFBA, 2008), 1:185–205.
362. António de Oliveira de Cardonega, *História geral das guerras angolanas*, 2 vols. (Agência Geral do Ultramar, 1972), 1:27.
363. Thornton and Heywood, *Central Africans*, 68–98.
364. John Thornton, "The Art of War in Angola, 1575–1680," *Comparative Studies in Society and History* 30, no. 2 (1988): 360–78; and Cadornega, *História geral*, 1:616.
365. Nafafé, *Lourenço*, 148–51.
366. David Birmingham, *Trade and Conquest in Angola* (Clarendon Press, 1966), 14.
367. Thornton, *Africa and Africans*, 59.
368. Thornton, *Africa and Africans*, 60.
369. Glasgow, *Nzinga*, 27.
370. Glasgow, *Nzinga*, 27.
371. Birmingham, *Trade and Conquest*, 37.
372. Glasgow, *Nzinga*, 27–28.
373. Glasgow, *Nzinga*, 28; Lopes, *Bantos*, 110.
374. Glasgow, *Nzinga*, 35; Cavazzi, *Descrição*, 2:66.
375. John Henrik Clarke, "African Warrior Queens," *Black Women in Antiquity*, ed. Ivan Van Sertima, (Transaction Publishers, 1992), 132, quoted in Glasgow, *Nzinga*, 177.
376. Original: "Rosa Aluanda, qui tenda, tenda / Qui tenda, tenda / Qui tem tororo!" Registered by Cascudo at a Maracatu party in Recife in 1909; see Cascudo, *Made*, 175.
377. Assis Júnior, *Dicionário*, 241, 243.
378. Freitas, *O escravismo*, 31.
379. This group of mercenaries is often referred to as the Jagas. Friar Cavazzi recounts the invasion of the "flesh-eater Jagas," who assaulted Kongo in 1568, resulting in devastating plunder, devastation, and slaughter. Cavazzi, *Descrição*, 1:173. A footnote from Cavazzi's translator, Padre Leguzzano, clarifies that the Jagas were not a unified group or nation but rather a "sect" formed from individuals captured in war and assimilated; see Cavazzi, *Descrição*, 2:72. Joseph Miller traced the Mbangala's origins from the outskirts of the Luba Empire and their migration northward, where they shifted to raiding and plundering for sustenance; See Joseph Miller, *Way of Death: Merchant Capitalism and the Angolan Slave Trade, 1730–1830* (University of Wisconsin Press, 1988). Anne Hilton's interpretation is that rather than a distinct ethnic group, they were foreigners who integrated militarized microstates and formed alliances as needed; see Anne Hilton, "The Jaga Reconsidered," *Journal of African History* 22 no. 2, (1981): 191–202. John Thornton agreed that "jaga" describes a way of life rather than a specific ethnic group; see John Thornton, "A Resurrection for the Jaga," *Cahiers d'Études Africaines* 18, no. 69/70 (1978): 223–27.
380. Assis Júnior, *Dicionário*, 120.
381. *Kilombo* referred to joint military forces as well as to a place for the gathering of workers; see Assis Júnior, *Dicionário*, 127.
382. Mariana Bracks Fonseca, "Nzinga Mbandi e as guerras de resistência em Angola. Século XVII" (MA thesis, Universidade de São Paulo, 2012), 138–46.

383. Birmingham, *Portuguese Conquest*, 31. Glasgow, *Nzinga*, 94.
384. Glasgow, *Nzinga*, 94.
385. Cavazzi, *Descrição*, 2:73. Nzinga also used cockfights to make her decisions: one black, one white, and the winner would indicate whether she should enter a battle or not. Cavazzi, *Descrição*, 2:82.
386. Cavazzi, *Descrição*, 2:73. According to Cavazzi, each province had its particular protective spirit; see Cavazzi, *Descrição*, 1:216.
387. Cavazzi documents a range of specialized roles and titles within Central African society. Among these are the Quitombe, supreme chiefs and advisors responsible for ensuring good harvests, and the Quitomba, distinguished by their long hair braided with amulets, who lead processions carrying wooden "fetish" sculptures. Others notable figures include the Ngombo, who walk on their hands; the Mpindi, who control the weather, particularly thunder and rain; the Ntinu-a-maza, king of the waters, who stores his magical objects underwater and retrieves them using spells and a bucket; the Nequita, known for creating protective "Kongo walls"; the Nganga Atambola, reputed to resurrect the dead; and the Nganga-ia-zumbi, priests, healers, or doctors who diagnose the causes of diseases. See Cavazzi, *Descrição*, 1:92–102, 1:200–203; 2:73.
388. Cavazzi, *Descrição*, 1:186.
389. Buakasa Tulu Kia Mpansu, "Le discours de la 'kindoki' ou 'sorcellerie,'" *Cahiers des Religions Africaines* 6, no. 11 (1972): 29, quoted in Bockie, *Death*, 43, 47.
390. Bockie, *Death*, 47.
391. Bockie, *Death*, 66.
392. Bockie, *Death*, 71.
393. Claridge, *Wild Bush*, 147.
394. Claridge, *Wild Bush*, 204.
395. Bockie, *Death*, 67.
396. Milagres, *Dicionário*, 102.
397. Milagres, *Dicionário*, 100. Assis Júnior, *Dicionário*, 326.
398. Milagres, *Dicionário*, 100.
399. Milagres, *Dicionário*, 100.
400. Cavazzi, *Descrição*, 1:184–86
401. Cavazzi, *Descrição*, 2:182.
402. Glasgow, *Nzinga*, 37–38.
403. Cavazzi, *Descrição*, 1:191.
404. Cavazzi, *Descrição*, 1:191–92.
405. Freitas, *O escravismo*, 32.
406. Glasgow, *Nzinga*, 83.
407. Glasgow, *Nzinga*, 83.
408. Glasgow, *Nzinga*, 84.
409. Lopes, *Bantos*, 113.
410. Glasgow, *Nzinga*, 93.
411. Glasgow, *Nzinga*, 94.
412. Glasgow, *Nzinga*, 122.
413. Anne Hilton, *The Kingdom of Kongo* (Oxford University Press, 1985), 112.
414. Birmingham, *Portuguese Conquest*, 34.
415. Glasgow, *Nzinga*, 133.
416. Glasgow, *Nzinga*, 136.
417. Glasgow, *Nzinga*, 149.
418. Glasgow, *Nzinga*, 149.
419. Glasgow, *Nzinga*, 160.

420. Jean Cuvelier and O. Boone, *Koningin Nzinga van Matamba* (Bruges, 1957), 141, quoted in Glasgow, *Nzinga*, 161.
421. Glasgow, *Nzinga*, 158–59.
422. Glasgow, *Nzinga*, 164.
423. Glasgow, *Nzinga*, 172.
424. Cavazzi, *Descrição*, 2:126.
425. Glasgow, *Nzinga*, 161–62.
426. Glasgow, *Nzinga*, 173. "The crosses started appearing on all houses and were also raised in front of the armies going to war." Cavazzi, *Descrição*, 2:144.
427. Glasgow, *Nzinga*, 170.
428. Cavazzi, *Descrição*, 2:156–57.
429. Cavazzi, *Descrição*, 2, 2:153.
430. John Thornton, "Legitimacy and Political Power: Queen Njinga, 1624–1663," *Journal of African History* 32, no. 1 (1991): 33.
431. Alberto Alesina, W. Easterly, and J. Matuszeski, "Artificial States," *Journal of the European Economic Association* 9, no. 2 (2011): 246. For ethnic borders, see George Peter Murdock's classic *Africa: Its Peoples and Their Culture History* (McGraw-Hill, 1959).
432. "Land acknowledgment is a traditional custom that dates back centuries in many Native nations and communities. Today, land acknowledgments are used by Native Peoples and non-Natives to recognize Indigenous Peoples who are the original stewards of the lands on which we now live." Smithsonian National Museum of the American Indian, "Honoring Original Indigenous Inhabitants: Land Acknowledgment," https://americanindian.si.edu/nk360/informational/land-acknowledgment.
433. Ieuan Griffiths, "The Scramble for Africa: Inherited Political Boundaries," *Geographical Journal* 152, no. 2 (1986): 206, https://doi.org/10.2307/634762.
434. Griffiths, "Scramble," 204.
435. "The Scramble for Africa: A History of Independence," *Al Jazeera*, September 5, 2010, https://www.aljazeera.com/features/2010/9/5/the-scramble-for-africa-a-history-of-independence.
436. "General Act of the Conference of Berlin Concerning the Congo," *The American Journal of International Law* 3, no. 1 (1909): 10.
437. "General Act," 25.
438. "General Act," 7–9.
439. According to Brazil's National System of Foreigners' Registration and Records (SINCRE), there is great diversity in Brazilian immigrants' countries of origin: more than 50 different nation-states. In this context, "Angola constitutes the main flow, with almost 13,500 registered immigrants during the period, representing 30 percent of the total registrations. Other significant countries include Cape Verde, Guinea-Bissau, Nigeria, Mozambique, Senegal, South Africa, Democratic Republic of the Congo, Morocco, and Egypt. It is worth noting the significant growth of countries that were scarcely represented in SINCRE in the year 2000, such as Libya, Benin, and Ivory Coast." See Rosana Baeninger, Natália Demétrio, and Luis Foiadelli, "Espaços das migrações transnacionais: perfil sociodemográfico de imigrantes da África para o Brasil no século XXI," in *Dossiê: migrantes africanos en América Latina: (in)movilidades y haciendo-lugar*, REMHU: *Revista Interdisciplinar da Mobilidade Humana* 27, no. 56 (May–August 2019): 41.
440. Carlos Serrano, "Ginga, a Rainha Quilombola de Matamba e Angola," *Revista USP: dossiê do Povo Negro*, no. 28 (1995–1996): 140.
441. According to historian Décio Feitas, Zumbi was born in 1655 in one of the villages of Palmares and was captured during an incursion in the same year. Entrusted to Portuguese priest Antônio de Melo, he was baptized as Francisco, received an education in Latin and Portuguese, and, at 15, escaped to Palmares. See Freitas, *O escravismo*, 30.

442. Marina de Mello e Souza, *Reis negros no Brasil escravista: história da festa de coroação de Rei Congo* (Editora UFMG, 2002), 329.
443. Moçambique chant, Rio Grande do Sul. Original: "Lá vem o Rei do Congo/ Com sua infantaria/ Coroa na cabeça/ E o rosário de Maria/(Coro) Ói, vamos nós s'imbora/ E não fica ninguém/ A Virgem do Rosário/ Vai com nóis também / (Mestre) Ó, minha Rainha Ginga/ Ói pisa de vaga/ Prás pedra miudinha/ Não sai do seu lugá." See Iosvaldyr Bittencourt Júnior, "Maçambique de Osório: entre a devoção e o espetáculo: não se cala na batida do tambor e da maçaquaia" (PhD diss., Universidade Federal do Rio Grande do Sul, 2006), 115, https://lume.ufrgs.br/handle/10183/12758.
444. Mariana Bracks Fonseca, *Nzinga Mbandi e as guerras de resistência em Angola, século XVII* (Mazza Edições, 2015), 305.
445. Mello e Souza, *Reis negros*, 315.
446. Fonseca, *Nzinga Mbandi*, 304.
447. Joel Rufino, "O mistério de Zumbi," *Comunicações do ISER* 5, no. 21 (1986): 67–69.
448. Rufino, "O mistério," 67.
449. Rufino, "O mistério," 67.
450. Rufino, "O mistério," 67.
451. Kamau Brathwaite, *Wars of Respect: Nanny, Sam Sharpe and the Struggle for People's Liberation* (Agency for Public Information for the National Heritage Week Committee, 1977), 7.
452. Roger Bastide, "The Other Quilombos," in *Maroon Societies: Rebel Slave Communities in the Americas*, ed. Richard Price (The John Hopkins University Press, 1979), 191.
453. Clóvis Moura, *Rebeliões da senzala: quilombos, insurreições*, guerrilhas (Editora Conquista, 1972), 87. See also Abdias Nascimento, ed., *O negro revoltado* (Nova Fronteira, 1982), 155, 163.
454. For some it means "small Angola," from *ia rianga* or *ia dianga*, meaning "first." See Agostinho da Silva Milagres, *Dicionário*, 21.
455. Décio Freitas, *Palmares: a guerra dos escravos* (Mercado Aberto, 1984), 65.
456. Kátia Mattoso, *Ser escravo no Brasil: séculos XVI–XIX*, (Brasiliense, 1982), 159. See also Moura, *Rebeliões*, 227.
457. Freitas, *Palmares*, 92.
458. Moura, *Rebeliões*, 181
459. Freitas, *Palmares*, 66–67, 94, 180.
460. Freitas, *Palmares*, 141. First published in exile in Uruguay as *Palmares: la guerrilla negra* (Nuestra América, 1971).
461. Freitas, *Palmares*, 157, 162–63.
462. Moura, *Rebeliões*, 28.
463. Nascimento, *O negro*, 160.
464. Nafafé, *Lourenço*, 245.
465. Nafafé, *Lourenço*, 244.
466. Nafafé, *Lourenço*, 244.
467. Nafafé, *Lourenço*, 245.
468. Nafafé, *Lourenço*, 244–45.
469. Rufino, "O mistério," 68–69.
470. Rufino, "O mistério," 68–69.
471. Bold added for emphasis and clarity. Kamau Brathwaite, Lecture at River City Writers' Series, The University of Memphis English Department, Memphis, Tennessee, 1995, https://www.youtube.com/watch?v=c1C3dDYdXik.
472. Carlos Hasenbalg and L. Gonzalez, *Lugar de negro* (Marco Zero: 1982), 58.
473. The Geledés Instituto da Mulher Negra (Black Women's Institute) was founded in 1988; see http://www.geledes.com.br. Other Black women's organizations established around the same time include Fala Preta! (1997) and Casa de Cultura da Mulher Negra (1990).

474. Sueli Carneiro, interview, *Revista Afirma*, March 11, 2002.
475. Carneiro, *Revista Afirma*.
476. Carneiro, *Revista Afirma*.
477. Carneiro, *Revista Afirma*.
478. Nascimento, *O negro*, 22.
479. Law no. 7668, of August 22, 1988, approved under the Presidency of José Sarney; see "L7668 Planalto," Legislação Federal Brasileira, https://legislacao.presidencia.gov.br/atos/?tipo=LEI&numero=7668&ano=1988&ato=868g3YU1UNBpWTe09.
480. Raquel Gerber and M. B. do Nascimento, *Ôrí*, Fundação do Cinema Brasileiro, 1989. Maria Beatriz do Nascimento was murdered at the age of 52. Prior to her untimely death, she was working on her thesis under the guidance of Professor Muniz Sodré at the Universidade Federal do Rio de Janeiro. On January 30, 1995, in the Botafogo neighborhood of Rio, Jorge Amorim Viana, known as "Danone," fatally shot her five times. The murderer was in an abusive relationship with a young woman who had sought help from Nascimento. In early 2000, after watching the documentary, I searched for Beatriz Nascimento, whom I hadn't known before. Eventually, I came across a record—a short article published the day after her murder titled "Professor May Have Been Murdered Due to Racism." No front page. No big headlines. See Paulo Gramado, "Professora pode ter sido morta por racismo." *Folha de São Paulo* (São Paulo), January 31, 1995.

In the last decades, the anthropologists Alex Ratts and Christen Smith, as well as Beatriz Nascimento's daughter, Bethânia Nascimento Gomes, have launched a series of publications providing access to and hemispheric contextualization for Nascimento's work. See Alex Ratts and Bethânia Nascimento Gomes, *Eu sou Atlântica: sobre a trajetória de vida de Beatriz Nascimento* (Instituto Kuanza: Imprensa Oficial do Estado de São Paulo, 2006); see also Alex Ratts and Bethânia Nascimento Gomes, *Todas (as) distâncias: poemas, aforismos e ensaios de Beatriz Nascimento* (Ogum's Toques Negros, 2015); Christen A. Smith, Bethânia N. F. Gomes, and Archie Davies, eds., *The Dialectic Is in the Sea: The Black Radical Thought of Beatriz Nascimento* (Princeton University Press, 2023).
481. Gerber and Nascimento, *Ôrí*.
482. Gerber and Nascimento, *Ôrí*.
483. Gerber and Nascimento, *Ôrí*. Frevo groups are street Carnaval ensembles from Pernambuco. Frevo is believed to have first appeared in 1909. Frevo performers follow a main singer known as the "tirador de loas" (literally, "Loa puller"). Evolving from the Congadas, the central figure is the Queen, who is typically protected and may carry a doll, a *calunga*. Ranchos have a place in the genealogical tree of the "Escolas de Samba": Cordões groups evolved into Ranchos, which then developed into "Escolas de Samba." According to Cascudo, at the beginning of the twentieth century some Cordões developed into Ranchos. See Cascudo, *Dicionário*, 346, 472, 220; see also Cascudo, *Dicionário*, 662.
484. Gerber and Nascimento, *Ôrí*.
485. Abdias Nascimento, *O genocídio do negro brasileiro: processo de um racismo mascarado* (Paz e Terra, 1978), 40; *Quilombismo: documentos de uma militância pan-africanista* (Vozes, 1980), 255.
486. Nascimento, *Quilombismo*, 255.
487. "As a town council, civic cult, and electoral college for selecting a new king and dethroning a bad or unpopular one." National Human Rights Commission (NHRC), correspondence from a representative to the Research Directorate, quoted in Research Directorate, Immigration and Refugee Board of Canada, "Nigeria: Ogboni Society, Including Structure, Rituals, Ceremonies, and Current Status; Membership and the Consequences of Refusing to Join or Trying to Leave; Relationship with Police and Judicial Authorities (2017–April 2019)," https://www.ecoi.net/en/document/2021322.html.
488. Bold added for clarity. Africanist John Pemberton III (1928–2016) explains that "'Onile' (written without a subscript below the 'e' and having a high tonal value) is the term that is used by the Ogboni and is to be translated as 'Owner of the house,' the ile referring to the Ogboni cult house.... Ajuwon

and Abiodun thought that the 'e' in Onile should be spelled with a subscript and have a low tonal value, thus being translated as 'Owner of the land,' ... Abimbola noted that there were very few references to Onile in Ifa texts, and, based on the few passages he could recall, Onile may have masculine connotations, as for example in the Oyo Yoruba tradition that refers to the land being 'owned by the king.'" See John Pemberton III, *African Arts* 18, no. 2 (1985), 89, https://doi.org/10.2307/3336205.
489. Sodré, *O terreiro*, 138.
490. Antônio Joaquim de Macedo Soares, *Dicionário brasileiro da língua portuguesa* (Leuzinger, 1954).
491. José de Moraes e Silva's *Dicionário da língua portuguesa* (Lisbon, 1779) and Alfredo de Sarmento's *Os sertões da África* (Lisbon, 1889), quoted in Soares, *Dicionário*, 120–21.
492. Assis Júnior, *Dicionário*, 80, 222.
493. Assis Júnior, *Dicionário*, 30.
494. Assis Júnior, *Dicionário*, 30.
495. Jan Vansina, *How Societies are Born: Governance in West Central Africa Before 1600* (University of Virginia Press, 2004), 163–67.
496. In the entry for *caboclo*, under geography, Macedo Soares includes the meaning "overall, in all provinces"; see Soares, *Dicionário*, 120.
497. Assis Júnior adds that Káboco "was formerly the residence of the soba (chief) of this name"; see Assis Júnior, *Dicionário*, 80.
498. Pierre Verger, *Orixás: deuses iorubás na África e no Novo Mundo* (Corrupio, 1992), 134–36. See also Mason, *Black Gods*, 56–59.

9. ÌTÀN: ANCESTRAL GENEALOGIES: OSHALA CAME BEFORE US

1. Sandra T. Barnes and P. B. Amos, "Benin, Oyo, and Dahomey: Warfare, State Building, and the Sacralization of Iron in West African History," *Expedition* 25, no. 2 (1983): 5.
2. John K. Thornton, "Traditions, Documents, and the Ife-Benin Relationship," *History in Africa* 15 (1988): 351–62. doi.org/10.2307/3171867.
3. Thornton, "Traditions," 359.
4. Thornton, "Traditions," 356.
5. Jacob Egharevba, *A Short History of Benin*, (Ibadan University Press, 1968), 23, quoted in Daniel Omoruan and F. O. Uzzi, "God's Chisel in the Hands of the Carver: An Esoteric View of Joseph Alufa Igbinovia," *Scholars: Journal of Arts, Humanities and Social Sciences* 4, no. 1, (2022): 50, doi.org/10.3126/sjah.v4i1.43054.
6. Adapted translation from Pierre Fatumbi Verger, "Olofin-Odudua cria o mundo em lugar de Oxalá," *Lendas africanas dos orixás* (Corrupio, 1985), 83–87.
7. While Verger's version, refers to "*imalés*," meaning Muslims, I am using "*imole*" instead. As "*Imole*" or "*Irunmole*" are beings (some believe they were Orishas) who inhabited the earth in the primordial times of creation. Reginaldo Prandi, *Mitologia dos orixás* (Companhia das Letras, 2001), 566.
8. Adapted translation. Pierre Fatumbi Verger, *Lendas*, 83–87.
9. Ulli Beier, *Yoruba Myths* (Cambridge University Press, 1980), 64.
10. Beier, *Yoruba Myths*, 64.
11. Beier, *Yoruba Myths*, 64.
12. Beier, *Yoruba Myths*, 64.
13. Babatunde Aremu Agiri, "Early Oyo History Reconsidered," *History in Africa* 2 (1975): 1–16, https://doi.org/10.2307/3171463.

14. Agiri is basing himself on an *Oriki* praise poem of Oranyan and Oduduwa that states that "the palace of the Ooni of Ife is known as He Igbo (House of the Igbo)." This text is recorded by the Rev. (Chief) Samuel Ojo, better known as Ojo Bada of Saki (1846–1901).
15. See also Ulli Beier, "Before Oduduwa," *Odu: Journal of Yoruba and Related Studies* 3, (1956): 25–32.
16. Opesanmi Esan, "Correspondence," quoted in Beier, "Before Oduduwa," 26.
17. Agiri, "Early Oyo," 7.
18. Agiri, "Early Oyo," 7.
19. Agiri, "Early Oyo," 7.
20. John Mason and G. Edwards, *Black Gods: Orisa Studies in the New World* (Yoruba Theological Archministry, 1985), 33.
21. Beier, *Yoruba Myths*, 67.
22. Beier, *Yoruba Myths*, 67.
23. Ulli Beier, *The Origin of Life and Death: African Creation Myths* (Heinemann, 1966), 72.
24. Excerpt of one Okanran Odu in William Bascom, *Sixteen Cowries: Yoruba divination from Africa to the New World* (Indiana University Press, 1980), 289.
25. Margareth Menezes, oficial website, https://margarethmenezes.com.br/internacional-en.
26. Adapted translation from Verger, "Oxaguiã," *Lendas*, 65–66.
27. José Beniste, *As águas de Oxalá: àwon omi Ósàlá* (Bertrand Brasil, 2009), 238.
28. Afolabi Epega and P. Neimark, *The Sacred Ifa Oracle* (Harper Collins, 1995), 5.
29. Beier, *The Origin*, 50
30. Beniste, *As águas*, 238.
31. Beier, *Yoruba Myths*, 72.
32. Pierre Verger, *Orixás: deuses iorubas na África e no Novo Mundo* (Corrupio, 1992), 257.
33. Leo Frobenius, *Mythologie de l'Atlantide* (Payot, 1949) 173, quoted in Verger, *Notas sobre o culto aos orixás e voduns na Bahia de Todos os Santos, no Brasil, e na antiga Costa dos Escravos, na África* (EDUSP, 2000), 451.
34. Thomas Mákanjúolá Ilésanmí, "The Traditional Theologians and the Practice of Orisa Religion in Yorubaland," *Journal of Religion in Africa* 21 (3): 219.
35. Ilésanmí, "Traditional Theologians," 219.
36. Vivaldo da Costa Lima, *A família-de-santo nos Candomblés Jeje-Nagôs da Bahia: um estudo de relações intra-grupais* (Universidade Federal da Bahia, 1977), 21.
37. Edlaine de Campos Gomes, *A tradição dos orixás: valores civilizatórios afrocentrados* (IPEAFRO, 2019).
38. Raphael Rodrigues Vieira Filho, "Folguedos negros no carnaval de Salvador (1880–1930)," in *Ritmos em trânsito: sócio-antropologia da música baiana*, ed. Livio Sansone e Jocélio Teles dos Santos (Dynamis, 1997), 51.
39. Definitions given by Raul Lody, Yeda Pessoa de Castro, Olabiyi Yai, and P. Fryer. Raul Lody, *Afoxé* (Funarte/ Cadernos de Folclore 7, 1976), 31. Yeda Pessoa de Castro, *Os falares africanos na Bahia: um vocabulário afro-brasileiro* (Topbooks, 2005), 144. Antonio Risério, *Carnaval Ijexá* (Corrupio, 1981), 12. Peter Fryer, *Rhythms of Resistance: African Musical Heritage in Brazil* (Wesleyan University Press, 2000), 23.
40. Previous versions of this chapter have been published as: Isis Costa McElroy, "A Transdiasporic Paradigm: The *Afoxé* Filhos de Gandhy," *Afro-Hispanic Review* 29.1 (2010): 77–100; and "A Transdiasporic Paradigm: The *Afoxé* Filhos de Gandhy," in *Religion, Theater and Performance: Acts of Faith*, ed. Lance Gharavi (Routledge, 2012), 127–54.
41. The Filhos de Gandhy official website indicates that "Vavá Madeira suggested the name for the *bloco*, which was inspired by the life of the pacifist leader Mohandas Karamchand Gandhi. The letter 'i' was changed into 'y' to avoid possible retaliations for using of the name of an important leader on

42. the world stage. See "Como tudo começou," *Filhos de Gandhy*, https://www.facebook.com/groups/eusoufilhodeghandy.
42. Original lyrics: "Omolu, Ogum, Oxum, Oxumaré / Todo o pessoal / Manda descer pra ver / Filhos de Gandhi // Iansã, Iemanjá, chama Xangô, / Oxóssi também / Manda descer pra ver / Filhos de Gandhi // Mercador, Cavaleiro de Bagdá / Oh, Filho de Obá / Manda descer pra ver / Filhos de Gandhi // Senhor do Bonfim, faz um favor pra mim / Chama o pessoal / Manda descer pra ver / Filhos de Gandhi // Oh, meu Pai do céu, na terra é carnaval / Chama o pessoal / Manda descer pra ver / Filhos de Gandhi." See Carlos Rennó, ed., *Gilberto Gil: Todas as letras* (Companhia das Letras, 1996), 146. Gilberto Gil's song "Filhos de Gandhi" (1973) was recorded on Gil and Jorge Ben Jor's album *Gil Jorge Ogum Xangô* (1975).
43. Antonio Risério, *Uma história da cidade da Bahia* (Versal, 2004), 564.
44. Marco Gérard, T. R. Ramos, and A. Côrtes, "Um olhar musical sobre a canção "Filhos de Gandhy" a partir da performance de Gilberto Gil na USP, em 1973," *Música Popular em Revista* 7, no. 1 (2020): 3.
45. Gérard, "Um olhar," 8.
46. Gérard, "Um olhar," 10.
47. Gérard, "Um olhar," 8.
48. Gilberto Gil, "Filho de Gandhi (Ao vivo)" Track 23, *Gilberto Gil ao vivo na USP* (GeGe Produções Artísticas, 1973), YouTube, https://music.youtube.com/playlist?list=OLAK5uy_mUikGIGTkiKZ-3yjoFw_m7jxv2Oip112k. Permission to reprint transcribed and translated excerpts of Gilberto Gils's performance granted by GeGe Produções Artísticas and Sony Music Publishing.
49. Gérard, "Um olhar," 14.
50. Gil, "Filho de Gandhi (Ao vivo)."
51. Gérard, "Um olhar," 16.
52. While many attribute the revival of a group on the brink of extinction to Gil, documentation by Anísio Félix reveals that Camafeu de Oxóssi and radio broadcaster Gerson Macedo were pivotal in rejuvenating the group. Gil's recordings of "Filhos de Gandi" (1975) and "Patuscada de Gandhi" (1977) played a crucial role in bringing this cultural reference to a national audience, previously limited to Salvador and Rio de Janeiro where the Filhos de Gandhy originated in 1952, welcoming both men and women. The melody of "Patuscada," originally titled "Papai Ojô," was composed by Carequinha (Arivaldo Pereira). Concurrently, Caetano Veloso aided in the resurgence of the "trios elétricos." Both Afoxé Filhos de Gandhy and Dodô and Osmar's "trio elétrico" were established in 1949, becoming significant hallmarks of the Bahian Carnaval, which saw a revival in the 1970s, as noted by Antonio Risério in *Uma história da cidade da Bahia*, 564.
53. Paulo Cesar Miguez de Oliveira, "A organização da cultura na cidade da Bahia" (PhD diss., Universidade Federal da Bahia, 2002), 303.
54. For Afrocentric or "root tourism," see Patrícia de Santana Pinho, *Reinvenções da África na Bahia* (Annablume, 2004). For the globalization and the commercialization of the Bahian Carnaval, see Christopher Dunn and Charles Perrone, eds. *Brazilian Popular Music and Globalization* (University of Florida Press, 2001).
55. Pravina Shukla, "Afro-Brazilian Avatāras: Gandhi's Sons Samba in South America," *Indian Folklore Journal* 1 (2001), 39.
56. Marc Hertzman, "Making Their Own Mahatma: Salvador's Filhos de Gandhy and the Local History of a Global Phenomenon," in *Race and Transnationalism in the Americas*, ed. David Sheinin and B. Bryce, (University of Pittsburgh Press, 2021), 140–58; McElroy, "A Transdiasporic" (2012).
57. Hertzman, "Making Their Own," 141.
58. "Isis Costa McElroy provides a more thoughtful consideration, even while confessing 'enchantment' with the group's 'certain incongruent metaphors' and symbolism." Hertzman, "Making Their Own," 141.
59. McElroy, "A Transdiaporic" (2012), 127.

60. Ana Maria Gonçalves, *Um defeito de cor* (Record, 2006). For Shukla's updated and more comprehensive analysis of the Gandhys, see Pravina Shukla, *Costume: Performing Identities through Dress* (Indiana University Press, 2015), especially the chapter "Festive Spirit: Carnival Costume in Brazil."
61. Term coined by Antonio Risério. See *Risério, uma história*, 562.
62. Muniz Sodré, *Samba, o dono do corpo* (Mauad, 1998), 36.
63. Nina Rodrigues, *Os africanos no Brasil* (Editora Universidade de Brasília, 2004), 208.
64. Rodrigues, *Os africanos*, 208.
65. Kim Butler, *Freedoms Given, Freedoms Won: Afro-Brazilians in Post-Abolition São Paulo and Salvador* (Rutgers University Press, 1998).
66. Rodrigues, *Os africanos*, 208.
67. Risério, *Uma história*, 563.
68. Fryer, *Rhythms*, 23.
69. "*Escolas-de-samba*: Literally, samba schools. The dozen or so large organizations in Rio and other parts of Brazil that compete with huge dancing parades. This is the model of carnival exported to the world and is certainly its most extravagant manifestation." Piers Armstrong. "The Carnaval of Bahia: 'From the Inside Looking Out'." BrazilMax, https://www.brazilmax.com accessed July 16, 2025; site inactive on July 16, 2025.
70. Lody, *Afoxé*, 13–14.
71. Lody, *Afoxé*, 10
72. Anísio Félix, *Filhos de Gandhi: a história de um afoxé* (Gráfica Central Ltda, 1987), 45.
73. *Babalotim*: "A large bottle was brought by the *Obá* as a symbol of his kingdom and worshipped by his vassals" Zeca Ligiéro, "Performances processionais afro-brasileiras," *O Percevejo* 12 (2003): 93. Félix, *Filhos*, 55
74. Risério, *Carnaval*, 52.
75. Félix, *Filhos*.
76. Edison Carneiro, *Folguedos tradicionais* (FUNART/INF, 1982), 52.
77. Lody, *Afoxé*, 6.
78. Lody, *Afoxé*, 6
79. Risério, *Carnaval*, 11–12.
80. Risério, *Uma história*, 563
81. Renato da Silveira, "Jeje-nagô, iorubá-tapá, aon-efan, ijexá: processo de constituição do candomblé da Barroquinha (1764–1851)," *Revista Cultura* 6 (2000): 80.
82. Agnaldo Silva, "Filhos de Gandhi: Entrevista por Emerson Nunes," *I Bahia: portal da Rede Bahia*, November 1, 2007.
83. Carole Boyce Davies, "Re-presenting Black Female Identity in Brazil: Filhas d'Oxum in Bahia Carnival," *Ijele: Art eJournal of the African World* 2.1 (2001): n/p. Africa Resource Center, November 1, 2007.
84. Davies, "Re-presenting."
85. J. Lorand Matory, *Black Atlantic Religion: Tradition, Transnationalism, and Matriarchy in the Afro-Brazilian Candomblé* (Princeton UP, 2005).
86. Ruth Landes, "Cult Matriarchate and Male Homosexuality," *Journal of Abnormal and Social Psychology* 35 (1940): 389.
87. Landes, "Cult Matriarchate," 390.
88. Landes, "Cult Matriarchate," 390.
89. J. Lorand Matory, *Black*,199.
90. Olga G. Cacciatore, *Dicionário de cultos afro-brasileiros* (Forense Universitária, 1988), 109.
91. Patrícia Birman, *Fazer estilo criando gêneros: possessão e diferença de gênero em terreiros de Umbanda e Candomblé no Rio de Janeiro* EdUERJ, 1995), 188–89.
92. Matory, *Black*, 212.

93. Félix, *Filhos*, 57
94. Shukla, "Afro-Brazilian," 40–41.
95. "In the 1930s, the era of the resurgence of the Afoxés, when the Filhos de Gandhy paraded for the first time in the streets, they were attacked by the police, who charged that the group consisted entirely of Blacks, many of whom were trade unionists." Pinho, *Reinvenções*, 125.
    "The police attacked the Filhos de Gandhy the first year they came out on the streets on account of the group's consisting mostly of Blacks, workers, and active trade unionists, and also because of their manner of dancing and singing, which upset all of Bahian society, who found the style too African, too Black. It disturbed people and was a political affirmation of Candomblé, Ijexá, and of the Blacks." Marco Aurélio Luz, *Identidade negra e educação* (Ianamá, 1989), 34.
96. Anamaria Morales, "O afoxé Filhos de Gandhy pede paz," in *Escravidão e invenção da liberdade*, ed. João José Reis (Brasiliense, 1988), 269.
97. Félix, *Filhos*, 41.
98. Félix, *Filhos*, 51.
99. Félix, *Filhos*, 13.
100. Félix, *Filhos*, 17.
101. Félix, *Filhos*, 62.
102. Félix, *Filhos*, 22.
103. *Gunga Din*, Dir. George Stevens, RKO, 1939.
104. The character Gunga Din is inspired by the poem by Rudyard Kipling. The film is about three British soldiers who, with the help from Gunga Din, a subservient Indian, overcome a rebellion that threatens British control of India. Gunga Din is a personification of a non-threatening presence within colonial dynamics. He is depicted as a weak childlike figure overly eager to please the British. In the filmic narrative, there is no way he "can be taken seriously, be treated as an equal of the heroes, or be in control of his destiny. He is, in every way, an Indian child in a world of British adults." David Birch, T. Schirato, and S. Srivastava, *Asia: Cultural Politics in the Global Age* (Palgrave, 2001), 6–7.
105. Verger, *Lendas*, 14.
106. Mason, *Black Gods*, 17–19.
107. In Rudyard Kipling's (1865–1936) poem "Gunga Din" that inspired the movie, Gunga Din is a water bearer serving the British Army at the end of the nineteenth century. He is beaten and looked down upon by the officers. ("You limping lump o' brick-dust, Gunga Din! / You squidgy-nosed old idol, Gunga Din // I'll *marrow* you this minute, / If you don't fill up my helmet, Gunga Din!") When he brings water to the soldier-narrator of the poem (Thomas Atkins), he is shot: "But of all the drinks I've drunk, / I'm gratefullest to one from Gunga Din." Rudyard Kipling, *Barrack-Room Ballads* (Heinemann, 1892), 30.
108. Félix, *Filhos*, 57.
109. Félix, *Filhos*, 32.
110. Félix, *Filhos*, 41.
111. Milton Araújo Moura points out a possible ambivalence in this aesthetic interpretation. According to Moura, the Carnaval revelers "were, however, aware of the political difficulties related to the militancy of the Left; an icon such as Gandhi was the antithesis of the Communist stigma. Although their outfits recalled those used by Gandhi, they were also similar to those used by some soldiers loyal to the British crown. The appearance of the revelers associated them with the world of Gandhi without making the distinction as to whether they were specifically those of the pacifist leader or those of the loyalist troops." Milton Araújo Moura, "World of Fantasy, Fantasy of the World: Geographic Space and Representation of Identity in the Carnival of Salvador, Bahia," in *Brazilian Popular*, Dunn and Perrone, 165.
112. Décio Freitas, *A revolução dos Malês: insurreições escravas* (Editora Movimento, 1985), 78.
113. Risério, *Uma história*, 335.

114. Risério, *Uma história*, 336.
115. According to Risério, "The success of the Afro-*bloco* Malê Debalê, together with the popular revalorization of the Islamic revolts, has created a type of myth around the Malês"; Nei Lopes, *Bantos, Malês e identidade negra* (Forense Universitária, 1988), 69. Nei Lopes states that Malê Islamism was a significant and effective factor in fostering unity among enslaved Africans in Brazil, helping them strengthen their bonds and unite. Through this movement, "all individuals, regardless of their differences, were unified under a single banner and identity: the Islamic nation." Lopes, *Bantos*, 58.
116. Castro, *Falares*, 235. Cacciatore, *Dicionário*, 126. "Lobo and Antônio Nássara, "Alá-lá-ô," Carnaval *marchinha* song, 1941. Author's translation of the original Portuguese lyrics: "It has arrived, our caravan has arrived / We come from the desert / Without bread, without banana / The sun was unbearable / It burned our faces / It made us sweat / We come from Egypt / And many times we had to pray / Allah, Allah, Allah, my good Allah / Send water for Ioiô (masta) / Send water for Iaiá (missy) / Allah, my good Allah." Full Portuguese text at Letra Mus, *Marchinhas de Carnaval*, accessed June 16, 2025, https://www.letras.mus.br/marchinhas-de-carnaval/497936/.
117. Castro, *Falares*, 135.
118. Shukla, "Afro-Brazilian," 39–40.
119. Raul Lody, *Cabelos de axé: Identidade e resistência* (Ed. Senac Nacional, 2004), 79.
120. Lody, *Cabelos*, 79.
121. Lody, *Cabelos*, 79.
122. "*Seli*: A woolen cord worn by Guru Nanak around his turban. It was worn as a symbol of living in the world but not in worldly matters. It was passed on to each successive guru up to Guru Hargobind who chose to wear the symbol of two swords of *meri* and *peri* instead." Sandeep Brar, "Glossary of Religious Terms," *Sikhism, Religion of the Sikh People*, accessed October 23, 2019, https://sikhs.org/glossary.htm.
123. Bhai Surinder Singh Ji and B. T. S. Ji, "El turbante de los sikhs," *Red Sikh Hispana*, n.d., http://www.redsikh.com.
124. Shukla, *Costume*, 269.
125. Shukla, *Costume*, 88.
126. Araújo Moura, "World of Fantasy," 173.
127. Shukla, *Costume*, 27.
128. Shukla, *Costume*, 27.
129. Shukla, *Costume*, 40.
130. Shukla, *Costume*, 256.
131. Shukla, "Afro-Brazilian," 42.
132. Félix, *Filhos*.
133. Anamaria Morales, "O afoxé Filhos de Gandhy pede paz," 274; João José Reis, ed., *Escravidão e invenção da liberdade* (Brasiliense, 1988).
134. Morales, "O afoxé," 268.
135. "Indian elements are representations of the representations of India made by outsiders . . . In Bahia, as in many parts of the world, images and caricatures of India created by the mass media become associated with symbols of deep spirituality and emotionality." Morales, "O afoxé," 42–43.
136. Oliveira, "A organização," 278.
137. Risério, *Carnaval*, 67.
138. *Filhos de Gandhy*, Dir. Lula Buarque de Hollanda, Latin American Video Archives, 2000.
139. Félix, *Filhos*, 31.
140. Moa do Catendê, "A política afoxesista," *Estudos Afro-Asiáticos* 8–9 (1983): 252.
141. Piers Armstrong, "Moralizing Dionysius and Lubricating Apollo: A Semantic Topography of Subject Construction in Afro-Bahian Carnival," *Luso-Brazilian Review* 38 (2001): 38–45.
142. Shukla, *Costume*, 67.

9. ÌTÀN

143. Basil Davidson, *The African Slave Trade Pre-colonial History 1450–1850* (Little, Brown & Company, 1961), 210–11.
144. Davidson, *The African*, 227.
145. Davidson, *The African*, 208.
146. Joseph Inikori and S. Engerman, *The Atlantic Slave Trade: Effects on Economies, Societies and Peoples in Africa, the Americas, and Europe* (Duke University Press, 1992), 2.
147. Alan Ryder, "The Re-Establishment of Portuguese Factories on the Costa da Mina to the Mid-Eighteenth Century," *Journal of the Historical Society of Nigeria* 1, no. 3 (1958): 157–83.
148. Ana Lucia Araujo, "Forgetting and Remembering the Atlantic Slave Trade: The Legacy of Brazilian Slave Merchant Francisco Felix de Souza," in *Crossing Memories: Slavery and African Diaspora*, ed. Ana Lucia Araujo, M. Candido, and P. Lovejoy (Africa World Press, 2011), 82.
148. Pierre Verger, *Trade Relations Between the Bight of Benin and Bahia from the Seventeenth to Nineteenth Century* (Ibadan University Press, 1976), 53–55.
150. Robin Law, "The Evolution of the Brazilian Community in Ouidah" *Slavery and Abolition* 22, no. 1 (2001): 23.
151. Verger, *Trade Relations*, 209, 257.
152. Verger, *Trade Relations*, 261–62.
153. Verger, *Trade Relations*, 406.
154. Verger, *Trade Relations*, 109–11.
155. Robin Law, *Ouidah: The Social History of a West African Slaving Port, 1727–1892* (The Ohio University Press, 2005).
156. Law, *Ouidah*.
157. M. J., Herskovits, *Dahomey: An Ancient West African Kingdom*, 2 vols. (J. J. Augustin, 1938), 1:3. Adegbulu Akinjogbin, "Hard and Soft Power Politics in Oyo-Dahomey Diplomatic Relations 1708–1791," *International Journal of Law, Political Science, and Administration* 1, no. 2 (2014): 34.
158. Archibald Dalzel, *The History of Dahomey, and Inland Kingdom of Africa: Compiled from Authentic Memoirs, with an Introduction and Notes* (Spilsbury and Son, 1793), quoted in Stanley Diamond, "Dahomey: The Development of a Proto-State" *Dialectical Anthropology 2* (1996): 130, https://doi.org/10.1007/BF00244520.
159. J. Alfred Skertchly, *Dahomey as It Is: Being a Narrative of Eight Months' Residence in That Country* (Chapman and Hall, 1874), 86–87.
160. Skertchly, *Dahomey*, 86–87
161. Suzanne Blier, "Razing the Roof: The Imperative of Building Destruction in Danhomè," 165, *Structure and Meaning in Human Settlements*," ed. T. Atkin and J. Rykwert, (University of Pennsylvania Press, 2005).
162. Cameron Monroe, "In the Belly of Dan: Space, History, and Power in Precolonial Dahomey," *Current Anthropology* 52, no. 6 (2011): 769.
163. Blier, "Razing," 165.
164. Igor Kopytoff, "The Internal African Frontier: The Making of African Political Culture," in *The African Frontier: The Reproduction of Traditional African Societies* (Indiana University Press, 1987).
165. Paul Mercier, "The Fon of Dahomey," in *African Worlds: Studies in Cosmological Ideas and Social Values of African Peoples*, ed. Daryll Forde (Oxford University Press, 1968), 48–49.
166. Leslie Desmangles, *The Faces of the Gods: Vodou and Roman Catholicism in Haiti* (University of North Carolina Press: 1992), 197.
167. Emmanuel Casséus Paul, *Panorama du folklore haïtien* (PortImprimerie de l'Etat, 1962), 271.
168. Jérôme C. Alladayê, "Cana, the Holy City of Danxomè," 1993, quoted in Usman Mama, "Cana, Benin, an Important piece of Black History," January 12, 2017, *The African Magazine*, https://myafricanmagazine.com.
169. Diamond, "Dahomey," 133.

170. Diamond, "Dahomey," 128.
171. Diamond, "Dahomey," 128.
172. Akinjogbin, "Hard," 33.
173. Diamond, "Dahomey," 132.
174. Diamond, "Dahomey," 132.
175. Adegbulu Akinjogbin, "Agaja and the Conquest of the Coastal Aja States, 1724–1730." *Journal of the Historical Society of Nigeria* 2, no. 4 (1963): 545.
176. Akinjogbin, "Agaja," 545.
177. Akinjogbin, "Hard," 37.
178. Akinjogbin, "Hard," 38.
179. Adegbulu Akinjogbin, *Dahomey and its Neighbours 1708–1818* (Cambridge University Press, 1967), 72.
180. Akinjogbin, "Hard," 40.
181. Akinjogbin, "Hard," 40.
182. Akinjogbin, "Agaja," 545–46.
183. Diamond, "Dahomey," 144.
184. Akinjogbin, "Hard," 44.
185. Akinjogbin, "Hard," 45.
186. Akinjogbin, "Hard," 46.
187. Verger, *Os libertos*, 71.
188. Akinjogbin, "Hard," 49.
189. Cascudo, *Dicionário*, 433.
190. Pierre Fatumbi Verger, *Os libertos: sete caminhos de liberdade de escravos na Bahia no século XIX* (Corrupio, 1992) 13–15.
191. Davidson, *The African*, 247.
192. The Fa is the Fon Ifa. As Ruth Finnegan notes, "similar or identical systems are found among the Fon of Dahomey and Ewe of Togo as well as some other Nigerian peoples." See Ruth Finnegan, *Oral Literature in Africa* (Oxford University Press, 1970), 191.
193. Davidson, *The African*, 242.
194. Verger, *Os libertos*, 13–15.
195. Verger, *Os libertos*, 9–12.
196. Alberto da Costa e Silva, *Francisco Félix de Souza, mercador de escravos* (Nova Fronteira, 2004), 12. Robin Law, "A carreira de Francisco Félix de Souza na África Ocidental (1800–1849)," *Topoi* 2, no. 2 (2001): 13–14.
197. Law, *Ouidah*.
198. Ana Lucia Araujo, "Forgetting," 79.
199. Luís Henrique Dias Tavares, *Comércio proibido de escravos* (Ática; CNPq, 1988), 59.
200. Tavares, *Comércio*, 59–61.
201. Araujo, "Forgetting," 88.
202. Verger, *Os libertos*, 69.
203. João José Reis, *Rebelião escrava no Brasil: a história do levante dos malês em 1835* (Companhia das Letras, 2003), 111.
204. Reis, *Rebelião*, 111–12.
205. Reis, *Rebelião*, 138.
206. Reis, *Rebelião*, 114.
207. Freitas, *A Revolução*, 35.
208. Freitas, *A Revolução*, 37.
209. Freitas, *A Revolução*, 37.
210. Freitas, *A Revolução*, 37–38.
211. Freitas, *A Revolução*, 42.

212. Reis, *Rebelião*, 145.
213. Reis, *Rebelião*, 145, 147.
214. Reis, *Rebelião*, 192.
215. Lopes, *Bantos*, 68.
216. Lopes, *Bantos*, 68.
217. Quoted in Lopes, *Bantos*, 69.
218. Pierre Verger reproduces this decree in its entirety in Verger, *Os libertos*, 137.
219. In addition to Porto Novo and Ouidah (or Ajudá), other Brazilian-African communities thrived along the shores of Nigeria, Togo, Benin, and Ghana. These communities can be found in the cities of Lagos, Lomé, Aguê, and Accra. Of interest is Renato Barbieri's controversial documentary, *Atlântico Negro: na rota dos orixás*, with research and script by Victor Leonardi, (São Paulo, Instituto Itaú Cultural Videografia, 1980). A vast bibliography on the subject includes Pierre Verger's *Os libertos*, Antonio Olinto's novel *A casa da água* (1969; Editorial Nórdica, 1988), Mariano Carneiro da Cunha's *Negros estrangeiros: Os escravos libertos e sua volta à África* (Brasiliense, 1985), Alberto da Costa e Silva's *Um rio chamado Atlântico: A África no Brasil e o Brasil na África* (Nova Fronteira, 2003), and various publications by Ana Lucia Araujo, as well as Robin Law.
220. Barbieri, *Atlântico negro*.
221. Araujo, "Forgetting," 84–85.
222. Araujo, "Forgetting," 85.
223. Araujo, "Forgetting," 86.
224. Araujo, "Forgetting," 80. In 1991, after more than twenty years of military dictatorship, Nicéphore Soglo was elected president of Benin.
225. Araujo, "Forgetting," 95.
226. Kevin Sieff, "African Country Still Slave to History: Benin Struggles to Resolve Legacies of Complicity in Trade," *The Washington Post*, January 29, 2018, https://www.washingtonpost.com/world/africa/an-african-country-reckons-with-its-history-of-selling-slaves/2018/01/29/5234f5aa-ff9a-11e7-86b9-8908743c79dd_story.html.
227. Kevin Sieff, "African Country."
228. Araujo, "Forgetting," 97.
229. Ana Lucia Araujo, quoted in Kevin Sieff, "African Country."
230. Olabiyi Yai, quoted in Kevin Sieff, "African Country."
231. Araujo, "Forgetting," 81.
232. Law, *Ouidah*, 168.
233. Araujo, "Forgetting," 90, 95–96.
234. Araujo, "Forgetting," 91.
235. Law, *Ouidah*, 177.
236. Araujo, "Forgetting," 97.
237. Milton Guran, *Agudás: os "brasileiros" do Benim* (Nova Fronteira, 1999), 203–04.
238. Araujo, "Forgetting," 94.
239. Edna G. Bay, "On the Trail of the Bush King: A Dahomean Lesson in the Use of Evidence." *History in Africa* 6 (1979), 9. Araujo, "Forgetting," 92.
240. Sieff, "African Country."
241. Araujo, "Forgetting," 94.
242. The De Souza Family Collective, https://chachaix.com.
243. Kevin Sieff, "African Country."
244. Kevin Sieff, "African Country."
245. Kevin Sieff, "African Country."
246. Edna Bay, "Protection, Political Exile, and the Atlantic Slave-Trade: History and Collective Memory in Dahomey," in *Rethinking the African Diaspora: The Making of a Black Atlantic World in the Bight*

of Benin and Brazil, Routledge Studies in Slave and Post-slave Societies and Cultures, ed. Edna Bay and Kristin Mann (Routledge, 2013), 53.
247. Bay, "Protection," 52–53.
248. Herskovits, Dahomey, 2:63.
249. Bay, "Protection," 54.
250. Quoted in Bay, "Protection," 55–56. Herskovits, Dahomey, 2:36.
251. Herskovits, Dahomey, 36.
252. Bay, "Protection," 56, 59.
253. Bay, "Protection," 56.
254. Vicente F. Pires, Viagem de África em o reino de Dahomé, ed. Clado Ribeiro de Lessa (Companhia Editora Nacional, 1957), 85, quoted in Bay, "Protection," 55.
255. Edna Bay, Wives of the Leopard: Gender, Politics, and Culture in the Kingdom of Dahomey (University of Virginia Press, 1998) 81–91.
256. Paul Hazoumé, Le pacte de sang au Dahomey (Institut d'Ethnologie, 1956), 31–32
257. Bay, "Protection," 56.
258. Édouard Dunglas, "Contribution à l'histoire du Moyen Dahome, de Kétou et de Ouidah," Etudes Dahoméennes 20, no. 19 (1957): 63–64; Herskovits, Dahomey, 2.64. Herskovits notes that Agontimé spent twenty-four years in the Americas and returned approximately eighteen years before Gezò's death in 1858. This timeline suggests that her period of exile lasted around forty-three years. Dunglas, Contribution, 35.
259. "Agossi yovo gboje agontime." Bay, "Protection," 57–58.
260. Arthur Ramos, Preface, A Casa das Minas: contribuição ao estudo das sobrevivências do culto dos voduns, do panteão daomeano, no Estado do Maranhão, Brasil, by Manuel Nunes Pereira (Vozes, 1979), 12.
261. Pereira, A Casa das Minas.
262. Pierre Verger, "Uma rainha africana mãe de santo em São Luís," Revista USP (June-July-August 1990): 151–58.
263. Verger, Os libertos, 66–77. Subsequent research has called into question Verger's findings.
264. M. J. Herskovits, Dahomey, 1:14.
265. Octavio da Costa Eduardo, The Negro in Northern Brazil: A Study in Acculturation (University of Washington Press, 1966), 77.
266. Luis Nicolau Parés, "The Jeje in the Tambor de Mina of Maranhão and in the Candomblé of Bahia," in Rethinking the African Diaspora: The Making of a Black Atlantic World in the Bight of Benin and Brazil, ed. Edna Bay and Kristin Mann (Routledge, 2013), 103.
267. Parés, "The Jeje," 104.
268. Verger, "Uma rainha," 155.
269. Barbieri, Atlântico negro.
270. Barbieri, Atlântico negro.
271. José Beniste, Dicionário yorubá-português (Bertrand Brasil, 2019), 539.
272. Lisa Earl Castillo and Luis Nicolau Parés, "Marcelina da Silva: A Nineteenth-Century Candomblé Priestess in Brazil." Slavery & Abolition 31, no. 1 (March 2009): 1–27.
273. Interview with Mestre Didi, in Haroldo Costa, Fala crioulo: o que é ser negro no Brasil (Record, 1982), 256–60.
274. Didi, in Costa, Fala, 256–60.
275. Didi, in Costa, Fala, 256–60.
276. Vivaldo da Costa Lima, "Ainda sobre a nação de queto," in Faraimará, o caçador traz alegria: Mãe Stella, 60 anos de iniciação, ed. Cléo Martins and Raul Lody (Pallas, 1999), 69.
277. Castillo and Parés, "Marcelina," 2.
278. Castillo and Parés, "Marcelina," 18.
279. Castillo and Parés, "Marcelina," 6.

280. Castillo and Parés, "Marcelina," 3.
281. Maria Inês Cortes de Oliveira, *Os libertos: Seu mundo e os outros* (Corrupio, 1988), 8, 41.
282. Castillo and Parés, "Marcelina," 3.
283. Verger, *Orixás*, 28–29; *Os libertos*, 89; Lima, "Ainda sobre," 77; Castillo and Parés, "Marcelina," 1.
284. Reis, *Rebelião*, 460, 466–67.
285. Castillo and Parés, "Marcelina," 7.
286. Castillo and Parés, "Marcelina," 18.
287. Castillo and Parés, "Marcelina," 5.
288. Castillo and Parés, "Marcelina," 5, 7.
289. Reis, *Rebelião*, 466.
290. Castillo and Parés, "Marcelina," 7.
291. Castillo and Parés, "Marcelina," 7. Reis, *Rebelião*, 464–66.
292. Renato da Silveira, *O Candomblé da Barroquinha: processo de constituição do primeiro terreiro baiano de keto* (Maianga, 2006), quoted in Castillo and Parés, "Marcelina," 7.
293. Castillo and Parés, "Marcelina," 7–8.
294. Castillo and Parés, "Marcelina," 14.
295. Oliveira, *Os libertos*, 43–44. Maria Inês Cortes de Oliveira, "Viver e morrer no meio dos seus: nações e comunidades africanas na Bahia do século XIX," *Revista USP*, no. 28 (1995–1996): 175–93.
296. Castillo and Parés, "Marcelina," 9.
297. Castillo and Parés, "Marcelina," 16.
298. Castillo and Parés, "Marcelina," 16. João do Rio, *As religiões no Rio* (Organização Simões, 1951), 20.
299. Castillo and Parés, "Marcelina," 16. Júlio Braga, *Na gamela do feitiço: repressão e resistência nos candomblés da Bahia* (Edufba, 1995).
300. Castillo and Parés, "Marcelina," 17–18.
301. Castillo and Parés, "Marcelina," 18. Matory, *Black Atlantic*.
302. Barbieri, *Atlântico negro*.
303. Interview with Emmanuel Karl-August, in Barbieri, *Atlântico negro*.
304. Inikori and Engerman, *The Atlantic*, 12.
305. Parés, "The Jeje," 93.
306. Ramos, preface Pereira, *A Casa das Minas*, 11.
307. João Reis explores how the Yoruba Orisha tradition has incorporated elements from other African spiritual systems, including Islam. He discusses the Ifa *itan* which recounts the origin of Ramadan. In this story, Nanã Buruku, the Orisha who presides over calm, murky, and enigmatic waters and is seen as the mother of all Muslims in Yoruba belief, falls ill. Her children, instructed to make offerings of cornmeal porridge to the Orishas, make offerings only to Nanã. By the end of thirty days, as Nanã's neared death, she commands her children to henceforth observe a thirty-day fast at the year's end. Reis highlights this syncretism, noting that the integration of Muslim elements into Orisha practice signifies not just a blending of traditions but an embrace of a faith increasingly prevalent among the Yoruba. See Reis, *Rebelião*, 153. Meanwhile, Margaret cites another example with the Odu "Otura Méjì," which predicts that a child born into the Yoruba culture will follow Islam. Margaret Thompson Drewal, "Embodied Practice/ Embodied History: Mastery of Metaphor in the Performances of Diviner Kolawole Ositola," in *Yoruba Artist: New Theoretical Perspectives on African Arts*, ed. Rowland Abiodun, Henry John Drewal, and John Pemberton (Smithsonian Institution Press, 1994), 189.
308. Risério, *Caymmi*, 177.
309. Influential works from this period include: Pinho, *Reinvenções da África*; Beatriz Góis Dantas, *Vovó nagô e papai branco: usos e abusos da África no Brasil* (Edições Graal, 1988); and Renato Ortiz, *A morte branca do feiticeiro negro: umbanda e sociedade Brasileira* (Brasiliense, 1991).

310. Influential works include: Júlio Braga, *Na gamela do feitico;* Marcos Antonio Lopez de niho, *Gaiaku Luiza* (Pallas, 2000); Fábio Batista Lima, *Os Candomblés da Bahia: Tradições e novas tradições* (UNEB, 2005); Gisèlle Cossard Binon, *Awô: o mistério dos orixás* (Pallas, 2007); Edmar Ferreira, *O poder dos Candomblés: perseguição e resistência no Recôncavo da Bahia* (EDUFBA, 2009); Luiz Claudio Nascimento, *Bitedô: Onde moram os nagôs: redes de sociabilidades africanas na formação do Candomblé jêje-nagô no Recôncavo baiano* (CEAP, 2011).
311. Roger Sansi and L. N. Parés. "The Multiple Agencies of Afro-Brazilian Religions." *Religion and Society* 3 (2012), 76–94.
312. Luis Nicolau Parés, *Joaquim de Almeida: a história do africano traficado que se tornou traficante de africanos* (Companhia das Letras: 2024); Pierre Verger, *Fluxo e refluxo do trafico de escravos entre o Golfo do Benin e a Bahia de Todos os Santos* (Corrupio, 1987); Manuela Carneiro da Cunha, *Negros estrangeiros;* Jerry Turner, "Les Bresiliens: The Impact of Former Brazilian Slaves Upon Dahomey" (PhD diss., Boston University, 1975).
313. Walter Hawthorne, *From Africa to Brazil: Culture, Identity, and an Atlantic Slave Trade* (Cambridge University Press: 2010); Robert Slenes "'Malungo, Ngoma vem!' África coberta e descoberta no Brasil," *Revista USP* 12 (1991/1992): 48–67; "A Árvore de Nsanda transplantada: cultos kongo de aflição e identidade escrava no Sudeste brasileiro (século XIX)," in *Trabalho livre, trabalho escravo: Brasil e Europa, séculos XVIII e XIX,* ed. Douglas Libby and Júnia Furtado (Annablume, 2006), 273–314; and *Na senzala uma flor: as esperanças e as recordações da família escrava—Brasil sudeste, século XIX* (Nova Fronteira, 1999); James Sweet, *Recreating Africa: Culture, Kinship, and Religion in the African-Portuguese World, 1441-1770* (University of North Carolina Pres, 2003); Elizabeth Kiddy, *Blacks of the Rosary: Memory and History in Minas Gerais, Brazil* (Penn State University Press, 2005); and Luis Nicolau Parés, *A formação do candomblé: história e ritual da nação jêje na Bahia* (Editora da Unicamp, 2007).
314. Nancy Naro, Roger Sansi, and David Treece, "The Atlantic, between Scylla and Charybdis," *Cultures of the Lusophone Black Atlantic* (Palgrave, 2007), 5.
315. Parés, "The Jeje," 95–96.
316. Parés, "The Jeje," 93.
317. Verger, *Fluxo,* 670
318. Verger, *Fluxo,* 14–15, 432.
319. J. L. Matory, "The Trans-Atlantic Nation: Reconsidering Nations and Transnationalism," Emory University, Atlanta, 17–18 April 1998), 13–14, quoted in Parés, "The Jeje," 95.
320. Pereira, *A Casa das Minas.* Parés, "The Jeje," 96–97.
321. Parés, "The Jeje," 99.
322. Parés, "The Jeje," 98–100.
323. Parés, "The Jeje," 101–02.
324. Leslie G. Desmangles, *The Faces,* 101.
325. Desmangles, *The Faces,* 101, 196.
326. Mercier, "The Fon," 210–21.
327. Mercier, "The Fon," 210–21. Desmangles, *The Faces,* 124.
328. Desmangles, *The Faces,* 187.
329. Mercier, "The Fon," 219–21.
330. Maya Deren, *The Divine Horsemen: The Voodoo Gods of Haiti* (Delta Publishing, 1972), 36.
331. Desmangles, *The Faces,* 104–05.
332. Mercier, "The Fon," 65–66.
333. Mercier, "The Fon," 219. Bay, "On the Trail," 6.
334. Desmangles, *The Faces,* 196.
335. Melville J. Herkovits, *Dahomean Narrative: A Cross-Cultural Analysis* (Northwestern University Press, 1958), 125.

336. Herkovits, *Dahomean*, 91.
337. Bay, "On the Trail," 6.
338. Mercier "The Fon," 219; Bay, "On the Trail," 6–7.
339. Mercier "The Fon," 107.
340. Diamond, "Dahomey," 146.
341. Herskovits, *Dahomey*, 1:316.
342. Diamond, "Dahomey," 147.
343. Diamond, "Dahomey," 182, 183–84.
344. Diamond, "Dahomey," 155–56.
345. Frederick Forbes, *Dahomey and the Dahomeans: Being the Journals of Two Missions to the King of Dahomey, and Residence at his Capital, in the Years 1840–1850*, 2 vols. (Longman, Brown, Green, and Longmans, 1851), 1:3, quoted in Diamond, "Dahomey," 193–95.
346. Mercier "The Fon," 233.
347. Bay, "On the Trail," 11.
348. Bay, "On the Trail," 11.
349. Bay, "On the Trail," 12.
350. Bay, "On the Trail," 2.
351. Bay, "On the Trail," 3.
352. Richard Burton, *A Mission to Gelele, King of Dahome: With Notices of the So-called "Amazons," the Grand Customs, the Yearly Customs, the Human Sacrifices, the Present State of the Slave Trade, and the Negro's Place in Nature* (C. W. Newbury, 1966), 268, quoted in Bay, "On the Trail," 3–4.
353. Skertchly, *Dahomey*, 271.
354. Bay, "On the Trail," 20.
355. Skertchly, *Dahomey*, 203, 208, quoted in Bay, "On the Trail," 10.
356. Skertchly, *Dahomey*, 272. For Bay, the name "Gaakpé," means "the week is sufficient." Bay, "On the Trail," 9.
357. Diamond, "Dahomey," 200.
358. Diamond, "Dahomey," 196–97.
359. Herskovits, *Dahomey*, 1.239.
360. Herskovits, *Dahomey*, 1.239.
361. Diamond, "Dahomey," 209–13.
362. Bay, "On the Trail," 12.
363. Bay, "On the Trail," 10–11.
364. Skertchly, *Dahomey*, 437.
365. Bay, "On the Trail," 13.
366. Ana Lucia Araujo, "Slavery, Royalty and Racism: Representations of Africa in Brazilian Carnaval," *Ethnologies* 31, no. 2, (2009): 140.
367. Araujo, "Slavery, Royalty," 143.
368. Armando Régis and Djalma Sabiá, *O navio negreiro* (G.R.E.S. Acadêmicos do Salgueiro, 1957) *Galeria do Samba*, https://galeriadosamba.com.br/escolas-de-samba/academicos-do-salgueiro/1957.
369. Araujo, "Slavery, Royalty," 143.
370. Araujo, "Slavery, Royalty," 148.
371. Araujo, "Slavery, Royalty," 144–63.
372. Cláudio Russo, J. Velloso, Gilson Dr, and Carlinhos do Detran, *Áfricas: do berço real à corte brasiliana* (G.R.E.S. Beija Flor de Nilópolis, 2007, https://www.beija-flor.com.br/2007.
373. Araujo, "Slavery, Royalty," 165–67.
374. Nei Lopes, *Xaxá de Ajudá e a rainha Mina do Maranhão* (Grêmio Recreativo de Arte Negra Escola de Samba Quilombo, 1984). Spirito Santo, " 'Xaxá de Ajudá' e a 'mancha branca' da nossa escravidão,"

August, 4, 2012, https://spiritosanto.wordpress.com/2012/08/04/xaxa-de-ajuda-e-a-mancha-branca-da-nossa-escravidao. Déo Caruso, Cleber, and Osmar, *A saga de Agotimé, Maria Mineira Naé* (G.R.E.S. Beija Flor de Nilópolis, 2001) *Galeria do Samba*, https://galeriadosamba.com.br/escolas-de-samba/beija-flor-de-nilopolis/2001. Russo, *Áfricas: do berço real à corte brasiliana*. Both sambas of Beija Flor de Nilópolis were performed by Luiz Antônio Feliciano Neguinho da Beija-Flor Marconde.
375. Verger, "Uma rainha," 158.
376. Ana Lucia Araujo, "History, Memory and Imagination: Na Agontimé, a Dahomean Queen in Brazil," in *Beyond Tradition: African Women and Their Cultural Spaces*, ed. Toyin Falola and Sati Fwatshak (Africa World Press, 2011), 59.
377. Victor Nowosh, Eduardo Tannus, Isac Ferreira, and Victor Fernandes, *O grande império Daomé-Maranhão e as não fronteiras da Encantaria do Querebetã de Zomadônu* (G.R.E.S.V. Império do Rio Belo, 2020). *Carnaval Virtual*, musical composition and lyrics, https://www.carnavalvirtual.com.br/site/discografia/cd-carnaval-virtual-2020-grupo-especial. https://www.youtube.com/watch?v=TAX97ejSqbk&list = carnaval-virtual-2020-grupo-especial/. Video of performance available at https://www.youtube.com/watch?v=TAX97ejSqbk&list=PL3NhGloAZEpabZVEnBzrB019eq1buQM4J&index=5.
378. "Meu leão virou pantera e tomou a avenida" and "As vodunsis entram na roda e vêm dançar / Chegam caboclos, tobossis e orixás." See Nowosh, *O grande império*. Tobosis are reincarnations of children, born anew in the waters of rivers or the ocean.
379. "Minha rainha, não fique a chorar / Seu rugido de pantera para sempre há de ecoar" Nowosh, *O grande império*.
380. "O meu eterno império de Daomé-Maranhão." Nowosh, *O grande império*.
381. Rono Maia, Jorge Melodia, and Alexandre Alegria, *Agudás, os que levaram a África no coração e trouxeram para o coração da África o Brasil!* (G.R.E.S. Unidos da Tijuca, 2003). *Galeria do Samba*, https://galeriadosamba.com.br/escolas-de-samba/unidos-da-tijuca/2003.
382. Bolaji Idowu, *Olódùmarè: God in Yoruba Belief* (Longman Nigeria, 1982), 76–77. Finnegan, *Oral Literature*, 191
383. "Na volta das espumas flutuantes, Mãe-África receba seus leões." Maia, *Agudás*.
384. "No rufar do tambor, atravessou o mar de Yemanjá. . . . É raça, é povo e se mistura." Maia, *Agudás*.
385. "Tem cheiro de benjoim no xirê, alabê. Prepare o acarajé, no dendê." Maia, *Agudás*.
386. "Salve o Chachá, salve toda negritude." Maia, *Agudás*.
387. See Miton Guran, *Agudás: os "brasileiros" do Benin* (Nova Fronteira, 2000).
388. Tavares, *Comércio*, 60.
389. Beier, *Yoruba Myths*, 61–62.
390. Luz, *Cultura*, 74.
391. Luz, *Cultura*, 74.
392. Luz, *Cultura*, 73–75.
393. Kamau Brathwaite, *Wars of Respect: Nanny, Sam Sharpe and the Struggle for People's Liberation* (Agency for Public Information for the National Heritage Week Committee, 1977), 4.

FINAL CONSIDERATIONS: DIKENGA AND OPÓN IFA: ANCESTRAL TIMES AND TECHNOLOGIES

1. Lawrence W. Fagg, *The Becoming of Time: Integrating Physical and Religious Time* (Scholars Press, 1995), 11.
2. Kimbwandènde Kia Bunseki Fu-Kiau, "Ntangu-Tadu-Kolo: The Bantu-Kongo Concept of Time," in *Time in the Black Experience*, ed. Joseph Adjaye (Greenwood Press, 1994), 20.

3. Fagg, *The Becoming*, 18.
4. Jan Vansina, "Memory and Oral Tradition," in *The African Past Speaks: Essays on Oral Tradition and History*, ed. Joseph Calder Miller (Archon, 1980), 264.
5. Original text: "Quando chegaram as Grandes Canoas dos Ventos (as caravelas portuguesas), tentaram banir o espírito do tempo, algemando-o no pulso do Homem da civilização. Desta época em Diante, o tempo passou a ser contado de modo diferente. Este modo de contar o tempo gerou a História, e mesmo a História passou a ser contada sempre do modo como aconteceu para alguns e não do modo como aconteceu para todos." In Kaká Werá Jecupé, *A terra dos mil povos: história indígena brasileira contada por um índio* (Editora Fundação Peirópolis, 1998), 71.
6. Vusa'mazulu Credo Mutwa, *Indaba My Children: African Folktales* (Grove Press, 1999), 590.
7. E. Bolaji Idowu, *Olódùmarè: God in Yoruba Belief* (Longman Nigeria, 1982), 78.
8. Fu-Kiau, "Ntangu," 17–34. Robert Farris Thompson, *Flash of the Spirit: African and Afro-American Art and Philosophy* (Random House, 1984), 109.
9. Fu-Kiau, "Ntangu," 30. Thompson, *Flash*, 109.
10. Olabiyi Yai, "In Praise of Metonymy: The Concept of 'Tradition' and 'Creativity' in the Transmission of Yoruba Artistry over Time and Space," in *The Yoruba Artist: New Theoretical Perspectives on African Arts*, ed. Rowland Abiodun, H. Drewal, and J. Pemberton III (Smithsonian Institution Press, 1994), 109.
11. Yai, "In Praise," 108.
12. Yai, "In Praise," 107.
13. Fu-Kiau, "Ntangu," 33.
14. Fu-Kiau, "Ntangu," 31.
15. Fu-Kiau, "Ntangu," 31.
16. Fu-Kiau, "Ntangu," 31.
17. Isis Barra Costa, "Afro-Brazilian Altar-Poems: The Poetic Text of Pontos-riscados, in "African Religions in the New World," ed. Narciso J. Hidalgo, special issue, *Afro-Hispanic Review* 26, no. 1 (2007): 103–20.
18. Robert Farris Thompson and J. Cornet, *The Four Moments of the Sun: Kongo Art in Two Worlds* (National Gallery of Art, 1981), and "Translating the World into Generousness: Remarks on Haitian Vèvè," *Res: Anthropology and Aesthetics* 32 (1997): 19–34.
19. George Hebert, "The Altar," (1633) Poetry Foundation, https://www.poetryfoundation.org/poems/44358/the-altar.
20. Hebert, "The Altar."
21. Olga Gudolle Cacciatore, *Dicionário de cultos afro-brasileiros* (Forense-Universitária, 1988), 214.
22. Makota Valdina Oliveira Pinto, "Pemba: Sacred Chalk of the Angola-Nation Candomblé," trans. Rachel Harding. Unpublished. n.d.
23. Pinto, "Pemba."
24. Miguel Barnet, *Cultos afrocubanos: la Regla de Ocha, la Regla de Palo Monte*. (Ediciones Unión, Artex, 1995), 127. The Spanish noun *firma* means "signature" or "seal."
25. Karen McCarthy Brown, "The Vèvè of Haitian Vodou: A Structural Analysis of Visual Imagery" (PhD diss., Temple University, 1975), 139.
26. Anna Wexler, "The Flags of Clotaire Bazile: A Description," *Callaloo* 20.2 (1997): 375.
27. Karen McCarthy Brown, *Tracing the Spirit: Ethnographic Essays on Haitian Art* (The Museum of Art; Distributed by the University of Washington Press, 1995), 31.
28. Barnet, *Cultos afrocubanos*, 127.
29. Thompson, *The Four*, 151.
30. Isis Barra Costa, "Other Forests: The Afro-Brazilian Literary Archive," in *Améfrica in Letters: Literary Interventions from Mexico to the Southern Cone*, ed. Jennifer Carolina Gómez Menjívar (Vanderbilt University Press, 2022), 129–49.

31. Edgar Morin, *Educar na era planetária: o pensamento complexo como método de aprendizagem pelo erro e incerteza humana* (Cortez, 2007), 58.
32. Maria Zilda da Cunha, "Naus frágeis e novos paradigmas em literatura e educação". *Perspectiva* 30, no. 3, Sept/Dec (2012): 775.
33. T. S. Eliot, "Tradition and The Individual Talent," *Selected Essays* (Faber and Faber, 1932), 21.
34. Eliot, "Tradition," 15.
35. Eliot, "Tradition," 13.
36. Eliot, "Tradition," 14.
37. Edimilson de Almeida Pereira, *A saliva da fala: notas sobre a poética banto-católica no Brasil* (Azougue, 2017), 173.
38. Pereira, *A saliva*, 49.
39. Antonio Candido, *Formação da literatura brasileira: momentos decisivos 1750–1880* (Fapesp, 2009), 24.
40. Candido, *Formação*, 153.
41. Candido, *Formação*, 24.
42. Pereira, *A saliva*, 32.
43. Pereira, *A saliva*, 144.
44. Pereira, *A saliva*, 23.
45. Pereira, *A saliva*, 145.
46. Pereira, *A saliva*, 23.
47. Pereira, *A saliva*, 67.
48. Pereira, *A saliva*, 67.
49. Pereira, *A saliva*, 149–50.

Works Cited

Adún, Guellwar. "Nota do editor." In *Traduzindo no Atlântico negro: cartas náuticas afrodiaspóricas para travessias literárias*, ed. Denise Carrascosa. Ogum's Toques Negros, 2017.
Agiri, Babatunde Aremu. "Early Oyo History Reconsidered." *History in Africa* 2 (1975): 1–16, https://doi.org/10.2307/3171463.
Aguiar, Marcos Magalhães de. "Historiadores e arquivos: testemunho de uma experiência." *Revista Múltipla* 5, no. 7 (December 1999): 109–16.
Akinjogbin, Adegbulu. "Agaja and the Conquest of the Coastal Aja States, 1724–1730." *Journal of the Historical Society of Nigeria* 2, no. 4, (1963): 545–53.
———. *Dahomey and Its Neighbours 1708–1818*. Cambridge University Press, 1967.
———. "Hard and Soft Power Politics in Oyo-Dahomey Diplomatic Relations 1708–1791," *International Journal of Law, Political Science, and Administration* 1, no. 2 (2014): 11–30.
Alencastro, Luiz Felipe de. *O tratado dos viventes: formação do Brasil no Atlântico Sul, séculos XVI e XVII*. Companhia das Letras, 2000.
Alesina, Alberto, W. Easterly, and J. Matuszeski. "Artificial States." *Journal of the European Economic Association* 9, no. 2 (2011): 246–77.
Alexandre, Cláudia. "Comissão da verdade sobre a escravidão negra no Brasil: relatório parcial inédito mostrará necessidade de reparações urgentes à população negra." *Portal Geledés*, June 23, 2015, https://www.geledes.org.br/comissao-da-verdade-sobre-a-escravidao-negra-no-brasil-relatorio-parcial-inedito-mostrara-necessidade-de-reparacoes-urgentes-a-populacao-negra/.
Almeida, Bira, and Mestre Acordeon. *Capoeira, a Brazilian Art Form: History, Philosophy, and Practice*. North Atlantic Books, 1986.
Alvarenga, Oneyda. *Música popular brasileira*. Livraria Duas Cidades, 1982.
Alvarez, Beethoven. "The Metamorphosis of the Giant Nicteroy in Brazilian Conservatism Since 1822." *Gremium: Studies in History, Culture and Politics* 15 (December 2021): 201–29. https://doi.org/10.34768/ig.vi15.358.
Alves, Albino. *Dicionário etimológico bundo-português*. 2 vols. Tipografia Silvas, 1951.
Anderson, Benedict. *Imagined Communities: Reflections on the Origin and Spread of Nationalism*. Verso, 1992.
Andrade, Mário de. "Os congos." In *Antologia do folclore brasileiro*, vol. 2, ed. Câmara Cascudo. Martins, 1965.
Antunes, Henrique Fernandes. "'It Is Not Solved Just by Writing It Down on Paper': Patrimonialization Policies and the Religious Use of Ayahuasca as a Brazilian Intangible Cultural Heritage." In *Religious Pluralism and Law in Contemporary Brazil*, ed. Paula Montero, C. Nicácio, and H. F. Antunes. Springer, 2023.

Araujo, Ana Lucia. "Forgetting and Remembering the Atlantic Slave Trade: The Legacy of Brazilian Slave Merchant Francisco Felix de Souza." In *Crossing Memories: Slavery and African Diaspora*, ed. Ana Lucia Araujo, M. Candido, and P. Lovejoy. Africa World Press, 2011.
———. "History, Memory and Imagination: Na Agontimé, a Dahomean Queen in Brazil." In *Beyond Tradition: African Women and Their Cultural Spaces*, ed. Toyin Falola and S. Fwatshak. Africa World Press, 2011.
———. "Slavery, Royalty and Racism: Representations of Africa in Brazilian Carnaval." *Ethnologies* 31, no. 2 (2010): 131–67.
———. "Zumbi and the Voices of the Emergent Public Memory of Slavery and Resistance in Brazil," *Comparativ* 22, no. 2 (2012): 95–111.
Armstrong, Piers. "The Carnaval of Bahia: 'From the Inside Looking Out.'" BrazilMax, July 13, 2003. https://www.brazilmax.com. Site inactive July 16, 2025.
———. "Moralizing Dionysius and Lubricating Apollo: A Semantic Topography of Subject Construction in Afro-Bahian Carnival." In "Memories of Slavery," ed. Michael Zeuske and Ulrike Schmieder, special issue, *Luso-Brazilian Review* 38 (2001): 29–60.
Assis Júnior, António de. *Dicionario kimbundu-português: linguístico, botânico, histórico e corográfico*. Santos, 1934.
Assunção, Matthias Röhrig. *Capoeira: The History of an Afro-Brazilian Martial Art*. Routledge, 2005.
Aubrée, Marion. "Brazil: Mental Health and the Magic-Religious Sphere." *Revue Tiers Monde* 187, no. 3, (2006): 547–56.
Augras, Monique. *O Brasil do samba-enredo*. Editora Fundação Getúlio Vargas, 1998.
Baeninger, Rosana, N. B. Demétrio, and J. Domeniconi. "Espaços das migrações transnacionais: perfil sociodemográfico de imigrantes da África para o Brasil no século XXI." *EMHU: Revista Interdisciplinar da Mobilidade Humana* 27, no. 56, (May–August 2019): 35–60, https://doi.org/10.1590/1980-85852503880005603.
Barbieri, Renato, dir. *Atlântico negro: na rota dos orixás*. Gaya Filmes, 1998.
Barbosa, Januário da Cunha. "Discurso." *Revista do Instituto Histórico e Geográfico Brasileiro* 1 (1839): 9–17.
———. *Nicteroy: metamorphose do Rio de Janeiro*. R. Greenlaw, 1822, https://digital.bbm.usp.br/handle/bbm/7704.
Barbosa, Wallace de Deus, ed. *Dossiê—Inventário para registro e salvaguarda da capoeira como patrimônio cultural do Brasil*. IPHAN, 2007.
Barnes, Sandra T., and P. B. Amos. "Benin, Oyo, and Dahomey: Warfare, State Building, and the Sacralization of Iron in West African History." *Expedition* 25, no. 2 (1983): 5–14.
Barnet, Miguel. *Cultos afrocubanos: la regla de Ocha, la regla de Palo Monte*. Ediciones Unión, Artex, 1995.
Bascom, William. *African Folktales in the New World*. Indiana University Press, 1992.
———. *Sixteen Cowries: Yoruba Divination from Africa to the New World*. Indiana University Press, 1980.
Bascom, William, and M. Heskovitz. *Continuity and Change in African Cultures*. University of Chicago Press, 1970.
Bastide, Roger. *As religiões africanas no Brasil*. Pioneira, 1960.
———. "The Other Quilombos." In *Maroon Societies: Rebel Slave Communities in the Americas*, ed. Richard Price. Johns Hopkins University Press, 1979.
Batsîkama, Patrício. *As origens do reino do Kôngo*. Mayamba Editora, 2010.
———. "As origens do reino do Kôngo segundo a tradição oral." *Sankofa: Revista de história da África e de estudos da diáspora africana* 3, no. 5 (2010): 7–41.
———. *O reino do Kôngo e a sua origem meridional*. Universidade Editora, 2011.
Batsîkama, Patrício, and R. Batsîkama. "Estruturas e instituições do Kongo." *Revista de História Comparada* 5, no. 1 (2011): 6–41.
Bay, Edna G. "On the Trail of the Bush King: A Dahomean Lesson in the Use of Evidence." *History in Africa* 6 (1979): 1–15, https://doi.org/10.2307/3171738.

———. "Protection, Political Exile, and the Atlantic Slave-Trade: History and Collective Memory in Dahomey." In *Rethinking the African Diaspora: The Making of a Black Atlantic World in the Bight of Benin and Brazil*, ed. Edna Bay and Kristin Mann. Routledge, 2013.
———. *Wives of the Leopard: Gender, Politics, and Culture in the Kingdom of Dahomey*. University of Virginia Press, 1998.
Beier, Ulli. "Before Oduduwa." *Odu: Journal of Yoruba and Related Studies* 3 (1956): 25–32.
———. *The Origin of Life and Death: African Creation Myths*. Heinemann, 1966.
———. *Yoruba Myths*. Cambridge University Press, 1980.
Bender, Gerald J. *Angola Under the Portuguese: The Myth and the Reality*. University of California Press, 1978.
Beniste, José. *As águas de Oxalá: àwon omi Ósàlá*. Bertrand Brasil, 2009.
———. *Dicionário yorubá-português*. Bertrand Brasil, 2019.
Benítez-Rojo, Antonio. *The Repeating Island: The Caribbean and the Postmodern Perspective*. Duke University Press, 1997.
Bentley, Callan, et al. "Palimpsest Outcrops." In *Historical Geology*. OpenGeology, 2020. https://opengeology.org/historicalgeology/case-studies/palimpsest-outcrops.
"Bento Teixeira." In *Enciclopédia Itaú cultural de arte e cultura brasileira*, 2023. http://enciclopedia.itaucultural.org.br/pessoa21740/bento-teixeira.
Berlin, Ira. "Time, Space, and the Evolution of Afro-American Society on British Mainland North America." *The American Historical Review* 85, no. 1 (1980): 44–78. doi.org/10.2307/1853424.
Bienal de São Paulo. "Between Ancestralities and the Diasporas, the 35th Bienal de São Paulo Announces the First List of Artists of the *Choreographies of the Impossible*." April 26, 2023. https://35.bienal.org.br/en/primeira-lista-de-artistas-coreografias-do-impossivel.
Biko, Steve. "Black Consciousness and the Quest for True Humanity." *SASO Newsletter* 1, no. 4 (May 1971): 17–21.
Binon, Gisèlle Cossard. *Awô: O mistério dos orixás*. Pallas, 2007.
Birch, David, T. Schirato, and S. Srivastava. *Asia: Cultural Politics in the Global Age*. Palgrave, 2001.
Birman, Patrícia. *Fazer estilo criando gêneros: Possessão e diferença de gênero em terreiros de Umbanda e Candomblé no Rio de Janeiro*. EdUERJ, 1995.
Birmingham, David. *The Portuguese Conquest of Angola*. Oxford University Press, 1965.
———. "Speculations on the Kingdom of Kongo." *Transactions of the Historical Society of Ghana* 8 (1965): 1–10.
———. *Trade and Conquest in Angola*. Clarendon Press, 1966.
Bittencourt Júnior, Iosvaldyr. "Maçambique de Osório: entre a devoção e o espetáculo: não se cala na batida do tambor e da maçaquaia." PhD diss., Universidade Federal do Rio Grande do Sul, 2006.
Blackmore, Josiah. *Moorings: Portuguese Expansion and the Writing of Africa*. University of Minnesota Press, 2009.
Blier, Suzanne. "Razing the Roof: The Imperative of Building Destruction in Dahomè." In *Structure and Meaning in Human Settlements*, ed. Tony Atkin and Joseph Rykwert. University of Pennsylvania Press, 2005.
Bockie, Simon. *Death and the Invisible Powers: The World of Kongo Belief*. Indiana University Press, 1993.
Bopp, Raul. *Poesia completa de Raul Bopp*. José Olympio, 1998.
Borges, Patrícia Souza. "O contato entre o português brasileiro e as línguas africanas na visão de Mendonça (1935[1933]) e Raimundo (1933): uma análise historiográfica." In *Cadernos de historiografia linguística do CEDOCH*, ed. Cristina Altman and O. Coelho. FFLCH/USP, 2015.
Braga, Júlio. *Na gamela do feitiço: repressão e resistência nos candomblés da Bahia*. Edufba, 1995.
———. *Sociedade protetora dos desvalidos: uma irmandade de cor*. Edições Ianamá, 1987.
Braga, Lourenço. *Umbanda, magia branca, Quimbanda, magia negra*. Editora Moderna, 1946.
Brar, Sandeep Singh. "Glossary of Religious Terms." *Sikhism, Religion of the Sikh People*. https://sikhs.org/glossary.htm.

Brasil. Supremo Tribunal Federal. "Crime de racismo e antissemitismo: Um julgamento histórico no STF." *Habeas Corpus*, no. 82.424/RS. STF, 2004.
Brathwaite, Kamau. *Barabajan Poems, 1492–1992*. Savacou North, 1995.
———. *Folk Culture of the Slaves in Jamaica*. New Beacon Books, 1981.
———. Lecture at River City Writers' Series, 1995. The University of Memphis English Department, Tennessee. Video, 1:02:15. Posted May 10, 2015. Originally posted by University of Memphis, YouTube. (Video no longer available.) Archived at https://www.are.na/block/20338115.
———. *Wars of Respect: Nanny, Sam Sharpe and the Struggle for People's Liberation*. Agency for Public Information for the National Heritage Week Committe, 1977.
Brown, Karen McCarthy. *Tracing the Spirit: Ethnographic Essays on Haitian Art*. The Seattle Museum of Art; distributed by the University of Washington Press, 1995.
———. "The Vèvè of Haitian Vodou: A Structural Analysis of Visual Imagery." PhD diss., Temple University, 1975.
Brown, Ras Michael. *African-Atlantic Cultures and the South Carolina Lowcountry*. Cambridge University Press, 2012.
Butler, Kim. *Freedoms Given, Freedoms Won: Afro-Brazilians in Post-Abolition São Paulo and Salvador*. New Rutgers University Press, 1998.
Cacciatore, Olga G. *Dicionário de cultos afro-brasileiros*. Forense Universitária, 1988.
Caldeira, Jorge. *Viagem pela história do Brasil*. Companhia das Letras, 1997.
Camões, Luís Vaz de. *Os Lusíadas*. Ed. Álvaro Júlio da Costa Pimpão and Aníbal Pinto de Castro. Instituto Camões, 2000.
———. *The Lusiads*. 2 vols. Trans. Richard Francis Burton, ed. Isabel Burton. Bernard Quaritch, 1880. https://burtoniana.org/books/1880-Os%20lusiadas/index.htm.
———. *The Lusiads*. Trans. L. White. Oxford University Press, 2008.
Campos, Haroldo de. *O sequestro do barroco na formação da literatura brasileira: o caso Gregório de Mattos*. Fundação Casa Jorge Amado, 1989.
Candido, Antonio. "Literature and the Rise of Brazilian National Self-Identity." *Luso-Brazilian Review* 5, no. 1 (Summer 1968): 27–43.
———. *Formação da literatura brasileira: momentos decisivos 1836–1880*. 2 vols. Martins, 1971.
———. "A revolução de 1930 e a cultura." *Novos Estudos CEBRAP* 2, no. 4 (1984): 27–32.
———. "Variações sobre temas da formação." In *Textos de intervenção*, ed. Vinício Dantas, 93–120. Duas Cidades/34, 2002.
———. *Formação da literatura brasileira: momentos decisivos 1750–1836*. 2 vols. Ouro sobre Azul, 2006.
———. *Formação da literatura brasileira: momentos decisivos 1750–1880*. 2 vols. Fapesp, 2009.
Capoeira, Nestor, and A. Ladd. *The Little Capoeira Book*. North Atlantic Books, 1995.
Cardonega, António de Oliveira de, and J. M. Delgado. *História geral das guerras angolanas 1680*. 3 vols. Agência Geral do Ultramar, 1972.
———. *Antologia do negro brasileiro*. Tecnoprint Gráfica S.A., 1967.
———. *Capoeira*. Ministério de Educação e Cultura, 1977.
———. *Folguedos tradicionais*. FUNART/INF, 1982.
———. *Religiões negras e negros bantos*. Civilização Brasileira, 1981.
Carneiro, Maria Luiza Tucci. *O preconceito racial no Brasil Colônia*. Brasiliense, 1983.
Carneiro, Sueli. Interview, *Revista Afirma*, March 11, 2002.
Carrascosa, Denise. *Traduzindo no Atlântico negro: cartas náuticas afrodiaspóricas para travessias literárias*. Ogum's Toques Negros, 2017.
Carvalho, José Murilo de. *Pontos e bordados: escritos de história e política*. Editora UFMG, 1999.
Carvalho, Marcos Antonio Lopez de. *Gaiaku Luiza*. Pallas, 2000.
Caruso, Déo, Cleber, and Osmar. *A saga de Agotimé, Maria Mineira Naé*. G.R.E.S. Beija-Flor de Nilópolis, 2001. *Galeria do Samba*, https://galeriadosamba.com.br/escolas-de-samba/beija-flor-de-nilopolis/2001.

Carybé, *O jogo da capoeira*. Livraria Turista, 1951.
Cascudo, Luís da Câmara. *Dicionário do folclore brasileiro*. Editora Itatiaia, 1993.
——. *Folclore do Brasil: pesquisas e notas*. Fundo de Cultura, 1967.
——. *Literatura oral no Brasil*. Editora da Universidade de São Paulo, 1984.
——. *Made in Africa: pesquisas e notas*. Civilização Brasileira, 1965.
Castro, Ruy. *O vermelho e o negro: pequena história do flamengo*. DBA Dórea Books & Art, 2001.
Castro, Yeda Pessoa de. *Camões com dendê: o português do Brasil e os falares afro-brasileiros*. Topbooks, 2022.
——. *Falares africanos na Bahia: um vocabulário afro-brasileiro*. TopBooks, 2001.
——. "Religions of African Origin in Brazil: Designation, Origins and New and Little-Known Cults." UNESCO *African Culture: Proceedings of the Meeting of Experts on the Survival of African Religious Traditions in the Caribbean and in Latin America*. São Luís, June 24–28, 1985. 137–50.
Catendê, Moa do. "A política afoxesista." *Estudos Afro-Asiáticos* 8–9 (1983): 251–53.
Cavalcanti, Pedro. "As seitas africanas do Recife." In *Estudos Afro-brasileiros: trabalhos apresentados ao Primeiro Congresso Afro-brasileiros do Recife em 1934*. 2 vols. Ed. Gilberto Freyre, René Ribeiro, Luís da Câmara Cascudo, and Waldemar Valente. Fundação Joaquim Nabuco; Editora Massangana, 1988.
Cavazzi, Padre João Giovanni António de Montecúccolo. *Descrição histórica dos três reinos Congo, Matamba, Angola*. 2 vols. Trans. Padre Graciano Mari de Leguzzano. 1687. Edição da Junta de Investigações do Ultramar, 1965.
Chalhoub, Sidney. *Visões da liberdade: uma história das últimas décadas da escravidão na corte*. Companhia das Letras, 1990.
Chamberlain, Henry, and R. B. Moraes, *Vistas e costumes da cidade e arredores do Rio de Janeiro em 1819–1820*. Livraria Kosmo, 1943. http://www2.senado.leg.br/bdsf/handle/id/227375.
Chamberlin, J. Edward. *Come Back to Me My Language*. University of Illinois Press, 1993.
Chatelain, Heli. "Geographic Names of Angola, West Africa." *Journal of the American Geographical Society of New York* 25, no. 1 (1893): 304–12. https://doi.org/10.2307/197042.
Chauí, Marilena de Sousa. *Brasil: mito fundador e sociedade autoritária*. Fundação Perseu Abramo, 2000.
Chiavenato, Júlio J. *O negro no Brasil: da senzala à Guerra do Paraguai*. Brasiliense, 1986.
Claridge, Cyril. *Wild Bush Tribes of Tropical Africa: An Account of Adventures and Travel Amongst Pagan Peoples in Tropical Africa, with a Description of Their Manners of Life, Customs, Heathenish Rites and Ceremonies, Secret Societies, Sport, and Warfare Collected During a Sojourn of Twelve Year*. Negro University Press, 1969.
Claro, Silene Ferreira. "Eugênia Anna dos Santos, a mãe Aninha do Ilê Axé Opô Afonjá." *Anais do 3 Encontro Internacional História & Parcerias*, ANPUHRJ, 1 (2021): 1–12.
Cobe, Francisco Narciso. *Novo dicionário Português-Kikongo*. Mayamba Editora, 2010.
Concone, Maria Helena Villas Boas and E. G. Rezende. "Umbanda in the Kardecist spiritualist novels." *Revista Eletrônica de Comunicação, Informação e Inovação em Saúde* 4, no. 3 (2010): 47–58. DOI: 10.3395/reciis.v4i3.385en.
Congresso Afro-Brasileiro. *O negro no Brasil: trabalhos apresentados ao 2° Congresso Afro-Brasileiro, Bahia*. Civilização Brasileira, 1940.
Costa, Emília Viotti da. *Da monarquia à república: momentos decisivos*. Brasiliense, 1985.
Costa, Haroldo. *Fala crioulo: o que é ser negro no Brasil*. Record, 1982.
Costa, Isis Barra. "Afro-Brazilian Altar-Poems: The Poetic Text of Pontos-riscados." In "African Religions in the New World," ed. Narciso J. Hidalgo. Special issue, *Afro-Hispanic Review* 26, no. 1 (2007): 103–20.
——. "Other Forests: The Afro-Brazilian Literary Archive." In *América in Letters: Literary Interventions from Mexico to the Southern Cone*, ed. Jennifer Carolina Gómez Menjívar, 129–49. Vanderbilt University Press, 2022.
——. "O Reino de Aruanda: De porto escravista luso-angolano a reino mítico afro-brasileiro." *Revista Scripta: Revista de Letras da Pontifícia Universidade Católica* 11 no. 20 (2007): 127–35.
Costa e Silva, Alberto da. *Francisco Félix de Souza, mercador de escravos*. Nova Fronteira, 2004.

———. *Um rio chamado Atlântico: a África no Brasil e o Brasil na África*. Nova Fronteira, 2003.
Costigan, Lúcia Helena. "A experiência do converso letrado Bento Teixeira: um 'Missing Link' na história intelectual e literária do Brasil-colônia." *Revista de Crítica Literaria Latinoamericana* 20, no. 40 (1994): 77–92.
Cunha, Cilaine Alves. "A meditação bíblica de Gonçalves Dias." *Revista Limiar* 3, no. 5 (2016): 91–125.
Cunha, Manuela Carneiro da. *Negros estrangeiros: os escravos libertos e sua volta a África*. Brasiliense, 1985.
Cunha, Maria Zilda da. "Naus frágeis e novos paradigmas em literatura e educação." *Perspectiva* 30, no. 3 (2012): 771–88.
Cusack, Igor. "From Revolution to Reflection: The National Anthems of the New Lusophone Worlds." *Luso-Brazilian Review* 45, no. 2 (2008): 45–67.
Dantas, Beatriz Góis. *Vovó nagô e papai branco: usos e abusos da África no Brasil*. Edições Graal, 1988.
Davidson, Basil. *The African Slave Trade Pre-colonial History 1450–1850*. Little, Brown & Company, 1961.
Davies, Carole Boyce. "Re-presenting Black Female Identity in Brazil: Filhas d'Oxum in Bahia Carnival." *Ijele: Art eJournal of the African World* 2.1 (2001): n./p. *Africa Resource Center*. November 1, 2007.
———. "Treasure in the Terror: The African Cultural Legacy in the Americas." *The Freedom Chronicle*, Northern Kentucky University's Institute for Freedom Studies 2, no. 1, Fall (2002). https://www.nku.edu/~freedomchronicle/treasureInTheTerror.
Debret, Jean Baptiste. *Voyage pittoresque et historique au Brésil*, 3 vols. Paris: Firmin Didot Frères, 1834–1839. https://digital.bbm.usp.br/handle/bbm/3813.
Deren, Maya. *The Divine Horsemen: The Voodoo Gods of Haiti*. Delta Publishing, 1972.
———. *Viagem pitoresca e histórica ao Brasil (1816–1831)*, 3 vols. Trans. Sérgio Milliet. São Paulo: EDUSP, 1972.
Desch-Obi, T.J. "Combat and the Crossing of the Kalunga." In *Central Africans and Cultural Transformations in the American Diaspora*, ed. Linda M. Heywood, 353–70. Cambridge University Press, 2002.
———. "Deadly Dances: The Spiritual Dimensions of Kongo-Angolan Martial Arts Traditions in the New World." In *Fragments of Bone: Neo-African Religions in a New World*, ed. Patrick Bellegarde-Smith, 70–89. University of Illinois Press, 2005.
———. "Engolo: Combat Traditions in African and African Diaspora History," PhD diss., University of California, 2000.
———. *Fighting for Honor: The History of African Martial Art in the Atlantic World*. University of South Carolina Press, 2008.
Desmangles, Leslie G. *The Faces of the Gods: Vodou and Roman Catholicism in Haiti*. University of North Carolina Press, 1992.
De Souza Family Collective. https://chachaix.com.
Diamond, Stanley. "Dahomey: The Development of a Proto-State." *Dialectical Anthropology* 2 (1996): 121–216. https://doi.org/10.1007/BF00244520.
Dias, Gastão de Sousa. *Os portugueses em Angola*. Agência Geral do Ultramar, 1959.
Dias, Gonçalves. *Cantos: Coleções de Poesias*, F. A. Brozkhaus, 1857. https://digital.bbm.usp.br/handle/bbm/4423.
———. *Poesia completa e prosa escolhida*. Ed. Manuel Bandeira, A. Houaiss and A. Herculano. Editora José Aguilar, 1959.
Dias, Gonçalves, and N. Ascher, "The Song of Exile." http://oldpoetry.com/opoem/122918-Antonio-Goncalves-Dias-The-Song-Of-Exile.
Diéguez, Carla Regina. "A masculinidade do trabalhador portuário: novas questões em tempo de automação." IX Seminário Fazendo Gênero: Diásporas, Diversidades, Deslocamentos. Universidade Federal de Santa Catarina, Florianópolis, August, 2010.
Dossar, Kenneth. "Capoeira Angola: Dancing Between Two Worlds." *Afro-Hispanic Review* 6, nos. 1–3 (1992): 5–11.
Doyle, Plínio. "Histórias de revistas e jornais." *Revista do libro* INL/MEC 32 (1968): 59–71.

Drewal, Margaret Thompson. "Embodied Practice/ Embodied History: Mastery of Metaphor in the Performances of Diviner Kolawole Ositola." In *Yoruba Artist: New Theoretical Perspectives on African Arts*, ed. Rowland Abiodun, H. J. Drewal, and J. Pemberton III. Smithsonian Institution Press, 1994.
Duarte, Eduardo de Assis. *Literatura, política, identidades*. FALE-UFMG, 2005.
———. "Úrsula e a desconstrução da razão negra occidental." In *Úrsula*, by Maria Firmina dos Reis, ed. E. A. Duarte. Editora PUC Minas, 2017.
Duarte, Evandro Piza, and Guilherme Scotti. "História e memória nacional no discurso jurídico: o julgamento da ADPF 186." *Universitas Jus* (Brasília) 24, no. 3 (2013): 33–45.
Duarte, Evandro Piza, Guilherme Scotti, and Menelick de Carvalho Netto. "Ruy Barbosa e a queima dos arquivos: as lutas pela memória da escravidão e os discursos dos juristas." *Universitas Jus* 26 (2015): 23–39.
Duarte, Luís Vítor. "De regresso à geologia de Angola: I. A zona costeira de Luanda ao Cuanza Sul." *Revista de Ciência Elementar* 7, no. 4 (2019): 1–8. http://doi.org/10.24927/rce2019.078.
Dunglas, Édouard. "Contribution à l'histoire du Moyen Dahome, de Kétou et de Ouidah." *Etudes Dahoméennes* 20, no. 19. Institut Français d'Afrique Noire/ Gouvernement du Dahomey/ Centre IFAN, 1957.
Dunn, Christopher, and C. Perrone, eds. *Brazilian Popular Music and Globalization*. University of Florida Press, 2001.
Eduardo, Octavio da Costa. *The Negro in Northern Brazil: A Study in Acculturation*. University of Washington Press, 1966.
Edwards, Adrian C. *The Ovimbundu Under Two Sovereignties: A Study of Social Control and Social Change Among a People of Angola*. International African Institute; Oxford University Press, 1962.
Eliot, T. S. "Tradition and The Individual Talent." *Selected Essays*. Faber and Faber, 1932.
Embaúba Filmes, "Live de lançamento de *A Rainha Nzinga chegou*." YouTube vídeo, June 24, 2021. https://www.youtube.com/watch?v=wpV-EStqdQI.
Enslen, Joshua Alma. *Song of Exile: A Cultural History of Brazil's Most Popular Poem, 1846–2018*. Purdue University Press, 2022.
Epega, Afolabi, and P. Neimark. *The Sacred Ifa Oracle*. Harper Collins, 1995.
Estrada, Joaquim Osório Duque, and F. M. Silva. "Hino Nacional." https://www.planalto.gov.br/ccivil_03/constituicao/hino.htm.
Fagg, Lawrence W. *The Becoming of Time: Integrating Physical and Religious Time*. Scholars Press, 1995.
Fanon, Frantz. *The Wretched of the Earth*. Trans. Constance Farrington. Grove Press, 1965.
Felinto, Renata. *Axexê da negra ou o descanso das mulheres que mereciam serem amadas*. São Paulo, 2017. https://renatafelinto.wordpress.com/axexe-da-negra.
Félix, Anísio. *Filhos de Gandhi: a história de um afoxé*. Gráfica Central Ltda, 1987.
Fellini, Federico. *E la nave va*. Concorde Film, 1983.
Feres Júnior, João and J. Zoninsein, eds. *Ação afirmativa e universidade: experiências nacionais comparadas*. Editora Universidade de Brasília, 2006.
Fernandes, Florestan. *A integração do negro na sociedade de classes*. Dominus Editôra, 1965.
Ferreira, Aurélio Buarque de Holanda. *Novo Aurélio século XXI: o dicionário da língua portuguesa*. Nova Fronteira, 1999.
Ferreira, Edmar. *O poder dos Candomblés: perseguição e resistência no Recôncavo da Bahia*. EDUFBA, 2009.
Filhos de Gandhy. Dir. Lula Buarque de Hollanda. Latin American Video Archives, 2000.
Finnegan, Ruth. *Oral Literature in Africa*. Clarendon Press, 1970.
———. *Oral Poetry: Its Nature, Significance and Social Context*. Indiana University Press, 1992.
———. *The Penguin Book of Oral Poetry*. Allen Lane, 1978.
Fonseca, Mariana Bracks. "Ginga de Angola: memórias e representações da rainha guerreira na diáspora." PhD diss., Universidade de São Paulo, 2018.
———. *Nzinga Mbandi e as guerras de resistência em Angola, século XVII*. Mazza Edições, 2015.

———. "Nzinga Mbandi e as guerras de resistência em Angola. Século XVII." MA thesis, Universidade de São Paulo, 2012.
Foucault, Michel. *Histoire de la folie à l'âge classique*. Gallimard, 1972.
———. "Two Lectures: Lecture One: January 7, 1976." In *Power/Knowledge: Selected Interviews and Other Writings*, ed. Colin Gordon. Vintage Press, 1980.
Freitas, Décio. *O escravismo brasileiro*. Mercado Aberto, 1991.
———. *A revolução dos Malês: insurreições escravas*. Editora Movimento, 1985.
———. *Palmares: A guerra dos escravos*. Mercado Aberto, 1984.
French, Jan Hoffman. "Race, Racism, and Affirmative Action in Brazil and the United States." *Latin American Research Review* 56, no. 4 (2021): 988–97.
Freyre, Gilberto. *Casa-grande e senzala: formação da família brasileira sob o regime da economia patriarcal*. Fundação Gilberto Freyre, 1992.
———. *The Masters and the Slaves: A Study in the Development of Brazilian Civilization*. Trans. Samuel Putnam. Alfred Knopf, 1946.
———. *O mundo que o português criou: aspectos das relações sociaes e de cultura do Brasil com Portugal e as colônias portuguesas*. José Olympio, 1940.
Fromont, Cécile. *Art of Conversion: Christian Visual Culture in the Kingdom of Kongo*. Chapel Hill, 2014.
Fryer, Peter. *Rhythms of Resistance: African Musical Heritage in Brazil*. Wesleyan University Press, 2000.
Fu-Kiau, Kimbwandende Kia Bunseki. *African Cosmology of the Bântu-Kôngo: Tying the Spiritual Knot—Principles of Life and Living*. Athelia Henrietta, 2001.
———. "Kapuera e cultura ancestral Bantu." Lecture, Salvador 1997. https://terreirodegrios.wordpress.com/2022/03/09/palestra-do-dr-fu-kiau-salvador-1997-kapuera-e-cultura-ancestral-bantu.
———. "Ntangu-Tadu-Kolo: The Bantu-Kongo Concept of Time." In *Time in The Black Experience*, ed. Joseph K. Adjaye. Greenwood Press, 1994.
———. *Self-Healing Power and Therapy: Old Teachings from Africa*. Vintage Press, 1991.
Galante, Rafael. "Construtores da liberdade: comunidades, lutas e identidades negras no Brasil do século XIX." Mukanda Cultural Course. July 1, 2020–September 2, 2020.
———. "'Essa gunga veio de lá': filosofias espirituais centro-africanas e narrativas históricas diaspóricas nos reinados de Minas Gerais." 1st ed. Mukanda Cultural Course. July 12–August 11, 2022.
———. "'Essa gunga veio de lá': filosofias espirituais centro-africanas e narrativas históricas diaspóricas nos reinados de Minas Gerais." 2nd ed. Mukanda Cultural Course. August 21–September 27, 2023.
———. "'Essa gunga veio de lá!': sinos e sineiros na África centro-ocidental e no Brasil centro-africano." PhD diss., Universidade de São Paulo, 2023. doi:10.11606/T.8.2023.tde-23052023-132320.
———. "História social das culturas da diáspora centro-africana no Brasil." Mukanda Cultural Course. April 8–May 20, 2021.
Galante, Rafael, and Marcos Cardoso, *Essa gunga veio de lá: tradição africana nos sinos do Brasil*, Canal USP, 2023. https://www.youtube.com/watch?v=TKOaAjd7bts.
Galeano, Eduardo, *Memory of Fire*. Vol. 3, *Century of the Wind*. Trans. Cedric Belfrage. Pantheon Books, 1988.
Geledés Instituto da Mulher Negra. http://www.geledes.com.br.
"General Act of the Conference of Berlin Concerning the Congo." *American Journal of International Law* 3, no. 1 (1909): 7–25.
Gérard, Marco, Tassio da Rosa Ramos, and A. Côrtes. "Um olhar musical sobre a canção 'Filhos de Gandhy' a partir da performance de Gilberto Gil na USP, em 1973." *Música Popular em Revista* 7, no. 1 (2020): 1–253.
Gil, Gilberto. "Filho de Gandhi (Ao vivo)." Track 23 on *Gilberto Gil ao vivo na USP*. GeGe Produções Artísticas, 1973. YouTube Music. https://music.youtube.com/playlist?list=OLAK5uy_mUikGIGTkiKZ-3yjoFw_m7jxv2Oip1i2k.
———. *Gilberto Gil: todas as letras*, ed. Carlos Rennó. Companhia das Letras, 1996.

Gil, Gilberto, and Jorge Ben Jor. "Filhos de Gandhi." On *Gil Jorge Ogum Xangô*. Philips Records, 1975.
Glasgow, Roy Arthur. *Nzinga: resistência africana à investida do colonialismo português em Angola, 1582–1663*. Editora Perspectiva, 1982.
Glosbe. *Glosbe Multilingual Dictionary*, https://glosbe.com.
Gomes, Edlaine de Campos. *A tradição dos orixás: valores civilizatórios afrocentrados*. IPEAFRO, 2019.
Gomes, Heloisa Toller. *As marcas da escravidão: o negro e o discurso oitocentista no Brasil e nos Estados Unidos*. Editora UFRJ, EdUERJ, 1994.
Gomes, Núbia Pereira Magalhães, and E. A. Pereira. *Negras raízes mineiras: os Arturos*. EDUFJF; MinC,1988.
———. *Arturos: Olhos do rosário*. Mazza Edições, 1990.
Gonçalves, Ana Maria. *Um defeito de cor*. Record, 2006.
Gondola, Ch. Didier. *The History of Congo*. Greenwood Press, 2002.
Gonzalez, Lélia, et al. *Festas Populares no Brasil/ Popular Festivals in Brazil*. Editora Index, 1989.
———. "A categoria político-cultural de Amefricanidade." In *Primavera para as rosas negras: Lélia Gonzalez em primeira pessoa*, ed. Raquel Barreto. Diáspora Africana, 2018.
Gordon, Cyrus and M. Stefon. "Solomon." *Encyclopedia Britannica*. https://www.britannica.com/biography/Solomon.
"Gottschalk, Louis Moreau." *The International Music Score Library Project (IMSLP)*. https://imslp.org/wiki/Category:Gottschalk,_Louis_Moreau.
Graham, Richard. "Technology and Culture Change: The Development of the 'Berimbau' in Colonial Brazil." *Latin American Music Review / Revista de Música Latinoamericana* 12, no. 1 (1991): 1–20
Griffith, Paul A. *Afro-Caribbean Poetry and Ritual*. Palgrave Macmillan, 2010.
Griffiths, Ieuan. "The Scramble for Africa: Inherited Political Boundaries." *Geographical Journal* 152, no. 2 (1986): 204–16. https://doi.org/10.2307/634762.
Grizoste, Weberson Fernandes. "Gonçalves Dias e a procura da identidade nacional brasileira." *Brasiliana: Journal for Brazilian Studies* 2, no. 2 (November 2013): 371–400.
Guillobel, Joaquim Cândido "Vendedor ambulante tocando berimbau." *Enciclopédia itaú cultural de arte e cultura brasileira*. Itaú Cultural, 2024. http://enciclopedia.itaucultural.org.br/obra65322/negro-vendedor-ambulante-tocando-berimbau.
Guimarães, Manoel Luís Lima Salgado. "Nação e civilização nos trópicos: O Instituto Histórico Geográfico Brasileiro e o projeto de uma história nacional." *Caminhos da Historiografia* 1, no. 1 (1988): 5–27.
Guimarães, Roberta Sampaio. "Patrimônios e conflitos de um afoxé na reurbanização da região portuária carioca." *Mana* 22, no. 2, (2016): 311–40.
Gunga Din. Dir. George Stevens. RKO, 1939. Film.
Guran, Milton. *Agudás: os "brasileiros" do Benim*. Nova Fronteira, 1999.
Harring, Harro Paul. "Danse de nègres musiciens jouant les instruments de leur pays," 1840. https://www.brasilianaiconografica.art.br/obras/19278/danse-de-negres-musiciens-jouant-les-instruments-de-leur-pays.
Hartman, Saidiya. "Secret Histories." Interview conducted by Alexis Okeowo, *The New Yorker*, October 26, 2020, 44–51.
———. "Venus in Two Acts." *Small Axe: A Caribbean Journal of Criticism* 12, no. 2, (2008): 1–14.
Hasenbalg, Carlos Alfredo. *Descriminições e desigualdades raciais no Brasil*. Edições Graal, 1979.
Hasenbalg, Carlos Alfredo, and L. Gonzalez. *Lugar de negro*. Marco Zero, 1982.
Hayner, Priscilla B. "Truth Commissions: A Schematic Overview." *International Review of the Red Cross* 88, no. 862 (2006): 295–310.
Hawthorne, Walter. *From Africa to Brazil: Culture, Identity, and an Atlantic Slave Trade*. Cambridge University Press: 2010.
Hazoumé, Paul. *Le pacte de sang au Dahomey*. Institut d'Ethnologie, 1956.
Hebert, George. "The Altar," (1633) *Poetry Foundation*. https://www.poetryfoundation.org/poems/44358/the-altar.

Henson, Bryce. "Communication Theory from América Ladina: Amefricanidade, Lélia Gonzalez, and Black Decolonial Approaches," *Review of Communication* 21, no. 4 (2021): 345–62.
Herskovits, Melville J. *Dahomean Narrative: A Cross-Cultural Analysis*. 2 vols. Northwestern University Press, 1958.
——. *Dahomey: An Ancient West African Kingdom*. 2 vols. Augustin, 1938.
Hertzman, Marc. "Making Their Own Mahatma: Salvador's Filhos de Gandhy and the Local History of a Global Phenomenon." In *Race and Transnationalism in the Americas*, ed. David Sheinin and B. Bryce. University of Pittsburgh Press, 2021.
Heywood, Linda. *Njinga of Angola: Africa's Warrior Queen*. Harvard University Press, 2017.
Hilton, Anne. "Family and Kinship among the Kongo South of the Zaïre River from the Sixteenth to the Nineteenth Centuries." *The Journal of African History* 24, no. 2 (1983): 189–206.
——. "The Jaga Reconsidered," *Journal of African History* 22, no. 2, (1981): 191–202.
——. *The Kingdom of Kongo*. Oxford University Press, 1985.
Hilton, John L. "Adamastor, Gigantomachies, and the Literature of Exile in Camões' *Lusíads*." *Journal of the Australasian Universities Language and Literature Association* 112 (2009): 1–23.
Hogendorn, Jan, and M. Johnson, *The Shell Money of the Slave Trade*. Cambridge University Press, 2003.
Huntley, Brian. *Ecology of Angola: Terrestrial Biomes and Ecoregions*. Springer, 2023. https://doi.org/10.1007/978-3-031-18923-4_4.
Ianni, Octávio. *A ideia de Brasil moderno*. Brasiliense, 1994.
Idowu, E. Bolaji. *Olódùmarè: God in Yoruba Belief*. Longman Nigeria, 1982.
Ilésanmí, Thomas Mákanjúọlá. "The Traditional Theologians and the Practice of Orisa Religion in Yorubaland," *Journal of Religion in Africa* 21, no. 3 (1991): 216–26. https://doi.org/10.1163/157006691X00032.
Inikori, Joseph, and S. Engerman. *The Atlantic Slave Trade: Effects on Economies, Societies and Peoples in Africa, the Americas, and Europe*. Duke University Press, 1992.
Instituto Estadual do Patrimônio Histórico e Artístico de Minas Gerais. *Dossiê de Registro da Comunidade dos Arturos, Contagem / MG*. IEPHA/MG, 2014.
Instituto Histórico, "Fim e objeto do objeto do instituto." *Revista do Instituto Histórico e Geográfico Brasileiro* 1 (1839).
——. "Prêmios popostos pelo Instituto na segunda sessão pública aniversária." *Revista do Instituto Histórico e Geográfico Brasileiro*, vol. 2. 3rd ed. 1840. https://ihgb.org.br/publicacoes/revista-ihgb.
Instituto Cultural Steve Biko. https://www.stevebiko.org.br.
Isichei, Elizabeth. *Voices of the Poor in Africa: Moral Economy and the Popular Imagination*. University of Rochester Press: 2002.
Jahn, Janheinz. *Muntu: African Culture and the Western World*. Grove Press, 1961.
Jecupé, Kaká Werá. *A terra dos mil povos: história indígena brasileira contada por um índio*. Editora Fundação Peirópolis, 1998.
Ji, Bhai Surinder Singh, and B. T. S. Ji. "El turbante de los sikhs." *Red Sikh Hispana*. http://www.redsikh.com.
Jordão, Lia Ramos. "Januário da Cunha Barbosa." https://bndigital.bn.gov.br/dossies/biblioteca-nacional-200-anos/os-personagens/januario-da-cunha-barbosa.
Kamel, Ali. *Não somos racistas: uma reação aos que querem nos transformar numa nação bicolor*. Nova Fronteira, 2006.
Kenny, Mary Lorena. *Deeply Rooted in the Present: Heritage, Memory, and Identity in Brazilian Quilombos*. University of Toronto Press, 2018.
Kent, R.K. "Palmares: An African State in Brazil." In *Maroon Societies: Rebel Slave Communities in the Americas*, ed. Richard Price. Johns Hopkins University Press, 1979.
Kiddy, Elizabeth. *Blacks of the Rosary: Memory and History in Minas Gerais, Brazil*. Penn State University Press, 2005.
Kipling, Rudyard. *Barrack-Room Ballads*. Heinemann, 1892.

Klein, Bernhard. "Camões and the Sea: Maritime Modernity in The Lusiads." *Modern Philology* 111, no. 2 (November 2013): 158–80.
Kopytoff, Igor. *The African Frontier: The Reproduction of Traditional African Societies*. Indiana University Press, 1987.
Kubik, Gerhard. *Africa and the Blues*. University Press of Mississippi, 1999.
———. *Extensions of African Cultures in Brazil*. Diasporic Africa Press, 2013.
Landes, Ruth. "Cult Matriarchate and Male Homosexuality." *Journal of Abnormal and Social Psychology* 35 (1940): 386–97.
Latin American Studies Association. "About LASA 2020," https://lasaweb.org/en/lasa2020/.
Law, Robin. "A carreira de Francisco Félix de Souza na África Ocidental (1800–1849)." *Tôpoi* 2, no. 2 (2001): 9–39.
———. *Ouidah: The Social History of a West African Slaving Port, 1727–1892*. Ohio University Press, 2005.
Lawrence, Natalie. "Making Monsters." In *Worlds of Natural History*, ed. Helen Anne Curry, N. Jardine, J. A. Secord, and E. C. Spary. Cambridge University Press, 2018. doi:10.1017/9781108225229.007.
Legislação Federal Brasileira, "Lei no. 7668, of August 22, 1988." https://legislacao.presidencia.gov.br/atos/?tipo=LEI&numero=7668&ano=1988&ato=868g3YU1UNBpWTe09.
Lewgoy, Bernardo. "A antropologia pós-moderna e a produção literária espírita." *Horizontes Antropológicos* 4, no. 8 (1998): 87–113.
Lewis, John Lowell. *Ring of Liberation: Deceptive Discourse in Brazilian Capoeira*. The University of Chicago Press, 1992.
Ligiéro, Zeca. *Corpo a corpo: estudo das perfomances brasileiras*. Garamond, 2012.
———. "O conceito de 'motrizes culturais' aplicado às práticas performativas afro-brasileiras." *Dossiê Religiões Afro-americanas* 8, no. 16 (2011): 129–44.
———. "Motrizes culturais: do ritual à cena contemporânea a partir do estudo de duas performances: Danbala Wedo (afro-brasileira, do Benin, Nigéria e Togo) e Sotzil Jay (Maia, da Guatemala)." *KARPA 10: Journal of Theatricalities and Visual Culture* (2017): n/p. https://www.calstatela.edu/al/karpa/karpa-10.
———. "Performances processionais afro-brasileiras." *O Percevejo* 12 (2003): 84–98.
———. "O que é performance." *O Percevejo* 11 (2003): 25–50.
Lima, Fábio Batista. *Os Candomblés da Bahia: tradições e novas tradições*. UNEB, 2005.
Lima, Vivaldo da Costa. "Ainda sobre a nação de queto." In *Faraimará, o caçador traz alegria: Mãe Stella, 60 anos de iniciação*, ed. Cléo Martins and R. Lody. Pallas, 1999.
———. *A família-de-santo nos Candomblés Jeje-Nagôs da Bahia: um estudo de relações intra-grupais*. Universidade Federal da Bahia, 1977.
Lipking, Lawrence. "The Genius of the Shore: Lycidas, Adamastor, and the Poetics of Nationalism." *PMLA* 111.2 (1996): 205–21.
Lipski, John M. "Portuguese Language in Angola: Luso-creoles' Missing Link?" Presented at American Association of Teachers of Spanish and Portuguese Conference (AATSP), San Diego, 1995. http://www.personal.psu.edu/faculty/j/m/jml34/angola.pdf.
Lody, Raul F. *Afoxé*. Funarte, 1976. *Cadernos de Folclore 7*.
———. *Cabelos de axé: identidade e resistência*. Ed. Senac Nacional, 2004.
———. *O povo do santo: religião história e cultura dos orixás, voduns, inquices e caboclos*. Editora Pallas, 1995.
Lopes, Nei. *Bantos, malês e identidade negra*. Forense Universitária, 1988.
———. *Novo dicionário banto do Brasil*. Pallas, 2003.
———. *Xaxá de Ajudá e a rainha Mina do Maranhão*. Grêmio Recreativo de Arte Negra Escola de Samba Quilombo, 1984.
Lopes, Victor. *Língua, vidas em português*. Costa de Castelos Filmes, 2007.
Luyaluka, Kiatezua Lubanzadio "Comparative Theology: Sumer, Memphis, Kongo Religion and Natural Systematic Theology." *Journal of Religion and Theology* 2, no 1 (2018): 31–45.
Luz, Marco Aurélio. *Cultura negra e ideologia do recalque*. Achiamé, 1983.

Luz, Marco Aurélio, ed. *Identidade negra e educação*. Ianamá, 1989.
Macedo, Ana Paula Rezende. "A capoeira angola: História, persistências e transformações." *História e Perspectivas* 1, no. 34 (2006): 425–61.
Macfarlane, Robert. "In London's Epping Forest, A Scientist Named Merlin Eavesdrops on Trees' Underground Conversations." *The New Yorker*, August 7, 2016. https://www.newyorker.com/tech/annals-of-technology/the-secrets-of-the-wood-wide-web.
MacGaffey, Wyatt. "The Black Loincloth and the Son of Nzambi Mpungu." *Research in African Literatures* 5, no. 1 (1974): 23–30.
———. *Kongo Political Culture: The Conceptual Challenge of the Particular*. Indiana University Press, 2000.
———. *Religion and Society in Central Africa: The Bakongo of Lower Zaire*. University of Chicago Press, 1986.
Machado, Maria Helena. "Maria Firmina dos Reis, Nineteenth-Century Maranhão (Brazil)." In *If She Were Free: A Collective Biography of Women and Emancipation in the Americas*, ed. Erica L. Ball, T. Seijas, and T. L. Snyder. Cambridge University Press, 2020.
Maia, Rono, Jorge Melodia, and Alexandre Alegria. *Agudás, os que levaram a África no coração e trouxeram para o coração da África o Brasil!* G.R.E.S. Unidos da Tijuca, 2003. Galeria do Samba, https://galeriadosamba.com.br/escolas-de-samba/unidos-da-tijuca/2003.
Maio, Marcos Chor, and C. E. Calaca. "New Christians and Jews in Brazil: Migrations and Antisemitism." *Shofar: An Interdisciplinary Journal of Jewish Studies* 19, no. 3 (2001): 73–85.
Mama, Usman. "Cana, Benin, an Important piece of Black History." January 12, 2017, *The African Magazine*. https://myafricanmagazine.com.
Marques, Wilton José. *Gonçalves Dias: O poeta na contramão: literatura e escravidão no romantismo brasileiro*. EDUFSCAR, 2010.
———. "Revista e ruptura." Paper presented at the II Congresso da História do Livro e da Leitura no Brasil, 2003, Campinas, Caderno de Resumos, 339–45.
Martins, Leda Maria. *Afrografias da memória: o reinado do Rosário no Jatobá*. Editora Perspectiva; Mazza Edições, 1997.
Martins, Maria Aparecida de. *Foram 17 anos*. Gravadora CID, 1976.
Mason, John, and G. Edwards. *Black Gods: Orisa Studies in the New World*. Yoruba Theological Archministry, 1985.
Matory, J. Lorand. *Black Atlantic Religion: Tradition, Transnationalism and Matriarchy in Brazilian Candomblé*. Princeton University Press, 2005.
Mattos, Ricardo Mendes. "Jongo: Travessias atlânticas e retorno ritual a Aruanda." *Letrônica* 15, no.1 (2022): 1–11. https://doi.org/10.15448/1984-4301.2022.1.40930.
Mattoso, Kátia. *Ser escravo no Brasil: séculos XVI–XIX*. Brasiliense, 1982.
Matuka, Yeno and A. Mawadza. *Dictionary and Phrasebook: Kikongo-English / English-Kikongo*. Hippocrene Books, 2021.
M'bokolo, Elikia. *África negra: história e civilizações*. 2 vols. EDUFBA, 2008.
McElroy, Isis Costa. "Poemas-altar afro-brasileiros: o texto poético dos pontos-riscados." In *Um tigre na floresta de signos: Estudos sobre poesia e demandas sociais no Brasil*, ed. Edimilson de Almeida Pereira. Belo Horizonte: Mazza Edições, 2010.
———. "A Transdiasporic Paradigm: The *Afoxé* Filhos de Gandhy." *Afro-Hispanic Review* 29.1 (2010): 77–100.
———. "A Transdiasporic Paradigm: The *Afoxé* Filhos de Gandhy." In *Religion, Theater and Performance: Acts of Faith*, ed. Lance Gharavi. Routledge, 2012.
Melo, Karine. "OAB cria comissão nacional da verdade sobre a escravidão." *Agência Brasil*, February 6, 2015. https://agenciabrasil.ebc.com.br/direitos-humanos/noticia/2015-02/oab-cria-comissao-nacional-da-verdade-sobre-escravidao.
Mello e Souza, Marina de. "Kongo King Festivals in Brazil: From Kings of Nations to Kings of Kongo." *African Studies Quarterly* 15, no. 3 (2015): 38–45.
———. *Reis negros no Brasil escravista: história da festa de coroação de Rei Congo*. Editora UFMG, 2002.

Mendes, Lorraine Pinheiro. "Minha história é suada igual dança no ilê, ninguém vai me dizer o meu lugar." *Políticas Culturais em Revista* 14, no. 2 (July/December 2021): 122–41.
Mendonça, Nilton. *3000 pontos riscados e cantados na Umbanda e Candomblé*. Editora Eco, 1974.
Mendonça, Renato. *A influência africana no português do Brasil*. MEC-Civilização Brasileira, 1973.
Menezes, Margareth. *Official Website*. https://margarethmenezes.com.br/internacional-en.
Mercier, Paul. "The Fon of Dahomey." In *African Worlds: Studies in Cosmological Ideas and Social Values of African Peoples*, ed. Daryll Forde. Oxford University Press, 1968.
Merrell, Floyd. *Capoeira and Candomblé: Conformity and Resistance in Brazil*. Markus Wiener Publishers, 2005.
Milagres, Agostinho da Silva. *Dicionário kimbundu/português/kimbundu: versão básica* (2021). https://www.academia.edu/43089182/Dicion%C3%A1rio_de_Kimbundu.
Miller, Joseph Calder. *Way of Death: Merchant Capitalism and the Angolan Slave Trade, 1730–1830*. University of Wisconsin Press, 1988.
——. "Central Africa During the Era of the Slave Trade, c. 1490s–1850s." In *Central Africans and Cultural Transformations in the American Diaspora*, ed. Linda M. Heywood. Cambridge University Press, 2002.
Molina, Diego A. "'A meditação' de Gonçalves Dias: a natureza dos males brasileiros." *Estudos Avançados* 30, no. 86 (2016): 235–52.
Monroe, Cameron. "In the Belly of Dan: Space, History, and Power in Precolonial Dahomey." *Current Anthropology* 52, no. 6 (2011): 769–98.
Morais, Mariana Ramos de. "Race, Culture, and Religion: The Afro-Brazilian Congresses and Anthropology in 1930's Brazil." *Bérose: encyclopédie internationale des histoires de l'anthropologie*. 2020. https://www.berose.fr/article2170.html.
Morales, Anamaria. "O afoxé Filhos de Gandhy pede paz." In *Escravidão e invenção da liberdade*, ed. João José Reis. Brasiliense, 1988.
Morin, Edgar, ed. *Educar na era planetária: o pensamento complexo como método de aprendizagem pelo erro e incerteza humana*. Cortez, 2007.
Morrison, Toni. *Beloved*. Alfred A. Knopf, 1987.
——. "Memory, Creation, and Writing." *Thought: A Review of Culture and Idea* 59, no. 235, (December 1984): 385–90.
Motta, Roberto. *Os afro-brasileiros: anais do III congresso afro-brasileiro*. Fundação Joaquim Nabuco, Editora Massangana: 2017.
Moura, Clóvis. *Dialética radical do negro no Brasil*. Anita, 1994.
——. *Rebeliões da senzala: quilombos, insurreições, guerrilhas*. Editora Conquista, 1972.
——. *Sociologia do negro brasileiro*. Ática, 1988.
Moura, Gloria. "A força dos tambores: a festa nos quilombos contemporâneos." In *Negras imagens: ensaios sobre cultura e escravidão no Brasil*, ed. Lilian Moritz Schwarcz and L. V. S. Reis. Estação Ciência / EDUSP, 1996.
Moura, Milton Araújo. "World of Fantasy, Fantasy of the World: Geographic Space and Representation of Identity in the Carnival of Salvador, Bahia." In *Brazilian Popular Music and Globalization*, ed. Christopher Dunn and C. Perrone. University Press of Florida, 2001.
Murdock, George Peter. *Africa: Its Peoples and Their Culture History*. McGraw-Hill Book Company, 1959.
Mutwa, Vusa'mazulu Credo. *Indaba My Children: African Folktales*. Grove Press, 1999.
Nabuco, Joaquim. *A escravidão*. Fundação Joaquim Nabuco, 1988.
Nafafé, José Lingna. *Lourenço da Silva Mendonça and the Black Atlantic Abolitionist Movement in the Seventeenth Century*. Cambridge University Press, 2022.
——. "Lourenço da Silva Mendonça: o primeiro ativista antiescravista?" *Modern Maroonage: The Pursuit and Practice of Freedom in the Contemporary World*, March 12, 2019: n/p. https://mmppf.wordpress.com.
Naro, Nancy, R. Sansi, and D. Treece, *Cultures of the Lusophone Black Atlantic*. Palgrave, 2007.
Nascimento, Abdias. *O genocídio do negro brasileiro: processo de um racismo mascarado*. Paz e Terra, 1978.

———. *O negro revoltado*. Nova Fronteira, 1982.
———. *Quilombismo: documentos de uma militância pan-africanista*. Vozes, 1980.
Nascimento, Luiz Claudio. *Bitedô: onde moram os nagôs: redes de sociabilidades africanas na formação do Candomblé jêje-nagô no Recôncavo baiano*. CEAP, 2011.
Nazareth, Paulo. *L'arbre d'oublier (Tree of Forgetfulness)* 2013, site.videobrasil.org.br/en/acervo/obras/obra/1801794.
Negrão, Lísias Nogueira. *Entre a cruz e a encruzilhada: formação do campo umbandista em São Paulo*. EDUSP, 1996.
Nowosh, Victor, Eduardo Tannus, Isac Ferreira, and Victor Fernandes. *O grande império Daomé-Maranhão e as não fronteiras da Encantaria do Querebetã de Zomadônu*. G.R.E.S.V. Império do Rio Belo, 2020. *Carnaval Virtual*. Musical composition and lyrics. https://www.carnavalvirtual.com.br/site/discografia/cd-carnaval-virtual-2020-grupo-especial/.
———. "O grande império Daomé-Maranhão e as não fronteiras da Encantaria do Querebetã de Zomadônu." YouTube video, 2020. https://www.youtube.com/watch?v=TAX97ejSqbk&list=PL3NhGloAZEpabZVEnBzrB019eq1buQM4J&index=5.
Okpewho, Isidore. *African Oral Literature: Backgrounds, Character, and Continuity*. Indiana University Press, 1992.
Olinto, Antonio. *A casa da água*. Editorial Nórdica, 1988.
Oliveira, Alan Santos de. "Círculos, espirais e rodas no mundo afro-atlântico: itinerários do pensamento rodante." PhD diss., Universidade de Brasília, 2021.
Oliveira, José Carlos de. "Os zombo e o futuro (Nzil'a Bazombo): na tradição, na colônia e na independência." PhD diss., Universidade de Coimbra, 2008.
Oliveira, Maria Inês Cortes de. *Os libertos: seu mundo e os outros*. Corrupio, 1988.
———. "Viver e morrer no meio dos seus: nações e comunidades africanas na Bahia do século XIX." *Revista USP* 28 (1995–1996): 175–93.
Oliveira, Paulo Cesar Miguez de. "A organização da cultura na cidade da Bahia." PhD diss., Universidade Federal da Bahia, 2002.
Omoruan, Daniel, and F.O. Uzzi. "God's Chisel in the Hands of the Carver: An Esoteric View of Joseph Alufa Igbinovia." *Scholars: Journal of Arts, Humanities and Social Sciences* 4, no. 1, (2022): 44–52. doi.org/10.3126/sjah.v4i1.43054.
Òrí Dir. Raquel Gerber and M.B. do Nascimento. Angra Filmes and Fundação do Cinema Brasileiro, 1989. Film.
Ortiz, Renato. *Cultura brasileira e identidade nacional*. Brasiliense, 1985
———. *A morte branca do feiticeiro negro: Umbanda e sociedade brasileira*. Brasiliense, 1991.
Oyěwùmí, Oyèrónkẹ́. *The Invention of Women: Making an African Sense of Western Gender Discourses*. University of Minnesota Press, 1997.
Parés, Luis Nicolau. *A formação do candomblé: história e ritual da nação jêje na Bahia*. Editora da Unicamp, 2007.
———. *The Formation of Candomblé: Vodun History and Ritual in Brazil*. University of North Carolina Press, 2013.
———. "The Jeje in the Tambor de Mina of Maranhão and in the Candomblé of Bahia." In *Rethinking the African Diaspora: The Making of a Black Atlantic World in the Bight of Benin and Brazil*, ed. Edna Bay and Kristin Mann. Routledge, 2013.
———. *Joaquim de Almeida: a história do africano traficado que se tornou traficante de africanos*. Companhia das Letras: 2024.
Parés, Luis Nicolau, and L.E. Castillo, "Marcelina da Silva: A Nineteenth Century Candomblé Priestess in Brazil." *Slavery & Abolition* 31, no. 1 (March 2009): 1–27.
Parés, Luis Nicolau, and R. Sansi "The Multiple Agencies of Afro-Brazilian Religions." *Religion and Society* 3 (2012), 76–94.

Park, Chris. "Religion and Geography." In *Routledge Companion to the Study of Religion*, ed. John Hinnells. Routledge, 2004.

Pastinha, Mestre. *Capoeira Angola*. Salvador: Escola Gráfica N. S. de Lorêto, 1964.

———. *Quando as pernas fazem miserêr: metafísica e prática da capoeira, Bahia, Pelourinho, 196, manuscritos e desenhos*. In *A herança de Pastinha*, ed. Ângelo Decânio. Estatutos do Centro Esportivo de Capoeira Angola (1956–1960). PDF Manuscritos de Mestre Pastinha. "Caderno Albo," https://www.capoeirashop.fr/en/blog/pdf-manuscritos-de-mestre-pastinha-n19.

Patrocínio, José. "Discurso na Gazeta de Notícias de 6 setembro de 1880." In *A campanha abolicionista*. Ministério da Cultura, Fundação Biblioteca Nacional, n/d. http://www.dominiopublico.gov.br/download/texto/bn000110.pdf.

Paul, Emmanuel Casséus. *Panorama du folklore haïtien*. Imprimerie de l'Etat, 1962.

Peixoto, Norberto. *Vozes de Aruanda: obra mediúnica*. Editora do Conhecimento, 2005.

Pemberton III, John. *African Arts* 18, no. 2 (1985): 88–91. https://doi.org/10.2307/3336205.

Penha-Lopes, Vânia. "Affirmative Action and Racial Identity in Brazil: A Study of the First Quota Graduates at the State University of Rio de Janeiro." In *The Melanin Millennium: Skin Color as 21st Century International Discourse*, ed. Ronald Hall. Springer, 2013.

Pereira, Avelino Romero Simões. "Hino nacional brasileiro: que história é esta?" *Revista do Instituto de Estudos Brasileiros* 38 (1995): 21–42.

Pereira, Edimilson de Almeida. *Lugares ares: obra poética 2*. Mazza Edições, 2003.

———. *A saliva da fala: notas sobre a poética banto-católica no Brasil*. Azougue, 2017.

Pereira, Lúcia Miguel. *A vida de Gonçalves Dias: contendo o diário inédito da viagem do Gonçalves Dias ao Rio Negro*. José Olympio, 1943.

Pereira, Manuel Nunes. *A Casa das Minas: contribuição ao estudo das sobrevivências do culto dos voduns, do panteão daomeano, no Estado do Maranhão, Brasil*. Vozes, 1979.

Philip, Marlene Nourbese. "The Absence of Writing or How I Almost Became a Spy." In *Out of the Kumbla: Caribbean Women and Literature*, ed. Carole Boyce Davies and E.S. Fido. Africa World Press, 1994.

Pigafetta, Filippo, and D. Lopes. *Relação do reino do Congo e das terras circunvizinhas: uma verdadeira história de navegações e aventuras do século XVI*. Alêtheia Editores, 2015.

Pinheiro, Márcia Leitão. "'The Sound of Silenced Voices': Mobilizations, Connections, and Demands in the Investigation of Slavery in Brazil," trans. Thaddeus Gregory Blanchette and David Rodgers. *Vibrant* 15, no. 3, 2018. doi.org/10.1590/1809-43412018v15n3d502.

———. "Uma comissão da verdade no Brasil: escravidão, multiculturalismo, história e memória." *Civitas*, Porto Alegre, vol. 18, no. 3 (September–December 2018): 683–98.

Pinheiro, Robson. *Aruanda: magia negra, elementais, Preto-Velhos e Caboclos sob a ótica espírita*. Romance Mediúnico, espírito: Ângelo Inácio. Casa dos Espíritos Editora, 2004.

———. WEBtv. https://www.youtube.com/@RobsonPinheiroWEBtv.

Pinho, Patrícia de Santana. *Reinvenções da África na Bahia*. Annablume, 2004.

Pinto, Valdina Oliveira. "Candomblé de Angola: uma recriação de tradições culturais Bantu sobreviventes entre nós." *II encontro de nações de candomblé setembro de 1995 anais*. Centro de Estudos Afro-Orientais da UFBa, 1997.

———. "Pemba: Sacred Chalk of the Angola-Nation Candomblé," trans. Rachel Harding. Unpublished. n.d.

Polanyi, Karl. *Dahomey and the Slave Trade: An Analysis of an Archaic Economy*. University of Washington Press, 1966.

Pollak, Michael. "Memória, esquecimento, silêncio." *Estudos Históricos* 2, no. 3 (1989): 3–15.

Pool, Deborah. "El estado y sus márgenes: etnografías comparadas. *Cuadernos de Antropología Social* 27 (2008): 19–52.

Portal do Poder Executivo Federal, "Serviços e informações do Brasil: Símbolos nacionais." https://www.gov.br/planalto/pt-br/conheca-a-presidencia/acervo/simbolos-nacionais.

Prado, Paulo. *Retrato do Brasil*. DP&C, 1928.

Prandi, Reginaldo. *Mitologia dos orixás*. Companhia das Letras, 2001.
Programa de Pesquisas sobre Povos Indígenas do Nordeste Brasileiro. *Documento final da conferência dos povos e organizações indígenas do Brasil*. April 21, 2000. https://pineb.ffch.ufba.br/downloads/1242404195Documento%20Final_Outros%20500.pdf.
Queiroz, Sônia. *Palavra banto em Minas Gerais*. Editora UFMG, 2019.
Quint, David. *Epic and Empire: Politics and Generic Form from Virgil to Milton*. Princeton University Press, 1993.
Quintão, Antonia Aparecida. *Irmandades negras: utro espaço de luta e resistência, São Paulo: 1870–1890*. Annablume; Fapesp, 2002.
Ramos, Arthur. *A aculturação negra no Brasil*. Companhia Editora Nacional, 1942.
——. *O negro brasileiro: ethnographia, religiosa e psychanalyse*. Companhia Editoria Nacional, 1940.
Ratts, Alex, and M. B. do Nascimento. *Eu sou Atlântica: sobre a trajetória de vida de Beatriz Nascimento*. Instituto Kuanza: Impr. Oficial do Estado de São Paulo, 2006.
——. *Todas (as) distâncias: Poemas, aforismos e ensaios de Beatriz Nascimento*. Ogum's Toques Negros, 2015.
Régis, Armando, and Djalma Sabiá. *O navio negreiro*. G.R.E.S. Acadêmicos do Salgueiro, 1957. *Galeria do Samba*, https://galeriadosamba.com.br/escolas-de-samba/academicos-do-salgueiro/1957.
Reis, João José. *Rebelião escrava no Brasil: a história do levante dos malês em 1835*. Companhia das Letras, 2003.
Reis, Maria Firmina dos. *Úrsula*. Editora PUC Minas, 2017.
Remédios, Joaquim Mendes dos. *Camões, poeta da fé*. Coimbra Editora Ltda., 1924.
Rennó, Carlos, ed. *Gilberto Gil: todas as letras*. Companhia das Letras, 1996.
Research Directorate, Immigration and Refugee Board of Canada. "Nigeria: Ogboni Society, Including Structure, Rituals, Ceremonies, and Current Status; Membership and the Consequences of Refusing to Join or Trying to Leave; Relationship with Police and Judicial Authorities (2017–April 2019)." https://www.ecoi.net/en/document/2021322.html.
Ribeiro, Darcy. *O povo brasileiro: a formação e o sentido do Brasil*. Companhia das Letras, 1995.
Ribeiro, Maria de Lourdes Borges. "O jongo." *Revista do Arquivo Municipal* 16, no. 216 (1960): 165–235.
Rio, João do. *As religiões no Rio*. Organização Simões, 1951.
Risério, Antonio. *Carnaval Ijexá*. Corrupio, 1981.
——. *Caymmi: uma utopia de lugar*. Editora Perspectiva; COPENE, 1993.
——. *Uma história da cidade da Bahia*. Versal, 2004.
——. *Textos e tribos: poéticas extra-ocidentais nos trópicos brasileiros*. Imago, 1993.
Roach, Joseph. *Cities of the Dead: Circum-Atlantic Performance*. Columbia University Press, 1996.
Robatto Filho, Alexandre. *Vadiação*, 1954. YouTube video. https://www.youtube.com/watch?v=rUO691y4F3A.
Rocha, João Cezar de Castro. "A lírica do exílio e a cultura brasileira." In *Leituras desauratizadas: Tempos precários, ensaios provisórios*, ed. Valdir Prigol. UFPE, 2017.
Rodrigues, Nina. *Os africanos no Brasil*. Editora Universidade de Brasília, 2004.
Romero, Sílvio. *Estudos sobre a poesia popular do Brasil*. Typ Laemmert & C., 1888.
——. *História da literatura brasileira*. 3 vols. José Olympio: 1943.
Rosa, Cristina. "Playing, Fighting, and Dancing: Unpacking the Significance of Ginga within the Practice of Capoeira Angola." *TDR: The Drama Review* 3 (Fall 2012): 141–66.
Rossi, Paolo. *O passado, a memória e o esquecimento*. Unesp, 2010.
Rudner, Jalmar. "An Archaeological Reconnaissance Tour of Angola." *The South African Archaeological Bulletin* 31, nos. 123–124 (1976): 99–111.
Rufino, Joel. "O mistério de Zumbi." *Comunicações do ISER* 5, no. 21 (1986): 67–69.
Russo, Cláudio, J. Velloso, Gilson Dr, and Carlinhos do Detran. *Áfricas: do berço real à corte brasiliana*. G.R.E.S. Beija-Flor de Nilópolis, 2007. https://www.beija-flor.com.br/2007.
Ryder, Alan. "The Re-establishment of Portuguese Factories on the Costa da Mina to the Mid-Eighteenth Century." *Journal of the Historical Society of Nigeria* 1, no. 3 (1958): 157–83.

Sansone, Livio. "The Dilemmas of Digital Patrimonialization: The Digital Museum of African and Afro-Brazilian Memory." *History in Africa* 40 (2013): 257–73.
Santana, Tiganá. "A cosmologia africana dos bantu-kongo por Bunseki Fu-Kiau: tradução negra, reflexões e diálogos a partir do Brasil." PhD diss., Universidade de São Paulo, 2019.
——. "Tradução, interações e cosmologias africanas." *Cadernos de Tradução* 39 (2019): 65–77.
Santos, João Henrique dos. "Gente da nação: os judaizantes e a preservação do judaísmo no Brasil." In *Identidade e cidadania como se expressa o judaísmo brasileiro*, ed. Helena Lewin. Centro Edelstein de Pesquisas Sociais, 2009.
Santos, Sales Augusto dos. *O sistema de cotas para negros da UnB: um balanço da primeira geração*. Paco Editorial, 2015.
Sartre, Jean-Paul. Preface to *The Wretched of the Earth*, by Frantz Fanon, trans. Constance Farrington. Grove Press, 1965.
Schechner, Richard. "O que é performance?" Translated by Dandara. *O Percevejo: Revista de Teatro, Crítica e Estética* 12 (2003): 25–50.
Schueman, Lindsey Jean. "Welcome to the Wood Wide Web." *One Earth*, October 25, 2021. https://www.oneearth.org/welcome-to-the-wood-wide-web.
Scott, David. "That Event, This Memory: Notes on the Anthropology of African Diasporas in the New World." *Diaspora: A Journal of Transnational Studies* 1, no. 3 (1991): 261–84.
Segatto, José Antônio, and M. C. Leonel. "Formação da literatura e constituição do estado nacional." *Itinerários* 30 (January/June 2010): 11–30.
Serrano, Carlos. "Ginga, a Rainha Quilombola de Matamba e Angola." *Revista USP: Dossiê do Povo Negro* 28 (1995–1996): 136–41.
Shakespeare, William. *The Tempest*. Ed. Barbara A. Mowat and Paul Werstine. Folger Shakespeare Library, 2015. https://folger.edu/explore/shakespeares-works/all-works.
Shukla, Pravina. "Afro-Brazilian Avatāras: Gandhi's Sons Samba in South America." *Indian Folklore Journal* 1 (2001): 35–45.
——. *Costume: Performing Identities through Dress*. Indiana University Press, 2015.
Silva, Agnaldo. "Filhos de Gandhi: Entrevista por Emerson Nunes." *iBahia: Portal da Rede Bahia*. Accessed April 28, 2011. URL no longer available.
Silva, Denise Ferreira da. *Toward a Global Idea of Race*. University of Minnesota Press, 2007.
——. *Unpayable Debt*. Sternberg Press, 2022.
Silveira, Renato da. "Jeje-nagô, iorubá-tapá, aon-efan, ijexá: processo de constituição do candomblé da Barroquinha (1764–1851)." *Revista Cultura* 6 (2000): 80–101.
Skidmore, Thomas. *Preto no branco*. Paz e Terra, 1976.
Skertchly, J. Alfred. *Dahomey As It Is: Being a Narrative of Eight Months' Residence in that Country*. Chapman and Hall, 1874.
Slenes, Robert. "Escravos, cartórios e desburocratização: o que Rui Barbosa não queimou será destruído agora?" *Revista Brasileira de História* 5, no. 10 (March/August 1985): 166–97.
——. "'Malungo, Ngoma vem!' África coberta e descoberta no Brasil" *Revista USP*, 12 (1991/1992): 48–67.
——. *Na senzala uma flor: as esperanças e as recordações da família escrava: Brasil sudeste, século XIX*. Nova Fronteira, 1999.
——. "'Malungu, Ngoma's Coming!': Africa Hidden and Discovered in Brazil," In *Mostra do redescobrimento: negro de corpo e alma: Black in Body and Soul. Exhibition catalog*, ed. Nelson Aguilar. Fundação Bienal de São Paulo, 2000.
——. "A Árvore de Nsanda transplantada: cultos kongo de aflição e identidade escrava no Sudeste brasileiro (século XIX)." In *Trabalho livre, trabalho escravo: Brasil e Europa, séculos XVIII e XIX*, ed. Douglas Libby and J. Furtado. Annablume, 2006.
——. "Metaphors to Live by in the Diaspora: Conceptual Tropes and Ontological Wordplay among Central Africans in the Middle Passage and Beyond." In *Tracing Language Movement in Africa*, ed. Ericka Albaugh and K. de Luna. Oxford University Press, 2016.

———. "'I Come from Afar, I Come Digging': Kongo and Near-Kongo Metaphors in Jongo Lyrics." In *Cangoma Calling: Spirits and Rhythms of Freedom in Brazilian Jongo Slavery Songs*, ed. Pedro Meira Monteiro and M. Stone. University of Massachusetts Press, 2013.

Smith, Christen A., B. N. F. Gomes, and A. Davies, eds., *The Dialectic Is in the Sea: The Black Radical Thought of Beatriz Nascimento*. Princeton University Press, 2023.

Smithsonian National Museum of the American Indian. "Honoring Original Indigenous Inhabitants: Land Acknowledgment." Accessed April 28, 2023. https://americanindian.si.edu/nk360/informational/land-acknowledgment.

Soares, Antônio Joaquim de Macedo. *Dicionário brasileiro da língua portuguesa*. Leuzinger, 1954.

Soares Filho, Daniel. *Aruanda: a morada dos orixás*. Anúbis, 2017.

Sodré, Muniz. *Samba, o dono do corpo*. Rio de Janeiro: Mauad, 1998.

———. *O terreiro e a cidade: a forma social negro-brasileira*. Vozes, 1988.

Souza, Albano de Neves e. *Da minha África e do Brasil que eu vi . . .* Lello, 1974.

Souza, Raquel de. "Salvo-conduto." In *Traduzindo no Atlântico negro: cartas náuticas afrodiaspóricas para travessias literárias*, ed. Denise Carrascosa. Ogum's Toques Negros, 2017.

Sperber, Dan. *Rethinking Symbolism*. Cambridge University Press, 1975.

Spirito Santo, "'Xaxá de Ajudá' e a 'mancha branca' da nossa escravidão," August 4, 2012. https://spiritosanto.wordpress.com/2012/08/04/xaxa-de-ajuda-e-a-mancha-branca-da-nossa-escravidao.

Sweet, James. *Recreating Africa: Culture, Kinship, and Religion in the African-Portuguese World, 1441–1770*. University of North Carolina Press, 2003.

Takamiya, Hiroto. "Introductory Routes of Rice to Japan: An Examination of the Southern Route Hypothesis." *Asian Perspectives* 40, no. 2 (2001): 209–26.

Talmon-Chvaicer, Maya. *The Hidden History of Capoeira: A Collision of Cultures in the Brazilian Battle Dance*. University of Texas Press, 2008.

Tavares, Luís Henrique Dias. *Comércio proibido de escravos*. Ática, 1988.

Teixeira, Bento. *Prosopopéia*. Typographia do Imperial Instituto Artistico, 1873. https://digital.bbm.usp.br/handle/bbm/4060.

Thiong'o, Ngũgĩ wa. *Decolonizing the Mind: The Politics of Language in African Literature*. J. Currey; Heinemann Kenya, 1986.

Thompson, Robert Farris. "Canons of the Cool: Interview with Robert Farris Thompson." Conducted by Fred Iseman, *Rolling Stone*, November 22, 1984. https://www.rollingstone.com/culture/culture-news/robert-farris-thompson-canons-of-the-cool-58823.

———. "Capoeira Tough Guys Do Dance." *Rolling Stone*, March 24, 1988.

———. *Flash of the Spirit: African and Afro-American Art and Philosophy*. Random House, 1984.

———. *Tango: The Art History of Love*. Knopf Doubleday Publishing Group: 2010.

———. "A Tango with Robert Farris Thompson: Interview with Ned Sublette." *AfroPop Worldwide*, October 20, 2005. https://afropop.org/articles/robert-farris-thompson-interview-2005.

———. "Translating the World into Generousness: Remarks on Haitian Vèvè." *RES: Anthropology and Aesthetics* 32 (1997): 19–34.

Thompson, Robert Farris, and J. Cornet. *Four Moments of the Sun: Kongo Art in Two Worlds*. National Gallery of Art, 1981.

Thornton, John. *Africa and Africans in the Making of the Atlantic World, 1400–1680*. The Press Syndicate of the University of Cambridge, 1995.

———. "The Art of War in Angola, 1575–1680." *Comparative Studies in Society and History* 30, no. 2 (1988): 360–78.

———. *A Cultural History of the Atlantic World, 1250–1820*. Cambridge University Press, 2012.

———. "The Kingdom of Kongo, ca. 1390–1678: The Development of an African Social Formation." *Cahiers d'Études Africaines* 22, no. 87–88 (1982): 330.

———. *The Kingdom of Kongo: Civil War and Transition, 1641–1718*. University of Wisconsin Press, 1983.

———. "Legitimacy and Political Power: Queen Njinga, 1624–1663." *Journal of African History* 32, no. 1 (1991): 25–40.
———. "Modern Oral Tradition and the Historic Kingdom of Kongo." In *The Power of Doubt: Essays in Honor of David Henige*, ed. Paul S. Landau. Parallel Press, 2011,
———. "The Origins and Early History of the Kingdom of Kongo, c. 1350–1550." *International Journal of African Historical Studies* 34, no. 1 (2001): 89–120, doi.org/10.2307/3097288.
———. "A Resurrection for the Jaga." *Cahiers d'Études Africaines* 18, nos. 69–70 (1978): 223–27.
———. "Traditions, Documents, and the Ife-Benin Relationship." *History in Africa* 15 (1988): 351–62.
Thornton, John, and L. Heywood. *Central Africans and Cultural Transformations in the American Diaspora*. Cambridge University Press, 2002.
Thornton, John, and A. Mosterman. "A Re-Interpretation of the Kongo-Portuguese War of 1622 According to New Documentary Evidence." *Journal of African History* 51, no. 2 (2010): 235–48.
Torres, Júnia, and I. Casimira, dirs. *A Rainha Nzinga chegou*. Documentary. Embaúba Filmes, 2019.
Turner, Jerry. "Les Bresiliens: The Impact of Former Brazilian Slaves Upon Dahomey." PhD diss., Boston University, 1975.
Turra, Cleusa e Gustavo Venturi, ed. *Racismo cordial: a mais completa análise sobre preconceito de cor no Brasil*. Ática, 1995.
UNESCO. "Declaration on Race and Racial Prejudice." https://www.un.org/ruleoflaw/blog/document/declaration-on-race-and-racial-prejudice.
———. "International Decade for People of African Descent (2015–2024)." https://en.unesco.org/internationaldecadeforpeopleofafricandescent.
University of São Paulo, Center for Astronomy Outreach (USP: Centro de Divulgação da Astronomia). "Painel do Cruzeiro do Sul." Accessed September 26, 2023. https://cda.jct/cruzeiro-sul/index.html.
Vansina, Jan. *How Societies are Born: Governance in West Central Africa Before 1600*. University of Virginia Press, 2004.
———. "Memory and Oral Tradition." In *The African Past Speaks: Essays on Oral Tradition and History*, ed. Joseph Calder Miller. Archon, 1980.
———. *Oral Tradition as History*. University of Wisconsin Press, 1985.
Velloso, Monica Pimenta. "A literatura como espelho da nação." *Revista Estudos Históricos* 1, no. 2 (1988): 239–63.
Ventura, Roberto. *Estilo tropical: história cultural e polêmicas literárias*. Companhia das Letras, 1991.
Verger, Pierre Fatumbi. *Fluxo e refluxo do tráfico de escravos entre o Golfo do Benin e a Bahia de Todos os Santos*. Corrupio, 1987.
———. *Lendas africanas dos orixás*. Corrupio, 1985.
———. *Notas sobre o culto aos orixás e voduns na Bahia de Todos os Santos, no Brasil, e na antiga Costa dos Escravos, na África*. EDUSP, 2000.
———. *Orixás: deuses iorubás na África e no Novo Mundo*. Corrupio, 1992.
———. *Os libertos: sete caminhos na liberdade de escravos*. Corrupio, 1992.
———. "Uma rainha africana mãe de santo em São Luís." *Revista USP* (June-July-August 1990): 151–58.
———. *Trade Relations Between the Bight of Benin and Bahia from the Seventeenth to Nineteenth Century*. Ibadan University Press, 1976.
Vianna, Hermano. *O mistério do samba*. Editora UFRJ, 1995.
Vieira Filho, Raphael Rodrigues. "Folguedos negros no carnaval de Salvador (1880–1930)." In *Ritmos em trânsito: sócio-antropologia da música baiana*, ed. Livio Sansone e Jocélio Teles dos Santos. Dynamis, 1997.
Von Martius, Karl Frederich. "Como se deve escrever a história do Brasil." *Revista do Instituto Histórico e Geográfico Brasileiro* 24, 1844. In *Livro de fontes da historiografia brasileira*, ed. Manoel Luiz Salgado Guimarães. EdUERJ, 2010.
———. *Como se deve escrever a história do Brasil*. EdUERJ, 2010.

Von Martius, Karl Frederich, and J. B. von Spix. "História da literatura e identidade nacional." In *Literatura e identidades*, ed. José Luiz Jobim. EdUERJ, 1999.
——. *Viagem pelo Brasil 1817–1820*. 3 vols. Trans. Lúcia Furquim Lahmeyer. Senado Federal, Conselho Editorial, 2017
Warner, Marina. *Alone of All Her Sex: The Myth and Cult of the Virgin Mary*. Knopf Doubleday, 1976.
Welcome to Angola Portal. "Black Rocks of Malanje." Accessed October 30, 2024. https://welcometoangola.co.ao/en/directorio/black-rocks-de-malanje.
Winter, Sylvia. "The Re-enchantment of Humanism: An Interview with Sylvia Wynter." Conducted by David Scott, *Small Axe: A Caribbean Journal of Criticism* 4, no. 2, (2000): 119–207.
Wolkmer, Antônio Carlos. "Paradigmas, historiografia, crítica e direito moderno." *Revista da Faculdade de Direito* 28, no. 28 (1994–1995): 55–67.
Xavier, Chico. *Parnaso de além-túmulo*. Federação Espírita Brasileira, 1932.
Yai, Olabiyi. "In Praise of Metonymy: The Concept of 'Tradition' and 'Creativity' in the Transmission of Yoruba Artistry over Time and Space." In *The Yoruba Artist: New Theoretical Perspectives on African Arts*, ed. Rowland Abiodun, H. Drewal, and J. Pemberton III. Smithsonian Institution Press, 1994.
Zeleza, Paul Tiyambe. "Rewriting the African Diaspora: Beyond the Black Atlantic." *African Affairs* 104, no. 414 (2005): 35–68.
Zilbermann, Regina. "Mito e literatura brasileira." In *Negros e índios: história e literatura*, ed. Moacyr Flores. Editora da PUC Rio Grande do Sul, 1994.
Zumthor, Paul. *Oral Poetry: An Introduction*. Trans. Kathy Murphy-Judy. University of Minnesota Press, 1990.

Index

Abiodun (Alaafin chief) (r. 1770–1789), 35, 274, 361n488
Abiodun, Rowland, 361n488
Abreu, Casemiro de, 186
Acadêmicos do Salgueiro, 301–302
An Account of Travels in Brazil at the Command of His Majesty, Maximilian Joseph I, King of Bavaria, in the Years 1817 to 1820 (Von Martius and Von Spix), 86–89
Adamastor (fictional character), 19–21, 23, 56, 59–71, 85, 115, 312
Adami, Humberto, 110
Adandozan (King of Dahomey) (r. 1797–1818), 35, 270, 274–277, 283–286, 298
Addokpon (King-as-Prince of Dahomey), 299–300
Adún, Guellwar, 161
The Adventures of Huckleberry Finn (Twain), 94
Afoxés, 301, 367n134; groups, 31–33, 244–268, 363n41, 364n51, 366n94, 367n114; origins, 243, 254
African American, 1–3, 14, 70, 95, 105, 130, 210, 321n1
African Arrival. *See* A Chegada Africana
African Brazil (*Brasil africano*), 2, 321n1
African-Brazilian (*brasileiro africano*), 2, 3, 8, 177, 321n1; civilizations, 10, 22, 26, 29, 31, 98, 116, 129–135, 210, 228–234; cosmologies explained by Carnaval griots, 244–268
African-Catholicism, 99, 102, 170
African civilizations, 1–2, 17–18, 25–26, 94–95, 150, 228–229
African Embassy. *See* Embaixada Africana
African Merrymakers. *See* Pândegos da África

Os africanos no Brasil (*Africans in Brazil*) (Rodrigues), 90, 92, 112
African tales of the orishas. *See Lendas africanas dos orixás*
Afro-American, 2, 321n1
afro-brasileiro. *See* Afro-Brazilian
Afro-Brazil, 6, 10, 36, 116, 293, 312
Afro-Brazilian (*afro-brasileiro*), 9–10, 12, 23, 93–94, 116, 293–294, 303, 312; Carnaval, 252, 253–256; as term, 2, 321n1
Afro-Brazilian congresses (1934, 1937, 1982), 2, 23, 103–105, 321n1
Afro-Brazilian Institute of Bahia, 104
the Afro-Brazilian and Indigenous History and Culture Law. *See* Law No. 10.639/2003
Afro-Caribbean Poetry and Ritual (Griffith, P.), 13, 16
afrodescendente (Afro-descendant), 2, 109, 321n1
Afro-(Euro)-Brazil, 10, 115–116
Afrografias da memória (*Afrographies of Memory*) (Martins, L. M.), 9, 340n15
Afro-Jamaican, 7, 12–13
Afro-Muslim-Brazilian Malê Rebellion (1807–1835), 262–263, 270, 278–279, 290–293
Agaja (King of Dahomey) (r. c.1718–1740), 35, 273, 297
Agassiz, Louis, 87
Agiri, Babatunde Aremu, 238, 363n14
agogô (sacred bell), 27, 139, 141, 247, 249, 255
Agonglo (King of Dahomey) (r. 1789–1797), 35, 274, 284–286
Agudas, 33–34, 280, 282, 303–304, 340

"Águas de Oxalá" (Obatala's Waters), 32, 239, 242, 244, 262
Akaba (King of Dahomey) (r. 1685–1716), 298
"Alá-lá-ô," 263, 367n115
Alegria, Alexandre, 303
Alencar, José de (1829–1877), 81, 96
Alencastro, Luiz Felipe de, 157, 268
the Algarves, 58, 219
O alienado no direito civil brasileiro (Rodrigues), 334n6
Alladayê, Jérôme, 272
Almeida, Joaquim de, 276
Almeida, José Antônio de, 87
altar-poems, 314
"The Altar" (Herbert), 313–314
Alufás, 132
Alvarenga, Oneyda (1911–1984), 171
Alvarez, Beethoven, 70, 73, 329n90
Alves, Castro (1847–1871), 186, 301–302
Alves, Thomé José, 290
"Always-Present-Ancestral-Whole" force. *See* Nzambi-a-Mpungu
Amado, Jorge (1912–2001), 95
Amaral, Braz do, 90
Amaral, Tarsila do, 47
"Améfrica Ladina," 322n21
"amefricanity," 11
Américo, Pedro, 44–46, 121, 190
amnesty laws, 223–224
Ampumandezu, Tata (1881–1946). *See* Folha, Tata Bernardo Bate
ancestral texts, 11–13, 19
Anderson, Benedict (1936–2015), 71
Andrada e Silva, José Bonifácio de (1763–1838), 112
Andrade, Mário de (1893–1945), 95, 96, 172
Andrade, Oswald de (1890–1954), 95, 96
"And the Ship Sails On." *See* "E la nave va"
Ângelo Inácio (spirit). *See* Pinheiro, Robson
Angola, 133, 139, 221, 349n118, 356n321, 358nn385–387, 359n426; Congo-Angola region, 30–31, 295, 341n35; Kongo, Mozambique and, 28, 159, 175, 176, 193, 194; *Tambores de Angola*, 188. *See also* Kongo-Angola
Angola Janga. *See* Quilombo dos Palmares
Angola-Konga, 26, 131, 132, 166, 170
O animismo fetichista dos negros baianos (Rodrigues), 334n6
Aninha, Mãe (Iyá Obá Biyi, Eugênia Anna dos Santos) (1869–1938), 103–104, 243
"Anthem of Brazil's Proclamation of the Republic," 72

anthropology, 16, 23, 90–96, 104, 107, 110–111, 158
anthropomorphism, 21, 56, 62, 78, 84
Anthropophagic Movement (1928–1929), 96
anti-Semitism, 111, 205–206
Antonil, André João, 86
ara-aiyê, 305–306
Arabic, 66, 67, 248, 290
Araketu (Carnaval group), 240
Araujo, Ana Lucia, 276, 281, 301, 302, 370n218
L'Arbre d'oublier. *See* Tree of Forgetfulness
architecture, 7, 13, 36, 188, 280
Armstrong, Piers, 267–268, 365n68
Aroeira (California Pepper) tree, 175, 350n141
O Arquivo (journal), 332n49
Aruanda, 6, 18, 28, 312; coronation of kings on both banks of Atlantic, 169–172; dance transcending space, time, bonds and history, 182–185; from inside out, 185–194; Kongo and, 194–206; legacy of colonial cartography, 218–220; Ndongo and Kongo contextualized, 194–196; poetics of Congadas, 172–181; Portuguese welcomed by Nzinga-a-Nkuwu, 199–205; from Pungo-a-Ndongo to, 160–165; Queen Nzinga and, 156–159, 210–217, 220–227; royal performances and exile of Ndongo royalty, 165–169; victories of the Mbundu and rose of, 207–217; *Vozes de Aruanda*, 187
Aruanda (Pinheiro, R.), 188–189
As coletividades anormais (Rodrigues), 334n6
ashe (*àṣe, axé*) 254, 305–307
"Asipá Borogun Elesé Kan Gongôô!" (Àṣípá Borógun, Eléṣèkan Gòngóò!), 288, 289
Assis Júnior, António de, 141, 164, 190–191, 232, 338n5, 344n107, 362n497
astronomy, 76, 309, 331n14
Atinsá (tree shrine, Vodun), 294
atabaque drums, 139, 140, 247, 249, 255–256
Atlântico Negro (documentary film), 370n218
Attenborough, Richard, 244
Aubrée, Marion, 186
Augustine (Saint), 310
Aurélio, Marco, 112
Autran, José Pedro, 289, 290, 291
Aveiro, João Afonso de, 235
Awole (Alaafin chief) (r. 1789–1796), 35, 274
Awolede (diviner), 240, 242

Babalawos, 7, 104, 179, 288, 312
Babassuê, 134
Bacchus (mythical figure), 55–56, 58, 62, 68
Bada, Maria, 103

Bahia, 103–104, 142, 335n55, 364n51, 367n134; Hindu-Muslim-Bahian *fantasia*, 263–268; from Pungo-a-Ndongo to, 165–169
baiano (in Umbanda), 189; *baiana* (woman vendor of *acarajé*, emblem of Afro-Brazilian culture) 247–248, 278, 265
Bakongo, 26–27, 132, 149, 182, 195–197, 200, 293; cosmogram, 30, 152, 164, 179, 181, 311; cosmology, 1, 152, 155–156, 163; culture, 140, 150. *See also* Dikenga
Balandier, Georges, 148
Banda. *See* Umbanda
Bandeira, Cavalcanti, 315
bandeirantes (colonial bounty hunters), 42, 50, 172, 179, 223
Bantu, 15, 67, 91, 124, 139, 146, 161, 227, 267; cultures, 127, 134, 144, 149, 190, 226, 243; languages, 66, 144, 166, 176–177, 190, 315
baptisms, 100–101, 214, 288, 355n315
Barbieri, Renato, 286, 370n218
Barbosa, Ruy, 25, 111–112, 114
Barbosa, Wallace de Deus, 140
barefoot philosophy, 3
Barnet, Miguel, 315
Bascom, William, 11
Batsîkama, Patrício, 155, 195–198
Batuque (Culto de Nação), 88, 133, 294
Bay, Edna, 285, 299
"Beads" ("Contas") (Pereira, E. de A.), 124–125
Behanzin (King of Dahomey) (r. c. 1890–c. 1894), 274
Beier, Ulli (1922–2011), 237–239
Beija-Flor samba school, 34, 302, 303, 374n373
bells, 27, 139–145, 179, 247, 249, 255
Beloved (Morrison), 4
Bender, Gerald (1941–2017), 94, 95, 201
benevolent spirits. *See nkisi*
Benítez-Rojo, Antonio, 13
Beowulf, 12
berimbaus, 27, 136–140, 144, 146–147, 158
Berlin, Ira, 14
Berlin Conference (1884–1885), 218–219
Biko, Steve (1947–1977), 108, 337n17
Bilac, Olavo, 186
bilongo (*bilôngo*, sacred medicine) 189, 193
Bimba, Mestre (Manuel dos Reis Machado) (1899–1974), 98, 139, 343n75
Birman, Patrícia, 258
Birmingham, David, 203–204, 207
Biyi, Iyá Obá (1869–1938). *See* Aninha, Mãe
Black (*negro, preto*), 2, 109, 321n1
Black Atlantic, 3, 11, 15–16, 168–169

Black Atlantic (documentary film), 286–287
Black bodies, 4, 47, 65
Black Brazilian Front. *See* Frente Negra Brasileira
Black Coalition for Rights. *See* Coalizão Negra Por Direitos
Black Consciousness Movement, 108
Black Elders. *See* Pretos Velhos
Black Lives Matter. *See* Vidas Negras Importam
Blackmore, Josiah, 57, 61, 64–65
Black movement, 19, 42, 43, 108, 110, 224–226
The Black Brazilian. *See O negro brasileiro*
Black Unified Movement (Movimento Negro Unificado, MNU), 43, 225
"black war." *See guerra preta*
Black Women's Institute. *See* Geledés Instituto da Mulher Negra
bloco (street parade group in Brazilian Carnaval) 246, 251, 254, 258–263, 363, 367
Bloco da Bicharada (Bloco of a Herd of Animals), 263
Boas, Franz (1858–1942), 92
Bockie, Simon (1944–1993), 212
bodies, xv, 15, 27, 32, 67, 134, 187; Black, 4, 47, 65; of Christ, 76, 141; decapitation, 167, 217, 241; feet, 3, 31, 37, 76, 138, 145, 163–164, 174, 176, 179, 239, 306; *ori*, 305–306; possessions, 191, 258. *See also* Capoeira; dance
boiadeiro, 118, 189; ox driver, 19, 118, 121; oxcart driver, 45–46, 121; cattle drover, 189
Bolsonaro, Jair, 73, 267
Bonfim, Martiniano Eliseu do (1859–1943), 243, 291, 292
bonfire, 10, 39, 116, 152, 216
Bopp, Raul (1898–1984), 96, 126, 136–137, 341n58
Bornus (Kanuris), 132
Braga, Júlio, 170–171
Braga, Lourenço (1900–1963), 191–192
branqueamento (whitening), 46, 47, 91, 93, 101, 107
Brasil, Vavá Pau, 103
Brasil africano. *See* African Brazil
brasileiro africano. *See* African-Brazilian
"O Brasil que a gente quer são outros 500." *See* "The Brazil We Want Is Another 500"
Brathwaite, Kamau, 2, 6–8, 11–13, 182, 222, 224, 307
Braz da Luz, Mário, 173, 176, 179
Brazil, 41–43, 94, 122; as giant, 21, 69–70, 73, 77, 85, 92; independence, 23, 44, 58–59, 71, 72, 83; military dictatorship, 72, 110, 121, 245–246, 251, 343n75, 370n223; national identity, 18, 48–49, 53, 71, 96–97, 100–101, 111–112; Portugal and, 11, 19, 23, 44, 48–51, 74–75; praise song for, 71–73

Brazilian Bar Association, 109–110
Brazilian Coalizão manifesto (2020), 108–109
Brazilian Geographical and Historical Institute. *See* Instituto Geográfico e Histórico Brasileiro
Brazilian Institute for Geography and Statistics (IBGE), 107
Brazilian literature, 53–54, 74, 85, 90–91, 154, 318
Brazilian National Truth Commission, 109–110
Brazilian Portuguese, 2, 177, 232, 321n1
"Brazilian Solemn March" ("Marcha solene brasileira"), 72
Brazilian-Yoruba-Ewe-Fon, 175, 180
"The Brazil We Want Is Another 500" ("O Brasil que a gente quer são outros 500"), 41–42
"Brief Explanation of the Congo Nation." *See* "Ligeira explicação sobre a nação Congo"
Brocos, Modesto, 46, 47, 121
Brown, Karen (1942–2015), 315–316
Brown, Ras Michael, 143–144
Brown/Mestizo. *See Pardo*
Bumba-meu-Boi, 165
Burton, Richard (1821–1890), 299
"Bush King." *See* "King-as-Prince" governance model
Butler, Kim, 253–254

Caboclo, 142, 172, 179–180, 189–192, 230–232, 248, 267
Cabral, Pedro Álvares, 42, 75–77, 100, 331n14
Cabula, 133
Cacciatore, Olga Gudolle, 175–176, 314
cachaça, 23, 86–90
Café, Humberto, 260
Caliban (fictional character), 20, 58–60, 63
California Pepper tree. *See* Aroeira tree
call-and-response, 146, 158, 247, 255. *See also* vissungo
calundunga, 177. *See ndunga*
Camilo, Geraldo, 176
Caminha, Pero Vaz de, 12, 100
Camões, Luís de (c. 1524–1580), 19, 55–56, 59, 65, 75, 79, 137. *See also The Lusiads*
Campos, Haroldo de (1929–2003), 54
"Canção de exílio." *See* "Song of Exile"
Cândida, Felisbina Rita, 173
Candido, Antonio (1918–2017), 53–54, 75, 78, 98, 318
Cândido Xavier, Francisco. *See* Xavier, Chico
Candombe, 31, 140, 150; musical instrument, 126–128, 175–176; practitioners, 148, 175, 268
Candomblés, 24, 187, 191, 226–227, 232, 240, 253, 288, 295, 336n81; "Águas de Oxalá" and, 32, 239, 242, 244, 262; ceremonies, 34, 255, 303, 304, 315; chants, 189, 190; dances, 158, 255; drums, 27, 75, 140, 175, 247, 255–256; Filhos de Gandhy and, 260–263, 266–267; leaders, 102, 103; origins, 175–176, 243; rhythms, 142, 254; rituals, 141, 257; schools or associations, 133–134, 294; temple, 254, 255, 290; women in, 257, 258, 262; Yoruba-speaking regions and, 130. *See also* Angola; Caboclo; Congo; Jeje; Ketu
candonga (candongueiro), 177–178
cangaceiro (in Umbanda), 189
canoes, 152–153, 178, 180, 268, 310, 338n5
cantopoetas. *See* "singer-poets"
Cão, Diogo (1452–1486), 200
Capoeira, 24, 98, 133, 148, 152, 165, 343n75; chants, 28, 150–151, 158–159, 160; fighting techniques, 138, 344n124; movements, 47, 121, 147, 149, 156–159, 178, 190; musical instruments, 137–140, 142–143, 144; N'golo and, 138–139, 342n74; wheel, 146–147, 150, 159
caravel(s), 10, 39, 42, 57, 116, 121, 137, 229, 376n5
Cardoso, Fernando Henrique, 43–44
Caribbean oral traditions, 16
Carnaval, 24, 210, 227, 366n110; futebol and, 97–100, 184; groups, 6, 31–34, 133, 143, 226, 240, 243–268, 302–304, 361n483, 363n41, 364n51, 366n94; songs, 263, 301–305, 367n115. *See also* Afoxés
Carneiro, Edison (1912–1972), 93, 103–104, 147, 255
Carneiro, Maria Luiza Tucci, 206
Carneiro, Sueli, 107, 225
cartography, 14, 218–220
Carvalho, José Murilo de (1939–2023), 48–49
Carvalho Netto, Menelick de, 111, 112
Carybé (1911–1997), 147
A casa da água (Olinto), 370n218
Casa Branca, 289, 290
Casa Grande das Minas. *See* Querebentã de Zomadonu
Casa-grande e Senzala ("The Master's House and the Slave Quarters") (Freyre), 94, 100–101
Cascudo, Luís da Câmara (1898–1986), 93–94, 139, 148, 171, 342n74, 352n193, 355n297
Casimira, Antônio (brother), 122–124
Casimira, Isabel, 122–124, 230
Castilho, J. Feliciano de, 329n90
Castillo, Lisa, 289–290
Castro, Ruy, 98
Castro, Yeda Pessoa de, 133, 161, 164, 175, 342n59
Catendê, Mestre Moa do (1954–2018), 267

INDEX

Catholic Church, 19, 43, 161, 200, 217, 288, 318; African-Catholicism, 99, 102, 170; bells, 141, 142; influence, 21, 53, 78, 167–169, 201, 205–206, 243, 280; Irmandades, 166, 170–171, 184, 256; Jesuits, 50, 209
Catimbó, 134
Cavazzi, João António (Friar) (1621–1692), 200, 208, 213, 356n321, 357n379, 358nn386–387, 359n426; on harps, 138; on Kongo celebrations, 169–170; Queen Nzinga and, 212, 216–217, 349n101, 349n118, 358n385
Caymmi, Dorival (1914–2008), 185
censorship, 82–83, 121
"central code" of Afro-Brazil, 293
chalk. *See pemba*
Chamberlain, Henry (1796–1843), 138
chants, 123–124, 172, 180, 189–190, 192–193, 210, 303; Capoeira, 28, 150–151, 158–159, 160; Congada, 156, 159, 174–178, 220; griots with healing, 246–253; poem-chants, 26, 160–161, 165, 268. *See also* Candombe; Candomblés; songs
Chauí, Marilena, 51
A Chegada Africana (African Arrival), 253
children, 42, 109, 156, 180–181, 213, 222, 280, 372n306; enslaved, 291; Feast of the Children of the Rosary, 170; Filhos da África, 253; infertility, 240–241; Moçambique Children of the Rosary, 31; sons and mothers, 257–258
Children of Africa. *See* Filhos da África
Children of Gandhy, 31, 233
Children of Our Lady of the Rosary. *See* Filhos do Rosário
"Choreographies of the Impossible," São Paulo Art Biennial, 128
chorus, singing, 64, 71, 146, 151, 159, 172, 220, 255
Christ, 76, 82, 141, 186–187, 245
Christianity, 79, 101, 200, 214, 216–217, 239
church tower, as sacred space, 142
Ciata, Tia (1854–1924), 34, 302
Cities of the Dead (Roach), 13, 16
The City of Women (Landes), 257–258
civilization, 43, 49, 50, 54, 86, 92, 105, 218; African civilization(s), 1, 2, 7, 16, 94, 95, 98, 129, 142, 228, 229; African civilizations in Brazil viii, 1, 17, 25, 117, 131, 150; African-Brazilian civilization, 10, 22, 29, 31, 116, 210, 228–230, 234; African matrix, 143; Afro-(Euro)-Brazilian, 10, 115; Afro-Brazilian, 98, 129, 133; Afro-diasporic (African diasporic) 137, 139; Bantu, 15, 127, 144, 226; Bantu-Yoruba, 134; Black, 133; Black Atlantic, 15; Brazilian, 95, 105; Dogon, 15; Euro-Afro-Brazil, 119; Eurocentric, 120; European civilization(s), vii, 4, 7, 54, 66–67, 120, 142; European civilization(s) in Brazil, 17, 19, 22, 26, 39, 51; Kongo (Bakongo), 137, 230, 311; Kongo-Angola (Angola-Kongo), 128, 132, 137, 145, 149, 164, 165; Nago-Jeje African-Brazilian (Nago-Ketu, Jeje-Mina), 31; Neo-African-Brazilian, 129; Roman and Greek (Greco-Roman)1, 60, 134; Western civilization, 15, 27, 30, 319; Yoruba, 15, 235, 238 [I included here all (or most) of the references to "civilizations." This needs to be checked, and it may be important to keep, but I am not sure.]
Claridge, Cyril (c. 1885–?), 212
Clarke, John Henrik (1915–1998), 210
Coalizão Negra Por Direitos (Black Coalition for Rights), 108
Cobra Norato (Bopp), 96
Cobrinha, Mestre, 149
codex, 26, 122, 124
coding (production), 27, 144
Coli, Jorge, 44–45
colonial bounty hunters. *See bandeirantes*
colonized-monster, hero-colonizer and, is something missing here? 19–20
A Color Defect. See Um defeito de cor
Columbus, Christopher, 34, 281
combats, mock, 138, 171–172, 174, 180, 213, 217, 242
Commission for Historical Reparations for Black People, 110
communion, 100–101, 141, 182, 184, 240, 242
Conceição, Djalma, 260
Concone, Maria Helena, 187, 188
confirmation, with baptism and communion, 100–101
conga, 150, 352n191
Congadas, 29, 31, 102, 147, 152, 190, 244, 312, 339n6; chants, 156, 159, 174–178, 220; conga, 150, 352n191; coronations, 26, 88–89, 166–167, 170–172; Filhos do Rosário, 180–181; mock combats within, 171–172, 180; musical instruments in, 27, 142, 144–145, 175; performances, 23, 88–89, 165, 170–173, 180–181, 213, 220–221, 243, 256–257, 323n52; poetics of, 172–181; role of, 166–171, 182–184. *See also* Afoxés
Congo, 98, 103, 122–123, 126, 145, 194, 323n52; dance style, 178–179; performers, 29, 173–174, 179–181. *See also* Guarda and Congadas.
Congo-Angola region, 30–31, 295, 341n35
Congress of the Latin American Studies Association (LASA), 322n21

Constitutions, 72, 97, 111, 338n1
"Contas." *See* "Beads"
"continuance theory," 296
Contreiras, Cristovão de Burgos de, 168
coronations, 26, 88–89, 166–167, 169–172
Correia, Raimundo, 186
cosmogram (Yowa), 146, 232, 313; Bakongo, 30, 152, 164, 179, 181, 311; Kongo, 124, 311, 316
cosmogramic altars, 316
cosmologies, 54–57, 175, 180, 285, 296; African-Brazilian, 244–268; Bakongo, 1, 152, 155–156, 163; Kongo, 151, 185–186, 192–193, 313; Kongo-Angola, 102, 145–146, 151, 164, 192, 232; Oyo, 271, 293; Yoruba, 28, 31–32, 179, 255–257, 305–306
Costa, Cláudio Manuel da, 75
Costa, Haroldo, 288
Costa, Manoel Vitorino da (1900–1980). *See* Falefá, Manuel
Costigan, Lúcia Helena, 78, 331n25
costumes, 174, 247, 249, 254, 257, 263–268, 366n110
coup d'états, 59, 73, 121, 270, 274, 285
Couto, Mia, 59
COVID-19 pandemic, 108, 303
cranioscopy method, 90
creolization, 94–101, 150, 279
crimes, 111, 113, 169
critical fabulation, 5, 12, 18, 28, 30, 85, 234,
crosses, 76, 164, 217, 316, 331n14, 359n426
crossings (oceanic, diasporic, transatlantic) 149, 229, 268, 292, 303, 310
Cruz e Silva, António Diniz da (1861–1898), 75, 80
The Cry of Ipiranga (*O grito do Ipiranga*). *See Independência ou morte*
Cuba, 1, 16, 186, 292–293, 341n38; *firmas*, 313, 315, 316–317; slavery and, 239, 275
Cucumbi, 172. *See also* Congadas
Culto de Nação. *See* Batuque
cultural archive, 7–8, 181
Cunha, Manuela Carneiro da, 294
Cunha, Mariano Carneiro da, 370n218
Cunha Barbosa, Januário da (1780–1846), 21, 49, 75–78, 80, 85, 115
currency shells. *See nzimbus*
curses, 20–21, 56, 59–65, 68–69, 80–86, 292, 308
Cusack, Igor, 70–71
Cuvelier, Jean (1882–1962), 198

Da Costa e Silva, Alberto, 370n218
Dadah Dedjalagni Agoli-Agbo (King of Abomey) (1934–2018), 282, 283

Da Gama, Vasco, 64, 132. *See also* Vasco Da Gama
Dahomey, 130, 271–272, 280, 293, 303; governance model, 34–35, 230, 275, 296–301; Oyo empire and, 273–275, 277, 285
Dahomey (Herskovits), 371n257
Dakodonu (Tacoodonou) (King of Dahomey) (r. c. 1620–1645), 35, 271–272, 297
Dama do Paço (Lady of the Palace), 255
Dan Ayido Hwedo (serpent), 35, 295
dance, 7, 26, 149–150, 158, 170, 255, 344n107; *cachaça*, wild hunts and royal, 86–90; dancers and, 135, 146, 153, 178–179; fighting and, 138–139, 342n74; transcending space, time, bonds and history, 182–186. *See also* Candombe; Candomblés; Capoeira; Congadas; Congo; Samba
Dance of Black Musicians Playing the Instruments of Their Country, 138
Danh (Vodun deity), 271–272
Da Silva, Carmelinda Maria, 173
Da Silva, Domingos, 290
Da Silva, Francisca (c. 1780–1859). *See* Nàsó, Ìyá
Da Silva, Marcelina (c. 1812–1885). *See* Tossi, Obá
Da Silva, Maria Magdalena, 289, 290
Davidson, Basil (1914–2010), 269, 275
Davies, Carole Boyce, 257
Dawson, Charles Daniel, 8–9, 147–149
"Deadly Dances" (Desch-Obi), 344n107
death, 44–45, 121, 149, 152, 190, 212, 305–306; funerals, 46, 72, 81, 138, 150, 217; Irmandade da Boa Morte, 256; tombs, 186, 217, 282, 301
Debret, Jean-Baptiste (1768–1848), 47, 70, 86, 138
Decânio, Mestre, 342n69
decapitation, 167, 217, 241
Declaration of Independence, Brazil, 44
Declaration on Race and Racial Prejudice, UNESCO, 4
decoding (interpretation), 27, 122, 124–125, 130, 144, 213, 316
Deeply Rooted in the Present (Kenny), 16
Um defeito de cor (*A Color Defect*) (Gonçalves, A. M.), 253
Deixa Falar ("Let them say whatever they want"), 99
Desch-Obi, T. J., 139, 147, 342n74, 344n107
Descrição histórica dos três reinos Congo, Matamba, Angola (Cavazzi), 349n118, 356n321, 358nn385–387, 359n426
"Description of the Recife of Pernambuco" (Teixeira), 79
Desmangles, Leslie, 272, 296

INDEX 405

De Souza, Francisco Félix (Chacha I) (c. 1754–c. 1849), 33–34, 36, 270, 275–276, 280–283, 285, 302–307
De Souza, Honoré Feliciano (Chacha VIII), 282
De Souza, Raquel, 161
De Souza, Roger Moise (Chacha IX), 34, 282, 283
Diamond, Stanley, 272, 297
Dias, Gonçalves (1823–1864), 75–76, 115, 186, 329n90, 330n3, 332n35, 332n49; national anthem and, 21, 74; with prophecy of cursed legacy, 80–85
Didi, Mestre (Deoscóredes Maximiliano dos Santos) (1917–2013), 35, 247–248, 287–292, 305
Dikenga (Yowa), 18, 124, 165, 193; Bakongo, 1, 26–27, 30, 132, 140, 149–150, 152, 155–156, 163–164, 179, 181–182, 195–197, 200, 293, 311; cross, 164, 316; Dingo-Dingo movement, 164, 311–312; Pan-African, 313–317
Dilogun (cowrie shell, Ifa) 304
Dingo-Dingo movement, 164, 311–312
"Diongo, Mundiongo," (Maria Aparecida Martins) 26, 118, 120–122, 152
diongo, mundiongo ((umndiongo, umndóngo, umnjongo) (house of the word, centers of knowledge) *See* Jongo. 18, 26, 118, 120–122, 152, 153, 346n19
diplomatic delegation. *See* Embaixada
Dodô and Osmar, 254, 364n51
Dom João Carlos de Bragança (Regent Prince of Portugal), 274
doppelgänger. *See* "King-as-Prince" governance model
Dos Anjos, Augusto, 186
Dossar, Kenneth, 146
doubling, 35, 296–297
Drewal, Henry, 372n306, 376n10
Drewal, Margaret Thompson, 372n306
drums, 128–130, 135, 151–153, 158, 178, 188; *atabaque*, 139, 140, 247, 249, 255–256; Candomblés, 27, 75, 140, 175, 247, 255–256; *tamboril*, 173, 190
Drums from Angola. See Tambores de Angola
Duarte, Evandro Piza, 111, 112, 113, 114
dunga, *See* ndunga
Duque Estrada, Joaquim Osório, 72, 73, 74, 75, 115
Durão, José de Santa Rita, 75
Dutra, Francisco, 329n90

Eddington, Arthur (Sir) (1882–1944), 309
Edict of Expulsion, 205
Eduardo, Octavio da Costa, 286
Egba, 130, 132, 271

Egbado, 130, 271
Egharevba, Joel, 235
Egun, 9, 36, 180, 257–258, 287, 305; Ipori, 306
Egungun, 247, 256–257
Ejigbo, 35, 239–242
Ekiti, 130, 271
E la nave va (film), 45–46
"E la nave va" ("And the Ship Sails On") (Coli), 45
Elegba (Orisha), 14, 34, 47, 142, 312
Elegun (medium, spirit-mounted), 258
Eliot, T. S., 12, 317–318
Eliseu do Bomfim Ajimúdà, Babalawo Martiniano (Ojé L'adê) (1859–1943), 104
Embaixada (diplomatic delegation), 171, 253, 263
Embaixada Africana (African Embassy), 253–254
Embanda. *See* Umbanda
Emi, 305
Empire of Brazil (1822–1889), 19, 49, 58–59, 72, 84
encantamento (enchantment) movement, 251–253; *encantado*, 251
enslaved people, 84, 88, 93, 125, 203–204, 223, 308; former, 17, 33, 87, 113, 270, 276, 280–284, 291, 294, 302, 304; political rivals as, 284–286; rebellions, 224, 262–263, 270, 278–279, 290–292
Enslen, Joshua Alma, 74–75, 330n3
"Entra em Beco, Sai em Beco" ("Go In Through an Alley, Come Out Through an Alley"), 263
epic poems, 12, 21, 75–79, 85. *See also The Lusiads*
"A escrava." *See* "The Slave Woman"
Eshu-Elegba (Èṣù-Ẹlẹ́gbára, Legba, Exu) (Orisha), 34, 142, 241
Estado Novo dictatorship (1937–1945), Portugal, 53, 97
ethereal realm. *See* Ile Orun
Ethiopia, 219, 353n216
Euro-Afro-Brazil, 9–10, 115–116, 312
Euro-Afro-Brazilian, 22, 23, 86, 103, 120, 131
Euro-Brazil, 10, 20, 25, 69, 116, 312
Euro-Brazilian, 18, 24, 54–57, 116, 120–121, 136
European languages, 28, 122, 229
Ewe-Fon, 103, 161, 164, 175, 179–180, 190–191, 294, 303
extraterrestrials, 2, 187–188

Fa. *See* Fon Ifa
Falefá, Manuel (Manuel da Formiga, Manoel Vitorino da Costa) (1900–1980), 103
"Family" (Hilton, A.), 355n297
family trees, 14–17, 30, 317–320
Fanon, Frantz (1925–1961), 184–185

fantasia, Hindu-Muslim-Bahian, 263–268
Fanti, 132
Faras, João de (Mestre João), 331n14
Father Joaquim from Aruanda. *See* Pai João da Aruanda
Feast of Our Lady of the Rosary of the Arturos Community, 173
Feast of the Children of the Rosary, 170
feasts, 170, 173, 175, 217; "Águas de Oxalá," 32, 239, 242, 244, 262; in *The Lusiads*, 68, 85; in "Meditation," 85
feet, bodies, 3, 31, 37, 76, 138, 145, 163–164, 174, 176, 179, 239, 306
Feitas, Décio, 359n441
Felinto, Renata, 47
Felipe I de Sousa (King of Ndongo). *See* Ngola-a-Hari I
Félix, Anísio (1936–2007), 260, 364n51
Fellini, Federico, 45–46
femicide, 109, 361n480
Fernandes, Victor, 303
Ferreira, Isac, 303
fighting, 138–139, 342n74, 344n124. *See also* Capoeira
Figueiredo, Maria Júlia (1890–1994), 256
Filhos da África (Children of Africa), 253
"Filhos de Gandhi," 244–251, 364n42, 364n51
Filhos de Gandhy (Sons of Gandhi), 31–33, 244–252, 254–268, 363n41, 364n51, 366n94
Filhos do Rosário (Children of Our Lady of the Rosary), 172, 174, 180–181
finda (mfinda), 144, 190
Finnegan, Ruth, 369n191
firmas (signature), 313, 315, 316–317
First Afro-Brazilian Congress (1934), 2, 103–104, 105, 321n1
First Indigenous Conference, Coroa Vermelha, 41–42
500th anniversary celebrations, Brazil, 41–44
flags, 21, 52, 76, 88, 224, 255
Flash of the Spirit (Thompson, R. F.), 15–16
Florentino, Manolo Garcia (1958–2021), 125
Folha, Tata Bernardo Bate (1881–1946) (Tata Ampumandezu, Manoel Bernardino da Paixão), 103–104
Folia de Reis (Revelry of the Kings), 158, 257
folklore, 54, 94, 96, 152, 228
Fon, 16, 131–132, 191, 271, 285, 369n191; ideology, 35, 296–297; Yoruba-Fon, 30, 33
Fon Ifa (Fa), 275, 369n191
Fonseca, Manuel Deodoro da (Marshal), 59

Fonseca, Mariana Bracks, 156–157
food, 67, 213, 242, 264, 299, 304. *See also* feasts
Foram 17 anos (It Has Been 17 Years), 121
The Formation of Brazilian Literature (*Formação da literatura brasileira*) (Candido), 53, 318
Formiga, Manuel da (1900–1980). *See* Falefá, Manuel
forts, 35, 131, 269–270
Foucault, Michel, 3, 45
foundational texts, 20, 80. *See also The Tempest*
foundation myths, 51, 95–96, 173, 199, 237, 271; African-Brazilian civilization, 228–233; Euro-Brazilian cosmology, 54–57; Brazilian cosmology, 17, 39; Luso-Brazilian cosmology, 20; Kongo, 30; Ndongo, 208; royal cultural traditions, 28
four moments of the sun, 124, 164, 311
Freitas, Décio, 223, 263, 348n72
French, Jan Hoffman, 107
French Artistic Mission (Missão Artística Francesa), 70
French Parnassianism, 186
Frente Negra Brasileira (Black Brazilian Front, FNB), 109
Freud, Sigmund, 93
Frevo Carnaval, 143, 226, 246, 361n483
Freyre, Gilberto (1900–1987), 23–24, 94–95, 100–101, 103–104, 112, 257
friendship hierarchy, 300–301
Frobenius, Leo, 242
Fruku (Prince), 284
Fryer, Peter, 254
Fu-Kiau, Bunseki (1934–2013), 36, 135, 164, 196, 309, 311, 313; Capoeira and, 146, 148–150; on Nzambi, 152, 161
Fulanis (Fulás), 132
Fundação Cultural Palmares (Palmares Cultural Foundation), 226
funerals, 46, 72, 81, 138, 150, 217
fungi, subterranean networks, 14
futebol (soccer), 97–100, 148, 158, 184
futú (sacred pouch, medicine), 189, 193

Gaakpé (King-as-Prince of Dahomey). *See* Gezó-Gaakpé
Galante, Rafael, 141–143, 335n68, 338n5
gameleira fig tree, 294, 295
Gandhi (film), 244
Gandhi, Mohandas Karamchand (1869–1948), 30, 36, 366n110; Children of Gandhy, 31, 233; "Filhos de Gandhi," 244–251, 364n42; Filhos

de Gandhy, 31–33, 244–252, 254–268, 363n41, 364n51, 366n94
Gandhi's Revelry. *See* "Patuscada de Gandhi"
"Le géant couché." *See* "The Reclining Giant"
Gege. *See* Jeje
Geledés Instituto da Mulher Negra (Black Women's Institute), 225, 360n473
Geledé societies, 256
geography, sacred, 164, 185–186, 272
Gerber, Raquel, 226, 361n480, 361n483
German Historical School, 51
Gézo (King of Dahomey) (r. 1818–1858), 33–35, 270, 273–277, 282–283, 285–286, 298–303, 371n257
Gezó-Gaakpé (King-as-Prince of Dahomey), 35, 298–301
Ghana, 33, 35, 37, 130–132, 269, 370n218
Ghede, 284
giants, 60; Brazil as, 21, 69–70, 73, 77, 85, 92; stone, 21, 22, 75–78, 312. *See also* Adamastor; Niteroi
"O Gigante de pedra." *See* "The Stone Giant"
Gil, Gilberto, 35, 244–251, 258–259, 287, 364n42, 364n47, 364n51
Gilroy, Paul, 16, 294
Ginga. *See* Nzinga-Mbandi-Ngola-Kiluanji
ginga movement, 156–159, 178, 255
Gleason, Judith, 283
Glele/Gelele (King of Dahomey) (r. 1858–1889), 299–300
God. *See* Nzambi
"Go In Through an Alley, Come Out Through an Alley." *See* "Entra em Beco, Sai em Beco"
Golden Law. *See* Imperial Law
Gomes, Heloisa Toller, 94, 352n194
Gomes, Bethânia Nascimento, 361n480
Gomes, Núbia Pereira Magalhães (1940–1994), 172–175, 181–182
Gomez, Diogo (Father), 209
Gonçalves, Ana Maria, 252–253
Gonçalves de Magalhães, 75
Gonzalez, Lélia (1935–1994), 11, 322n21
Gottschalk, Louis Moreau (1829–1869), 72
graphocentrism, 319
Graham, Maria, 87
"a grande máquina do Mundo." *See* "World-Machine"
"Grande fantasia triunfal sobre o hino nacional brasileiro." *See* "Great Triumphal Fantasy on the Brazilian National Anthem"
Great Britain, 217, 219

"The Great Empire of Dahomey-Maranhão and the Boundless Borders of the Spiritual Enchantment of Querebetã of Zomadônu," 303
"Great Triumphal Fantasy on the Brazilian National Anthem" ("Grande fantasia triunfal sobre o hino nacional brasileiro"), 72
Greco-Bantu, 134
Grêmio Recreativo de Arte Negra Escola de Samba Quilombo, 302
Grêmio Recreativo Império do Rio Belo, 34, 303
Griffith, Paul, 13, 16
Griffiths, Ieuan, 218
griots, 138, 244–268, 301–305, 307
O grito do Ipiranga (*The Cry of Ipiranga*). *See Independência ou morte*
Guarda (Guarda de Moçambique; Guarda de Congo) 29, 122–123, 145, 255, 340n15, *See* Congadas
Guanabara (Niterói) Bay, 21, 70, 77
O Guanabara (*The Guanabara* [*Bay*]) (journal), 80, 82–83
Guarda de Moçambique e Congo Treze de Maio ("The May Thirteenth Moçambique and Congo Guard"), 122–123, 145
guerra preta ("black war"), 167, 203–204, 223
guerrillas, 33, 214, 220, 223, 254, 280
"guerrilla scholarship," 16
Guild, Fellowship, or Brotherhood of Martyrs. *See* Irmandade dos Martírios
Guillobel, Joaquim Cândido (1787–1859), 138
Guimarães, Bernardo, 329n90
Guimarães, Roberta Sampaio, 33
gunga berimbau, 140, 146
Gunga Din (film), 260, 261–262, 366nn102–103
"Gunga Din" (Kipling), 261, 366n103, 366n106
gungas, 27, 139–140, 143–145, 174–175
Gurunsis, 132

ha-goyim (nations), 205–206, 356n333
Haiti, 16, 224, 313, 315–316
Haitian Revolution (1791–1804), 131
Ham's Redemption. See A redenção de Cam
Hangbe (Queen of Dahomey), 298
Hargobind (Guru), 367n121
Harlem Renaissance, 95
harps, 27, 136–140, 143–146, 174–175
Harring, Harro Paul (1798–1870), 138
Hartman, Saidiya, 5, 14
Hasenbalg, Carlos (1942–2014), 107
Hawthorne, Walter, 294
Hayner, Priscilla, 337n21

head. See ori
healing, 142, 189, 191–192, 246–253, 282, 336n78
Helios (sun god), 70
Henrique (Prince of Kongo), 201
Henson, Bryce, 11
Herbert, George, 313–314
herbs, xvi–xviii, 265, 320, 350n141, 352n194
hero-colonizer, colonized-monster and, 19–20
heroes, 12–13, 33, 56–57, 96, 302, 307
Herskovits, Melville (1895–1963), 7, 11, 15–16, 105, 284, 286, 297, 371n257
Hertzman, Marc, 252, 364n57
Hilton, Anne, 200, 355n297, 357n379
Hilton, John Laurence, 60
Hinduism, 191, 261–262, 264, 266–268
Hindu-Muslim-Bahian *fantasia*, 263–268
History of Brazilian Literature (*História da literatura brasileira*) (Romero), 53, 90–91
Hollanda, Lula Buarque de, 267
Holy Office, 78, 206
"A Hora do Brasil" ("The Time of Brazil"), 99
horses, 45, 115, 192, 241, 258, 315
Houmasse, Adjahô, 286–287
How the History of Brazil Should Be Written (Von Martius), 50–51
human rights, 97, 109–110, 113, 169–170, 182, 337n21, 361n487
hungu, 137
hunts, *cachaça*, royal dances and, 86–90
The Hyssop (Cruz e Silva), 75

Iabaday, Henrique, 18–19, 22, 41
Ianni, Octávio (1926–2004), 97
Iansã. See Oya-Yansan
Ibadan, 132
Ibeju (Iebu), 132
Iberian Union (1580–1640), 202, 203
IBGE. See Brazilian Institute for Geography and Statistics
iconography, 6, 164, 264
Identidade negra e educação (Luz), 366n94
ideology, 35, 57, 92–93, 101, 121, 296–297
Iebu. See Ibeju
Iemanjá. See Yemaya
Ifa oracle (Ifá), 104, 243, 361n488, 372n306; diviners, 147, 241, 242, 289, 291; Odu verse, 239–241; Opón, 311–313; Orunmila, 236, 303, 311–312
Igbo people, 131
IHGB. See Instituto Geográfico e Histórico Brasileiro

Ijebu, 130, 271
Ijesa region, 130, 271
Ijesha (Ijexá), 132, 133, 235, 246, 255–256, 266, 292
Ikù (Orisha), 305–306
Ile Aiye (Ilé Aiyé) (house of the living, the Earthly World) 236, 237
Ilê Aiyê ((*bloco afro* from Salvador), 254
Ile-Ifé (Ilé-Ifẹ̀ / Ile Ifẹ), 31–32, 34, 230, 232, 234–239, 241–244, 271–272
Ile Orun (Ilé Ọ̀run) (House of the ancestors and spirits, the Spiritual World), 236–237
Ilésanmí, Thomas Mákanjúọlá, 243
Illiteracy. See literacy. 319
imagery, 53, 57, 60; of Aruanda, 160; Brazilian national anthem, 20, 73, 76, 84, 85, 122. See also visual arts
immigrants, 109, 136, 359n439
Imperial (Golden) Law, 45, 302
Imprensa Régia. See Royal Press
Inácio, Ângelo. See Pinheiro, Robson
inclusion, 24–25, 108, 139, 179, 191, 228, 265, 267
Independência ou morte (*Independence or Death, O grito do Ipiranga, The Cry of Ipiranga*), 44–45, 121
India, 55–57, 60, 67, 261, 264–268, 367n134
Indigenous: movements, 19, 41–42; people, 25, 41–43, 81, 84, 90, 100, 112–113, 168, 179–180, 204, 223, 225, 231, 248, 267, 310, 335n55, 359n432; as racial category, 107
infertility, 240–241
Inquices. See Nkisis
the Inquisition, 21, 78, 168, 205–206
Instituto Geográfico e Histórico Brasileiro (IHGB, Brazilian Geographical and Historical Institute), 19–22, 25, 49–51, 77, 80, 86, 119–120
insurrections, 84, 131, 263, 270, 278–279, 289–290, 325n4
interpretation. See decoding
Introdução à antropologia Brasileira (*Introduction to Brazilian Anthropology*) (Ramos), 93
IPHAN. See National Institute of Historic and Artistic Heritage
Iracema (Alencar), 96
Irmandade da Boa Morte ("Sisterhood, or Sorority of Good Death"), 256
Irmandade dos Martírios (Guild, Fellowship, or Brotherhood of Martyrs), 256
Irmandades, 166, 170–171, 184, 256
Isaac (biblical figure), 84
Isabel (Princess) (1846–1921), 44–45, 72, 302
Isichei, Elizabeth, 11, 31, 36

Islam, 239, 278–279
Islamism, Malê, 367n114
itan (*itàn*) (oral texts, history), 18, 36; Danh, 271–272; Ejigbo kingdom, 239–242; Obatala, 240–242, 305–306, 312; Ramadan origins, 372n306; *pa itàn*, 312
It Has Been 17 Years. *See Foram 17 anos*
Iyámi Agbá (female ancestral powers, Geledé)
Iyá Nassô (high priestess, Casa Branca, Candomblé Ketu)

Jagas, 208, 211, 215, 357n379
Jahn, Janheinz, 15
Jamaica, 7, 12, 13
Janus (mythical figure), 20, 71
Jatobá Brotherhood of Our Lady of the Rosary, 126, 127, 194, 340n15
Jecupé, Kaká Werá, 310
Jeje (Gege), 34; Ewe-Fon, 103, 294, 303; Nago-Jeje, 30–31, 132, 243, 285, 292–295; Nago-Jeje-Ketu, 232
Jeje-Mina, 26, 131
Jeje Vodun, 294–295
Jesuits, 50, 209
Jews, 21, 22, 75, 78, 111–112, 168, 205–206
Jinga. *See* Nzinga-Mbandi-Ngola-Kiluanji
João, Mestre. *See* Faras, João de
João de Sousa (King of Ndongo). *See* Ngola-a-Hari II
João I (King of Kongo). *See* Nzinga-a-Nkuwu
João II (King of Portugal) (1455–1495), 200
João III (King of Portugal) (1502–1557), 202, 207
João VI (King of Portugal) (1767–1826), 44, 58, 70, 80, 89
Jongo (Ndiongo, Ndongo, Ndiongo, Njongo) 31, 147, 152–153, 158, 178, 190
Judaism, 78, 79. *See also* diongo
Jung, Carl, 93
Junqueiro, Guerra, 186

Kagame, Alexis, 15
kalunga, 144, 180, 190, 192; boundary line, 155–156, 163, 165, 176, 193, 311, 316; *Mundiongo* in, 146–153
Kanuris. *See* Bornus
Kardec, Allan (Hippolyte Léon Denizard Rivail) (1804–1869), 186, 187
Kardecist Spiritualism, 186
Karl-August, Emmanuel, 292
Kasanje, 29, 207, 210–217, 221, 222
Kenny, Mary Lorena, 16

Kenya (Melinde/Malinde, Mombasa), 20, 55, 61, 66, 67
Ketu (Ketou, Queto), 103, 132, 235, 240, 271, 289, 291; Candomblé, 133, 255; Nago-Jeje-Ketu, 232; Nago-Ketu, 26, 131, 288, 295
Khoisan people, 20, 66–67, 310
Kidder, Daniel Parish, 87
Kiddy, Elizabeth, 294
kijiko (war prisoners), 169, 208
Kikongo, 131; etymology and connotations, 140–141, 143, 150, 156, 161, 175–178, 190, 213, 222, 232, 315, 340n16, 342n59, 352n194; proverbs, 195, 196, 230
Kilombo, 28, 357n381; Queen Nzinga with, 29, 35, 211–214, 217, 220–227, 275, 297; rituals, 210, 211, 213
Kimbundo, etymology and connotations, 26, 121, 137, 140–141, 143, 148, 152, 175–177, 181, 210, 211, 213, 342n59
Kimbundu, 232; etymology and connotations, 141, 152, 164, 174, 177–178, 191, 195, 340n16, 348n72, 349n126; speakers, 131, 222
Kimpanzu family, Bakongo, 196, 197
"King-as-Prince" ("Bush King," doppelgänger) governance model, 34–35, 230, 275, 296–301
Kindoki (force, protective/destructive), 212
King of the White Cloth. *See* Obatala
Kinganga (Nganga practice, healing, philosophy), 212
Kimpasi (Kongo philosophical schools), 156
Kinenga (balance of life), 135
Kinguri-kya-Bangela, 210
Kinsaku family, Bakongo, 196, 197
kinship, 178, 198–199, 222, 272, 291, 297, 301
Kinzinga family, Bakongo, 196, 197
Kipling, Rudyard (1865–1936), 261, 366n103, 366n106
Klein, Bernhard, 57, 63, 65–67
Kongo, 28, 30, 169–170, 176, 197, 206, 323n52; contextualization of, 194–196; cosmogram, 124, 311, 316; cosmology, 151, 185–186, 192–193, 313; *makanda* clans, 194, 198–199; philosophies, 16, 148, 156, 312–313; Portugal and, 199–205; proverbs, 143–144, 196
Kongo-Angola, 103, 147, 160–161, 189–191, 203, 318–319, 349n101; Candombe, 140, 175; civilization, 148–149, 165, 194, 231; cosmology, 102, 145–146, 151, 164, 192, 232; cultural region, 130; culture, 98, 243; Dikenga, 312; Greco-Bantu, 134; harp and, 137; sacred geography, 164
Kongo-Angola-Mozambique, 28, 159, 175, 176, 193, 194

Kpengla (King of Dahomey) (r. 1774–1789), 274, 284
Kubik, Gerhard, 26, 129–130, 165–166, 191, 341n35
Kuntu (modalities of experiencing and expressing), 15

L'adê, Ojé (1859–1943). *See* Eliseu do Bomfim Ajimúdà, Babalawo Martiniano
Lady of the Palace. *See Dama do Paço*
Lágrimas de Nossa Senhora. *See* Tears of Our Lady
Landes, Ruth (1908–1991), 257–258
languages, 26, 53, 125, 160, 172, 293; Arabic, 66, 67, 248, 290; Bantu, 66, 144, 166, 176–177, 190, 315; Brazilian Portuguese, 2, 177, 232, 321n1; European, 28, 122, 229; musical instruments and, 27, 135, 137, 144; Yoruba, 130–131, 243, 271, 288, 312. *See also* Kikongo; Kimbundo; Kimbundu; *specific languages*
LASA. *See* Congress of the Latin American Studies Association
Law, Robin, 270, 281–282, 370n218
Law No. 10.639/2003 (the Afro-Brazilian and Indigenous History and Culture Law), 2, 321n1
Lawrence, Natalie, 60–61
Lemba, 148, 230–231
Lendas africanas dos orixás (African tales of the orishas), 236
Leonardi, Victor, 370n218
Leonel, Maria Célia, 48, 53
Leopoldina (Princess) (1797–1826), 44
"Let them say whatever they want." *See* Deixa Falar
Lewgoy, Bernardo, 187
LGBTQI+ (LGBTTQI+) community, 33, 109, 259
Os libertos (Verger), 370nn217–218, 371n262
"Ligeira explicação sobre a nação Congo" ("Brief Explanation of the Congo Nation") (Folha), 103–104
Ligiéro, Zeca, 27, 134–135, 158, 365n72
Lima, Raimundo Queiróz "Raimundo Gandhy" (1925–2006), 255
Lipkin, Lawrence, 61
literacy. *See* illiteracy. 12, 25, 123, 125, 313
Lobo, Haroldo, 263, 367n115
Lody, Raul, 254–255, 265
Loko, 294, 295
Lombroso, Cesare (1835–1909), 90
Lopes, Duarte, 148, 344n125
Lopes, João (1930–2004), 29, 126–128, 173, 175, 194, 234, 340n15
Lopes, Nei, 176, 177, 279, 340n16, 367n114

Lord of the Good End (Nosso Senhor do Bonfim), 245, 259
Lourenço da Silva Mendonça (Prince) (1620–1698), 29, 167–169, 217
Louverture, Toussaint, 224
Luccock, John, 87
Lukeni-lua-Nimi, 194
Lukeni-Luansanze (Queen of Mbata), 194
Lula da Silva, Luiz Inácio, 73
lungungu, 137–137
The Lusiads (Camões), 12, 58, 75, 78, 85, 115, 326n19; Adamastor in, 19–20, 56, 59–71; founding myths and, 54–57; "World-Machine" in, 20, 68–69. *See also* Vasco Da Gama
Lusitania, ancient, 55–56, 66, 68, 78
Luso-Brazilian literature, 75
Lusotropicalism, 3, 20
Lusus (mythical figure), 55, 56, 70
Luvèmba (sunset, transformation), 311
Luyaluka, Kiatezua Lubanzadio, 156
Luz, Marco Aurélio, 133, 366n94
Lwas. *See* Vodun
lyrics, Brazilian national anthem, 21, 69, 71–72, 74

Macedo, Gerson, 364n51
Macedo Soares, Antônio Joaquim de, 232, 362n496
MacGaffey, Wyatt, 178
Machado, Manuel dos Reis. *See* Bimba, Mestre
Macumba. *See* Umbanda
Macunaíma (Andrade), 96
Madeira, Vavá (Durival Marques da Silva), 260, 363n41
magic, 5, 20, 57–59, 172, 179, 284, 336n78. *See also* curses; prophecies
Maia, Rono, 303
makanda clans, Kongo, 194, 198–199
Makota (council of elders) 167, 197, 208.
Makota, (title, role) *See* Ritual Elders
"Makukwa matatu malâmb'e Kôngo" ("Minkuka mitatu mia Kongo") (the three pots in which the Kongo Kingdom was "cooked"/sustained), 193, 196
Malê Debalê, 263, 367n114
Malê Islamism, 367n114
Malê Rebellion, 262–263, 270, 278–279, 290–292
Malês, 132
malícia, 147–148
Malinde. *See* Kenya
Malinke people, 131
malungo(s), 116, 153, 198, 222, 345n142, 351n167, 373n312, 373n312, 395

Mameto (Prince of Kongo), 172, 349n126
Mandingas (Mandês), 132
Mandinga, 152, 159, 346n39
Manuel, Geraldo Zilote, 355n297
Manuel I (King of Portugal) (1469–1521), 12, 100, 201, 206
Maracatu, 165, 190, 210, 226, 255–256
Marcha, 72, 99, 246
"Marcha solene brasileira." *See* "Brazilian Solemn March"
Mardi Gras, 36, 304
Maria Jesuína (Queen). *See* Na Agontimé
marinheiros. *See* sailors
Maroons (Quilombolas), xv, xvi, 113; communities, 102, 109, 158, 168, 179, 220, 222, 224, 227, 278, 348n72; heroes, 12–13. *See also* Quilombo
Marques, Wilton, 81, 83
Martins, Domingos José, 276
Martins, Leda Maria, 9, 126, 128, 319, 340n15
Martins, Maria Aparecida (1939–1985), 26, 118, 120–122, 152
martyrs, 95–96
Marujada, 165
Mason, John, 179, 238–239
master-movement (*movimento-mestre*), 195, 196, 198
masters. *See mestres*
"The Master's House and the Slave Quarters." *See Casa-grande e Senzala*
Matamba, 167, 170–171, 195, 207–211, 214–217, 220, 230
Matory, Lorand, 257, 258
matrices, 26, 126, 129–135, 254
Mattos, Ricardo, 153, 345n142
maturity. *See* Tukula
Mawe, John, 86
Mawu-Lisa (creator godess), 35, 230, 272, 295–301
"The May Thirteenth Moçambique and Congo Guard." *See* Guarda de Moçambique e Congo Treze de Maio
Mayombe, 186, 316
Mbanza Kongo, 10, 29, 116, 123, 155, 169, 194–201, 230
Mbumba-Lowa (creator god), 156, 159
Mbundu, victories, 207–217
McElroy, Isis Costa, 363n40, 364n57.
media, 2, 99, 266, 315–316, 321n1, 364n51, 367n134
meditation, 138, 314, 330n3
"Meditation" ("Meditação") (Dias), 21, 80–85, 332n35, 332n49
mediums, 186–194, 314–316
Melinde. *See* Kenya
Mello e Souza, Marina de, 166

Melo, Antônio de, 359n441
Melodia, Jorge, 303
memory, 9, 11, 129–130, 310, 340n15; collective, 15, 28, 36, 43, 71, 114, 171, 194, 220, 230, 307; re-membering, 3–5, 22, 287
men, 256–259
Mendes (Friar), 209
Mendes, Lorraine Pinheiro, 47, 121
Menezes, Margareth, 240, 363n25
mental maps, of history, 310–311
Mercadores de Bagdá (Merchants of Baghdad), 266–267
merchants, 219, 248, 266–267, 274, 282; Portuguese, 201–202, 204–206, 208–210, 214; with slave trade, 204, 281, 283
Merchants of Baghdad. *See* Mercadores de Bagdá
Mesquita, Gaspar da Costa, 169
Os mestiços brasileiros (Rodrigues), 334n6
mestres (masters), 134, 139, 146
metaphors, 25, 27, 29, 36–37, 119, 140–141, 163–164; canoes, 178, 268; with national identity of Brazil, 18; trees, 14
"Metaphysics and Practice of Capoeira" (Pastinha), 139
Middle Passage, 124, 127, 137, 292, 301
Miguez, Leopoldo, 72
military, xvi, 19, 43, 138, 169–170, 273; coup d'états, 59, 73, 121, 270, 274, 285; dictatorship in Brazil, 72, 110, 121, 245–246, 251, 343n75, 370n223
Miller, Joseph, 357n379
milonga, 147–148, 152
Minki (pl. Nkisi), 131, 190
miscegenation, 23, 93, 97, 101, 103, 112
Missão Artística Francesa. *See* French Artistic Mission
MNU. *See* Black Unified Movement
Moçambique, 126, 171, 177, 179, 194, 323n52; chants, 176, 178, 180; Guarda de Moçambique e Congo Treze de Maio, 122–123, 145; Our Lady of the Rosary and, 174–176, 178, 181; performers, 29, 172–174, 244
Moçambique Children of the Rosary, 31
Mocambo. *See* Quilombo
modalities of experiencing and expressing. *See* Kuntu
Modern Art Week. *See* Semana de Arte Moderna
Modernists, 95–96, 136
Molina, Diego, 81, 84
Mombasa. *See* Kenya
monsters, 19–20, 60–61. *See also* Adamastor
Morais, Mariana, 104, 105

Morales, Anamaria, 260, 367n134
Morin, Edgar, 317
Morrison, Toni (1931–2019), 4–5
Moses (biblical figure), 76, 79, 187
mothers, sons and, 257–258
Mother Susana (fictional character), 154
motion, energy and, 134
m(o)trices, 26, 129–135
Motta, Roberto Mauro, 104
Motta, Virgulino, 126
Moura, Clóvis (1925–2003), 92
Moura, Milton Araújo, 265, 366n110
movimento-mestre. See master-movement
Movimento Negro Unificado. *See* Black Unified Movement
Moçambique. *See* Guarda and Congadas.
Mozambique (Sofala), 126–129, 132, 166, 177, 200, 217, 234, 308; Angola, Kongo and, 28, 159, 175, 176, 193, 194; cultural region, 131; in *The Lusiads*, 65–67
Mpansu, Buakasa Tulu Kia (1937–2004), 212
Muçumis (Muçumurin), 132
Mukambu-Mbandi Bárbara (Queen of Ndongo and Matamba), 217
Mundiongo, 18; Afro-Brazilian civilization m(o)trices and matrices, 129–135; different ways of writing, reading, teaching and learning, 122–125; "Diongo, Mundiongo," 26, 118, 120–122, 152; in *kalunga*, 146–153; talking bells, 140–145; talking harps, 136–140; two parties on parallel water banks, 125–129 *See also* Diongo
Musa Bin Bique (Muça Al Bique) (Muslim sultan), 132
music, 6, 33, 99, 100, 140, 149, 319; Brazilian national anthem, 72, 75; with royal processions, 88–89. *See also* Samba
musical instruments, 26, 135; bells, 27, 139–145, 179, 247, 249, 255; *berimbaus*, 27, 136–140, 144, 146–147, 158; Candombe, 126–128, 175–176; Congadas, 27, 142, 144, 145, 175; *gungas*, 27, 139–140, 143–145, 174–175; harps, 27, 136–140, 143–146, 174–175; rattles, 27, 88, 89, 144–145; tambourines, 88–89, 139; *viola*, 139, 140. *See also* drums
Muslims, 33, 67, 132, 277, 280–281, 362n7; Hindu-Muslim-Bahian *fantasia*, 263–268; Malê Rebellion, 262–263, 270, 278–279, 290–292
Musoni (southern sun, mysteries, perfection), 193, 311
Mvemba-a-Nzinga Afonso I (King of Kongo) (1456–1542), 29, 157, 200–202, 207, 217

Mvemba-a-Nzinga Afonso II (King of Kongo), 157
Mvemba-a-Nzinga João I (King of Kongo), 200
mysteries. *See* Musoni
myths, 2, 13, 90, 96, 183; national, 51, 111; Our Lady of the Rosary, 126–127, 173, 176. *See also* foundation myths

Na Agontimé (Maria Jesuína) (Queen), 33–34, 36, 277, 282–295, 301–307, 371n257
Nabuco, Joaquim (1849–1910), 113
Nafafé, José Lingna, 167–168, 223
Nago-Jeje, 30–31, 132, 134, 243, 285, 292–295
Nago-Jeje-Ketu, 232
Nago-Ketu, 26, 131, 288, 295
Nago-Vodun, 295
Nana Buluku, 103
Nascimento, Abdias do (1914–2011), 225, 227, 279
Nascimento, Beatriz (1942–1995), 11, 29, 171, 226–227, 322n21, 361n480, 361n483
Nascimento, Ciro, 226–227
Nàsó, Ìyá (Francisca da Silva) (c. 1780–1859), 35, 36, 287–291, 305, 307
Nássara, Antônio, 263, 367n115
national anthem, Brazil, 20–23, 52, 69–76, 84–85, 122
National Black Consciousness Day, 109
National Historic Landmarks, 103
National Human Rights Commission (NHRC), 361n487
National Institute of Historic and Artistic Heritage (IPHAN), 140, 338n1
National Museum of Fine Arts, 47
national myth, 51, 111
National System of Foreigners' Registration and Records (SINCRE), 359n439
nations. *See* ha-goyim
nation-state, 48, 53, 71, 218, 359n439
Natural History (Pliny the Elder), 61
"Navio negreiro" ("Slave Ship") (Alves, C.), 302
Nazareth, Paulo, 308
Ndongo, 165–169, 194–196, 208. *See also* Nzinga-Mbandi-Ngola-Kiluanji
ndunga (dunga, calundunga), 177, 311.
Negras (Gomes, H. T., and Pereira, E. de A.), 352n194
Negritude, 34, 95, 304
negro. See Black
"Negro" (Bopp), 136–137, 341n58
Negro church, processions, 88–89
O negro brasileiro (*The Black Brazilian*) (Ramos), 93

Negros estrangeiros (Cunha, Mariano Carneiro da), 370n218
Neguinho da Beija-Flor Marconde, Luiz Antônio Feliciano, 374n373
Neo-African-Brazilian civilization, 129–135
Neo-African cultural zones, 26, 129, 341n35
Nepomuceno, Alberto, 72
Netto, Menelick de Carvalho, 111–114
Neves, Tancredo, 72
New Christians, 78–79, 168–169, 205–206, 331n25
New (Nova) Lusitania, 79, 115
nganga ("priest doctor"), 212–213, 231
ngangela (cardinal point, fire), 155, 191
Ngola-a-Hari I (Felipe I de Sousa) (King of Ndongo), 167
Ngola-a-Hari II (João de Sousa) (King of Ndongo), 163, 167, 217
Ngola-Kanini João Guterres, 217
Ngola-Kiluanji (King), 163
Ngola-Kiluanji-Kia-Ndambi (King of Ndongo) (1556–1561), 209
Ngola-Kiluanji-Kia-Samba (King of Ndongo) (1515–1556), 208, 209
N'golo (Zebra Dance), 138–139, 342n74
ngoma, 151, 152, 181
ngunga(s), 140–141, 143, 174–175, 345n142
NHRC. *See* National Human Rights Commission
Nimi-a-Lukeni-lua-Mvemba Álvaro I (King of Kongo) (1568–1587), 209
Nimi-a-Nzima (King of Mpemba), 194
Niteroi (mythological figure), 21, 76–77, 115
Niterói Bay. *See* Guanabara Bay
Niterói or the Metamorphosis of Rio de Janeiro (Cunha Barbosa), 21, 75–78, 85, 115
Nkanga-a-Mvika Pedro II (King of Kongo), 207
nkisi (*nkita*, *simbi*, benevolent spirits). *See* Inkisi. 43, 144, 212
Nkita, 156. *See also* nkisi
Nkumbi Mpudi-a-Nzinga Diogo (1546–1561), 157
nonviolence, 31, 252
Nossa Senhora do Rosário. *See* Our Lady of the Rosary
Nosso lar (Our Home) (Xavier), 186–187, 189
Nosso Senhor do Bonfim. *See* Lord of the Good End
Notas sobre os comestíveis africanos (*Notes on African Edibles*) (Aninha), 104
Novais, Paulo Dias, 209, 210
Nova Lusitania. *See* New Lusitania
Nowosh, Victor, 303
Nsaku-Mpanzu-Nzinga (founding siblings), 159
Nsanda tree, 196–206

Nuestra América, 322n21
Nupês. *See* Tapas
Nzambi (God, Zambi), 152, 159, 161, 180, 192–193, 230, 316
Nzambi-a-Mpungu ("Always-Present-Ancestral-Whole" force), 164, 175, 231
nzila ya ntangu. *See* sun's path
nzimbus (currency shells), 28, 145, 155, 208, 209
Nzinga-a-Nkuwu (João I) (King of Kongo) (1440–1509), 29, 157, 199–205
Nzinga-Mbandi-Ngola-Kiluanji (Rainha Jinga, Ginga) (Queen of Ndongo and Matamba) (1582–1663), 102, 123, 163, 172, 230–231, 302; Capoeira movements and, 157–159; Cavazzi and, 212, 216–217, 349n101, 349n118, 358n385; with *Kilombo*, 29, 35, 211–214, 217, 220–227, 275, 297; as leader, 28–30, 156, 170–171, 209–212, 214–217

Obatala (Oxalá, Oshagiyan, King of the White Cloth), 34, 230–231, 296, 302–303; "Águas de Oxalá," 32, 239, 242, 244, 262; Filhos de Gandhy and, 257, 259, 263–264; *itan*, 239–242, 305–306, 312; as Oshalufan, 240, 266; Yoruba creation narrative and, 235–239
Obatala's Waters. *See* "Águas de Oxalá"
Obras poéticas de Glauceste Satúrnio (Costa), 75
Oduduwa (king of Ile-Ife), 34, 235–238, 271, 363n14
Odu verse, 239–241
Ogun (Ogum) (Orisha) 175, 179, 236, 245, 251, 261, 264, 302
Ojigi (Alaafin chief) (r. 1724–1735), 35, 273
Ojo Bada of Saki (Samuel Ojo) (1846–1901), 363n14
Old Christians, 206
The Old African and His Instrument, the Oricongo, 138
Olinto, Antonio, 370n218
Oliveira, Alan Santos de, 159
Oliveira, Alberto de, 186
Oliveira, João de, 275–276
Oliveira, José Carlos de, 156
Oliveira, Manuel Botelho de, 75
Olódùmarè, xvii, 236–237, 239, 242
Ondo, 130, 271
one-string harp. *See* urucongo
One Thousand and One Nights (film), 267
Onilé, 180, 230–232, 361n488
Opón Ifa, 311–313
oracles. *See* Ifa oracle

oral literature, 6, 8, 12–13, 194, 285, 313, 319
oral texts. *See itan*
oral traditions, 1, 163, 207, 211, 260, 271, 283; African-Brazilian, 132, 177; Caribbean, 16; Casa Branca, 289; chants, 123–124; history, 7; Kongo culture, 194–195; Oba people, 238; text performances, 4; veracity of, 6, 11; Yoruba people, 243
oraliture (*oralitura*), 319
Oranyan (founder of Oyo), 235, 271, 363n14
O Rappa, 106
Òrí (documentary film), 226–227, 361n480, 361n483
ori (head), 305–306
Oriki(s), 178, 190, 238, 240, 288, 363n14
ori-inu (orí-inú) (inner self, person's potential), 305–306
Orishas (Òrìṣàs, *Orixás*), xvi, xvii, 131, 236, 294, 372n306. *See also specific Orishas*
Oro societies, 256–257
Olodumare (Olódùmarè, Olodumaré), 17, 236–237, 239, 242
Ortiz, Renato, 96
òrun (spiritual plane), *See* Ile Orun, xvii–xviii, 236–237, 306, 320
Orunmila (Orumilá) (Ifa), 236, 303, 311–312
Osayin (Ossaim), xvi, xviii
Oshagiyan. *See* Obatala
Oshalufan, 240, 266. *See also* Obatala
Oshosi (Orisha), 179, 245, 289
Oshumare (Orisha), 245, 251
Oshun (Orisha), 245, 251, 255
Ouidah, 272, 274–275, 280, 292, 308
"Ouidah 92" festival, 281
Our Home. *See Nosso lar*
Our Lady of the Rosary (Nossa Senhora do Rosário), 31, 126–127, 172–176, 178, 180–181, 194, 340n15
oxcart driver (ox driver) See *boiadeiro*
Oxalá. *See* Obatala
Oxóssi. *See* Oshosi.
Oxóssi, Camafeu de, 364n51
Oxum. *See* Oshun.
Oxumará. *See* Oshumare.
Oya-Yansan (Òyá, Ìyánsàn, Oiá, Iansã) (Orisha), 36, 245, 251, 304
Oyěwùmí, Oyèrónkẹ́, 32, 238
Oyo empire, 32, 34–35, 131, 230, 263, 270, 287, 288; cosmology, 271, 293; Dahomey and, 273–275, 277, 285; Ile-Ifé and, 234–239
Ozolua (King of Benin), 235

Pai João da Aruanda (Father Joaquim from Aruanda), 190
Paixão, Manoel Bernardino da (1881–1946). *See* Folha, Tata Bernardo Bate
Pajelança, 133
Palmares Cultural Foundation. *See* Fundação Cultural Palmares
Palo Mayombe, 315. *See* Mayombe
Pan-African dikengas, 313–317
Pândegos da África (African Merrymakers), 253, 254–255
Pão de Açúcar. *See* Sugarloaf Mountain
parables, 64, 239–244
Paraguayan War (War of the Triple Alliance) (1864–1870), 72
Pardo (Brown/Mestizo), 107, 336n8
Parés, Luis Nicolau, 285, 289–290, 293, 294
Park, Chris, 185
Parnaso de além-túmulo (*Parnassus from Beyond the Tomb*), 186
parrots, 181, 352n193
Pastinha, Mestre (Vicente Ferreira Pastinha) (1889–1981), 136, 139, 147, 343n75, 344n124
patangome (patangoma, patangonga) 145
Patrocínio, José do (1854–1905), 113
patronage system, 80, 81, 169
"Patuscada de Gandhi" (Gandhi's Revelry), 260, 364n51
Paulistas, 48
Pedro I (Emperor of Brazil) (1798–1834), 44–45, 48, 58–59, 71, 77, 84
Pedro II (Emperor of Brazil) (1825–1891), 48, 49, 59, 71–72, 74, 80, 84. *See also* Nkanga-a-Mvika Pedro II
Peixoto, Norberto, 187
Peleus (mythical figure), 56, 64
Pêlo, Miguel Tércio, 355n297
pemba (chalk), 191, 314–315
Pemberton, John III (1928–2016), 361n488
Penal Code (1890), 336n78
Penha-Lopes, Vânia, 106, 107
Pentecostalism, 293
Pereira, Arivaldo Fagundes "Carequinha," 260–261, 364n51
Pereira, Avelino Romero Simões, 72
Pereira, Edimilson de Almeida, 8, 115, 124, 318–319, 352n194; Congadas and, 172–175, 181–182; limitations of Western languages and, 26, 125
Pereira, Lúcia Miguel (1901–1959), 82, 332n49
Pereira, Manoel Nunes (1893–1985), 285, 294
perfection. *See Musoni*

INDEX   415

peristil (ritual courtyard, the community of Vodou and other Afro-Haitian life practices), 295–296, 316.
Philip, M. NourbeSe, 6
Philip II (King of Spain), 78–79
Picturesque and Historical Voyage to Brazil (*Voyage pittoresque et historique au Brésil, ou séjour d'un artiste français au Brésil*) (Debret), 70
Pierson, Donald (1900–1995), 105
Pinheiro, Cônego Fernandes (1825–1876), 80
Pinheiro, Márcia Leitão, 110, 337n20
Pinheiro, Robson (Ângelo Inácio), 188–189
Pinto-Bailey, Cristina, 154
Pliny the Elder, 61, 63
"plurifunctional," 107
poem-chants, 26, 160–161, 165, 268
poems: altar-poems, 314; Orikis, 178, 190, 238, 240, 288, 363n14
"poemusic," 100, 319
poetics, 11, 13, 17, 75–79, 121, 312, 317; Brazilian-Kongo-Angola-Catholic, 318; of Congadas, 172–181; Dias and prophecy of cursed legacy, 80–85
poetry: *Afro-Caribbean Poetry and Ritual*, 13, 16; praise, 178, 190, 238, 240, 288, 363n14
"The Poet Against the Flow" (Marques), 81
police, 19, 43, 104, 259–260, 262, 336n81, 366n94
pontos-riscados, 313–317
Portrait of Brazil. See Retrato do Brasil
Portugal, 53, 70, 97, 206, 208–210; Brazil and, 11, 19, 23, 44, 48–51, 74–75; Kongo and, 199–205; Queen Nzinga and negotiations with, 214–217
Portuguese Empire, 16, 53, 55, 58, 84
possessions, bodily, 191, 258. *See also* trance and elegun.
Prado, Paul (1868–1943), 94
praise poetry, 178, 190, 238, 240, 288, 363n14
praise songs, 34, 70, 71–73, 146, 288, 289
Presidential Decree (1934), 104
preceito, 146
preto. See Black
Pretos Velhos (Black Elders), 189, 190
"priest doctor." *See nganga*
O problema negro na América do Sul (Rodrigues), 334n6
production. *See* coding
"Professor/Instructor May Have been Killed Due to Racism," 361n480
Projects for Brazil. See Projetos para o Brasil
Projetos para o Brasil (*Projects for Brazil*) (Andrada e Silva), 112

prophecies, 20–21, 56–57, 60, 68, 78–79, 308; of Adamastor, 62–63, 69; Dias with cursed legacy, 80–85; Ifa oracle, 104, 147, 236, 239–243, 289, 291, 303, 311–313, 361n488, 372n306
Prosopopoeia (*Prosopéia*) (Teixeira), 21, 78–79, 85, 331n25
Prospero (fictional character), 20, 57–59, 63, 71
Proteus (sea god), 21, 78–79, 115
proverbs, 143–144, 149, 182, 195–196, 230, 232, 300, 316
Pungo-a-Ndongo, 10, 116, 29, 160–169, 217, 220, 230, 311, 349n101; Pedras Negras, 162–163
punishment, divine, 20, 84, 85
pwen, 316

Queen Nzinga Arrived. See A Rainha Nzinha chegou
Querebentã de Zomadonu (Casa Grande das Minas), 34, 286, 295, 303
Querino, Manuel (1851–1923), 90
Queto. *See* Ketu
Quilombo (Mocambo), 16, 29, 31, 171, 172, 179, 348n72; Aruanda and, 190; resistance, 220–227, 302
Quilombo dos Palmares (Angola Janga, Republic of Palmares) (c. 1605–1695), 28, 131, 165, 168, 222, 225, 302, 311
Quilombolas. *See* Maroons
quilts, African-American, 130
Quimbanda. *See* Umbanda
Quitombe (supreme chiefs and advisors), 170, 358n387

racism, 2, 4, 24, 92–93, 101, 106–109, 361n480; anti-Semitism, 111, 205–206; scientific, 97, 186
radio, 99, 315–316, 364n51
A Rainha Nzinha chegou (*Queen Nzinga Arrived*) (documentary film), 123
Rainha Jinga. *See* Nzinga-Mbandi-Ngola-Kiluanji
Ramatis (spirit), 187–188, 353n216
Ramos, Arthur (1903–1949), 23, 93–95, 103–105, 170, 257, 285
rasteira Capoeira movement, 47, 121
rattles, 27, 88, 89, 144–145
Ratts, Alex, 361n480
"re-Africanization" process, 243, 254
rebellions, 65, 129, 224, 262–263, 270, 278–279, 290–292, 366n103
"The Reclining Giant" ("Le géant couché"), 70
Recreativo da Beija-Flor de Nilópolis, 302
A redenção de Cam (*Ham's Redemption*), 46, 47

red sun. *See* Tukula
Regimento, 201
Régis, Armando, 301
Rei, Chico, 34, 302
Reinados, 123–128, 335n68, 338n5, 339n9, 340n15
reinóis, 21
Reis, João José, 277, 278, 372n306
Reis, Maria Firmina dos (1822–1917), 154–155
Reisados, 170–171
re-learning, the world, 6–9
"The Religious World of Blacks in Bahia" (Falefá), 103
re-membering, 3–5, 22, 287
Republic of Palmares (c. 1605–1695). *See* Quilombo dos Palmares
reterritorialization, 182–183, 253
Retrato do Brasil (*Portrait of Brazil*) (Prado), 94
returnees, 33, 270, 280–284, 294, 304
Revelry of the Kings. *See* Folia de Reis
the Revolta dos Malês (1835), 278, 325n4
Rezende, Eliane, 187, 188
rhythms, 13, 129–130, 135, 139, 142, 174, 246, 255
Ribeiro, Maria de Lourdes (1912–1983), 152–153
Risério, Antonio, 95, 99, 263, 279, 293, 365n60, 367n114; Carnaval and, 254, 256, 364n51; "poemusic" and, 100, 319
Ritual Elders and Priestesses: Makota (Macota); Mametu Nkisi (Mameto Nkisi); Mãe de Santo; Ialorixá (Iyalorixá, Ìyálòrìṣà)
Ritual Elders and Priests: Tata Nkisi; Pai de Santo; Babalorixá (Bàbálòrìṣà); Ogã (Ògá)
Rivail, Hippolyte Léon Denizard. *See* Kardec, Allan
Roach, Joseph, 4, 11–13, 16, 36
rocks, 20, 77, 160–165, 193–194. *See also* stone giant
roda. *See* wheel
Rodrigues, Nina (1862–1906), 95, 112, 139, 285, 293, 334n6; Afro-Brazilian anthropology and, 23, 90–93; Afro-Brazilian Carnaval and, 253–254
Röhrig Assunção, Matthias, 139, 147
Romanticism, 53, 73, 81, 82, 96, 101, 189
Romero, Sílvio (1851–1914), 23, 53, 90–91, 331n25
Rosa, Cristina, 158
Royal Press (Imprensa Régia), 80
royal processions, with music, 88–89
Rufino, Luiz, 11
Rufino dos Santos, Joel (1941–2015), 221, 224
Rugendas, Johann-Moritz, 87
The Ruler of Ejigbo: An Ifa Story. *See* "Uma História de Ifá: Elegibo"
rum-rumpi-lé drum trio, 75, 140

Sabiá, Djalma, 301
sagaras. *See* sangamentos
sailors (*marinheiros*), 24, 57–58, 65–70, 153, 173, 176, 274
A saliva da fala (*The Spit of Speech*) (Pereira, E. de A.), 318
Samba, 24, 143, 190, 246, 253, 280; blues music and, 129; futebol, Carnaval and, 97–100; movements, 158, 178; schools, 33–34, 99, 226–227, 254, 263, 301, 302–304, 365n68, 374n373
"Samba de Caboclo," 142
sangamentos (*sagaras*), 138, 169–170
Sankofa (mythical bird), 31, 37
Sansi, Roger, 293
Sansone, Livio, 338n1
Santana, Tiganá, 161
Santería, Cuban, 293
Santo, Claudiana do Espírito, 287
Santo, Maria Bibiana do Espírito (1890–1967), 287
Santos, Deoscóredes Maximiliano dos. *See* Didi, Mestre
Santos, Eugênia Anna dos (1869–1938). *See* Aninha, Mãe
Santos, Juana Elbein dos, 288
Santos, Manoel dos "Guarda Sol," 260
Santos, Nelson dos "Lobisomem" (1925–2009), 260
Santos, Sales Augusto dos, 109
São Paulo Art Biennial (2023), 128
Saraiva, Ovídio, 71–72
Sartre, Jean-Paul (1905–1980), 184–185
SASO. *See* South African Students' Organization
Schechner, Richard, 135
science, 4, 14, 90, 97, 186. *See also* social sciences
Scott, David, 14–15
Scotti, Guilherme, 111, 112, 113, 114
Scramble for Africa (1884–1914), 29, 218, 219
Second Afro-Brazilian Congress (1937), 103–104, 105
Secret Knowledge, 187
seeds, 27, 36, 145
Segatto, José Antônio, 48, 53
Semana de Arte Moderna (Modern Art Week) (1922), 95
Senegal, 131, 359n439
Serrano, Carlos, 220
sertanejo (in Umbanda), 189
sertão, 118. *sertões*, 189.
Shakespeare, William, 19, 20, 58, 59, 137. *See also* The Tempest
Shango. *See* Xangô

Sharpe, Nanny, 12
Sharpe, Sam, 12
shells, 154–156, 204, 212, 304. *See also nzimbus*
Shukla, Pravina, 244, 252–253, 259, 264–268
Sieff, Kevin, 281
signature. *See firmas*
Silva, Agnaldo (1949–2021), 257, 266
Silva, Chica da (c. 1732–1796), 302
Silva, Denise Ferreira da, 128
Silva, Durival Marques da. *See* Madeira, Vavá
Silva, Francisco Manuel da, 71–72
Silva, Itamar Ferreira da. *See* Tropicália, Ythamar
Silva, Jacques Raimundo Ferreira da, 177
Silva, Leônidas da ("Black Diamond," "Rubber Man") (1913–2004), 98
Silva, Maria Madalena da (c. 1829–1892), 287
Silva, Orlando, 98
Silva, Reinivaldo. *See* Zulu, Rey
Silveira, Oliveira, 218
Silveira, Renato da, 291
Silvério, Arthur Camilo (father), 173
Silvério da Silva, Arthur Camilo (1885–1956), 173
Simard, Suzanne, 323n40
Simas, Luiz Antonio, 11
simbi. See nkisi
SINCRE. *See* National System of Foreigners' Registration and Records
sing-dance-drum-tell, 135, 158
"singer-poets" (*cantopoetas*), 318
singing, 68, 135, 158, 247, 249, 313; Brazilian national anthem, 22, 70–71, 73; chorus, 64, 71, 146, 151, 159, 172, 220, 255
"Sisterhood, or Sorority of Good Death." *See* Irmandade da Boa Morte
Skertchly, Josiah (1850–1926), 299, 300
slave ports, 28, 33, 160, 270, 282
Slave Route Project, UNESCO, 4, 34, 277–279, 281
slavery, 2, 8, 14–15, 21, 48–49, 94, 120, 149, 283; abolition of, 13, 45, 90, 97, 113–114, 168–170, 219, 248, 253, 275, 291, 302; burning of archives, 25, 112–114; critics, 80–81; *guerra preta* and, 167, 203–204, 223; heroes and, 12–13, 307; Middle Passage, 124, 127, 137, 292, 301; Truth Commission on Black Slavery in Brazil, 18, 25, 110–111
slaves. *See* enslaved people
"Slave Ship." *See* "Navio negreiro"
slave ships (tumbeiros), as "floating tombs," 7–8, 136–137, 218, 284, 301–302
"The Slave Ship" (Acadêmicos do Salgueiro), 301–302

"The Slave Woman" ("A escrava") (Dias), 85
slave trade, 201–203, 205, 207, 215, 283; parable for, 239–244; transatlantic, 4, 17, 35, 131, 169, 185, 200, 204, 222, 270, 275, 280–282, 292, 294, 297, 303–304, 307–308
slave traders, 33, 34, 275–278, 280–282, 304
sleeping king, 83–85
sleeping stone giant, 75–76
Slenes, Robert, 152, 178, 294
Smith, C. A., 361n480
Smithsonian Institution, 281
Soares Filho, Daniel, 189–191
soccer. *See futebol*
social sciences, 2, 23, 86–91, 321n1; diagnosis and clinical trials, 92–105; futebol, Samba and Carnaval, 97–100
sociological research, Afro-Brazilian, 293–294
Sodré, Muniz, 131, 180, 182–185, 253, 361n480
Sofala. *See* Mozambique
Soglo, Nicéphore, 370n223
Solanke, Ladipo (1886–1958), 104
Song of Exile (Enslen), 330n3
"Song of Exile" ("Canção de exílio") (Dias), 21, 74–75, 330n3
songs, 121, 178; Carnaval, 263, 301–305, 367n115; praise, 34, 70, 71–73, 146, 288, 289. *See also* national anthem; singing; *specific songs*
sons, mothers and, 257–258
Sons of Gandhi. *See* Filhos de Gandhy
Sousa, Hilton Bruno de Almeida, 342n69
South African Students' Organization (SASO), 108
Southern Cross, 76, 331n14
southern sun. *See* Musoni
Souza, Albano Neves e, 138
Souza, Eduarlino de "Dudu," 260
space, 142, 146, 289, 316; time and, 6, 15, 37, 150, 163, 179, 182–185, 230, 233, 243, 309–310, 312; Vodun divinities in physical, 282
space capsules, slave ships as, 7–8
spiritism, 186–188, 191, 336n78
Spiritists, 6, 28, 186–189
Spiritist Union of Umbanda in Brazil. *See* União Espírita de Umbanda do Brasil
spirits, 144, 160, 187–188, 190–191, 256, 258, 353n216
Spiritualist novels, 6, 28, 186–187
spiritual plane. *See òrun*
The Spit of Speech. See A saliva da fala
State University of Rio de Janeiro (UERJ), 107
Statute of Indigenous Societies, 19, 41
Stevens, George, 366n102

stomach, head and, 305
rocks (African and Afro-diasporic imagination) 162–163, 164, 193–194, 220, 228, 230, 239; *pedra* (stone) 353n243, 360n443; *pedrinha* (pebble) 160, 162, 193, 354n245; bedrock, 160–165, 193–194, 228; outcrops, 162, 163, 165; hill, 185, 196; mountain, 15, 119, 128, 156, 162–165, 196, 197, 222, 230–234, 237, 295
rocks (European and Europeanized imagination), 20–21, 60, 63–64, 77, 160–165
stone giant, 21, 22, 75–78, 312
"The Stone Giant" ("O Gigante de pedra") (Dias), 21, 75
storytelling, 135, 138, 190, 246
structural racism, 2, 24, 108
Sugarloaf Mountain (Pão de Açúcar), 77
Sultan of Malindi (fictional character), 67–68
sun, 70, 124, 150–151, 164–165, 193, 311
sunset. *See* Luvèmba
sun's path (*nzila ya ntangu*), 150–151
supreme chiefs and advisors. *See* Quitombe
Supreme Court (Supremo Tribunal Federal), 25, 102, 111–112, 190
Suruí Nation, chief of, 18–19, 22, 41
Sweet, James, 294
symbols, 13, 28, 29, 310–311

Tacoodonou. *See* Dakodonu
talking bells, 140
talking drum, 137
talking harp, 126, 136–137
Talmon-Chvaice, Maya, 159
Tambor de Mina, 133, 294
Tambores de Angola (*Drums from Angola*) (Pinheiro, R.), 188
tamboril drums, 173, 190
tambourines, 88–89, 139
Tango, 149–150
Tannus, Eduardo, 303
Tapas (Nupês), 132
Taprobana, 57, 326n19
Távora, Francisco de, 217
Tears of Our Lady (Lágrimas de Nossa Senhora), 27, 145
technology, 14, 27, 57, 65, 128, 310
Tegbesu (King of Dahomey) (r. 1740–1742), 274
Teixeira, Bento (1560–1600), 21, 78–79, 85, 115, 331n25
Teles de Menezes, Joaquim, 276
Temba-Ndumba (first chief of the Kasanjes), 29–30, 210–211, 213

The Tempest (Shakespeare), 19–20, 54, 57–60, 62–63, 71, 326n24, 327n27
Terecô, 133
terreiro (ritual courtyard, and by extension the community of Candomblé, Umbanda, and other Afro-Brazilian life practices), 240, 242, 249, 288–290, 294–295; communities, 102–104, 118, 180; ground, 122, 153, 227; Yoruba, 180, 243, 315
Tethys (titaness, mother of the Oceanids), 70
Thetis (nereid, sea goddess), 56, 64, 68–70
Third Afro-Brazilian Congress (1982), 104
Thompson, Robert Farris, 3, 9, 11, 15–16, 146, 150, 294, 313
Thornton, John, 15, 138, 169, 207, 235, 357n379
Tidalectics, 13
time, 47, 313; space and, 6, 15, 37, 150, 163, 179, 182–185, 230, 233, 243, 309–310, 312; symbols, 310–311
"The Hour of Brazil." *See* "A Hora do Brasil"
Toco, 190
Togo, 1, 26, 33, 130–131, 369n191, 370n218
tombs, 186, 217, 282, 301. *See also* slave ships
"Toque de Barravento," 142
Toré, 134
Tossi, Obá (Marcelina da Silva) (c. 1812–1885), 35, 36, 287, 289–292, 305, 307
Toward a Global Idea of Race (Silva, D. F. da), 128
"Tradition and the Individual Talent" (Eliot), 317–318
trance, 184, 191–192, 194, 246, 293
transformation. *See* Luvèmba
translation(s), 13, 137, 150, 155, 160–161, 229, 275, 329, 340, 356, 362–363, 367
travel accounts, 86–90
Treaty of Tordesillas (1494), 219
Tree of Forgetfulness (*L'Arbre d'oublier*), 292, 308
trees, 175, 294, 295, 323n40, 350n141; family, 14–17, 30, 317–320; Nsanda, 196–206
tricksters, 95–96, 181, 236, 312, 352n193
Trio Elétrico, 254, 364n51
tripod metaphor, 27, 140
Tropicália, Ythamar (Itamar Ferreira da Silva), 240
truth commissions, 18, 25, 109–111, 337nn20–21
Tschudi, Johann Jakob von, 87
Tukula (red sun, zenith, maturity), 311
tumbeiros ("floating tombs"). *See* slave ships
turbans, 68, 244, 247, 249, 254, 257, 264–265, 367n121
Turner, Jerry, 294
Twain, Mark, 94
twins, 295–301

UERJ. *See* State University of Rio de Janeiro
Uma história da cidade da Bahia (Risério), 364n51
"Uma História de Ifá: Elegibo" (The Ruler of Ejigbo: An Ifa Story), 240
Umbanda (Quimbanda, Embanda, Banda, Macumba), 99, 133, 158, 186–188, 226–227, 246; chants, 189, 190, 192–193; as philosophical and religious expression, 24, 98, 191, 267; *pontos-riscados*, 313–317
umbrellas, 1, 27, 299
umgunga, 137
Um rio chamado Atlântico (Da Costa e Silva), 370n218
UNESCO. *See* United Nations Educational Scientific and Cultural Organization
União Espírita de Umbanda do Brasil (Spiritist Union of Umbanda in Brazil), 98
Unidos da Tijuca (Carnaval group), 33, 34, 303–304
United Kingdom of Portugal, 58
United Nations Educational Scientific and Cultural Organization (UNESCO), 4, 34, 105, 243, 277–279, 281, 288
United Nations International Decade for People of African Descent (2015–2024), 3–4
United States, 1, 16, 72, 101, 106–107, 129, 180, 218–219
universe, wheel of, 164, 165, 180, 313
Unpayable Debt (Silva, D. F. da), 128
Úrsula (Reis, M. F. dos), 154
urucongo (one-string harp), 137

Vai-Vai, 226–227
Valdina Pinto, Makota Zimewaanga (1943–2019), 133, 149, 163–164, 315
Vansina, Jan, 30, 36, 310
Varella, Fagundes, 329n90
Vargas, Getúlio (1882–1954), 52, 73, 97–99, 104, 343n75
Varnhagen, Francisco Adolfo de, 348n72
Vasco Da Gama (fictional character), 19–20, 55–69
Vatican, 167–169, 201
Velho, Domingos Jorge (c.1641–1705), 223
Veloso, Caetano, 364n51
Ventura, Roberto (1957–2002), 52
Verger, Pierre Fatumbi (1902–1996), 147, 235, 276, 291, 362n7, 370nn217–218, 371n262; on Queen Na Agontimé, 34, 277, 285–286, 303; with research, 288, 294; on Samba lyrics, 302
vèvè, 313–316,
Viana, Jorge Amorim "Danone," 361n480

Vianna, Hermano, 95, 101
Vidas Negras Importam (Black Lives Matter), 108
Vieira, António (Father), 205
Vieira Filho, Raphael, 263
Vila Rica (Costa), 75
Vilokan, 185–186, 296, 316
viola (*violinha*), 139, 140
violence, xv, 25, 31, 109, 111, 252; police, 104, 259–260, 262, 366n94; racist, 205. *See also* rebellions; slavery
Viotti da Costa, Emília, 101
vissungo (field hollers), 121
visual arts, 3, 36, 44–47, 121
visual forms of expression, rhythmic patterns with, 129–130
Voduns (Vodouns, Vodous, Lwas), 36, 103, 131, 190, 280–281, 285, 292; deities, 34–35, 271–272, 282, 286, 292–296, 303; Haitian, 315–316; Querebentã de Zomadonu, 34, 286, 295, 303
Voices from Aruanda. *See Vozes de Aruanda*
"The Voice of Brazil." *See* "A Voz do Brasil"
Von Binzer, Ina, 87
Von Martius, Karl Friedrich Philipp (1794–1868), 50–51, 85–91, 101, 122, 171, 213
Von Spix, Johann Baptist (1781–1826), 23, 86–90, 171, 213, 223
Voyage pittoresque et historique au Brésil, ou séjour d'un artiste français au Brésil. *See* Picturesque and Historical Voyage to Brazil
"A Voz do Brasil" ("The Voice of Brazil"), 99
Vozes de Aruanda (Voices from Aruanda) (Peixoto), 187

Walsh, Robert, 87
War of the Triple Alliance. *See* Paraguayan War
war prisoners. *See kijiko*
"We Are Not Racists" (study), 106–107
Western films, 267
Western languages, 26, 125
wheel (*roda*), 146–147, 150, 159, 164–165, 177, 180, 313
whitening. *See branqueamento*
white problem, 101–102
women, xv, 85, 242, 255–258, 262, 291; Black, 47, 104, 109, 360n473; femicide, 109, 361n480
Wood Wide Web, 14, 323n40
"World-Machine" ("a grande máquina do Mundo"), 20, 68–69
The Wretched of the Earth (Fanon), 184–185
writing, 122–125, 187, 191, 314–315
Wynter, Sylvia, 5

Xambá, 133
Xangô (Candomblé system), 134, 294
Xangô (Shango) (Orisha), 34, 233, 241, 245, 287–288, 290, 302
Xavier, Chico (Francisco Cândido Xavier) (1910–2002), 186–187, 189, 352n212

Yai, Olabiyi (1938–2020), 256, 281, 312
Yala Nkuwu council, 197
Yansan. *See* Oya-Yansan
"Years of Lead" (1968–1978), 246
Yemaya (Yemọja, Iemanjá) (Orisha), 99, 245, 251, 303
Yoruba, 15–16, 92, 175, 180, 241–242, 304, 315; cosmology, 28, 31–32, 179, 255–257, 305–306; creation narrative, 235–239; language, 130–131, 243, 271, 288, 312; people, 91, 126–127, 139, 234, 243, 246, 257–258, 291
Yoruba-Ewe, 91, 132
Yoruba-Ewe-Fon, 161, 164, 179, 190–191
Yowa. *See* cosmogram; Dikenga
Yuka, Marcelo, 106

Zambi. *See* Nzambi
Zangronis, Juan José, 276
Zebra Dance. *See* N'golo
Zeleza, Paul, 3
zenith. *See* Tukula
Zilberman, Regina, 52, 95–96
Zimbo (king of the Ndongo), 29, 208, 210–211
zimvila clan mottos, Kongo, 198
Zulu, Rey (Reinivaldo Silva), 240
Zumbi dos Palmares (c. 1655–1694), 30, 34, 36, 109, 307, 311; early years, 359n441; as resistance leader, 28–29, 220–227, 302

GPSR Authorized Representative: Easy Access System Europe, Mustamäe tee
50, 10621 Tallinn, Estonia, gpsr.requests@easproject.com

www.ingramcontent.com/pod-product-compliance
Lightning Source LLC
Chambersburg PA
CBHW031228290426
44109CB00012B/202